Luis Buñuel

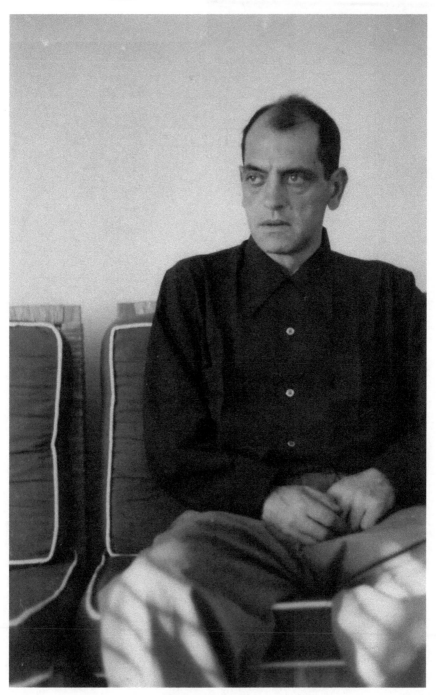

Figure 1 Luis Buñuel in Mexico City, *c.* 1948.

Luis Buñuel

A Life in Letters

Edited by
Jo Evans and Breixo Viejo

BLOOMSBURY ACADEMIC
NEW YORK • LONDON • OXFORD • NEW DELHI • SYDNEY

BLOOMSBURY ACADEMIC
Bloomsbury Publishing Inc
1385 Broadway, New York, NY 10018, USA
50 Bedford Square, London, WC1B 3DP, UK

BLOOMSBURY, BLOOMSBURY ACADEMIC and the Diana logo
are trademarks of Bloomsbury Publishing Plc

First published in the United States of America 2019

Cover design: Eleanor Rose
Cover image: Luis Buñuel in 1982 © Gabriel Figueroa Flores

Library of Congress Cataloging-in-Publication Data
Names: Buñuel, Luis, 1900-1983, author. | Evans, Jo, 1963- editor. |
Viejo, Breixo, editor.
Title: Luis Buñuel: a life in letters / edited by Jo Evans and Breixo Viejo.
Description: New York, NY : Bloomsbury Academic, 2019. |
Includes bibliographical references and index. |
Identifiers: LCCN 2019011689 (print) | LCCN 2019015887 (ebook) |
ISBN 9781501312595 (ePDF) | ISBN 9781501312601 (ePub) | ISBN 9781501312571
(hardback : alk. paper) | ISBN 9781501312588 (paperback : alk. paper)
Subjects: LCSH: Buñuel, Luis, 1900-1983–Correspondence–Translations into
English. | Motion picture producers and directors–Spain–Correspondence.
Classification: LCC PN1998.3.B86 (ebook) | LCC PN1998.3.B86 A4 2019 (print) |
DDC 791.4302/33092 [B] –dc23
LC record available at https://lccn.loc.gov/2019011689

ISBN: HB: 978-1-5013-1257-1
         PB: 978-1-5013-1258-8
         ePDF: 978-1-5013-1259-5
         eBook: 978-1-5013-1260-1

Typeset by Integra Software Services Pvt. Ltd.
Printed and bound in Great Britain

To find out more about our authors and books visit www.bloomsbury.com
and sign up for our newsletters.

This research was generously funded by a Research Project Grant (2015–18)
awarded by The Leverhulme Trust, London, UK.

LEVERHULME
TRUST _____

In memory of Juan Luis Buñuel (1934–2017)

Contents

Figures

Note on this edition

Many of the letters selected for this edition have not been published previously, and almost all of them appear for the first time here unabridged and in English. We have, for reasons of space, included only a small selection of the extensive collection of Luis Buñuel correspondence with Pierre Braunberger, Jean-Claude Carrière, Eduardo Ducay, Carlos Fuentes, Ricardo Muñoz Suay, Georges Sadoul, Serge Silberman and the organizers of the Cannes Film Festival and the Venice Film Festival (including Robert Favre Le Bret and Luigi Chiarini). We have also included letters – to date only partially published, or unpublished – from smaller, but equally important, collections from the archives of: Max Aub, José Donoso, Oscar Lewis, Dalton Trumbo, Zachary Scott and Pierre Unik, as well as unpublished letters from Buñuel to José Francisco Aranda, Corpus Barga, Robert Benayoun, André Breton, Alexander Calder, Jean Cocteau, Jean Giono, Ado Kyrou, Joseph Losey, Louis Malle, Ivor Montagu, Jean Painlevé, Man Ray, Pedro Salinas and François Truffaut. A significant part of his correspondence with friends and collaborators (from Luis Alcoriza and Julio Alejandro to Hugo Butler and Gabriel Figueroa) is also published here for the first time. However, *Luis Buñuel: A Life in Letters* is essentially an anthology: the complete Buñuel correspondence would amount to more than two thousand letters, even without the couple of hundred more letters that must have existed (as they are referred to at various points in this collection), but that are presently considered 'lost'.

This edition also includes an extremely important collection of letters that have appeared in other books, journals and catalogues. Amongst the most relevant of these are the letters between Buñuel and the Viscount and Viscountess de Noailles edited by Jean-Michel Bouhours and Nathalie Schoeller, and published in French by the Pompidou Centre, Paris, in 1993; a complete collection of letters exchanged with Ricardo Urgoiti in Spanish, included in an appendix to *Ricardo Urgoiti: Los trabajos y los días* by Josetxo Cerdán and Luis Fernández Colorado, published in 2007; and the equally important correspondence between Buñuel and Juan Larrea, also in Spanish, published by Gabriel Morelli in the same year. Letters written to José Rubia Barcia and to Francisco Rabal (although not their replies to Buñuel) appeared in book form in 1992 and 2001, respectively. This edition would not have been possible without the essential investigative work of these and other researchers (and their work is sourced in the selection headed 'Previous Publication' at the end of this note).

Although the major part of the present edition is made up of letters, we have included other forms of written communication, such as postcards, telegrams, draft notes, invitations, *pneumatiques,* interdepartmental memos from the time Buñuel spent working in the Office of the Coordinator of Inter-American Affairs in New York and at Warner Brothers in Los Angeles, as well as various handwritten dedications that appear on photographs and in books. This has allowed us to bridge a number of gaps, as there is still limited public access to some material (the correspondence between Buñuel and Lulú and Hernando Viñes, for example). There may well also still be fairly extensive collections of letters whose present location is unknown – such as the majority of the professional correspondence generated by Buñuel's work in Mexico with Oscar Dancigers and Gustavo Alatriste, or the correspondence Buñuel must have exchanged with his French agent, Paulette Dorisse.

In relation to general questions of style, we have added in some missing punctuation and homogenized the spelling of names and places and the dates that appear at the beginning of letters rather than reproducing their many original variations. We have included postal addresses wherever possible, but only on the first occasion. Once this has been indicated, the same postal address has not been repeated. The address that appears at the opening of letters is always that of the addressee, the address of the sender has been included after their signature if it was included in the original.

Buñuel was in the habit of opening letters on the same line, for example, 'Muy querido Carlos: encantado de haber tenido carta suya' (Dear Carlos: delighted to get your letter). For reasons of legibility, we have replaced these colons with a comma and continued each letter (using a capital letter for the first word) on the line below.

Likewise, for legibility, when transcribing telegrams, we have also substituted words like 'STOP' with the relevant punctuation marks, although we have retained the capital letters used in telegrams. Where a letter was written originally in English – and has been reproduced here in the original – we have indicated this by placing the entire letter in italics in order to distinguish this fact immediately from the vast majority of letters that were originally written in Spanish, and, on occasion, in French, Italian and Portuguese. Footnotes have been kept to a minimum and are only included, for example, the first time a particular individual is mentioned (when in doubt, readers are advised to use the index for the relevant reference and to be advised that where no nationality has been indicated, the individual in question is Spanish). Square brackets have been used, in the cases of sources, to indicate a letter once held in an archive, the location of which is now unknown. Square brackets have also been used, more occasionally, to indicate a word in a letter that is illegible, or nearly illegible in the original.

Each letter is then followed by abbreviations indicating the original language, physical description, location and the source in cases where a complete transcript of that particular letter has been published previously. (A full list of abbreviations is included after the 'Note on Translation'.) Where the previous publication was a facsimile reproduction of the original an *f* has been included after the page number. We have omitted references to partial transcriptions, previously erroneously dated and/or poorly translated letters. If a letter has appeared in its entirety in different texts, we refer here only to the facsimile publication or, where that does not exist, to the earliest publication we have found. Letters where no publication is listed have not, to our knowledge, been published previously. In the case of autograph (handwritten) dedications, the technical description includes in parentheses the title and edition of the original source; in the case of postcards, the location shown as an image on the front of the postcard.

We should like to express our deeply sincere thanks to everyone who has made this project possible. To Juan Luis Buñuel, first of all, who welcomed us so warmly to his flat in Paris on behalf of the Buñuel family on various occasions, and who was so constant in facilitating our access to his father's letters. Our thanks are also due – for allowing us to access and reproduce so many letters – to Federico Álvarez and Teresa Álvarez Aub, Homero and Betty Aridjis, Yvonne Baby and Roger Salloch, Asunción Balaguer, Laurence Braunberger, Aube Elléouët Breton, Michael Butler, Jean-Claude Carrière, Fernando Casado Campolongo, Catherine and Nathalie Chouchan, Héctor Delgado, Sylvie Durbet Giono, Eduardo Ducay and Alicia Salvador, Gabriel Figueroa Flores, Paula Gluzman, Juan Goytisolo, Carmen Hernández-Pinzón Moreno, Claudio Isaac, Eduardo Laborda and Iris Lázaro, Silvia Lemus de Fuentes, Justine Malle, David Novais, Antony Penrose, Susan Marie Rigdon, Jacqueline Roblès Macek, Roxane Silberman, Giorgio Tinazzi, Margot Pepper, Eleni Samarakis, Ana and Carlos Saura, Laura, Eva, and Joséphine Truffaut, Mitzi Trumbo, Luce Vigo and Steven Vogel.

We would like to offer our sincere thanks, also, to the members of the Steering Committee for this project – Mario Barro, Carmen Carrara, Javier Espada, Peter W. Evans, Guadalupe Ferrer, Ian Gibson, Román Gubern, Julián Daniel Gutiérrez Albilla, Paul Hammond, Rosario López de Prado, José María Prado, Antonia Rojas, Agustín Sánchez Vidal, Paul Julian Smith and Rob Stone for their invaluable help during the early stages of this research. Similarly, without funding from The Leverhulme Trust in the form of a three-year research grant this project would have been impossible. Thanks are also due to colleagues at the School of European Languages, Culture and Society, University College London, and to our patient editors, Raúl García (Ediciones Cátedra) and Katie Gallof (Bloomsbury Publishing).

In Spain, we were fortunate enough to receive considerable support from staff at the Filmoteca Española and, in particular, from Eduardo Sastre and Miguel Ángel Martínez López, who responded with patience and good humour to endless queries relating to the Archivo Buñuel. Thanks also to the Agencia Carmen Barcells, Barcelona; Montse Aguer, Fundación Gala-Salvador Dalí, Figueras; Antonio Bayona and Julián Gómez, Fundación Pilar Bayona, Zaragoza; Esther Bentué, Archivo Histórico de la Universidad, Zaragoza; Antonio García-Rayo, Madrid; Luis Gasca, San Sebastián; Emilio Casanova, Fundación Ramón y Katia Acín, Zaragoza; Rosa Illán, Fundación García Lorca, Madrid; Nieves López Menchero and Alicia Hérraiz, Institut Valencià de l'Audiovisual i la Cinematografía, Valencia; Amparo Martínez Herranz, Universidad de Zaragoza; Francisco J. Millán, Diario de Teruel; Esteve Riambau, Filmoteca de Catalunya, Barcelona; María José Rucio Zamorano, Biblioteca Nacional de España, Madrid; Daniel Sánchez Salas, Universidad Rey Juan Carlos, Madrid; John D. Sanderson, Universidad de Alicante; Francisco Tortajada, Fundación Max Aub, Segorbe; Alfredo Valverde, Residencia de Estudiantes, Madrid; Jaime de Vicente, Otoño Cultural Iberoamericano, Huelva; and Jordi Xifra, Centro Buñuel, Calanda.

In France, we should like to extend our thanks to staff at the archives of the Cinématheque francaise, Paris, as well as to Sylvie Colla, Fonds Cortázar, University of Poitiers; Guy Dugas, Université Paul Valéry, Montpellier; Guillaume Fau, Bibliothèque nationale de France, Paris; Nathalie Fressard and Paul Cougnard, Bibliothèque Littéraire Jacques Doucet, Paris; Marie-Françoise Garion, Bibliothèque Historique de la Ville, Paris; Marie Jager, Archives Jean Painlevé, Paris; and François Ruault, Bibliothèque francophone multimedia, Limoges. In Italy, thanks to Nicola Bassano, Fondazione Fellini, Cineteca di Rimini, Rimini; Marica Gallina, ASAC Fondazione La Biennale di Venezia, Venice, and to Debora Demontis, Centro Sperimentale di Cinematografia, Rome; in the UK, to Jonny Davies, British Film Institute, London; and in Switzerland, to Elisabeth Martin-Brachet and Annie Massot, Archives départementales des Alpes-de-Haute- Provence, Digne-les-Bains.

In the United States, we owe thanks to Fernando Acosta-Rodríguez, Firestone Library, Princeton, New Jersey; Susan Brauer Dam and Alexander Rower, Calder Foundation, New York; Alessia Cecchet, Syracuse University Library, Syracuse; Elizabeth Garver and Steve Wilson, Harry Ransom Center, Austin, Texas; Mary Haegert, Houghton Library, Cambridge, Massachusetts; Louise Hilton, Margaret Herrick Library, Los Angeles; Aaron Lisec, Morris Library, Carbondale, Illinois; Julianna Jenkins and Cesar Reyes, University of California, Los Angeles; Jennifer Lee, Rare Book and Manuscript Library, Columbia University, New York; Sarah McElroy, The Lilly Library, Bloomington, Indiana; Sarah Moazeni, Tamiment Library, New York; Mona Nagai and Jason Sanders, Pacific Film Archive, Berkeley, California; Carly Sentieri, King Library, Oxford, Ohio; Brett Service, Warner Brothers Archive, Los Angeles; Amanda Stow, American Heritage Center, Laramie, Wyoming; and Ashley Swinnerton, Museum of Modern Art, New York.

We should also like to extend our gratitude to staff who responded so kindly to our queries at other international archives and libraries: the custodians of the Sir Michael Redgrave Archive, Victoria and Albert Museum, London; Susan Brady (Jerzy Kosinski Papers), Beinecke Library, New Haven, Connecticut; Concha Fernández Candau, Fundación Rafael Alberti, Puerto de Santa María; Alberto Ferraboschi (Archivio Zavattini), Biblioteca Panizzi, Reggio Emilia; Tatiana Goryaeva and Natalya Strizhkova, Russian State Archive of Literature and Art (RGALI), Moscow; Joan Miller (Frank Capra Papers), Wesleyan Cinema Archives, Middletown, Connecticut; Caroline Neeser, Cinémathèque Suisse, Penthaz; Vera Rumyansteva, Musei Kino, Moscow; Orna Somerville (Dan O'Herlihy Papers), University College, Dublin; Kerry Watson, Roland Penrose Archive, Edinburgh; and Claire Wotherspoon (Sir Alec Guinness Archive), The British Library, London.

We are also grateful to Iria Bermúdez, for her invaluable help with the transcription of letters; to Mathieu Boutang, for his help with accessing documents at the Silberman Archive in Paris; and to Stephen Fay and Gaëlle Suñer, for their arduous and tireless work on translation. Our thanks also to Jomi and Florencio Delgado in Mexico City; to Erica and Bill Clark and to Jessica and Andrés Rosende in Los Angeles; to Jim Pepper in Santa Barbara, to Kevin Johnson in Baltimore; to Alex Branger, Anne Boyman and John Rajchman, Arthur Fournier, Ross Hamilton, Odile and Robert Hullot-Kentor, and Rob King in New York; to Katia and Amine Moussi in Paris; to Diana Saldaña and David Cortés and to Victoria Contreras and Alex Torregrosa in Madrid; thanks to all of you for your warm hospitality and friendship during our periods of research in those locations. Thanks, finally, to our families and friends – and in particular to Iria and Vera, and to David and Marie – for the constant support they have provided during the long process of completing this project.

Jo Evans and Breixo Viejo

Note on the English translation

What makes this correspondence so invaluable as a first-hand account presents a singular challenge when it comes to translation: the first-hand Buñuel is nothing if not idiosyncratic and this version of Buñuel in English has inevitably undergone a process of adaptation and compromise. We have prioritized Buñuel's tone and register at all times, and while that means we have taken some liberties with word choice, we have retained the original sentence structure where possible. As with the identification of speakers and names, we have kept footnotes to a minimum, inserting them only at points where English is particularly inadequate to convey Buñuel's sense of humour and increasing use of light-hearted allusions to well-known Spanish quotations and refrains.

Along with these more general questions of register and colloquial in-jokes, letters present some immediate problems to do with greetings and farewells. There is no adequate English equivalent, for example, to the widely used ending, *abrazos*, in Spanish. The literal translation ('hugs') implies a more intimate relationship and is, still today, more colloquial. Similarly, the word *amigo*, which frequently appears at the beginning of Buñuel's letters, sounds slightly odd to anglophone ears ('Friend, León', for example). After some consideration, and with some regret, we have adjusted letters beginning 'Amigo León' to 'Dear León', but have otherwise translated the 'friends' literally (where a letter opens 'Querido amigo León', for example, we have used: 'Dear friend Léon). The ubiquitous *abrazos*, on the other hand, we have restricted to close correspondents. A three-word telegram sent on 14 September 1967 ('Un abrazo, Dalí') illustrates the problem with the Spanish 'hug'. Buñuel's estrangement over the years from Dalí (and *vice versa*) seemed to rule out an '(English) hug', but we felt that 'regards', which we have sometimes used as a substitute elsewhere, might suggest an irony Dalí did not intend at this point in his life. We settled, in the end, on the compromise: 'Greetings, Dalí'. But to add to the complication, and the debate, the date indicates that this telegram was sent in response to the success of *Belle de jour*, so 'congratulations' might well have been more to the point.

Two other slightly problematic words with myriad implications are: *espiritual* and *moral*. In Spanish, these have multiple shades of meaning related to ethical, aesthetic, artistic, creative and intellectual engagement and we have tended to adjust their translation into English to avoid any unintentional association (on Buñuel's part) with religious sentiment or bourgeois morality. We offer these three simple words here – *abrazos, espiritual* and *moral*– as a *caveat* to highlight some of the compromises we have had to make, and to acknowledge that we consider this translation to be primarily informative (and formative) rather than definitive.[1]

---

[1] Spanish readers may want to consult the letters in (what is in most cases) the original Spanish in *Luis Buñuel: Correspondencia escogida*, ed. Jo Evans and Breixo Viejo (Madrid: Cátedra, 2018).

Buñuel's register, particularly in the later letters, is startlingly contemporary, but we have updated the occasional archaic reference to dates and places, reintroducing the noun for clarity on occasions where the original Spanish may have been 'en ese', meaning 'this [month]'. With regard to addresses: we have, for obvious reasons, kept the original ('calle' or 'rue') to indicate street names, while translating the relevant town or city into English. Italics have been used for words underlined in the original as well as for foreign terms, including the French words and phrases that Buñuel uses so frequently, such as *metteurs en scene, scénario* and *découpage*. We have used the Spanish (Residencia) and the more familiar nickname (Resi) for the famous Madrid University Halls of Residence, and we have also left in Spanish the word *putrefacto*. This is in order to signify that this term was particularly favoured by Buñuel and close friends from the *Resi* to indicate disgust: so that, although there is a straightforward English equivalent (putrid), this word and its various permutations appear here in italics and in Spanish to indicate that their implications for this group of friends exceed the literal translation. All titles and honorifics have been translated into English, except the more occasional use of *Don* or *Doña*. We have also kept the Spanish title *Fray* (Brother, or Friar), traditionally used in English to refer, for example, to the famous Spanish Golden Age writer, Fray Luis de León.

Italics have been used throughout for all letters originally written in English (to distinguish them from our own translation). The titles of films, books and journals also appear in italics and in their original language. Whether or not they were originally written in the original correspondence in quotation marks or capital letters. Titles of poems or articles are indicated with quotation marks. With the exception of *Gran Casino*, which we felt was self-explanatory, *Belle de jour* and other one-word titles that refer to individual characters, such as *Viridiana*, all films directed by Buñuel are referred to by their English titles throughout. A full list of these is included in the 'Filmography'. The index also includes references to the Spanish and French title of these films, with a link to the English title for the relevant page references.

Jo Evans and Stephen Fay

Filmography

An Andalusian Dog (*Un Chien andalou,* 1929)
The Golden Age (*L'Âge d'Or,* 1930)
Land Without Bread (*Las Hurdes: Tierra sin pan,* 1933)
Gran Casino (1947)
The Great Madcap (*El gran calavera,* 1949)
The Young and the Damned (*Los olvidados,* 1950)
Susana (1950)
Daughter of Deceit (*La hija del engaño,* 1951)
A Woman Without Love (*Una mujer sin amor,* 1951)
Mexican Bus Ride (*Subida al cielo,* 1951)
The Brute (*El bruto,* 1952)
Robinson Crusoe (1952)
This Strange Passion (*Él,* 1953)
Wuthering Heights (*Abismos de passion,* 1953)
Illusion Travels by Streetcar (*La ilusión viaja en tranvía,* 1953)
The River and Death (*El río y la muerte,* 1954)
The Criminal Life of Archibaldo de la Cruz (*Ensayo de un crimen,* 1955)
That is the Dawn (*Cela s'appelle l'aurore,* 1955)
Death in the Garden (*La Mort en ce jardin,* 1956)
Nazarín (1958)
Fever Mounts at El Pao (*La Fièvre monte à El Pao,* 1959)
The Young One (1960)
Viridiana (1961)
The Exterminating Angel (*El ángel exterminador,* 1962)
Diary of a Chambermaid (*Le Journal d'une femme de chambre,* 1964)
Simon of the Desert (*Simón del desierto,* 1965)
Belle de jour (1967)
The Milky Way (*La Voie lactée,* 1969)
Tristana (1970)
The Discreet Charm of the Bourgeoisie (*Le Charme discret de la bourgeoisie,* 1972)
The Phantom of Liberty (*Le Fantôme de la liberté,* 1974)
That Obscure Object of Desire (*Cet obscur objet du désir,* 1977)

Abbreviations

Original Languages

Spa   Spanish

Fre   French

Eng   English

Ita   Italian

Por   Portuguese

Physical Description

Ad   Autograph draft

Add   Autograph dedication

Als   Autograph letter signed

Alu   Autograph letter unsigned

Ans   Autograph note signed

C   Copy of the original

Exh. Cat. Exhibition catalogue

f   Fax copy

fp   Fax partial copy

I   Incomplete

Iocs   Inter-office communication signed

L   Letterhead

np   No page references

Od   Original Drawing

Olu   Original location unknown

Pas   Postcard autograph signed

Pau   Postcard autograph unsigned

PS   Postscript

pu   Publisher unknown

Tda   Typed draft with autograph notes

Tel   Telegram

Tls   Typed letter signed

Tlsps   Typed letter with autograph signature and postscript

Tlts   Typed letter with typed signature

Tlu   Typed letter unsigned

Tps   Typed pneumatique signed

Archives

AB   Archivo Luis Buñuel, Filmoteca Española, Madrid

ABC   Archivo Luis Buñuel (Cartas), Filmoteca Española, Madrid

ABR   Archivo Luis Buñuel (Recortes), Filmoteca Española, Madrid

AC   Alexander Calder Foundation, New York

ACP   Art in Cinema Papers, Pacific Film Archive, Berkeley

AF   Archivo Alejandro Finisterre, [León]

AG   Archivo Antonio Gálvez, Barcelona

AGP   Fonds Anne Gérard Philipe, Cinémathèque française, Paris

ALC   Archivo Luis Alcoriza Española, Madrid, Filmoteca

AMEC   Archivo Central del Ministerio de Educación y Cultura, Madrid

ASV   Archivo Agustín Sánchez Vidal, Zaragoza

ARA   Archivo José Francisco Aranda, Filmoteca Española, Madrid

AV   Amos Vogel Papers, Columbia University, New York

BIE   ASAC Fondazione La Biennale di Venezia, Venice

BK   Bibliothèque Kandinsky, Centre Pompidou, Paris

BNE   Biblioteca Nacional de España, Madrid

BNF   Archives et Manuscrits, Bibliothèque nationale de France, Paris

BRT   Fonds André Breton, Bibliothèque litteraire Jacques-Doucet, Paris

CB	Archivo Corpus Barga, Biblioteca Nacional de España, Madrid
CBC	Centro Luis Buñuel, Calanda
CCF	Fonds Comité de Défense, Cinémathèque française, Paris
CCP	Casa de Cultura, Puebla
CF	Carlos Fuentes Papers, Princeton University, Princeton, New Jersey
CI	Archivo Claudio Isaac, Mexico City
CIN	Cinémathèque française, Paris
CL	Carlton Lake Collection, The University of Texas, Austin
COL	Archivo del Colegio de México, Mexico City
CS	Archivo Carlos Saura, Madrid
DT	Dalton Trumbo Papers, University of California, Los Angeles
ED	Archivo Eduardo Ducay, Madrid
EL	Archivo Eduardo Laborda, Zaragoza
EG	Elena Garro Papers, Princeton University, Princeton, New Jersey
EP	Erwin Piscator Papers, Southern Illinois University, Carbondale
ER	Fonds Emmanuel Roblès, Bibliothèque francophone multimedia, Limoges
ERM	Emir Rodríguez Monegal Papers, Princeton University, Princeton, New Jersey
FG	Fondo Goya, Archivo Histórico de la Universidad de Zaragoza, Zaragoza
FGL	Fundación Federico García Lorca, Madrid
FR	Archivo familiar de Francisco Rabal, Madrid
FSD	Fundació Gala-Salvador Dalí, Figueres
FT	Fonds François Truffaut, Cinémathèque française, Paris
GA	George Antheil Papers, Columbia University, New York
GAS	Archivo Luis Gasca, San Sebastián
GCI	Guillermo Cabrera Infante Papers, Princeton University, Princeton, New Jersey
GD	Fondo Gustavo Durán, Residencia de Estudiantes, Madrid
GF	Archivo Gabriel Figueroa Flores, Mexico City
GP	Grove Press Records, Syracuse University Library, Syracuse
GS	Fonds Georges Sadoul, Cinémathèque française, Paris

GT	Giorgio Tinazzi Archive, Padua
HA	Archivo Homero Aridjis, Mexico City
HB	Hugo Butler Papers, University of Wyoming, Laramie
IM	Ivor Montagu Collection, British Film Institute, London
JBB	Fonds Jacques-Bernard Brunius, Cinémathèque française, Paris
JC	Fonds Jean Cocteau, Bibliothèque historique de la Ville de Paris, Paris
JCC	Jean-Claude Carrière Archive, Paris
JD	José Donoso Papers, Princeton University, Princeton, New Jersey
JG	Fonds Jean Giono, Archives des Alpes de Haute Provence, Digne les Bains
JL	Jay and Si-Lan Leyda Papers, New York University, New York
JLB	Juan Luis Buñuel Archive, Paris
JLC	Joseph Losey Collection, British Film Institute, London
JP	Jean Painlevé Archives, Paris
JV	Fondo Juan Vicens, Residencia de Estudiantes, Madrid
LL	Colección Laborda-Lázaro, Zaragoza
LM	Fonds Léon Moussinac, Bibliothèque nationale de France, Paris
LMA	Fonds Louis Malle, Cinémathèque française, Paris
LSC	Fondo León Sánchez Cuesta, Residencia de Estudiantes, Madrid
MA	Fundación Max Aub, Segorbe
MJA	Museu Joan Abelló, Mollet del Vallés
MoMA	Luis Buñuel Papers, Film Study Center, Museum of Modern Art, New York
OL	Oscar Lewis Papers, Susan Marie Rigdon Archive, Urbana, Illinois
PB	Pierre Braunberger Archive, Paris
PBA	Fundación Pilar Bayona, Zaragoza
PK	Paul Kohner Agency Records, Academy of Motion Picture Arts and Sciences, Los Angeles
PP	Archivo Pere Portabella, Barcelona
PS	Pedro Salinas Papers, Houghton Library, Harvard University, Cambridge, Massachusetts
PU	Pierre Unik Archive, Paris
PV	Archivo Pere Vehí, Cadaqués

RMS   Archivo Ricardo Muñoz Suay, Institut de Cultura, Valencia

RS   Roxane Silberman Archive, Paris

RU   Archivo Ricardo Urgoiti, Filmoteca Española, Madrid

RUA   Rodolfo Usigli Archive, Miami University, Oxford

SS   Archivo Emilio Sanz de Soto, [Madrid]

TFF   Telluride Film Festival, Academy of Motion Picture Arts and Sciences, Los Angeles

VH   Fundación Vicente Huidobro, Santiago de Chile

VL   Archivo Víctor Lahuerta Guillén, Zaragoza

WB   Warner Brothers Archives, University of Southern California, Los Angeles

ZJRJ   Sala Zenobia y Juan Ramón Jiménez, Universidad de Puerto Rico, Río Piedras

ZS   Zachary Scott Papers, Lilly Library, Indiana University, Bloomington, Indiana

ZSA   Zachary Scott Archive, Harry Ransom Center, The University of Texas, Austin

Previous Publication

ABC   *ABC*, 25 February 1931

AGE   Jean-Michel Bouhours and Nathalie Schœller (eds), *L'Âge d'Or: Correspondance Luis Buñuel-Charles de Noailles. Lettres et documents (1929–1976)* (Paris: Centre Pompidou, 1993)

ARM   Pierre Lherminier (ed.), *Armand Tallier et le studio des Ursulines* (Paris: Association française des Cinémas d'Art et d'Essay, 1963)

AROJ   Román Gubern and Paul Hammond, *Los años rojos de Luis Buñuel* (Madrid: Cátedra, 2009)

ART   Scott MacDonald (ed.), *Art in Cinema: Documents toward a History of the Film Society* (Philadelphia, PA: Temple University Press, 2006)

AUG   Yasha David (ed.), *¡Buñuel! Auge des Jahrhunderts*, Exh. Cat., Kunst- und Ausstellungshalle der BRD, Bonn, 1994

BDM   *Buñuel entre dos mundos*, Exh. Cat., Cenart, Mexico City, 2008

BLD   Agustín Sánchez Vidal, *Buñuel, Lorca, Dalí: El enigma sin fin* (Barcelona: Planeta, 1988)

BMS   Yasha David (ed.), *¡Buñuel! La mirada del siglo*, Exh. Cat., Museo Reina Sofía, Madrid, 1996

BOL   *Boletín de la Fundación Federico García Lorca,* no. 27–28 (December 2000)

BRU   *Brújula* 8, no. 1 (Spring 2010)

BSD   Augusto Martínez Torres, *Buñuel y sus discípulos* (Madrid: Huerga y Fierro editores, 2005)

BUL   *Bulletin of Spanish Studies* 93, no. 4 (May 2016)

BREL   Antonio Gálvez, *Buñuel: Una relación circular* (Barcelona: Lunwerg Editores, 1994)

BVMC   Biblioteca Virtual Miguel de Cervantes [www.cervantesvirtual.com]

CAC   *Les Cahiers de la Cinémathèque,* no. 30–31 (Summer-Autumn, 1980)

CAH   *Cahiers de L'Herne,* no. 87 (January 2009)

CINE   Scott MacDonald (ed.), *Cinema 16: Documents Toward a History of the Film Society* (Philadelphia, PA: Temple University Press, 2002)

CILB   *Ciclo Luis Buñuel,* Cinemateca Portuguesa, Lisbon, 1982

CLB   José Rubia Barcia, *Con Luis Buñuel en Hollywood y después* (Sada: Edicións do Castro, 1992)

CUA   *Cuadernos de la Academia: En torno a Buñuel,* no. 7–8 (August 2000)

DAF   *Dalí & Film,* Exh. Cat., Tate Publishing, London, 2007

DAL   Rafael Santos Torroella, *Dalí Residente* (Madrid: Residencia de Estudiantes, 1992)

EC   *Études cinématographiques,* nos. 20–21 (cuarto trimestre de 1962)

EE   Fernando Gabriel Martín, *El ermitaño errante* (Murcia: Tres Fronteras Ediciones, 2010)

ELB   Manuel López Villegas (ed.), *Escritos de Luis Buñuel* (Madrid: Páginas de Espuma, 2000)

FA   Fundación Ramón Acín [www.fundacionacin.org]

FB   Robert Hughes (ed.), *Film: Book 1. The Audience and the Filmmaker* (New York: Grove Press, 1959)

FGL   Ian Gibson, *Federico García Lorca,* tomo 1 (Barcelona: Grijalbo 1985)

FTC   Gilles Jacob and Claude de Givray (eds), *François Truffaut: Correspondence* (Rennes: Hatier, 1988)

GOY   Luis Buñuel, *Goya. La Duquesa de Alba y Goya: Guión y sinopsis cinematográfica de Luis Buñuel* (Teruel: Instituto de Estudios Turolenses, 1992)

HJP   *Homenatge a Joan Prats,* Exh. Cat., Fundació Miró, Barcelona, 1975

ICO   Alba C. de Rojo (ed.), *Buñuel: Iconografía personal* (Mexico City: Fondo de
          Cultura Económica, 1988)

ILE   Gabriel Morelli (ed.), *Ilegible, hijo de flauta: Argumento cinematográfico
          original de Juan Larrea y Luis Buñuel* (Seville: Renacimiento, 2007)

JRJ   Alfonso Alegre Heitzmann (ed.), *Juan Ramón Jiménez: Epistolario II,
          1916–1936* (Madrid: Residencia de Estudiantes, 2012)

JOH   Luis Buñuel and Dalton Trumbo, *Johnny Got His Gun: Johnny cogió su fusil*
          (Teruel: Instituto de Estudios Turolenses, 1993)

LAT   *Latente*, no. 5 (April 2007)

LBAR   Javier Herrera, *Luis Buñuel en su archivo* (Madrid: Fondo de Cultura
          Económica, 2015)

LBFC   Ian Gibson, *Luis Buñuel: La forja de un cineasta universal* (Madrid: Aguilar,
          2013)

LBNR   Peter William Evans and Isabel Santaolalla (eds), *Luis Buñuel: New Readings*
          (London: British Film Institute, 2004)

LBOC   Agustín Sánchez Vidal, *Luis Buñuel: Obra cinematográfica* (Madrid:
          Ediciones JC, 1984)

LBOL   Juan José Vázquez (ed.), *Luis Buñuel: El ojo de la libertad* (Madrid:
          Residencia de Estudiantes, 2000)

LBS   Emmanuel Guigon (ed.), *Luis Buñuel y el surrealism* (Teruel: Museo de
          Teruel, 2000)

LET   *Letras peninsulares* 22, no. 1 (2009)

LOGD   Carmen Peña and Víctor Lahuerta (eds), *Los olvidados: Guión y documentos*
          (Teruel: Instituto de Estudios Turolenses, 2007)

LOLB   Agustín Sánchez Vidal *et al*, *Los olvidados: Una película de Luis Buñuel*
          (Mexico City: Fundación Televisa, 2004)

MED   Claudio Isaac, *Luis Buñuel: A mediodía* (Mexico City: Conaculta, 2002)

MGEN   *La música en la generación del 27: Homenaje a Lorca*, Exh. Cat., Ministerio
          de Cultura, Madrid, 1986

NCL   *Nuevo Cine Latinoaméricano*, no. 5 (Winter 2003)

NOV   *Novedades*, 9 April 1958

NUE   *Nuestro Cine*, no. 65 (September 1967)

PB   Jacques Gerber (ed.), *Pierre Braunberger, Producteur: Cinémamémoire*
          (Paris: Centre Pompidou, 1987)

PAS   *Pasarela: Artes plásticas,* no. 10 (December 1999)

POS   *Positif*, no. 10 (May 1954)

PUT   *Los putrefactos por Salvador Dalí y Federico García Lorca: Dibujos y documentos*, Exh. Cat., Fundació La Caixa, Barcelona, 1998

REV   *Revista de Catalunya*, no. 112 (November 1996)

RR   *RR Auction 16 September 2015*, auction catalogue, RR Auction House, Boston, 2015

QUE   Pedro Guerrero Ruiz (ed.), *Querido sobrino: Cartas a Francisco Rabal de Luis Buñuel* (Valencia: Pre-Textos, 2001)

RLB   Pedro Christian García Buñuel, *Recordando a Luis Buñuel* (Zaragoza: Diputación Provincial, 1985)

RUTD   Josetxo Cerdán and Luis Fernández Colorado, *Ricardo Urgoiti: Los trabajos y los días* (Madrid: Filmoteca Española, 2007)

SPA   *Cinema Sparta: Revista cinematográfica*, Yr. II, no. 29 (15 January 1936)

SSR   *Le Surréalisme au service de la révolution*, no. 3 (December 1931)

SUR   Jaume Pont (ed.), *Surrealismo y literatura en España* (Lleida: Universitat de Lleida, 2001)

TEM   Denise Tual, *Le Temps décoré* (Paris: Fayard, 1980)

TIE   Alfredo Guevara, *Tiempo de fundación* (Madrid: Iberautor, 2003)

UNI   Alicia Salvador, *De ¡Bienvenido, Mr. Marshall! a Viridiana: Historia de UNINCI* (Madrid: Egeda, 2006)

VID   Ian Gibson, *La vida desaforada de Salvador Dalí* (Barcelona: Anagrama, 1998)

VIR   Amparo Martínez Herranz (ed.), *La España de Viridiana* (Zaragoza: Prensas de la Universidad de Zaragoza, 2013)

Except where otherwise indicated, photographs have been reproduced with the kind permission of the Buñuel family and the Filmoteca Española. Every effort has been made to trace the copyright holders and obtain permission to reproduce material published in this edition. Please do contact the editors with any enquiries or information relating to this material or to the rights holder.

Introduction

'La inteligencia no tiene remedio'

Max Aub[1]

Film scholars, unlike literary historians, have not tended to produce critical editions of letters. We now have annotated editions of the correspondence of the major writers of the twentieth century (the impeccable, four-volume edition of Samuel Beckett's letters, for example)[2] and yet we still have no access to the letters of similarly revered filmmakers like Charles Chaplin, Fritz Lang, Sergei Eisenstein, Alfred Hitchcock or Akira Kurosawa, to mention but a few. With some exceptions,[3] this absence has deprived Film Studies of a resource as original and relevant as accounts of film shootings, autobiographies and collections of interviews: it is an absence that has deprived readers of essential primary source material in which the filmmakers speak in the first person and in their own voice.

There are two major reasons for this. The first is theoretical: the struggle to raise the art of making films to the level of more established art forms meant that Film Studies was dominated for many years by *auteur* theory, an approach that tends to concentrate on the aesthetic rather than the social, economic and legal factors surrounding the making of films (the latter being precisely the aspects that characterize the correspondence of filmmakers like Luis Buñuel). Even the least mythologizing versions of auteurism tend to focus on the *modus operandi* of the director in a way that diminishes the impact of salaries, contracts, censorship, box office results, etc. This approach, although undeniably enlightening, also tends to suggest by omission that the director's style is somehow unaffected by material conditions and collective

---

[1] M. Aub, 'There is no remedy for intelligence' (1971), in *La gallina ciega: Diario español*, ed. M. Aznar Soler (Barcelona: Alba, 1995), p. 602. The title of Aub's book is a reference to the children's game Blind Man's Bluff and, by association for Spanish readers, to Goya's famous painting of a group of adults playing the game. Aub uses this as a metaphor to suggest that Spain was left reeling and blind-folded by nearly thirty years of dictatorship, an allusion that is, of course, lost in the literal translation of the title into English. Unless otherwise indicated, all translations into English are by the authors.

[2] *The Letters of Samuel Beckett*, ed. M. Fehsenfeld, L. More Overbeck, G. Craig and D. Gunn (Cambridge: Cambridge University Press, 2009–16).

[3] See *Pasolini Lettere, 1940–1975*, ed. N. Naldini (Turin: Einaudi, 1986); *François Truffaut: Correspondance*, ed. G. Jacob and C. de Givray (Paris: Hatier, 1988); *Jean Renoir: Letters*, ed. L. Lobianco and D. Thomson (London: Faber, 1994); *Glauber Rocha: Cartas ao mundo*, ed. I. Bentes (São Paulo: Companhia das Letras, 1997); *The Selected Letters of Elia Kazan*, ed. A. Devlin and. Devlin (New York: Knopf, 2014).

decisions, as if it exists in some kind of super-structural limbo that is particularly inappropriate for the industrial art *par excellence* that is filmmaking.[4]

The second reason is practical. It is difficult to gain access to and make sense of the material held in film archives, and it is almost always incomplete. That is why the process is so often described as a form of archaeology: each archive is also, in many ways, a ruin. In the case of correspondence, the work of reconstruction is further complicated by the fact that inevitably the letters will be dispersed. Unless a director kept copies of their own letters, which is the exception, if they survive at all their archives will contain only the letters they received: a vital source of information, but only half of it. The papers held at the Buñuel Archives of the Filmoteca Española in Madrid include a wonderful collection of letters written to Luis Buñuel, but few, naturally, from the director himself. This archive was, therefore, a major inspiration for the search for the 'missing' other half that has led to *Luis Buñuel: A Life in Letters*.

These two theoretical and practical reasons behind the lack of published correspondence of filmmakers are tightly interwoven, making it particularly difficult to access the life behind the constructed image of the *auteur*. Or at least, this has generally been the case with Luis Buñuel: a man now regarded as one of the great twentieth-century *auteurs*, who lived through no fewer than three periods of (self-)exile and worked under no fewer than four different film industries (Spain, France, the United States and Mexico), and who therefore had to employ numerous different strategies over the six decades of this fully transnational career, to secure work in an industry that is complex and subject to a process of continual transformation.

Myth

Forged from the mid-1950s onwards, the 'myth of Buñuel' was, as one of the director's first biographers describes it, a 'necessary' myth.[5] In France in the aftermath of the Second World War (1939–45), it was linked to an attempt to recuperate the apparently vanished *auteur* of two key works of surrealist film, *An Andalusian Dog* (1929) and *The Golden Age* (1930), the latter having been boycotted immediately after its premiere by the anti-Semitic far right and all but removed from circulation from that point onwards. This was one of the major reasons why in the late 1950s, French intellectuals, film theorists and filmmakers (André Bazin and colleagues at the *Cahiers du cinéma*, Ado Kyrou and the young critics of the *L'Âge du Cinéma*, the film historian Georges

---

[4] Naturally, the auteurist approach is neither homogenous nor the only approach to the life and work of the director and there are numerous examples of excellent work in this field, including *Chaplin: His Life and Art* by David Robinson (London: Collins, 1985); *David Lean: A Biography* by Kevin Brownlow (London: Richard Cohen Books, 1996) and, more closely related to the present volume, *Luis Buñuel* by Virginia Higginbotham (London: Twayne, 1979) remains an authoritative early approach in English to the life and work of the director.

[5] J. F. Aranda, 'Buñuel entre nosotros' (1983), in *La fabulación de la pantalla: Escritos cinematográficos*, ed. Breixo Viejo (Madrid: Filmoteca Española, 2008), pp. 227–231 (p. 227).

Sadoul, and the director of the Cannes Film Festival Robert Favre Le Bret) found in 'Buñuel' an ideal challenge to the commercial and cultural hegemony of Hollywood.[6]

In Spain during the second half of the Franco Regime (1939–75), to reclaim Buñuel was to reclaim the surrealist documentary style of *Land Without Bread* (1933) and attempt to mitigate, albeit only symbolically, the effects of the Republican defeat by Nationalists at the end of the Spanish Civil War (1936–39) and the haemorrhaging of left-wing Spanish artists that 'guillotined the promising rise of the Spanish film industry'[7] in the 1930s. The trauma of the Spanish Civil War for Buñuel's generation should not be forgotten nor underestimated: no fewer than three of the director's closest friends were assassinated, barely weeks apart in July and August 1936 (Juan Piqueras, Ramón Acín and Federico García Lorca). To speak of Buñuel, in the 1950s and at the height of the Franco Regime, was therefore to honour the victims of Civil War and to attempt to bridge the gap between Spanish film and Spanish film in exile, so it is not surprising that it was at this point that the name 'Buñuel' began to symbolize a heterogeneous group of film professionals in exile including Julio Alejandro, Manuel Altolaguirre, Federico Amérigo, Max Aub, Gustavo Pittaluga, Eduardo Ugarte and Carlos Velo.[8]

In Latin America, the re-release of *The Young and the Damned* in 1951 demonstrated that it was possible to make films from, and for, the continent without kowtowing to Hollywood or to the predominant alternative at that time of Italian neorealism. This film had a singular blend of the documentary and the oneiric that inspired a new wave of Ibero-american films released during the 1960s. It influenced a generation of filmmakers working in the style now known as 'Third Cinema' or 'Imperfect Cinema', and it is no coincidence that the Mexican film journal *Nuevo Cine*, founded in 1961, dedicated an early volume to Buñuel's career.[9] Nor that shortly after the Cuban Revolution, the representatives of the newly created Instituto Cubano de Arte e Industria Cinematográficos would write to Buñuel from Havana, seeking advice on the development of a post-revolutionary film industry.[10] Nor that the *enfant terrible* of Brazilian *Cinema Novo*, Glauber Rocha, would express his public admiration for the director he met and interviewed in Venice in 1968.[11]

The myth of Buñuel was also nurtured by a number of singular feats: the addition, for example, of subversively parodic interludes to otherwise generic and commercial Mexican films – the most original, and often the most comical sequences in films like *Mexican Bus Ride* (1951), *This Strange Passion* (1953) and *The Criminal Life of Archibaldo de la Cruz* (1955) – or the infiltration and mockery of the Franco Regime that is summed up so humorously in

---

[6] See, for example: the chapter on Buñuel in A. Kyrou, *Le Surréalisme au cinema* (Paris: Arcanes, 1953), pp. 211–243; the interview with A. Bazin and J. Doniol-Valcroze, 'Entretien avec Luis Buñuel', *Cahiers du cinéma*, no. 36 (June 1954), 2–14.

[7] R. Gubern, *Cine español en el exilio* (Barcelona: Lumen, 1976), p. 217.

[8] See, for example, early texts on Buñuel, Velo and Aub published by J. F. Aranda, J. García Atienza and M. Rabanal Taylor in *Cinema Universitario*, no. 4 (December 1956).

[9] See articles by Salvador Elizondo, Emilio García Riera, José de la Colina, Jomi García Ascot, Nancy Cárdenas, Octavio Paz and Alberto Gironella in *Nuevo Cine*, no. 5–6 (November 1961).

[10] See letters from Alfredo Guevara to LB (in 1959 and 1960) in *Tiempo de fundación* (Madrid: Iberautor, 2003), p. 65 and 69.

[11] A. M. Torres, 'Echoes d'une conversation: Luis Buñuel et Glauber Rocha', *Cinéma 68*, no. 123 (February 1968), 48–53.

Alberto Isaac's cartoon, where the polemical 'case' of *Viridiana* (1961) literally backfires on General Franco.[12] This 'Buñuel', revisiting his anti-bourgeois and anti-ecclesiastical roots in *The Exterminating Angel* (1962) and *Simon of the Desert* (1965), was by now gaining public acclaim along with the attention of international film critics, and even prizes, during the final stages of his career, at the most prestigious film festivals: a Golden Lion at the Venice Film Festival for *Belle de jour* (1967); an Interfilm prize at the Berlinale for *The Milky Way* (1969); and an Oscar for *The Discreet Charm of the Bourgeoisie* (1972).

This myth of 'Buñuel', founded on a series of undeniable yet embellished facts, gradually became consolidated in a way that threatened to vacate the content, and the day-to-day concerns, of a man increasingly envisaged as a genius, set apart from an ignominious film industry, who had somehow managed to secure international fame without leaving the Mexican street, the Cerrada Félix Cuevas, on which he built his home in Mexico City: to the point where, as his sons have signalled with the laconic irony so characteristic of their father, by the 1990s 'Buñuel' was becoming no more than a 'figure in a museum' for tourists.[13]

By contrast and more recently, a number of studies based on original and diverse archival research – by writers including Agustín Sánchez Vidal, Román Gubern, Paul Hammond, Fernando Gabriel Martín and Ian Gibson – has reinvigorated the Buñuel legacy with scholarly rigor. As Sánchez Vidal points out, there is no longer any reason to cover up 'the hidden sides of a personality that needs no such compromise to convey its humane and creative scope'; these studies now also provide a vital counterweight to others whose attempt to demystify the figure of Buñuel is now 'as much to be rejected as the saintly official versions'.[14]

Each of these important studies makes assiduous use of three texts based on conversations with the director that have become the most important and most frequently consulted primary sources in the by now vast secondary literature on Buñuel. These three texts are: the interviews Max Aub recorded between 1969 and 1971 that were published after the deaths of both participants as *Conversaciones con Buñuel* in 1985; the interviews conducted between 1975 and 1977 with José de la Colina and Tomás Pérez Turrent, that were also published after some delay as *Luis Buñuel: Prohibido asomarse al interior* in 1986; and, finally, the conversations Luis Buñuel had with his great friend and co-scriptwriter, Jean-Claude Carrière, in 1981. These were transcribed by Carrière and published in the form of an autobiography, *Mon Dernier soupir*, in 1982.[15] These books are still vital to any understanding of Buñuel's world, but they do need to be read with some caution as numerous people, not least the director himself, have acknowledged his tendency to spin a yarn and,

[12] For a detailed description of this cartoon, see J. F. Egea, *Dark Laughter: Spanish Film, Comedy and the Nation* (Madison: University of Wisconsin Press, 2013), p. 81.

[13] See J. L. Buñuel and R. Buñuel, 'Afterword', in L. Buñuel, *An Unspeakable Betrayal: Selected Writings of Luis Buñuel* (Berkeley: University of California Press, 2002), p. 265.

[14] A. Sánchez Vidal, 'Prólogo', in F. G. Martín, *El ermitaño errante* (Murcia: Tres Fronteras Ediciones, 2010), 15–26 (p. 16 and p. 18).

[15] M. Aub, *Conversaciones con Buñuel* (Madrid: Aguilar, 1985), published in English as *Conversations with Buñuel*, ed. and trans. J. Jones (Jefferson, NC: McFarland, 2017). Material from these conversations was subsequently re-edited for the publication M. Aub, *Luis Buñuel, novela*, ed. C. Peire (Granada: Cuadernos del Vigía, 2013). The original publication of the interviews with J. de la Colina and T. Pérez Turrent, *Luis Buñuel: Prohibido asomarse al interior* (Mexico City: Mortiz, 1986)

of course, as Aub points out, to 'callar lo que le conviene' (not to say what did not suit him).[16]

Luis Buñuel: A Life in Letters contributes to this renewed focus on primary source material and rigorous archival research some 750 letters written and received by Luis Buñuel between 1909 and 1983. These are published here together – in almost all cases – for the first time in English and they help to fill an inevitable gap between the way Buñuel expressed himself in front of a tape recorder, or in interviews destined for publication, and the way he expressed himself in day-to-day communication with a frankness that both differs from and complements the existing primary sources. Additionally, the inclusion here of messages to Buñuel from dozens of recipients also provides direct testimony from family, friends and collaborators on the production and reception of his lengthy filmography, filling yet more historiographical gaps and providing a more collective, polyphonic 'reconstruction' of the director.

Buñuel rarely saved copies of his own letters, and frequently declared himself a dreadful correspondent. This has nurtured a (self-penned) cliché of the director as 'ágrafo' (word- blind)[17] that is quickly redressed by more detailed archival investigation. Buñuel appears to have used a certain disinclination to put pen to paper as an excuse to postpone correspondence he considered unnecessary. Just as, on other occasions, he would use his well-known hearing problems to excuse himself from public appearances: 'you don't need to raise your voice' he confessed to Aub at the beginning of their conversations, 'I hear well with my hearing aid'.[18] Naturally, Buñuel did not always say (or write) exactly what he meant, as is clearly demonstrated in this edition by the number of letters from 1961 onwards in which he announces his definitive retirement from filmmaking, before going on to make no fewer than nine more feature films including the three for which he is perhaps still best remembered (*The Exterminating Angel, Belle de jour* and *The Discreet Charm of the Bourgeoisie*).

History versus myth

Extensive research in over a hundred public and private archives, in Spain, France, Italy, England, Mexico and the United States, indicates that the far from 'word-blind' Buñuel wrote hundreds of letters throughout his life. Some are long and revealing of his work

was reissued in Spanish as *Buñuel por Buñuel* (Madrid: Plot, 1993) and translated as *Objects of Desire*, ed. and trans. P. Lenti (New York: Marsilio, 1992). The memoirs, transcribed by Carrière and first published as *Mon Dernier soupir* (Paris: Laffont, 1982) have also appeared in Spanish as *Mi último suspiro*, trans. by A. M. de la Fuente (Barcelona: Plaza & Janés, 1982), and in English as *My Last Breath: The Autobiography of Luis Buñuel*, trans. A. Israel (London: Jonathan Cape, 1984).

[16] M. Aub, *Diarios, 1967–1972* (Mexico City: Conaculta, 2003), p. 177. See also Gibson, *Luis Buñuel: La forja de un cineasta universal* (Madrid: Aguilar, 2013), pp. 25–26.

[17] Buñuel often refers to himself as 'ágrafo', a relatively common Spanish adjective derived from the far less commonly used noun 'agraphia' (that Buñuel also uses with some frequency). Agraphy, or agraphia, is the medical term for various complex neurological conditions that impair writing skills. In this edition, we have used the English term 'agraphy' to replicate Buñuel's use of the less common term 'agraphia' but have substituted the adjective (used more commonly in Spanish) with the slightly less medically related English phrase 'word-blind'.

[18] Aub, *Conversaciones con Buñuel*, p. 34.

methods (particularly those written during the early stages of his career, before 1950), others are succinct, concrete and frequently ironic (particularly those written from the 1950s onwards). They trace the various ways in which Buñuel adapted and developed his approach to an industry in a state of continual flux, and throughout a career that would result in not only the thirty-two feature films he directed, but in a significant number on which he appears as producer and/or supervisor of editing and dubbing. If, as has been noted elsewhere, the film industry evolves in response to various crises associated with the rapid obsolescence of each new technological innovation,[19] what this edition offers is first-hand insight into the strategies Buñuel adopted to face a series of crises that were both individual and industrial, and with varying degrees of success relative to his location and historical context, not to mention, of course, to the social, financial and legal conditions that affected so many of the lives of his generation of Spanish left-wing artists.

Few letters survive from his adolescence in Calanda (the small town in Aragon, north-eastern Spain where he was born) and in Zaragoza (the Aragonese capital where his family also had a home). Frustratingly few survive also from his young adulthood in student accommodation at the Residencia de Estudiantes in Madrid.[20] From 1925 onwards, when he moved to Paris, the young Buñuel wrote often to his friends from the Residencia (including Lorca, Salvador Dalí, Pepín Bello, Juan Vicens and León Sánchez Cuesta – the friend whose bookshops in both capital cities were an important point of cultural exchange for French and Spanish artists).[21] These friendships, like so many youthful relationships, were subject to prevailing passions and rivalries, and the letters show a young adult Buñuel tackling a new life: his father having died before he completed his degree in Madrid, Buñuel had abandoned the Spanish capital in search of new stimulation (he would later describe this period as 'a voluntary exile. [...] I was fed up [with Spain] and felt stifled').[22] This 'early' Buñuel wanted to become a writer. He wrote poems and short stories before beginning to discover a vocation for film, as a critic (writing film reviews to journals like *La Gaceta Literaria* and *Cahiers d'Art*); as a film programmer for the film club at the Madrid Residencia; and then, from 1929, as assistant director to the French filmmaker Jean Epstein.

Although we still have no information about the technical training Buñuel may have received as a student at the Académie du Cinéma in Paris or as an assistant on various highly successful productions, these early letters do reveal preoccupations that would recur throughout his career: the struggle to become a filmmaker in his own right ('I'm not a critic' – he wrote to Pepín Bello in November 1927 – 'I would rather have my own work criticized by others');[23] the search for creative and financial collaborators (from Lorca, to Ramón Gómez de la Serna and Claudio de la Torre); his

---

[19] R. Altman, 'Crisis Historiography', in R. Altman, *Silent Film Sound* (New York: Columbia University Press, 2004), pp. 15–23.

[20] See Gibson, *Luis Buñuel*, pp. 80, 149, 203 and 261.

[21] For more on Sánchez Cuesta, see A. Martínez Rus, *San León Librero: Las empresas culturales de Sánchez Cuesta* (Gijón: Trea, 2007). Between 1925 and 1930, Buñuel must also have written from Paris to Ramón Gómez de la Serna, Ernesto Giménez Caballero, Rafael Sánchez Ventura and José Ignacio Mantecón, but this correspondence has not been preserved.

[22] See Aub, *Diarios, 1967–1972*, p. 309.

[23] Letter to J. Bello, 8 November 1927, in *Buñuel, Lorca, Dalí*, p. 166.

stubborn perseverance with projects that would eventually go nowhere (the un-filmed scripts of *El mundo por diez céntimos*, or the biopic on *Goya* that was cancelled first by the Aragonese government and then by the Julio César production company); his early appreciation of the difficulty of combining the creative impulse (and an overriding desire to triumph in the European capital) with the need to make money (thus Buñuel calls Dalí's early triumph in Barcelona 'easy' by comparison with the no doubt 'terrible disappointments' that would await him in Paris).[24]

These difficulties may well have influenced Buñuel's self-defined 'plan of attack'.[25] Having patched up his squabble with Dalí and 'more united than ever', Buñuel would go on to write with him the script for *An Andalusian Dog* that he describes as 'without precedent in the history of film'.[26] This plan of attack would, we now know, have been impossible without vital financial family support. *An Andalusian Dog* was financed by a loan from his mother of 25,000 pesetas at a time when the average salary in Spain was around 2,400 pesetas a year, and it served as a 'calling card' to the French intelligentsia. Its considerable success put him in touch, not only with the Parisian surrealists, but also with the financial support provided by the Viscount and Vicountess de Noailles. In the space of a few brief months, Buñuel went from dreaming of literary success on the cultural periphery of the French capital (reading and listening to Benjamin Péret, André Breton and Louis Aragon) to a role, as a film director, at the heart of the Parisian cultural élite. In an expansive letter to Dalí on 24 June 1929, Buñuel says that *An Andalusian Dog*:

> will be shown at a luxury beach resort for three days this summer. The Viscount of Noailles has hired it for a screening at his palace on 2 July, and he is opening his salon on the 3rd for me to invite anyone I like. Picasso wants to come. I've met all the surrealists and they are delightful, especially Queneau, Prévert, Max Morise, Naville, they are all 'stupendous', and just the way we imagined them. On Saturday they borrowed the film to conclude a programme Artaud and Roger Vitrac were organizing at Studio 28. The theatre was full. The (very mixed) audience reacted marvellously. There was applause and whistling at the end. But they all howled and laughed in the right places. Afterwards they put on poor Deslaw's film, which was booed. You could hear people making fun of him, saying 'isn't this vanguard!' It left me firmly convinced that people can't stand [films with] upside-down houses and car wheels passing by.

An Andalusian Dog was clearly intended as a challenge to what Buñuel and Dalí considered to be the 'putrefacción' of avant-garde filmmaking. Their interest was in 'anti-artistic' film, inspired by newsreels and popular American comedies produced by Buster Keaton, Mack Sennet and Ben Turpin. The idea of Buñuel as an avant-garde 'artist' is perhaps one of the most enduring misinterpretations of the director, who made it clear in 1929 that: 'traditional ideas about art applied to film seem to me

[24] Letter to J. Bello, 5 September 1927, in *Buñuel, Lorca, Dalí*, p. 162.
[25] Letter to S. Dalí, 24 June 1929, in V. Fernández Puertas, 'Sobre una amistat: Dalí i Buñuel', *Revista de Catalunya*, no. 112 (November 1996), 85–112, p. 96.
[26] Letter to J. Bello, 10 February 1929, in *Buñuel, Lorca, Dalí*, p. 189.

monstrous. Whether we are talking about a film or a car. It is the artist who sullies the purest objects of our time.'[27]

The financial patronage of the de Noailles provided Buñuel with what he describes in a letter in May 1930 as 'complete spiritual freedom' to make *The Golden Age*.[28] This was the kind of creative control it would take him a full two decades to recover. Thanks to the extensive correspondence Buñuel exchanged with his producers during the making of this film,[29] we also have access to information that goes beyond the immediate topic to provide a unique introduction to film production in Europe at the point of the transition from silent to sound film. Buñuel's letters on the production of *The Golden Age* offer information on all aspects: from budgets and salaries to the process of writing the literary and technical scripts; from the selection and directing of the actors to the cost of hiring equipment and sets; from practical problems with shooting in exterior locations to complex post-dubbing processes and so on.

The Buñuel–de Noailles correspondence also provides insight into Buñuel's visit to the Hollywood film 'mecca' at the end of 1930, coinciding with the Soviet filmmaker Eisenstein's abortive visit to Los Angeles. Buñuel's view of US studio system was that 'they just go on making the same old films where the star is the only object and the only subject.' In December 1930 he writes:

> All the directors are controlled directly and at all times by supervisors whose job it is to safeguard moral values, public taste, political ideas, good sense, and every kind of routine human convention. They are marvellously well set up to quash any new ideas, unless they are purely technical ones. I don't mean the practical side of things, that is even more impressive than I imagined. However, I am learning to despise such levels of perfection and marvellous organization at the service of the worst kind of imbecility.[30]

It has been assumed there was a gap in Buñuel's film activities from 1931 to 1938, but the letters show just how actively he was working during what Gubern and Hammond eloquently describe as his 'red years'.[31] He did only direct one complete film during this period, *Land Without Bread*, but we now know that while he was becoming more politically aware and aligning himself with the Communist Party, he was also working on scripts (such as a preliminary adaptation of *Wuthering Heights* co-signed by his close friends Georges Sadoul and Pierre Unik); he held various roles in dubbing departments at Paramount Pictures and Warner Brothers, in Paris and Madrid; he had his first experience as partner and executive producer on four features made by Ricardo Urgoiti's Spanish production company, Filmófono and, when Civil War broke

---

[27] Cited in an interview with S. Dalí published as 'Luis Buñuel', *L'Amic de les Arts*, 4, no. 31 (31 March 1929), p. 16. See also S. Dalí, 'Film arte, film anti-artístico', *La Gaceta Literaria*, no. 24 (15 December 1927), 4.

[28] Letter to J. Bello, 11 May 1930, in *Buñuel, Lorca, Dalí*, p. 246.

[29] *L'Âge d'Or: Correspondance Luis Buñuel – Charles de Noailles*, ed. J.-M. Bouhours and N. Schoeller (Paris: Centre Georges Pompidou, 1993).

[30] Letter to Charles de Noailles, 2 December 1930, in *L'Âge d'Or: Correspondance*, p. 90.

[31] R. Gubern and P. Hammond, *Los años rojos de Luis Buñuel* (Madrid: Cátedra, 2009); *Luis Buñuel: The Red Years* (Madison: University of Wisconsin Press, 2012).

out in Spain in 1936, he supervised the editing of two propaganda films in Paris, in defence of the Republican government: *España 1936* (1937) and *España 1937* (1938). From unpublished letters Buñuel exchanged with the French producer and distributor Pierre Braunberger, we also know that in 1938 they were planning to make a feature for United Artists 'a film in favour of Republican Spain, intended to show the on-going struggle of the Spanish people'.[32]

Buñuel's progress during these years was also related to the fact that his first three films made so little money. He may have had total or near-total creative control over them, but whether it was because they were not intended to be commercial or due to the effects of censorship on the distribution of *The Golden Age* and *Land Without Bread*, Buñuel was left frustrated by attempts to market them, as can be seen from the fact that he would attempt to market different version of both these films as the 1930s progressed.[33] His work at Filmófono, on the other hand, which emulated the Hollywood studio model,[34] was intellectually unsatisfying, or so we assume at least, from the fact that Buñuel did not put his name on the credits of the Filmófono productions he was associated with, and sent an open letter to the Madrid journal *Cinema Sparta* in January 1936, to reject their notion that he was the 'putative or hidden'[35] father of those films. Both of these actions suggest that Buñuel felt torn between his left-wing political affiliation and financial reality.

He tried to resolve this conflict at various points during his exile in the United States. Shortly after arriving in Los Angeles, in an effusive letter written to the founder of Filmófono, Urgoiti, in January 1939 he announces that 'Buñuel is dead. [...] And now, without the artistic prejudices, I think I could be more useful than before'.[36] But this second trip to America only exacerbated the conflict. Buñuel's experience in the United States was mixed. It led to an enduring love-hate relationship with the Hollywood film industry, for which he would work sporadically and in a variety of roles over eight years. Buñuel had travelled to the United States on the pretext of a contract with MGM in 1938, in the end, however, he was not taken on as an advisor by the studio, but he did manage to secure work – from Spring 1941 and with the help of Iris Barry – in the Office of the Coordinator of Inter-American Affairs, based at the Museum of Modern Art in New York. Then, having lost that position as a result of pressure from the ultraconservative American press, he found work at the Loew's Theatres in New York, and in May 1944 was briefly signed up as director of dubbing at Warner Brothers in Los Angeles until the section closed down the following year. The letters he wrote during this period also

---

[32] Letter from P. Braunberger, 30 August 1938 (Paris: Braunberger Archive).

[33] For information of the attempt to release a commercially viable version of *The Golden Age* and for detail on his attempts to market *Land Without Bread* from 1933, see Gubern and Hammond, *Los años rojos de Luis Buñuel*, pp. 135–197.

[34] Documents held in the Buñuel and Urgoiti Archives at the Filmoteca Española indicate that Buñuel invested some 75,000 pesetas in the production of *Don Quintín el amargao* (dir. L. Marquina, 1935), which cost 330,000 pesetas to make and brought in over 900,000 in its first season, and that he contributed to funding *La hija de Juan Simón* (dir. J. L. Sáenz de Heredia, 1935), which cost 380,000 pesetas to make and brought in over 1 million.

[35] 'Carta abierta de L. Buñuel', *Cinema Sparta: Revista cinematográfica*, no. 29 (15 January 1936), p. [8].

[36] Letter to R. Urgoiti, 30 January 1939, in J. Cerdán and L. Fernández Colorado, *Ricardo Urgoiti: Los trabajos y los días* (Madrid: Filmoteca Española, 2007), p. 198. From 1939 to 1946, financial transactions between Buñuel and his relatives in Spain were frustrated, in part at least, by the autarky imposed on the country during the first half of the Franco Regime.

outline problems with his legal status and with the English language that had a further negative impact on his struggle to find work in the United States.

These were important and turbulent years: Buñuel was invited to present *Land Without Bread* at Columbia University and was secretly investigated by the FBI; he was asked to screen the surrealist films at the San Francisco Art Museum and plagiarized by Robert Florey in *The Beast with Five Fingers* (1946). Various projects fell through – including a story about the Los Angeles rubbish dumps co-written with Man Ray, and the script of *La novia de los ojos deslumbrados* with José Rubia Barcia –, but then, in May 1946, at a meeting in Mexico City with the Russian-French producer Oscar Dancigers, an opportunity arose to direct a commercial feature under the Mexican studio system. This project would result in *Gran Casino* (1947) starring the highly popular Jorge Negrete and Libertad Lamarque, and Buñuel's response to this opportunity highlights his need to find some form of ideological/financial compromise: 'Now more than ever', Buñuel writes in June 1946, 'I want to do interesting things and take on new adventures, like this film with Jorge Negrete, this time in order to succeed at them though, rather than to mock them as I used to from my ivory tower.'[37]

Gran Casino was the start of a new era. In spite of its lukewarm reception at the box office, it initiated a working relationship with Dancigers that would produce nine films between 1947 and 1956, and, more importantly, that would allow Buñuel to alternate commercial films such as *The Great Madcap* (1949) with more personal projects like *The Young and the Damned*. Finally, Buñuel was beginning to resolve the conflict between the creative and the commercial, a division he notes when describing his films as 'alimenticios' (bread and butter) or 'de interés' (interesting films).[38] The luxury of the early patronage he enjoyed in Paris was no longer an option, and he states emphatically in a letter to Iris Barry from Mexico City in July 1948 that 'the de Noailles no longer exist […]. But I can't go backwards and leave here. *Victory or die trying.*'[39]

Between 1950 and 1956, Buñuel made no fewer than fourteen feature films for the Mexican studios subject to similar conditions: rapid production schedule (of no more than three or four weeks); an average or lower-than-average budget; fixed director's salary (of around 25,000 pesos); and no control over the final cut.[40] It is important to note that these tendencies – towards the commercial and the personal – did not so

---

[37] Letter to R. Urgoiti, 23 June 1946, in Cerdán and Colorado, *Ricardo Urgoiti*, pp. 215–216. Dancigers also mentions to Aub that Buñuel was reluctant, at first, to have his name listed as the director of the first film he made in Mexico (see Aub, *Conversaciones con Buñuel*, p. 369).

[38] Buñuel uses the term 'alimenticio' (bread and butter) in de la Colina and Pérez Turrent, *Luis Buñuel*, p. 71; for his films 'de interés' ('of interest'), see his letter to G. Tinazzi, 11 June 1975 (Padua, Archivo Tinazzi).

[39] Letter to I. Barry, 7 July 1948 (New York, Museum of Modern Art Archive, Buñuel /12.04) (italics added).

[40] The sum of 25,000 pesos was equivalent at that time to US$3,000; established Mexican directors, such as Julio Bracho or Emilio Fernández, were receiving salaries of 70,000 pesos (see E. García Riera, *Historia del cine mexicano* [Mexico City: Secretaría de Educación Pública, 1986], p. 125). Buñuel's salary, even for higher budget films, was modest. His fee for *Robinson Crusoe* (1954), with a budget of around US$350,000, was only around US$10,000; the production cost is low by comparison with other Hollywood productions: *20,000 Leagues under the Sea*, the colour feature directed by Richard Fleischer and also released in 1954, cost US$5 million; *Rear Window*, filmed in 1954 by Alfred Hitchcock, cost US$1 million.

much clash (as the auteurist narrative has tended to assume) as work in productive synergy. The prestigious prize awarded to *The Young and the Damned* at the Cannes Film Festival in 1951 ensured the successful re-release of the film in Mexican cinemas. The intense rhythm of commercial film production (two, even three features a year) allowed Buñuel to return to Europe for the premiers of films like *This Strange Passion* and *Robinson Crusoe*, which, in turn, brought him to the attention of the critics of *Cahiers du cinéma* and *Positif* and ensured an invitation to the Cannes Film Festival jury in 1954. During this period, his letters to George Sadoul, and to Janet and Luis Alcoriza are particularly revealing about this compromise: in a letter to the Alcorizas in May 1954, he indicates his astonishment at the 'dirty tricks' played by the Cannes jury and, at the same time, his enthusiasm for screenings of *This Strange Passion* to a group of psychiatrists in Paris (famously including Jacques Lacan), and of *Land with Bread* and *The Young and the Damned* to a group of workers at the Renault factory.[41]

Of course, the phenomenon that was 'Buñuel' in the mid 1950s was not simply the result of a change in career strategy and some positive film reviews: the film industries of the Americas and Europe were also changing, and sectors of the viewing public along with them. Post-war film viewers influenced by Italian neorealism found the so-called 'cruelty' of films such as *The Young and the Damned* far more to their taste than escapist Hollywood films. And the fact that the film sold so well in France[42] is a clear indication that it was not just Buñuel, but the industry itself that was going through a process of important historical change. Numerous factors – the decline in the studio system, the introduction of more affordable film equipment, the arrival of television and the eruption onto the Western market of films by non-Western directors like Akira Kurosawa and Satyajit Ray – were influencing change on an international level. That Buñuel was asked by Aurora Bautista (in 1953) to come and work in Spain during this period on a film adaptation of *The House of Bernarda Alba*[43] is a clear indication of the effect of industry change even on a country so completely dominated by the Franco Regime: Buñuel was now both recognized and sought after.

Towards the mid-1950s, just as the 'myth' of Buñuel was becoming more crystallized, the 'polyphonic' quality of the correspondence increases. In Italy, there was growing interest in his work from scriptwriters such as Cesare Zavatini and theorists such as Guido Aristarco; in Belgium and Scotland, there were invitations to participate in the Brussels and Edinburgh film festivals; in London, the National Film Theatre held the first retrospective of his work; in New York, critics and film programmers such as Amos Vogel and Gideon Bachmann began to screen his films. Buñuel's return to a Spanish-language working environment and his resolution to pursue work in Mexico City ('*Victory or die trying*') brought Mexican citizenship, a more regular income, success within the Mexican film industry and a place, as a Mexican film director, at numerous international festivals.

During this stage, the letters selected for *Luis Buñuel: A Life in Letters* from some of his co-writers are particularly enlightening, not only for the information they provide on the shared creative process of filming (Hugo Butler and Miguel Álvarez

---

[41]   Letter to L. Alcoriza, 9 May 1954, in *Brújula*, vol. 8, no. 1 (Spring 2010), p. 27.
[42]   Letter from C. Brückner, [1951], Madrid, Buñuel Archive, Filmoteca Española (AB/691.53).
[43]   Letter from A. Bautista, 9 April 1953, Madrid, Buñuel Archive, Filmoteca Española (AB/625.1–3).

Costa) but also for what they reveal about frictions over content and authorship during pre- and post-production (Juan Larrea and Jean Ferry). Buñuel also began to contest the construction of his public image, writing to correct accounts published in various reviews (*Novedades* in Mexico City and *Philm* in Paris) and by certain critics (José Francisco Aranda). These letters also reveal the extent to which he was now preoccupied with the distribution and restoration of *An Andalusian Dog* and *Land Without Bread*, and (in the letters he exchanged with Jaime García Terrés and Robert Hughes) the production of two short texts that still offer vital insight into his work as a director: his 1954 lecture 'El cine, instrumento de poesía', published by *Revista de la Universidad de México* in December 1958, and his answers to a questionnaire in *Film*, a yearly publication by Grove Press, that came out the following year.[44]

After the success of *Nazarín* in 1959, Buñuel resolved the conflict between commercial demands and personal inclination: he regained control over the final cut and would maintain this, with isolated exceptions,[45] throughout the rest of his career. He had established a new way of working with independent producers who were able to market his work successfully on the international circuit whilst respecting, and protecting, his right to creative control. Buñuel turned 60 years old in 1960, and over the decade that followed he would work with various producers: George Pepper (*The Young One*, 1960), Gustavo Alatriste (*Viridiana, The Exterminating Angel, Simon of the Desert*), Eduardo Ducay and Joaquín Gurruchaga (on initial attempts to film *Tristana*), Serge Silberman (*Diary of a Chambermaid*, 1964; *The Milky Way*), and the brothers Robert and Raymond Hakim (*Belle de jour*). This meant he could finally balance his options in a volatile industry and take on new opportunities that would distance him from the now beleaguered Mexican studio system.[46]

The extensive correspondence he exchanged with producers during the 1960s documents the complex process of negotiation and renegotiation that characterizes his career from this point onwards. Buñuel kept to his contractual habits: a fixed salary rather than a percentage of the box office takings (although the salary was increasing), and rapid shooting and editing (although this was generally extended to between six and eight weeks). He would present ideas to a producer who would take the final decision on financial viability and thus 'commission' Buñuel. This intricate process qualifies Buñuel's slightly disingenuous claim that: 'I'm just a director for hire, all I do is turn down the ones I think are too bad.'[47] Buñuel certainly did continue working as if he were still tied to the studio system, taking offers and committing to deliver the finished product according to a strict contract: his own self-imposed restrictions

---

[44] L. Buñuel, 'El cine, instrumento de poesía', *Revista de la Universidad de México* 13, no. 4, (December 1958), 1–2 and 15; and 'Luis Buñuel', in *Film: Book 1. The Audience and the Filmmaker*, ed. R. Hughes (New York: Grove Press, 1959), pp. 40–41.

[45] Buñuel was convinced the Hakim brothers had influenced cuts to *Belle de jour*, for example.

[46] For a case study of other unrealized film projects during this period, see J. Evans and B. Viejo, '"No hay creación sin maldición": Los proyectos cinematográficos de Luis Buñuel y Carlos Fuentes', *Turia*, no. 123 (June–October 2017), 249–258. For more on the crisis in Mexican filmmaking at this stage, see E. de la Vega, *La industria cinematográfica Mexicana* (Guadalajara: Universidad de Guadalajara, 1991).

[47] Declaration to François de Montferrand, June 1954, cited in M. Drouzy, *Luis Buñuel: Architecte du Rêve* (Paris: Lherminier, 1978), p. 100.

regarding salary and timescale made him an attractive proposition for producers, who were now open to allowing him the final cut. The letters written in relation to *Viridiana* show just how effectively Buñuel was now pursuing his creative independence and the challenge that this represented to state censorship, which is illustrated by the award of the Palme d'Or to *Viridiana* at Cannes in 1961 and the immediate prohibition of the film by the Franco Regime in Spain.

The negotiation process was not over, but from the 1960s onwards Buñuel was in a far more advantageous and experienced position. This is highlighted by his frank expressions of annoyance and frustration to producers about publicity for *Viridiana* and to the editorial board of *Nuestro Cine* over their publication of an interview in which he saw himself misrepresented. It is also shown by his willingness to reject projects that did not interest him and take a lower salary for those that did. These letters reveal myriad tensions over funding for *Simon of the Desert*; censors' cuts imposed on *Belle de jour*; a boycott by students at the Escuela Oficial de Cine in Madrid over his decision to film *Tristana* in dictatorship Spain; and over various projects that would not come to fruition – the compilation film *Cuatro misterios* and adaptations of Matthew Lewis's gothic novel *The Monk*; Dalton Trumbo's *Johnny Got His Gun*; Malcolm Lowry's *Under the Volcano*; and José Donoso's *Hell has no Limits*.

At the same time, these letters also demonstrate his success at this mature stage in his career, his preoccupations as a filmmaker, the evolution of his style and how he managed to sustain, with the assistance of numerous co-workers, what he described as 'a continual margin of dissidence'.[48] He received many moving letters at this stage: from former friends (José Bergamín, Álvaro Custodio, Wenceslao Roces, Joaquim Novais Teixeira); key novelists of the so-called Latin American *Boom* (Julio Cortázar, Carlos Fuentes, Álvaro Mutis, José Donoso); co- scriptwriters and collaborators (Luis Alcoriza, Julio Alejandro, Jean-Claude Carrière, Pierre Lary); and from some of his favourite actors (Jean-Claude Brialy, Catherine Deneuve, Jeanne Moreau, Muni, Michel Piccoli, Francisco Rabal, Fernado Rey, Monica Vitti), not to mention important messages from other filmmakers (Federico Fellini, Louis Malle, Carlos Saura). These letters convey, from their many different geographic locations, multiple impressions and emotions of gratitude and congratulations in response to screenings of *The Exterminating Angel*, *Simon of the Desert* and *The Discreet Charm of the Bourgeoisie*. And they were clearly of immense value to Buñuel, who explains in a letter to Emmanuel Roblès: 'You could say that when I make a film, I never think about the public, but only the group of close friends whose opinion really matters to me.'[49]

It is still something of a paradox that the 'last Buñuel' (as we have chosen to refer to the always-evolving director in Chapter 10) would go on to direct three features in his seventies: *The Discreet Charm of the Bourgeoisie*, *The Phantom of Liberty* (1974) and *That Obscure Object of Desire* (1977). Each was produced with a relatively tight-knit group of collaborators (including Siberman, Lary, Carrière, Suzanne Durrenberger, Hélène

---

[48] Cited in C. Fuentes, 'Luis Buñuel: El cine como libertad', in *Casa con dos puertas* (Mexico City: Mortiz, 1970), pp. 197–215, p. 214; to which Buñuel added: 'These small weapons, a book, or a film, may still be useful for exposing the fascist potential that lies at the heart of capitalism' (p. 214).

[49] Letter to E. Roblès, 14 May 1962, Limoges, Fonds Roblès, Bibliothèque francophone multimedia.

Plemiannikov, Edmond Richard) and with complete creative freedom. Each was also received with almost unanimous praise from viewers and the international press alike. Always suspicious of a success he dubbed 'a bad thing'[50] (in relation to *Belle de jour*), and despite his frequent reiteration in the letters of his inclination towards a life of '*dolce far niente*' ('Nothing interests me', he writes to Ducay in September 1975 'except my sterile leisure'[51]), towards the end of this extremely productive career, Buñuel was finally enjoying an arduously fought-for autonomy. When he did finally retire at 77, he still worked on a script with Carrière about a group of terrorists (provisionally entitled *Agony, or A Sumptuous Ceremony*, 1978), and on two books, his so-called 'memoirs', with Carrière, and the edition of his *Obra literaria* that was published towards the end of 1982.[52]

This final chapter also offers new insights into his relationship with Hollywood (where he was photographed in disguise in 1973 holding the Oscar awarded to *The Discreet Charm of the Bourgeoisie*), and with a new generation of Mexican filmmakers (Buñuel agreed to write letters of recommendation for Homero Aridjis and Claudio Isaac). His position in relation to twentieth-century film history was now assured, but he also told the directors of the Casa de Cultura de Puebla in Mexico, who were launching the new Cinemateca in his name, that he would prefer they didn't name it after any director in particular, and that film should be preserved 'not as a sacred cow or museum piece, but as something living and liberating that serves to disrupt the conventional workings of thought and culture'.[53] Always provocative, Buñuel also looked back at this point on 'that mildewed and mummified corpse formerly known as *The Golden Age*' and reflected wryly on the effect of time on once radical aesthetic and political acts: 'Who would have thought fifty years ago that viewers would now watch it with an untroubled digestion and a smile on their faces. Maybe they will react the same way, and far sooner, to the Baader-Meinhof gang.'[54]

Myth versus history versus myth

Buñuel's reaction to the 'resuscitation' of *The Golden Age* is a useful reminder that it is not enough to go back to the primary source, to compile and present facts: myth will always outpace history, galvanized by our partial interpretations and biased readings of that same source material. 'I am always on the side of those who search for the truth,' Buñuel said, in this respect, 'but I drop them as soon as they think they've found it.'[55] Perhaps it was predictable then, that such a successful and committed

---

[50] Letter to F. Rabal, 29 July 1967, in *L. Buñuel, Querido sobrino: Cartas a Francisco Rabal*, ed. P. Guerrero Ruiz (Valencia: Pre-Textos, 2001), p. 67.

[51] Letter to E. Ducay, 18 September 1975, Madrid, Archivo Eduardo Ducay.

[52] A. Sánchez Vidal (ed.), *Luis Buñuel: Obra literaria* (Zaragoza: Ediciones de Heraldo de Aragón, 1982).

[53] Letter to P. Á. Palou and F. Osorio Alarcón, Mexico City [December 1975], Puebla, Archivo Casa de Cultura.

[54] Letter to E. Ducay, 17 April 1978, Madrid, Archivo Eduardo Ducay.

[55] L. Buñuel, 'Pesimismo' (1980), in *Recordando a Luis Buñuel*, ed. P. C. García Buñuel (Zaragoza: Ayuntamiento de Zaragoza, 1985), pp. 172–174 (p. 172).

iconoclast was, and will continue to be canonized; that his entertaining anecdotes and the erotic publicity stills of some of his last films prove more attractive than his life-long investigation of sexual taboos, religious hypocrisy, and social injustice; that critics pay more attention to psychoanalysing his surrealist poetics than to his interest in the fluidity of the cinematic relationship between space and time (the use of false cuts and the disjuncture between sound and image);[56] and that many will be tempted to seek the final word on what is undoubtedly an open debate. As summed up by Carrière in 1994:

> I find it impossible to say how Buñuel's mind worked [...]. There is something completely secret, completely hidden, completely unknown in Buñuel's character and it is from that part of him that his subjects arose, his way of imagining. You really can't describe it, you can't sum it up in words. You can talk about his work and try to get towards the centre of it, but the centre itself remains a mystery.[57]

Anyone looking for intimate confessions or artistic revelations in *Luis Buñuel: A Life in Letters* will be disappointed, because Buñuel was as opposed in his correspondence as he was in his films to all forms of self-involved self-expression. His approach to writing is not unlike his approach to filming: concrete, stripped of unnecessary decoration, predisposed towards humour, irony and antiphrasis (deliberately stating the opposite of what is meant). The letter-writing Buñuel challenges the traditional codes of communication in the same way that the filmmaking Buñuel challenges the institutional mode of representation. The severed eye in *An Andalusian Dog* was a statement of intent: deliberately intended *not* to please. Anti-seductive, counter-hypnotic, disenchanted with the world, Buñuel believed in film that did not believe in film (Pedro, enraged, throwing an egg at the camera in *The Young and the Damned*). And this needs to be borne in mind when reading the correspondence of this self-proclaimed 'dreadful correspondent' and 'born anti-essay-writer' (who elsewhere lamented that 'I may have some importance as a filmmaker, but I would have given up everything to be a writer'[58]). The voices heard in *Luis Buñuel: A Life in Letters* testify to the limitations of *auteur* theory. In this edition, a multitude of 'Buñuels' trace the underlying threads of a life inextricably linked to all these interlocutors: directors, scriptwriters, producers, actors, commissioning editors, film critics, distributors, novelists, poets, artists, all contribute to our understanding of the production and reception of Buñuel and his films within their historical and cultural context.

This correspondence has much to reveal: about Buñuel's life and work and the various film industries he worked under at different stages of his life, and in different countries and languages; about his experiments with conventional and subversive film discourses; about the lucrative, and sometimes ruinous, cost of production, distribution and screenings; and about the subtle, and the not so subtle, ways of censors and how to elude them. Buñuel forged a career through diverse and competitive commercial

---

[56] See the section dedicated to Buñuel in G. Deleuze, *L'Image-temps* (Paris: Minuit, 1985), pp. 134–135; *Cinema 2: The Time Image*, trans. by H. Tomlinson and R. Galeta (Minneapolis: University of Minnesota Press, 1989), pp. 102–103.

[57] J.-C. Carrière, 'Testimonios sobre Luis Buñuel', *Turia*, no. 28–29 (1994), p. 198.

[58] Luis Buñuel, *Obra literaria*, p. 18.

systems and, having started out with such exceptional patronage and creative control, he fought consistently over decades to regain control over the final product.[59] His correspondence says a lot about the on-going friction between the would-be independent *auteur* and the film industry, and the way this evolved, not as a process of head-on confrontation, but in a gradual, continual process of negotiation.

Aranda's astute and early insight into the 'real' Buñuel hints at the career path we trace in this edition of letters:

> Buñuel was famous for being impulsive, fierce and intransigent. He was, however, always capable of giving way on things of secondary importance in order to get to what was fundamental. His life was a cilice of limitations, attempts, disguises, renunciations and self-censorship.[60]

Of course, Buñuel's career was, in many ways, no exception. A detailed study of any director of Buñuel's own or any other generation, would no doubt uncover a similar process of struggle and mortification – Lindsay Anderson, Michelangelo Antonioni, Ingmar Bergman, John Cassavetes, Liliana Cavani, Miklós Jancsó, Serguéi Paradjanov, Alain Resnais, Maya Deren, Ousmane Sembene, Hiroshi Teshigahara, the list could, and does, go on. This is what Deleuze means, perhaps, when he refers to the history of film as a 'long martyrology', and notes that:

> The vast proportion of rubbish in cinematographic production [...] is no worse than anywhere else, although it does have unparalleled economic and industrial consequences. The great cinema directors are hence merely more vulnerable – it is infinitely easier to prevent them from doing their work.[61]

In some ways Buñuel was fortunate. He was not prevented from doing his work – or at least, not all of it – but, as this edition illustrates, he certainly had to contend throughout his life with the 'vulnerable' position of the film director. We hope, therefore, that the account of this process provided in *Luis Buñuel: A Life in Letters* will prove useful to all those who are interested in getting a little closer to what Carrière described as the 'mystery' at the heart of the work of the man from Calanda.

Jo Evans and Breixo Viejo

---

[59] Unlike many directors contracted to studios at that time, Buñuel co-wrote almost all his films and directed almost all the scripts he wrote. There are only four on which he is not listed as a scriptwriter: *Gran Casino, The Great Madcap, Daughter of Deceit* (1951) and *Illusion Travels by Streetcar* (1954). Scripts he was involved in directed by others at this point are: *Si usted no puede, yo sí* (If You Can't, I Can) (dir. J. Soler, 1951), co-written with Luis and Janet Alcoriza; *Johnny Got his Gun* (dir. D. Trumbo, 1971), co-written with Trumbo; and *The Monk* (dir. A. Kyrou, 1970), co-written with Carrière. For a list of unfilmed scripts see P. C. García Buñuel, 'Los proyectos de Buñuel', in *Luis Buñuel: El ojo de la libertad*, exh. cat. (Madrid: Residencia de Estudiantes, 2000), pp. 283–292.

[60] Aranda, 'Buñuel entre nosotros', p.229; the 'cilice' is a Catholic self-mortification device, usually tied to and causing pain to the upper thigh, but also linked to the use of more general methods of self-mortification associated with hair shirt and sackcloth and ashes.

[61] G. Deleuze, *Cinema 1: The Movement-Image*, trans. H. Tomlinson and B. Habberjam (London: Continuum, 1986), pp. xix–xx.

The early years: Madrid and Paris (1909–29)

Figure 2 Buñuel, top row centre, at the Jesuit school, El Salvador, Zaragoza, 1911.

To two classmates[1]

[Zaragoza, 1909]

Tomorrow, at three o'clock, I'll be waiting for you both in the alley at the Faculty. If you don't come, you'll be sorry.

Luis Buñuel

Spa Ans, AB/588; *RLB* 60 f

[1] Diego and Fernando Madrazo, pupils at the Jesuit school, El Salvador, where Luis Buñuel [henceforth LB] studied from 1908 to 1915.

To his mother[1]

[Calanda[2], 2 January 1910]

Dear Mama,

I went to a performance at the nuns' last night, with the little gypsy girl, and everyone said you were much better, although the girl from Magallón was very good. The fake thunderstorm made me laugh.

Uncle[3] and I send our regards to don Macario, kisses from me for my sisters and Churumbelo,[4] I can't wait to hug him myself, and goodbye, little gypsy girl.

Luis

Spa Als, AB/587; *ICO* 15 f

[1] María Portolés Cerezuela (1881–1969).
[2] LB was born in Calanda and spent Christmas and summer holidays there as a child.
[3] Santos Cerezuela, priest and maternal uncle of María Portolés, who added a note to this letter: 'Wishing you a Happy New Year, your uncle Santos.'
[4] Leonardo, LB's younger brother, born March 1909; his sisters, María, Alicia and Concepción (Conchita) born 1901, 1902 and 1904 respectively.

From his father[1]

Zaragoza, 1 December 1922

Dear son,[2]

Several days have gone by now since they discharged your fellow conscripts and I assume they haven't kept you at the barracks as an example.[3] Your silence puzzles us. What can be keeping you in Madrid? A sweetheart?[4] It can't be your studies, because everywhere including the university is now closed.

Love from your father,
Leonardo

PS After I wrote the above, your letter arrived saying your military service has come to an end. We are happy to hear that, although we don't understand why you are still in Madrid, with nothing to do there. There are no classes, and they will not begin for a long time, so you will only be able to study in your room. You could do that here.

Sort this out soon.

Spa Als, AB/591; *LBFC* 140–141

[1] Leonardo Buñuel González (1854–1923).
[2] Autumn 1917, LB moved to the halls of residence at Madrid University (known as the Residencia de estudiantes or 'Resi') to study Agricultural Engineering.
[3] Cuartel Daoiz y Velarde near Atocha station where LB did military service in 1921–22.
[4] Concepción Méndez Cuesta (1898–1986), LB's girlfriend from 1919 to 25.

From his father

Zaragoza, 18 April 1923

My dear son,

We agree with all the points in your letter. For your own peace of mind and ours, we must resolve the question of your degree soon, because we have now been going backwards and forwards on this issue for many years.[1] You are 23, and of an age to take life very seriously.

María[2] seems to be completely recovered. I heard that her husband paid you a visit.

Alicia y Galán[3] enjoyed Calanda, although not as much as Leonardo y Alfonsito[4] who would not leave the drums alone for a moment. This year there were 340 drums, and even three kettledrums![5] A real Judgement Day. Although we did miss the irreplaceable Juanete, who died of pneumonia just a few days earlier.

The *putuntunes*[6] put on a good show, they even saluted me for the flagon of wine Campos took to the guard post. They had also suffered a noteworthy loss: Uncle Melena, the general I gave the baton to, who did such marvellous tricks with it at the changing of the guards.

That's all. Best wishes from all, and love from your father,
Leonardo[7]

Spa Als, AB/593; *BMS* 300

[1] After giving up Agricultural Engineering, LB began a degree in Philosophy and Letters specializing in History in September 1921.
[2] LB's sister.
[3] Pedro Galán, LB's brother-in law, married to Alicia.
[4] Alfonso, younger brother of LB, born 1915.
[5] The famous Calanda drums, played at Catholic Easter processions. The reference to Judgement Day is intended to link the tremendous noise of the drums to Doomsday.
[6] Calanda residents who dress up as Romans on Good Friday.
[7] LB's father died two weeks later, 1 May 1923.

From Federico García Lorca[1]

[Madrid, 13 June] 1923

The Festival of San Antonio[2]

The first festival the good Lord sent
was for San Antonio de la Florida.
Luis: at the enchanted light of dawn
my always flourishing friendship sings.
The full moon turns and shines
in the high and tranquil skies.
And my heart turns and shines
in the green and yellow night.

Luis: my zealous friendship
crisscrosses with the breeze.
The boy plays the barrel organ
so sad, and ill at ease.
Under the paper arches,
    my hand and your hand meet.

Federico

Spa Ans, Od; *RLB* 67 f

[1]   Poet and dramatist (1898–1936), met LB at the Residencia in 1919.
[2]   '*Verbena de San Antonio*', poem by Lorca, copied by LB onto the back of photograph of the two of
      them taken in Madrid at the same festival.

To Pilar Bayona[1]

Pilar Bayona
San Miguel 12, Zaragoza

Paris, 10 October 1925

My dearest friend Pilar,
    Congratulations! May the festivities you share with Zaragoza be merry.[2] Do you
have any musical excursions planned for this winter? We could arrange something
here if you let me know in good time. A Spanish programme, perhaps, from Falla[3] to
Halffter,[4] leaving some room for Poulenc[5] and Milhaud.[6] Think it over.

A cordial handshake from your friend,
Luis Buñuel

Spa Pau (Cité y Pantéon, Paris), PBA

[1]   Pilar Bayona y López de Ansó (1897–1979), pianist, and friend of LB from 1915, born on the same
      day as the Patron Saint of Zaragoza (see below).
[2]   Yearly festivals held on 12 October to celebrate the patron saint of Zaragoza, the Virgen del Pilar.
[3]   Manuel de Falla (1876–1946), composer.
[4]   Ernesto Halffter (1905–89), composer, pupil of Falla.
[5]   Francis Poulenc (1899–1963), French composer.
[6]   Darius Milhaud (1892–1972), French composer.

To León Sánchez Cuesta[1]

Paris, 17 October 1925

Dear León,
    After a silence that now feels almost like a year, I'm writing my first letter. I blame
indolence, not me. Although I'm sure Moreno Villena and other friends who have
visited me will have sent my best wishes on their return.

I am still enchanted by this wonderful city. Paris is so welcoming you very quickly come to feel like a native. The first few months, I devoted all my time to entertainment and *dolce far niente*,[2] but now that I have completely settled in, I spend all my time reading and working. You will have heard that my plans with CICI[3] came to nothing, the simple reason being that, for now, the dire economic situation means the French government is not providing them with any funding. That said, I'm still pleased that I decided to move out of the Residencia[4] because at least I've found an environment here that is conducive to work, which, as you know, wasn't the case in Madrid. Although, now, I don't lay the blame for this so much on Madrid as on myself. This Christmas, I will probably spend a couple of weeks over there with you all, and I may publish my first book.[5] Although that will depend how much progress I've made by then.

I have attached a small book order. I would be very grateful if you could send them to me as soon as possible. As for the bill, I could either pay it in person at Christmas or, if I don't make it to Madrid, I could send it when I'm at home in Zaragoza.

Are you considering any trips to Paris yourself? Do please let me know.

Love from your affectionate friend,
Buñuel

PS Benjamin Palencia[6] sends his greetings.

[*Order*]
    Wells, *The Outline of History*.
    Spanish Authors (vol. XV: Castilian Prose pre C15)[7]
    Bible: concise edition.
    Thomas Hardy:[8] your choice, any two novels.
    Collection of Spanish folk songs with 'El vito',[9] and anything else interesting.
    A decent English grammar, in Spanish of course.
    English–Spanish, Spanish–English dictionary.
    Publishers' catalogues (Calpe etc.): novels, stories, essays and poetry.[10]

Spa Als, LSC/1a-c

[1] Bookshop owner (1892–1978), arrived at the Residencia in 1916, ran a bookshop in Madrid from 1923 to 1936.

[2] To the 'love of doing nothing'.

[3] CICI (International Committee on Intellectual Cooperation), founded in 1922 as an advisory body to the League of Nations on intellectual exchange.

[4] Halls of residence at Madrid University (known as the Residencia de estudiantes or 'Resi').

[5] Likely reference to LB's unpublished book, *Polismos (Narraciones)*.

[6] Painter (1894–1980), former student at the Residencia, with a studio in Paris from 1926.

[7] Pascual de Gayangos (editor), *Escritores en prosa anteriores al siglo XV*, M. Rivadeneyra, Madrid, 1860 (2nd edition, published by Sucesores de Hernando, Madrid, 1922).

[8] English novelist (1840–1928).

[9] Traditional Andalusian dance.

[10] Calpe (Compañía Anónima de Librería y Publicaciones Españolas) (Anonymous Company of Spanish Bookshops and Publications) founded by Nicolás María de Urgoiti in 1918.

From Salvador Dalí[1]

[Figueres, January 1926]

Dear Buñuel,

I've spent a while in Cadaqués semi-savage, swimming and painting a lot. Then another spell in Barcelona; Ballets Russes, Stravinski, Picasso, Juan Gris!!!,[2] etc.

Back in Figueres now, in the middle of carnival, where Ballet takes to the streets.

Ingres,[3] Rafael,[4] it was inevitable. If we only had the patience to learn to draw again, it could be the beginning of a great age; although I think we should still pay attention to, or better still, delight in Ozenfant[5] and metallic bridges …

[Dalí]

Spa Ad I, Od; *DAL* 133 f

[1] Salvador Dalí i Domènech (1904–89), painter and friend of LB's at the Residencia from September 1922.
[2] Sergei Diaghilev's *Ballets Russes* (1909–29), performed in Barcelona in 1925; composer Igor Stravinsky (1882–1971) and painters Pablo Picasso (1881–1973) and Juan Gris (1887–1927) collaborated with Diaghilev at various points in their careers.
[3] Jean-Auguste-Dominique Ingres (1780–1867), French neoclassical painter.
[4] Italian Renaissance painter (1483–1520).
[5] Amédée Ozenfant (1886–1966), French cubist painter and friend of Corbusier with whom he co-founded the Purist Movement.

To Federico García Lorca

Paris, 2 February 1926

Dear Federico,

It's such a shame we've let our friendship become so completely moth-eaten! You are at least partly to blame, because I've noticed you have not the slightest interest in hearing about me. You haven't troubled to inquire of any friends who might have passed on my news. I don't think the blame is all mine. As a weapon in my defence, I'm sending you this delightful portrait.[1] I imagine you will put it on one of those traditional Grenadine fabrics you always hang on your walls. My only request is that you hide me discreetly from the gaze of our mutual friend Paquito Soriano,[2] should he visit.

Are you working a lot? What are you up to? Useless questions, I'll save them for Judgement Day, if poets turn up to that particular shambles, because I know you won't answer, but 'I pardon you through God's Holy Justice.'[3]

It's a pity you don't come and spend some time over here, or at least get a change of air. You of all the people would benefit most. At least I would be able to see you all the time and patch up our old friendship. I'll never forget the intense moments we shared over those years. Madrid would seem so empty now, without any of you there and without the Residencia … As I'm sure you'd agree.

I'm working hard. At the moment, on a book soon to be published, all about cinema: aesthetics, theory, biographical sketches, and distribution, etc.[4] I'm also going to help Epstein[5] with *mise en scène*.[6] In a couple of years, I may well be just another labourer in the film industry, which is, in addition to the purely creative possibilities, very well paid. Mainly I'm working a lot and the lethargy I felt those last few months when I was living in Madrid has completely gone.

If you were in Madrid this spring, I would come and see you. I think Dalí will also be there then. We write to each other often.

Hinojosa[7] has published another book, much better than the first. It's illustrated by Manolo.[8] And he's a case in point. Paris has changed don José María into quite a different person. He has truly found himself here.

I don't want to bore you any longer. If you write, I'll send a long reply 'artfully, and with great style'.[9] But for now I limit myself to these tear-soaked lines to see if they move you to write me a long letter by return post.

Much love
Luis

Spa Als, FGL COA/144; FGL 434–435

---

[1]　Photograph of LB dedicated to Lorca (*BOL* 166).

[2]　Francisco Soriano Lapresa (1893–1934), politician and intellectual.

[3]　Quote from the 1844 play by José Zorrilla, *Don Juan Tenorio Part 1, Act 1, Scene XII*.

[4]　Possible reference to a new version of *Polismos*.

[5]　Jean Epstein (1897–1953), French director and film theorist.

[6]　*Mauprat* (1926) film on which LB worked as assistant director and played a small role.

[7]　José María Hinojosa (1904–36), poet, first book *Poema del campo* (Madrid: Imprenta Maroto, 1925); second, *Poesía de perfil* (París: Imprenta Le Moil y Pascaly, 1926).

[8]　Manuel Ángeles Ortiz (1895–1984), painter.

[9]　In Gregorio Mayan's introduction to the life of Cervantes; the words 'ingeniosamente escribió con estilo' refer to the French Archbishop Fénelon, author of *The Adventures of Telemachus* (1699).

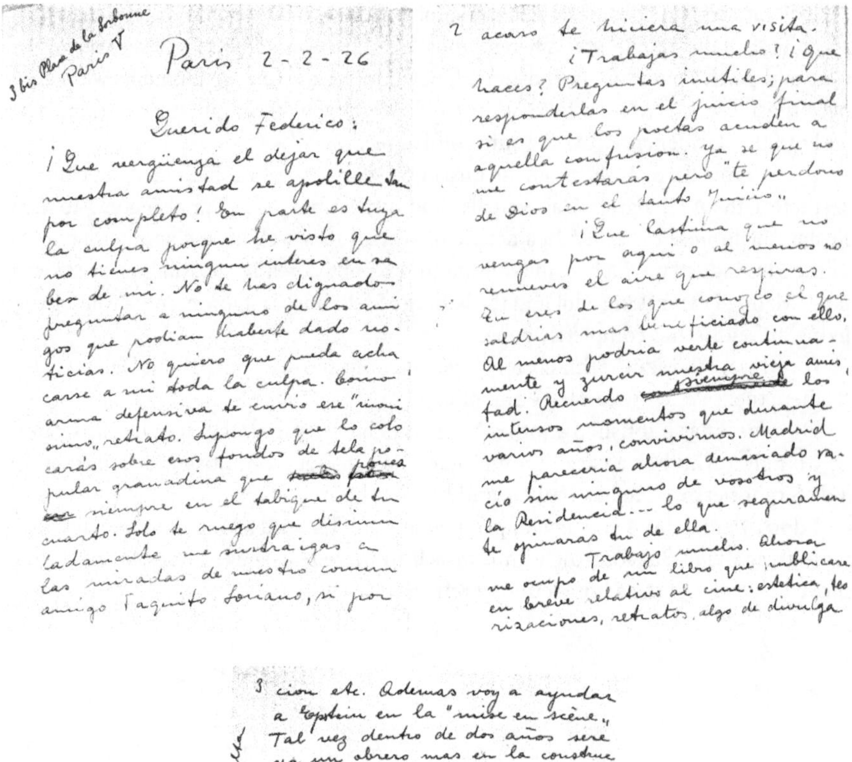
3 bis Place de la Sorbonne
Paris V

Paris 2-2-26

Querido Federico:
¡Que vergüenza el dejar que
nuestra amistad se apolille tan
por completo! En parte es tuya
la culpa porque he visto que
no tienes ningun interes en sa
ber de mi. No te has dignado
preguntar a ninguno de los ami
gos que podian haberte dado no-
ticias. No quiero que pueda acha
carse a mi toda la culpa. Como
arma defensiva te envio ese "inoni
simo" retrato. Supongo que lo colo
carás sobre esos fondos de tela popular granadina que ~~sueles~~ ~~faten~~ pones
~~ccc~~ siempre en el tabique de tu
cuarto. Solo te ruego que disimu
ladamente me sustraigas a
las miradas de nuestro comun
amigo Paquito Soriano, si por

2 acaso te hiciera una visita.
¿Trabajas mucho? ¿Que
haces? Preguntas inutiles; para
responderlas en el juicio final
si es que los poetas acuden a
aquella confusion. Ya se que no
me contestarás pero "te perdono
de Dios en el Santo Juicio"
¡Que lastima que no
vengas por aqui o al menos no
remueves el aire que respiras.
Tu eres de los que conozco el que
saldrias mas beneficiado con ello.
Al menos podria verte continua-
mente y zurcir nuestra vieja amis
tad. Recuerdo ~~continuamente~~ siempre los
intensos momentos que durante
varios años, convivimos. Madrid
me pareceria ahora demasiado va-
cio sin ninguno de vosotros y
la Residencia... lo que seguramen
te opinaras tu de ella.
Trabajo mucho. Ahora
me ocupo de un libro que publicare
en breve relativo al cine: estetica, teo
rizaciones, retratos, algo de divulga

3 cion etc. Ademas voy a ayudar
a Epstein en la "mise en scène"
Tal vez dentro de dos años seré
ya un obrero mas en la construc
cion de "films". Esto ademas de lo
que tiene de pura creacion, esta muy
bien pagado. Sobre todo, trabajo mu
cho y se me fue por completo aque
lla especie de hastio que me entro
en Madrid, los ultimos meses que
lo habité.
Si esta ~~primavera~~ primavera fueses
a Madrid iria a verte. Dali creo
que ira tambien alli, por esa
epoca. Nos escribimos con frecuencia.
Hinojosa publica otro
libro, mucho mejor que el pri
mero. Lo ilustra Manolo. Ahi
tienes un caso. Paris a converti
do a Dn. Jose Maria en otra per
sona muy diferente. Aqui se ha
encontrado consigo mismo.
No quiero darte mas
el latazo. Si me escribes te res-
ponderé largo, "ingeniosamente, con
estilo". Ahora me limito a lagri-
mear unas lineas para ver si
te conmueven y me escribes muy largo a vuelta
de correo. Un abrazo muy fuerte de Luis

Figure 3 Letter from Buñuel to Lorca, 2 February 1926.

To León Sánchez Cuesta

Paris, 10 February 1926

Dear León,

Juanito Vicens[1] has written, and he says you were asking after me. My address, by the way, is still the same: 3 Place de la Sorbonne, Paris V.

I waited for your reply for a long time and only found out much later that you had the great misfortune to lose your mother. And it didn't seem appropriate to write then, because a letter would have taken a month and a half to arrive and in that kind of situation it is often better to remain silent when the person suffering knows that his friends feel his pain. But now some time has passed, and you will have found some consolation, I wonder if you would have a few spare minutes to tell me something of your life and give me news of your plans? I would be grateful if you would.

I was in Spain at Christmas. I decided to spend it in Zaragoza with my mother, who kept me fully occupied – continually reminding me how generous she is to allow me to live so far away. I will travel to Madrid in May to publish a book. My life has taken an unexpected and definitive turn. I am now working in the film industry. I will soon start helping Jean Epstein with *mise en scène* to learn the trade. At the same time, I will publish on cinema: theory, *scénarios*,[2] etc. And perhaps in a couple of years, with some publications and the experience of working such a wonderful teacher, I will be able to work independently. Spain is truly virgin territory for a filmmaker, I'm sure you won't mind me saying. What is there already is so *putrefacto*[3] as to send any cultured man running from the screen. But ultimately, it is better, is it not, to see things, rather than just hear about them?

I would be very grateful if you could send me the attached list of books. As I won't be there until May and paying in francs is something of a nuisance, you might want to send the bill to my mother in Zaragoza, Independencia 29.

With fondest regards, your friend,
Luis Buñuel

> *Books*
> Spengler, *Decline of the West,* vol. III[4]
> Wells, *The Outline of History,* vol II Bibles
> Pepito Ortega, *La deshumanización del arte*[5]
> *Revista de Occidente,*[6] from and including no. 3 and all future monthly editions (*s'il vous plaît*)
> Has anything on cinema been published in Spain? Anything serious, that is
> *Cinelandia,* Ramón Gómez de la Serna.[7]

Spa Als, LSC/2a-c, 1d; *GOY* 127–130 f

---

[1] Juan Vicens de la Llave (1895–1959), bookshop owner and associate of Sánchez Cuesta, whom LB met at the Residencia.

[2] LB often uses the French term *scénarios* for film scripts, reproduced here in the original French throughout.

[3] *Putrefacto* (putrid): much favoured pejorative term, adopted by LB and his friends at the Residencia to refer to almost anything they disliked and/or disapproved of.

[4] Oswald Spengler, *La decadencia de occidente* (Madrid: Calpe, 1923).
[5] José Ortega y Gasset (1883–1955), philosopher, author of *La deshumanización del arte e Ideas sobre la novela* (Madrid: Revista de Occidente, 1925).
[6] Journal founded by Ortega y Gasset in 1923.
[7] Writer and journalist (1888–1963), published *Cinelandia (Novela grande)* (Valencia: Editorial Sempere de Valencia, 1923).

To Federico García Lorca

Amsterdam, 24 April 1926

Dearest Federico,

A quick note from over here as a prelude to a longer letter to follow on my return to Paris. I'm here as stage director and puppet-operator for a production of *El retablo del Maese Pedro*,[1] which opens here the day after tomorrow.[2] I'll send you the programme.[3] I spent a few days in Paris with Dalí; far fewer than we would both have wished.

Much love,
Luis

Spa Pau (Kloveniersburgwal, Amsterdam),
FGL COA/145; *BOL* [188] f

[1] Musical by Manuel de Falla based on an episode in *Don Quijote*, premiered in Paris, 1923.
[2] 26 April, at the Hollandsche Schouwburg theatre, with Willem Mengelberg as musical director and set designs by the painter, Joaquín Ruiz-Peinado Vallejo (1898–1975), who was a friend of LB.
[3] Published by Druk van Munster, Amsterdam, 1926 (AB/563).

To Federico García Lorca

Châteauroux, 18 June 1926

Dearest Federico,

Just a few lines. I'm working non-stop. The film is not particularly interesting (commercial, a crowd-pleaser), but a very useful learning experience.[1] We'll finish it in the autumn. And … I plan to start my own early next year. Now, listen carefully (and send me an honest reply): would you like to write a few *scénarios* to show on the *écran*[2] of my debut. It's very well paid, as you know, and I know you're keen to make money – however possible? That's enough for now; if you agree, I'll send more information. Write to me at my Paris address as soon as you can.

Much love,
Luis

PS They haven't even bothered to reply to me from *El Sol*.[3]

Spa Pau (rue Gambetta, Argenton-sur-Creuse),
FGL COA/146; *BOL* [189] f

¹   *Mauprat*, filmed in Paris, Romorantin and Châteauroux.
²   *Écran* (film screen), French in the original. LB raised this question again with Lorca, unsuccessfully, in postcards dated 26 June and 8 October 1926, FGL COA/147 and 148.
³   Liberal newspaper founded by Nicolás María de Urgoiti and published in Madrid from 1917 to 1936.

To León Sánchez Cuesta

Leon Sánchez Cuesta (Bookshop)
Calle Mayor 4, Madrid

Paris, 30 June 1926

Dear León,

   I got back to Paris yesterday and found, waiting for me, the book I requested from Châteauroux. Thank you. Now, I would be grateful if you could send me, as soon as possible, a cheap edition (Calpe would be best) of Cervantes' twelve *Novelas ejemplares*.¹ I'll definitely be staying in Paris until the end of the summer, by which time we will surely have finished the film.

Fond regards,
Buñuel

PS Garfias² has published a book. Would you be able to get it for me? Eternally grateful.

Spa Pau (Amstel Magere brug, Amsterdam), LSC/5; *GOY* 132 f

¹   Short stories written 1590–1612.
²   Pedro Garfias Zurita (1901–67), Spanish poet.

Figure 4 Dalí, Moreno Villa, Buñuel, Lorca and José Antonio Rubio Sacristán, Madrid, 1926.

To León Sánchez Cuesta

Paris, 14 September 1926

Dear friend León,

Just a few lines to greet you and to ask, at the same time, if you could send as soon as possible, by mail or whatever route seems quickest, the following books: *Pan y toros*,[1] *El barberillo de Lavapiés*,[2] *Las glorias del torero* (by Fernández y González),[3] *Goya* (by Laurence Matheron, published by Biblioteca Universal).[4]

Also, I think Salcedo, the author of *Historia de España*, wrote another book specifically on the reigns of Carlos IV and Fernando VII.[5] If I'm right, could you send it with the others. And if you know of any other books that focus mainly on the lifestyles, customs and traditions, major events, anecdotes, etc. of the same era, please also include them. But the most urgent are the titles above.

Yesterday, I received the official commission from the Goya Centenary Committee[6] to prepare the screenplay for a major biographical film about the painter that we will probably start in January. I'll come to Madrid sometime mid-October.

Fond regards from,
Buñuel

Spa Als, LSC/6; *GOY* 133 f

[1]   José Picón, *Pan y toros*, libretto of a *zarzuela* (comic opera) by Francisco Asenjo Barbieri premiered in Madrid, 1864, based on the life of the painter Francisco de Goya (1746–1828).

[2]   Luis Mariano de Larra, *El barberillo de Lavapiés* (Madrid, 1874); libretto of a *zarzuela* by Barbieri premiered in Madrid the same year.

[3]   Manuel Fernández y González, *Las glorias del toreo* (Madrid, 1879).

[4]   Laurence Matheron, *Goya* (Madrid: Biblioteca Universal, 1890).

[5]   Ángel Salcedo Ruiz, *La época de Goya: Historia de España e Hispano-América desde el advenimiento de Felipe V hasta la Guerra de la Independencia* (Madrid: Saturino Calleja, 1924).

[6]   A Regional Commission with links to the University of Zaragoza, in charge of coordinating activities to commemorate the centenary of the death of Goya.

To Emilio Ostalé[1]

Madrid, 18 January 1927

Dear Ostalé,

I am attaching a list of my expenses. I would be grateful if you could let me know whether you agree with it and the most convenient way for you to reimburse me. I will be in Madrid for a few more days: you can write to me at the address on the letterhead.[2]

I am working frantically to prepare a financial inventory for the film. When it's ready, I will send you a copy so that Mr Royo Villanova[3] can be sure the project is financially viable before contracting anyone. I will also send a copy to the officials of the Special Centenary Committee involved in producing the film. You will remember,

I think, that this is what we agreed at our last meeting with Mr Montserrat and the other gentlemen.

I have arranged all this at my own expense, to make sure that both the artistic and financial side of the film are as perfectly legal and correct as they would be for any other kind of business. If things do not work out this time, I shall consider my role in this venture to have come to an end.

Naturally, wherever financial backing comes from in the end, the film will remain under the control of and dependent on the Centenary Council.

I ask you please to respond to this letter as soon as you are able, your dear friend,

Luis Buñuel

Account of expenses
Paris–Irun (11 November 1926) = 372 francs, exchange at 23% = 85 pesetas
Irun–Zaragoza (*idem*) = 50
Zaragoza–Madrid (27 November 1926) = 50
Madrid (Hotel Nacional, 4 days at 14 pesetas) = 56
Madrid (9 meals at 6 pesetas) = 54
Madrid–Hendaye (2 December 1926) = 98
Hendaye–Paris (*idem*) = 372 francs, exchange at 25% = 93
Paris (4 days at Trianon-Palace, at 55 francs) = 220 francs, exchange at 25% = 55
Paris (9 bis Pl. Sorbonne, 17 days at 27 francs) = 459 francs, exchange at 25% = 114
Paris (21 days with 42 meals at 20 francs) = 840 francs, exchange at 25% = 21
Paris (typist, 4 days at 30 francs) = 120 francs, exchange at 25% = 30
Paris (automobile rental, 4 days at 20 francs) = 80 francs, exchange at 25% = 20
Paris (assistant, 2 days at 50 francs) = 100 francs, exchange at 25% = 25
Paris–Irun (22 December 1926) = 372 francs, exchange at 26% = 96
Irun–Zaragoza (*idem*) = 50
[Total =] 1086

Notes[4]
1) The accounts begin with my first trip from Paris for the reading-through of the *scénario*, and end with my trip to Zaragoza of 22 December 1926.
2) All expenses incurred gradually worked out at a *de facto* exchange rate of 25%.
3) All figures rounded down by default, except for travel, which has been rounded up.

Spa Als M, FG/III/1927(18-B.7); *GOY* 136–140 f

[1] Emilio Ostalé Tudela, journalist and secretary to the Regional Council for the Goya Centenary.
[2] Hotel Nacional, Madrid.
[3] Ricardo Royo Villanova (1868–1943), doctor and rector of Zaragoza University, 1913–28, and Council President.
[4] Notes by LB.

Figure 5 Buñuel, first on left, with cast of *Master Peter's Puppet Show*, Amsterdam, April 1926.

To Emilio Ostalé

Paris, 30 March 1927

Dear Ostalé,

As the time I set aside for the successful conclusion of the film project has come to an end, I consider my role in this to have come to an end also. I am writing, therefore, to advise you that I am distancing myself from the project and that I regret, as we all do, that it has been impossible to proceed due to lack of funds. The measures I undertook with the assistance of my friend don José Ignacio Mantecón,[1] as specified in the report, and with your support, have also come to nought.

I therefore ask that you kindly to reimburse the 1,086 pesetas that – as was agreed – I am owed for travel undertaken at the beginning of last December. You may deliver the money to my family home and my mother will ensure it gets to me.

I ask you please to reply to this letter, so I may put my mind at rest on this matter.

With cordial greetings from,
Luis Buñuel

Spa Als, FG/III/1927(18-B.7); *GOY* 147–148 f

---

[1]   José Ignacio Mantecón Navasal (1902–82), historian and politician, childhood friend of LB.

To León Sánchez Cuesta

Madrid, 21 April 1927

Dear friend León

I hope you will forgive me for not having written or sent the money yet, but I have been so dreadfully busy these first three days of my stay in Madrid. If it is not too much trouble, I would prefer to send you the money as soon as I receive my salary towards the end of the month. I could pay you now, but if the delay is not too much of an inconvenience for you, it would be much easier for me to pay in a few days. Thank you.

Now for news. People ask after you constantly. I have described the *boutique*[1] in such glowing terms some wonder if I am getting it confused with Notre Dame. I had lunch today with don Alberto,[2] who is very interested in the screening, but the films have still not arrived yet.[3] What can be happening to them? We have hounded the Ministry of State here, and they have finally written a letter the person bringing the films will be able to present at the border, so the customs officials will let them through. Do you know if anyone is planning to travel in the coming days? Corpus[4] hasn't written, and we don't even know if he has the films.

Ramón is delighted with the project I have asked him to be involved in.[5] He is going to write an original script and is dedicating most of his energies to raising money for *Goya*, based on his *scénario*. We shall see.

Pittaluga's[6] film, according to the current plan, will cost 125,000 pesetas!!! One of Conchita Méndez's brothers was going to give him 15,000, but he has left the city and no one has heard from him. They want to meet up with MacKinley now, to get him involved in the project. Those fellows really do have a feverish imagination!

Don Alberto and I would be extremely grateful if you could do us the following favour. In Place de la Madeleine, as you approach along the Rue Royale and immediately on the right, there is an important music shop. Could you please ask them to look for the Erik Satie's[7] score for *Entr'acte* by René Clair,[8] not the score itself, but Darius Milhaud's adaptation for violin and orchestra. That is all, simply to make the request and the payment. They will make the arrangements to send it.

I saw Palencia, so pleasant and 'eager to please'. He's leaving for Paris on Sunday.

I haven't seen Juanito yet: I'm going to spend the whole morning with him tomorrow. My address is: Ram,[9] 8 Plaza de Bilbao.

Fond regards,
Luis Buñuel

Spa Als, LSC/9a-b

---

[1]   Likely reference to the Spanish Bookshop Sánchez Cuesta was about to open in Paris at 10, rue Gay-Lussac.

[2]   Alberto Jiménez Fraud (1883–1964), professor and director of the Residencia from 1910 to 1936.

[3]   Experimental films LB wanted to screen for the Sociedad de Cursos y Conferencias at the Residencia in May 1927.

[4]   Andrés García de Barga (1887–1975), writer known by the pseudonym Corpus Barga, uncle of Ramón Gómez de la Serna.

⁵ LB contracted Gómez de la Serna to write a screenplay based on some of de la Serna's own short stories initially entitled *El mundo por diez céntimos*, then *Caprichos* after Goya's set of eighty prints by that name.
⁶ Gustavo Pittaluga González del Campillo (1906–75), composer.
⁷ French composer (1886–1925).
⁸ *Entr'acte* (*Intermission*, 1924), a film influenced by DADA and directed by René Clair (1898–1981).
⁹ Hotel in Madrid.

To León Sánchez Cuesta

Madrid, 24 April 192[7]

Dear León,

On behalf of Don Alberto, could I ask you to go to the Vieux-Colombier theatre,[1] at no. 21 in the street of that same name, between 11 and 12 o'clock, and ask them to send to the Residencia the slow-motion studies 'Revolver bullet', 'soap bubble', 'bull catching the bullfighter', by post or any other means, paying the duty on them. We need it before the 4th. It's a small amount of footage so the duty should not be too high. If they offer you Renoir's dream[2] sequence you can say no, because that is arriving in Madrid on Wednesday with the other films. Ortiz Echagüe, from *La Nación*,[3] is bringing them.

As you can see, it won't be too much bother; it should only take half an hour. You should tell them where the films are going and let them know that we got the dream and *Rien que les heures*[4] for 1,500 francs just in case they ask you for a lot of money. Although I don't think they will ask for more than 500 francs. We would be happy with the three slow-motion studies mentioned above, around 40 metres of film in total that, if possible, should be separated from the rest of Vieux-Colombier's short film. One last thing: if they ask you to name a price, you should offer 250 francs and, if they can only give the full film, go up to 500 francs. Corpus has some money left over.

I saw Juanito yesterday and invited him to lunch on Tuesday.

I will get the money very soon and will send it to London straight away.

Fondest regards, your friend
Buñuel

PS Any news of the score? I promise we won't bother you anymore. If it is too much trouble for you to go to the Vieux Colombier, ask Peinado, who knows Jean Tedesco,[5] the director, very well.

I found the pre-war films here in Madrid.

I will pass by your house on Monday to see Luis.[6]

Spa Als, LSC/3a-c; *LBOL* 334–335 f

¹ Theatre and location of numerous avant-garde film screenings in Paris during the 1920s.
² Slow-motion dream sequence from *La Fille de l'eau* (1925) dir. Jean Renoir (1894–1979).
³ Fernando Ortiz Echagüe (1893–1946), Spanish correspondent for the Buenos Aires newspaper, *La Nación*.

4 *Rien que les heures* (1926), experimental film by Brazilian director Alberto Cavalcanti (1897–1982).
5 French director (1895–1958) and director of the Vieux-Colombier Theatre from 1924 to 1934.
6 Brother of León Sánchez Cuesta.

To the Zaragoza Regional Commission for the Goya Centenary

Zaragoza, 24 June 1927

I hereby confirm receipt of 750 pesetas from the Zaragoza Regional Commission for the Goya Centenary as payment in full for preparatory work undertaken, on behalf of the Commission, towards the making of a film about Goya.

Luis Buñuel

Spa Tls, FG/III/1927(18-B.7); *GOY* 15 f

To León Sánchez Cuesta

Paris, 28 June 1927

Dear León,
Could you enquire about any other interesting books on banditry? Alternatively, which of the Zugasti[1] volumes do you think would be the most useful – in terms of action, narrative, information, etc. – for my *scénario*? I'm surprised there are so many volumes. I would be grateful if you could give this your full attention. I will write from Brittany with my address for the summer.

Regards,
Buñuel

PS The bookshop, *wonderful*.

Spa Pau (Jardín del Palacio Real, París), LSC/12; *GOY* 152 f

1 Julián de Zugasti y Sáenz (1836–1915), politician and author of *El bandolerismo: Estudio social y memorias históricas* in 10 vols. (Madrid: T. Fortanet, 1876–80).

To León Sánchez Cuesta

St. Michel-en-Grève, 28 July 1927

Dear León,
Your letter arrived today. I'm replying in haste so that, for one thing, you don't write back to this address, because I'm leaving for Paris the day after tomorrow. Along with your letter, I received another offering me the position of 'assistant

director' on a film that Alex Nalpas[1] is making with Josefina Baker.[2] I accepted, naturally, and will send my new address (*pas*[3] Place de la Sorbonne). They're even paying me for this *engagement* (I don't mind telling you), though not a lot. Plus, board and lodging although I won't believe it until I see it, or at least until the money's in the bank. I'm also preparing something to be presented in Madrid and Barcelona. Until that's accepted, I shall continue working over here as an assistant director, which is an important role, although one that, in my particular case, is not well paid. And, while I think of it, if you happen to see Ramón, could you try to find out, diplomatically, whether he is still writing the script for me. He accepted when I proposed it in May and I've written to him subsequently, but as is always the case when I'm expecting something interesting to happen, I've heard nothing more.

Other news. Bores[4] has sold 17 paintings to Paul Rosenberg.[5] Incredible! I don't have the details. The others are still in Paris, stalking dealers and critics. Cossío,[6] a 1,000-peseta prize in a poster competition run by an insurance company from Zaragoza. Hernando,[7] making model puppets for a film by Henri Gad,[8] the director I might work with if Ramón ever sends me his screenplay.

I'm working on a book for October providing I have, as I have up until now, some free time. I'm about halfway through. Title: *Polismos (Narraciones),*[9] which I know you won't like, although admittedly, I've never read any of it to you. I'll publish it in *Litoral*[10] or in *La Gaceta.*[11] It's dedicated to Vicens, Sánchez Ventura[12] and Pepín.[13] Do you ever publish anything yourself?

The parcel arrived with your usual punctuality, for which I am truly grateful.

Everyone at the restaurant was asking after you. I do believe they have lost their best customer. Do whatever you can to get here in October. Remember you promised me an evening 'without prejudice or theology',[14] and you haven't made good on that yet. By then, I shall be a close friend of Josefina Baker, and we'll spend the night at her *petite boite*[15] in Montmartre. Also, you left without visiting a single studio, although Mr Don Francisco Goya was, of course, still driving me mad then. I don't know whether I told you I was on the brink of suing Royo Villanova and his puppets. Still, I managed to get 750 pesetas of the 1,000 or so they owed me.

Please send my greetings to Luis, and to Juanito if he writes to you. And for you, fondest regards from

Luis Buñuel

Als, LSC/14a-d; *GOY* 154–157 f

---

[1]   French director, also known as Mario Nalpas.
[2]   *La Sirène des tropiques* (The Siren of the Tropics, 1927), co-directed by Nalpas and Henri Étiévant (1870–1953), with Josephine Baker (1906–75).
[3]   French in the original, 'pas' (not) and 'engagement' (job).
[4]   Francisco Bores López (1898–1972), painter and illustrator, moved from Madrid to Paris in 1925.
[5]   French art dealer and agent of artists including Picasso (1881–1959).
[6]   Francisco Gutiérrez Cossío (1894–1970), painter, moved to Paris in 1923.

[7] Hernando Viñes Soto (1904–93), painter, shared a Paris studio with Joaquín Peinado.

[8] Pseudonym of Henri Fischman (1885–1930), experimental Romanian filmmaker, dir. *Le Cabaret épileptique* (1928).

[9] '*Polismos*', LB's neologism for 'various – poly – isms', '*narraciones*' (narrations, narratives, stories or tales).

[10] Literary magazine founded in Malaga in 1926 by poets Emilio Prados Such (1899–1962) and Manuel Altolaguirre Bolín (1905–59) along with with a number of Spanish poets of the Spanish literary movement known as the 'Generation of 27'.

[11] *La Gaceta Literaria*, cultural review in which LB published a number of articles on film, edited by Ernesto Giménez Caballero (1899–1988) and published in Madrid from 1927 to 1932.

[12] Rafael Sánchez Ventura (1897–1990), university professor and childhood friend of LB.

[13] José "Pepín" Bello Lasierra (1904–2008), writer, and friend of LB from the Residencia from 1917.

[14] Biblical allusion to Luke the Evangelist.

[15] French in the original (small nightclub).

To José Bello

Brittany, 28 July 1927

Pepín,

I've received an *asquerosa*[1] letter from Federico and his acolyte Dalí. He has him enslaved. I'm returning to Paris as the *assistant*[2] on the film Henri Étiévant is making with Josefina Baker. I'll write from there. Why haven't you replied yet? I'm writing a book called *Polismos (Narraciones)* to be published in September if the job leaves me any free time. I think it's going to turn out really well. I'm dedicating it to Sánchez Ventura, Vicens and to you. I'm about half-way through.

Fond regards and see you in Paris,
LB

Spa, Od; *BLD* 158

[1] Spanish word 'asqueroso' – left untranslated in this letter, and the one below, as LB's wordplay depends on the connection between the Spanish adjective (disgusting) and the town, 'Asquerosa', where Lorca lived as a child (renamed Valderrubio in 1943).

[2] French in the original.

To José Bello

[Paris,] 22 August 1927

Dearest Pepín,
    Your letter arrived.
    Congratulations on your job
    I'm still the assistant on *La Sirène des tropiques*.
    Working 10-hour days.

Neglecting my book for lack of time.

Have come up with two stupendous scripts.

But no time to write them.

I'll be making a film in Greece in the spring.

In Spain this winter:

Project with Ramón.

Project with Sánchez Mejías[1] (top secret).

Josefina Baker's arse is piston-powered.

My director is, mentally and physically, very similar to Don Ricardo de Orueta.[2]

Dalí has written me some *asquerosas* letters.

He is an *asqueroso*.

And Federico is doubly *asqueroso*.

For being from Asquerosa and *asqueroso*.

I've seen your engineer-diplomat twice in the Dome.[3]

He's so ugly!!

And, worse still, he knows it.

I'm waiting for a reply from that nice Mejías.

If things work out, I'll let you know.

But for now, don't breathe a word!!!

Problem:

$x^2 + 2x - x = 3b$, $3b = x$, $x = $ me and you.

I'll send you photos of the film.

Write.

Our theatrical *Polismo*[4] is masterful

Tell me about your life in Seville.

But, come back to Madrid!![5]

I always remember our early mornings in Madrid and at the Prado.

LOVE,
Buñuel

PS I'd like to read you bits of the book. It's your kind of thing.

Spa Als, Ou; *BLD* 157 f

---

[1] Ignacio Sánchez Mejías (1891–1934), bull-fighter and dramatist.
[2] Ricardo de Orueta y Duarte (1868–1939), art historian.
[3] The *Dôme*, famous café in Montparnasse.
[4] Reference to *Hamlet (tragi-comedia)*, a four-act play co-written by LB and Bello, performed at the Café Select, Paris, possibly in July 1927.
[5] Bello was working for the Ibero-American World Fair held in Seville, 1929.

Figure 6 Buñuel, bottom row second from the right, with Baker and the crew of *Siren of the Tropics*, Paris, August 1927.

To José Bello

Paris, 5 September 1927

Dearest Pepín,

Your letter arrived, so delectably rich in news. I'd almost forgotten the barrel-belly story[1] and I obsessed about it again for several hours. Uzelay,[2] who was with me at the time, had to listen to me telling the story of the Sharif of Morocco's troops a hundred times. He couldn't stop laughing at my splendid rendition. You are so right, and so astute, to call it the children's story *par excellence*. Here is the story of the Moroccan troops:

'There was once a troop and it was Moroccan. And I was there, and I was already there with them. And a little Arab fella died, then the prickly pear and the troops too. And then there were some shots, and a woman and I died too, so I wasn't there anymore. And then it got very scary with the Moroccan troops and *I think that's it.*'

Paris, crummy. Allué Salvador[3] came yesterday with 500 sons of bitches … to play football. They brought a band with them from Zaragoza (wouldn't your skin just crawl to hear, directly after eating out in all the dust and filthy denizens of the Paseo de la Independencia, a hospice band playing Marina's *La fenestra se ubre*?[4]). They played *jotas*[5] throughout the game. A lot of rot from a lot of rotten rabble.[6]

It's very good that things are over with Araceli.[7] You have a lot to tell me. Although I won't be coming to Spain unless something definite turns up.

I've finished the interiors. We leave for Dieppe tomorrow and then to Fontainebleau.

That is unless I can find another *metteur en scène*[8] to work with, which is what I want. I'll send you a photo of me with Baker and the *metedores*.[9] But for now I'm sending you this one taken between filming.

Federico really pisses me off. I knew the boyfriend was a *putrefacto*,[10] but Federico is even worse. His dreadful aestheticism has driven a wedge between us. His rampant narcissism already made it difficult for him to have pure friendships. Well, I'm done with him. The worst of it is that his work may even suffer.

Dalí is head-over-heels. He thinks he's a genius now, all puffed up by Federico's affections. He writes saying 'Federico is better than ever. He's the real thing. His drawings are incredible. I'm doing extraordinary things, etc., etc.' Well, it's easy to say that when you're in Barcelona. He is going to find Paris a terrible disappointment. I'd love to see him come over here and start again, away from García's perverse influence, because there is no doubt that Dalí is very talented.

Congratulations on your job. It goes without saying that it would be much better for you to finish your studies[11] then get whatever kind of job you choose. Still, it's your decision. You'll see.

Send me Sánchez Mejías's permanent address. I'm not sure if he got my letter. Pepín, be very careful with him, because all my business arrangements with him are up in the air. It would be best not to say you've heard I wrote to him. If he accepts my proposition, the film could be a big success. I just addressed my letter to him at the Club Joselito, Seville.

And that's that and me with it,[12] love and goodbye,

Luis

PS You can always write to rue de la Glacière.[13] If I leave, they will forward my correspondence on daily. I've put in a note for you to give to our friend J. I.[14]

Spa Als, Od; *BLD* 160–162 fp

---

[1] Probable reference to a sarcastic story Bello tells about Hinojosa, referred to as a 'vil colodra carpetovetónica' (common wine barrel), and whose Andalusian accent LB mocks in the nonsense story that follows in a way that is impossible to replicate in the English translation.

[2] José María Uzelay (1903–79), painter.

[3] Miguel Allué Salvador (1885–1962), Mayor of Zaragoza from January 1927 to June 1929.

[4] Joke, with sexual innuendo, on the Spanish phrase 'la ventana se abre' (the window opens), replacing *abre* (opens) with *ubre* (udder).

[5] Folk dance from Northern Spain.

[6] The original 'Qué horrendo carnuzismo el de esa gentuza' uses a favourite word of Bello's – derived from *carnuzo* meaning 'rotting', or 'rotten flesh' and by extension, 'people'. This also echoes the friends' use of 'putrefacto' (rotting) as a catch-phrase for general distaste.

[7] Araceli Durán Martínez, girlfriend of Bello and sister of the composer Gustavo Durán (1906–69), whom LB met at the Residencia in 1922.

[8] French in the original (film director).

[9] Spanish wordplay on the French *metteurs*, used to differentiate Nalpas and Étiévant from more distinguished filmmakers.

[10] 'Putrefacto' one of Buñuel and Resi friend's favourite pejorative terms.

[11] Bello is giving up studying Medicine in Madrid.

[12] LB reverts to untranslatable mock-Andalusian here: 'ya etá y yo con eto'.

[13] LB is staying at the Hôtel des Terrases, 74 rue de la Glacière, Paris, XIII.
[14] Jose Ignacio Mantecón, working with Bello at the Ibero-American World Fair.

To José Bello

Paris, 8 November 1927

Dear Pepín,

I've received both your letters and, as you can see, am replying immediately as requested. I'm extremely busy. I've been appointed editor of the new cinema section for *La Gaceta Literaria,* responsible for compiling, requesting contributions, rejecting articles, reporting news, interviews, etc., etc.. I've already sent in the material for the first edition: it will have an article by Giménez Caballero introducing the new section and me, a long piece by Epstein, an article of mine with two great photos, an article by Dalí, literary-film news, etc., etc., etc. It's going to be splendid, because it will be the only cinema section in Europe with no advertisements and with articles that explore cinema from a theoretical and unbiased perspective.[1] It will also include protest pieces and interviews about the shortcomings of the cinema in Madrid, etc. Giménez Caballero writes almost every day; he has been extremely friendly and has given me complete editorial freedom.

Also, and this is even more serious, the day before yesterday I was offered a job at *Cahiers d'Art*.[2] There, I'll also be responsible for compiling the cinema section and requesting, selecting and rejecting contributions. That should really open doors for me in Paris. I start with the next edition. As you know, it's the best modern art review in the city. I'm very grateful to Mr Zervos[3] for the honour. But in spite of this success as a critic, I am not, God forbid, a critic! I would prefer my own work to be criticized by others. Still, it's a useful start.

I'll be working with Epstein again soon,[4] hoping that Ramón will send me his script. That son of a … promised I would have it by the 15th of last month, and I've heard nothing so far. I've put all my hopes for a screen debut into that project. I have an excellent financial plan, as you will see. It will be a Franco-Spanish film. But without the *scénario* I'm stuck. Once I've got it, I will still have to work on it for a month, plus another two to set up the company and then start filming. So even if all goes well, I won't be able to start on my first film until March. It will include German, French and Spanish actors, and a friend or two, including you, if you like, and Santa Cruz.[5]

I think my book will turn out well. It's half-finished. I've pushed on with it over the last few days, but the criticism is killing me.[6] I'll chop my own ear off if I don't get it out one way or another this winter!

I published Dalí's article *out of pity*. I look at everything from my position as an editor, but I can see straight through his theories and his vanguard-eze. My article, the one I published in *Cahiers d'Art*, already says everything he's trying to say now.[7] And there's really no need for him to exaggerate. There are some extraordinary and ingenious German films. And some, though fewer, French ones. *L'image* by Feyder,[8] *Coeur fidèle* by Epstein,[9] *Feu Mathias Pascal* by L'Herbier,[10] etc. He's right, of course, but none of this is new. Poor Dalí is definitely beginning to lag behind. I know full well he's sending photos to the dealers around here. Rosenberg says that he doesn't draw badly and Pierre,[11] the surrealist, says he's influenced by Miró.[12] No one has bought anything from him yet and that's the extent of his success. In Spain, though, everyone is still saying 'How brilliant! How very modern.' He's being left behind. It's Federico's fault. His banquet was a big deal of course: you can read all about it in *La Gaceta.*[13]

Paragraphs:
Our editor-in-chief organized the banquet, not for him, but so that the guests could express their opinions out loud rather than whispering them under the tables.
Ramón stood up:
–Of all those present, I am the only one who has seen the work.
Laughter.
–And I can assure you that it exudes great freedom, great freedom, great freedom.
Laughter.
Of course – he adds – none of those present here today have seen the play.
Etc.

Poor old Federico must have felt like crying. The guests, revolting: Margarita Xirgu,[14] Natalio Rivas,[15] Benavente,[16] the Ambassador of Paraguay, Dalí, etc.
It serves him right and I am infinitely happy for him. The work has been a complete failure. Fernández Ardavín and Villaespesa[17] are the only ones who could possibly envy him. Still, it did earn him 12,000 pesetas.
Sánchez Mejías has behaved very badly. He hasn't replied to any of my letters. Don't say anything to him. I don't need him anymore.
Sota's[18] son-in-law, from Bilbao, has written to ask me to make a film for him and has sent me the play he wants me to adapt. With customary bluntness, I wrote back saying it needed a lot of editing and adaptation. I'm waiting for his reply. But I fear he may have taken offence or got cold feet. Grant me patience, and may we resist the temptation to do a Mariana Pineda!![19]
And what about you, Pepín? Now it's your turn to reply to this letter with all the details of your life.

Much love
Luis

PS If you write me something about cinema for *La Gaceta, I will publish it*. I am still in charge. Write four or five good pages. I'll put it next to a long piece by L'Herbier on the second page.[20] Write something about Menjou[21] and send it to me here. I'll add the photos.

Spa, Od; *BLD* 166–167

---

[1] See *La Gaceta Literaria*, no. 24 (15 December 1927), pp. 4–5 for the articles LB mentions including Dalí's 'Film-art, Anti-artistic Film' and a 'Note' by LB about Charles Chaplin's (1889–1977) proposed biopic about Christ.
[2] Cultural review founded in Paris in 1926.
[3] Christian Zervos (1889–1970), art historian and founder of the journal *Cahiers d'Art*.
[4] On *La Chute de la maison Usher* (1928), based on the story by Edgar Allan Poe (1809–49).

[5] Friend of Pepín Bello's from the Medical Faculty.

[6] Joke: play on words involving criticism and his job as a critic.

[7] In 1927 LB published reviews of three film premieres in a supplement, 'Feuilles volantes' (Flying Leaves) for *Cahiers d'Art: Napoleon*, dir. Abel Gance (Year II, no. 3, p. 3); *The Way of All Flesh*, dir. Victor Fleming (Year II, no. 10, p. 6); and *College*, dir. Buster Keaton (Year II, no. 10, pp. 6–7).

[8] *The Image* (1926) dir. Jacques Feyder (1885–1948), Buñuel played a small role in Feyder's *Carmen* (1926).

[9] *Faithful Heart* (1923).

[10] *The Late Mathias Pascal* (1925), dir. Marcel L'Herbier (1888–1979).

[11] Pierre Loeb (1897–1964), French art dealer and owner of Galerie Pierre, where an exhibition of surrealist painting was held in November 1925.

[12] Joan Miró (1893–1983), Spanish painter.

[13] See *La Gaceta Literaria*, no. 21 (1 November 1927), p. 5, 'Homage to García Lorca' was hosted by the journal at the Villa-Rosa restaurant on 22 October to celebrate the premiere, a few days earlier, of Lorca's play *Mariana Pineda* at the Fontalba Theatre, Madrid.

[14] Margarita Xirgu Subirá (1888–1969), actress whose company staged the majority of Lorca's plays.

[15] Natalio Rivas Santiago (1865–1958), conservative politician.

[16] Jacinto Benavente y Martínez (1866–1954), dramatist, Nobel Prize for Literature, 1922.

[17] Luis Fernández Ardavín (1892–1962) and Francisco Villaespesa Martín (1877–1936), dramatists.

[18] Ramón de la Sota y Llano (1857–1936), shipping magnate/entrepreneur, whose son Manuel de la Sota Aburto (1897–1979), promoted the Bilbao *Cineclub* from 1929.

[19] Mocking reference to Lorca's play, *Mariana Pineda*.

[20] L'Herbier, 'Arte vivo', *La Gaceta Literaria*, no. 27 (1 February 1928), p. 3.

[21] Adolphe Menjou (1890–1963), US film actor.

To José Bello

Paris, 14 February 1928

Dear Pepín,

I've been in Paris for ten days now, getting my business affairs going again. They are coming along very well, and your likeness will shortly appear on the world's *écran*.[1] Within the week, I will have signed a contract agreeing to make a film this summer. The other signatories will do the same, committing to pay 10,000 *duros*.[2] I can't tell you the name of the other 'party', although you know them well.[3] Once the contract is signed, I'll be able to tell you all the details. I put it all together drinking *whisky*[4] in the Ambassy [*sic*] and listening (can you believe it!) to the old negroes from the Rector's Club.[5] Our unforgettable saxophonist has hired new musicians and improved the orchestra so dramatically it's now one of the best I've heard.

By the way: why don't you send me a good photo of you? I might be able to get you some *ad hoc* acting. In Epstein's film that we start shooting next Monday, there might have been a part for you.

A Moral Tale

Carmencita was very well-behaved. Carmencita's innocence was legendary. Her mother watched over her day and night, building a wall of vigilance between her daughter and all worldly temptation. When Carmencita reached her twelfth birthday, her mother became sorely afraid. 'On the day my daughter menstruates *for the first time*,' she thought, 'it's goodbye to her precious innocence.' But she came up with a solution. When she saw Carmencita grow pale *for the very first time*, she ran out into the street like a madwoman, returning soon afterwards with a large bunch of red flowers. 'Take these, my child, for you are now becoming a woman.' And Carmencita, delighted and fooled by those flowers, forgot to menstruate. Every month, twelve months a year, for many years, Carmencita was fooled in this way and protected from the ruinous truth. When the tell-tale shadows appeared under her eyes before the 30th of every month, her mother would hand her a bunch of red flowers.

Carmencita reached her fortieth year. Her mother, now a very old woman, still called her Carmencita, but everyone else referred to her as Mistress Carmela. At that age, a month came when the shadows did not appear under her eyes and so then her mother gave her a *bouquet* of white flowers. 'Take these, my child, it is the last bouquet I shall give you, for now you are no longer a woman.' Carmencita protested, 'But mother, I never realised I was one.' To which her mother replied: 'All the worse for you, my child.' And that white *bouquet*, by then withered, leafless, tattered and dry, was the one they placed on the Carmencita's coffin.

An Immoral Tale

When Mariquita reached the critical age, her mother wanted to do the same for her as Carmencita's mother had done for her daughter, so when she saw her daughter turn pale and sallow-eyed, she gave her a *bouquet* of red roses. But Mariquita was more brazen than Carmencita. She took the *bouquet*, opened the window, tossed it out and set to menstruating like good old Maruja,[6] whom you saw triumph, Pepín, in that unforgettable competition.

Well, Pepín, just like Hernani, I salute you with three blasts of the cornet. The month of February fades. I shall await your money order of 100 pesetas. Do not forget our pact … I need not remind you of the rigor of my methods.

Love,
Luis

PS Joking aside, I really need your 100 'smackers' to buy an actinoscope for the film I'm starting with Epstein. I've been penniless for two days now.

Spa, Ou; *BLD* 173–174

---

[1]   French in the original (screen).
[2]   Spanish in the original: *duros* (old 5 peseta piece, or general reference to money).
[3]   Manuel de la Sota, friend of Severino Bello, Pepín's brother.
[4]   English in the original.
[5]   The Rector's Club, at the Palace Hotel, Madrid, where LB and friends went to listen to jazz bands including the Jackson Brothers.
[6]   Maruja Mallo (1902–95), painter with whom LB had a close and joking relationship; LB had planned to end the screening of avant-garde films at the Residencia in May 1927 by saying: 'The menstruation competition will now begin. Maruja Mallo has the floor' (*BLD* 174).

To José Bello

Paris, 21 March 1928

Dear Pepín,

Your 100 pesetas have arrived, somewhat delayed, although I had at least received your explanatory note beforehand. I am truly grateful, not for the money itself now, but because you have shown yourself to be so correct. I would never have imagined you could show such *respect* for your word of honour. Immoral as you are! Bravo, Pepín.

I've been working for a month and a half on the Poe film, as *assistant*-subdirector to Jean Epstein. A few days ago, I fell out with *my boss*[1] over a panegyric I'd written about American cinema; I handed my notice in the following day, and it was cheerfully accepted. So much the better. My business affairs are going very badly. I never imagined starting out would be this difficult. The Greek film is not going to get made now, even though it was all arranged. Ramón still hasn't sent me his script!! You'll remember that we worked on it together in Madrid and it was supposed to be finished. And to top it all off … Vicens has sold the mill.[2] I found out and wrote him a wonderfully serious and carefully-planned business proposition (when I tell you the details, you will think it was splendid, like everyone else); I told him that I would also invest shares of 20,000 pesetas, etc. Well, he wrote back saying I was mad, that he couldn't get over his shock at such foolishness, that I should go to bed and sleep it off, and all kinds of things. Scolding me like an old man. I'm sorry to say I sent him back a letter by return post that would make your hair stand on end. He is bitter, and full of ill will, and he sees us all as idiots or thieves. As far as he's concerned, and I have the documents to prove it, our friends are all riffraff; the southerners, riffraff; the youth of today, (literally) riffraff; and the film people he should have been working with for our project, also riffraff. The poor man is expecting another child in June and it must have deranged him. I never expected such foolish and un-called-for behaviour from Vicens.

And so, Pepín, I now find myself not knowing what to do. Of course, I'm not losing hope and I'm carrying on. The experience I'm gaining from this as-yet-to-begin career is making me see the world quite differently from the days when we used to drink rum in my room. The project I mentioned so mysteriously was with Claudio de la Torre[3] and the son of Sota, from Bilbao. I had supper with them the other evening, making the most of Sota's visit and … well, another project slipped through my fingers.

So here you find me in my room 'knowing not what to do'.

Love,
Luis Buñuel

PS Write to me!!

Spa, Od; *BLD* 174–175

[1] English in the original; LB and Epstein fell out when Epstein took offence at LB's defence of US film and his attack on Gance in the review of *Napoleon* published in *Cahiers d'Art*.
[2] Vicens sold a flour mill in Cifuentes (Guadalajara) for 50,000 pesetas to fund his Spanish Bookshop in Paris.
[3] Claudio de la Torre Millares (1895–1973), writer and film-maker.

To León Sánchez Cuesta

Zaragoza, 12 June 1928[1]

Dear León,

I would be very grateful if you could send, with all possible speed, photographs of the Goya paintings listed below. My *scénario* is on the up: an important film studio[2] has asked me to have it ready in five days.

Here is the list: *Majas on a Balcony, The Meadow of San Isidro, Blind Man's Buff, Stilts*, two or three different photos versions of *Procession, The Inquisition, Portrait of Goya* by Vicente López,[3] *Portrait of María Luisa, Portrait of Charles IV*, one maja, two of the Duchess of Alba, *Portrait of Moratín, The Bandits*,[4] two or three etchings, *Portrait of a* Monk,[5] *Village* Bullfight,[6] *The Picnic* and one or two others of your choice, as long as they have some kind of narrative and architectural content if possible. Send me the bill with the photos.

I am truly grateful. I will write again with more information. Everything is working out very well.

Fond regards,
Luis Buñuel
Costa 6

PS If you can't do it, send me a telegram. I definitely need the photos by Saturday. I repeat: Thanks (with a capital T).

Spa Als L, LSC/15a-b; *GOY* 158–159 f

[1] Written on letterhead with LB's name.
[2] Julio César Productions considered funding LB's *Goya* screenplay towards the end of 1928.
[3] Oil painting by Vicente López Portaña (1826).
[4] One, or maybe all, of Goya's Bandit trilogy (1808–11).
[5] Likely reference to *The Monk's Visit* (1808–12) from the *Disasters of War*.
[6] Presumably Goya's *A Village Bullfight* (1812–14), rather than *Capea de pueblo* (the title LB provides here) by Eugenio Lucas Velázquez (1855).

Figure 7 Jeanne Rucar, centre, outside Sánchez Cuesta's bookshop, Paris, 1928.

To León Sánchez Cuesta

Zaragoza, 22 June 1928

Dear León,

The photos have arrived and I'm so grateful. The etchings were no good, too big and too little content I can use for my *scénario*. I am returning them to you. If the publisher will take them back, please credit my account, if not, which would be a shame, you can give them away, or throw them away or whatever you think best. I am sending you 70 pesetas to settle my account, unless they take back the etchings, in which case I would be 13 pesetas in credit. But I should say again, please do not give the discount a moment's thought unless it's absolutely no bother.

Julio César Productions have accepted my *scénario*. I'm also negotiating a position as technical director. Keep this to yourself though, there's a lot of interest and quite a few people who might be put out – film people, that is.

I leave tomorrow for Paris.

Fond regards to you and Luis, from your friend,
Buñuel

PS I'm putting four copies of the new review, *Feuilles volantes*, in with the etchings.[1] One is for the *Resi*, one for Moreno Villa, and you can decide how best to use the others to promote the magazine.

Spa Als L, LSC/16a-b; GOY 160–161 f

[1] Edited by Zervos, 10,000 copies at 5 francs each were published in June 1928, with the same title Feuilles volantes as the *Cahiers d'Art* supplement. It contains a piece by LB, 'Variations sur Menjou' (p. 14), later published in a slightly revised version as 'Variaciones sobre el bigote de Menjou' in *La Gaceta Literaria*, no. 35 (1 June 1928), p. 4.

To José Bello

Saint Michel-en-Grève, 1 August 1928

Dearest Pepín,

I don't know whether you are in Seville, so I'm sending this brief note. Reply by return.

I'll be in Spain in October for the Film Congress.[1]

It's very likely that I'll sign a contract with Julio César Productions, their president holds me in high regard.

Julio César have accepted my *Goya* script: they will pay me 45,000 pesetas.

I'm working on the *découpage*[2] of my next film, *Caprichos*, based on a *scénario* by Ramón. The film is made up of six stories.[3] I'll begin shooting in September or October, working with a production company from Paris.

I have 25,000 pesetas in my bank account to make *Caprichos*.[4]

On 1 September I'll take on an apartment in Paris that I'll furnish myself. I'll send you the new address. There will be *two beds*.

I'll be a little tight for money, so I won't be able to pay for your trip, but if you were in Paris I would give you an important part in one of the stories.

The jockey's death is Maruja's fault. As he rode past the stands where Maruja was sitting, his member reared up of its own accord and he suffered the most fatal of falls.

That's all,

Love,
Luis

Spa, Od; *BLD* 175–176

[1] Primer Congreso Español de Cinematografía (First Spanish Film Congress), Madrid, 12–20 October 1928.
[2] French in the original: LB uses *découpage* here as distinct from *scénario* to refer to the technical script indicating camera positions, framing, etc.
[3] Gómez de la Serna published various mini short stories under this title, *Caprichos*, in *La Gaceta Literaria*, no. 21 (1 November 1927), p. 3, and no. 24 (15 December 1927), p. 7.
[4] Possible reference to the sum (25,000 pesetas) LB's mother contributed to *An Andalusian Dog*.

To José Bello

Paris, 14 September 1928

Dear Pepín,

Let's make more effort to write to one other. What a foolish way to end a letter, Pepin, and for you, a Sevillan, of all people to speak like that. Your letter arrived with the photos, which are very disappointing. How un-photogenic, Pepín. And there was I, picturing you as a blend of Menjou and Pollard.[1] But I see now that you are more of an *Anthropopitecus erectus*: a frivolous and moustachioed Bécares,[2] that's our Pepín. Still, all effort will be made to get you a role, *bout d'essai*[3] depending. In fact, I have a part in my film for you if the screen test goes well. I might begin in October. Right now, I'm finishing the *découpage* and starting on the budget. We'll talk about it more soon. I'll be in Spain at the beginning of October with a more definite plan. As well as my first film, I don't know if I told you that I am negotiating with Julio César for a position as a director. I shall meet their President, Mr Palles, here in Paris, to try to come to a final arrangement. It would be wonderful for me because it would involve contracts over a number of years and I would be filming all the time. They produce films in France, Germany and England.

Our brilliant friend Perojo[4] works for them.

I saw Federico in Madrid and patched up our friendship, so you'll know I'm not being prejudiced when I say that, in my view and those of people who have travelled a bit further than Seville, his book of ballads is very bad.[5] It has the finesse and *approximate* modernity that any contemporary poet needs to appeal to the Andrenios, the Baezas and to the queer and *cernudos* poets of Seville.[6] But there is an abyss between that and the true, beautiful and important poets of today. Opening the book at random:

San Miguel all covered in lace
In the alcove of his tower
Shows off his beautiful thighs
Girded by bright lanterns   (so what?).[7]

Preciosa drops her tambourine

And runs without a pause   (so what?).
Preciosa is full of fear,
As she walks into the house
Where high above the pines
the English consul lives   (so what?).
Silences of dark rubber
and fears of fine sand   (this makes Baeza come).

There is drama, for people who like that kind of flamenco drama; there is the spirit of classical ballads for people who still enjoy the classical ballads century after century; there are even some magnificent and truly novel original images, but few and far between and mixed with a *storyline* I find unbearable that has filled Spanish beds with menstrual blood. That said, I do prefer him to Alberti,[8] who is reaching the outer limits of lyrical absurdity and whose poems are now more or less just:

Tataracha tatarera
Barabacha Platko[9] yank
Putupuntun tuputun
Perrian plan plan plan, pataplan.

Our most exquisite poets, our authentic elite, our anti-crowd pleasers, are: Larrea,[10] first of all; Garfias (a shame about his sparse and limited imagination; his outpourings would be truly divine if he had only half of Federico's fancy); Huidobro;[11] and the histrionic Gerardo Diego,[12] at times. The rest, frankly, don't *excite* me the way they do the Mediodía[13] group.

I haven't seen María Luisa[14] yet. She's had another child, and I'm not sure when she's going to stop. Vicens hidden away in his bookshop, as always, and me with my films, my articles and the preparations for my upcoming debut. *La Gaceta* of October 1st is wholly dedicated to cinema.[15] You must read it.

Love (you used to be so much more, etc., than you seem in the photos you sent me),
Luis

Spa, Od; *BLD* 178, 180

[1] Harry Pollard (1879–1934), American silent-film actor.
[2] Galician, who studied medicine at the Residencia with Pepín Bello.
[3] French in the original (screen test).
[4] Benito Perojo González (1894–1974), film-maker.
[5] Federico García Lorca, *Romancero gitano* (*Gypsy Romances*) (Madrid: Revista de Occidente, 1928).
[6] Andrenio, pseudonym of journalist and literary critic Eduardo Gómez de Baquero (1866–1929), reviewed Lorca's *Romancero gitano* for *La vanguardia*; Ricardo Baeza (1890–1956), journalist and translator, reviewed *Romancero gitano* for *El Sol* (29 July 1928); 'cernudo' is a reference to the poet Luis Cernuda (1902–63), and possible play on the Spanish word *cornudo* (cuckold).
[7] Comments from LB in brackets on lines transcribed from *Romancero gitano*.
[8] Rafael Alberti Merello (1902–99), poet.
[9] Franz Platko (1898–1983), Hungarian goalkeeper, to whom Alberti dedicates his 'Oda a Platko' in his collection *Cal y canto* (Sand Lime and Song) (Madrid: Revista de Occidente, 1929), written 1926–27.
[10] Juan Larrea Celayeta (1895–1980), Spanish poet.
[11] Vicente Huidobro (1893–1948), Chilean poet.
[12] Gerardo Diego (1896–1987), Spanish poet.
[13] Literary group from Seville including Rafael Laffón, Rafael Porlán and Joaquín Romero, published (from June 1926) a journal with the same name.
[14] María Luisa González Rodríguez (1900–98), linguist and wife of Vicens.
[15] Special issue of *La Gaceta Literaria*, no. 43 (1 October 1928) called 'El séptimo arte: Cinema, 1928', in which LB published texts including '*Découpage*: o segmentación cinematográfica' (p. 1).

To José Bello

Paris, January 1929

Dear Pepín,

I'm writing this letter in duplicate, because I'm not sure if you're in Seville or Madrid.

Tomorrow or the day after I'm going to Dalí's house for a couple of weeks to work on some film ideas with him.[1] The world may collapse, but I am determined to start this film in early April with the money I have left, adapting it as I go along to make sure I stay on budget and don't have to ask anyone else for money. Write to us at Monturiol 24, Figueres.[2] I sent Dalí your Athenaeist thing.[3] He liked it so much he's going to publish it along with something of mine on cinema in the next edition of *L'Amic de les Arts*.[4]

I've heard nothing else from Mantecón. It's really too much. Try to find out what you can then write to me. I'd be really grateful if you would.

Effusive and abusive love,
[Luis]

PS I've dedicated my book in press to you: here is one of the its prose poems (a few of them will be coming out soon in *La Gaceta*).

Mojigatería[5]

The puddles make headless dominoes of the tall towers, one of which I had been told about as a child. From a single window as high as the eyes of a mother leaning over a cradle. Near the window a hanged man swings, balancing over an abyss enclosed by eternity, howling into space. IT IS ME. It is my skeleton, with only the eyes still intact. Now they are smiling at me, now they are squinting at me, NOW THEY ARE GOING TO EAT A BREADCRUMB INSIDE MY BRAIN. The window opens, and a lady appears filing her nails. When she is sure they are sufficiently gratuitous, she plucks out my eyes and throws them into the street. Only my eye sockets are left: no gaze, no desires, no sea, no fledglings, nothing.

A nurse comes and sits beside me at the café table. She opens a newspaper from 1856 and reads out loud:

'When Napoleon's troops entered Zaragoza, they found nothing but the wind blowing through the deserted streets. Alone in a puddle croaked the eyes of Luis Buñuel. Napoleon's soldiers finished them off with their bayonets.'

Spa, Od; *BLD* 184–185

[1] Script of *An Andalusian Dog*.
[2] Dalí family residence from 1912.
[3] Calligram by Pepín Bello.
[4] Art and literature review edited by Josep Carbonell and published in Sitges from 1926–29; Bello's calligram, and an interview with Dalí by LB, were published in the journal, *L'Amic de les Arts*, Year IV, no. 31 (31 March 1929), p. 14 and p. 16, respectively.
[5] The Spanish title could be translated variously as: 'sanctimoniousness', 'hypocrisy', 'prudery' or 'priggishness'. The book LB refers to was never published, but 'Mojigatería' was published under an alternative title, 'Palacio de Hielo', in *Helix*, no. 4 (May 1929), p. 5.

To Juan Ramón Jiménez[1]

[Figueres, January 1929]

Our most distinguished friend,

We feel it is our duty to tell you – yes – without bias, that your work is deeply repulsive to us for its immorality, its hysteria, its pestilence, its arbitrariness.

In particular:

MERDE!![2]

On your *Platero y yo*,[3] on your facile and malicious *Platero y yo*, the least donkey-like of donkeys, the most *odious* of donkeys we have ever come across.

And on you, for your pernicious performance, another:
SHIT!!!!

Yours sincerely,
Luis Buñuel and Salvador Dalí

Spa, Od; *BLD* 189

¹ Very highly regarded Spanish poet and writer (1881–1958), awarded the Nobel Prize for Literature in 1956.
² French in the original (Shit).
³ Jiménez's enormously popular children's story about a donkey, Platero, was initially published in 1914 in Madrid by Ediciones de la Lectura.

From Juan Ramón Jiménez

[Madrid, February 1929]¹

My most well-known and dear *surréalistes*,
    I agree completely with you both and the third person hiding behind you:² everything I have published to date is worthless, and as I have myself said many times I am ashamed of most of my written work. Whatever you might say about my work, I have already said, in my own words, despite the fact that, to my dismay, according to critics of both sexes and the opposite sex from you, my work is the foundation of almost all contemporary Spanish and Hispanic American writing in poetry and prose, verse and criticism. But you are, as well as *surréalistes*, cowardly idiots. Your Franco-Catalan patter reveals you to be incapable of the most basic command of Spanish; *merde* is meaningless to me and, as you must have known, I would never stoop to respond to your particular brand of gutter language. Nor would I succumb to the ridicule of engaging my supporters, male, female or 'pansies' (as my Moguer³ locals call you). You should also know that my friends were delighted with your letter, and they judge you to have made a fine job within it of depicting the most vibrant portrait of yourselves.

Many thanks from this admirer of your abilities,
J. R. J.

Spa Tda, ZJRJ J-1/134(1); *JRJ* 500 f

¹ Draft with notes written in the 1940s.
² Lorca is the likely 'third' person indicated here.
³ JRJ's birthplace in the province of Huelva.

To José Bello

Paris, 10 February 1929

Dear Pepín,
    You are right, we should have written to you from Figueres, but they were so many things to tell you we decided it was better not to write at all. We didn't write to anyone

in fact, not even a postcard. And I can only repeat that there were so many things to say we decided to say nothing. Also, since I arrived here I've been so overwhelmed with work I've had no time for anything. Dalí and I, more united than ever, have been working very closely on a splendid *scénario*, unprecedented in the history of film. It's going to be really big. I think you are going to love it. I will start filming in March. I'm now getting everything ready. I will keep you posted. We were going to call it *Marist with a Crossbow*, but for now it has the provisional title of *Dangereux de se pencher en dedans*.[1] The replies you sent Dalí were very good. I think he's going to publish them in *L'Amic*. Buy the latest edition of *La Gaceta*, the 1 February one. Bergamín[2] mentions you; and your name also appears in the publicity for the next edition of *L'Amic*.[3]

I'm including a copy of the letter Dalí and I sent to Juan Ramón Jiménez from Figueres.[4] If you hear anything about it, do let me know.

My book is in press. It is dedicated to you and starts with the Athenaeist thing. There are quite a few things you haven't seen before, and although now slightly *demodés*,[5] they're not bad. It's an opening salvo. I will publish more weighty things later. I'm going to write a book with Dalí this summer in Cadaqués. And you and I should do another together as soon as the opportunity arises. The title of my book is now *The Andalusian Dog*, which made Dalí and me piss ourselves laughing when we came up with it. There isn't a dog in the entire book, by the way, but it looks OK and is very well behaved. It's also happy and idiotic. It should be out within the month and I'll send you a copy. Now turn this page and read one of the poems that will appear in it. I sent you one already in my previous letter.

The Rainbow and the Poultice

How many Marists fit on a footbridge? Four or five.
How many quavers does a Don Juan have?
1,230,424.
These are easy questions.

Is a piano key a louse?
Will I catch a cold on my lover's thighs?
Will the Pope excommunicate pregnant women?
Does a policeman know how to sing?
Are hippopotamuses happy?
Are all pederasts sailors?
And these questions, are they also easy?

In a few moments two salivas
will come down the street leading
a school of deaf-dumb children by the hand.
Would it be rude of me to vomit a piano on them
from my balcony?

I prefer to say nothing about Alberti because I have nothing good to say. I think he's slandering us in public and in private. His declarations in *La Gaceta* made it quite clear.[6] If I were in Madrid I'd soon put him straight.

What do you think of these poem titles Dalí and I came up with recently. Here are a few.

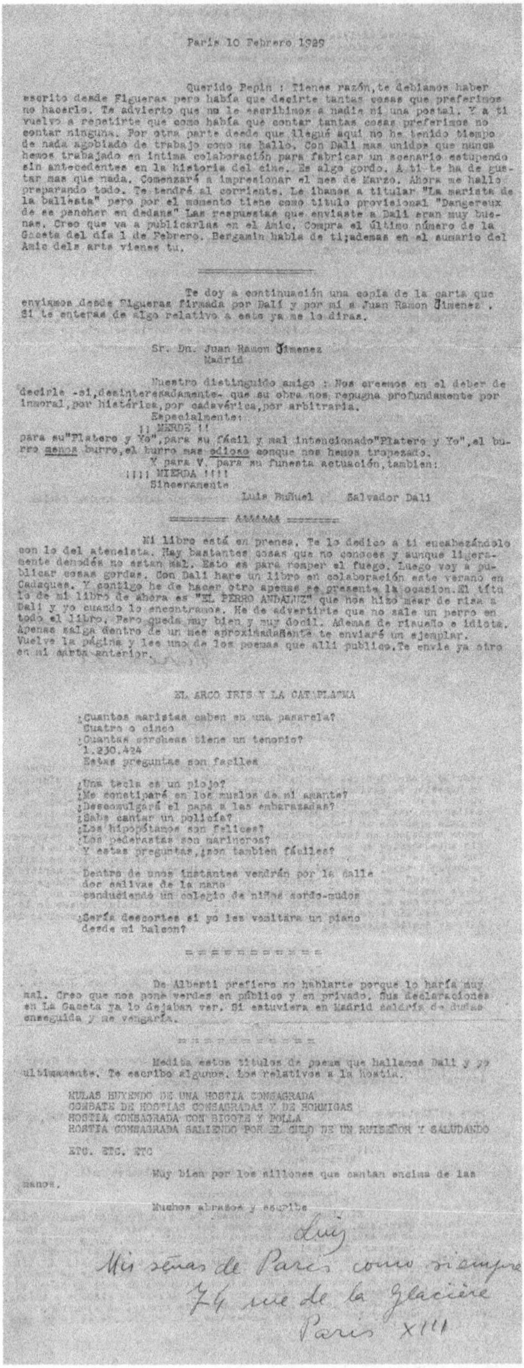

París 10 Febrero 1929

Querido Pepín : Tienes razón, te debíamos haber escrito desde Figueras pero había que decirte tantas cosas que preferimos no hacerlo. Te advierto que no le escribimos a nadie ni una postal. Y a ti vuelvo a repetirte que como había que contar tantas cosas preferimos no contar ninguna. Por otra parte desde que llegué aquí no he tenido tiempo de nada agobiado de trabajo como me hallo. Con Dali mas unidos que nunca hemos trabajado en intima colaboración para fabricar un scenario estupendo sin antecedentes en la historia del cine. Es algo gordo. A ti te ha de gustar mas que nada. Comenzaré a impresionar el mes de Marzo. Ahora me hallo preparando todo. Te tendré al corriente. Le ibamos a titular "La marista de la ballesta" pero por el momento tiene como titulo provisional "Dangereux de se pancher en dedans" Las respuestas que enviaste a Dali eran muy buenas. Creo que va a publicarlas en el Amic. Compra el último número de la Gaceta del día 1 de Febrero. Bergamin habla de ti;ademas en el sumario del Amic dels arts vienes tu.

Te doy a continuación una copia de la carta que enviamos desde Figueras firmada por Dalí y por mi a Juan Ramon Jimenez . Si te enteras de algo relativo a esto ya me lo diras.

Sr. Dn. Juan Ramon Jimenez
Madrid

Nuestro distinguido amigo : Nos creemos en el deber de decirle -si,desinteresadamente- que su obra nos repugna profundamente por inmoral,por histérica,por cadavérica,por arbitraria.

Especialmente:

¡¡ MERDE !!

para su"Platero y Yo",para su fácil y mal intencionado"Platero y Yo",el burro menos burro,el burro mas odioso conque nos hemos tropezado.

Y para V. para su funesta actuación,tambien:

¡¡¡¡ MIERDA !!!!

Sinceramente

Luis Buñuel   Salvador Dali

======= &&&&&& =======

Mi libro está en prensa. Te lo dedico a ti encabezándolo con lo del ateneista. Hay bastantes cosas que no conoces y aunque ligeramente denodés no estan mal. Esto es para romper el fuego. Luego voy a publicar cosas gordas. Con Dali hare un libro en colaboración este verano en Cadaques. Y contigo he de hacer otro apenas se presente la ocasion. El titulo de mi libro de ahora es "EL PERRO ANDALUZ" que nos hizo mear de risa a Dali y yo cuando lo encontramos. He de advertirte que no sale un perro en todo el libro. Pero queda muy bien y muy docil. Ademas de risueño e idiota. Apenas salga dentro de un mes aproximadamente te enviaré un ejemplar. Vuelve la página y lee uno de los poemas que alli publico. Te envie ya otro en mi carta anterior.

EL ARCO IRIS Y LA CATAPLASMA

¿Cuantos maristas caben en una pasarela?
Cuatro o cinco
¿Cuantas sorcheas tiene un tenorio?
1.230.424
Estas preguntas son faciles

¿Una tecla es un piojo?
¿Me constiparé en los muslos de mi amante?
¿Descomulgará el papa a las embarazadas?
¿Sabe cantar un policía?
¿Los hipopótamos son felices?
¿Los pederastas son marineros?
Y estas preguntas,¿son tambien fáciles?

Dentro de unos instantes vendrán por la calle
dos salivas de la mano
conduciendo un colegio de niñas sordo-mudos

¿Sería descortes si yo les vomitara un piano
desde mi balcon?

= = = = = = = = = = = =

De Alberti prefiero no hablarte porque lo haría muy mal. Creo que nos pone verdes en público y en privado. Sus declaraciones en La Gaceta ya lo dejaban ver. Si estuviera en Madrid saldría de dudas enseguida y me vengaría.

= = = = = = = = = = = =

Medita estos titulos de poema que hallamos Dali y yo ultimamente. Te escribo algunos. Los relativos a la hostia.

MULAS HUYENDO DE UNA HOSTIA CONSAGRADA
COMBATE DE HOSTIAS CONSAGRADAS Y DE HORMIGAS
HOSTIA CONSAGRADA CON BIGOTE Y POLLA
HOSTIA CONSAGRADA SALIENDO POR EL CULO DE UN RUISEÑOR Y SALUDANDO

ETC. ETC. ETC

Muy bien por los sillones que cantan encima de las manos.

Muchos abrazos y escribe

Luis

Mis señas de París como siempre
74 rue de la Glacière
Paris XIII

Figure 8 Letter from Buñuel to Bello, 10 February 1929. Courtesy of Agustín Sánchez Vidal.

About the host: *Mules fleeing from a consecrated host. Battle of the consecrated hosts and the ants. Consecrated host with moustache and cock. Consecrated host emerging from the arse of a nightingale and waving.* Etc., etc., etc.

Well done with the arm chairs singing on the palms of the hands.

Love, and write,
Luis

PS My address in Paris, as always: 74 rue de la Glacière, Paris XIII.

Spa Tlsps, Od; *DAL* 219–221 f

[1]   Reference to the first draft of *Andalusian Dog*. The title (*Dangereux de se pencher en dedans*) is a play on French train signs warning that it is 'Dangereux de se pencher en dehors' (dangerous to lean out).
[2]   José Bergamín (1895–1983), poet, defines Bello a an 'extra-literary master' of Lorca and Dalí in his article 'Literatura y brújula', *La Gaceta Literaria*, no. 51 (1 February 1929), p. 1.
[3]   A copy of the letter sent to Juan Ramón Jiménez (see above).
[4]   Publicity, by Dalí, for the upcoming edition announcing work by writers including LB and Bello in 'Un número violento de L'Amic de les Arts', *La Gaceta Literaria*, no. 51 (1 February 1929), p. 7.
[5]   French in the original (dated or outdated).
[6]   Alberti criticizes, amongst other things, the 'pazguatismo boquiabierto del cine' (cinema's dumb amazement) in *La Gaceta Literaria*, no. 49 (1 January 1929), p. 2.

To José Bello

Paris, 17 February 1929

ATTENTION! Everything underlined in red is worth ruminating after an initial careful read-through.[1]

Dearest Pepín,

I got your laconic letter asking me to tell you what topics to write on in your article for *L'Amic de les Arts*. I've already said we very much enjoyed the list of the things you are interested in, and that Dalí was going to send it to *L'Amic*. I told him to cut out a couple of things, like the one about the Holy Christ's arses, not because it was in bad taste, because it seemed in excellent taste to me (bearing in mind those aforementioned arses are the only ones you can take out to play without them running off and getting run over by a tram), but rather because the censors might have stepped in and given you a hard time. *I think that is precisely the kind of work you should be doing, confident that you will do great things.* When you write, rid yourself of all prejudice, forget what people think is literary or in good taste, or idiotic, etc., and give free rein to your instinct. Of course, *there will be days when you do nothing*, but one day you'll be inspired, your irrationality will break free, and that's when great things will happen, you'll see. Then it's just a question of a few stylistic revisions (which are very easy), eliminating anything superfluous and leaving just the essential. Never set out to write about something specific, just take up your pen and paper and allow your hand to write freely. Also, never, ever, contemplate writing to a preconceived plot. That's enough advice for now. I'm sure when we're together again I'll be much more help. I'm also sure you will produce great things. You have always been a surrealist and only a surrealist at heart, which is already enough, because surrealism *IS THE ONLY INTERESTING THING IN ARTISTIC(?) CREATION.* I'll translate some Benjamín Péret[2] for you below; he's Dalí's and my idol, *the best poet* of our age, maybe of all ages. I'll also put in one of Dalí's recent essays and, finally, an extract from a very long and magnificent story I wrote a while ago and that will be included in the book. I'm sure you will love it: it's infinitely better and more ambitious than our *Hamlet*.

BENJAMIN PERET: I'm writing a supplement on him (with examples) for *La Gaceta*, which you, Dalí and I will sign.[3]

Péret is the big thing in surrealism. If you were here with us, you'd really love reading him. What I'm putting in here for you is just a pale reflection. Bear in mind the difference between the surreal and the simply idiotic that does, however, have some of the same inclinations. Surrealism animates day-to-day reality with all kinds of dark symbols and the strange life in the depths of our subconscious that intelligence, good taste and all that traditional *poetic shit* has suppressed altogether. That's why it's so alive, so close to the primal life-source, to the savage and the child. *It is authentic reality*, without *a posteriori* deformation. When we say that Menjou's moustache does this or that, we are saying more than when we look at the latest torpedo and talk about how fast it can go. For that, you need culture and experience. And honestly, Menjou's moustache is faster than 50-horse power. *We must fight*, with our scorn and our rage, all traditional poetry from Homer to Goethe[4] via Góngora[5] – *the foulest creature ever born* – to the ruinous little turds produced by today's poets. I'm sorry these suggestions are so unhelpful and so badly expressed, but I'll make up for them when we're together.

I'm too lazy now to write out the extract from my story. Anyway, I'd prefer you read the whole thing together. The book will be out in about three weeks and I'll send you a copy at once. You'll see, modesty aside (and modesty is beside the point anyway, because I only wrote down what I saw), that it's wonderful. It's about a *soirée* at my house that ends in disaster. I'm compelled to visit a wise friend, where strange things happen. From there I end up in hospital on the outskirts of Toledo, where other things happen. In the end I die, not before making my last testament – and what a testament, as you will see – and finally ....

'It was barely said and done in time for me to expire decorously. Four pallbearers took my body and carried it to the church next door to be buried. They lifted the pestilent lid of Cardinal Tavera's[6] tomb and, taking out his carrion corpse and throwing it on a dung heap as even the poor no longer cared for it, they placed me in there for all eternity. MAY ALL THE LOINCLOTHS REST IN PEACE!!!'

It ends on this line, which is also the title. You should have seen the state the carrion corpse of the Cardinal was in *as even the poor no longer cared for it*. You'll piss yourself laughing at everything that goes on with me and *the priests*, as much as I pissed myself writing it. The poem I sent you in my last letter was based on some lines from this story. By the way, in your last letter you said I hadn't written for ages. Mine must have crossed yours in the post.

You will appreciate the distance that separates you, me and Dalí from all of our poet friends. Incompatible worlds, the north pole of Earth and south pole of Mars, and they are all in the most rancid crater of *putrefacción*, with no exceptions. Federico *wants* to write surrealism, but it's fake, written with intelligence, WHICH IS INCAPABLE OF DISCOVERING WHAT INSTINCT DISCOVERS. The latest excerpt published in *La Gaceta* shows just how bad.[7] It's just as artistic as his 'Ode to the Most Holy Sacrament', a fetid ode to stiffen the weak pricks of Falla and his artistic kind.[8] Although, when it comes to the irremediably traditional, Federico is one of the best if not the best of them. Alberti disturbs me even more than the idea God exists; than the thought of faeces flowing in the bellies of pretty women; than the Society of Conferences and Courses;[9] the Aragonese *jota*, concerts by the Symphony Orchestra[10], than Aladrén;[11] I find Alberti repulsive through and through. The poor thing is trying to make fools of us. If only he could. Alberti, *anti-vital* and *garrulous* Alberti. Piu piu currucutupiu tiu tiu tiu.[12]

Our film gets stuck into all of this. Moves in the same world. I begin next month. That's it.

Much love from,
Buñuel

PS *Write something and send it to me.*

Spa Tlsps, Od; *DAL* 224–226 f

---

[1] Indicated here with italics, which are also used for words underlined in blue and black in the original.

[2] French surrealist poet (1899–1959).

[3] Various extracts from Péret's 1928 collection *Le Gran jeu* (The Big Game), translated into Spanish, (*BLD* 194–197).

[4] Johann Wolfgang von Goethe (1749–1832), German poet and novelist.

[5] Luis de Góngora y Argote, much-admired Spanish Golden Age poet (1561–1627).

[6] Juan Pardo de Tavera (1472–1545), cardinal, Inquisitor General of Spain, whose tomb in the Toledo Cathedral appears in *Tristana*.

[7] F. García Lorca, 'Degollación de los inocentes', illustrated by Dalí, no. 50 (15 January 1929), p. 1. LB published 'Redentora' and 'Bacanal' in the same edition, p. 2.

[8] Lorca's 'Oda al Santísimo Sacramento del Altar', dedicated to Falla, published in *Revista de Occidente*, no. 66 (December 1928), pp. 294–298, includes the line 'el mundo de ruedas y falos que circula' (a world of wheels and phalluses turning).

[9] Cultural society, founded in 1924, to organize lectures at the Residencia.

[10] Madrid Symphony Orchestra, founded in 1903.

[11] Emilio Aladrén Perojo (1906–44), sculptor, friend of Dalí's at the Escuela de Bellas Artes, and Lorca's lover from 1927–28.

[12] Nonsense verse, transcribed verbatim.

2

Surrealism and Hollywood (1929–31)

Figure 9 Dalí, Buñuel, Mareuil, Rucar and Hommet during filming of *An Andalusian Dog*, Le Havre, April 1929.

To Salvador Dalí

[Paris,] 22 March 1929

Dear Salvador,

Very busy and completely preoccupied with my film.[1] So I'm only going to write to you about that. *L'Amic de les Arts*,[2] stupendous. We'll talk more.

I now have a studio to start working in on 2 April.[3] Batcheff,[4] and a German, young, strong, blonde, square-jawed, fit, very elegant, who has agreed to play the role of the young man waiting on the beach and will do it for nothing.[5] He's worked for a year with

Ufa.[6] So he knows what he's doing. On Monday, the production manager[7] and director of photography[8] arrive and will start getting everything ready. I haven't got anything yet. I've found a girl I used to know, with a wonderful head, to play the role of the girl who picks up the hand in the street.[9] And the girl I want to star is coming over now.[10] I won't say any more about this until I can tell you how it works out. I've only seen a photo of her.

   You will have to take care of the ants. It's impossible to get them around here. Try to get them on the day you leave, and you can bring them to the studio as soon as you get to Paris and I'll film them. You have up until the end of the 9th to get them and get here. It'll be too late after that. I'm relying on you not to have to put caterpillars or flies or rabbits in the hole in the hand. You can bring the ants in a small wooden box, seal it completely except for a little hole covered with fine metal mesh. Put cotton inside the box. As you'll get them on the day you travel, I think they'll survive for a couple of days. Ask one of the locals in from Cadaqués to help you, and you can pay him well because it's included in the budget. Your father[11] will be able to advise on how much to pay and what you should do. I think it should be straightforward in Cadaqués. You could test it out by collecting a few ants and keeping them for a couple of days in cotton to see if they die. I'm counting on you, which is not to say I won't keep trying to get some round here, although I don't think it will be easy.[12]

   The star was just here. She'll do. Provocative little body. Pretty good expression. You may not like her much. But I think I can work with her. I'll give her half what she's asked for. She's the best of a bad lot.

Love, and write to me,
Luis

PS Batcheff has asked for 10,000 francs, which is a serious discount. I considered not accepting it, but with so much going on I'm half crazy, so I think I'll take it in the end. I called him. I'll know for certain tomorrow.

                                                                Spa Tls, PV; *PUT* 42 f

---

[1] *An Andalusian Dog.*
[2] See letter from LB to Pepín Bello, January 1929, note 4.
[3] Billancourt Studios, Paris, founded by Henri Diamant-Berger in 1922.
[4] Pierre Batcheff (1901–32), French actor of Russian origin LB met while working on *Siren of the Tropics.*
[5] Role played, in the end, by Robert Hommet (1909–58), French actor.
[6] Universum Film, major German film studio, established in Berlin in 1917.
[7] Marval, production assistant and actor.
[8] Albert Duverger (1899–1971), French director of photography, whom LB met working on *Mauprat.*
[9] Fano Messan (1902–98), French sculptor and actress.
[10] Simone Mareuil (1899–1954), French actress.
[11] Salvador Dalí i Cusí (1872–1950), solicitor.
[12] Biologist Carlos Velo Cobelas (1909–1988) eventually supplied the ants for the film.

To José Bello

Paris, 25 March 1929

Dear Pepín,

This behaviour is beneath you. My long letters have been for nothing.

On the 2nd I start work on what will be your favourite film in the world. All our ideas up on screen. I'm really sorry I can't get you over here to help out, play a part, or screw the hot, plump, daft and not ugly star. I should be finishing it by the beginning of May.

The edition of *L'Amic de les Arts* with your work in it will be out the 30th. It's going to be wonderful. Dalí and I are going to start a magazine.

Goodbye,
Luis

PS Dalí is coming to Paris in a few days and plans to stay for a long while.

Spa Od; *BLD* 203

To Jacques-Bernard Brunius[1]

Jacques-Bernard Brunius
34 rue Trezel, Paris XVII

Paris, 19 June 1929

Dear Sir,

First of all, I hope you will forgive this request, because it was Mr Zervos who urged me to write on his behalf. *Cahiers d'Art* is going to publish a page of photographs from my film *An Andalusian Dog*[2] and I had the audacity to ask whether you, as the most appropriate person, might write the text.[3] I may have over-stepped though, so for my own peace of mind I would very much like to know whether it would be too much trouble for you. I should also very much like to meet with you and Pierre Kéfer[4] one of these days. If you are free, would you like the three of us to meet up tomorrow, Thursday, at Francis at around 6:30pm?[5] If you are not able to make this meeting, please call me tomorrow morning before 11:00 on Invalides 03–54.

Most cordially yours,
Luis Buñuel
Rue du Laos 7

Fre Asp, JBB/13–B4

---

[1] Pseudonym of Jacques Henri Cottance (1906–67), French critic and film director.
[2] Premiere of *An Andalusian Dog* held at a special screening at the Ursulines Studio, Paris, 6 June 1929.

[3] See photographs and reviews from writers including J. Bernard Brunius, *Cahiers d'Art*, Year IV, no. 5 (July 1929), pp. 230–231.

[4] French artistic director and photographer; set designer on *Mauprat*, where he met LB.

[5] Chez Francis, Parisian restaurant in Place de l'Alma.

To Salvador Dalí

Paris, 24 June 1929

Dear Salvador,

I sent you a selection of photographs a few days ago, some pretty good ones, considering they are just stills from a particularly interesting bit of film. I'm very keen to know if you liked them.

The film is doing well. Thanks to the machinations of the director of *Studio 28*, Mauclaire,[1] the censors are not going to veto it and Mauclaire wants to hold on to it for a two-month screening in the Autumn *saison*.[2] It will be shown at a luxury beach resort for three days this summer. The Count of Noailles[3] has hired it for a screening at his palace on 2 July and he's opening up his salon on the 3rd for me to invite anyone I like. Picasso wants to come. I've met all the surrealists and they are delightful especially Queneau,[4] Prévert,[5] Max Morise,[6] Naville,[7] they are all 'stupendous', and just the way we imagined them. On Saturday they borrowed the film to finish off a series Artaud[8] and Roger Vitrac[9] were organizing at *Studio 28*. The theatre was full. The (very mixed) audience reaction was marvellous. There was applause and whistling at the end. But they all howled and laughed in the right places. Afterwards they screened poor old Deslaw's[10] film, which was booed. You could hear people making fun of him, saying 'this is so vanguard!' It left me firmly convinced people can't stand upside-down houses and car wheels passing by.

I've been asked for some photographs, *Variétés*,[11] *Cahiers d'Art*, *Cahiers de Belgique*,[12] *Bifur*,[13] *Du cinéma*,[14] etc., etc., etc. I've reminded everyone I've been able to speak to about your central role in the *conception* of the film. As you know, the only people discussed in relation to films (so far at least) are the director or the actors. Auriol,[15] Desnos,[16] Brunius, etc., will mention both our names, so we'll be presented as a team. The article by Montes[17] is not bad: it's a shame he mentioned the vile *jota* and the filthy Ebro. Every day I meet more people who want to be introduced to us.

I shall buy and send on the jacket for your sister[18] in the next two or three days, when I have the money. I'll write to you on the day I send it so please let me know the best address.

That son of a bitch Federico has not turned up. But his pederastic news has reached me. That wily fox, Concha Méndez, wrote to Vensssensss[19] saying: 'Federico was in London and he's told me all about Buñuel and Dalí's great failure. What a shame, poor boys.'

As you can see, the world is so full of whores they'll be taking over soon.

Alberti *m'a fait chier*[20] and it's time to do something about it. I'll wait until we're together to put together a plan of attack. I can't wait to see you again under more favourable circumstances.

I'll be with you by mid-August. Plans: all of them, in particular BOOK, magazine and film.

I'm sending some articles from *Pour Vous*,[21] *Intran*[22] and *Ami du Peuple*.[23] The most important ones haven't come out yet.

Much love,
Buñuel

PS Hinojosa is writing the vilest little poems and is in charge at *Litoral*.

The other day Zervos asked me: 'Who do you know in Spain who could write a good article on Dalí?' (that's significant and is at least partly related to your growing reputation in Paris, intensified by the film). I asked Goemans,[24] who agrees it should be done, he says Éric de Haulleville[25] will write it. I'll tell Zervos today. If you don't like the idea, let me know. But I do think everyone has the right to their opinion and that one should stay very much on the side-lines. It would be very different if the piece were signed by you. The other day someone said to me: 'If Breton[26] knew you were giving your film to Vitrac and Artaud, he would be furious'. Of course, I feel personally closer to Breton (who is now surrounded by foul little surrealists like Thirion,[27] Megret[28] and friends), but the film will be shown wherever they pay for it. So, I'm giving it to Noailles, because he's offering 1,000 francs. That said, I haven't *accepted his invitation to dine* at the reception.

Magritte[29] liked some things in it a lot and was annoyed by others. The film does mock his painting a bit of course.

Spa Als, MJA; 4745; *REV* 94–97 f

[1] Theatre in Montmartre specializing in avant-garde film and established, February 1928, by Jean Mauclaire.

[2] French in the original (reason).

[3] Viscount Charles de Noailles (1891–1981), French aristocrat and art dealer; he and his wife, Marie-Laure, had a projection room at their mansion, no. 11, Place des États-Unis.

[4] Raymond Queneau (1903–76), French writer, joined the surrealist group in 1924.

[5] Jacques Prévert (1900–76), French writer and film-maker.

[6] French artist and translator (1900–73).

[7] Pierre Naville (1904–93), French writer and sociologist.

[8] Antonin Artaud (1896–1948), French poet, actor, dramatist and director.

[9] Roger Vitrac (1899–1952), French poet and dramatist, who co-founded the Alfred Jarry Theatre in Paris with Artaud in 1927.

[10] Eugene Deslaw (1898–1966), pseudonym of Levhen Slavchenko, Ukrainian film-maker; the film is probably *La Marche des machines* (The March of the Machines, 1927).

[11] Cultural review founded by Paul-Gustave van Hecke in Brussels, May 1928, published review by André Delons, '*Un Chien andalou*', *Variétés* (15 July 1929), p. 222.

[12] Art review founded by Pierre Janlet in Brussels, February 1928.

[13] Cultural review founded by Pierre Lévy and Georges Ribemont-Dessaignes in Paris, May 1929; the photographs from *An Andalusian Dog* were published in *Bifur*, no. 2 (July 1929), p. 209.

[14] Journal founded in Paris in 1928 (title later changed to *La Revue du cinéma*) published review by J. B. Brunius, '*Un Chien andalou*', *La Revue du cinéma*, no. 4 (15 October 1929), pp. 67–68.

[15] Jean-George Auriol (1907–50), French film critic and founder of *Du cinéma*.

[16] Robert Desnos (1900–45), French surrealist poet and film critic.

[17] This article by Eugenio Montes Domínguez (1900–82), poet and Catholic journalist, was published in *La Gaceta Literaria*, no. 60 (15 June 1929), p. 1.

[18] Anna María Dalí i Domènech (1908–89).

[19] Possibly Juan Vicens.

[20] French in the original (is a real pain in the arse).

[21] Weekly film journal founded in Paris, November 1928, published reviews by J. Lenauer, 'Deux noveaux films: *Le Mystère du château du Dé* et *Un Chien andalou*', *Pour vous*, no. 30 (13 June 1929), p. 4, and by J. Vincent-Bréchignac, '*Un Chien andalou*', *Pour vous*, no. 47 (10 October 1929), p. 5.

22 *L'Intransigent*, French newspaper founded by Eugène Mayer in 1880.
23 Conservative newspaper, founded in Paris in 1928, published article by J-.G. Auriol, '*Un Chien andalou*', *L'ami du peuple* (21 June 1929).
24 Camille Goemans (1900–60), Belgian surrealist writer and gallery owner, who held the first Dalí exhibition in Paris, November 1929.
25 Éric de Haulleville (1900–41), Belgian poet.
26 André Breton (1896–1966), French poet and writer, principal theorist of surrealism.
27 André Thirion (1907–2001), French writer.
28 Frédéric Mégret (1909–75), French artist.
29 René Magritte (1898–1967), Belgian surrealist painter.

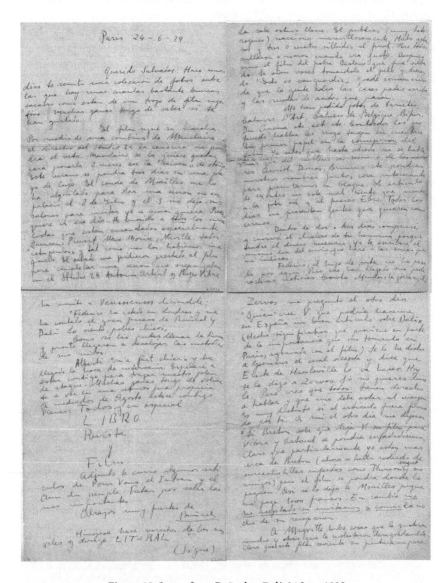

Figure 10 Letter from Buñuel to Dalí, 24 June 1929.

From Charles de Noailles

[Paris,] 7 July [1929]

My dear sir,

It is my great pleasure to inform you that the screening here of *An Andalusian Dog* the day before yesterday was a great success.

My friends were so impressed they have asked me to show it again.

Among those present were Carl Dreyer,[1] Jean Lods,[2] Léon-Paul Fargue,[3] René Crevel,[4] Michel Leiris,[5] Moussinac,[6] Jean Tedesco and various others who I am sure will promote your film. I am now thinking of other friends who might well be interested, because I should like to screen it again for them on Wednesday the 10th. I sent word to Mr Braunberger,[7] although he is so non-committal I am quite terrified he may not be ready by then. If you could stand in for him, you would be doing me a considerable favour. Congratulations again.

Most cordial greetings,
[Charles de Noailles]

Fre Tlu, BK; *AGE* 33

[1] Carl Theodor Dreyer (1889–1968), Danish film-maker, whose *La Passion de Jeanne d'Arc* (Passion of Joan of Arc, 1928) LB reviewed in *La Gaceta Literaria*, no. 43 (1 October 1928), p. 3.
[2] French film-maker (1903–74).
[3] French writer (1876–1947).
[4] French surrealist poet (1900–35).
[5] French poet and art critic (1901–90).
[6] Leon Moussinac (1890–1964), French film historian, founder, with Lods, of the Paris film club, Les Amis de Spartacus, in March 1928.
[7] French producer and distributor (1905–90).

To Charles de Noailles

Viscount Noailles
11 Place des États-Unis, Paris

San Sebastián, 18 July 1929

My dear sir,

I left Paris about two weeks ago and only received your letter of 7 July with the second cheque, forwarded from my Paris address, the day before yesterday. I am touched by your interest and the support you have shown for my film, you have done so much more that I could alone. I did not expect, as well as financial backing, the very effective publicity that the screenings at your home most definitely provided, and under – as I myself was able to appreciate – the most favourable conditions. I hope to be able to convey my intense gratitude in person as soon as I return to Paris.

Meanwhile, I offer you my most cordial greetings,
Luis Buñuel

Fre Tls, BK; *AGE* 34

To Jean Painlevé[1]

Jean Painlevé
14 rue Saint-Dominique, Paris

Cadaqués, 27 August 1929

Dear friend,

I hope to see you as soon as I get back to Paris to arrange the screening of your films this winter at in the Madrid Cineclub.[2] Our first session is in November. Have you been working on anything new recently? I am preparing a film for next winter.

Best wishes from
L. Buñuel

Fre Pau (Puerto de Cadaqués), JP/11834

[1] French biologist and film-maker (1902–89).
[2] Cineclub Español founded December 1928 and co-directed by Giménez Caballero and LB.

Figure 11 Postcard from Buñuel to Painlevé, 27 August 1929.

From Jean Cocteau[1]

[Paris,] Sunday [22 September 1929]

My dearest Buñuel,

My doctor is ill (these things happen), so my operation has been postponed. They are probably going to lock me up in a clinic tomorrow. I telephoned Ariane. She still had certain hopes. If I'm not there on Tuesday,[2] bad luck will have intervened (the delay was the good luck). Ariane will show me the film, but I really wanted to see you before I lose you again.

Fond regards,
Jean Cocteau

PS If they lock me up on Tuesday, would you let the directors of Studio 28 know, because they were waiting to hear from me.

Fre Als, AB/603

[1]　French writer, artist and film-maker (1889–1963).
[2]　The commercial premiere *of An Andalusian Dog* was held at Studio 28 on Tuesday, 1 October 1929.

To Jean Cocteau

Paris, Friday [27 September 1929]

My dear Cocteau,

All my best wishes for an immediate recovery from the operation. I often have news of you from friends I share with Ariane.

I'm showing the film on Tuesday at 9pm in *Studio 28*, but if you can't make it, I'll lend you a copy, so you can watch it whenever you like. I'll leave it with Ariane.

Very cordial greetings,
Luis Buñuel

Fre Als, JC

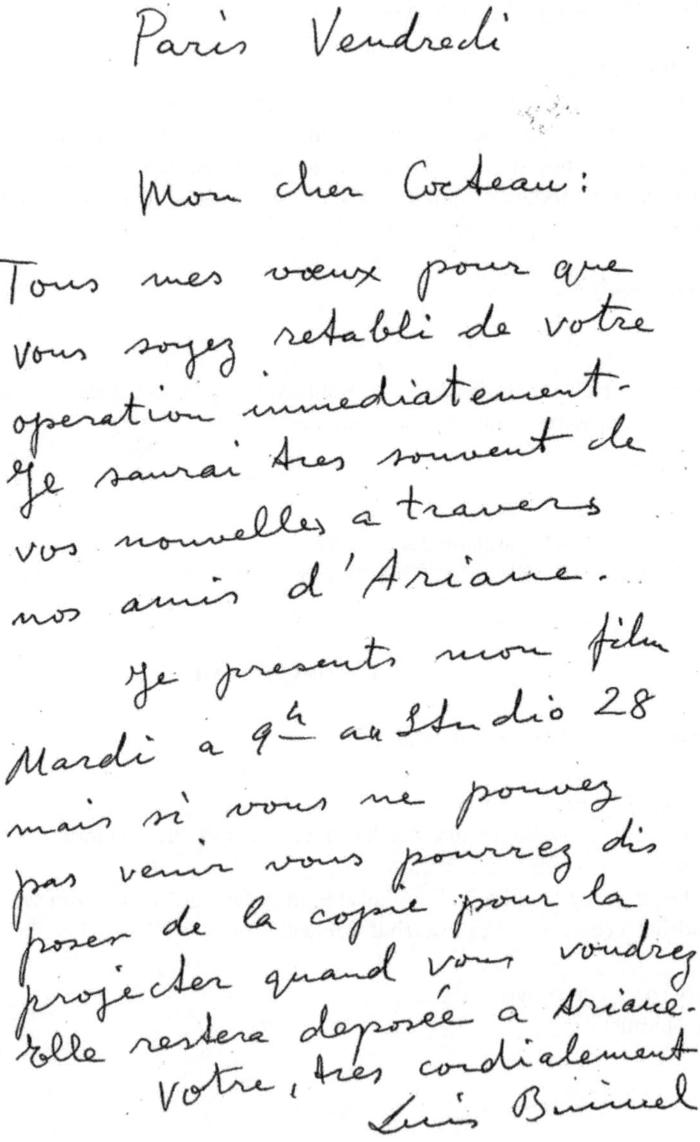

Paris Vendredi

Mon cher Cocteau:

Tous mes vœux pour que
vous soyez retabli de votre
operation immediatement.
Je saurai tres souvent de
vos nouvelles a travers
nos amis d'Ariane.

Je presents mon film
Mardi a 9ʰ au Studio 28
mais si vous ne pouvez
pas venir vous pourrez dis
poser de la copie pour la
projecter quand vous voudrez
Elle restera deposée a Ariane.
Votre, tres cordialement
Luis Buñuel

Figure 12 Letter from Buñuel to Cocteau, 27 September 1929.

To André Breton

Paris, 2 October 1929

Dear friend,

I stopped for a moment in the lobby after yesterday's screening to greet some friends. When I left later, everyone had disappeared: I looked for you everywhere in vain. So do please send everyone my apologies and thank them for me.

I can't go to Radio[1] today, but will be there tomorrow, Thursday, from 7pm.

My sincere friendship to you and Suzanne,[2]
Luis Buñuel

Fre Als, BRT/C/371

[1] Café Radio, in Rue Coustou, where Breton advised LB to stop the script of *An Andalusian Dog* being published in *La Revue du cinéma*, on the basis that is was a bourgeois publication.
[2] Possible reference to Suzanne Muzard (1900–92), Breton's lover at that time.

To the editors of several Parisian newspapers[1]

Paris, 19 November 1929

Mr Director,

May I count on your benevolence kindly to publish the following letter in your newspaper?

I most strongly protest against the abuse of my trust on the part of Mr Gallimard,[2] who has published not only without my permission, but also against my wishes, the *scénario* of my film *An Andalusian Dog* in *La Revue du cinéma* by NRF publishers. Mr Gallimard has sent me written confirmation of the publication of the text,[3] acknowledging that this is contrary to my wishes. I would take legal action were this not the kind of behaviour I abhor, and did I not find it preferable to let the public judge for themselves an unquantifiable infraction that clearly shows the extent to which the interests of those in power still take precedence.

Luis Buñuel

Fre Tls, LM 4o Col 10/10 (19)

[1] In protest at the unauthorized publication of the script of *An Andalusian Dog*.
[2] Gaston Gallimard (1881–1975), French editor, co-founder of Éditions de la Nouvelle Revue française in Paris in 1911.
[3] The script was published in *La Revue du cinéma*, no. 5 (15 November 1929), pp. 2–16, translated by Maxime Zvoinski; the same version, without acknowledging the translator, was published in *La Révolution Surréaliste*, no. 12 (15 December 1929), pp. 34–37, with an introductory note by LB.

Figure 13 Photomontage published in the edition of *La Révolution Surréaliste* No. 12 (December 1929, p. 73) which includes the script of *An Andalusian Dog*. Clockwise from top left, Alexandre, Aragon, Breton, Buñuel, Jean Caupenne, Éluard, Fourrier, Magritte, Albert Valentin, Thirion, Tanguy, Sadoul, Paul Nougé, Goemans, Ernst and Dalí.

To Marie-Laure and Charles de Noailles

Zaragoza, 14 December 1929

Dear friends,

I've been in Zaragoza for a while now, and having completed the *scénario*, I'm now working on the *découpage*. I'm very pleased with the *scénario*, which I think is much better than *An Andalusian Dog*. I'll set off for Hyères on 1 January, where I hope to be able to read it to you and hear what you think. Would you be so kind as to let me know my exact itinerary? I plan to arrive at Cerbère (at the French-Spanish border) on 2 January at midday and would like to know what train I should take for the closest station to your residence. I am very sorry to bother you and thank you in advance for the information.

I wanted to suggest two actors who will add 50 per cent value and creative expression to the film. I don't yet know if they are available, but if they were, and you agreed, it would benefit the film greatly.

Cordial greetings,
Luis Buñuel
Costa 6, Zaragoza

PS I forgot to send this letter and have just received your own, dated the 10th of this month and forwarded from Cadaqués, where I left about 8 days ago.[1] I shall follow your suggestions about publishing the photographs of Dalí's paintings in *Documents*.[2] I think I've already mentioned the hostility of the surrealists towards Bataille.[3] As for Dalí, I have it on good authority he has true sympathy for you (and with good reason). I hope to see you again on the 28th, as I mean to spend a day in Cadaqués on my way to Hyères, and I'll be able to give you an account of my conversation with him. We can discuss it further, but your reply to Éluard[4] seems very fair to me.

Fre Tls, BK; *AGE* 40

[1] On 8 December, LB attended the premiere of *An Andalusian Dog* at the Royalty Cinema in Madrid.
[2] Review founded Paris 1929, co-directed by Georges Bataille, Carl Einstein and Georges Henri Rivière.
[3] Georges Bataille, French philosopher and literary critic (1897–1962), refers briefly to *An Andalusian Dog* in his 'Dictionnaire', *Documents*, no. 4 (September 1929), p. 216.
[4] Paul Éluard (1895–1952), French surrealist poet; de Noailles told him they had given Bataille permission to reprint photographs of two Dalí paintings from their private collection in *Documents* (*AGE* 39).

To Corpus Barga

Madrid, 15 December 1929
(9am at the station)

My dear friend,
   It is impossible to prolong my stay in the city, despite my great interest in your proposal: I have a project on hold I must return to without delay. I hope you can forgive me and that you will deal directly with Giménez Caballero in relation to the film screening, tell him to put back in the two frames that were cut. The film should be projected slowly.[1] I hope that if there is any trouble you will be good enough to let me know. Until Paris,

your very cordial friend,
Luis Buñuel

PS It is a shame the Spanish copy of the film is not just badly printed, but in such poor condition. I think they are going to exchange it for a new one.

Spa Als, CB/1/34

[1] By adjusting the speed of the projector, generally set at 16–24 frames a second.

From Charles de Noailles

[Hyères,] 19 December 1929

Dear friend,

Many thanks for your letter.

We are delighted to receive such good news about the *scénario*; it is very often on our mind. In fact, it is quite difficult to think of anything else as one cannot open a single newspaper, not even a paper like *Le Figaro*,[1] without coming across advertisements for *An Andalusian Dog* at the *Théâtre des Champs-Elysées*,[2] for example. As for *La Revue du cinéma*, *Formes*,[3] and *La Révolution surréaliste*,[4] you are mentioned every third line.

I imagine you have copies of all of these, but if not, you will find them here. We are very much looking forward to seeing you and hearing which actors you have in mind.

2 January is very convenient for us and we will be expecting you, unless you send word to the contrary. I don't think the journey should be too long, but if you find it is, I have heard the hotel in Tarascón is very acceptable, you could spend the night there and carry on the next day.

The itinerary is as follows: take the 13:45 train from Cerbère (the one that leaves Barcelona at 9:55). Change trains at Narbonne even though your train does go on to Tarascón, otherwise you'll lose an hour there, and you will arrive at Tarascón at 18:51. There will be a car waiting for you outside the station in Tarascón (either a beige or green Rolls) that will bring you here. If possible, bring suitcases rather than trunks; it will be much more comfortable, because you will be able to take them with you in the car; also, I don't think you can move checked baggage to the other train at Narbonne, and so it wouldn't get to Tarascón until much later.

However, if you would prefer to bring a trunk, send me a telegram and I will take care of it. You will find a couple of large capes in the car to throw over your shoulders if it is very cold. It takes about three hours to get here from Tarascón. I think the best way to save time would be to stop for dinner in Aix-en-Provence, you should arrive there at around 8:30. If you prefer to stay over in Tarascón, the driver will wait for you at the *Hôtel Terminu*s to continue the journey the following day.

I should let you know that a few friends, who are coming to spend Christmas with us, may still be here when you arrive. I mean Georges-Henri Rivière,[5] Jean Cocteau, Jean Desbordes,[6] Georges Auric[7] and Christian Bérard.[8] Some, or even all of them may well have left by then, but I can't be sure. We have just spent two weeks completely alone. If you would rather not coincide with them, let me know and we can delay your trip by a week or so: everyone will have left by then and we are not expecting any more guests until the end of January.

We hope you will stay for a few days and, needless to say, that you will train with me every morning; I have no illusions about the athletic prowess of the group of friends just mentioned.

As I will not see you until the New Year, I send you our very best Christmas wishes and, finally, I enclose a cheque as, if I remember correctly, the first payment was due towards the end of the year.

With our most sincere friendship,
[Charles de Noailles]

Fre Tlu, BK; *AGE* 40–41

[1] Conservative French newspaper, founded in 1826.
[2] Founded by entrepreneur, Gabriel Astruc, in 1913.
[3] International journal of plastic arts, founded by Shigetaro Fukushima in Paris in 1929.
[4] Surrealist review, founded in Paris in 1924, directed by Pierre Naville and Benjamin Péret and, from 6 January, by André Breton.
[5] French art historian and restorer (1897–1985).
[6] French poet (1906–44), Jean Cocteau's lover.
[7] French composer (1899–1983).
[8] French set designer (1902–49).

To Charles de Noailles

Zaragoza, 27 December 1929

My dear friend,
   Your charming letter was handed to me on my return from Calanda, from where I sent you a postcard. I hope it arrived and that you will therefore excuse this delayed reply.
   I'm truly delighted by your invitation and it will be a great pleasure to exercise with you.
   I've not practised any sports since winning the 1920 Spanish amateur boxing championships,[1] and it's something I really enjoy.
   Your letter alluded to the possibility of delaying my journey to Hyères. I'm happy to do so, as it will allow me not only to spend some time alone with you both to discuss the film freely, but also to spend a few days in Paris preparing the contracts for the assistant director, the director of photography and the production manager. The assistant director may well be Bernard Brunius, who has been working for a while now in sound and talking films. For the director of photography, Duverger. He was the cinematographer for my first film and I get on very well with him. As for the production manager, I've not yet completely decided, but I hope to get an excellent one called Maurice Morlot.[2] These are my suggestions so far, but if you want more names or have other people in mind, do let me know. Of course, it will be useful for us to accept any kind of French partnership to help us out should we need it with the legal requirements.

I'll finish the first draft of the *découpage* tomorrow and as soon as I am back in Paris I'll start on the second. If it suits you, I will follow your instructions and definitely be in Tarascón on 10 January at 18:51. So I will leave Paris on the 8th and spend a day in Cadaqués discussing the changes we have made to the *scénario* with Dalí. On the 10th, I'll take the Cerbère train that leaves for Tarascón at 13:45.

I will confirm all these plans from Paris and unless you indicate otherwise, I'll stick precisely to this itinerary.

I don't want to end this letter without thanking you for your New Year's greetings. For my part, I send my best wishes to you and Mrs de Noailles.

Affectionately,
Luis Buñuel
Librairie Espagnole
10 rue Gay-Lussac, Paris V

PS I leave for Paris the day after tomorrow, on the 29th. I am very grateful for your cheque, sent so far in advance, and I am enclosing a receipt.[3]

Fre Tls, BK; *AGE* 42–43

---

[1] LB practised boxing in his youth, but there is no evidence yet to suggest he won a national competition.
[2] Production assistant on *La Chute de la maison Usher*, where he met LB.
[3] Receipt attached for 12,000 francs (*AGE* 43).

To Jacques-Bernard Brunius

Paris, 31 December 1929

My dear friend,

I've just got back from Spain and will start work soon on a film. I'd like to see you as soon as possible and, if you are available and willing, would like you to be my assistant director. You can drop me a line to arrange a meeting. I hope you will like the film. It's much better than *An Andalusian Dog* and I have complete financial and creative freedom to make it.

Looking forward to your reply, I send my best wishes,
Luis Buñuel

Fre Tsp, LL; *AROJ* 36 f

Figure 14 Auric, Buñuel and Noailles, Hyères, January 1930.

To Marie-Laure and Charles de Noailles

Paris, 24 January 1930

Dear friends,

A thousand apologies for this delayed reply, but I was waiting until I could find the small Japanese flowers for my little friend Laure.[1] I've been so busy these last few days that I had no time to get them until yesterday. I can't describe how many fond memories I still treasure of the marvellous days I spent with you. Your warmth has moved me deeply and I only hope I shall one day have an opportunity to demonstrate my great affection for you both.

I set to work on the budget yesterday. I'm doing everything I can to save money wherever possible and I hope we will always agree on the results. As a last resort, we could always reduce the number of reels. By my calculations, the budget should be ready towards the end of the month.

I'm sending, along with this letter, a registered envelope with the declaration the former surrealists published against Breton and his reply.[2] This copy of the declaration is quite old and in a fairly bad state, but I couldn't find another one. It doesn't really deserve to be clean anyway. I bumped into Breton: he was very friendly and is delighted I'm making the film.

I met Marc Allégret[3] today at Billancourt's studio. He's very nice; we spoke a lot of you both and of Saint-Bernard. He invited me to lunch and I found myself all of a sudden at the truly luxurious home of Mr Paul[4]... in Rue Lisbonne, another of your friends was also invited: Mr Randal. If I carry on like this, I shall soon be a man of the world, and as I know I could never dream of becoming an Ángeles Ortiz[5] from now on will carefully avoid all further temptation.

Both Mr and Mrs Paul (whose surname I don't recall) and Maurice Randal are truly charming.

With best wishes, dearly hoping to see my little friend Laure again soon, your firm friend
Luis Buñuel

PS I'm sending the 'terrible' declaration by registered post, and in a little box, also registered, the Japanese flowers.

I have opened a current account at Banco Español de Río de la Plata.

Fre Tls, BK; *AGE* 45

---

[1] Laure de Noailles (1924–79), daughter of the de Noailles.
[2] Anti-Breton pamphlet, '*Un Cadavre*' signed by Bataille, Leiris and Desnos and others on 15 January 1930; Breton's immediate reply 'Avant, Aprés' is included in the revised second edition of the *Second manifeste du surréalisme* (Paris: Éditions Kra, 1930).
[3] French-Swiss film director (1900–73).
[4] Paul Chadourne, member of the DADA group, married to photographer Georgette Chadourne (1899–1983).
[5] Famous Parisian high-society gallant.

To Marie-Laure and Charles de Noailles

Paris, 8 February 1930

My dear friends,

Above all, please forgive this delayed reply, but I find myself busy all day and sometimes into the night. I received little Laure's letter and her hugs with no problem and send mine back; I miss her and am keen to see her again. I'm also grateful for your letter, truly kind. It was indeed Paul Chadourne's house Marc Allégret took me to. His wife is not just beautiful, she is also charming, which is more or less the same thing.

The preparations and the budget for the film are almost all in place. I hired the set designer,[1] the second assistant director and the production manager a week ago and we are all working together. The *découpage* has changed a little, it now has some new gags[2] I thought up that I'm afraid I can't explain in writing because I wouldn't be able to do justice to the desired effect. There are two in particular, the best in the whole film, that will really surprise you: these will be one of the very few elements in the film you are not already aware of.

We will start work at the Billancourt studio on the 24th. Mr Feldman,[3] who is a great help, has let me have the largest studio for 2,000 francs a day, whereas he charges all other film directors 3,500. Mr Modot[4] charges 10,000 francs a week, but he's only charging me 5,000. The star[5] charges 4,000 francs a week, but I've got her to work for me for half that. With these three deals alone, I'm saving 80,000 francs of the overall budget. I'm also delighted to say that I have reduced the studio rental for recording dialogues down to just two days.[6] Of course, we will still need to add in the cost of the soundtrack. It would take too long to explain all the cuts and modifications I've had to make to avoid problems and save as much as possible. There's no point spending money on anything unless it improves the overall effect. I've booked the Billancourt studio for a month. You will receive the overall budget and photos of the two lead actors in a couple of days. The budget will be supervised free of charge by Mr Woog,[7] a specialist with considerable experience already: he oversaw the budget for films like *The Road is Fine*.[8]

I am providing you with a list here of all those who have offered considerable discounts on their wages or fees, it's the least I can do for them: the Billancourt studio; Claude Heymann,[9] unsalaried assistant director (Brunius is charging); Modot; Suzanne Christy; Vigneau,[10] the photographer (who has worked for nothing); Schildknecht, the set designer (a discount); and Woog, budget supervisor (free). Other matters: Max Ernst[11] will almost certainly play the chief bandit. He has a marvellous face. His wife[12] wanted to play the lead role, but she doesn't have the right expression unfortunately.

I now know the overall cost of the film almost exactly. I'm only missing a few relatively minor details. On Tuesday, you will receive the full budget with the photos and a copy of the *découpage* in French. Although I can send you the overall costs now with very little margin for error:

Although I've factored in 30 per cent of the overall budget for unforeseen miscellaneous expenses, there are some guarantees, such as having found the exterior locations, we will be in Spain mostly (sun and good weather for shooting) and, even more importantly, the arduous work on pre-production, so I can be very sure I won't go over budget. The contribution for Tobis is also missing,[13] which is why I've included a higher figure than they will actually request. I've also included the fees you've already paid me, as well as the exterior locations in Spain (bandits, founding of Rome, etc.). To sum up: these figures are for the complete negative of the film with sound.

If you think the cost is excessive, I have an excellent solution. Firstly, I'll cut out location shooting in Spain, at Cap de Creus, which is all very expensive and, as a result, the studio set design for the bandits' cabin. So the film would start with the documentary about Rome you already know about, and that would include the inauguration ceremony where the lead actors make their appearance. Cutting the film to 600 metres[14] will bring the budget down by at least 200,000 francs.

Complete silent film (negative)	
20%	470,000 francs
	94,000
	564,000
Sound, studio orchestra, etc.	150,000
Total	714,000

I would be grateful if you could send me a telegram as soon as you receive this letter to let me know whether you agree in principle to the budget, so that I can, one way or another, take the necessary steps regarding hiring the studio, the modification of the *découpage*, the outstanding contracts, etc. I've been reluctant to sign off on anything up until now except the weekly contracts of the production manager, assistant director and set designer. Lastly, I should add that, at this price, the film would be made very correctly in terms of the crew, sets, extras, stars, etc.

I'm very sorry this is all just about numbers: with any luck, this will be the first and last time. Once we have agreed the budget, I would prefer to discuss other things.

Some news

The Goemans Gallery is finished. His girlfriend,[15] who was smitten with Rott, the principal shareholder, has become his ... mistress. Goemans, who was in love with Yvonne and is very distraught, has taken himself off no one knows where. Breton, Aragon[16] and Fourrier[17] have ethical objections – I think – to taking over the gallery. And Rott and Yvonne can't take it over, because it might look as if they threw Goemans out when in fact, of course, it was he who disappeared. The gallery is in the hands of a Catalan swindler Goemans took on out of pity (when the man was destitute) a month before the romantic split. This all happened over three weeks ago. Naturally, all payments to the gallery's painters may well now be suspended.

With all friendship,
Luis Buñuel

PS I've read back through this letter. I'm sorry it is so rambling, but it must be sent today and I've no time to re-write it. Thank you.

Fre Tlsps, BK; *AGE* 46–48

1   Pierre Schildtknecht (1892–1968), French-Russian set designer.
2   English in the original (gags).
3   Michel or Simon Feldman, French-Russian owners of the Billancourt Studios.
4   Gaston Modot (1887–1970), French actor.
5   Possible reference to the Belgian actress Suzanne Christy (1904–74), although the female lead in *The Golden Age* was eventually played by French-German actress Lya Lys (1908–86).
6   *The Golden Age* was devised as a *film sonore et parlant* (with sound and dialogue).
7   Roger Woog, Head of Production at Billancourt; LB writes his name as 'Vogue'.
8   *The Road is Fine* (1930), a commercially successful film made in London, directed by Robert Florey and produced by Pierre Braunberger.
9   French assistant director, script-writer and director (1907–94).

[10] André Vigneau (1892–1968), French cinematographer.

[11] German painter (1891–1976).

[12] Marie-Berthe Aurence (1906–60), French painter and second wife of Ernst.

[13] German film studio founded in 1927, specializing in sound techniques, with an outlet in Paris from 1929 (*Les Films Sonores Tobis*).

[14] Twenty-two minutes, when projected at twenty-four frames per second.

[15] Yvonne Bernard, partner of gallery owner, Camille Goemans.

[16] Louis Aragon (1897–1982), French poet and essay writer.

[17] Marcel Fourrier (1895–1966), communist lawyer, in charge of the Galerie surréaliste.

From Salvador Dalí

[Carry-le-Rouet, February 1930]

Dear Luis,

Very good to get rid of the skyscraper, I was liking it less by the day, the man who kicks the violin does it really badly, but that could be funny, Picotin-style.[1]

In the love scene, he could kiss the tips of her fingers and then rip off one of her nails with his teeth, and you could film the mouth ripping off the nail by attaching a bit of paper to the mannequin's fake hand to show the tearing close up, and she would give a short, sharp, but spine-chilling and piercing shriek at this point, then everything would continue as normal.

I think this bit of horror would be very good, much more powerful than the severed eye; I was not in favour of including horror, but we should use this idea which is *superior* to the earlier one; not if it were the same intensity or less, and especially not in *that* love scene, but this is the perfect touch!

My oh-so-mysterious life … oh shit! My projects are now many and vague. I'll tell you about them some time.

I trust you will include in the film the scene you promised would make me exclaim: 'Oh shit!'

Turn the page because I've come up with a way of achieving your long dreamt-of cunt on screen

In the love scene, she has her head tilted back at one point like this.[2] I see all this a bit like Windermer's [*sic*] fan.[3] He gazes at her and we see her lips trembling. There are two solutions here:

1) her face blurs slightly and her lips gradually stand out until we see the lips of a real *cunt, shaved* to look more like the previous lips, or instead

2) close up of the lips against the white background of the face; and on that background and *around the lips* gradually superimpose shots of a feather boa (cunt hair) around the neckline (white, like the face, the background to the mouth). Fade-in continues to close up showing the mouth has now disappeared completely and rapid heaving of her breast. The feathers are swaying in the breeze. The bust is moving.

The impression of a cunt-mouth will be very clear, but impossible to cut because, of the two shots, one is an actual mouth and the other is just a neckline surrounded by real feathers.

Moment of maximum impact. The *wet* and drooling mouth should open slightly, without showing any *teeth*, just the tongue.

I'm dying to see their faces. Can you send me a photo? I'd be eternally grateful. Or at least let me know if you are happy with them.

In the love scene, *she* is practically naked, there must be a lot of bust and *arse*. I see the neckline like this,[4] without that. Shoulders completely bare. He, of course, will be wearing a dinner jacket in the love scene.

Aesthetic: Louise Brooks.[5] With the little mirrors.

Much love,
[Dalí]

PS You're right about the coffins, they're in keeping with a quite different kind of film.

I probably won't go with you all to Cadaqués, because I'm likely to be here with Gala,[6] who has just sent me a telegram with the details of her arrival. However, do let me know in good time just in case.

Spa Als Di, ABC/01/05; *AGE* 51–52 f

---

[1]   Picotin: French name for the comic character played by Stan Laurel (1890–1965).
[2]   Letter includes numerous drawings by Dalí.
[3]   *Lady Windermere's Fan* (1925), silent film by Ernst Lubitsch, based on the play by Oscar Wilde; LB mentions the film in an article influenced by Deluc and Epstein's concept of 'photogénie' (the theory that a shot might capture the 'spirit', or 'soul' of the film): 'Del plano fotogénico', *La Gaceta Literaria*, no. 7 (1 April 1927), p. 6.
[4]   See note 2.
[5]   US actress (1906–85).
[6]   Elena Ivanovna Diakonova, known as Gala (1894–1982), wife of Éluard, married Dalí in 1934.

From Salvador Dalí

Carry-le-Rouet, [February 1930]

[Dear Luis,]
I've been thinking a lot about tactile cinema, it would be easy and really amazing if we could use it in our film, as a basic illustration. The spectator rests their hand on a board on which, one after the other, different materials appear; a character strokes someone's skin, the board moves past with skin, etc. It would have a completely surreal and spine-chilling effect. A character touches a dead body and on the board the spectators' fingers sink into putty! If we could manage six or seven well-chosen tactile synchronizations (we should at least bear it in mind for the future), the public would go wild.[1]

A train rushes past with *French people at every window*, but very, very *fast*. But this can wait for another film.

Someone could have their flies slightly unbuttoned (just a little!), so that you can see their shirt, but only so slightly that people will think it's been done *inadvertently* and with no wish to offend;[2] this person could appear *a lot* and even at times very close to the camera.

REALLY GOOD

In the love scene, before the lights go out, we should *hear* the sound of pissing in the toilet bowl (sound of the bidet, water); one long stream of piss and two or three short ones, and then the sound of the kiss, etc. All this, with the beautiful, sexy woman, the garden, etc, will be very poetically erotic.

A characteristic sound that *every man and his dog* will recognize. Beforehand, she could say something to make it absolutely clear, like 'Just a moment, I'm coming right back' or '*In a moment* I'll be with you'.

Done properly, it really could have the most ingenious eroticism, don't you agree? I like it a lot.

During the dialogue in the love scene we should hear a bed creaking if possible; this is, of course, a very subtle, perhaps excessive, touch.

I LIKE OUR FILM MORE EVERY DAY.

Send my regards to little Duverger and to Mareuil, if she is with you.

[Dalí]

Spa Alu L Od, ABC/01/07; *BLD* 242–243

---

[1] Dalí illustrates this with various drawings.
[2] Suggestion included in the brief shot of the slightly unbuttoned flies of the character played by Gaston Modot.

To Marie-Laure and Charles de Noailles

Paris, 28 February 1930

Dear friends,

I've just received your telegram and I think you are quite *right*. My rationale was purely commercial and, as this is of little matter to you, everything will proceed as planned. Many thanks and do forgive me for bothering you.

If you want me to send you the balance of accounts with receipts etc. on a monthly or even weekly basis, do let me know. I still have money in the bank, but as I have significant payments to make at the beginning of March, I would grateful if you could make a transfer.

I have taken on Artigas,[1] the potter, to play the part of the governor. He's going to do it as a favour; and as I see it, there is no question his is by far the most interesting character in the entire film. Did Max Ernst or his wife tell you that even Eisenstein[2] wanted to play a small role in our film? The studio rental began yesterday, and the set is being built now. I'll start with the bandits on Monday at 8am. As we begin to take photos, I will send them to you. That way you can follow the whole film in progress.

It was very difficult to get insurance for the film. The cost is much higher than Mr Woog calculated. Luckily, and because of various offers available at the moment, I was able to insure it with Lloyds[3] for an initial 10,000 francs. On all other aspects of the budget, I'm saving money.

With all friendship,
Luis Buñuel

Fre Tls, BK; *AGE* 58–59

[1]   Josep Llorens i Artigas (1892–1980), ceramicist and art critic.
[2]   Sergei M. Eisenstein (1898–1948), Russian film-maker.
[3]   UK bank founded in 1865.

To Marie-Laure and Charles de Noailles

Paris, 7 March 1930

Dear friends,

I am infinitely grateful for your generosity. I received both transfers, one almost immediately after the other, and precisely at the time I truly needed them. I've now paid all the bills and still have 152,000 francs. I am also very proud to announce that I've made savings on all areas of the budget. And now I shall tell you about the film.

Firstly, the camera work is much better than in *An Andalusian Dog*. I have now watched the scenes with the bandits and the mansion, and I've filmed the pine tree and other things falling from the window. For the last two days I've been shooting the garden scene, which is where I encountered my first serious difficulties. The female lead, who is indeed reasonably pretty, lied when she said she had worked on several films, because I now see she barely knows how to put on her own make-up.[1] Still less act! She has no temperament, and temperament is exactly what is needed for this role. Yesterday was her second day on set and I got so annoyed I was on the point of firing her in spite of her contract. After all, as I have no money and no flat, if she wanted to take me to court, she would get nothing out of me. But I shouted at her as much as I could, and with superhuman effort managed to get her to throw herself into the role. I think we'll get there in spite of everything though. The poor girl was a wreck by the end of the day's filming. I'm sure you will both appreciate the enormous responsibility she has on her shoulders; if she doesn't get it right, the film will only be half as good. Modot is fairly good but a bit old school unfortunately. I'm keeping an eye on him. I think his part will turn out very well.

Another problem is that Modot does not like his co-star. The love scene in the garden should convey unimaginable anguish and violence. Three more ideas for terrible gags came to me. If we manage to get this scene right, it alone will have far greater impact than the whole of *An Andalusian Dog*. I intend to finish shooting in the garden the day after tomorrow (Tuesday). I'm still on schedule, despite the time and film stock wasted thanks to the leading lady. To bring you right up to date: I'm also adding in some numbers that weren't in the original *découpage*. I'm very happy with all the bandit scenes. What you'll see is some very odd bandits doing strange things. It came to me as soon as I saw them in costume, although I hadn't envisaged it at all in the *découpage*. All the bandits were Spanish painter friends, except Max Ernst, Prévert and Marie-Berthe's brother. Do you recognize Cossío in among the bandits, the cripple from *An Andalusian Dog*? I've put a note on the back of each photograph.[2]

I'm worried I'll bore you if I go on much longer. To conclude, let me simply say that, overall, I am quite happy with everything I've filmed so far.

Affectionately,
Luis Buñuel

Fre Tls, BK; *AGE* 60–61

[1] Lya Lis had played small roles in *Maman Colibri* (1929) dir. Julien Duvivier and *Moral um Mitternacht* (1930), dir. Marc Sorkin.
[2] Reproduced in *AGE* pp. 121–128 and 137–144.

To Marie-Laure and Charles de Noailles

Paris, 15 March 1930

Dear friends,

Your letter arrived safely, and I'm delighted to hear you liked the news and photographs of the film so much. In a few days I'll send a third lot of photographs from the love scene with the orchestra in the garden. I finished the final garden set yesterday and I'm absolutely on schedule. Everything is going well despite the significant problems that sometimes arise. For example, the performance of the fake orchestra conductor,[1] an old man with an incredibly stupid-looking face, gave me a great deal of trouble. The leading lady on the other hand, all but hypnotized, gets better by the day. Hugo's[2] wife (not Valentine,[3] but a relative who is a doctor) plays the wife of the governor and you wouldn't believe what a startling couple they make. Ernst's wife is also playing one of the women invited to the castle. I think that the carefully chosen extras have worked out quite elegantly.

I've now shot on ten different sets and I'll be filming all next week in the *hall*.[4] Yesterday I had a real orchestra with 20 musicians and a conductor in the studio, together with 35 extras and the cast. The set was the rear facade of a grand Roman villa, with large garden, topiary hedges and cypresses. The guests were sitting in the garden while the orchestra played on the terrace. I can confirm that *The Andalusian Beast*[5] is a is a real super-production. You can't tell that the garden is a set, especially when you don't know, otherwise it would be terrible. The camera work is still very good.

Let me tell you some anecdotes that will amuse you. Yesterday the woman who plays the marquise[6] came to ask me for a 100-franc raise for the scene where she is slapped. Now that's what I call a marquise! The marquis[7] is no less ambitious: he asked me to double his fee for applying false moles to his face. The leading lady is not of quite such refined aristocracy, but she still has her weak points. She was supposed to kiss the fake orchestra conductor, who as I mentioned is an old fossil, on the mouth. But she flatly refused. She only agreed when I said: 'People with the soul of an artist accept no limits.' This is a woman who really *wants to succeed*. Hugo's wife is really very pleased with her brand-new husband. And not without good reason, because he really is quite extraordinary. I won't describe him here. You will soon see a photograph of the happy couple for yourselves. Marc Allégret has been really wonderful: he has taken it upon himself to find the young woman who comes out of the castle.

The costs are as anticipated in the budget. Only the sections listed as 'negative' and 'processing' are going to increase by 50 per cent; on the other hand, I will save 15,000 francs on the sections marked 'furniture', 'sets' and 'extras'. I should warn you that this month I will have to use two thirds of the budget, in particular on the sections marked 'Billancourt studio', 'Tobis sound', 'sets', 'furniture', 'accessories', 'costume', 'set designer', 'assistant set designer', most of the cost of the negative and development, and the on-going cost of the actors and other employees. I still have 110,000 francs. I will send you a telegram when I have only 30,000 or 40,000 left. I say 'telegram' because my bank takes two days to cash cheques and then two more to send the money.

With all affection,
Luis Buñuel

Fre Tls, BK; *AGE* 62–63

[1]   Played by French actor A. Duchange.
[2]   Jean Hugo (1894–1984), French painter, great-grandson of Victor Hugo.
[3]   Valentine Gross (1887–1968), French painter and illustrator, married to Jean Hugo.
[4]   English in the original.
[5]   *La Bête andalouse*, or *La bestia andaluza* (in the feminine) was a title LB rejected, along with ¡*Abajo la Constitución!* for the film that would eventually become *The Golden Age*.
[6]   French actress Germaine Noizet.
[7]   Played by B. Ibáñez.

Figure 15 Filming *The Golden Age*, Paris, March 1930: standing, Modot, Lys and Brunius; sitting, Heymann, Buñuel and Rucar.

From André Meyer[1]

[Paris, March 1930]

We undertake to supply Mr Buñuel with a Normande cow[2] for a fee of 600 francs in total plus 50 francs commission, to appear in a cinematographic representation. In case of accident, the cow is valued at 3,500 francs. The animal will be delivered to the Quai du Point du Jour de Billancourt on Tuesday, 25 March, at 10 o'clock.

A. Meyer

Fre Als, Od; *AUG* 412 f

[1] Co-owner of the firm Joseph et André Meyer, suppliers of livestock.
[2] Reference to the cow that appears in *The Golden Age*.

To José Bello

Paris, 11 May 1930

Dearest Pepín,

I received your letter and I truly believe, as the swine-Christ might say, that our silence is offensive as well as shameful. But I offer the excuse from my side that since November I've not had a single day's rest, not even on Sundays. I don't know if you heard that Noailles has given me a million francs to make him a talking film with absolute complete creative freedom, and I hope for that reason it will make everyone who sees it blush with shame. It's a great spectacle over an hour long. I was thinking of calling it *The Andalusian Beast*, but now I prefer *Down with the Constitution!* Of course, neither the Cadiz Courts nor any other constitutional courts appear in the film. I worked with Dalí on the plot as we did for *An Andalusian Dog*. I would be so pleased if you could come to the premiere, which will be mid-June.[1] Then we could go to Toledo for a week. And even if you can't come, do let me know if you would like to plan a trip. I would write at once to Hinojosa. And Dalí would come too.

You wouldn't believe how much I've changed and the progress I feel I've made, especially in terms of ideology and application. But better to wait until we meet up and our long conversations will leave you in no doubt.

I heard you have a girlfriend. You, on the other hand, tell me nothing. Instead you speak only of your grand exploits. What's this? Pepín with enough money to buy a car? Tell me at once where it came from. Although I assume it's from the exhibition and the canal. Anywhere rather than from our friend Mantecón. Not that I mean to suggest he's tight-fisted. I mean for your work for Vías and Riegos.

I have no news of your plans, what you intend to do, your life, your family, etc., etc. And what's more, I feel there's no point trying to explain things like that in a letter, especially after all the time that has elapsed since we last met up or even wrote. Really, our letters should have no purpose other than to show we are up to date, that our friendship is still alive, and that the day for excuses or explanations can wait. I'm so removed from our other friends by now that I have no feelings either way, positive or negative. When I was in Madrid last November I was back home by 7pm because there was no-one to spend time with. The only person I saw regularly was Moreno Villa, and even then, I only still felt close to him because of the memories, ideologically, we have nothing in common. In spite of this, I still think of my friendship with him as one of the few that has survived. And as for Federico, I've almost no idea who he is. If I saw him now, I wouldn't know what to say to him, I would find him as alien as Doucloux,[2] do you remember? I have broken ties with *everyone* in Madrid. Particularly since the return of that filthy faggot, son of a bitch, gouty old bastard they call Unamuno.[3] I wept with rage at that old fart of a man on a train coming back into Spain shouting: GOD, HOMELAND AND LAW.[4] I thought Bergamín's[5] article was particularly abject and now consider him worthy of my utter contempt and future scorn. Basically, I've broken off contact permanently WITH EVERYONE. You, Hinojosa, Moreno Villa and I'm sorry to say Dalí, are the only real friends I have left. Oh! I was forgetting Sánchez Ventura. Of Vicens, I can tell you he's the epitome of commercial abjection and spiritual poverty. He is still the same man, the same good friend, but his life is probably the most regrettable of all. And I'll stop now because I'm making myself miserable. I hope to see you as soon as possible,

with much love
Luis

Spa Od; *BLD* 246–247

[1] LB planned to hold a private premiere of *The Golden Age* at the de Noailles's mansion in Paris.
[2] Acquaintance from the Residencia of whom LB was not fond.
[3] Miguel de Unamuno (1864–1936), writer and philosopher.
[4] The words Unamuno pronounced, an adaptation of the Carlist motto: 'Dios, Patria, Rey' on his arrival at Irún on 9 February 1930, after having been exiled to France during the Dictatorship of Primo de Rivera.
[5] José Bergamín, 'Contra éstos y aquéllos. Dios, Patria and Ley', *La Gaceta Literaria*, no. 78 (15 March 1930), p. 13.

To Jean Painlevé

Paris, 5 June 1930

Dear friend,

Forgive me for not answering your letter before now, but I was waiting for news of Miratvilles,[1] whom I hadn't seen for a while. He's still at the same address and I've now telephoned and asked him to get in touch with you. You have every right to be concerned and to ask them to return your films as soon as possible.[2] The Madrid Film Club is very correct when it comes to payment, but not at all when it comes to returning films. It's two years now since I worked for them.

Hoping to see you again soon, my best wishes,
Luis Buñuel

Fre Tls, JP/649

[1] Jaume Miratvilles (1906–88), writer and extra in *An Andalusian Dog*.
[2] Possibly, the short films *Hyas et stenorinques, crustacés marins* (1927), *Les oursins* (1927), and *Bernard, l'hermite* (1927) by Painlevé, screened in the thirteenth session (May 1930) of the Cineclub Español, Madrid.

To Charles de Noailles

Paris, 16 June 1930

My dear friend,

At midday today, I'll hear the entire soundtrack for the first time. I listened to part of it on Friday and was reasonably satisfied with the results. The film is better, if that's possible, than I could have imagined. Of course, I was only listening to the soundtrack without the images, but I have a perfect sense of the way they synchronize. Anyway, according to the contract, I will need to make the second payment today. To avoid disturbing you every couple of days, we could if you like settle all the outstanding accounts now. This is how they stand at the moment:

All payments for the silent film (the negative) have been made. After paying everything, there were 4,074.70 francs left. The insurance company owes approximately 2,000 francs no-claim bonus. Also, as I did the musical and sound adaptation myself, we saved the 5,000 francs in the budget for the musician. Frankly, if I had hired a musician, we would have had to pay him about three times that. So, you have approximately 11,000 francs left. I will provide paper accounts for this on Wednesday.

Still outstanding were: 80,000 francs for the soundtrack, 16,500 for Tobis's operating licence on the basis of 1,400 metres of film (ours is 1,700 metres) and 5,000 francs for the musician. In total, 101,500 francs. Other significant costs we still have to pay: GM Film, about 7,000 francs for the copy of the soundtrack and for the first synchronized copy for distribution plus 2,237 francs labour costs (extras), transport and sound costs. Also, if you agree, I would be strongly in favour of renewing the 750,000-franc insurance on the negative for three more months, which should come to no more than 3,000 francs. All these costs come to a total 113,737 francs. Bearing in mind the 11,000 francs we are in credit, that leaves around 103,000 francs.

Important: the sound copy, and the original sound-image copy are included in the exhibition expenses so they weren't in the original budget. I'll have the accounts for all the payments you've made towards the silent copy, that is, 576,000 francs, for you on Wednesday. As I will as soon as I have the invoices (in ten days or so) for the 40,000 francs from the other day and the 103,000 francs mentioned above. So, the cost of the film will come to 715,000 francs (not including the 3,500 for the sound-image copy), an overall saving of 32,000 on the initial budget I prepared of 747,409 francs in total.

If you are happy with these figures, could you send me two cheques sometime today: one for 40,000 francs to pay Tobis tomorrow; the other for 63,000 francs to be paid into my current account.

Please forgive this BUSINESS letter and, until we meet on Wednesday, I am at your service.

Affectionately,
Luis Buñuel

PS I saw the Eisenstein film financed by Rosenthal, called *Romance*.[1] It's a disgrace. If the director were in Paris, I would go and give him a good thumping. I'll tell you more about this scandalous production later. Mrs Rosenthal[2] is the only actress in it, and there's only one small set and some images of clouds and a piano. The film cost 700,000 francs. Mr Eisenstein has charged half a million to make one of the most miserable films I've ever seen.

Fre Tls, BK; *AGE* 72–73

---

[1] *Romance sentimentale* (1930), co-directed by Eisenstein and Grigori Alexandrov, produced by Russian jeweller Léonard Rosenthal.
[2] Mara Griy (1894–1975), Lithuanian actress, Rosenthal's lover.

To Jacques-Bernard Brunius

Paris, 28 June de 1930

Monday 30 June, at 9:30 sharp, film screening at the Noailles's, Place des États-Unis 11. I look forward to seeing you there,

Buñuel

PS It will be a terrible copy. You can bring someone with you, your sister, if she likes.

Fre Asp, JBB/13-B4

To Charles de Noailles

Paris, [30 June 1930]

My dear friend,

We weren't able to show the film[1] because the projector broke down. But don't worry. It's not important. We'll show it at the Panthéon Cinema,[2] after the main session if possible. I'll bring it tomorrow at around 2:30. People made do with orangeade and spirits at the bar.

Affectionately,
Buñuel

Fre Als, BK; *AGE* 73

---

[1] At the de Noailles residence.
[2] Cinéma du Panthéon, acquired and run by Pierre Braunberger from 1929.

From Charles de Noailles

Paris, 10 July 1930

My dear Luis,

Last night we screened *The Golden Age* for the final time. To an intelligent audience: Édouard Bourdet,[1] Carl van Vechten,[2] Julien Green,[3] Lipchitz,[4] etc. It was a triumph.

It's as if the film is all anyone in Paris can talk about at the moment.

We've been completely overwhelmed with requests to see it; I'm delighted, no film has ever been more sought after.

As our room here is too small, I intend to screen it for all those who have asked at a public theatre in mid-October (by which time most people will have returned to Paris). We shall send out invitations for a specialist screening.

I'll talk to Allégret and see if we can use the Panthéon; I think the best thing would be to have a morning screening at 11 or 11:30. Perhaps we could combine it with a press screening the evening before, or the following day.

Cordially,
[Charles de Noailles]

Fre Tlu, BK; AGE 74–75

1   French dramatist (1887–1945).
2   US writer and photographer (1880–1964).
3   US writer, who published primarily in French (1900–98).
4   Jacques Lipchitz (1891–1973), French sculptor.

To Marie-Laure and Charles de Noailles

Zaragoza, 16 July 1930

Dear friends Marie-Laure and Charles,
    Your letters arrived safely and gave me great pleasure. Infinite thanks. The article in *L'Illustration* is truly an odd coincidence.[1] It's on a much grander scale than our film, but so alike in aspiration and spirit. What's more, there was a very similar location in Cap de Creus that I didn't choose because of the size. As you saw, even with 25,000 people the place in the article looks far from full and for a location that size I only had a crowd of 100. Many thanks for thinking of me and for sending the photograph.
    I'm delighted the screenings at your home are now over. And even more pleased you are happy with the results. Let's agree towards the end of September on a plan to hold screenings for the public and the censors along the lines you propose in your letter.
    I've not yet been to San Sebastián, I relax much more easily here, despite the heat. I hardly move from my arm chair all day long. I'm taking intense revenge on all the activity last winter.
    When are you going on holiday? And where? You must be keen to leave Paris, which must be rather sad by now. Perhaps you've left already?
    I should like Charles's opinion on something I've been giving thought to over the last few days. The money I had in my current account while making the film was not earning interest.
    You'll know better than I do whether banks pay some kind of interest in this sort of circumstance. Should I write to the bank manager to ask for interest on the money that was in my current account over those six months? If they were to pay, the money would at least cover the cost of Tobis's licence.

Yours,
Luis Buñuel

PS No sign of life from Dalí. He's probably lost in some blissful idyll with the invisible man and 'Her'![2] And I doubt whether the Civil Guard will be able to put a stop to that whatever Dalí's father demands.[3]

Fre Als, BK; AGE 75–76

1   *L'Illustration*, no. 4546 (19 April 1930), an illustrated article on an Easter Week procession in a valley near Hollywood (*AGE* 74).
2   *El hombre invisible* painting by Dalí made between 1930 and 1933; 'Her' refers to Gala Éluard.
3   Dalí was visited by the Spanish Civil Guard after his father denounced the couple.

From Charles de Noailles

Paris, 14 August 1930

Dear Luis,

We are in Paris, recently arrived from Trouville, for 24 hours and are about to leave for my mother-in-law's[1] house near Orléans.

Your postcard was waiting, thank you very much, as was Mr Mauclaire's *pneumatique*,[2] which I enclose here.

I telephoned him yesterday; I told him I take no decisions without you and that, moreover, we have no wish to screen *The Golden Age* in a vanguard theatre.[3]

He told me the censors will pass the film as long as Mr Lautier[4] is still at Fine Arts.

I told him I would pass this on to you, but that I did not think we would be able to do anything until your return in October. If you agree, we can talk it over at a later date, if not please write to me.

My faith in Mr Mauclaire is, in any event, rather limited, and bearing in mind what he paid you for *An Andalusian Dog*, I feel we owe him no charity.

I've just heard that Mr Bailby,[5] the editor of *L'Intransigeant*, is setting up a Western Electric[6] sound system in the *L'Intransigeant* building that will be ready in October when he intends to screen *Hallelujah*,[7] *Der blaue Engel*,[8] etc. I think it's wonderful and I'm sure it will mean they can no longer prevent screenings of foreign or interesting films.

In fact, those two films were screened last week by Philippe de Rotschild[9] at the Pigalle theatre, to a select group, it seems.

I am not sure if I've already told you this, but as Philippe de Rotschild sent us so many different people who were keen to see the film we let him come to the final screening of *The Golden Age* we held after supper.

Paris is as lifeless, in fact, as every other place we've visited over the last month. I have a terrible cold, which would not matter had Laure and Nathalie not both caught chicken pox in Trouville, which is really sad. Laure recovered while we were there, but Nathalie only caught it three days ago and is still ill.

You are wise to stay in San Sebastián.

Regards,
[Charles de Noailles]

Fre Tlu, BK; *AGE* 76–77

¹   Marie-Thérèse de Chevigné (1880–1963), French aristocrat.
²   A handwritten note sent via pneumatic tube system, very common in France at that time.
³   Studio 28.
⁴   Eugène Lautier (1867–1935), undersecretary to the Ministry of Culture.
⁵   Léon Bailby (1867–1954), French journalist.
⁶   Les Miracles film theatre, in Réaumur Street, with sound system by US Western Electric.
⁷   *Hallelujah* (1929), dir. King Vidor.
⁸   *Der blaue Engel* (1930), dir. Josef von Sternberg.
⁹   French art dealer and collector (1902–88).

To Marie-Laure and Charles de Noailles

San Sebastian, 15 August 1930

Very dear friends,

First of all, I want to say how touched I was by your gift.¹ I love it. And with your kind dedication it's a memento I shall always cherish. After finding out it had arrived at the customs office in San Sebastián, I had to wait another two days for it to arrive here finally, you can imagine my impatience. They only delivered it yesterday. I really don't know how to thank you enough for your generosity.

I also received the beautiful postcard from London and the letter on Marquis paper,² in the style of *The Golden Age*, with the tiny cardboard bouquet. And as for the Sunday Majorcans,³ if we are ever in Toledo together I'll show you a hundred of them in the old church of San Román.⁴ They are hidden behind an altar by El Greco,⁵ and the only way in is through a hole in the altar itself. Very few people know about it. Of course, there are quite a few Majorcans here in San Sebastián, very much alive and kicking, or at least they seem to be. But I much prefer to see them in their Sunday best and silent, like the ones from Cuenca Marie-Laure sent me.

I only arrived here from Zaragoza about eight or nine days ago. I spent a day in San Juan de Luz, where I sent you a postcard. The weather is quite bad here, lots of rain. I saw Braunberger on San Juan beach. He's coming with me tomorrow to see a bullrun. Very kindly, he says you can use the Panthéon for the press screening.

René Crevel has written asking about the article Marie-Laure mentioned. I will write back one of these days accepting the commission. He says he goes to the cinema in a wheelchair.⁶

I don't know if I told you I was due to travel to Russia this summer with Aragon and Ella.⁷ Well, I had to pull out in the end, because I was feeling unwell and afraid of embarking on such a long trip. And what of your paddle steamer cruise? It must have been great fun. I hope Laure and Nathalie are well. I think of them often and can't wait to see them again.

I'll go back to Paris on September 20. I am very bored here in San Sebastián and I hardly go out, except to the beach. The worst thing is the apathy that keeps me prostrate in an arm chair, inert for hours on end.

I must say again how happy I am with your gift. And I send you my very best wishes,
Luis Buñuel

PS I've just received Charles's letter. I was asking about Laure and Nathalie above, and now I discover they have chickenpox. Although according to your news they should now be on the mend. I very much hope so. I think you are right not to trust Mauclaire. He would like to screen the film for the censors, so he can take advantage of it afterwards. The room at *L'Intransigeant* would be much better for the screenings or the Panthéon, even. Anything but the vanguard. As for the censors, from today I'm entirely at your disposal to present the copy whenever you like, even if I have to travel to Paris expressly for the purpose. Mauclaire wrote to me after your refusal as if the film belonged to me. I shall write back saying that the film is not mine and that I should not, in any event, like to see it screened at Studio 28. I repeat, let me know your plans for the film and do not give my holiday a moment's thought: I am at your disposal.

Whatever decision you take will be fine by me. My only role is to facilitate.

Affectionately,
L. B.

Fre Tlsps, BK; *AGE* 77–78

[1] Copy of *Les infortunes de la vertu* (1787) by the Marquis de Sade (1740–1814), dedicated to the de Noailles and published by Fourcade in Paris in 1930 (AB/465); Marie-Laure de Noailles's maternal relatives were direct descendants of de Sade.
[2] *'Papier marquis'*, referring to the trademark, Marquis, paper.
[3] Reference to the bishops and their skeletons in *The Golden Age*, and, more generally, LB's term for bourgeois and right-wing Spanish supporters of Mussolini.
[4] Thirteenth-century *Mudéjar* (post-Moorish) church.
[5] Doménikos Theotokópoulos (1541–1614), Cretan painter based in Toledo from 1577.
[6] Crevel was suffering from tuberculosis.
[7] Ella Kagan (1896–1970), French writer of Russian origin, wife of Aragon.

To Charles de Noailles

Paris, 18 October 1930

My dear friend Charles,

I'll be staying in Spain until next Saturday to spend some time with my mother before I leave for America.[1] So I'll be back in Paris on the 26th and 27th; I set sail for New York on the 28th. I should like to see you before I leave. I will, however, send a long and detailed letter from Spain so that when I return you will have all my news and be able to offer me some advice, in person or by letter. For now, I just have time – I'm leaving within the hour – to let you know about the copies for the screening.[2]

I listened to the new copy yesterday and, for the most part, it is quite good. GM Film will deliver it to the Panthéon on Tuesday afternoon. A person I trust will be responsible for ensuring this happens before the early evening. Also, if anything were to go wrong with the screening, I took a back-up copy today and handed it personally to the projectionist at the Panthéon.

I will pass by your house later to leave a copy of the contract and another document that I'll explain by letter later.

Many thanks for your kindness in receiving my friends. I've just sent you a telegram.

Please forgive this hurried and somewhat confused letter. My next, from Spain, will be much more detailed.

With best wishes to Marie-Laure, and at your service as always,
Luis

Fre Als L, BK; *AGE* 82

¹ To spend six months working at the MGM Studios in Los Angeles.
² *The Golden Age* premiered to an invited audience at the Panthéon, 22 October.

From Jean Vigo¹

Paris, 25 October 1930

I will be in Paris for a few days. Could we meet?
I saw two consecutive screenings of *The Golden Age* last Wednesday. BRAVO.
Your film is immanent justice.
THANK YOU,

Jean Vigo
Hotel Corneille
5 Rue Corneille, Paris VI (in the Odéon)

Fre Als, AB/572.11; *BDM* 49 f

¹ French film-maker (1905–34).

To Sergei M. Eisenstein

Hollywood, California, [November 1930]¹

Dear Eisenstein,
 I came to see you, but you were out. I would be very happy to meet again. Would you like to call me one morning before 10am on CR 6468?

Until then, yours
Luis [Buñuel]

Fre Ans, AER/1923/1691; *LBBC* 132

¹ On Hotel Hollywood letterhead.

To Marie-Laure and Charles de Noailles

Culver City, 2 December 1930¹

Very dear friends,
 First, I must thank you for sending the two letters, the one from Drieu² and the other one,³ as well as the press cuttings, all of which arrived in good time.⁴ I see the

critics are still prattling on and lecturing you about charity (donating that million for a retirement home), instead of promoting a film against charity. My friendship and admiration for you increase by the day. You are unique among those of your class for having produced a work like that. And I hope that when more reviews come out they will confirm what I've just said. Let's hope!

I've been here for a month now and I've achieved nothing. I arrive at Metro at about midday and have lunch, then I leave at around 3pm and don't go back until the following day. If I had hopes of doing anything they are beginning to fade. All I can say is that there is an immense list of untouchable topics. And all the topics that interest me are on that list. They just go on making the same old films where the star is the only object and the only subject. Eisenstein, to give a fine example, is leaving tomorrow having achieved absolutely nothing. And not because he proposed any overtly revolutionary scripts. They rejected the idea of him making *L'Or* by Cendrars.[5] There is more talking in films every day and Metro alone has over sixty writers charged with inventing, writing, adapting or translating scripts. And you've already seen what they produce. For example: Yves Mirande[6] is the first French writer and Martínez Sierra[7] will be the first Spaniard. All the directors are controlled directly, and at all times, by supervisors whose job it is to safeguard moral values, public taste, political ideas, good sense, and every kind of routine human convention. They are marvellously well set up to quash any new ideas, unless they are purely technical ones. I don't mean the practical side of things, that is even more impressive than I imagined. However, I am learning to despise such levels of perfection and marvellous organization at the service of the worst kind of imbecility. For my part, in order to justify my salary, I've asked to be put in charge of dialogues in Spanish or the adaptation of foreign films. It involves very little responsibility and will allow me to get through the first six months of my contract without being noticed. I shall return to Paris in May.

We had no idea how impressive Los Angeles would be. It is ten, maybe twenty times as big as Paris. It is a vast garden with palm trees, lawns and flowers, on which they've built avenues where the house numbers go up to seven or eight thousand. Each one is a *bungalow*.[8] And the standard of living couldn't be more perfect. Even with my outgoings, I've been able to buy myself the latest Ford and live in an apartment I could not have dreamt of. Particularly in terms of the comforts. Even with the garage, monthly payments on the car, etc., I'm still saving almost 100 dollars a month. I play miniature golf every day, which is much more entertaining than normal golf. I spend Sundays at Chaplin's house. He's very likeable, but not particularly clever. He never spends any time with the Americans and he's always with us (us = two young Spaniards[9] and me). When he's out in public, he only likes to joke around, doing the bread roll dance,[10] miming and performing other charming tricks. When he gets serious, he shows us a postcard from London and tells us all about his childhood with his mad mother begging on the streets. And then he suddenly goes back to performing the bread roll dance. He is only ever still for a moment, at the Turkish baths, perhaps meditating. However, he does have human qualities and a quite straightforwardly warm personality.

I'm sending you a magazine with photographs from the police archives over here. It is quite remarkable, completely dedicated to gangsters and their crimes. I hope you find it interesting.

I see all the famous stars every day, male and female, at the Metro canteen. They are extremely disappointing. Joan Crawford[11] is truly ugly. Greta Garbo[12] keeps herself to herself and dresses very plainly. Norma Shearer[13] is insignificant. Lily Damita,[14] on the other hand, is very pretty, but she sticks her tongue out whenever she notices people looking at her. Menjou and Lewis Stone[15] are just as they appear in the films. Buster Keaton is not particularly interesting either. And many others. The Metro canteen is like a DEAR LITTLE MALAMPIA'S GROTTO.[16] But the film magazines have fooled us all, one way or another.

I honestly envy you when I think of Saint-Bernard. I often remember my visit there and it makes me sad to think I won't be able to visit this winter. Nonetheless, I shall save your kind invitation for next winter. I can just imagine Charles in his coat and Marie-Laure taking the flowers outside at night. And playing with Laure and Nathalie from 5 to 7 in the evening. Send them both my love.

Yours affectionately,
Luis
Metro-Goldwyn-Mayer Studios
Culver City, California

PS Why don't you come to Los Angeles and Hollywood in the Spring? The climate is wonderful, and the city is truly beautiful. It would be a wonderful trip ... and I would be able to spend a few days with you. So, it's a very selfish suggestion on my part. If you were to come, I would delay my return to Europe.

The photo: my car, Georgia[17] and me (Georgia is Charlot's friend, the lead in *The Gold Rush*, where she was a brunette).

Fre Tlsps L, BK; *AGE* 90–91

---

[1] Written on MGM letterhead.

[2] Letter from the French writer Drieu la Rochelle (1893–1945) to Charles de Noailles, commenting on his response to *The Golden Age* (AB/572.13).

[3] Possibly the French politician, Gaston Bergery (AB/572.25).

[4] Album with press cuttings on *The Golden Age* (AB/1515).

[5] Blaise Cendrars, pseudonym of Frédéric-Louis Sauser (1887–1961), French-Swiss writer, author of the novel *L'Or* (1925), adapted for cinema by Eisenstein as *Sutter's Gold* (1930) but never filmed.

[6] Pseudonym of Anatole Charles Le Querrec (1876–1957), French scriptwriter and director.

[7] Gregorio Martinez Sierra (1881–1947), dramatist, scriptwriter and film director.

[8] English in the original.

[9] Possible reference to the authors and scriptwriters Eduardo Ugarte (1901–55) and José López Rubio (1903–96), also under contract with MGM.

[10] From the famous sequence in *The Gold Rush* (1925).

[11] US actress (1904–77).

[12] US actress of Swedish origin (1905–90).

[13] US actress of Canadian origin (1902–83).

[14] French-US actress (1904–94).

[15] US actor (1879–1953).

[16] Phrase adapted from 'mon cher grand fond Malampia', used by a young French woman, Blanche Monnier, to describe the room in which her mother imprisoned her from the age of 25 for 24 years; André Gide uses this phrase in his account of the trial 'La Séquestrée de Poitiers' (Paris: Gallimard, 1930), p. 67.

[17] Georgia Hale (1905–85), US actress.

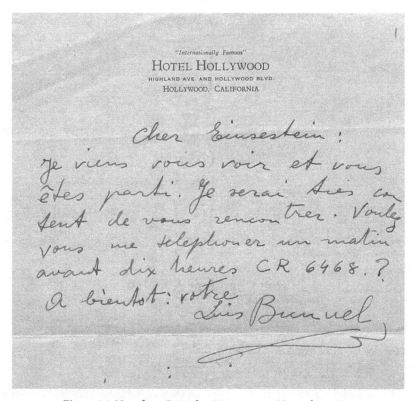

Figure 16 Note from Buñuel to Eisenstein, *c.* November 1930.

Figure 17 Buñuel and Eisenstein, Los Angeles, 1930.

To André Breton

André Breton
42 rue Fontaine, Paris IX

Culver City, 13 December 1930

RECEIVED FILM PROGRAMME.[1] MAGNIFICENT MANIFESTO. WITH YOU ALL ALWAYS. WILL WRITE,

BUÑUEL

Fre Tel, CIN; *AUG* 255

[1] Pamphlet on *The Golden Age* published by Studio 28, with text signed by Breton, Aragon, Crevel, Dalí, Éluard, Peret, Sadoul and other members of the surrealist group.

From Charles de Noailles

[Hyères,] 13 December [1930]

Luis Buñuel
Metro-Goldwyn-Mayer

I SEE FROM THE PRESS THAT *THE GOLDEN AGE* HAS BEEN BANNED IN PARIS.[1] I FEAR SERIOUS PROBLEMS. THINK IT NECESSARY TO DEMAND RETURN OF ALL COPIES TO RUE GAY-LUSSAC.[2] I ASK THIS OF YOU AS A PERSONAL FAVOUR. I PREFER NOT TO BE NAMED,

[CHARLES]

Fre Ba, BK; *AGE* 104

[1] 12 December, following the attack on Studio 28 carried out by member of the extreme right groups on 3 December 1930.
[2] Address of the Librairie Espagnole where Juan Vicens and Jeanne Rucar (1908–1994) were working; Rucar married LB in June 1934.

To Charles de Noailles

Culver City, 14 December 1930

TELEGRAM RECEIVED. ORDERING COLLECTION OF COPIES. LEAVE EVERYTHING TO ME. YOURS,

LUIS

Fre Tel, BK; *AGE* 104

From Charles de Noailles

[Paris,] 14 December [1930]

[Dear Luis,]

We received your telegram, infinite thanks. We knew we could count on your friendship.

The Golden Age is slowly becoming poisoned. It pains me that Studio 28 has become a site for *political* demonstrations, rather than, as we wanted, a space to screen a remarkable film.

Your reputation (even your name, as you will see from the programme and the press cuttings) has been (deliberately, I think) increasingly marginalized in an attempt to court more scandal by highlighting the group and our own name.[1]

The same thing has happened with Cocteau's film,[2] so we feel obliged to avoid any kind of scandal from now on. We need to make them forget about us.

The papers are saying Mauclaire will be sued, but I don't think it will be anything serious. Could you please ask him not to mention my name again! My only contact with him, apart from the telephone calls, was in response to his letter sending me the programme and asking me if I wanted to make any changes; I replied correcting Artigas's name and urging him to delete the phrase 'the Count of B is clearly JC'.[3]

He telephoned me to say that as it was Dalí's phrase he couldn't change it. The day after the *Action française*[4] protest, I received a letter from Dalí telling me about the protest and saying that Mauclaire had only just communicated my objections to him.[5]

Since then, I've had no news, except from the papers.

As long as all the copies of the film are with your friends at rue Gay-Lussac I won't worry.

And of course, the ban means our contract with Mauclaire is dissolved.

You cannot imagine the relief we felt when we received your telegram, to know that we could count on your assistance.

Of course, if you wish to have a couple of copies sent to America, I would be happy to arrange that. My only request is that you protect my name in France.

[Charles de Noailles]

Fre Ba, BK; *AGE* 104–105

---

[1] Reference to the surrealist group and to the de Noailles themselves.
[2] *Le Sang d'un poète* (1930), also financed by the de Noailles and shown at a private premiere in their Paris residence in November 1930.
[3] B (Blangis), JC (Jesus Christ); the Duke of Blangis, a character in de Sade's novel, *Les 120 journées de Sodome* (1785), who appears, dressed up to look like Christ, at the end of *The Golden Age*.
[4] Extreme right nationalist group founded in 1899; Noailles is referring to the vandalizing of Studio 28 on 3 December.
[5] Letter from Dalí to de Noailles, 4 December 1930 (*AGE* 92–93).

From Jean Cocteau

Paris, [December 1930]

My dear Buñuel,
     I have spent terrible, wonderful and unforgettable days (and nights) with your film.
     Some of the takes (like taking blood) have left me empty and weak. With strength only to admire and embrace you, with Charles[1] (our Pope) as our intercessor.

Yours,
Jean

     Fre Ad (J. Cocteau, *Opium: Journal d'une désintoxication* (*Diary of an Opium Eater*)
                                      (Paris: Librairie Stock, 1930), AB/411

[1]   De Noailles, who sent LB a copy, with this note, of Cocteau's *Opium*.

To Marie-Laure and Charles de Noailles

Beverly Hills, 26 December 1930

Very dear friends,
     I am so sorry about the news just arrived from Paris. The level of collective stupidity is unbelievable. Naturally, I'm not sorry for myself; on the contrary, I feel quite proud. But the thought that this upset might affect you both, if only slightly, makes me sick. After demonstrating such selfless and noble intentions, for you to become embroiled in any way in this scandal, would be truly unfair and must be avoided. It has occurred to me to write a letter to the Paris press – without quoting you – to make it clear that you have nothing to do with all of this, and that if you screened the film it was only out of friendship for me and to demonstrate the latest innovations in film. I would say this very briefly, leaving the rest of the letter to reiterate that I am the sole author, director and distributor of the film. Which is no more or less than the strict truth. I won't send you a copy though, until I know what you think. You could always write the letter yourselves and send it to me to sign.
     This scandal goes far beyond anything I could have imagined. If what I've heard about the various incidents is true, some of them sound as if they would have made excellent gags in the film itself. For example: the Italian complaint that their royal family is being mocked in the scenes with Hugo's wife and Artigas.[1] Unbelievable! I've also heard there is some speculation about whether you will be excommunicated for having supported such a film. It's beyond comprehension. And there are other things like the closing of and considerable fine levied on Studio 28; the confiscation of copies of the film by the police; the film theatre being practically destroyed; the injuries sustained during the confrontation; the cowardly censors suggesting the version screened had been altered. (That last point is absolutely false.)
     This is the result of a film I believed to be heartfelt, in spite of its violence, a film that would make its viewers reflect, not plunge them into a nightmare. It is, on the other hand, exactly the kind of response I would have expected to *An Andalusian Dog*.

All this has made me feel even closer to you both and even more prepared to do whatever I can to ensure you are spared any anguish. If you need me to come back, you need only let me know. Although I think that by now the scandal must be dying down and people will have begun to forget about *The Golden Age*. I think it's very sensible to cancel the screenings.[2] Following your instructions, I sent a telegram to Vicens telling him not to renew the contract with Studio 28. He was also able to save the original copy. We had a request for the film from England (from Cunard,[3] I think), but I turned it down. Better to let some time pass and for you to come to a decision. If you need anything, you can always contact rue Gay-Lussac directly, without consulting me first. You really have been very kind.

I impatiently await the letter you promised in your last telegram. I trust it will contain better news than I received today from Paris.

Many thanks to Marie-Laure for her letter and the press cuttings. I also received the book from Cocteau with its kind dedication. Could you please pass on to him my most sincere thanks. The statement in the programme for *The Golden Age* is magnificent.[4] Thank you for sending it to me.

I'm still idle over here. Now more convinced than ever that I won't carry on working with them. The films they make are too foolish. Also, I've been told that as a result of the scandal in Paris they may cancel my contract early and pay me the remaining months. It's just a rumour for now. We'll know more in a few days when Lawrence arrives. I should also let you know that the American press has picked up on the fighting over *The Golden Age*. I read about it here in the *Los Angeles Examiner*.[5]

Much love to Laure and Nathalie, and my admiration and friendship to you both,
Luis

PS Should you agree with my suggestion about writing to the press, I would prefer you draft it yourselves. That would help me better convey your feelings and avoid mistakes. It is rather too delicate for me to do it alone.

Fre Tls L, BK; *AGE* 107–108

[1] 9 December 1930, after the premiere, the Italian Embassy in Paris wrote to the French Ministry for Foreign Affairs demanding the censorship of sequences showing Artigas's character founding the new Imperial Rome (*AGE* 94).
[2] In a telegram of 29 December 1930, Noailles asks LB not to renew the contract with Mauclaire (*AGE* 109).
[3] Nancy Cunard (1896–1965), British writer.
[4] Included in the pamphlet to accompany the screening of *The Golden Age* published by Studio 28.
[5] Newspaper founded by William Randolph Hearst in 1903.

From Charles de Noailles

[Paris,] 29 December [1930]

NEW SCREENINGS ANNOUNCED BY MAUCLAIRE. PROPOSE SENDING TELEGRAM TO CASTAIGNET,[1] LAWYER, 281 RUE SAINT HONORÉ. PLEASE

RESPECT CONTRACT. DO NOT PERMIT NEW COPY WITHOUT NEW CONTRACT.

[CHARLES]

Fre Ba, BK; *AGE* 109

[1] P. Castaignet, trial judge.

To Marie-Laure and Charles de Noailles

Beverly Hills, 7 February 1931

Very dear friends,

Firstly, I thank you kindly for the photo you sent of Marie-Laure and little Laure. They both look lovely and I was delighted to see them. I am so very far away that a letter or a memento from friends like you helps to fill some lonely hours with happiness.

Thanks to the press cuttings I've received from you and Argus,[1] I am up to date with the press campaign and reviews of the film. Your name would have been left completely out of it had it not been for *Le Figaro* and those spiteful comments in *Aux Écoutes* in particular.[2] That magazine has taken cowardice to the point of publishing anonymous articles. If I were in Paris, I would track down that vile anonymous myself.

That apart, I've also received some long and positive reviews. Painlevé sent me one in Dutch and Argus sent others in English, Russian and German. I've made an album I'll show you when I have a chance. I quite agree with you though that for now the film is a lost cause in France. I am sure that the passing of time will correct this.

In some of the cuttings (in particular an excessively ignorant article by Charensol,[3] and in *Aux Écoutes*) I read that Cocteau's film is also considered *dangerous*. So it seems that if we want to make films that stay within the boundaries set by the legal system, the censors, tradition and general loathing for poetry, etc., we are limited to Ruttman-esque films or *charming* American comedies. That is: to abstain from making films altogether.

That is what is happening to me here. It is so difficult to explain, but you can't imagine what it means to make a film over here, especially at Metro-Goldwyn. Even Eisenstein, who didn't come up with any excessively revolutionary projects, was forced to leave after ten months without producing anything. There is nothing more predictable, outdated, banal and *honest* than the films made over here. For what it's worth, they have a level of technical perfection that Europeans attempt to imitate in vain. For my part, I just observe and in no way intervene in production. Which is not to say they are not friendly, because they do pay me and do not expect anything in return.

I followed your instructions not to sell the film to anyone else. Where England was concerned it was too late and by the time my telegram arrived, the deal had already been done.[4] The arrangements with Strasbourg, Brussels and Spain though were all cancelled. On my instructions, Vicens went to the laboratory and collected the complete film negative. He wrote to say he had taken it to your home, correctly stored in two large boxes. The copy that was not seized is securely stored and will not be released without your permission. We are now going to demand the other two copies from the police: I hope they will return them.

My friends on the rue Gay-Lussac are just waiting for Mauclaire's cheque before sending you the accounts. I think they wrote to you about this a few weeks ago.[5] As the film was banned though, I imagine there won't be much money. GM Film have sent invoices I've already paid, the receipts for these are in the file you have in Paris. I've told them I will bring them over to show them when I get back. As for Tobis, I think he has made a copy of the damaged negative in his laboratory.

I am sorry you can't come to Hollywood. I will see you back in France then, as I don't plan to stay in America much longer. I would love to tell you about all my adventures and misadventures since our last meeting.

Best wishes to Auric if he is still with you. I'm envious.
To you and Laure and Nathalie, all my friendship and fond regards,
Luis

PS I am sending an envelope with the cuttings you asked me to return. Thank you.

Fre Tls, BK; *AGE* 130–131

[1] *L'Argus de la presse*, press agency founded in 1878.
[2] French nationalist weekly, founded by Paul Lévy in 1918.
[3] Article by film critic, Georges Charensol (1899–1995) in the magazine *La Femme de France*, 18 January 1931.
[4] *The Golden Age* was screened at the Gaumont Theatre, London, 2 January 1931.
[5] Letter from Vicens to de Noailles, 22 January 1931 (*AGE* 129).

To the editor-in-chief of *ABC* newspaper[1]

Hollywood, February 1931

[To the Editor-in-chief,]

In the issue of *ABC* of 10 December last year, you published an article entitled 'The Surrealist Protest against Luis Buñuel'.[2] The article began by describing the events that occurred in Paris during one of the screenings of my latest film, *The Golden Age*. It went on to add:

All the French newspapers are publishing this story, but without alluding to the cause. Buñuel has deceived the surrealists. When it comes to money, there is no such thing as an artistic school or inclination and Buñuel, like so many others, has signed a contract with a North American studio to go to Hollywood to work as an assistant to a Spanish director.

As this is so clearly detrimental both to the truth and my own interests, I should like to state that:

The attack on my film was organized by a political faction of the far right, situated at precisely the opposite end of the spectrum from surrealism.

The surrealists, of whose group I am still a member, defended my film at every possible opportunity.

I have not come to Hollywood to work as an assistant director, but as a director, as stipulated in the contract I signed in Paris last October. Nor am I working as a Spanish director, as I do not participate in any way in Spanish production.

There should be no speculation on the alleged sale of my ideals for American gold until such time as I produce something to prove it. In the meantime, however, I am happy to confirm that I am, and intend to remain, fully committed to them,

[Luis Buñuel]

Spa Od; *ABC* 14–15

[1]   Juan Ignacio Luca de Tena (1897–1975), director of the Spanish newspaper *ABC* from 1929 to 1936.
[2]   Anonymous, 'Protesta surrealista contra Luis Buñuel', *ABC*, 10 December 1930, p. 15.

From Frank Davis[1]

Culver City, 27 Feb 1931

Dear Mr Buñuel:

It is only the fact that it has become the policy of this company to suspend the production of pictures in the Spanish language that forces me with deep regret to say, Hasta la vista.[2] Yours has been one of the most pleasant associations this department has experienced and the fact that you anticipated our situation by voluntarily relieving us of our contractual obligation to you has shown us aside from your many talents, that you are the kind of person that we want with us when we go into production again.

Please let us know how you fare on the many voyages you are planning and if there is ever a time when we can help you in any way I hope you will not hesitate to communicate with us.

Very sincerely yours,
Frank Davis
Supervisor of Spanish Productions
Metro-Goldwyn-Mayer

Eng Tls L, AB/629; *RLB* 87 f

[1]   US producer and scriptwriter (1897–1984); letter published in italics to indicate that this version has been reproduced in the original English-language version.
[2]   Spanish in the original.

To Marie-Laure and Charles de Noailles

Beverly Hills, 27 February 1931

Dear friends,

Just a few words to let you know I'll be leaving here on 16 March. There are still three months left on my contract, but I asked for permission to leave and it was granted. They have really been very good to me, because I've been able to study their work methods without having the least contribution demanded of me.

I had considered travelling from San Francisco to Sydney, stopping along the way at the Pacific islands – Fiji, Tahiti, the Virgin Islands, Samoa, etc. However, this would have been an extremely long journey as there are very few boats. At points, I would have had to wait for two months on a deserted island for the next ship to pass by. And I had neither the time nor money for that.

So I shall return by the North Pacific. I sail from San Francisco bound for Marseille, stopping at Hawaii, Japan, China, Manila, Singapore, Ceylon, Alexandria, Naples and Marseille. I arrive at my final destination on 27 May. A two and a half-month voyage in all.

I don't think you will still be in Saint-Bernard towards the end of May. I'm truly sorry, because I would have visited you. As well as the pleasure of seeing you again, I feel I need to talk to you and seek your advice before returning to Paris. I don't even know how you may feel now about our friendship, as it is my fault (albeit in good faith) that you have had so much trouble.

If for any reason you wish to communicate with me during my voyage, please see the addresses below. At Singapore, only telegrams, but telegrams and letters to Alexandria. I would, in any event, be truly happy to have news of you at one of these ports.

Send my love to Laure and Nathalie: I think of them often. And for you, my friendship,

Luis
Mr Luis Buñuel, passenger on the SS President Adams
Dollar Steamship Lines, Singapore, Straits Settlements
Departure: 30 April 1931
Or: Alexandria, Egypt
Departure: 20 May 1931

PS I think Mauclaire is unlikely to respond, even if you ask him for the money he still owes. Or so I gather from the last letter I received from Paris. They are waiting to close all the accounts before sending them to you. If this has not happened by the time I return, I will take care of it at once.

Fre Tls, BK; *AGE* 132–133

3

Second Republic and Civil War (1931–8)

To Marie-Laure and Charles de Noailles

Paris, 30 April 1931

Very dear friends,

I want to apologize, first of all, for this delayed reply; I do hope you will believe me when I say I only received your letter the day before I left. I sent a telegram at once.

For my part, nothing has changed and I'm happy to meet up wherever you suggest, as long as that does not involve changing your current travel plans of course. I really don't want to inconvenience you.

I've now met up with a number of people, who have brought me up to date with all the events I was completely unaware of. I do think, in general though, that people are beginning to forget the whole issue.

I'm looking for work now and hoping to join the Spanish section.[1] I've put myself forward for everything, except director.

I won't write much more here as I am hoping to see you soon. If that's not possible, I shall write you a long letter.

My love to Laure and Nathalie, and all my friendship to you.
Luis
Hôtel Lutétia

PS Please reply to the bookshop, because I'll be leaving this hotel tomorrow.

Fre Als L, BK; *AGE* 145

[1] Section for Spanish-language versions and dubbing established by Paramount Pictures (founded in 1914) in Joinville, on the outskirts of Paris, in April 1930.

From Vicente Huidobro

Paris, 20 May 1931

Mr *don* Luis Buñuel,

First of all, speaking of shit, we are now I believe in a mutual shitstorm.[1]

So now, with regard to the alleged attacks you claim I have made on Surrealism, I declare that:

1) I am not disputing those accusations to ingratiate myself with the Surrealists, nor because I feel myself compelled to sing their praises, but in order to honour the truth. I do not believe in intangible sects (and am certainly not afraid of them). I do believe in one or another man from a group, but not in the group as a whole.

   Moreover, remembering that you felt you had the right to attack the Surrealists as you did in the days of your friendship with Zervos, what can you possibly say to me now for doing the same thing?

2) It may well when you and Dalí were at the Dôme, I attacked certain acts, certain individuals and certain ideas of Surrealism – particularly its painting – but not the movement itself, as it has many of the characteristics I have always defended, particularly its vital opposition to the usual conventions. If I am not mistaken, Tzara was there and he supported my position. Hela Hein was also with us.

3) I said, and I reiterate this here, because it is the truth, that when we wrote a poem each of us a line at a time, with Éluard, at my house, 41 Rue Victor Massé, I wrote the first line. This poem still exists, with Éluard's lines in his own hand. I would not have said this to attack Éluard, as I have always enjoyed much of his work (and have said as much whenever I have had occasion to write about him). I knew him and was his friend when you were still eulogizing García Lorca, before you set foot in Paris. What is more, had I criticized him, it would still mean nothing, because Breton, such a close friend of Éluard's, suggested when discussing the poets of that group that Desnos and Péret were the most interesting and far superior to Éluard (as I am sure you know, Éluard and Péret's poetry was, in essence, exactly the same for Dada[2] as for Surrealism. That much is perfectly clear).

4) I have never attacked Breton personally, as he has always seemed to me one of the worthiest of contemporary writers, and one I have often defended, even against people who are now his friends, both when he wrote *Le Coeur à barbe*[3] and previously. Tzara could tell you something about those discussions, which took place only two years ago, or a little longer. This does not mean that I feel obliged to find all Breton's work perfect, nor he himself sacrosanct.

5) Nor is it true that I claimed the Surrealists invited me to join their group and offered to publicize my work. I remember exactly what I said. I said that in the early days the Surrealists opened an office to promote their ideas, and that on one occasion when I was there, they said I was always welcome and Breton gave me one of his books with a very gracious dedication (a book I still possess). I then added that whenever a new school is born it presents the rest of us with the choice to join in and count on the support of the whole group or remain apart and risk being considered hostile or indifferent. That is what I said, and I repeat it now, although I was referring principally, I'm sure, to *Le Coeur à barbe* and Dada, because cubism[4] and Creacionismo[5] are the only groups I have ever been involved in, albeit always retaining my own independence.

6) I have not attacked Freud[6] (you refer to everything as an attack); what I said
was that Freud saw the sexual complex behind every phenomenon and that I
considered the death complex to be just as important to the life of mankind; just
as important, if not more important, than the sexual complex. This I reiterate now.
And do not think that I am making excuses for myself, for I do not believe Freud
or anyone else, to be inviolable.

Have no fear that I will hide your letter away and only produce my own; that is not
in my nature. When I do show mine, I will also show yours, and I only hope we'll soon
find a way of publishing them together.

As regards the term 'failed artist', you may be correct; indeed, this may be my only
source of pretension. I do believe that only two or three of my close companions are
fully able to enjoy my poetry, but the curious thing is that, instead of making me sad,
this is in fact a source of happiness that consoles me for the success of some of my
other books, especially those that I had to write to make a living. Only success makes
me doubt myself, as it makes me doubt all other men. And we shall never see eye to
eye, because I believe the opposite is true for you: you are interested only in success
and seek only success. This is precisely what makes me doubt you. I join Rimbaud and
Lautréamont[7] in my failure, and they are fine company. They were the great failures
of their time, whilst the celebrated poet, who graced the salons patronized by the
Viscounts and Viscountesses de Noailles of the day, was one Rollinat,[8] whom no one
now remembers. I am quite sure that the Rimbauds and the Lautréamonts will always
be the great and unknown failures of their day. And that this will always be the case.

With regard to my inferiority complex, you are again mistaken. For any true initiate
in psychoanalysis, the first symptom of inferiority is demonstrated by the need to
belong and an inability to stand alone, a need to take refuge in groups, to feel sick, weak
and meagre when not shoulder-to-shoulder with the rest. Rimbaud and Lautréamont,
whom the surrealists quite rightly so much admire, were not members of a group,
they were, on the contrary, solitary souls, not drawn to the herd or to the squad. An
'inferiority complex' consists precisely in suffering the vertigo of loneliness. One finds
it in those men of effeminate character, so abundant in this beautiful city of Paris, men
who cannot take a single step without leaning on and being supported by others. This
is what is known as making a strength of many weaknesses.

I now consider this matter to be at an end and have just two things to add. Your
words and your actions reveal you to be a clinical case of the succubus and prototype of
the Catholic who, having abandoned his religion, has to follow other idols and submit
himself absolutely to another Pope. I have no such idolatry, nor do I believe in infallible
sects (if you could only know how well I feel), nor do I need to consult anyone in order
to reply to you. I respond by and for myself.

It is not my place to speak of Cossío and Castanyer.[9] I shall forward your letter to
them.

[Vicente Huidobro]

Spa Tlu f, VH; *SUR* 137–140

[1] Reference to a previous (lost) letter from LB to an earlier one by Huidobro dated 13 May 1931; the Chilean poet concluded this earlier letter: 'And all that is left to add, in conclusion, is that I also shit on you and on the next five generations of your descendants' (*SUR* 137).
[2] Vanguard artistic movement founded in Zurich in 1916.
[3] Magazine co-founded by Tzara in Paris in April 1922 (in response to attacks on Breton); Huidobro, Éluard and Péret were among those who contributed to its single issue.
[4] Vanguard artistic movement that emerged from 1907.
[5] Literary movement developed by Huidobro from 1912.
[6] Sigmund Freud (1856–1939), Austrian neurologist and founder of psychoanalysis.
[7] Isidore-Lucien Ducasse, Comte de Lautréamont (1846–70), Uruguayan-born French poet much admired by the surrealists.
[8] Maurice Rollinat (1846–1903), French poet.
[9] Joan Castanyer (1903–72), painter, set designer, scriptwriter; an extra in *The Golden Age*.

To Marie-Laure and Charles de Noailles

Paris, 17 September 1931

Very dear friends,

Many thanks for your letter and the copy of Rosenblueth's. I've written back to him already but would like your opinion before I send it. I'm asking 1,300 dollars for the film[1] and 8,000 additional francs for every copy. I'm sure we could have asked for more but given the difficult situation in Germany and the terms of his letter in particular, I think it's wise to leave it at that. Theoretically, we should have asked for at least 3,000 dollars. I'll await your views on the matter.

I'm also negotiating the sale of the film in Spain. I've asked for the same amount as from Germany. Also, Mrs Victoria Ocampo[2] (a friend of Mrs Cuevas[3]) wants it for the Buenos Aires film club.[4] I asked 15,000 francs for five screenings and 25,000 francs for a single copy. This is what we did with Holland and the agent did ask if they could screen it, but I had no money unfortunately at the time and did not even write back. Mrs Ocampo paid the other day. She wants to see it again, so I'll get the Dutch agent to come along as well.

I am looking forward to seeing you both again, especially now I have a fair amount of gossip to share. All quite inoffensive, of course. There is some about the taxi, its *clients*, and other people who have their own *private cars*.

I'm still inactive and looking for work, but so far I've been unable to find anything I like. As you can imagine, I'm extremely keen to work and have some money at my disposal. I don't think it will take long. In the meantime, I'm working on a book project and strolling the streets. Nothing spectacular.

My best wishes and friendship,
Luis

Fre Tls, BK; *AGE* 147–148

[1] *The Golden Age*, which LB and the Noailles were seeking to market outside France.
[2] Argentine writer and intellectual (1890–1979), founder, in 1931, of the magazine *Sur*.

[3] María Adela 'Tota' de Atucha (1887–1970), Countess of Cuevas de Vera, Argentine aristocrat, surrealist, communist, feminist co-founder of the Sociedad de Cursos y Conferencias de Madrid.

[4] Founded in 1929.

To Charles de Noailles

Paris, 19 October 1931

Dear Charles,

I am enclosing the letter from Rosenblueth I had translated although, frankly, not brilliantly. I think I understand he wants us to send him the copy and that the terms of hire are acceptable. I'll write back asking him to pay for the cost of the copy as a guarantee against damage, loss, etc. I'll also arrange delivery and return at his expense. I'm also going to seek advice on the terms normally set by editors in this kind of situation.

As I thought this letter would be all about business, I've addressed it just to you, but Marie-Laure will no doubt be interested to know we went to the Panthéon with the Aurics[1] last night and the place was packed. Everyone who was at yours for lunch recently was there: Gide,[2] Milhaud and other friends of the Aurics. Also, Mrs Fellowes,[3] whom I'd never met. I was expecting a lot more, given what I'd heard about her personality and her looks. Nora and I stationed ourselves by the staircase to the balcony so as to see her. When she passed by, I covered my head, so my haircut wouldn't bring back bitter memories for her. It was a Marx brothers' film,[4] and although everyone else was delighted, I found it rather *too* funny. And to conclude this brief chronicle of the mundane, may I say that Crevel is now in Paris and that Auric, next time he sees you, intends to appear before you sporting a plagiarized copy of my own hairstyle.

I've delayed my trip to Madrid for one week, because I want to wait for Dalí to get back, so we can settle the German issue. I'll talk to him about the event at Hyères.[5] I had something feasible in mind, but it's too individual to work as a group spectacle. I'll definitely drop it if we decide to do our *number* together. I'll tell you all about it when we next meet. It's very good, because it is infinitely adaptable and yet still works.

As my trip will be rather difficult without some help, I'll accept the advance Charles mentioned to Giacometti[6] and me the other day. I thought I could manage, but the truth is I can't. Sincere thanks.

All my best wishes,
Luis

Fre Tls, BK; *AGE* 148

[1] Georges and his wife Nora Auric (1903–82), an Austrian-French painter.

[2] André Gide (1869–1951), French writer.

[3] Daisy Fellowes (1890–1962), French aristocrat, patron of the arts, and Paris editor of *Harper's Bazaar*.

[4] Premiere of *Monkey Business* (1931), dir. Norman McLeod.

[5] Artistic event organized by the de Noailles at their villa in Hyères, April 1932, at which LB presented an installation called 'Giraffe'.

[6] Alberto Giacometti (1901–66), Swiss artist.

To Marie-Laure and Charles de Noailles

Zaragoza, 5 December 1931

Very dear friends,

I have to confess my silence since leaving Paris is inexcusable. I left over a month ago and this is the first time I've written. Many of my friends will be annoyed with me at the moment, and I can only ask you to accept my apologies.

I screened *The Golden Age* in Madrid, at an unadvertised private session, owing to the formal ban from the police. Naturally, there was no question of selling it. Most of the audience (about 300) did not like it at all; and as always, there was a small group of enthusiasts. We'll be showing it in Barcelona soon, where its reception will no doubt also be less than favourable.[1]

I've been thinking about your Spring spectacle. I hope Crevel, Dalí and Giacometti have already discussed their projects and explained them to you. I've told them they can count on me. I look forward to hearing more details and finding out the exact date you want to hold it. The week you suggested would be perfect.

I spent one month in Madrid, six days here, and I go back to Toledo tomorrow. I'll be there for eight days. I intend to work there on a script for Braunberger.[2] He's determined to get me to do something for him. I'll be in Zaragoza towards the end of the year and then back in Paris.

I am truly sorry I wasn't able to celebrate the *little party* at my house with you. I never thought I would be in Spain for so long. But I'm hopeful that it's just a postponement.

In Madrid, I was able to organize an invitation for Breton to speak at the Society of Courses and Conferences run by Carmen Yebes,[3] Countess Cuevas, etc. He will, of course, arrive by taxi. This will be the pretext to address a larger audience at a later date. I'm hoping it will happen this month.

No news from Paris. Not even from Dalí. And no idea about the magazine that was supposed to be due to come out.[4] Thanks to my ineffable lethargy, I did not send in my contribution. They must be annoyed with me.

And what of Auric's film?[5] I'll write to Nora and to J. M. Frank[6] from Toledo.

Please accept my apologies and constant regards,
Luis
27 Independencia, Zaragoza

Fre Als, BK; *AGE* 149

---

[1]   Possibly the screening at the Lido cinema, Barcelona, 13 January 1933.
[2]   Film adaptation of *Wuthering Heights* (Emily Brontë, 1847).
[3]   Carmen Muñoz Rocatallada (1901–88), Countess of Yebes, historian and co-founder of the Sociedad de Cursos y Conferencias.
[4]   Possible reference to a plan LB and Dalí had to co-edit a surrealist review in Spain.
[5]   Possible reference to *À nous la liberté* (1931), dir. René Clair, with music by Auric, premiered in Paris, December 1931.
[6]   Jean-Michel Frank (1895–1941), French designer, who decorated the de Noailles's Paris mansion.

Figure 18 Sadoul, Unik and Buñuel, Paris, *c.* 1931.

From Maurice Heine[1]

[Paris, December 1931]

Open letter to Luis Buñuel[2]

I implore you, Buñuel, not to compare this text to those *critiques* that do no more than critique their own authors. Your work, I believe, belongs to a realm quite separate from those detestable moral writings that macerate 'good' and 'bad' judgements like unfortunate foetuses in an unwholesome womb. Works that strive not to leave the 'common people' at peace with their unclean consciences are all too infrequent... This letter then, written the day after the screening of *The Golden Age*, comes from a simple spectator with no technical, nor any (I repeat) critical pretensions, whose intention is merely to present before you some reflections not so much on the Sado-Freudianism present in your film as a whole, as on the exclusively Sadean inspiration behind its final part.

We are dealing here, clearly, with an event the consequences of which we are only just beginning to glimpse: the introduction of de Sade, and of his most representative work moreover, to the cinematic repertoire. The episodic nature and the brevity (which are striking, incidentally) of your adaptation are of no great importance. The film carries the date – 1930 – and no one will therefore be able to deny you the honour of being the first to have dared to attempt such a feat. You spatter with real blood a screen that has for too long been accustomed to drip rose water and blackcurrant syrup. We could see from the moment you evoked *Les 120 Journées de Sodome* that this new *école de libertinage*[3] would become conjoined in our hearts, finally and fatally, with that spirit of essential and vital freedom that is the cinema and against which the greed of the film industry, a brutalized public, and the tyranny of the censors continue to conspire today.

It must have been your painful desire for emancipation, Buñuel, that inspired you to attempt a synthesis that still overwhelms me. How will we ever be able to forget, amongst so many others, that astonishing sequence of supreme moral Sadism? When, immediately upon leaving Sillig Castle,* the Duke of Blangis walks onto that rope drawbridge like a man 'treacherous from birth, cold, authoritarian, barbaric, selfish, as prodigious in the pursuit of his own pleasure as miserly in the service of others, a lying, gluttonous, drunken, cowardly, sodomitic, incestuous, murderous, and thoroughly wicked thief',** who is, we discover in a moment of heart-wrenching revelation, the very image of Christ ... The leader appears first, but we already know which three accomplices will follow: 'Your Jesus is no better than Mohammed, Mohammed no better than Moses, and all three together are no better than Confucius, who came up with a few good principles, while the other three were still raving; but all are no more than impostors, mocked by philosophers, believed by the masses, whom the law should have strung up by their necks'.***

So, Buñuel, having extended your own interpretation to this point, why not pursue it to its natural end? Why not provide Jesus with some worthy rivals? Why not hurl a quadruple blasphemy simultaneously against the four great religions? Does attacking one of them not by default implicate the other three? Sade was careful to rally before himself a united front of believers.

Also, and finally, there is in de Sade a mysterious numerical harmony that it would be best not to break: it is no accident that the whole of *Les 120 Journées de Sodome* is built on one square foundation. But: why bore you with abstractions? Is this brief sketch of these perspectives not enough to justify to you the importance of preserving them?

May this letter at the very least convince you of my impassioned interest and committed support,

Maurice Heine

*Name, in *Les 120 Journées de Sodome*, of the castle in the middle of the Black Forest built for voluptuous torture and executions.
**Marquis de Sade, 'Introduction', *Les 120 Journées de Sodome*, Stendhal et Cie, Paris, 1931, vol. I, p. 11.
***Marquis de Sade, *Dialogue entre un prêtre et un moribond*, Stendhal et Cie, Paris, 1926, p. 51.[4]

Fre, Od; *SSR* 12–13

[1] French writer (1884–1940), editor and scholar of the Marquis de Sade.
[2] Published in *Le Surréalisme au service de la révolution*, no. 3 (December 1931), pp. 12–13; asterisked notes by Heine.
[3] Subtitle of *Les 120 Journées de Sodome*; Heine was, with the permission of the de Noailles, preparing a new edition of the text in three volumes Editions Stendhal, Paris, from 1931 to 1935.
[4] Written in 1782.

To Marie-Laure and Charles de Noailles

Paris, 27 January 1932

Very dear friends,

Just arrived after a long stay in Spain. At the moment, things are very exciting there and had I not taken a drastic decision, I might well have stayed longer.[1]

The day after I arrived, I had word of you both from Giacometti, who had just left you. He told me you were well, but little more as he'd only been able to spend a few hours with you. He had no more information about the spectacle you discussed with us in some detail. So we await your instructions.

After a lot of wrangling and negotiation over *The Golden Age*, the censors would not allow us to screen it in Spain.[2] I got the copy back yesterday. As I think I mentioned, I only held one private screening at a cinema in Madrid. By invitation only … but at 5 pesetas, which exactly covered the cost of transport and customs.

The Marseille film club have asked for the film: one session, 2,000 francs.[3] May I send it to them? Van Hecke[4] wants it for Belgium, and a company in Holland has also inquired.

The production of the film in Paris is going terribly.[5] Braunberger is looking for new funding: he doesn't have enough money to finish *Fantômas*[6] and, when it is all over, he's going to close the studios for a few months. Something similar is happening at Pathé-Natan.[7]

Paramount's Spanish production has been on hold for a while now. So, I'm going to try to get a job as a director in Russia, which some well-placed sources have told me should not be too difficult.[8]

I would be delighted to have news of you both, and hope for more detail than Giacometti provided. I would love to know whether Marie-Laure is still singing Wagner[9] and whether Charles is still wearing his overcoat. If the Aurics are still with you, do please send them my most cordial greetings. I shall write to them soon, I owe Nora a letter.

Love to Laure and Nathalie, whom I haven't seen in a long time, but always remember fondly.

My best wishes to you both,
Luis

Fre Tls, BK; AGE 149–150

[1] The Constitution of the Second Republic was ratified on 9 December 1931, and on 29 January 1932 LB attended a meeting in Paris of the Association des Écrivains et Artistes Révolutionnaires (AEAR).
[2] In commercial cinemas.
[3] *The Golden Age* was shown near Marseilles, at the cinema L'Éden de la Ciotat, 15 February 1932.
[4] Paul-Gustave van Hecke (1887–1967), Belgian patron of arts and film promoter.
[5] Probable reference to *Wuthering Heights*.
[6] Feature directed by the Hungarian film-maker, Pál Fejos, premiered in May 1932.
[7] The Pathé studios in France, established in 1896, were taken over by the magnate Bernard Natan from 1929 and, under the name Pathé-Natan, produced over sixty features between 1930 and 1935.
[8] This may be a reference to Ella and Louis Aragon and a proposed adaptation of Gide's novel *Les Caves du Vatican* (1915) for Soviet producer Sojuskino.
[9] Richard Wagner (1813–83), German composer, much appreciated by LB, whose music is used in *An Andalusian Dog* and *The Golden Age*.

From Salvador Dalí[1]

[Cadaqués, March 1932]

Dear Luis,

I've just received your letter, which I consider to be very serious indeed. I see you have completely abandoned all the ideas (surrealist) that we shared until now, and all for the sake of party discipline.

I am surprised that the simple fact of joining the Communist Party should eliminate all vestiges of intelligence, even in individuals such as Aragon and yourself who (although no proof of this existed previously) might now be mistaken for the most elementary and infantile obscurantists.[2] I am going to address in haste (because it would take ten more letters) the points in your letter that I regard as the most fundamental and the most monstrous. The most striking of which is your absolute lack of dialectic.

You talk of your *unspeakable* plan to go on with the magazine *as if nothing had happened*, and to make it strictly surreal and experimental with no political articles (!); when it is not the communist articles the communists object to, but the strictly surrealist ones (the Kharkov resolution);[3] in fact, the communist articles were introduced by the communist-surrealist faction. This all seems nonsensical to me, especially the unimaginable sentence with which you conclude your explanation that I cite here verbatim: 'This approach may not be brilliant, but time will prove us right.' No, this will never prove us right because *surrealist experimentation* is, and always will be (*if genuine*), regarded as very subversive by today's society (that is to say, by the bourgeoisie), and as infinitely more subversive by today's communists, as they are paving the way for a bourgeois state of mind and ideology that is *far inferior* in evolutionary terms.

As for the films, I beg you not to undermine the gravity of this issue with yet another phrase that, again, is absolutely inexplicable coming from you: 'Do not forgive their artistic errors.' Artistic errors!! It's not about those errors (which do exist). Those films, shitty proletarian literature, etc., etc., are *polemical* works, with entirely propagandistic ends; they are the *faithful* expression of the spirit and ideology *to which they aspire*; these are *polemics* that are not only permitted (PERMITTED) by the government but made by that same government. Those films and that literature are *abominations*, made in the spirit of ideological shit, on grubby mysticism, on *veiled* sanctity, etc., etc.. That was what made Aragon cry when he saw *Earth*, Dovzhenko's infamous film,[4] not its artistry, but its *ideological content*. It is all unforgiveable; we are not talking, therefore, about artistic errors (I for one will never forgive the indecent optimism of that poem 'Red Front',[5] I find it shameful, poetically speaking. Poppies are red flags! It sounds Andalusian! It could almost, almost be Catalan!!!).

However, the most unbelievable phrase in your letter is this one: 'This new spirit of communism will reach future generations when the imperialist threat has passed, the dictatorship of the proletariat will come to an end with the disappearance of the social classes'. This phrase is exactly the kind of *reformist fatalism* in the realm of politics that you all (and rightly) used to hate so much; it is the equivalent of saying: 'There is no need to protest now nor prepare for the revolution because communism will arise inevitably out of the development of history and inherent contradictions of capitalism'(!). 'This is what the future generations will get'!!! This is your anti-dialectical reasoning when faced with the most transcendental and most human spiritual questions.

As this new state of mind and morality is the inevitable consequence of social and economic revolution, we do not need to concern ourselves with them any longer. WHAT SHIT! Those of us who have defended ideological and spiritual subversion honestly demand intervention, violent, incessant and urgent intervention in this sphere, as in the political sphere, through the most effectively revolutionary actions.

Historical materialism based on the constant assimilation of scientific evolution raises serious questions today: there are endless indications that this new obscurantism suggests that significant aspects of modern knowledge have not been incorporated into Marxism, nor into proletarian culture, and even that a significant amount of that knowledge has been brutally rejected. They do analyse with some objectivity the case for psychoanalysis as today's Marxists perceive it. But it is truly shameful.

There are some completely erroneous ideas in Marx and Engels[6] (on love) that may have been due to shortcomings in scientific knowledge at the time, but that are still held today. These ideas have been subjected to absolutely no modification to date, in spite of the overwhelming existence of Freud.

Had Marx, who appreciated as if it were his own the saying that 'nothing human is alien to me', and who turned even the meagre insights of his time to good effect when constructing his theories; had Marx known Freud, do you not think that he would have modified his timid theories of love? Everything is being violently rejected by the Stalins[7] of today who are organizing the most *chaste*, most REPRESSED society in history: playing checkers (?); physical exercise and only the kinds of love they consider to be natural and healthy (!!).

They are conjuring up the most horrendous form of spiritual slavery.

The rejection of everything that seems to be subversive in modern natural sciences is the same as the rejection of surrealism, instead all efforts will be channelled into the creation, little by little (alongside the great and magnificent economic revolution) of a bourgeois spirit, starting with the current shit of proletarian art and eventually raising 'future generations of ever more perfect spirit'.

Juan Ramón Jiménez, for example,* will surely be modified, but it will be for a more gentle Juan Ramón Jiménez, one that is less aggressive and more bourgeois as in the future communist society he will not have been influenced by our aggressive age of class and economic struggle.

In your case and in Aragon's, your absolute lack of appreciation for historical responsibility is monstrous. We may forgive the millions of revolutionaries who have no knowledge of surrealism, but in your case, you KNOW what surrealism represents for this age (particularly now, in the age of Russia's moral brutalization): THE ONLY POSSIBLE FUTURE FOR THE WORLD, FOR THE SPIRIT, AND FOR TRULY SUBVERSIVE MORALITY, I say your attitude is unforgiveable for we have a unique historical mission that depends on our own activities and conscience.

I know that you are both sincere people and that may well make it worse. With your new communist stance, you are as distant from me as Federico was when he published his *Gypsy Ballads*.** All of this reflects a frightening spiritual weakness that makes me think you never felt surrealism *as I did*. Surrealism will be strengthened by this future split because it was being held back by that unfortunate political dilettantism, from now on we shall denounce all shit, even if it is proletarian. In fact, Aragon has not existed as a surrealist for a while now. And you have contributed nothing to surrealism, *theoretically*, despite *my very high hopes of you*.

Surrealism is the only moral consolation left: you cannot imagine how strongly I condemn your attitude.

Down with the bourgeois and reactionary optimism of the five-year plan!
LONG LIVE SURREALISM!

This time, I violently demand a reply from you: there are no legitimate excuses; you cannot leave me with no news again for three months. It is very important for our friendship. I await your immediate reply with all the candour and *violence* you think necessary.

Regards,
Dalí

PS If we could talk, you would see that I am able to expand on and justify everything that I've just said here, because I am surrounded by notes and extremely well informed on all these matters, they are as familiar to me as to any communist. I've done nothing but read Marx (or 'about Marxism'?) for the last three months. I am preparing a long article on what Marx called *bestial love* and *modern sexual* love, full of documentary evidence and enormously objective. In it, I conduct an extensive analysis of *perversion* as an essential characteristic and condition of *human love* in that it (perversion) presupposes the intervention in love of intelligence and imagination. What we call *human* love is in fact bestial: but I demonstrate all of this with reference to quotations well known to everyone and with a precise methodology.

* Juan Ramón Jiménez is, in Spain, the representative of pure poetry, of the ivory tower, removed from all social struggle and revolutionary concern. He is the great poet of the upper class and the aristocracy.
** Federico García Lorca is a young Spanish poet (a former friend of mine and Dalí's), Catholic, queer, counter-revolutionary and arch-individualist.

Fre CmfL, PU

---

[1] Translation into French of a letter from Dalí to LB (the original of which has been lost), replying to one from LB (also lost); the asterixed notes are LB's.
[2] LB joined the Spanish Communist Party at the turn of 1931–1932.
[3] Reference to the conference Aragon attended of the Union internationale des écrivains révolutionnaires (UIER) in the Ukranian city of Kharkov, USSR, September 1930.
[4] Aleksandr Dovzhenko (1894–1956), Russian film-maker and director of *Zemlyá* (Earth, 1930).
[5] P. Éluard, 'Front rouge', poem published in *Littérature de la révolution mondiale*, no. 1, July 1931, UIER journal that provoked the 'Aragon affair' that divided the surrealist group.
[6] Karl Marx (1818–83) and Friedrich Engels (1820–95), authors of the *Communist Manifesto* (1848).
[7] Joseph Stalin (1878–1953), leader of the USSR from 1925 until his death in 1953.

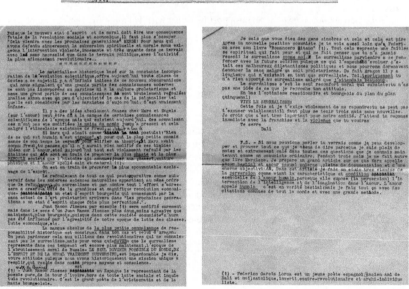

Figure 19 Copy of letter from Dalí to Buñuel, *c*. March 1932.

To Marie-Laure and Charles de Noailles

Paris, 17 March 1932

Very dear friends,

I've been wanting to write to you for some time now – since receiving Charles's letter – but these last few days I've been very busy with endless surrealist complications. I'm also tied up with 'dubbing' work for Paramount.

I spoke to Giacometti the other day about the *surprise* Charles mentioned in his letter: he has agreed to prepare it with me and we'll keep you informed.[1] As for Crevel, he told me he would write to you. He came for supper at my home on Sunday, with Mrs Cuevas and Ortiz.

Naturally, we spoke of nothing all night but the latest complications with the group. For rather complicated reasons, a new splinter group has formed consisting this time of Aragon, Sadoul,[2] Unik,[3] Alexandre,[4] Giacometti and me. This split was caused by the publication of Breton's *Poetry's Misery*.[5] Dalí wrote to me from Cadaqués: he now represents the extreme right wing of surrealism. It's all so sad and you can imagine the terrible time we are having.

Frankly, the Marseille business did not go well. That Mr Castelli took two months to decide to pay me 2,000 francs, and I see from your letter that the takings came to 13,000. The same with Belgium and Holland. As they don't want to pay me more than 1,000 francs per screening, I've spent the last month writing to them. Everyone has the same excuse: limited screenings due to censorship. I should like to know what you think, and whether you would prefer I just keep the film with me here, rather than let it go at that price. I still think that had the censors not intervened we would have recovered the production costs; Braunberger was saying the same thing a few days ago. The film has also been requested by Prague.

If you have a moment to write, I'd be grateful for more specific details about the kind of *surprise* you would like so that we can get on with our preparation. It goes without saying that we'll try to do the best possible job.

The other evening after dinner we played some poetic games and René was lamenting that Marie-Laure was not with us, because she would have loved it. Mrs Cuevas was truly inspired and wanted to carry on and wash the dishes. Only a titanic struggle on our part dissuaded her.

There are no major novelties as far as films go. There was a magnificent Eddie Cantor film, *Palmy Days*.[6] Renoir's film *The Bitch*, is *very well* made and has a very good cast.[7] In my opinion, it's the best French film in recent years. I went to see *Orpheus* by Offenbach[8] and found it admirable. A play, *Pains of Youth*,[9] has caused great commotion among the surrealists, especially Breton; but I prefer Wedekind.[10] It's the same genre, of course, but with that unpleasant so-called 'post-war' touch. Wedekind filtered through the Treaty of Versaille.

I got Nora's letter and want to write back at once. Do let her know and send her my thanks in advance.

Love to Laure and Nathalie and all my friendship to you both,
Luis

Fre Tls, BK; *AGE* 150–151

¹ 'Giraffe' installation LB and Giacometti made for the event at the de Noailles's residence in Hyères, mid–April 1932.
² Georges Sadoul (1904–67), French film historian.
³ Pierre Unik (1909–45), French poet.
⁴ Maxime Alexandre (1899–1976), French poet and dramatist.
⁵ Breton, *Misère de la poésie: L'Affaire Aragon devant l'opinion publique* (Paris: Éditions surréalistes, 1932).
⁶ *Palmy Days* (1931), dir. Edward Sutherland, starring US comic actor Eddie Cantor (1892–1964).
⁷ *La Chienne* (1931), co-producided by Braunberger, starring Michel Simon and Janie Marèse.
⁸ Jacques Offenbach (1819–80), French composer of German origin, whose comic opera *Orphée aux enfers* premiered in 1858.
⁹ *Krankenheit der Jugend*, play by Ferdinand Bruckner, premiered in Hamburg in 1926.
¹⁰ Frank Wedekind (1864–1918), German dramatist.

Figure 20 At the Noailles's villa, Hyères, April 1932: left to right, back row, Markevitch, Poulenc, Buñuel, Christian Bérard, Giacometti and Desbordes; front, Boris Kochno, Pierre Colle, Désormière and Henri Sauguet.

To André Breton

Paris, 6 May 1932

My dear Breton,

I do believe that in spite of my delay there is still time in this letter to state my position with regard to the surrealist group and to address the latest events that have marked a particularly serious phase for the very future of surrealism.

When some years ago I wanted to join forces with you, I saw that – leaving aside other purely poetic qualities – the great and truly subversive ideological consolation offered by surrealism was its implacable resistance to the intellectual sterility of the bourgeoisie, from which I myself originated and against which some time previously, I had rebelled. Only the fact that I had bound my ideological destiny to that of surrealism led me sometime later to join the PCE,[1] and in this choice I see, both subjectively and objectively, clear evidence of the revolutionary qualities of surrealism, my current position being the natural consequence of our collaboration over recent years. Until just a few months ago, I would never have thought it possible that an apparently violent contradiction would arise between these two disciplines, surrealism and communism: or that these latest events would demonstrate them now to be mutually incompatible. You will appreciate that, were it not for my recent affiliation with the PC (with all that entails, both practically and ideologically), the problem would never have arisen, and I would have continued to work with you all. However, given the current state of events, there is no room for a communist to doubt himself or to question for a moment the choice between his party and any other activity or discipline. I do not consider myself particularly politically gifted and I still believe my abilities would be put to better use within surrealism, but I doubt that I would be of more service to the revolution by remaining with you than by continuing to belong to a party for which I can at least make some contribution.

My separation from your activities does not mean that I completely abandon ALL your ideas, but only those that TODAY present an obstacle to the acceptance of the surrealist movement by the PC; obstacles that are, I want to believe, of a purely formal and transient nature. For example, poetically speaking, there is no doubt that my ideas may differ from your own, especially in my conviction that it is currently impossible to sustain a 'closed' notion of poetry over and above the class struggle. It is this word 'closed' that provokes the discrepancy between you and me. The subversive value of poetry removed from the context of class can only be subjective, although this does not prevent me thinking that insofar as emotion and love are concerned your poem 'Union libre'[2] is wholly admirable. It is not for me to resolve this difficult problem and I am happy to accept in the meantime (alongside poetry as you understand it or rather, as surrealism permits me to understand it), a less pure form of expression with propagandistic merit that may reach the masses more directly. This is why I have always liked the poem 'Front rouge' or at least its intentions.

Before finishing this letter, which I have pared down to say only what is essential, I want also to express my profound and absolute rejection of the manifestos and libellous writings that have followed the publication of *Misère de la poèsie* above all, *Paillasse!*.[3] As always, I continue to believe in the sincerity of your revolutionary stance, but this does not prevent me when I look at the 'circumstances' that led to your accusation of Aragon in *L'Humanité*[4] and the 'strict and literal' sense of that accusation, from distancing myself from the surrealist position that seeks to spoil Aragon's revolutionary activity in an 'affair' that is *far from* over.

Yours, in friendship,
Buñuel

Fre Tls, BNF/NAF25094/102; *AROJ* 117–118 f

[1] Partido Comunista de España, founded 14 March 1921.
[2] Love poem by Breton, first published in his book, *Le Revolver à cheveaux blancs* (Paris: Éditions des Cahiers Libres, 1932).
[3] Reference to the anti-Aragon pamphlet, *Paillasse! Fin de 'l'Affaire Aragon'*, published by Éditions Surréalistes in Paris, March 1932, with co-signatories including Char, Crevel, Dalí, Éluard, Ernst, Péret and Tzara.
[4] French communist newspaper, founded in 1904; on 10 March 1932; Aragon calls Breton's text 'counterrevolutionary'.

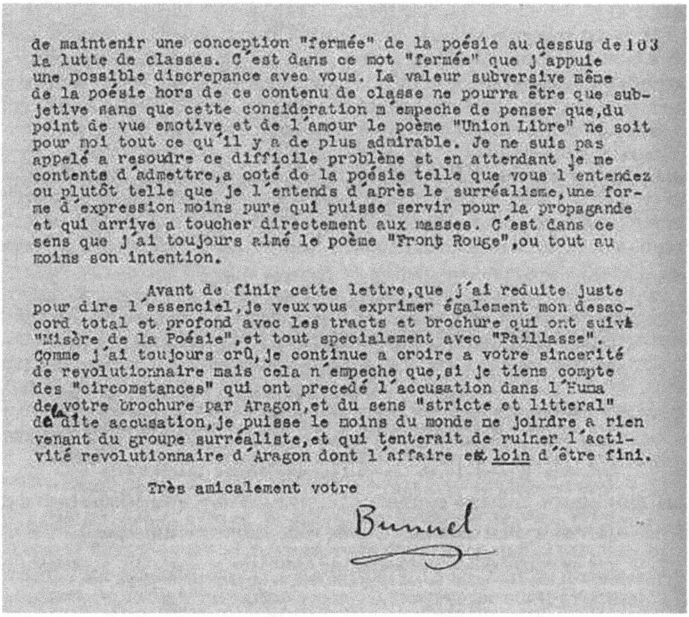

Figure 21 Letter from Buñuel to Breton, 6 May 1932.

To Pierre Unik

Near Sabiñánigo and Sallent de Gállego (Huesca), 19 June 1932

My dear Unik,

I hope you got my telegram and have now applied for your passport.

Even though I've no money, I can still send you 100 pesetas (200 francs), which should be enough to buy you a third-class return ticket to Pau. Take the train from Orsay station at 7:20 sharp and you will be in Pau by 8 am. I'll pick you up at around 10. Wait for me on the platform. Send me a telegram to let me know which day you'll be leaving Paris. If you don't want to come, write to me so that I can quickly send you the *scénario* I've now finished, adding new dialogues, etc.[1] I would still like to change quite a few things, but we can work on it here and you could take it back with you and deliver it to Braunberger. As for me, I'll have to return to Madrid.

Everything is so beautiful around here. Bring warm clothes because it can be hellishly cold at times. You'll be staying in a hotel. I'm at my mother's house, under close supervision.

I look forward to hearing from you.

Regards,
Buñuel

Fre, Tls, PU

[1]   Script of *Wuthering Heights* co-written by LB Unik and Sadoul.

To Pierre Unik

San Sebastian, 16 August 1932

My dear Unik,

Your letter arrived safely and by dint of this *desperate effort* I am managing to reply.

Firstly, thank you for the information and news, which are not as disturbing as we imagined on our way to Pau. The only really disappointing news is about Wenstein and M. T. Georges. They may face the firing squad over there.

Let's discuss the *scénario*. I had finished it all, including the epilogue, when Braunberger turned up at my house three days ago to pick it up. I'd sent a telegram to Paris and the people at Billancourt told him I was here. I went to Saint-Jean[1] yesterday and we discussed the script, because he had already read it. He thinks it's very good and says he has now made up his mind to make the film. He will start organizing everything when he gets back to Paris. I'm afraid though that even if all goes well, we won't start filming for another couple of months. It's vital to speak to the sponsors, etc., and reassure them that this is a *commercial film*. Braunberger had a reasonable suggestion, which was to add to the tension by finishing with the cemetery scene and inserting some extra material between the love scene and Lisbeth's[2] death. It won't be easy but I'm going to try. Conclusion: I'm sure there will be two or three months' work for you this winter.

I've seen a few comrades down here and meet new ones every day. It's a wonderful country, especially as there is so much still to be done. I'm still hoping to go to Madrid, but I don't have any money. At least I get fed here. I'm thinking of borrowing some money and leaving within the week. If you need to write to me though, you can still use this address. The monarchist plot was quite serious, and if it failed it was only thanks to the workers.[3] The Republicans thanked them, however, with the barrel-end of a gun the very day after the coup.

They are now more sickening than ever, and they all seem to think they're great Don Quijotes (Braunberger really liked Richard's heroic gesture). I hope they'll get what they deserve someday soon. I'm imagining the crowd jostling Largo Caballero[4] in the middle of a riot as I, forcefully opening up a path, save him from the people's rage. He then thanks me with great emotion and I, with a heinous smile, say: 'I trust you are not confusing me with Don Quijote?' And pull his teeth out two at a time.

I've no news of anyone, except what you sent in your letter. There are lots of pretty girls around here, but I am still fasting. I don't have anyone to introduce me and they are all decent women. Nothing to be done.

I've read *Babahouo*.[5] It's got some good bits and some very funny moments. But nothing really new and impossible to make after what happened with *An Andalusian Dog* and *The Golden Age*. The theoretical side is even funnier. I saw Man Ray[6] at Saint-Jean and he told me that Dalí has high hopes that some director will decide to film it.

I'm thinking of coming back at the beginning of next month. I'll let you know.

Regards from,
Buñuel

PS Let me know if you want to come to San Sebastian. Campos remembers you fondly even though he can't stand the French because of the Napoleonic Wars. And send Cerquant[7] my anti-Trotskyist regards.

Fre Tlsps, PU

[1] Saint-Jean-de-Luz, French Basque town about 30 km from Braunberger's home in San Sebastian.
[2] Female protagonist of *Wuthering Heights*.
[3] Thwarted political coup against the Second Republic led by General Jorge Sanjurjo on 10 August 1932.
[4] Francisco Largo Caballero (1869–1946), left-wing politician, president of the Spanish Socialist Workers' Party and Minister for Work in 1932.
[5] Film script by Dalí, subtitled *Scénario inédit précédé d'un histoire critique du cinema et suivi de Guillaume Tell, ballet portugais.*
[6] Pseudonym of Emmanuel Radnitzky (1890–1976), US photographer and film-maker.
[7] Émile Cerquant (1913–68), French journalist and film critic.

To Marie-Laure and Charles de Noailles

San Sebastian, 18 August 1932

Dear Marie-Laure and Charles,

I got the letter you wrote on-board and I envy your beautiful journey. I remember our meetings last summer and the small library, so perfectly chosen for a paddle steamer trip. Is Stendhal[1] still the favourite?

Are you already in Saint-Bernard? I would love to hear from you again.

I spent two weeks in a village in the Spanish Pyrenees that was truly impressive and anti-touristic. Impossible to find more absolute and bleak solitude. I've enclosed some photos. Pierre Unik came to visit me there. He really is a clever and good man. After the mountains, I went to Jaca, to Zaragoza and then finally came here ten days ago. At the end of August I mean to travel to Madrid then go back to Paris around 10 September. What a shame I won't see you until October. Our 'philosophical' meetings were interrupted so abruptly …

I've now given Braunberger my adaptation of *Wuthering Heights*: he liked it a lot and is planning to film it when he has the money. It could be a good romance. It won't have music, which is a shame because I would have liked to involve some of our musical friends, especially Markevitch and Nabokov.[2] I was talking to them recently at your house. So it would probably be better not to mention it to them.

I have no news from friends, not even from Aragon, who must have been in the Urals for a month now. And although everything was going well, I've heard nothing from Sojuskino either.

Dalí and Gala wrote to invite me to Cadaqués, where Crevel is also staying. Unfortunately, I won't be able to go due to lack of time and resources. They sent me *Babahouo*; there were fragments I found amusing, but the theoretical side is rather odd.

Last night, at around 11pm, I was thinking of you; remembering that is the time you take the flowers out to the garden. I would have liked to be there to lend a hand as I used to.

Yours,
Luis

Fre Als, BK; *AGE* 158

¹ Pseudonym of French writer, Marie-Henri Beyle (1783–1842).
² Igor Markevitch (1912–83) and Nicolas Nabokov (1903–78), Russian composers LB met at Hyères in April 1932.

To Marie-Laure and Charles de Noailles

Paris, 24 September 1932

Dear Marie-Laure and Charles,

Marie-Laure's news-filled letter arrived while I was in Spain. I got back to Paris shortly afterwards. I still haven't seen any of our mutual friends; I hope and assume you will have more news than I do.

As soon as I arrived, I began work on my next film.[1] It's all going very well and we should start shooting in a couple of months. I am passionately committed to this one. And I think I've kept the script very true to the spirit of the book.

A bit of bad news. Braunberger handed over my *new* film, *In the Frozen Waters of Selfish Calculation* to the censors three days ago. For two days, although they had already seen it, they gave no hint as to their decision. They must have consulted with all the Chiappes,[2] etc. Finally, yesterday, they told us they were definitely refusing it a licence. I think it's a small act of vengeance on that lady's[3] part, because there is nothing in the film to justify censorship. I even cut out the scene where the blind man is kicked recently, because I no longer agree with it. This should perhaps lead me to conclude that having made *The Golden Age*, I should never make another film? I'm sure that, objectively, there was nothing to censor and what's more there have been a number of requests for screenings in October. If I had any influence, I would campaign vigorously against such wholly fascist arbitrariness. As I have none, no one will find out about this latest 'castor oil purge' on their part.

When Ortiz came to see me, he told me all about the old-fashioned, novelesque romance taking place at Saint-Martin d'Ardèche featuring the Ernsts, Breton, Ortiz, Valentine, and starring one Miss Colette.[4] Apparently, Breton has proposed to her, but she is in love with Ortiz.[5] Valentine stormed like enraged Juno out of Ardèche for Paris. Followed by Manolo, who found himself excluded by the Ernsts, who play the role in this tale of the defenders of Miss Colette's honour. The epilogue is yet to come. Perhaps we will soon hear wedding bells and see Breton advancing, appropriately dressed in black, over dry leaves, his arm extended, very pale, etc., etc.

When are you planning to return? It must be soon, and it makes me happy to think I'll see you again.

With all my affection,
Luis

Fre Tls, BK; *AGE* 159–160

[1] *Wuthering Heights.*
[2] Jean Chiappe (1878–1940), Paris Chief of Police, involved in the banning of *The Golden Age.*
[3] Censorship (feminine noun in Spanish).
[4] Possibly Colette Jerameck, daughter of a French industrialist and first wife of Roland Tual.
[5] Breton ended his relationship with Valentine Hugo in 1932.

From José Bello

Madrid, 30 January 1933

Dear Luis,

You left before we could take that trip to Toledo. It's a shame, because who knows when we'll get another opportunity like that.

I bumped into the Vile Barrel-Belly[1] yesterday; he was in Madrid for that conference and I enclose his photograph here. He told me he's trying to organize a fascist party in Malaga.

I'm leaving for Seville tonight, I'll write you a long letter from there to see if we can pick up on our old correspondence.

I'm leaving without having seen Federico.

The piece of roasted meat sleeps under an olive tree next to the road from San Feliu to San Guíxols, covered with a newspaper and under a gravestone that reads 'The Norms'.[2]

Much love,
Pepín

Als, AB/601; *BLD* 256

[1] José María Hinojosa.
[2] Reference to a short story (starring a piece of meat), '*La agradable consigna de Santa Huesca*', co-written by LB and Bello in the Café Castilla, Madrid, December 1932.

To Man Ray

Paris, 26 March 1933

My dear friend,

I leave for Spain at the end of the week and wanted to see you beforehand to ask if you would like to come along.[1] Do you want to come for supper at my house next

Wednesday at 8pm? Lotar[2] and Unik will be there. We can discuss the 'excursion' over dinner and prepare our departure, the itinerary, budget, etc., etc. I'd be delighted if you could make this little get–together. If I don't hear to the contrary, I'll see you on Wednesday.

Yours,
Buñuel,

Fre Als, CL/204.6

[1] To Las Hurdes, Extremadura, to film *Land without Bread*.
[2] Éli Lotar (1905–69), French photographer and film-maker of Rumanian origin, director of photography on *Land without Bread* and co-director with Yves Allégret of the documentary *Tenerife* (1932).

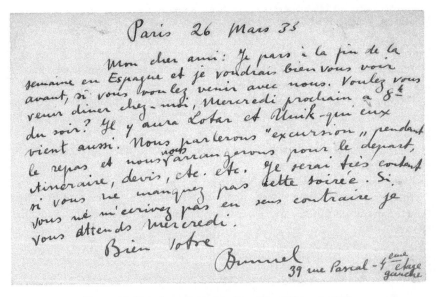

Figure 22 Note from Buñuel to Man Ray, 26 March 1933.

To Éli Lotar and Pierre Unik

Las Batuecas,[1] 16 April 1933

Dear Lotar and Unik,[2]

You need to bring your journey forward.

I hope you got the telegram that preceded this letter.

Leave Paris on the 20th *at the latest* (and if possible on the 19th); on the 21st (or even better the 20th) you will arrive at Canfranc. Ask for Mr Agulló, administrator of the Spanish customs office, and introduce yourselves as friends of ours (Acín[3]

Madrid 10 Janvier 1934

Mon cher Pierre: Tu as mis longtemps à m'ecrire
et moi aussi,mais malgré ça je savais bien,comme toi,que "cela ne
voulait rien dire". De toutes façons il serait preferable d'avoir
des nos nouvelles plus souvent. J'attendais toujours le moment pro-
pice pour t'inviter,que je voyais très prés,et celle-ci est la pri-
cipale raison de mon silence.

Maintenant je peux t'avancer quelque chose sûre
mais avant il faut que je te fasse une petite histoire"clinique"de
ma vie depuis que je t'ai vu la dernière fois.

Tu sais que je suis venu en Espagne exclusive-
ment parce que je me trouvais mal de santé et que le moyens de vie
devenaient difficiles à Paris. J'ai passé sept mois tenant debout
mais avec des douleurs à la jambe et craignant toujours la crise
aigüe de sciatique. Il y a deux mois j'ai eu enfin cette crise qui
m'a jeté au lit où je continue encore aujourd'hui malgré que
je me trouve beaucoup mieux. J'ai eu de sales moments pas seulement
phisiques mais morales. A la fin je decidais de m'instaler à Madrid
et attendre que ma santé soit entierement retabli et en me consolant
de Paris pensant que la guerre allait éclater bientôt. Donc......

J'ai dit a Jane de donner congé pour l'apparte-
ment à Paris et de faire venir à Madrid les meubles. A partir du
mois de Fevrier je serai completement installé et tu peux choisir
l'époque qui te conviens le plus pour venir passer un ou deux mois
en Espagne. Si tu as l'argent pour le voyage tu n'a pas besoin d'un
sou de plus. Lacasa veux aussi t'inviter dans une maison très sympha
tique qu'il vient de se construire à coté de Madrid. Donc,tu as
déjà deux endroits pour passer des longs séjours. Maintenant j'ai une
petite bagnole et très peu de travail:nous voyagerions tout le temps.
Seulement je prefererait que tu arrives quand je serai completement
guerit. Pour finir:j'insiste que pour venir à Madrid tu as besoin
d'avoir SEULEMENT le prix du billet ALLER à Madrid. Maintenant c'est
à toi la parole.

Je ne sais pas si etant donnés les conditions
de mauvaise santé où je me trouve vont m'accepter en U.R.S.S. Cela
va sans dire que ce projet me plait extraordinairement et que si je
peux j'irai travailler la bas.

and Buñuel). He will have been asked to help you with the customs paperwork. If
Mr Agulló is not there, find the owner of the hotel at the station, who is a friend.
He'll give you the money to pay the customs office, if necessary. I'll write to him
later on.

You'll leave Canfranc for Zaragoza at 4pm and arrive at 8pm. The next morning, that
is, on the 21st, take the 9am train for Madrid; you'll be there by 3pm. We'll be waiting for
you at the station. If for any reason there's no one there, go straight to the Hotel Dardé,
7 Constantino Rodríguez Street. At the hotel, ask for Acín or for Sánchez Ventura (this
timetable is only a rough guide),

          Tu ne dois pas savoir que le film "HURDES" a
été defendu partout,en Espagne& et à l´etranger et que j´ai appris
que la prohibition viens de l´ambassade d´Espagne à Paris. Il pa-
rait que Vogel a voulu faire un chantage avec ton article et souti-
rer d´argent a l´ambassade pour ne pas le publier. L´ambassade a été
mise en eveil et par sa demande le ministère de l´interieur içi a
defendu le film. J´ai eu ces renseignements de sources absolument
veridiques.

          Ecris-moi bien long en me racontant le genre
de vie que tu menes.Je pense très souvent a nos repas et reunions
et vraiment je vois qui comptent beaucoup pour moi. En attendant
que je retourne à Paris nous renouvelèerons tout ça à Madrid,Batue-
cas,etc. Tu dois me dire vers quelle époque tu prefererais venir içi
te reposer.

          La situation en Espagne est très indecise et
on peut difficilement prevoir la sortie inmediate. Nous sommes toujours en etat de guerre et cela par peur qu´on puisse parler sur
l´infame repression du mouvement. Hitler a fait beaucoup moins que
nos Lerroux et Gil. J´ai envoyé a Hernando pour te la passer une
lettre d´un deputé radical-socialiste a Lerroux,et qui a mon avis
est un document precieux pour aider la campagne internationale con
tre la repression. Je dois dire qu´avec ███████████ ma maladie et
mon alitement je suis actuellement un peu dehors de la politique.

          Breton m´a ecrit l´autre jour pour que je lui
prête "L´age d´or";il doit aller faire une conference a Tenerife et
il en a besoin. Ces sont toutes les nouvelles surréalistes que j´ai
eu après mon depart.

          Je voudrais que tu me donnes des nouvelles
de "tes amours" toujours un peu misterieux. Mais je ne voudrais pas
te demander trop de choses pour qu´elles ne te donnent pas la paresse
de m´ecrire.

                    Grandes abrazos de *Luis*

          Je repondrai a tes lettres.

          As tu demenagé de chez tes parents? Tu habites
dans un atelier,appartement,ou quoi?

Figure 23 Letter from Buñuel to Unik, 10 January 1934.

That's all. But … do exactly as I've asked.

It's a wonderful place, much better than we could have imagined. On the 24th, there is an extraordinary feast day we really must film.[4]

See you both soon,
Buñuel[5]

PS When you get to Canfranc, send a telegram to Acín at the Hotel Dardé, 7, Constantino Rodríguez Street, Madrid.

Communist greetings,
Buñuel.
Anarchist greetings,
Acín.
Greetings!
Sánchez Ventura

Fre Als, PU

---

[1] Valley in the southern Salamanca region, about 30 km from Las Hurdes.
[2] Unik, together with Sánchez Ventura, is assistant producer on *Land without Bread*.
[3] Ramón Acín Aquilué (1888–1936), artist, writer, teacher and co-producer of *Land without Bread*.
[4] 'El Día del Trago', festival celebrated in La Alberca, in which recently married young men on horseback pull the heads of cockerels, as shown in *Land without Bread*.
[5] Letter dictated by LB and written by Sánchez Ventura with postscripts from all three, including Acín.

To Pierre Unik

Madrid, 10 January 1934

My dear Pierre,

You took your time writing to me, as I did to you. But I know, as do you, that this 'signifies nothing'. Still, it would be better to be in touch more often. The main reason for my silence was that I kept waiting for the most propitious moment to invite you here, which always seemed only just on the point of arriving.

I now have concrete news, but first I should give you a brief 'clinical' history of my life since I last saw you.

You know I only came to Spain because my health was very bad and life in Paris was becoming difficult. I put up with it for seven months, but my leg was painful, and I was living in fear of an acute attack of sciatica. A couple of months ago that attack finally came confining me to my bed, where I remain, although I'm feeling much better. I had some terrible times, not just physically, but also in terms of morale. In the end, I decided to move to Madrid and stay there until I was completely better; my consolation for not being in Paris was the thought that war was about to break out. So …

I told Jeanne to cancel the contract on the Paris apartment and send the furniture to Madrid. I'll be fully installed from February and you'll be able to decide when it best suits you to come and spend a month or two in Spain. If you have enough money for the journey, you won't need a peseta more. Lacasa also wants to invite you to stay at a very beautiful house he has just had built near Madrid. So, you already have two places to stay on long visits. I have a small car now and very little work: so we could travel all the time. Although I would, of course, prefer you to come when I am completely recovered. So – I repeat – you ONLY need the cost of your fare TO Madrid. Now, it's up to you to say when.

I don't know whether, given my current state of health, they will take me on in the USSR. Although I'm really enthusiastic about the project and will, if possible, go and work over there.

You may not know that *Land without Bread*[1] was banned everywhere in Spain and abroad, and I'm told the ban came from the Spanish Embassy in Paris. It seems Vogel[2] wanted to use your article to do a little blackmailing and get some money out of the Embassy not to publish it. This alerted the Embassy and they sent word to the Ministry of the Interior over here, who then banned the film. I have all this from an absolutely reliable source.

Write back at great length telling me all about your life. I often think about our lunches and get-togethers – they really mean a lot to me. While I await my return to Paris, let's continue them here in Madrid, Las Batuecas, etc. Let me know roughly when you would like to come here for a break.

The situation in Spain is very unstable and it's very difficult to envisage an immediate solution. We are practically at war, and all because they are scared someone will speak out against this shameful repression.[3] Hitler[4] has done far less than our own Lerroux[5] and Gil.[6] I sent a letter for Hernando to pass on to you; it's a letter from a radical-socialist member of parliament to Lerroux that is, in my opinion, an incredibly valuable document for the international campaign against repression here. I should say though that being ill and confined to bed has somewhat distanced me from politics for now.

Breton wrote the other day to ask if I would lend him *The Golden Age*; he needs it for a talk he's giving in Tenerife.[7] That is the only surrealist news I've heard since I left.

I'd like to hear news of your always rather mysterious 'loves'. But I don't want to ask too many questions in case it puts you off writing back.

Much love
Luis

PS I will reply to your letters.

Did you move into your parents' house? Are you living in a studio, an apartment, or somewhere else?

Fre Tls, PU

---

[1] The film was screened with live commentary from LB at the Palacio de la Prensa in Madrid, December 1933, but was banned from general release by the Spanish government.
[2] Lucien Vogel, owner of the review *Vu*, for which Unik had written an article on *Land without Bread*.

[3] Reference to the Anarchist uprising in December 1933 that was violently repressed by the new coalition government made up of the Partido Republicano Radical (PRR) and the Confederación Española de Derechas Autónomas (CEDA).

[4] Adolf Hitler (1889–1945) was elected chancellor of Germany in January 1933.

[5] Alejandro Lerroux García (1864–1949), leader of the PRR and president of the cabinet from December 1933 to April 1934.

[6] José María Gil-Robles (1898–1980), leader of CEDA and Member of Parliament from1931 to 1939, attended the Nuremberg Rally in September 1933 as an observer.

[7] For the Second Universal Surrealist Exhibition in Tenerife, postponed until May 1935.

From Guillermo de Torre[1]

[Madrid,] 26 May 1934

Mon cher Louis,[2]

I now know you were in Madrid a while ago and made no attempt to visit me. That's fine. But because I am more of a friend to you than you realize, I shall now pay you back as follows by asking you to send me some photographs from your film about Las Hurdes. I realize that our 'very clever' government has banned it in Spain. But I don't think that veto extends to the reproduction of a few scenes in the press. Let's risk it together anyway, because I'm very interested in publishing some photos from the film and have the perfect conditions under which to do so. I have at my disposal and subject to absolutely no restrictions of any kind a weekly column in a magazine, *Diablo Mundo*[3] (edited by Corpus Barga, very wide-ranging, intellectually tied to no particular political flag; and I should say Alberti contributed to the latest edition[4] to soothe any scruples you may have). I am due to review your film in my column – as far as I am able without having seen it – and to make some appropriate comment on its prohibition. I'm not the only one who wants you to send the photos. Corpus Barga and other mutual friends are also interested. So, please humour us as soon as you can.

And send news, if possible, of your current and future *activities*,[5] as they say in America. I write with the steadfast faith of *naguère*,[6] steadfast in my conviction that this is all that matters. I shall be passing through Paris mid-July, on my return from The Hague, where I'm going back this year to give some lectures. Let me know if you'll be there then and I'll be sure to get in touch.

I await the photos. Be a 'good man' and send them to me. Regards from Norah[7] and love from your old friend,

Guillermo de Torre
130 Velázquez, Madrid

Spa Tls L, ABC/03/31

[1] Guillermo de Torre (1900–71), poet, essayist and chief editor of *La Gaceta Literaria*.

[2] French in the original (My dear Luis).

[3] Literally, 'Devil World', weekly magazine published in Madrid from April to June 1934.

[4] Alberti published the poem 'Geráneos' in *Diablo Mundo*, no. 5, 26 May 1934, p. 9.

[5] English in the original.

6   French in the original (of yesteryear).
7   Norah Borges, pseudonym of Leonor Borges Acevedo (1901–98), Argentinian artist and art critic, Torre's wife, and sister of writer Jorge Luis Borges.

From Salvador Dalí

[Paris, May 1934]

Dear Buñuel,

I have just seen *An Andalusian Dog* in Studio 28, and imagine my *stupefaction*, my *indignation*, to see that there was *absolutely no* reference to my participation. You will no doubt appreciate that this is such an outrageous *moral* and *material* injustice that I have put the matter in the hands of a solicitor at once, as there is more than sufficient reason to do so and as I can claim significant compensation for the days it has been screened without any indication of *my participation* when there are existing documents to prove the participation in question (*La Révolution surréaliste*, etc.).

In Barcelona[1], the program also glosses over two essential facts: 'surrealist film' and *my participation*. I am even more surprised by this as I believe *The Golden Age* still belongs to you, that is, that you haven't sold it yet, as you have *An Andalusian Dog*.

I am ready, moreover, to turn this into the most phenomenal scandal. When do you arrive?

I hope you will help with my suit if necessary; you know *better than anyone* that neither *An Andalusian Dog* nor its successor *The Golden Age* could have existed *without me*. This incomprehensible brushing aside of my participation is therefore quite monstrous.

I shall take this to its furthest limits.

REGARDS,
Dalí

PS *I am really livid! All friends and acquaintances also indignant.*

Spa Als, ABC/01/02; *LBFC* 565

1   Screening of *The Golden Age* at the Cine Fantasio, Barcelona, 18 May 1934.

From Jeanne Rucar

Paris, 26 May 1934

Dear Luisito,

Your letter arrived on Thursday and I gave it to Mohos at once.[1] Now, let me tell you what happened to me that same Thursday afternoon: I went to Montmartre with Georgette[2] to buy some things and on our way we bumped into Dalí who said: 'Imagine, they're screening *An Andalusian Dog* at Studio 28 and it is dreadful – my name doesn't appear anywhere, so I've made an appointment with my lawyer and I'm going to sue the director; we're going to sort him out good and proper.' When he had finished, I told him that it wouldn't be necessary because the matter had been resolved; he was very happy. As for his threat to sue, he still doesn't see the funny side and thinks it should stand. I went to see Mohos this morning, mostly to collect the 500 francs, but also to ask him what Gross[3] (Studio 28) is planning to do, and he's going to ask GMF at once for a few more metres of film. And as for the threat to sue, Mohos agrees with Dalí that it can stay as it is, and the manager of a cinema has every right to tell his customers it has nothing to do with the film. Argus is starting to send his articles through. Still no letters. Well, there is one from Braunberger, he wants to see you, so I'm going to telephone or send him a note to let him know you're not here.

I saw Nuniez yesterday, the man who came for the Las Hurdes film: on behalf of Studio Éclair. Is that the same company that you were dealing with before you left?

Still no news from you.

I hear Piqueras[4] is out of the clinic; how is he doing?

I went to see Mr Bardinet yesterday to ask him exactly what documents we need,[5] because I was told you would need written consent from *your parents*. I thought that couldn't be right, but I wanted to consult with Mr Bardinet. We need your birth certificate, your identity card, a certificate of residency from the concierge, and maybe even a Certificate of Custom/Law for Marriage, although I'm not sure about this last one. In short, Luis, you must hurry because time is of the essence; don't forget your ID card and birth certificate.

I think yours will be enough for the town hall. But I'm worried that we'll have to go to the bride's town hall, because there are still some things to take care of.

I am very happy to be marrying you too, mostly because I love you very much and, well, I don't know what else, but I'll tell you something my Luisito, we need to hurry, a lot. I went for supper at Hernando's on Thursday and I'm worried we won't be able to count on them to be our witnesses, because they are planning to go to the Midi soon, you'll need to get your documents organized fast. Hernando is going to get you a tailcoat and Lulu,[6] a pretty dress???

But Luisito, where will I go if you stay in Madrid? I'm sure I could be with you for a few months, no? What do you think? Then later you could say 'Push off, Juanita' and I would leave … We'll discuss all this again when we're together.

I'm going to see the doctor on Monday, because I should, apparently,[7] Lulu was really insistent that I go.

My Luisito, I should like the first 500 francs to be for me, do you think I can have them? It would make me very happy.

Don't forget your *identity card*, whatever you do.

I will leave you now, Luisito. Until very soon now.

Much love from your
Juanita

PS Send my best to Conchita. Any news from her? I'll reply as soon as I get your letter.
Lots of kisses

Fre Als, ABC/05/19

1   Zoltán Mohos, film distributor of Hungarian origin, from Paris-based Intercontinental Films.
2   Georgette Rucar, sister of Jeanne, secretary at Sánchez Cuesta's Librairie Espagnole.
3   Édouard Gross, owner of Studio 28 from 1932.
4   Juan Piqueras Martínez (1904–36), film critic and editor of the Spanish journal *Nuestro Cinema* from 1932 to 1935, hospitalized that month with stomach ulcers.
5   For their marriage.
6   Lulu Jourdain, wife of Hernando Viñes; the couple were witnesses at LB and Jeanne Rucar's wedding in Paris, on 23 June 1934.
7   Jeanne is pregnant with their first child.

From Salvador Dalí

[Paris, May 1934]

Dear Buñuel,
   Your letter seems to me to suffer from a *terrifying* lack of objectivity.

1) You said: '*An Andalusian Dog* doesn't *belong* to me; I've sold it to I don't know whom; it leaves a nasty taste in my mouth; he can do with it whatever he wants, etc.' But now it transpires that it does still belong to you.

2) I have seen *two* lawyers who *assure* me in no uncertain terms that I can win *damages* (there are *precedents*), [even] without a contract or the evidence from *La Révolution surréaliste* and in letters where you mention our collaboration, etc., etc. and all kinds of personal testimonies. The most *surprising* thing is that according to your letter you were prepared, if the case went ahead, to *deny our collaboration*, which seems to me a colossal betrayal.

3) I bumped into Juanita by chance,[1] and she explained that the film was now yours, that I shouldn't do anything, that everything would be sorted out, and naturally I put the matter on hold.

4) You say that [the copy of] *An Andalusian Dog* being screened at Studio 28 features neither your name nor mine; excuse me for correcting you, but I have *seen the film for myself*, as have others, and my name is not there, whereas yours is. There was a large sign saying 'Film by BUÑUEL' and nothing else, no actors, no Duverger, nothing.

But the worst thing in all of this is your lack of objectivity that, as you will have seen when you began to read this letter, I perceive to be *terrifying*, because, despite the fact that I've been obliged to *discuss* these *lamentable* incidents *on many occasions*, you continue to *resist* in a way you may not even be aware of as you appear to be speaking in good faith.
   You try to justify the description of the film *The Golden Age, film by Buñuel*, with no mention of my participation, as just another of the foolish customs of normal film programming.[2] That is phenomenal!! And phenomenal for the following reasons:

1) *The Golden Age* is not a *normal* film nor is it an *exception*, which would justify exceptional programming.

2) Normal programming never says *film by so-and-so director*, but gives the title and names of the *stars*, with no mention of the director, unless it is one of the greats (Murnau,[3] etc., and *I am sending an example*); in other words, your programme is not normal, but extravagant, given that you don't even mention the *stars* etc.

Conclusions:

Given that you announce the film in a way that is completely out of the ordinary, why the *fuck* would you not go just *a little further*, as it wouldn't cost you a single centime, and put that I collaborated on the *scénario*, which is the *truth*? As you know, *this is very important to me* and, moreover, our friendship would seem to justify this, even if there were no more objective reasons, because, as you know, in a *surrealist film* the *scénario*, the *plot*, is more important than in normal films where, the plotting is usually non-existent.

You are the most thoughtless man in the world. I am amazed how blind you are to your own motives. Deep down, you want, unconsciously, to erase my part in the two films and you are attempting to do so by consciously invoking all manner of childish and ridiculous pretexts.

Your confused use of the word *author* in its *exclusive* sense, rather than *author-director*, as I am also an *author* (look up the meaning of that word, which you use in such a strange way), is symptomatic. You will remember that you admitted yourself when discussing this sorry subject that it was monstrous to attach the same degree of importance to my participation as to Braunberger,[4] Simone Mareuil or the obnoxious Batcheff, who appeared in the beach scene,[5] because in the film we see 'Film by Luis Buñuel', followed by, and all in the same font, '*scénario* by Dalí and Buñuel; with: Pierre Batcheff, Simone Mareuil, etc.; camera operator, Braunberger,[6] etc. really incredible and, if you remember correctly, you said so yourself.

To conclude: this is all very serious and I promise you that had I been in your shoes I would have taken care of and handled your participation far more scrupulously.

You find my moral and material principles funny; but they are *only fair* and it is shit that people I am *interested in* do not know that I collaborated on the film and that I have explain it to them myself, etc., etc.

If you were suddenly to see the film presented as '*The Golden Age, film by Dalí*' I'm sure you would be far from indifferent.

Without me, these films would never have existed, remember your vanguardist projects with Gómez de la Serna when I was writing the first version of *An Andalusian Dog* and inventing *surrealist film* for the very first time.

Dalí

Spa Als, ABC/01/03; *BMS* 215–216

---

[1] Jeanne Rucar is sometimes referred to as Jane, Juana or Juanita.
[2] *The Golden Age* was shown in Barcelona at private session for the Agrupació 'Amics de l'Art Nou', 7 June 1934.
[3] Friedrich Wilhelm Murnau (1888–1931), German film-maker.
[4] Dalí appears to be confusing Braunberger with Duverger.
[5] Robert Hommet plays the man on the beach.
[6] See note 4.

To Nora[1] and Georges Sadoul

Madrid, 16 August 1934[2]

Dear Nora and Georges,

I was away from Madrid for a few days and found your letter on my return. What a surprise to discover you are in Spain, although unfortunately a little far away for me. I never go to Barcelona.

Do you have a fixed or open return? If it's open, I would love to see you in Madrid. I promise I would entertain you here to the best of my abilities. And it wouldn't be expensive. I may still live hand-to-mouth, but I have the means to alleviate your costs considerably. You can count on me to pick up the bill for any excursions and most of the meals. If it were winter, I would be able to put you up with friends, but that's not possible at the moment.

I've had no news from Aragon, although I did know that he had left for the USSR. Unik sent me a letter from Toulon.

My life at the moment is quite gloomy and most of all stultifying, because of the work I have to do.[3] Luckily, I go out as little as possible and sometimes have days when I'm completely free. My boss in is Barcelona, what's more.[4] I'm in Madrid for health reasons: I've spent the last five months with a sciatica problem that has made it impossible for me to do anything. I sometimes feel like a 'great invalid' who has 'gone to war'. I hope that this winter won't cripple me completely and confine me to my bed.

As I don't much like to write, I'll finish now. If you can come, let me know so I can save up a little and keep a few days free for some excursions.[5]

Warmest regards,
Luis Buñuel

Fre Tls L, GS/64

[1] Jacqueline 'Nora' Sadoul (1912–39), first wife of Sadoul and sister of Henri Cartier-Bresson.
[2] Written on Residencia de Estudiantes letterhead.
[3] Supervisor of dubbing for Madrid branch of Warner Brothers (US studios founded in 1923) established in Spain from January 1934.
[4] René Huet, supervisor of French dubbing.
[5] The Sadouls visited Madrid and attended, with LB, a joint meeting of the Socialist and Communist Youth at the University Stadium on 16 September 1934.

To Elie Lotar

Madrid, 30 September 1934

My dear Lotar,

Your letter has arrived, and I am delighted to have news of you.

I see you have serious 'work' plans and I promise I'll do whatever I can to help you get to Madrid. At the moment it's not easy because film production has only just begun and the five or six local operators are hogging all the work. That said, there are a few foreign operators here. If I hear of any opportunities, I'll let you know at once.

You also did the right thing meeting with Grémillon,[1] he has worked in Spain and is thinking of doing so again.[2] He will be able to help you, and we could both look for something you could do. If not on a film, then with me[3]

Spa Ba, ABC/04/09

[1]   Jean Grémillon (1901–59), French film-maker, met LB at the Billancourt Studios in 1929.
[2]   Grémillon directed *La Dolorosa* (1934) for Falcó Films at the CEA Studios in Madrid.
[3]   Unfinished draft on Residencia de Estudiantes letterhead (hence no final fullstop above).

From Jeanne Rucar

[Paris,] Sunday 11 [November 1934]

My Luisito,

It's all done, and well done; I have a precious son who, in spite of his scant eight months already weighs more than some full-term babies.[1] Just imagine my Luisito, 2.85kg, and very handsome … He takes after you, completely, I no longer exist. My Luisito, I'm so happy I can't tell you how happy I am, but I know you understand. And you, Luisito? Are you happy, even though you can't stand babies? Although this one is adorable and he's crying right now (which is rare, by the way), he's in his Moses basket next to me and he's just gone back to sleep now. Imagine, he has your hands, you know how when you drink, I mean when you have a glass in your hand, your little finger is always raised? Well, your little boy, when he's sucking his thumb, raises his little finger. Exactly the same way as you do, you can see the end of his finger sticking up.

Hélène[2] says he's going to be intelligent. Everyone is bowled over by this little one, who already has an Aragonese appetite.

The birth was very quick, two hours of pain and, if the little devil had only come out head first, everything would have been over in an hour, but he came out bottom first and peed while his head was still inside. The doctor says that it's better he came at eight months, because at nine months he would have been very big and I would really have had something to scream about. Yesterday the midwife showed me a baby born on the same day as mine, who is also only eight months too: and mine's a colossus! But the midwife says it's quite normal, the other baby is wrapped up in cotton wool and is very small.

So, we should be very proud, because he's very handsome. Mama is happy now, she's always saying 'he gets that from Luis'. My father never stops telephoning and will probably come around this morning.

It was Mrs Casnou who helped with the arrival of the illustrious little man. I'll tell you more about it all when we're together.

I wish you could see Aunt Georgette's face, 'how handsome he is', etc., etc.

Figure 24 Rucar and Juan Luis Buñuel, Paris, November 1934.

My Luisito, I could talk to you about him for pages and pages. And you, my poor Luis? Is your leg hurting? I can't stop thinking about the barrel of whisky. Please look after yourself … make your son proud. Is Conchita happy? Tell her I'm very happy and that next summer there'll be one more devil at the Retiro with her children.[3]

I'm very comfortable here in the clinic. I'm settled in a big white room and you can just imagine how many flowers I've already received.

Let's get down to more serious matters: as you asked Georgette, the clinic costs 1,500 francs for 11 days, plus a 200-franc tip for the midwife and 100 francs for other expenses (I think 1,800 will be enough).

I'm back with you again; my son has just eaten with a hearty appetite, although it was quite hard to wake him. Let's get back to what we were discussing. The best thing, if you can send the money, is to send it to Georgette's address.

The second transfer you made might be returned to you because it arrived on the day I left, and the postman was naturally reluctant to hand it over to mama.

Have you told your mother you have a son? I don't know if I should write to her, I would love to see you but in some ways it's better you come in December when I'll be back on my feet and little Juanito-Luisito will be more interesting (he won't be speaking to you yet), but he'll be awake.

JB

PS Here is the address: Maternity Clinic, 20–22 rue de Turenne, Paris.

Fre Als, ABC/05/06

[1] Juan Luis Buñuel, born on 9 November 1934.
[2] Hélène Casnou, close friend of Jeanne Rucar.
[3] Address of Conchita Buñuel's family, Doctor Castelo 13, opposite the Retiro park in Madrid.

From Louis Aragon

[Odessa,] 20 December [1934]

My dear Luis,

I was very happy to receive news of you, albeit indirectly. As I don't have your address, I'm writing to you via Pierre;[1] he will forward this letter to you.

I remember two years ago, when you were about to leave for America, you told me that if an opportunity came up elsewhere, you would leave America. Well, at that time I wasn't able to sort anything out immediately. But now it's different. Now I'm on the ground and working for a studio[2] that is extremely keen for you to come and work with them. But we can't do anything of course, without knowing whether you would be prepared to leave the job you have at the moment, which must be interesting: if you are interested, you can let me know through Pierre because I travel around a lot and my current address would be no use to you.

The studio, to be honest, is quite rudimentary in terms of resources: but it's nothing we couldn't sort out. I don't think that's the most important thing for you anyway. As for a script, you could write one of your own or choose one ready-prepared: we could discuss that when you are here. At the moment, an ultra-modern Spanish operetta, a kind of '¡Olé, Olé!', '¡Caramba!', a *Carmen*,[3] in other words, would go down really well; although that's not absolutely necessary, father Ubu.[4] We could arrange for you to use a script of mine (a little love story from 1904), or whatever you like.

Personally, I would encourage you to accept, unless of course it would mean leaving a job you really want to keep. I'm sure all our friends in Madrid would be delighted by any film you might make over here and if they try to convince you, you should let yourself be persuaded. You would only have to pay for the travel, which wouldn't be too expensive. Then you would have everything you need: room, allowance, etc. You could come alone or with Jeanne, whichever was better for you both. As you're going to Paris, bear in mind that I'll be back at the beginning of February and I could explain everything better than I can in a letter. I think the best thing for you would be to come in March.

But for that to happen, I need a firm answer, so that I can negotiate over here before I leave. Send me a quick note in any case. Because as you'll understand, if you don't want to come now I also need to know: it would be very awkward to have no answer.

Best wishes to everyone. And regards from us[5] to you both. Very ceremoniously yours, Louis

Fre Als, ABC/04/20

[1]   Unik.
[2]   Ukrainfilm, on a film adaptation of his unpublished novel *Les Cloches de Bâle*.
[3]   Reference to the Georges Bizet opera, *Carmen*, premiered in March 1875 and based on the Mérimée novella (1845).
[4]   Reference to *Ubu Roi*, play by Alfred Jarry, premiered December 1896.
[5]   Aragon is in Odessa with his wife, Elsa Triolet.

From André Breton

Paris, 27 December 1934

My dear friend,

I have an opportunity to give a lecture[1] on surrealism in Tenerife in the near future, where I'll be able, among other things, to rest for a few days, which is something I now require as a matter of extreme urgency (my complete lack of money has kept me in Paris for over a year now). This lecture *depends*, however, on my securing a loan of *The Golden Age* for a public screening over there (invitation-only, I assume). Cordier,[2] from Brussels, told me you sent him a copy of the film for the *Club de l'Écran* a few months ago.[3] Would you mind giving your consent for that copy to be sent to me? Alternatively, and providing you have no objections of course, could you tell me whom I should approach?

As I'm unsure of your address, I am writing to you as before, at 13 Doctor Castelo. May I ask you to reply urgently, whatever your decision.

And do not forget that I should very much like to hear your news and above all to see you again.

Your friend,
André Breton

Fre Als, ABC/02/43

[1]   'Arte y política', paper delivered by Breton at the Ateneo, Santa Cruz, Tenerife, 16 May 1935.
[2]   Stéphane Cordier, pseudonym of Jean Stéphane, editor of the Brussels review *Documents*, 1933–1936.
[3]   Film club founded by Piet Vermeylen and André Thirifays in Brussels in 1932.

To André Breton

Madrid, 2 January 1935

My dear friend,

I got your letter and I'm delighted to hear from you. You can count on that copy of *The Golden Age*. You should phone the Spanish Library, 10 rue Gay-Lussac, and speak to Miss Rucar,[1] I've written to ask her to make it available to you.

Don't forget though that to take a film outside France, you have to comply with a number of infuriating formalities. So, it would be better to take the film to some shipping company like the Agence Michaux, at 2 rue Rocroix. I've attached a list of the details the agency will require from you to get the export licence. I understand you'll be covering transport costs.

I haven't considered screening the film again because of the sound track, which is very poor quality, as with all films made in 1930 at the beginning of sound. Do please warn the audience about this, also, could you ensure posters etc., for all venues and screenings, indicate, as follows: *The Golden Age*, a surrealist film by Luis Buñuel, based on a script by Buñuel and Dalí.

Please forgive all these instructions, but I think they will be useful for you. If you pass through Madrid on your way to Tenerife, do let me know. I would be very happy to see you again.

For several months I was suffering from arthritis in the spine that left me bed-ridden. I am feeling somewhat better now though, so if you did come, I could accompany you around and show you a little of Castile. Do at least pass through Madrid on your return journey.

Yours,
Luis Buñuel

> [*List*]
> Title = *The Golden Age*
> Metrage = 1,700 metres
> Reels = 6
> Author and editor = Buñuel

You will need to supply 6 photos from the film, one for each reel. Please ask Miss Rucar to give them to you.

Fre Als, BRT/C/372

---

[1] Georgette Rucar.

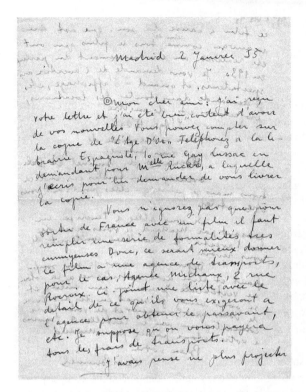

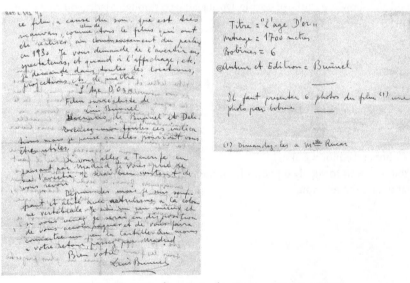

Figure 25 Letter from Buñuel to Breton, 2 January 1935.

From his brother Alfonso

Zaragoza, 17 January 1935

Dear Luis,

I'm writing because I should very much like to know if you are still thinking of going to Russia. Tell me what you've written. Try to make them wait until April or March, because you will be feeling better by then.

I see Sánchez Ventura quite often. He wanted to make a book of *collages* with me. I've already got quite a few nice ones.

I know mama told you some nonsense about me doing I don't know what kind of 'artistic' things. Pay no attention. It's only a few of us getting together to discuss whatever we please, but they are all anti-fascists and lovely people of course; some of them are from *Noreste*,[1] which, as you know, is nonsense, but not that bad. If you have any clichés or anything from Paris when they take you there, send them to me; I won't say they're yours; I'll pretend they're mine. Some of them subscribe to *Minotaure*[2] and

Figure 26 Banquet in honour of Hernando Viñes in Madrid, May 1935: standing, José Caballero, Ugarte, Eva Thaïs, Salazar, Alfonso Buñuel, García Lorca, Vicens, Buñuel, Lupe Condoy, Acacio Cotapos, Alberti, Guillermo de Torre, Miguel Hernández, Neruda, Sánchez Ventura, María Antonieta Hagenaar and Honorio Condoy; sitting, Alberto Sánchez, Delia del Carril, Bayona, Viñes, Jourdain, León, Durán and Ángeles Dorronsoro; in front, Domingo Pruna, Hortelano, Bergamín, Bello and Santiago Ontañón.

they would really like to publish things by Max Ernst or Dalí or Tanguy[3] in *Noreste*, or anything else you might have.

Don't forget to write and let me know about Russia.

Regards to Perico,[4] Conchita and the boys, and a big hug from your brother,
Alfonso

Spa Als, ABC/03/49

[1] Avant-garde literary review edited by Tomás Seral in Zaragoza from 1932 to 1936.
[2] Surrealist review edited by Albert Skira in Paris from 1933 to 1939.
[3] Yves Tanguy (1900–55), French surrealist painter.
[4] Air Force Commander Pedro García Orcasitas (1897–1951), LB's brother-in-law, married to Conchita.

From Ricardo Urgoiti[1]

Filmófono[2]
27 Avenida de Eduardo Dato

Madrid, 7 May 1935

Dear Sir,

In light of our conversations, it is our pleasure to confirm the terms of your participation in the film *Don Quintin the Bitter*.[3]

1) Mr Luis Buñuel contributes to the capital the amount of 75,000 pesetas, for which he will be provided with the appropriate receipt.
2) Filmófono will provide, either alone or with other investors, the outstanding amount needed to cover the budget.
3) When the total cost of the film has been determined, Filmófono will provide *don* Luis Buñuel with a definitive title of participation, which will provide a record of his exact percentage of the ownership or capital of the film, this percentage being calculated in relation to the 75,000 pesetas contributed and total cost of the film.
4) According to this agreement, Filmófono, the majority share-holder, will be obliged to invite the opinion of Mr Buñuel on any decision-making process and, in particular, on any decisions affecting control over, or ownership of the film and its sale abroad.
5) Filmófono will distribute the film in Spain and throughout the Protectorate,[4] for a fee of 30 per cent, and will assume all costs related to this distribution, including the appropriate promotion of the film. The sum of 30 per cent will be calculated based on the net income generated by the film after the deduction of 7.5 per cent tax.
6) The number of copies of the film required for distribution in Spain and in the Protectorate will be determined by Filmófono. Their cost will be met by Filmófono and will not be included in the overall cost of the film but will be deducted from the first repayments of the capital fund.

7) Within the first 15 days of each trimester, Filmófono will present Mr Buñuel with a detailed account of the revenue generated by the film and will make payment of the amount corresponding to his participation. To this effect, the first payment will be made within the first 15 days of January 1936. Filmófono is required to present Mr Buñuel with all receipts pertaining to the monthly revenue and any such figures as he may request regarding the wider distribution of the film.

8) Filmófono guarantees that from the sale of the film, Mr Buñuel will receive no less of two thirds of the capital invested (in other words, 50,000 pesetas).

9) Filmófono will be responsible for the sale of the film overseas and all costs related to these sales and will receive an additional fee of 20 per cent on all sales made.

In the hope that the above is a faithful reflection of matters previously discussed, Your humble servant,

R. M. de Urgoiti, Managing Director
Filmófono

PS We have received the aforementioned 75,000 pesetas.

Spa Tlsps L, AB/568.63–64; *ICO* 50–51

[1] Ricardo María de Urgoiti Somovila (1900–79), engineer and founder of Union Radio in 1924.
[2] Film sound and distribution company set up by Urgoiti in 1929, which moved into film production from 1935 and employed LB to supervise the making of four feature films.
[3] *Don Quintín el amargao*, first film produced by Filmófono, directed by Luis Marquina and based on a *sainete* (one act comic opera piece) by Carlos Arniches and Antonio Estremera, filming began on 20 May, and the film premiered on 3 October 1935.
[4] Spanish Moroccan territory from 1912 to 1956.

From his sister Alicia

Zaragoza, [December 1935]

Dearest Luis,

I can imagine your surprise when you arrived and saw Juan Luis walking! And how well he walks!

I went to see *La bien pagada*[1] at the Circo[2] yesterday with Perico.[3] It was completely full, and I don't know if it's because it ends badly, or for some other reason, but the balcony got angry and whistled and stamped their feet. I should have liked to have seen it with you. I like *Don Quintín el amargao* more every day. Tomorrow we're going to see *La hija de Juan Simón*.[4] On the radio they're saying it's ten times better than *Don Quintín*. I'll write and let you know if it goes down well and what I think of it. Make sure you ask for a good percentage of the takings.

Are you Saénz de Heredia?[5]

I think you'll like Perico's story.[6] It also has some gorgeous landscapes … and it ends well!

Tell Juana I think of her often, and, of course, Juan Luis. My very best wishes to you and big hugs from me to the little one,

Love from your sister,
Alicia

Spa Tls L, ABC/02/04

[1] Feature film directed by Eusebio Fernández Ardavín for CEA-Portago Studios in 1935.
[2] Popular theatre for variety shows, plays and film at Calle de San Miguel, 12.
[3] Pedro Galán Bergua, Alicia Buñuel's husband, a paediatrician and member of the Zaragoza Academy of Medicine.
[4] *La hija de Juan Simón*, second Filmófono production directed by José Luis Sáenz de Heredia (1911–92), based on a play by José María Granada and Nemesio Sobrevila, filmed Autumn 1935.
[5] Reference to the rumour that LB directed the film after the first director, Sobrevila, was sacked.
[6] '*El hijo del diablo*', an original script by Pedro Galán for Filmófono, set in the Pyrenees.

From Tota Atucha, Countess de Cuevas de Vera

Buenos Aires, [1935]

You must be dazed by all these letters[1] Luis, but I've been to several *private views*[2] of Argentine cinema recently and wanted to tell you about them.

I've got to know the directors of SIFAL,[3] Río de la Plata studios,[4] etc., and I sense they don't have a clue. They have no money either, but they do have endless admiration for you, and although the results are not that good they are all very influenced by *An Andalusian Dog*, which is the only one of your films they've shown over here.[5]

A first-rate photographer, Coppola,[6] has made a film about the dams on the Seine that is simply marvellous and another about the English countryside[7] that made me think straight away of *Wuthering Heights*. I think you could work with him. But he's also looking for money to do something. Films are all anyone talks about. If I could find enough money to pay you well, I'd tell them to invite you over to give them the guidance they need. Some are let down by aesthetics; others (the ones I prefer) by vulgarity. It's all just starting up over here. South America is crying out for films in Spanish (which should interest Spain). Gardel's[8] films are so popular they now come with the words of the songs, so they don't have to stop, rewind and play them again, as they had to in Costa Rica when the crowd went wild.

I went to La Boca last night, at the far end of the harbour. Outside the cabaret (purest of pure tango) was a ship called the Barcelona, just there, level with the pavement, so close I could have jumped right on it. I could imagine how it might feel just to climb on board and let it carry me away.

Very far away and lonely these days, I've condensed my desperation into a questionnaire that, if it's not too much of an affront to your habits, you might fill out with a yes or a no and send it back by airmail.[9]

Love, Luis, *darling*,[10]
Tota

Spa Als, ABC/04/50; *LET* 177–178

1   An extensive collection of letters from Atucha to LB is held in the archives of the Filmoteca Española, Madrid.
2   English in the original.
3   Sociedad Industrial Fotográfica Argentina Limitada, production company founded by film-makers Luis Saslavsky and Alberto de Zavalía in 1934.
4   Argentine production company established by Francisco Canaro, Jaime Yankelevich and Juan Cossío in 1934.
5   Screened at the Cineclub de Buenos Aires, Spring 1930.
6   Horacio Coppola (1906–2012), Argentine photographer and film-maker.
7   *Un dique en el Sena* (1934) and *Un domingo en Hampstead Heath* (1935), experimental films.
8   Carlos Gardel (1890–1935), composer and much admired singer of tangos, star of various popular musicals in the 1930s.
9   Copy lost.
10 English in the original.

To the *Cinema Sparta*[1] magazine

Cinema Sparta
Palacio de la Prensa

4 Plaza de Callao, Madrid
[Madrid, 15 January 1936]

My very dear sir,

I would be very grateful if you could include the following lines in the magazine you edit.[2]

In the edition of *Cinema Sparta* dated this 28 December, my name was mentioned in an article by Mr Hernández Girbal called 'The Outsiders are Coming'.[3] With the best of intentions, and one for which I would be grateful were I not averse to such accolades, Mr Girbal attributes to me the parentage of two recent Spanish films.[4]

I should like to correct the inaccuracies in that assertion. Each of these films is the responsibility of their own director.[5] And neither is unknown in the small world of cinema; one for his experience in studios; the other for having made a film previously.[6] Both are fully capable of directing the films in question. If I had any role in the making of these films it was as studio production manager, a purely technical and administrative role, providing financial oversight. I had no creative, intellectual or artistic role. For that reason, therefore, I cannot be the hidden or putative father of these two productions.

Thanking you in advance for any trouble the publication of these lines may cause,

Your affectionate and courteous servant
Luis Buñuel

Spa, Od; *SPA* [8]

1   Madrid film review published from 1932 to 1936.
2   Letter published under the heading: 'Una rectificación de Luis Buñuel'.
3   Florentino Hernández Girbal, 'En torno al cinema nacional. De fuera vendrán…', *Cinema Sparta*, Year II, no. 28 (28 December 1935), np.

⁴ *Don Quintin the Bitter* and *Juan Simon's Daughter.*
⁵ Marquina and Sáenz de Heredia, respectively.
⁶ *Patricio miró a una estrella* (1934) directed by Saénz de Heredia for Estudios Ballesteros.

From his brother-in-law Pedro Galán

Zaragoza, 23 February 1936

Dear Luis,

With a view to achieving the greatest possible dynamism, the basic ingredient of cinema, I have managed to find several sets for the adaptation of *El último mono*.[1] It was fairly difficult at first, bearing in mind the play takes place in a general store.

This adaptation includes new characters, such as Bibiano's step-father, Zenón, Bibiano's mother, Francisca; Bruno and Ceferina, Zenón's children; Ramón, the farm hand, etc.

If you're happy with what I've done, I think you could get a lot out of the farm sequences at the beginning of the film and the ones in the café at the end. Bibiano's dream in the LAND OF MARVELS could be really original, with your talent you could do a lot with it.

Arniches's dialogue is hilarious. I think this could be the most popular Spanish film so far.

You should give the musical interludes to Guerrero.[2]

My first choice for Bibiano would be Antonio Vico, Nicolás Rodríguez or Galleguito.[3] Alfonso Muñoz[4] would be wonderful as Mr Nemesio (as would Arbó[5]). And Alfayate[6] would be excellent as Liborio.

Alizucha[7] has typed it all up for me ... and some of the words have gone astray! My best to Juana and kisses for the cub reporter.[8]

Love from your brother,
Perico

PS Greetings to María, Leonardo and Alfonso.[9]

Spa Tls L, ABC/02/06

¹ Literally 'The Last Monkey', project with Filmófono to adapt a *sainete* by Carlos Arniches Barrera (1866–1943), published in 1926.
² Jacinto Guerrero Torres (1895–1951), composer of *zarzuelas*, who wrote the soundtrack to *Don Quintín the Bitter.*
³ Contemporary Spanish actors of whom Antonio Vico (1903–72) was the best known.
⁴ Actor (1889–1957) who played Don Quintin in *Don Quintin the Bitter.*
⁵ Manuel Arbó del Val (1898–1973), actor, who played parts in *Don Quintin the Bitter, Juan Simon's Daughter* and *¿Quién me quiere a mí?* (1936), the third Filmófono production directed by Sáenz de Heredia.
⁶ José Alfayate (1900–71), actor who played Safiní in *Don Quintin the Bitter.*
⁷ Alicia Buñuel.
⁸ Juan Luis Buñuel.
⁹ LB's siblings.

From Roland Penrose[1]

Hampstead, 9 May 1936

Dear Buñuel,

Some friends and I are organizing a surrealist retrospective to be held in London this June and we hope to have at least one session of film screenings.[2] But only, of course, if we can show one of your films.

Unfortunately, Noailles does not want to give us permission to show *The Golden Age*, which means our only hope is that you might be prepared to loan us *An Andalusian Dog*, if you have a copy with you or in Paris.

I think it is extremely important, because an exhibition such as ours would be far from complete without the opportunity to see at least one of your films. And in London, the mere suggestion of films has generated a lot of interest and naturally we do hope to include *A Dog...* in the programme.

The curator of the exhibition would organize all transport costs and customs fees.[3] But what we are short of now is time, as the exhibition is due to open mid-June. Would it be possible, therefore, for you to send me a copy to London directly, or to let me know where I might find a copy in Paris? The copy would, of course, be appropriately insured during transit and returned to whatever destination is most convenient for you.

I sincerely hope that you are well and that I shall have the pleasure of seeing you again soon in London or in Paris.

I thank you in advance for the remarkable screening of *An Andalusian Dog* in London.

With my most cordial regards,
Roland Penrose
21 Downshire Hill, Hampstead NW3

PS I was told at the Librairie Espagnole, where I got your address, that all the copies of the film are in Spain. If you wish to let me know in advance how much the shipping will cost, I would wire you the amount immediately or you could send it freight collect.

Fre Als, ABC/04/01

---

[1]   British poet, artist and writer (1900–84), and extra in *The Golden Age*.
[2]   The International Surrealist Exhibition, New Burlington Galleries, 11 June–4 July 1936 did not in the end include film screenings.
[3]   Possibly, David Gascoyne (1916–2001), British surrealist poet, and head of the committee formed to organize the exhibition.

Figure 27 During filming of *On Guard, Sentry!, c.* April 1936: unknown, Buñuel, Urgoiti, unknown, Grémillon, Ugarte, unknown, Angelillo and Luis Heredia.

To Leo Fleischman[1]

Madrid, 25 August 1936

I have received from Leo Fleischman the sum of four hundred and ninety pounds sterling for the purchase of cinematographic materials,[2] and pledge to repay them at an appropriate moment.

Luis Buñuel

Spa Ans, JV; *AROJ* 271 f

[1] US mining engineer, brother-in-law of Juan Vicens, enlisted in the Fifth Regiment, died during the Spanish Civil War in October 1936.
[2] Probably intended for Republican propaganda films.

To Pierre Braunberger

Paris, 23 April 1937

My dear Braunberger,

The organizers of a series of films touring Denmark will be in touch with you in the next few days; the tour is organized under the auspices of the Arbejdernes Oplysningsforbund, which is a Danish trade union organization for the education of workers.[1]

You may extend to them the habitual cordiality with which you conduct all transactions relating to *Land without Bread*.

With thanks, I send you, dear Braunberger, my most cordial greetings,
Luis Buñuel

Fre Tls L, PB

[1] Founded in Copenhagen for the Communist Trade Union by Marie Nielsen and Inger Gamburg.

To Pierre Braunberger

Paris, 14 June 1937

Dear Braunberger,

As discussed, I would be grateful if you could urgently ensure that the reference in the introduction to: 'Savoy, Czechoslovakia, Italy, Switzerland'[1] be removed from all copies of *Land Without Bread* currently distributed.

I also ask you make the same cuts to any future copies.

My most cordial greetings,
Luis Buñuel

PS Could you make sure that cuts made to the copy for Marseille are also communicated to Lyon, so that the same cuts can be made to the copy that will be screened in and around Lyon. The censors have demanded these cuts, vehemently, and particularly for Savoy and Upper Savoy. I am counting on your assistance.

Fre Tls L, PB

[1] Shot of a map establishing a connection between these regions and Las Hurdes.

LA PROPAGANDE PAR LE FILM

26, RUE DE LA PÉPINIÈRE
BUREAUX 514-515 - TEL.: LABORDE 76-92

PARIS, le **14 juin 1937.**

Monsieur Braunberger
c/o Bté du Cinéma du
Panthéon,
13 rue Victor-Cousin
P a r i s . -

RECOMMANDEE.-

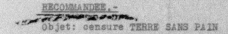

Objet: censure TERRE SANS PAIN

Cher Monsieur Braunberger,

      Comme suite à notre conversation, je vous
prie de bien vouloir faire d'urgence tout le nécessai-
re pour que sur toutes copies en cours de TERRE SANS
PAIN soit supprimée la mention, dans l'introduction, de
"SAVOIE, TCHECO-SLOVAQUIE, ITALIE, SUISSE".

      Je vous prie également de faire cette sup-
pression pour toutes copies ultérieures.

      Veuillez recevoir, cher monsieur, mes salu-
tations les meilleures.

Luis Buñuel

PS.-Je vous prie instamment de faire en sorte que les coupures faites dans la copie envoyée à Marseille, soient
transmises à Lyon afin que ces mêmes coupures soient effec-
tuées sur la copie qui doit passer à Lyon et dans la région.
A la censure, on a insisté très vivement pour que ces cou-
pes soient faites, surtout pour la Savoie et la Hte Savoie.
Je compte donc sur vous à ce sujet.

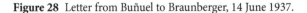

Figure 28 Letter from Buñuel to Braunberger, 14 June 1937.

To Pierre Braunberger

Paris, 9 November 1937

My dear Mr Braunberger,

We have just received an offer of 8,000 francs from England for *Land without Bread*, to include the rights to screening and first copy of the film.[1]

We are informing you of this in accordance with the terms of our contract. In anticipation of your response, my most cordial greetings,

Luis Buñuel
51 rue Saint-Georges

Fre Tls, PB

1 On behalf of the British film critic and director, Ivor Montagu (1904–84), and the Progressive Film Institute, London.

From Ricardo Urgoiti

Mexico City, 28 December 1937

Dear Luis,

The arrival of the new year, always a catalyst to shake off sloth, has inspired me to break our long silence.

You will already know that I am still hopping around America[1] trying to rebuild Filmófono. I don't know if I will be successful, but it won't be for lack of trying.

This is a marvellous country and so interesting in every way, even for its currently somewhat prodigious earth tremors. I will not recount my travels here because they are so numerous a letter could not hope to do them justice.

I wrote to Remacha[2] a few days ago. I don't know if he's still in Paris, but if not, I imagine you will have forwarded it on.[3]

I'm leaving for Havana now, but will be back soon so if when you get this you reply by airmail to Aspa Films,[4] 33 Uruguay, Mexico D.F., your letter will coincide with my return. I aim to pass through France at the beginning of March, decide what to do with my family, and begin the Buenos Aires-Mexico *tournée*[5] again, hoping to combine selling the films with working on a couple of productions if things take off.

I hope to hear from you soon; love to Ugarte and a warm embrace to you from your good friend
[Ricardo]

Spa Tlu, RU/01/04/01; *RUTD* 187

1 Left Spain in February 1937 accused of being a 'red' by Falangist film-maker Florián Rey.
2 Fernando Remacha (1898–1984), Spanish composer, collaborated on soundtracks for Filmófono including *¡Centinela, alerta!* (*On Guard, Sentry!*) filmed in April 1936 and premiered 12 April 1937.
3 Remacha collaborated in activities for the Spanish Pavilion at the Paris International Exposition (May to November 1937), for which LB was in charge of the film programme.

⁴   Mexican production company behind various feature films by Cuban director Ramón Peón, and
    Galician actor and director, Juan Orol.
⁵   French in the original (tour).

To Ricardo Urgoiti

Paris, 2 February 1938

Dear Ricardo,

Although they were very delayed, I took the opportunity of a recent trip to Barcelona to deliver your letters by hand to Remacha. He gave me in return the ones I enclose here.

I got your letter and the cheque for $200. I'll let Remacha know.

I saw your family in Biarritz, although I did not dare greet them because of all that 'you're red' or 'he's white'. Your daughter is adorable, and the little fellow has grown a lot. I didn't see Aurora,[1] because she wasn't on the beach at the time.

Ricardo, I have to tell you something 'very tragi-comic' that shows just what the *Generalissimo*'s[2] lot think of you. They may well cause you trouble. But you will always have a place with us. As you will soon be here, I'll explain when I see you.

Warm regards and see you soon,
Luis

[PS] My postal address: Spanish Embassy, 13 Avenue Georges V.

Spa Als, RU/01/04/03; *RUTD* 189

[1]   Aurora Gutiérrez, Urgoiti's wife.
[2]   Francisco Franco Bahamonde (1892–1975), one of the generals who instigated the military coup in
      July 1936 that led to the Spanish Civil War, dictator of Spain from the end of the Civil War in 1939
      to 1975.

To Pierre Braunberger

Pierre Braunberger

15 rue Lord Byron, Paris

Paris, 18 February 1938

Dear friend,

I should say first of all that I've yet to receive your reply to the memo I sent about the film we're interested in.

Secondly, I shall be leaving for London on an official mission[1] and imagine I will be away for about a week.

I'm very happy that our friends from London are interested in the project and as far as I'm concerned this seems like the best combination.

With regard your trip to Spain, I'll need to introduce you to the person I told you about, but at the moment they are out of the country.

I understand that this Monday, as agreed, you will send me a cheque for 3,000 francs as an advance on the total due. Thanking you in advance.

Affectionate greetings,
Luis Buñuel

Fre Tls, PB

[1]   As a representative of the Republican government.

From Pierre Braunberger

Paris, 9 March 1938

My dear friend,

I attach documentation concerning finances relating to *Land without Bread* as of 28 February to provide you with an up-to-date record.

Affectionate greetings, Pierre Braunberger

General situation regarding the film Land Without Bread *as of 28 February 1938*

Balance in favour of Mr Buñuel as of 31 October: 8,420.55			
Takings in Cineliberté[1]	November:	900	
	December:	375	
	January:	<u>472.50</u>	
		1,747.50	
25% commission:		<u>- 436.85</u>	
		1,310.65	1,310.65
Éclair Tirage[2] invoice number 16.057:		33.60	
number 16.058:		39.90	
number 16.059:		<u>176.40</u>	
		249.90	
Balance of sale to England:		3,709.25	
15% commission:		<u>- 556.40</u>	
		3,152.85	
		<u>249.90</u>	
		2,902.95	<u>2,902.95</u>
		12,634.15	

On 4 February cheque no. 245.164 was sent to Sainte Parisienne de Banque	3,000	
And at the end of February cheque no. 245.896 was sent to the same bank	1,500	4,500
Balance in favour of Monsieur Buñuel	8,134.15	

Fre CmfL, PB

[1] Production and distribution cooperative with links to the French Communist Party, co-producers of *Espagne 1936* (1937), a documentary supervised by LB with co-written commentary by LB and Unik.
[2] Éclair studios's film laboratory.

To Pierre Braunberger

Pierre Braunberger

95 avenue des Champs-Elysées, Paris
Paris, 4 May 1938

Dear friend,

I received your cheque, which, frankly, I was not expecting. Many thanks. I'm sure this liberal gesture will not be the last.

I am very sorry not to be able to send you the English soundtrack of *Land without Bread*.[1] As you know, I was not involved in the addition of the soundtrack to the film, so I don't know what has happened to that material. I'm also very busy at the moment and my secretary, who knows where everything is, is currently out of Paris. As for the *speech*,[2] I can send you the French[3] if it's any use to you.

Affectionate greetings,
Luis Buñuel

PS I didn't respond to your request earlier because I was waiting for my secretary to get back, as she's the only person who may know about the soundtrack.

Fre Tls, PB

[1] Leopold Maurice was in charge of the English translation of the commentary for *Land without Bread*.
[2] English in the original.
[3] French commentary co-written by LB and Unik in March 1934.

To Ricardo Urgoiti

Paris, 11 August 1938

Dear Ricardo,

It's been a long time since I've had news of you from any source, although I'm assuming things have worked out well and that you are happy to have your family with you. I would appreciate a few lines from you though to let me know how things are with you.

I've heard little news from our Filmófono friends. Remacha is still in Barcino,[1] very thin I believe. I'm still waiting for the moment, as always, when I can prove to him that he would be more useful over here than over there, because he's still not doing anything. I really wish he were here with us. Bautista[2] was in London for a concert. He came back a while ago. Halffter was here for a similar reason. The person who has extended his stay and has now been here for a couple of months is the director of *¿Quién me quiere a mí?*[3] He's been following his usual blind impulses, leading him into the most absurd adventures. He still speaks of you with great affection: he is, above all, a sentimental man. As always, we rarely see Grémillon.[4] He's not doing anything right now. Eduardo,[5] in his agency.

From a personal perspective, things are not going well for me and I may be called up before long. In case that happens, I would like to leave a number of issues settled including our *official* or *commercial* relationship, as the other, our friendship I mean, is the same as always. You will understand when I say this that I am thinking of my wife and son. Two outcomes are possible: that things go badly for you, in which case so much the worse for all of us; or that they go well, as I hope and anticipate. So I should like to reach a fixed and agreed decision as to the share that either my family or I might expect from your films currently being screened. The first thing is to establish, in pesetas, my participation from before the war. It is approximately as follows:

Participation as production manager in four films: 40,000 [pesetas].

Salary owed from the second film: 8,000.

Payment outstanding, as agreed, was a *minimum* of 40,000 pesetas, plus my salary for June and July, but I am happy to discount that.

Broadly speaking, we are talking about an agreed sum of around 90,000 pesetas. You can make your own calculations using this figure as a basis and get back to me with a precise figure, compatible with our friendship and your own financial affairs. I would abide by your decision with respect to any future collaborations. You mentioned something to this effect on your last trip, but at that time I saw no need for a formal arrangement.

Awaiting your reply and your news. My regards to Aurora and a hug for the children.

Cordially,
Luis

Spa Als, RU/01/04/05; *RUTD* 192

---

[1] Latin for Barcelona.
[2] Julián Bautista Cachaza (1901–61), composer.
[3] Eduardo Ugarte, scriptwriter for a film based on a plot by Enrique Horta.
[4] Director of *On Guard, Sentry!*
[5] Eduardo García Maroto (1903–89), editor of *Don Quintin the Bitter.*

From Pierre Braunberger

Paris, 30 August 1938

Dear sir,

Following our conversation today, we have discussed the possibility of collaborating on a film in support of Republican Spain, to demonstrate the current struggle of the Spanish people.

I confirm that I am able to obtain from the US company United Artists,[1] a contract guaranteeing distribution of the aforementioned film in all the offices that, as you know, they have established across the world (in South America, the United States, Canada, England, France, Belgium, Switzerland, etc.), under the same terms as the contract I've already signed with said company for previous productions, that is, 50 per cent of the distribution (revenue) on condition that the *scénario*, the principal actors and the artistic direction are acceptable to them and to me.

I am at your disposal should you wish to see copies of the contract that has already been signed.

Should you wish to proceed, it would be useful to be able to present a *scénario*, that would allow us to draw up a more precise plan and considerably improve on the existing contract.

My most cordial greetings,
Pierre Braunberger

Fre CmfL, PB

[1] US film studio founded in 1919.

To Marie-Laure and Charles de Noailles

Paris, 9 September 1938

Dear friends Marie-Laure and Charles,

I shall be leaving for Hollywood in a few days on a supposedly 'official' mission.[1] I'll be there for several months. So I am writing today in relation to this trip.

The full cost of my travel and accommodation is already covered, but under the current circumstances I do not want to leave my wife and son behind. To bring them with me, I need $425.

I've always been reluctant to borrow money, but the solution to this problem is of the utmost importance to me and obliges me to set aside all former prejudices.[2]

I'm asking you for this amount should you be able to lend it, but please know my friendship with you would be all the stronger should you have to decline. It is my faith in this that allows me to overcome the shame I feel writing this letter to you.

In America I will be able to save approximately $100 a month and so could repay my debt to you towards the month of February.

Very affectionately yours,
Luis Buñuel

Fre Als, BK; *AGE* 164

¹   As historical consultant for features relating to Spain.
²   LB also borrowed money from Ione Robinson and Rafael Sánchez Ventura.

From Charles de Noailles

Hyères, [12 September 1938]

My dear Luis,
   Please do not apologize for asking a favour of us when we are delighted to help. I have no doubt whatsoever that I can rely on you and I was delighted to hear in your letter the good news about your departure. We would all do well to live in America rather than our sad Europe!
   I shall be in Hyères for 24 hours then back in Paris on Saturday or Sunday after travelling through Switzerland.
   You didn't say how you would prefer the dollars. I think the best thing would be to send them via cheque to New York. I have an account there. Unless you would prefer French francs should you need them before you leave.
   Unfortunately, I don't have my American chequebook here, but unless I hear to the contrary, I shall send the cheque to New York when I arrive in Paris on Saturday. If you prefer francs, send me a note at the Place des États-Unis and I will send a cheque to Paris.
   Marie-Laure came back the day before yesterday from Stockholm, where she has just spent a month; she loved the city. I will forward your letter to her at the same time as I send this one.
   I do hope we can meet before you leave.

Love,
[Charles de Noailles]

Fre Tlu, BK; *AGE* 164

To Éclair Tirage

Éclair Tirage
12 rue Gaillon, Paris

Paris, 15 September 1938

Dear sirs,
   I hereby ask that you make available to Mr Pierre Braunberger, on his request, the negative with sound in English and all other negatives of the film *Land without Bread* stored in your archives.

Cordial greetings,
Luis Buñuel

Fre Tlu C, PB

To Marie-Laure and Charles de Noailles

Paris, 16 September 1938

Dear friends Marie-Laure and Charles,

Charles's letter did not arrive until last night and I leave for America with my family in the next few hours. I had written to you in case, although I knew you were not in Paris. I was delighted to have your news as well as this latest proof of your friendship.

I should have loved to see you, we have so many things to talk about. At times like these, we need our friends. I am deeply disturbed by what is going on and although I do not think there will be a war (I did not think that the last time either[1]), I do think that peace might well be even more painful for people like us.

I shall think of you when I'm over there more than you can imagine. I'll write and hope that you'll not leave me too long without news of you. I'm going back to cinema again and with luck on my side that is where I shall stay.

I think, following Charles's suggestion, that the best thing would be to send a cheque to New York, in the name of Luis Buñuel Portolés and to the address below. With your help, the great burden of the cost of three trips has been lifted.[2]

Very affectionately yours,
Luis

Consul General of Spain (for the attention of Luis Buñuel)
Spanish Consulate, New York

Fre Als, BK; *AGE* 166

[1] Reference to the Spanish Civil War (1936–39).
[2] LB left for New York, via London, from Le Havre on 17 September 1938.

4

Exile in the United States (1938–46)

To Ricardo Urgoiti

Britannic,[1] to New York, 20 September 1938

Dear Ricardo,

Here I am, on my way to America with my distinguished wife and adorable son. It's an official, though honorary trip, as I'm funding myself, or rather, I'm being funded by some good friends who've lent me money.[2] I'm going to Hollywood, hoping to find work if possible on the films being made about Spain. I have enough to support me, car included, for four months. But if I'm not gainfully employed by then I'll be completely cut off on the other side of the world, because I will have used up all my credit with my friends. Between now and then though the world may go under.[3]

I organized a supper with friends before I left. Grémillon was there and said he'd had a letter from you with bad news. Is that true? According to him, you are becoming discouraged and thinking of going back to Europe. Please don't under any circumstances. You would not believe the levels of confusion and corruption over there, although you must have some idea from the newspapers. It's all iniquity, cowardice and infamy. They think they are helping to prevent war, when all they are actually doing is squandering any advantage they had and preparing the way for an even more terrible one.[4]

I wish you would write and tell me about your life in every possible detail. But, most importantly, please take my advice and stay there.

I hope we shall stay in touch from now on. Who knows whether we may be able to help one another out in the future.

Write to me at the Consulate in New York, they'll forward my letters. As soon as I have an address, I'll send it to you.[5]

My very best to Aurora and the children, and love to you from
Luis

PS I'd be grateful if you could find out where Tota, Condesa de Cuevas de Vera, is staying and send me her address. She's over there at the moment.

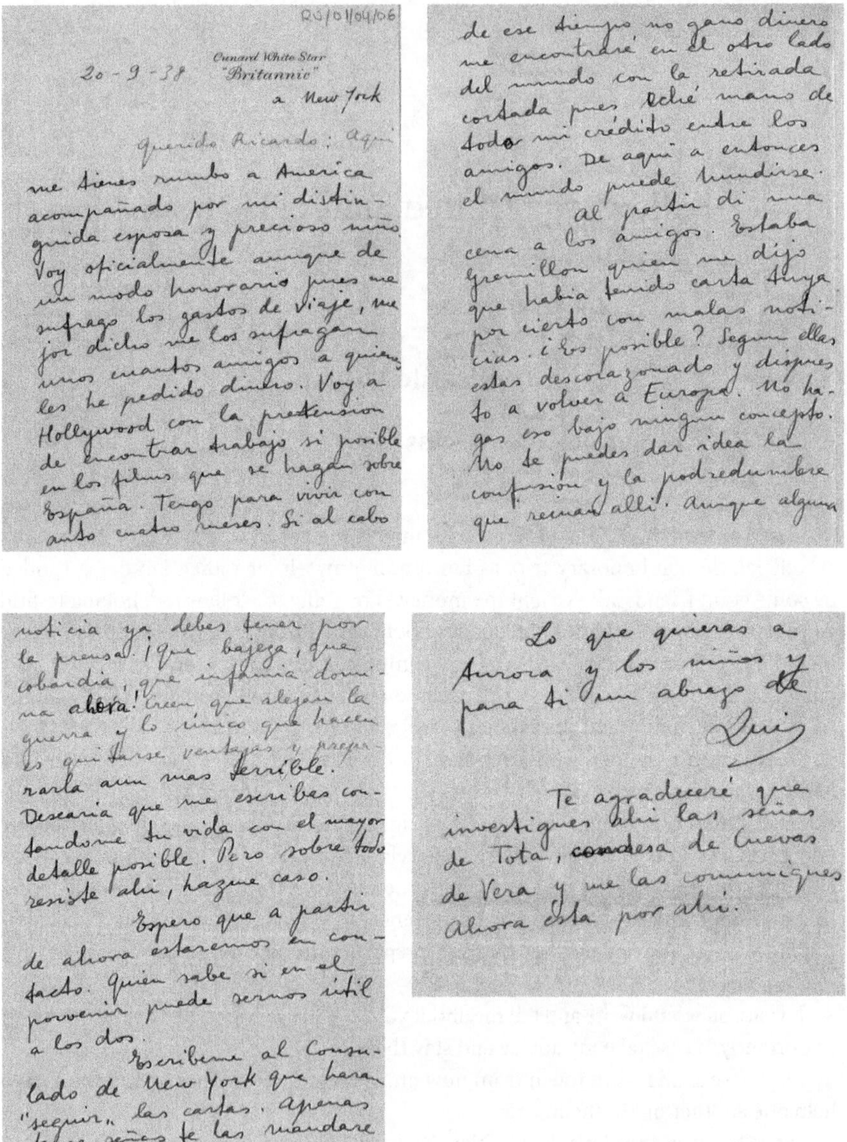

RU/01/04/06

Cunard White Star
"Britannic"
20 - 9 - 38
a New York

Querido Ricardo: Aquí
me tienes rumbo a America
acompañado por mi distin-
guida esposa y precioso niño.
Voy oficialmente aunque de
un modo honorario pues me
sufrago los gastos de viaje, me
jor dicho me los sufragan
unos cuantos amigos a quienes
les he pedido dinero. Voy a
Hollywood con la pretensión
de encontrar trabajo si posible
en los films que se hagan sobre
España. Tengo para vivir con
ello cuatro meses. Si al cabo

de ese tiempo no gano dinero
me encontraré en el otro lado
del mundo con la retirada
cortada pues eché mano de
todo mi crédito entre los
amigos. De aquí a entonces
el mundo puede hundirse.
Al partir di una
cena a los amigos. Estaba
Gremillon quien me dijo
que había tenido carta tuya
por cierto con malas noti-
cias. ¿Es posible? Según ellas
estas descorazonado y dispuesto
to a volver a Europa. No ha-
gas eso bajo ningún concepto.
No te puedes dar idea la
confusión y la podredumbre
que reinan allí. Aunque alguna

noticia ya debes tener por
la prensa. ¡Que bajeza, que
cobardia, que infamia domi-
na ahora! Creen que alejan la
guerra y lo único que hacen
es quitarse ventajas y prepa-
rarla aun mas terrible.
Desearia que me escribas con-
tandome tu vida con el mayor
detalle posible. Pero sobre todo
resiste allí, hazme caso.
Espero que a partir
de ahora estaremos en con-
tacto. Quien sabe si en el
porvenir puede sernos útil
a los dos.
Escribeme al Consu-
lado de New York que harán
"seguir" las cartas. Apenas
tenga señas te las mandaré

Lo que quieras a
Aurora y los niños y
para ti un abrazo de
Luis

Te agradeceré que
investigues allí las señas
de Tota, condesa de Cuevas
de Vera y me las comuniques
Ahora está por allí.

Figure 29 Letter from Buñuel to Urgoiti, 20 September 1938.

[1] Cunard-White Star Line transatlantic ship.
[2] In addition to de Noailles, LB borrowed money from the American painter Ione Robinson and Sánchez Ventura.
[3] The expression in Spanish: 'De aquí a entonces, el mundo puede hundirse' is ambivalent, it may well mean, simply, that (with the Second World War starting) the world may come to an end. However, it could mean, more ironically, that, with the help of his friends LB can afford, between now and then, not to care.
[4] Annexation of Austria into Germany in March 1938 and, on 29 September, the signing of the Munich Agreement.
[5] LB arrives in New York on 25 September 1938.

To Ricardo Urgoiti

Los Angeles, 2 January 1939

Dear Ricardo,

I've read your letter and all I can say is you are a *frivolous* person. You'd have to be not to show any signs of life at times as 'adventurous' as these and after the less than rosy news of you I had from Grémillon in Paris. Fortunately, your letter suggests things aren't that bad even if you haven't hit the jackpot yet.

I was amazed by your news of E. P.[1] I 'looked out' for him over the last months I was in Paris, but when I left for the States he had no money, no friends, and a very dubious passport. And now he's popped up in Bolivia, chopping down forests. He must be the world's luckiest man ... and the most shameless. By the way, I really need you to send me his address by return mail, I have something important to tell him.

I'm still *unoccupied* here: there's a lot of potential work, but it's difficult to get started, although I have faith in my lucky star and my own efforts. Everything has to be sorted out before March, because I only have $350 left to live on and pay for the car. Of course, I know I can find work, it's just a question of holding out and not spending too much until I get started. If I've still found nothing by the end of March though, for the first time in my life, I'll be in a truly terrible state. But God disposes, and I shall just have to hope the Virgin I never forget in my prayers will intervene effectively on my behalf.

I'm always thinking about friends, I miss them terribly. If things end up going well here and I manage to make some money, I shall appoint myself their collective father (there are not so many of them, after all) and provide for them if things take a turn for the worse in Spain. That was 70 per cent of the reason I came to Hollywood. And of course, I count Remacha among that little family.

I haven't seen López Rubio[2] and I don't even know if he's here. I'd be grateful if you could send me his address if you have it, because I'd like to see him. I live a very quiet life and see very few people. An agent is looking into a *job*[3] for me.

That wretched Spanish film production is really taking off here.[4] In a few months it will be raining films made in Hollywood. Might that interfere with your opportunities to find production work in this city?

Finally, knowing how busy you are, I'll just ask you to send the addresses I've asked for ..., which will also let me know you are still alive.

Send Aurora and the children appropriate greetings on my part; I assume they are still virgins when it comes to the 'Argentine accent'. Take care with that.

Jane and the boy are well. The former asks me to send her very affectionate greetings,

Best regards,
Luis

Spa Als, RU/01/04/11; *RUTD* 197

¹ Enrique Pelayo co-screenwriter of *Who Loves Me?* (¿Quién me quiere a mí?).
² After spending some years in Hollywood, in 1939 López Rubio was living in Mexico and Cuba.
³ English in the original.
⁴ Spanish-language films made in Hollywood for distribution to Spanish-speaking countries.

To Ricardo Urgoiti

Los Angeles, 30 January 1939

Dear Ricardo,

There's no point in our mentioning the terrible events and the tragedy faced by so many of our good friends! Being completely alone over here makes the days even more unbearable.

All I want now is to be able to get by and be of some use to my friends, my few old friends, although at the moment things are not going as well as I hoped.

It's all still promises and *bluff*¹ over here. They've been announcing Spanish production as the next big thing for months now, but it still hasn't happened. There's only one Spanish-language film being made in Hollywood right now, and that has Mexican actors and a Mexican director.² I've been 'on the point' of joining MGM as a *technical advisor*,³ but that's as far as I've got. The film with Chaplin fell through, along with a few other things. If I had enough money to get by, I'm *sure* I could achieve something, but I've only got enough money to cover one more month with the car.

The main reason I'm writing is to let you know that:

1) I'm ready to leave as soon as the money runs out and, if possible and if you are working on something, I should like to come back to Filmófono, but as a film-maker this time, or whatever. Buñuel is dead, I can now be any old Joe-Bloggs director. And now, without the artistic prejudices, I think I could be more useful than before. As soon as we have a hit, which would be immediately, we could bring Remacha on board. What is he doing now?⁴ I dread to think.
2) If you aren't working on anything and can't 'hire' me, send me as much money as you can over 10 dollars.
3) If you can't 'hire' me or send any money, write to let me know and send the contacts I asked for: for Tota and Enrique.

Please also – and I trust your friendship – destroy this letter and keep its contents to yourself.

Love
Luis

PS I've not mentioned something important I'm following up here that would bring in enough money for us to film in Argentina. I'll let you know if and when it happens.

Spa Als, RU/01/04/12; *RUTD* 198

[1] English in the original.
[2] Probably *Los hijos mandan* produced by Ramos Cobián, directed by Gabriel Soria, starring Mexican actors Arturo de Córdova and Fernando Soler.
[3] English in the original.
[4] Ostracized by Falangist supporters in Filmófono, Remacha had moved to Tudela in Navarre.

To José Moreno Villa

Los Angeles, 14 March 1939

Dear Pepe,

Just couple of lines to make contact, because I'm still not sure whether this will reach you, although I imagine if you are still in Mexico that this is the best way to reach you, at la Casa de España,[1] poor Spain.

Will you write back by return post so I can send you a longer letter?

I've been in America for six months and have decided to stay on indefinitely. I'm trying to find film work in Hollywood, which is not easy, although I'm sure I'll find something soon. For the first time in my life, I'm having to seek out my 'daily bread' with wife and children on board. As soon as I earn anything, I'll invite you to come and stay for as long as you want (it's an amazing country, it feels like the last remaining island of peace).

If you see Salazar,[2] tell him I got his letter and was grateful for it. Also that, if the opportunity arises, I will not forget him.

Dear Pepe: my only ambition now – and I don't know if it's too late – is to make a name for myself and some money to help out my good friends, who will need it. If I don't succeed, it will be worse for everyone.

Best wishes, and hoping for news of you.
Luis Buñuel

PS Could you do me a favour, and see if you can find a copy of the *Diccionario de la lengua Española* in Mexico, published by Calleja, the 1932 edition or one close?[3] If you can, could you get them to write to me, or send it cash on delivery? And put in some catalogues of South American histories and novels.

Do you have any news of don Ricardo? Any information you have about anyone or anything would be news to me, because I'm 'languishing' in the most terrible isolation over here.

Spa Als, COL 17/10

¹ La Casa de España, Mexico City, founded in 1938 to receive refugees from the Spanish Civil War.
² Adolfo Salazar, musicologist and composer (1890–1958), exiled to Mexico in 1939.
³ The *Nuevo diccionario manual, ilustrado, de la lengua castellana*, published by Saturnino Calleja in Madrid in 1914, reissued various occasions (undated) over subsequent decades.

To George Antheil[1]

Los Angeles, 11 April 1939

Dear Georges,
    Only a few words to explain my situation in USA briefly, so that your brother[2] could speak about my case in Washington, as you so kindly proposed.
    Here is my historia:
    1) I landed in New York, September 16th, [19]38[3] as a diplomatic attaché of the Spanish government. I have been here, therefore, for seven months.
    2) The Counselor of the Spanish Embassy in Washington wrote to me some time before the recognition of Franco,[4] saying that a negotiation had been made so that all the Spanish Government appointees could remain in USA as refugees after the recognition. So, I think I am a refugee, now.
    My only wish would be to have a place within the Spanish quota whose amount is about 250 individuals. If it is not possible your brother could speak about me and do his best.
    I'm very sorry to inconvenience both of you but this problem is so vital to me that I dare as much.
    I'm shamefaced about my English and must stop.

Thank you, George, for all.
Amitiés,[5]
Luis Buñuel

Eng Als, GA/I/01; *EE* 201 f

¹ American composer (1900–59), provided soundtrack for *Ballet mecánique* (Mechanical Ballet, 1924) co-dir. Fernand Léger and Dudley Murphy.
² Henry Antheil (1912–40), US diplomat.
³ Correct date: 25 September 1938.
⁴ Franco's government, recognized on 25 February 1939 by France and UK, and on 1 April by the USA.
⁵ French in the original (with friendship).

From Salvador Dalí

New York [April 1939]

    WRITE TO ME, for God's sake, don SIMÓN!
    Señor don Simón, life is fleeting…[1]

    What greater pleasure
    can there be than to

tell one's
dying FATHER
he's an arsehole.
QUEVEDO[2] (Spanish classic)

My dear little son,

Delighted with the songs you sang in your letter, I shall reply in an orderly fashion.

First, no divorce from Gala; on the contrary, our mutual understanding is *absolute,* and we've never been as happy together as we are together now, but as I've just spent four months at Chanel's[3] (with Gala) in Monte Carlo,[4] the inevitable *potins mondains rituals*[5] have arisen.

You know I don't believe in World War. We may well be experiencing some moments of *objective danger,* but I'm convinced that in under two months we'll see an abrupt change (already arranged and decided). France and Italy will sort themselves out, and once the *Axis* is disbanded, Stalin will agree to Hitler consuming the juicy roast rib of the UKRAINE. At that point, *Japanese* imperialism will automatically feel threatened (Russia-Germany), and conflict will break out in the United States.

I have to go and spend two weeks in Monte Carlo working on my spectacle, it will be at the Paris opera in June then, immediately afterwards, in London, so says the sacramental bread of Tristan.[6] Oliwood[7] has always interested me in theory, but as my economic situation improves by the day and I don't need to go, I'm investing all my *prowess* in waiting and rejecting all offers until the day (which will *inevitably* arrive due to the acceleration of my *prestige* and *popularity*) when they make me DICTATOR. *So many dollars* to make whatever fucking film I want in however many days I want is the only contract I shall even *consider,* and this would be impossible were I to accept anything *provisionally.* You see the rub now?[8]

Your new approach seems far more realistic than your old Marxist idealism. As a piece of friendly advice from Dalí of Toledo, disinfect yourself of every Marxist thought because Marxism, philosophically and from every other perspective, is the most moronic theory of our civilization. It is all wrong, and Marx himself was probably a paragon of abstract stupidity. It would be terrible if you stopped being a political Marxist and carried on thinking like a Marxist in all other ways, because Marxism blinds you to the phenomena of our age. A really wonderful young science: 'morphology', the meeting of morphology with psychoanalysis, even older, even more beautiful, with one of the most melancholic smiles the world has ever seen![9]

Good day to you, write to me, and if you do come to New York we shall meet up at once.

Love,
Dalí
St Moritz on the Park[10]
50 Central Park South

PS The end of the Negrins[11] and the Pasionarias[12] has turned my stomach a bit. Couldn't they have got themselves killed? Or made peace two months before the fall of Tarragona?[13] The apotheosis of mediocrity. Never to be forgiven!

Another thing, my individualism is now exacerbated, and I work with furious intensity on whatever comes into my *tête*;[14] so, it would be impossible for me to work with anyone else. Gala is the only person I listen to, for she has *mediunique* gifts, objective CHANCE,[15] and the paranoid interpretation of fortuitous events needed to follow the thread of my frenetical-critical activities.

A good day indeed, one incredible thing after the other is happening here. The reds put my sister in prison in Barcelona for three weeks (!) and martyred her, she's gone mad, she's in Cadaqués, they have to force feed her and she *shits the bed*.[16] Imagine my father's tragedy; they've stolen *everything* from him and he's living in *a boarding house* in Figueres. I am sending him dollars, of course; he's turned into a fanatical admirer of Franco, sees him as a demi-god, mentions our glorious *leader*, on every line of his delirious letters (they saved all my things from the Cadaqués house). The revolutionary experiment has been such a disaster that everyone prefers FRANCO. It's incredible: life-long Catalan loyalists, federal republicans, die-hard anti-clerical activists write to me over the moon with the new regime! At least they can eat, sleep and not worry about being robbed or murdered; it has to be said the left made a real mess of it.

Spa Als L, AB/572.53–55; *AROJ* 381–384 f

---

[1] Allusion to the lines of the character, Procopio, from the Spanish zarzuela *Buenas noches, señor don Simón* (1852): 'Don Simon, sir, life is fleeting, and no-one knows when their final moment will come'.

[2] Allusion to scatological, burlesque text by one of Spain's most celebrated Golden Age writers, Francisco de Quevedo y Villegas (1580–1645), *Gracias y desgracias del nobilísimo señor ojo del culo* (1628), which translates as 'The Fortunes and Misfortunes of the Most Noble Mr Arsehole'.

[3] Gabrielle 'Coco' Chanel (1883–1971), French fashion designer.

[4] In Autumn 1938, Dalí was working on his ballet *Bacchanale* (1939), based on music by Wagner, for the Monte Carlo Ballets Russes.

[5] French in the original (usual mundane gossip).

[6] Reference to Wagner's *Tristan and Isolde* (1865) and possibly to Dalí's ballet, *Mad Tristan*, eventually premiered in 1944; the reference to the Holy Communion bread, or sacramental host is unclear: 'la hostia de Tristán que explica' translates, literally, as 'Tristan's sacramental host explains'; 'hostia' is also used as an exclamation, or to add emphasis in Spanish, so Dalí's elliptical phrase may be an exclamation to do with his interest in Wagner and his own work, in which sacramental host is a recurring motif.

[7] Hollywood.

[8] Response to an unknown proposal; LB's letter to Dalí has not survived.

[9] Dalí visited Freud in London on 19 July 1938; he drew the portrait of Freud, now on display at the Freud Museum, the same year.

[10] Hotel opposite Central Park; Dalí's letter has hotel's letterhead.

[11] Juan Negrín (1892–1956), philosopher, politician, and last prime minister of Republican Spain from 1937 to 1939.

[12] Dolores Ibárruri, nicknamed 'La Pasionaria' (1895–1989), Communist Party MP between 1936 and 1939.

[13] The Catalan city of Tarragona, taken by Franco's troops in January 1939.

[14] French in the original (head).

[15] The neologism 'mediúnico' combines 'unique' with '(psychic) medium', and Dalí describes their relationship in Breton's terms as an 'hazard objectif' (an example of 'objective chance' or a 'fortuitous encounter').

[16] Anna María Dalí, imprisoned between 4 and 20 December 1938.

To Ricardo Urgoiti

Los Angeles, 11 August 1939

Dear Ricardo,

I sent you a registered letter last 30 January, to which, like the previous ones, I've had no reply. I decided you must have gone back to Europe, or that there must be a political reason for your inexplicable behaviour. I've known you long enough now though to know you would be quite incapable of using an excuse like that to avoid answering my very specific questions. I now know for certain that you are there in the city[1] and ask you urgently to reply.

Amorim, who was over here and will be conveying my verbal greetings to you on his return, told me something of your life. I now know you have thrown yourself into production already, contributing to the progress of humanity that 'Juan Simonian' pearl, *La canción que tú cantabas*.[2] I wish you every success, which you will doubtless achieve.

Do you have any news of Remacha? I am very concerned about his fate. Grémillon had a telegram from him in February from Tudela. He was begging him to take care of his wife and child, because he was in a French concentration camp. But since then no one has heard from him, although my friends in Paris have done everything they can to help his family. Let me know whatever you've heard. And what of Garrigós, Corujo and Moreno?[3] Ugarte, in Mexico, as you must know. He likes it and has already begun work in films locally.[4]

I still have no work over here. I'm very close to some great opportunities, but they haven't come together yet. I'm working hard, and my career and my immediate future are all I think about right now. The Rockefeller Institute has invited me to work for them and I've already presented whatever documents, CV, etc. they requested.[5] I hope they will take me on. They want to hire me to make 'psychological' documentaries, with significant resources and freedom. It won't make me a millionaire, but it does fit perfectly with my background as an independent film-maker and it would be a great start in the United States.

Although we haven't yet gone short of anything, I still live almost miraculously from hand to mouth. French friends, selling some personal effects, etc., have helped put bread on the table. My family are in no position to help. I'm going to repeat the request I made in my last unanswered letter. If you have just enough to live on, I withdraw it. But if you have anything left over, I want to claim, officially and amicably, my part of the films you've sold in South America. Leaving to one side my role as an investor, I should like the 3 per cent I'm due from each film, except *Juan Simón's Daughter*, which comes to 5 per cent. Over to you, if only to hear from you.

Regards,
Luis

Spa Tls, RU/01/04/14; *CUA* 567 f

---

[1] Buenos Aires.

2   Feature produced by Urgoiti with Filmófono Argentina, dir. Miguel Mileo, based on a story by
    Carlos Arniches, premiered in Buenos Aires on 7 July 1939.
3   Pedro Garrigós, Ignacio Corujo and Bartolomé Moreno, fellow collaborators with Filmófono;
    Corujo was shot in Barcelona in June 1938.
4   As co-scriptwriter on *El secreto de la monja* (1940) by Raphael J. Sevilla.
5   LB applied to the American Film Center, financed by the Rockefeller Foundation, directed by the
    academic Donald Slesinger and founded in 1938.

From Iris Barry[1]

Luis Buñuel,
c/o Mrs George Antheil[2]

[New York] 13 September 1939

Dear Mr Buñuel,

I was so sorry not to have the chance of meeting you again before leaving Hollywood, but we had to come back hurriedly in view of the European situation.[3] Would it be possible, do you suppose, for us now to obtain the print of The Golden Age *and* Land without Bread? *I fear, too, that it may seem impractical for us to obtain the Dali portrait of which we spoke.[4] Would it be possible for you to write me and let me know?*

We were both very happy indeed to meet you and I hope that we may see you again soon. If by any chance you do come to New York – either in connection with the film project for Schlesinger or otherwise – we should be very happy to put you up if you wished.

With kind regards,
Yours sincerely,
[Iris Barry]

Eng Tlu, MoMA/12.02

1   Film Critic (1895–1969), Head of the Film Library at the Museum of Modern Art (MoMA), New
    York, married to John Abbot, director of MoMA.
2   Elizabeth 'Boski' Markus (1903–78), married to Antheil.
3   3 September 1939, outbreak of the Second World War.
4   Salvador Dalí, *Portrait of Luis Buñuel* (1925), property of LB.

To Iris Barry

Los Angeles, 25 September 1939

Dear Mrs Barry,

Boski has passed on your letter and I am very grateful for your warm offer of hospitality. If I travel to New York, I would be delighted to see you; for the moment, I'm sorry to say I have no plans to travel. I thank you again though.

Under the current circumstances, I've abandoned any idea of bringing my films to the United States. So, I am very sorry to say that my offer to the Film Library will have to be postponed indefinitely, or until the connections interrupted by war can be re-established.

Regarding the portrait by Dalí, which is in Spain, I've written to my family to see whether it would be possible to ship it. If the outcome is positive, I will let you know.

Yesterday, as requested by Mr Schlesinger, I sent a copy of the account[1] I presented to the Rockefeller Institute by registered post. I sent it to your home address to make the dispatch more official. I am grateful to Mr Abbot for the gracious interest he has shown in these documents and, if possible, would like to know his opinion of them.

My most cordial greetings,
Luis Buñuel
1245 North Doheny Drive, Hollywood

Fre Tls, MoMA/12.02; *EE* 216 f

[1] Likely reference to LB's short bio 'Autobiography', 28 July 1939, thirty-five page typed copy (MoMA/12.05).

To Pedro Salinas[1]

Pedro Salinas
1160 Fifth Avenue, 402

New York, 4 March 1940

Dear Salinas,

I hear from mutual friends that you are now at the *college*,[2] so I am taking this opportunity to send you very warm greetings and the pages attached,[3] which I should like you to do me the favour of reading. You will find in them the outline of a lecture and some information about myself that may be useful for what I am about to tell you.

If you think the lecture might be of interest to your *college*, would you do me the favour of passing it on to the appropriate person? It is about some centres of quasi-neolithic civilization distributed across Europe with a film (in English) about one that is located in Spain.

Although the subject may seem very specialized and of interest only to anthropologists, it does have a wider appeal, the film was on release to the general public of the grand boulevards for eight months in Paris. Another important point: there is no possibility whatsoever that it in any way diminishes the reputation of Spain (and I'm not referring, here, to the Spain of *Arriba*[4]), as I take the Unamuno-esque view that the heroic struggle of humanity against a hostile environment is one of the great feats of our race rather than a cause of shame.

I hope I'll have an opportunity to see you one day in the not too distant future, and until then, I remain cordially yours (until then and always),

Luis Buñuel

[Lecture]

Luis Buñuel, European film producer whose biographical material is appended, has undertaken to exhibit before college groups one of his educational films, Land Without Bread. *This picture, shown originally in the Panthéon Theatre in Paris, runs a course of forty minutes. Mr Buñuel will introduce it with a fifteen-minute talk covering certain regions of Europe about which no literature has been written, where the layer of life has been too scanty for scientific or anthropological investigation. Las Hurdes, the setting of* Land Without Bread, *is one of these regions.*

An explanation of the film follows:

Land Without Bread *(English Version)*

There exists in Spain a section almost unknown by the Spanish, until King Alfonso made a trip to it in 1922. It still remains on the outskirts of Spanish life and civilization, its obstinacy a social enigma.

This section, called 'Las Hurdes', is one of the most miserable on the face of the globe, isolated from the outside world by mountains difficult to pass and with a population of 6000 inhabitants distributed in 52 hamlets.

It originated at the beginning of the XVI century, when some of the survivors of the Jewish expulsion and persecution, ordered by the Catholic Kings, went to inhabit it. Its population was increased later by outlaws who were seeking refuge in the mountains, fleeing the rigors of justice.

Only 100 kilometers from Salamanca, one of the centers of European culture, and 3 kilometers from Las Batuecas, one of the most interesting centres of paleolithic culture, Las Hurdes, nevertheless, has remained unbelievably backward.

Bread is almost unknown in Las Hurdes Altas. The inhabitants have to work, with great effort, their fields, which barely yield enough to sustain them for nine months. They almost completely lack utensils or work implements. There are no domestic animals. There is no folklore. During the two months Buñuel and his friends stayed there they didn't hear one song, nor see a single picture, in their little shacks and hovels. Impoverishment, hunger, incest, a product of the horrible misery, have made many inhabitants cretinous. Nevertheless, the majority possess normal mental faculties, being rather quick in intelligence.

The pathetic thing about this country, and for this reason its psychological and human interest is very superior to that of barbaric tribes, is that, though its material civilization is rudimentary and almost prehistoric, its religious and moral culture and ideas are like those of any civilized country. There are Hurdanos who speak French because they have emigrated. Why don't these people entirely abandon their country? Geographers are agreed that it is uninhabitable. Nobody has been able to explain the reason of their continuance there.

Luis Buñuel – A Biography

Born February 22, 1900, in Calanda, Spain, he received his primary education in Zaragoza. In 1917, he went to Madrid where he studied natural sciences under Dr Bolívar.[5]

Three years later his interest shifted from science to literature, and he became an active member of the advance guard group in Madrid. Meanwhile he studied philosophy at the

University of Madrid from which he graduated in 1924. Upon graduation, he went to Paris to study stage direction in the theatre.

As a director he made his debut in Amsterdam two years later with the puppet opera, El Retablo de Maese Pedro, *composed by Manuel de Falla and conducted by Mengelberg. Then, returning to Paris, he studied cinematic technique under the director Jean Epstein. During this period, he was the author of critical articles and poems for such reviews as 'La Gaceta Literaria', 'Cahiers d'Art', and 'La Révolution Surréaliste'.*

In 1929, he produced his first film An Andalusian Dog, *recognized as the first surrealist film ever made. This picture was deliberately made as a violent departure from the usual run of pretentious advance guard films, and the subject itself was quite new. With so bold an experiment, Buñuel anticipated failure and was amazed at its success. It ran nine months in a Paris picture house and started an avalanche of polemics in virtually all magazines and newspapers throughout Europe. Two or three imitators met with little success.*

Then the Vicomte de Noailles offered Buñuel the means for the making of another picture, with the understanding that Stravinsky make the musical score. For reasons of his own, Buñuel objected to the use of Stravinsky and won his point. The second film was named The Golden Age.

The Golden Age *depicts the eternal conflict in human society between the surging forces of love and the sentiments that interfere with it. Though the background and characters are realistic, the chief protagonists are motivated exclusively by the egoistic propulsion of the love impulse. And the quintessential motivation of the film is the interplay of the instinct of love and the instinct of death. The picture was an outcrop of the surrealistic frenzy of the period. In 1932 Buñuel left the Surrealist group.*

The film The Golden Age *was the subject of much controversy and after being exhibited before select groups, as well as the public, it was withdrawn by the Comte de Noailles for his private library. One of the consequences of this picture was the filming of Cocteau's* Blood of a Poet.

In 1933,[6] Buñuel produced a picture, which was not released until three years later. This picture, Land Without Bread, *was made in two versions – English and French. Its theme is everyday life in one of the most miserable regions in the world – how the inhabitants live, how they die, their moral and religious ideas. It is a story of the struggle for survival on a barren land recognized as uninhabitable by the geographers. Why the inhabitants don't quit this land constitutes one of the social enigmas of our time.*

The making of this film was a labor of love, and Buñuel was actually financed by the savings of a Spanish workman.[7] The budget was almost unbelievably small.

The picture was exhibited for four months in the Panthéon Cinema of Paris, and subsequently was shown on the Grands Boulevards. It was also shown in Belgium, Holland and England.

In recent years, Buñuel, to earn his livelihood, was employed as writer in Paramount studios of Paris and supervisor in Spain for Warner Brothers. He has also produced several films for Spanish- speaking countries: Don Quintin the Bitter, Don Simon's Daughter, Who Loves Me? *and* On Guard, Sentry!

Buñuel arrived in America in 193[8]. He intends to remain in this country.

Spa/Eng Tls, PS/I/83

[1] Poet and essayist (1891–1951), exiled to the US in September 1936.
[2] 'College', in English in the original, may refer to Wellesley or Middlebury, as Salinas was teaching at both at this time.
[3] Both typed appendices in English in the original.
[4] Spanish fascist weekly and official publication of the Falangists, founded in 1935.
[5] Ignacio Bolívar y Urrutia (1850–1944), naturalist and entomologist.
[6] Buñuel's mistaken claim, elsewhere, that *Land Without Bread* (filmed in 1933) was filmed in 1932 has subsequently been repeated.
[7] Acín co-financed *Land Without Bread* with 20,000 pesetas he won in a lottery.

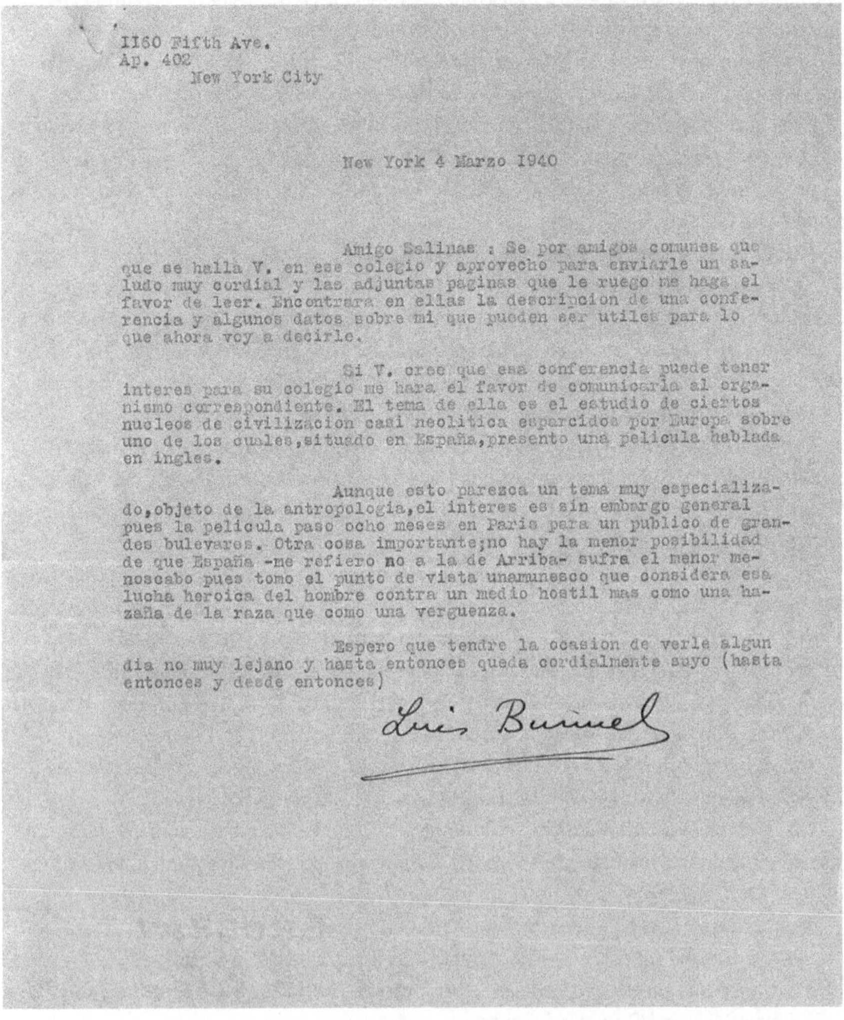

1160 Fifth Ave.
Ap. 402
New York City

New York 4 Marzo 1940

Amigo Salinas : Se por amigos comunes que que se halla V. en ese colegio y aprovecho para enviarle un saludo muy cordial y las adjuntas paginas que le ruego me haga el favor de leer. Encontrara en ellas la descripcion de una conferencia y algunos datos sobre mi que pueden ser utiles para lo que ahora voy a decirle.

Si V. cree que esa conferencia puede tener interes para su colegio me hara el favor de comunicarla al organismo correspondiente. El tema de ella es el estudio de ciertos nucleos de civilizacion casi neolitica esparcidos por Europa sobre uno de los cuales, situado en España, presento una pelicula hablada en ingles.

Aunque esto parezca un tema muy especializado, objeto de la antropologia, el interes es sin embargo general pues la pelicula paso ocho meses en Paris para un publico de grandes bulevares. Otra cosa importante; no hay la menor posibilidad de que España -me refiero no a la de Arriba- sufra el menor menoscabo pues tomo el punto de vista unamunesco que considera esa lucha heroica del hombre contra un medio hostil mas como una hazaña de la raza que como una verguenza.

Espero que tendre la ocasion de verle algun dia no muy lejano y hasta entonces queda cordialmente suyo (hasta entonces y desde entonces)

Luis Buñuel

Figure 30 Letter from Buñuel to Salinas, 4 March 1940.

To Ricardo Urgoiti

New York, 1 April 1940

Dear Ricardo,

Your letter arrived when I was least expecting it, and it has successfully erased all resentment, because I fully accept your apologies. I understand the inhibition you mention, because I've also felt it at times, although never quite as *criminally* as you.

Castillo[1] wrote and said he had also given you a friendly ultimatum after fruitless attempts to discover how you were. It looks as if you've finally replied. Castillo is a good friend to you and from what I've always seen, a true friend. I was glad you wrote to him.

I tried various ways to get news of you. Amorim, as you know, was one. Among others, the last was Angelillo, who was in New York for a few hours, but I found out too late and didn't get to see him. Ugarte also wrote saying you hadn't replied to him either.

I can see now that you are still battling on in the hope of producing films. I'm surprised you are not already a master producer in that city, coming from such a good, penny-pinching, artistically and morally bankrupt school as that of Buñuel-Remacha. I am sure that sooner or later 'you will triumph', although that triumph would be more assured if you had the aforementioned gentlemen at your side. I'm not even going to attempt to ask for news of our friend, as he's the only one about whom I've heard nothing for such a long time.

Thanks to the vital energy that drives me, I've not yet fallen into despair. Since arriving in America, I've not earned a single cent. I've survived thanks to good friends. It was absurd of me to attempt to get anything done in Hollywood. After a year there, I moved to New York last November and here, although I still haven't found a job, I do have high hopes. Better not to discuss them though, in case they are dashed. I can say that they have to do with film and radio.

If my situation is not resolved by June, I plan to travel to Argentina to 'produce films' Urgoiti style. I shall install myself right in front of Filmófono Argentina and make films at half the price, and far viler than the infamous Juan Simón's daughter. The only difference will be that the characters will call themselves 'vos' instead of 'tú'.[2] I hope you will rush over to join forces with me, but I shall refuse. More seriously: I may have access to some capital over there to produce films and, if that happens the money would be up front. I'll be in touch with you in due course.

Spanish Filmófono has been good for its debts, my mother has written to say that they are going to pay her 5,000 pesetas a month until they've returned her investment. I'm sure she could do with it.

I forgot to say earlier that my idea for starting negotiations with Argentina would be to ask for a small cash advance to spend three months studying the possibilities in Buenos Aires. I would, of course, get in touch with you straight away and would be really delighted if we could work together again. I've changed somewhat as far as the practicalities go, and in a way that would suit any studio, although I am still as committed, ideologically, as I was in my twenties. I owe this new sense of the practical side of life partly to our 'Juan Simón-esque collusion' in Madrid and partly to the hard times I've faced in this country. The idea of being able to work the way we did in Madrid would seem like the ultimate prize to me now and the best thing that could possibly happen.

Send Aurora appropriate greetings from me and tell her that my wife is trying to emulate her, for at the end of June I am hoping she will give me a 'robust daughter'.[3] Trouble always comes in twos (threes). Kisses for the children, and for you, my warmest regards,

Luis
741 West End Avenue, 3E

Spa Tls, RU/01/04/17; *RUTD* 202

[1] Carlos Castillo, lawyer who worked with Urgoiti at Unión Radio, exiled to Mexico 1938.
[2] 'Vos', 2nd-person singular pronoun used in Argentina, unlike 'tu' in Spain and most other Spanish-speaking countries.
[3] LB and Jeanne's second son, Rafael Buñuel, was born in New York on 1 July 1940.

From Iris Barry

New York, 6 April 1940

Dear Luis,

Before your letter arrived, I had already shown *Land Without Bread* to Robert Flaherty[1] and his wife,[2] but only to them. I'm sure you will have heard of Flaherty. He was absolutely amazed and moved by the film. He was on his way to Washington (he's about to start a film on agricultural and farming problems[3]), where I'm sure he will speak of you in glowing terms that may be of some benefit to you and that will, at the very least, promote your name in an environment where people take cinema seriously.

Mrs Flaherty was so impressed she called me yesterday to ask me to let her know if we will screen the film again. Flaherty says it's the most powerful film he has ever seen, he was very impressed with your use of close-up, and he regards you as a serious and intelligent man with heart and talent in equal measure. As do I! He is sure you will make a film here in America that no one else would be capable of making.

In short, please forgive me for having shown the film.

I cannot agree with you, but for now, if you insist, I will not show the film again. I do wonder, however, if you would consider giving a lecture to my students, completely in private, allowing me to screen the film just this once?[4] I would of course explain that the first reel is missing, and would say whatever is necessary, but, I implore you, come, if possible, next Wednesday; or if not, as soon as possible, and speak for half an hour. If you wanted, we could also show *An Andalusian Dog*. I should like to invite Ivens,[5] who has great admiration for you, and Jo Losey,[6] his wife[7] and sister[8], but the decision is yours.

I am *sure* that screening the film, even in its present, imperfect state, would be very good for you. I forgot to say that we pay $25 – it's not much, but it's what we always pay – per lecture.

Please call me. In the meantime, Dick[9] has just returned and sends his regards, as do my mother and father-in-law. I'm sorry that it is difficult to see Mrs Buñuel and I send her my best wishes. And please forgive my spelling mistakes ... I'm embarrassed by them, but I had to write.

[Iris]

Fre Tlu, MoMA/12.02

[1] US documentary filmmaker (1884–1951).
[2] Frances Hubbard Flaherty (1883–1972).
[3] *The Land* (1942).
[4] *Land Without Bread* was shown, with a talk by LB, at MoMA to Barry's Columbia University students on 10 April 1940.
[5] Joris Ivens (1898–1989), Dutch documentary film-maker, met LB in Paris during pre-production of his film on the Spanish Civil War, *The Spanish Earth* (1937).
[6] US filmmaker (1909–84).
[7] Elizabeth Hawes (1903–71), fashion designer.
[8] Mary Losey (1911–95), film critic and historian.
[9] John Abbott.

To Ricardo Urgoiti

New York, 19 July 1940

Dear Ricardo,

Just a few lines to which you are under no obligation to reply, to let you know the following:

1) In their wisdom and mercy, the ever-bountiful and fertile heavens have sent another heir to my vast fortune. Although as the little one is a second-born, I shall make him a soldier, which will always bring great glory, if not to him, to the Fatherland and the Faith. He and his mother are in rude health.

2) Before the end of the summer, I shall discover whether, yea or nay, I will find the capital to produce films over there. If it is a yea, collaborative proposals will be forwarded to you. But they will be tyrannical, because I intend to abuse my financial superiority. I shall require shares of at least 51 per cent in order to be able to boss everyone around.

3) I have a job, temporary, but well paid, on *The March of Time*.[1] Also more interesting things on the horizon. We shall see.

4) I dare not inquire about your business or your life, as I have already given you permission not to reply. Nevertheless, you know how happy I would be to hear your news.

5) Polaty,[2] the 'ex-Ulargui employee'[3] has secured a contract for distribution from United Artists and is going to produce in Cuba. We are in negotiations.

My best wishes to Aurora (is she happy in that tango-dancing country?) and your four little ones, who must be young men already.

I remain more a friend than ever, your
Luis

PS My new address: 244 East 86th Street, New York.

Spa Tls, RU/01/04/19; *RUTD* 204

[1] On the Spanish version of a brief newsreel, *The Vatican of Pius XII* (Vol. 6, episode 7), broadcast, in English, February 1940.
[2] Geza Polaty (1908–91), US producer and co-producer of *Embrujo antillano* (1946), Mexico-Cuba, dir. Juan Orol.
[3] Saturnino Ulargui Moreno (1894–1952), film producer and distributor.

To Ricardo Urgoiti

New York, 4 October 1940

Dear Ricardo,

I'll get straight to the point. I've secured capital in dollars to produce over there, that I shall have access to from November. Obviously, I would like to join forces with you. Before going into more detail, I'd like you to write to me about the options for producing over there: cost of films, available studios, chances of success, your opinions on the matter, etc. Your letter will be *crucial* in determining whether I make a definitive move towards producing in Argentina, or whether I stay here and work on a new project on Pan-American films[1] funded by Rockefeller,[2] they've approached me, but there's been no discussion of fees yet, etc. The Argentine plan, with the capital available, would be to produce three films, we would need more money, but with your experience over there I imagine it wouldn't be too difficult. Also, Tota Cuevas de Vera is over here and has promised to help in the search for funding.

I hope that this time I won't have to wait for your letter. I need, urgently, to make my decision.

Best wishes,
Luis

PS The dictatorship of Filmófono is over. As I will have 51 per cent of the shares, I shall be the big boss and Mr Ricardo will be the humble *assistant* to Mr Buñuel. Such are the times: some rise up while some of you fall.[3]

In my next letter, when I reply to yours, I shall provide any information and details you ask for.

My address for the next year: 301 East 83rd Street, New York

Spa Als, RU/01/04/21; *LBNR* 54 f

[1] Office of the Coordinator of Inter-American Affairs (OCIAA), founded August 1940.
[2] Nelson Rockefeller (1908–79), first coordinator of the OCIAA.
[3] LB is still joking, as in the previous letter, about the 51 per cent that will give him the majority of shares.

To Ricardo Urgoiti

New York, 12 November 1940

Dear Ricardo,

Your letter arrived a few days ago, and I can now provide the details you require. The elements I am able to contribute to our possible collaboration are as follows:

1) Ricardo Urgoiti as associate producer and manager of the project
2) 40,000 Argentine pesos in cash
3) Luis Buñuel as director
4) Rosita Díaz[1] to star, although this does not rule out engaging local stars according to market demands, and
5) help and assistance with whatever we may need from Tota Cuevas de Vera, starting with an investment of 5,000 pesos (already included in the 40,000).

Regarding the plot, as that is one of the most important issues, we shall discuss this Filmófono-fashion, when we've agreed on our reunion. The distributor you mention would have to be involved in any decision and, as you point out, they would have to have significant commercial reach. Polaty secured United Artists distribution in Cuba. I wouldn't be involved in that because I'm not a businessman, so it would be your job to find a good local distributor. I've never considered producing independently, so I leave that up to you.

These, succinctly, are the terms of my collaboration. If you can bring in more investors, so much the better. Tota will help us find others, and she is setting an example by investing some of her own money. She says it's not financially viable for her to put in any more *at the moment*. She has been over here for a couple of months. I thought she would have access to a lot more, but that wasn't the case. Nevertheless, given the way things are these days, it's quite an achievement.

I now know what they are proposing as a *job*[2] in the United States. The State Department has created a Pan-American propaganda department, based in Washington and led by Nelson Rockefeller.[3] Film is one of their thousands of other activities and the famous millionaire, John Whitney[4], is in charge. That gentleman, as well as being the King of the American Airways[5] is, among other things, one of David O. Selznick's[6] financial backers in Hollywood. His right-hand men, the directors of the Film Library of the Museum of Modern Art in New York,[7] were the ones who suggested me, and they have already introduced us. They have offered me a job in the organization that would be something like *technical advisor*[8] and occasional director. Whitney will travel to South America in January and it appears I would form part of this expedition. Their offices are not up and running yet as everything is still being organized. There is a six million dollar budget.

Under normal circumstances I would see this job as winning the lottery. Not today.

Every man and his dog over here now assume America will join the war next year and I intend to put some distance between us before then. I only have to imagine myself defending the American flag in Hong Kong or lounging in a concentration camp for a few years and, of course, I'm out of here.

I look forward to an immediate and definitive response, so I can get moving.

Send Aurora our warmest regards, and the same to your sons. I don't dare send them hugs because they will be men by now.

Affectionately yours,
Luis

PS Reparaz, from Filmófono, is coming this week. I shall try to see him.

The information about my *job* is not beside the point. I have a project in mind that would work with our plans and Whitney's. I'm seeing him this week to discuss it. If it works out, I'll let you know. If not, there is enough to be going on with here.

Spa Tlsps, RU/01/04/23; *LBNR* 56

¹   Rosita Díaz Gimeno (1911–86), Spanish actress; she and her husband Juan Negrín Fidelmann (son of the Spanish Republican President Negrín), were god-parents to Rafael Buñuel.
²   English in the original.
³   The OCIAA.
⁴   John Hay Whitney (1904–82), president of MoMA, and head of the Motion Picture Division at the OCIAA, founded in October 1940.
⁵   John Whitney's cousin, Cornelius Whitney, is co-owner of Pan American Airways.
⁶   US producer (1902–65) and founder, with John Whitney, of Selznick International Pictures, which won the Oscar for Best Picture in 1939, for *Gone with the Wind*, and for *Rebecca* in 1940.
⁷   Barry and Abbott introduced LB to Whitney at a reception at MoMA in October 1940.
⁸   English in the original.

To a friend or relative[1]

New York, [Autumn 1940]

Recognize this one? Photo taken a week ago at the country estate[2] of the president of the Museum where I shot this vulture. The photo has exaggerated my physical condition a little [I've lost weight],[3] but only a little.

[Luis]

Spa Ans, Od; *ICO* 55 f

¹   Handwritten note on back of photograph of LB with vulture.
²   Temora Far, the Abbott and Barry residence in Bucks County, Pennsylvania.
³   Original not entirely legible, the word appears to be 'reduje (lost)'.

Figure 31 Buñuel at the home of Abbott and Barry in Pennsylvania, Autumn 1940.

To John Abbott

New York, 14 January 1941

Dear Dick,

I suppose Iris has told you our last talk about my intention of finding some work that will permit me to wait for the start of your motion pictures project.[1]

In the new panamerican activities of the Museum, as I told Iris, I could be of use in some way. To specify this, I am now writing to you.

Translation of books and pamphlets.

Spanish correspondence.

General research.

I am a doctor of history[2] and speak and translate Spanish, French, English and I can translate Portuguese and Italian.

Besides all this I have direct contacts with writers and artists of different Latin America countries with whom, if you do not want to get in touch officially I should get about any question of interest to you.

Cordially yours,
Buñuel[3]

Eng Tls, MoMA/12.2

[1] OCIAA production and distribution of newsreels, approved in January, began March 1941.
[2] LB had a History degree not a doctorate.
[3] Between January and March 1941, LB edited shortened versions of *Triumph des Willens* (Leni Riefensthal, 1935) and *Feldzug in Polen* (Fritz Hippler, 1940) for a project on Nazi propaganda at MoMA.

Figure 32 Buñuel, Jeanne and Rafael, Stamford, New York, 1941.

To Louisa and Alexander Calder[1]

New York, 16 July 1941

Dear Luisa and Sandy,

Just a few words, to ask a favour of you. Jane and I are working on the documents for our immigration visa at the moment. The Museum[2] is taking care of everything (affidavits, lawyers, etc.), but we still need two more letters of personal recommendation. This is what the lawyer says: 'The letter from your friend should state that he is a citizen of the United States, the length of time he has known you and your wife, and any other flattering comments in your favour he is prepared to make.' We have known one another in person only a short time, but by name for a while now. Would you be able to write a letter for Jane and another for me? We would be very grateful. I've asked Paul Nelson[3] if he would write the other letter, as we've known each other for ten years. If you can write the letters, send them to me here, although the address at the top of the letter should be:

> *Office of Immigration*
> *Visa Section*
> *Department of State, Washington DC*

As for everything else – how are things with you? We are hoping to see you in September and just the thought of it makes us happy. I am also hoping to pay a few urgent debts I owe you for the apartment on 244 East 86th Street.[4]

Hugs for the little ones and, for you both, my friendship,
L. Buñuel
Film Library, Museum of Modern Art

Fre/Eng Als L, AC

---

[1]   US sculptor (1898–1976), married to Louisa James (1905–95).
[2]   LB began work for the OCIAA as chief editor at MoMA in March 1941.
[3]   US architect (1885–1979), studied at the École de Beaux-Arts, Paris, in the 1920s and 30s, where he met LB.
[4]   The Calder apartment in New York, where LB and his family lived at the beginning of 1940.

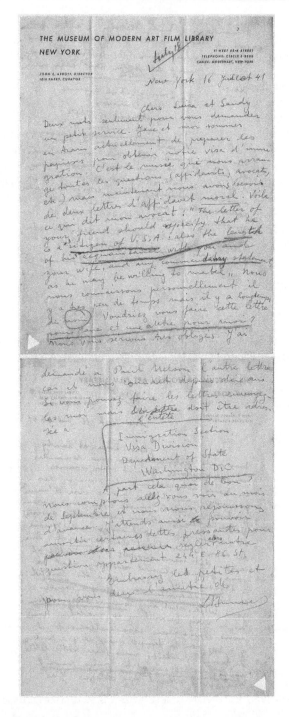

Figure 33 Letter from Buñuel to the Calders, 16 July 1941.

To Richard Griffith[1]

New York, 8 August 1941

I have read your note on the film Fièvre[2] *and found it correct – there is nothing that I could add to it or change.*

[Luis Buñuel]

Eng Iocs L, MoMA/12.02

[1] US film historian (1912–69), Assistant Head of the MoMA Film Library.
[2] Notes for the projection at MoMA of the French film *Fièvre* (Lois Delluc, 1921).

To Iris Barry

New York, 24 June 1943

With the purpose of having direct knowledge as to the reactions that the films edited by the Museum for the Coordinator were prone to produce on a genuine Latin American public, this department has organized in a private way a number of screenings for several distinguished South American personalities. All of them are friends of ours, so they expressed their impressions to us most openly and sincerely. Below is a list of the persons who have come to our shows:

His Exc. Dr Jose Santos,[1] ex-President of Colombia and well-known South American intellectual figures.

His Exc. Jorge Zalamea,[2] Secretary of Public Education in Colombia and now Colombia's Ambassador to Mexico.

Mr Pablo Neruda,[3] one of the greatest Spanish-speaking poets. Now Chilean Consul General in Mexico.

Countess Cuevas de Vera, member of one of the most outstanding Argentine families.
Dr. Jose Sabogal,[4] Director of the School of Fine Arts of Lima, Peru.

Mr Oscar Correia,[5] Consul General of Brazil in New York.

Mr Serge Milliet,[6] Director of the Cultural Department of Brazil.

Mrs Maria Correa, Cultural Attaché to the Chilean Embassy in Washington.

Mr Chamudez,[7] Chilean congressman.

Miss Maria Rosa Oliver,[8] prominent intellectual from Argentina and adviser to the Coordinator of Inter-American Affairs.

Miss Victoria Ocampo, Director of the literary magazine 'SUR' in Buenos Aires, and one of the intellectual leaders in Argentina.

The opinions received have been unanimous in the sense that these films are far superior in the manner of conveying propaganda than the other media employed by the Coordinator, such as radio, press, etc.

Some of them, like President Santos, have spoken to Mr Rockefeller in this connection.

They all consider that the films best appreciated by the Latin American public are cultural films, devoid of obvious political or economical propaganda and those in which no boastful claims are made.

In fact, we have often observed that the military and industrial film are less interesting to them than those purely scientific and cultural.

Important: None of these personalities nor their friends or colleagues, according to them, knew not only that our films were available through the United States Consulates and Embassies in Latin America, but even that this project was being carried out at all.

The programs presented have covered a number of films from the different types we have produced. The basic program has included the following titles:

Tanks	California junior symphony
Soldiers of the sky	Fugue in g minor
The cicada	Parachute athletes
High over the borders	Victory in the air[9]

[Sincerely,]
L. Buñuel

Eng Iocs L, MoMA/12.02

[1] Eduardo Santos Montejo (1888–1974), president of Colombia from 1938 to 1942.
[2] Columbian writer and diplomat (1905–69).
[3] Chilean poet (1904–73).
[4] Peruvian painter and essayist (1888–1956).
[5] Brazilian Ambassador to New York between 1938 and 1945.
[6] Sérgio Milliet (1898–1966), Brazilian poet and painter.
[7] Marcos Chamúdez Reitich (1907–98), Chilean politician and photographer.
[8] Argentinian writer and activist (1898–1977), editorial board member for literary journal *Sur*.
[9] Titles of newsreels produced, or supervised, by the OCIAA for distribution in Latin America.

Figure 34 In the projection room at the Museum of Modern Art, New York, 1943: Ed Kerns, Macgowan, Barry, Pittaluga, Mercedes Merwinoff, Duarte and Buñuel, next to the projector; front row, Norbert Lust and Arthur Kross.

To Iris Barry

New York, 30 June 1943

Dear Miss Barry,

In view of the continued references made in the Motion Pictures Herald[1] *of a prejudicial nature to me,[2] and in consequence of my conversation with you of this date, I feel that I have no alternative but to resign from my position as chief editor and chief of the writer department of the Museum's film adaptations for the office of the Coordinator of Inter-American Affairs.*

It seems evident to me that some person or a group of persons is determined to stir up trouble about me, presumably with the intention of embarrassing or discrediting the Coordinator[3] and the work of his film division, using for that purpose the tendencies represented in one of my pictures, made in 1930 in Paris, and entitled The Golden Age.

As you are one of the few persons in this country who have seen this film, you will understand, no doubt, that it could never be regarded as an anti-religious picture. Certainly, are in it symbolized the obstacles which religion, as well as society, oppose to the attainment of love. The film was a surrealistic poem. At that time, I used to give to the words poetry and love the same meaning that the surrealists did, because I was one of them. Surrealism, to my knowledge, has never been irregular or illegal.

As to the reference made to my 'left wing' feelings, let me bring to your attention the following fact: After being thoroughly investigated by different Government agencies, on June 18, 1942, I appeared before a tribunal at the State Department in Washington. This tribunal was composed by representatives of the different Government departments and agencies, i.e., State Department, Labor, Justice, Navy, Army and FBI As a result of this examination, which was entirely satisfactory, I was able to obtain thereafter the first papers for my American Citizenship.

Before finishing this letter, I wish to assure you that on leaving the Museum, after two and a half years, I carry with me the pleasantest memories. I have always found here a spirit of sincere cooperation for my work, together with the greatest comprehension and cordiality in our relations. All this, Miss Mary, has been possible because of you.

Sincerely yours,
Luis Buñuel

Eng Tls L, MoMA/12.03; *LBOC* 26–27 f

---

[1] Film journal founded by the US Catholic journalist, Martin Quigley, in 1931.
[2] An anonymous writer described LB as 'a storm center of submerged inquiries and discussions for more than a year, growing out of his left wing and surrealist film activities in France some years ago' in 'Museum's Pact with Coordinator Pends', *Motion Picture Herald* 151, no. 13 (26 June 1943), p. 40.
[3] Nelson Rockefeller.

From Iris Barry

Mr Luis Buñuel
Maple Farm Inn,
Stanford, New York

New York, 30 June 1943

Dear Mr Buñuel,
   It is with very sincere regrets that I accept your resignation of today's date. It gives me an opportunity to say, however, how warmly I have appreciated your loyalty and devotion to your work for the Coordinator's office these past two years and to put on record my recognition or your very great competence in handling all the various operations necessary to carry through the film adaptations. That it will be difficult or impossible to find anyone your equal either in ability or in enthusiasm I know very well: above all, your knowledge of Latin American taste and of the nuances of language gave to your work here a specially valuable quality, above and beyond your long experience and talent in this particular field.
   That your resignation, too, is a consequence of your interest in the success of the Coordinator's film work I also realize, and I can only say that I deplore the existence of a situation which made it seem advisable.

Sincerely,
[Iris Barry]
Curator

Eng Tlu C, MoMA/12.04; *RLB* 99 f

From Roy Obringer[1]

Mr Luis Buñuel
1311 No. Sycamore Ave.
Los Angeles, Calif.

Burbank, 18 October 1944

Dear Mr Buñuel,
   With reference to your contract of employment[2] with us dated May 15, 1944 and referring particularly to subdivision (a) of paragraph 25 thereof, please be advised that the undersigned elects to and does hereby exercise the right or option granted to the undersigned in said subdivision (a) of paragraph 25 of said contract.
   Therefore, the term of your employment is extended for an additional period of twenty-six (26) weeks from and after the expiration of the present term of said contract, upon the same terms and conditions as are contained therein, except that the compensation to be paid you for such first extended period shall be the sum of Two Hundred Twenty-five Dollars ($225) per week.[3]

Very truly yours,
By R. J. Obringer, Assistant Secretary
Warner Bros. Pictures, Inc. West Coast Studios

Eng Tls L, WB/2845a

[1] US producer and secretary at Warner Brothers.
[2] LB's contract with Warner to work as 'Dubbing Producer' in California for 26 weeks, 15 May 1944 (WB/Buñuel 2845A); LB moves his family to Los Angeles to take up this job in July 1944.
[3] From May to October LB earned 200 dollars per week.

From Gordon Hollingshead[1]

Burbank, 19 October 1944

Dear Luis:
Just received the following wire from Schneider regarding Spanish dubbing:[2]

COPY OF WIRE
NEW YORK, N.Y. OCT. 19, 1944

FROM: SCHNEIDER AND WOLFE COHEN[3]
TO: GORDON HOLLINGSHEAD

REFERENCE SPANISH DUBBING HAVE GONE OVER MATTER WITH JACK WARNER[4] *AND WISH TO DUB PICTURES IN THE FOLLOWING ORDER:*

TO HAVE OR TO HAVE NOT, OBJECTIVE BURMA, ROUGHLY SPEAKING, MEN WITHOUT DESTINY, CONFLICT, MY REPUTATION, THE CORN IS GREEN[5]

WE ARE ALSO CONSIDERING:
GOD IS MY CO-PILOT *AND* PILLAR TO POST[6]

ON WHICH WE WILL ADVISE YOU IN FEW DAYS. REASON FOR ABOVE PROCEDURE IS THAT WE WISH TO DUB SPANISH VERSIONS IN ORDER OF DOMESTIC RELEASE THEREFORE POSTPONE FOR THE PRESENT RHAPSODY IN BLUE AND SARATOGA TRUNK[7] *WHICH WILL NOT BE RELEASED FOR SOME TIME. WOULD APPRECIATE CONFIRMATION AND ALSO APPROXIMATE TIME FIRST THREE SUBJECTS WILL BE COMPLETED*

[Gordon]

Eng Iocs L, WB/2731

[1] US film producer (1892–1952), worked for Warner between 1944 and 1953.
[2] Warner's Spanish Dubbing Unit had undertaken to dub some of their films into Spanish, under LB's direction.
[3] US producer and executive at Warner.
[4] US producer (1892–1972), president of Warner Brothers.

[5] Features made or premiered by Warner in 1945: *To Have and Have Not*, dir. Howard Hawks; *Objective, Burma!* dir Raoul Walsh; *Roughly Speaking*, dir. Michael Curtiz; *Men Without Destiny* (provisional title for *Escape in the Desert*), dir. Edward Blatt; *Conflict* and *My Reputation*, dir. Curtis Bernhardt; *The Corn Is Green*, dir. Irving Rapper.

[6] *God is my Co-Pilot*, dir. Florey, and *Pillow to Post*, dir. Vincent Sherman, both made in 1945.

[7] *Rhapsody in Blue*, dir. Rapper, and *Saratoga Trunk*, dir. Sam Wood, both made in 1945.

To Phil Friedman[1]

Burbank, 27 December 1944

Dear Mr Friedman,

Miss Dora del Rio[2] was contracted by me in New York with a salary of $100.00 a week. As you know it was necessary to contract here the rest of the actors at a minimum salary of $175.00 a week. It is a fact that Miss del Rio is our best actress and is earning much less than the rest of her co-workers. I would like to avoid the demoralization that this produces. Could you obtain an identical contract for her to those the others have? Her option is to be renewed on January the 2nd.

I will appreciate it if you will inform me as soon as possible, the possibilities of arranging this matter.

Very truly yours,
Luis Buñuel

Eng Iocs L, WB/2738B

[1] Head of casting at Warner.
[2] Mexican actress and dubbing actress.

To Gordon Hollingshead

Burbank, 29 January 1945

Dear Gordon:

According to our conversation this morning, I have assigned Miss Juana Rucar for the translation and adaptation of our Spanish script of Objective Burma[1]. *Her total rate will be $575.00, to be payable after having finished her work. This picture has 15 reels but there is scarcely 11 to be translated, for that reason she will not be payed the rate of $50.00 a reel.*

Yours truly,
Luis Buñuel

Eng Iocs L, WB/2731

[1] Warner Brothers contract with 'miss' Juana Rucar, 29 January 1945 (WB/2371).

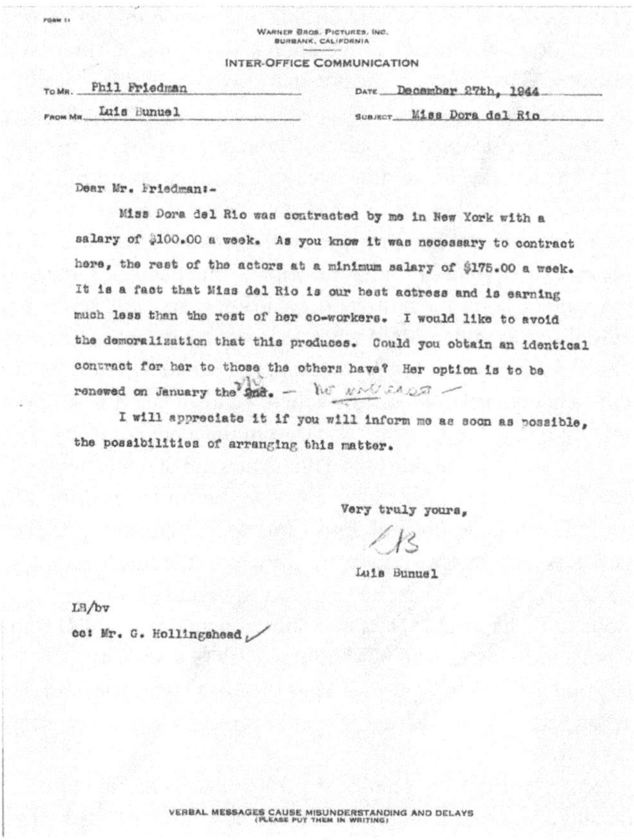

Figure 35 Memo from Buñuel to Friedman, 27 December 1944.

To Gustavo Pittaluga

Ollibood,[1] 15 February 1945

Dear Gustavo,

This is the third letter I've written since arriving at this cultured metropolis, not counting the one I wrote to Don Paulo[2] to compliment him on his triumphant voyage.

Portuguese gentlemen are bombastic, not to mention touchy and apt to feel stung if one does not respond to their epistles. While genteel Italian men such as yourself[3] are also liable to get tetchy and write insulting comments on menus to obscure their own idle penmanship.

I know a little of everyone except you. What are you up to? What are you doing to get by and what to prevail? What are your plans? You have to reply at once and no pleading excuses, because I've now opened fire. Tell me about your life too, the more minute the detail the better.[4] You can imagine just how much I crave news from my position of great solitude, without a single friend. Even my 'acquaintances' have given up on me as a result of my sheer apathy. I work, and I work hard and that way I can at least drug my nostalgia hypnogogically (Demetrio[5] will be able to untangle this weird word for you that is not in the dictionary). I await our liberation and return to the homeland. What is your view, those of you over there, of the possible proximity of this return?

Now, something about my work: it has wind in its sails. I am forming another new company. They have doubled my salary although there was no provision for that in my contract.[6] Incidentally, as we now need four writers we are running a kind of competition in Mexico and I've encouraged Ana María's[7] brother to put his name forward. I'm bringing Zulueta[8] on as my personal *assistant*.[9] They have also 'lifted' my title to *dubbing executive producer*.[10] I have complete independence, etc. If you would be interested in coming along as a musician, let me know and we'll see.[11] There are lots of possibilities to do other things. Mr Warner, as I said in a letter to Demetrio, is happy for me to make films in English, but he doesn't want me to leave the department; so until it is completely organized, I won't be able to go ahead, and when I do, it would have to be something that doesn't stray too far from the ideological line he has always followed. I can't see why you shouldn't have the same kind of opportunities? We could make this count in Spain, not financially, obviously, but in terms of prestige, so that Spanish films of the future do not sink into *Perojoismo*.[12] I'm surrendering myself to Hollywood as a necessary phase in my plan to work in the future on improving our own cinema. Frankly, I don't dare invite Cruz[13] over, because he is used to other roles in life and I don't think he would welcome a subordinate one in a film studio, even if his boss were someone like me, who holds him in such high esteem.

I got a telegram yesterday from Iris, who is down here. She's coming to have supper with us on Saturday with René Clair and Bronja.[14] We shall see what that great monument has to tell us.

I am fully recovered from the sciatica thanks to the monastic lifestyle they have prescribed me and a wonderful chiropractor. People who don't know me think I'm 35. Forgive me for saying how healthy and handsome I am at the moment. The only thing holding me back now is my deafness, which, if it carries on, will soon have me composing a *patétique* or painting a series of *caprichos*.[15] Or, more likely, asking you to let me design the sets for your next ballet. Apart from the couple of glasses of wine I drink when I get home from work, I never touch alcohol. My diet consists of dried fruits or raw vegetables, with meat twice a week. I sleep on a board and if I don't say morning prayers, it's only because we don't celebrate them in my house.

Don Paulo's book of recipes has arrived, and I have concluded he only wrote it to get at you. First: the author favours quality over quantity. Second: he says that Portuguese wine is good. Third: he only mentions Sherry in passing, along with Madeira, which he showers in glory. Four: he prefers Swiss cooking to Spanish. Five: aware of your preference for Monje, he speaks of decanting fine wines. Personally, what offended me most was his claim that oysters *portuguaises*[16] are the best in the world. Long live God Don Rascal, weary of Versailles, your worships the *Claires* of *Marennes*[17] and all those other crustaceans Mr Pittaluga so appreciates![18] It's enough to drive you crazy. I now see Don Paulo never ventured further than Duval's[19] or *Chez Dupont Tout Est Bon*[20] when he was in Paris. The only evidence of any good taste in his book is his observation that I make a splendid paella. In response, I am composing another book called *The Primitive Palate of Brazilians*, subtitled: *The French Influence in Certain Backwater*

Villages. I should be grateful if you would transmit these delicate impressions to Don Paulo; I shall be sending him others to follow directly.

Tell José Luis[21] I'm still waiting impatiently for the letter he promised in his New Year's card. I'll answer him at once. Warmest regards to him and my 'maña' Moncha.[22]

More, most affectionate, greetings to Cruz Marín. I can still see him elevating with his presence those Harvard Club[23] gatherings where the doormen took him for the member and Demetrio for his guest. Do not even say good day from me to that wretched Demetrio until he sends me a letter, and then I'll see what I have to say. You may give Mercedes[24] on the other hand, my warmest regards.

This letter is to you [and] Ana María; the fact that it is more comfortable to write in the third-person singular makes it look incorrectly as if I am just writing to you. I have more news of Ana María than of you, although still in less detail than I would like.

Much love to you both,
Luis

Spa, Od; *MGEN* 181–182

[1] Hollywood.

[2] Paulo Duarte.

[3] Reference to Gustavo's father, Gustavo Pittaluga Fattorini, an Italian doctor who took Spanish citizenship in 1904.

[4] Pittaluga is in exile in Mexico with his wife Ana María Muñoz Custodio (1908–76), an actress with roles in *Don Quintin the Bitter* and *On Guard, Sentry!*

[5] Demetrio Delgado de Torres (1900–84), undersecretary of the Ministry of Finance during the Spanish Republic and personal adviser to Juan Negrín, in exile in New York.

[6] Presumably a joke, as LB's salary at Warner is still 225 dollars.

[7] Álvaro Muñoz Custodio (1912–92), Spanish film director and writer, exiled to Mexico in 1944.

[8] Luis de Zulueta y Escolano (1878–1964), writer and Spanish Republican State Minister between 1931 and 1933, moved into exile to Colombia after the outbreak of the Civil War.

[9] English in the original.

[10] English in the original.

[11] Pittaluga would go on to compose sound tracks for LB's *The Young and the Damned*, *Mexican Bus Ride* and *Viridiana*.

[12] Reference to Perojo, major figure in the Spanish film industry known for literary adaptations, and films with folkloric appeal despised by LB.

[13] Antonio de la Cruz Marín.

[14] Bronja Perlmutter, actress married to Clair.

[15] Ironic references to works by Beethoven and Goya, both of whom became deaf.

[16] French in the original (Portuguese).

[17] Reference to Marennes-Oléron oyster beds.

[18] The original phrase is a comic blend of inaccurate Portuguese and English, LB is still joking about the oysters Duarte does not appreciate.

[19] Pierre-Louis and his son, Alexandre Duval (1847–1922) established a number of popular Parisian restaurants.

[20] Slogan of the Dupont chain of restaurants ('Everything is good at Duponts').

[21] Josep Lluis Sert i López (1902–83), architect and town planner; designed, with Lacasa, the Spanish Pavilion at the Paris International Exposition, 1937; exiled to the United States.

[22] Ramona 'Moncha' Longás, wife of Sert; 'Maña' is an affectionate colloquial reference to someone from Aragon.

[23] Private club in New York, founded by Harvard Alumnae in 1865.

[24] Mercedes Salvador Álvarez Carballo, wife of Delgado.

To Phil Friedman

Burbank, 14 September 1945

Dear Mr Friedman,

I have seen the last takes this morning of the Spanish version of All This and Heaven Too[1] *with the actor loaned by MGM Guillermo Acosta[2] and found them satisfactory.*

Therefore, Mr Acosta has finished his assignment today with us and is free to go back to New York tomorrow.

Please have his last check prepared as per my memo of September 6th. He will go to your office tomorrow, Saturday, at about 11 am, and I should appreciate it if Mr Acosta could have the return ticket to New York at that time.

Also, he will ask the cashier for the above-mentioned check.

Many thanks in advance for taking care of this matter.

Best regards.
Luis Buñuel

Eng Iocs L, WB/2731

---

[1]   Dir. Anatole Litvak, 1940.
[2]   Guillermo Portillo Acosta (1917-2004), Mexican singer, actor, and dubbing actor.

To José Rubia Barcia[1]

[Hollywood, October 1945]

Dear Comrade,

Phone or call at the house[2] today to discuss a possible project.[3] It will at least help us forget our regrettable lack of work. Full of loving kindness, I wanted to lend a hand.

Cheers,
LB

Spa Ans, CBC; *CLB* 207 f

---

[1]   Writer (1914-97) exiled to Cuba in 1939 and to the US in 1943; works for the US Office of War Information (OWI).
[2]   5642 Fountain Avenue, West Hollywood, LB's residence at this time.
[3]   Script titled *El umbral*, in English *The Threshold*, co-written pseudonymously by LB and Rubia, as L. Brunell and A. Aragon, registered with Screen Writers Guild in 1945 under the title *The Great Abyss* (PK/19 f.302).

To Vladimir Pozner[1]

Hollywood, 16 November 1945

My dear Pozner,

My dubbing work for Warner has come to an end, for now at least.[2] It goes without saying that personally I won't miss it. But I don't want to pass up a chance to be of some help to you, so I'm recommending some people I've worked with, who would make a magnificent contribution to your company.[3]

I'll start with Mr José Rubia Barcia, who has directed most of our films. He has dubbed actors, like Gary Cooper in the latest one we finished, *Saratoga Trunk*. As well as directing and acting, he is an even more outstanding dubbing script-writer. He knows everything about it, and you know people with that specialism are the most difficult to find. He is also highly educated and an expert in the complexities of dialogue.

Among the actors and actresses, three stand out:

1) Evita López[4] 18 years old. Great instinct for acting, excellent diction, no trace of regional accent. She dubs the complicated young woman in *The Corn Is Green* and Joan Leslie's[5] part in *Rhapsody in Blue*.
2) Roberto Ramírez.[6] Leading man. Lovely baritone. Good actor with good diction, undoubtedly a great theatrical talent. Examples: *Roughly Speaking* and *Objective, Burma!*
3) Rosita Dorca.[7] Qualities similar to the other two. She can adapt to different leading roles without being recognizably the same woman. She dubbed Rosalind Russell[8] in *Roughly Speaking* and Lauren Bacall in *To Have and Have Not*.

I hear things are going very well with you and I'm very glad. Things are not so bad with me, although I'm thinking of going back to Paris, maybe this Spring

With my warmest regards for the great Lopert,[9] and additional ones for you.
Luis Buñuel

Fre CmfL, CBC; *CLB* 201–202 f

---

[1] Writer and Russian spy (1908–75), worked for the OWI (US Office of War Information) between 1943 and 1945; arranged work for LB after he left MoMA dubbing for Loews Incorporated in New York.
[2] Warner closed the Spanish Dubbing Unit at beginning of November 1945.
[3] NGN International Film Corporation, New York, dubbing and distribution company.
[4] Eva López (1927–2017), Mexican-American actress, Rubia Barcía's wife.
[5] US actress (1925–2015).
[6] Roberto Ramírez Tafur (1915–2005), Colombian actor.
[7] Mexican dubbing actress.
[8] US actress (1907–76).
[9] Ylia Lopert (1905–71), US producer and distributor of Italian descent, coincided with LB at Paramount in Paris.

From Pierre Braunberger

Paris, 19 November 1945

My dear Luis,

I usually get my news of you from our many mutual friends, as you must get mine. But the purpose of this letter is to inform you precisely what happened, and what is happening to *Land Without Bread*.

When I got back to Paris after the Liberation,[1] the market for documentaries was more interesting than before the war, because cinemas are no longer allowed to project a single feature film, they have to meet quotas to include accompanying films.[2] That made me think of ways to make the most of *Land Without Bread*.

It had just one obvious drawback – its length – this mattered, because the new law dictates that a programme cannot exceed 3,400 metres, meaning it would not be possible to screen *Land Without Bread* at over 2,500 metres.

I looked for the negative straight away, but discovered the Germans had confiscated and destroyed it.

I then began an overly long, and overly complicated investigation, that I shall recount as follows.

One of the many crooks who emerged during the Occupation stole my *stock*[3] of copies and, in particular, my copy of *Land Without Bread*, knowing nothing about the film, but thinking there might be some profit to be made from it. He duplicated that copy and presented it to the German censors as his own.

Of course, the Propagandastaffel[4] *did* understand the film, seized the copy and started looking for the negative immediately, which they must have found in the laboratory. They may have requisitioned it and destroyed it, or maybe they sent it to the film archive in Berlin. But the crook in question kept his copy, because the Germans didn't realize he had a second one in addition to the negative.

After much writing backwards and forwards, I discovered the existence of that copy through another one the crook sold to the film archive in Rome.[5] I then convinced the con man in question to sell me his copy, which he threatened to destroy if I reported him or if I did not pay the price he was demanding. So, I thought it was best to go ahead and buy it.

This copy was nowhere near a complete version of the film, so I finished it with sections taken from the copy held at the Cinémathèque.[6]

I must say that the image quality is good and that I screened it privately at the Panthéon where only the most attentive spectators realized it was a copy.

Afterwards, thanks to Jean Painlevé, I acquired not only permission from the censors to licence the film, but also a special dispensation from Mr Painlevé to screen the documentary with a new film (because there are also new regulations that theoretically prohibit the screening of old documentaries with new films).

I have made plans to market the film, and as I've not been able to find our old contract, I am wondering about a 50 per cent split with you. I think I will soon have some interesting offers to discuss.

By my calculations, selling the film in France could easily bring in 100,000 to 200,000 francs. I've just sold it in North Africa for a lump sum of 10,000 francs, and I am negotiating sale of a re-edited version in Belgium.

What would you like me to do with your share of the money?

I've given a copy of this letter to Lulu Viñes, who was here while I dictated it.

Are you planning to come back to Europe? I would love to produce something with you.

How? One of your old team is now working for me: Jacqueline Sadoul.

Until very soon,
Pierre Braunberger
66 rue de Miromesnil

PS My feeling is that the current copy is almost identical to your own version of the film and that the only cuts are those ordered by the censors in 1938. However, to be quite sure we have the most faithful version possible, would you allow us to compare it to your sister-in-law Georgette Rucar's copy?

Fre Tls, AB/568.1; *BMS* 318

[1] August 1944, after the Occupation of France by Germany between 1940 and 1944.
[2] New film legislation from 1945.
[3] English in the original.
[4] Nazi agency in charge of press and film during the Occupation.
[5] Centro Sperimentale di Cinematografia, founded in 1935.
[6] Cinémathèque française, founded in Paris in 1936.

To Jerry Wald[1]

[Los Angeles, January 1946]

Dear Mr Wald,

I want first to remind you who I am. In France and Spain, I produced or directed a dozen films and the last two years I was head of the Spanish Department at Warners Studios.

Before that I was associate producer with Kenneth Mac Gowan in New York and Gordon Hollingshead and Bob Florey at the studios can tell you about me better than myself.

I have learned that you are now preparing a version about the life of Don Juan,[2] a subject which has always interested me very much. I would like to get an interview with you on this question and if you were interested maybe I could collaborate in your production as a writer – not for dialogue but just to help create situations and back ground – and also as a technical advisor.

Hoping I will hear from you sometime, I remain
Very truly yours
Luis Buñuel

PS One year ago, when I was still employed at the studios, I began with Florey a friendly collaboration on Don Juan and I established for him a plan of the town of Madrid in the seventeenth century before the fire of the Royal Palace.[3]

Eng Tls, WB/1717; *EE* 658 f

[1] US producer and scriptwriter (1911–62), working for Warner from 1935.
[2] Preliminary work on *The Adventures of Don Juan* (1948), dir. Vincent Sherman.
[3] WB replied to LB confirming postponement of production on 21 January 1946, WB/1717; EE 657.

To the Head of the Department for Legal and Revalidation of Studies

Mexico City, 3 June 1946

I, LUIS BUÑUEL PORTOLÉS, Spanish national, 46 years old, producer and director, resident of Fountain Avenue, Hollywood, United States and, in this city, at the Hotel Calvin, Azueta 33, hereby respectfully request your permission to register my literary work, *La luz que deslumbra* [Blinding Light], an adaptation of the novel *Wuthering Heights* by Emily Brontë, originally published in England between 1838 and 1840.[1] I wish to reserve the rights to its publication and reproduction of any kind for 30 years. This literary work is so far unpublished.

SYNOPSIS OF THE WORK: Randolph is rescued from the streets by the father of Richard and Isabel,[2] and grows up with them. When his father dies, Richard humiliates his adopted brother forcing him to become a mule-driver. Isabel and Randolph fall in love. The latter, unable to endure his poor treatment, leaves home and returns after some years having made his fortune. Isabel has married Edgar. But the love she shares with the former mule-driver lasts throughout the film until her death. Randolph marries Beatriz, Edgar's sister, to take out on her his hatred for Edgar. As for his former master, Richard, who has become a degenerate alcoholic, Randolph controls him with financial loans and an iron will. Randolph has no good, noble or humanitarian ideals beyond his love for Isabel, whose body he disinters after her death.

In anticipation of your favourable attention, I remain

Yours sincerely
Luis Buñuel

Spa Tls, CBC

[1] Written between October 1845 and June 1846 published in 1847.
[2] Lisbeth, in the 1932 adaptation.

To Ricardo Urgoiti

Hollywood, 23 June 1946

Dear Ricardo,

I was delighted to get your letter yesterday, although not surprised because my mother had mentioned you were on your way over to this atomic country. I'm intrigued to hear you're living in Rye[1] and curious to know why you've come over.[2] I am also, of course, FURIOUSLY keen to talk to you. We have so many things to discuss! But if you can't get over here, it will be difficult to fulfil this wish. You know you're welcome to come and stay here and if you were to come, you would have no living costs, because we can provide a room and a slice of the flavourless bread they make over here.

I've just got back from a month and a half in Mexico. A successful trip. I've taken on a film[3] I'm working on now, with … brace yourself, Negrete,[4] and I've also signed up to go to France in November to make a French version of *La casa de Bernarda Alba*[5] with Synops studios.[6]

What are your plans? To go back to Spain? Are you still working in film and radio?[7] I've not given up all hope of working with you again, although I don't know when or where. I have very fond memories of our 'Filmophonic' days. Although there is a crisis in film production in Mexico at the moment, I still think you would do very well here. There is a really positive atmosphere and a real desire to produce great work. But as I don't yet know your plans or why you are here, it may be pointless for me to go on about possibilities for you over there. I've discussed you a lot with Carlos Castillo. He is one of your true friends, you can count on him for anything. When he heard you were coming to America, he got very excited about the possibility you might come to Mexico. *Idem*[8] Ana María Custodio, who is as charming as ever.

I had legal documents drawn up in Mexico to allow my brother Alfonso to collect those Filmófono pesetas, should they ever come through.[9] I'd be very grateful to hear your views on this if only briefly. It would be really useful if I could transfer part of that debt over here because, although the work proposals are good, I don't have a cent in reserve.

What are your thoughts on the immediate future for Spain? This question alone we could discuss for hours. I know it's delicate, especially for you, to comment in a letter. But you could sum up your views in a single sentence without compromising yourself too much, for example: 'I think you will soon be over there producing films with me' or, on the contrary, 'Unless it's in China, Luis, I don't see us working together again, not in Spain at least.' In short, tell me something, even if it's in Sibylline code. I have no great hopes of returning to Spain any time soon, which is why I'm looking for new avenues in Latin America and France. I've changed somewhat in some ways. I've removed myself from all political activity, although I'm still true to my old beliefs. I despise the world and this technological society I live in and have a morbid tendency to take refuge in the past. As a last resort, although without much faith in it, I cling to cinema to avoid slipping too deeply into a life of contemplation. Now more than ever I want to do interesting things and take on new adventures like this film with Jorge Negrete, this time in order to succeed at them though, rather than to mock them as I used to from my ivory tower.

I hope, Ricardo, that you will write back, if only telegraphically, that is, very briefly, about the various topics in this letter. I am most interested in your plans and whether there is any chance I might interpolate myself among them.

My warmest regards,
Luis

PS I'll be back in Mexico from the second half of July to October. Then to France. And then back to America again. Although, of course, Buñuel proposes and destiny disposes ...

Spa Tls, RU/01/04/27; RUTD 215–216

[1] New York State, 40 km north of Manhattan.
[2] Visiting his sister, María Luisa, and brother-in-law, Guillermo Angulo.
[3] *Gran Casino*, feature produced by Dancigers; filming started December 1946.
[4] Jorge Negrete (1911–1953), Mexican actor and singer, known as the 'charro cantor' (singing Mexican cowboy).
[5] *La casa de Bernarda Alba*, play by Federico García Lorca, written in 1936 and premiered in Buenos Aires in 1945.
[6] Denise and Roland Tual's studio; the adaptation did not go ahead.
[7] After the premier of *Mi cielo de Andalucía* in 1942, Urgoiti retired from cinema.
[8] Latin (the same), here, 'as did'.
[9] From 1941, Urgoiti attempts to claim back money owed, including that owed to LB, from the new, pro-Franco administration at Filmófono.

Figure 36 Tual, sitting with two unknown people, opposite Buñuel and Dancigers, Mexico City, May 1946.

To Ricardo Urgoiti

Hollywood, 30 July 1946

Dear Ricardo,

In the face of your threat to consider me a good friend no longer I am making a supreme effort to write, although, if I did not do so 'only you would understand the hidden, subconscious, reasons why the pen or the *typewriter*[1] might fall from my hands' (your words, from a letter you wrote from Argentina in 1939. What a phenomenal memory I have! But I assure you I was convinced by your explanation and forgave your stubborn silence).

It would be pointless to try and hide from you the fact that your letter[2] made me very happy but also very sad, and I won't attempt to explain that paradox. Sad, because I can see what you must have been going through in Spain,[3] where so many owed you so much for your work on their behalf, or your friendship. Your flight to New York, as Castillo and I have discussed, is a clear indication of your current sense of unease, especially when you say you're going to study new techniques[4] in order to apply them back in Spain 'when it is possible to do serious work there again'. When will it be possible to do serious work there again? If you let me know your thoughts, it would help me see your view of the national and international world we live in. And that's why I get lazy and discouraged about keeping up with my correspondence.

You never really know what is going on with absent friends however many letters you exchange. But something is better than nothing and, from that point of view, these missives are a good thing.

I think you are being excessively pessimistic about the possibility of our future collaboration. I know it won't be tomorrow, or the day after, but if two people really want something they can make it happen. All it takes is for one of them to become successful then help the other out. If not for now in Spain, then somewhere else. But something tells me we will work together again. What a shame our Madrid days are over! Imagine what we could have achieved by this stage! I have such wonderful memories of our work and our friendship in those days. Thinking of which, you don't mention Remacha. What became of him?

I don't know if I told you about my current projects in my last letter. I'm leaving the United States. I'm going to make a film in Mexico, and I'm just waiting for Negrete to OK[5] my adaptation[6] (and I don't know if he will OK[7] it yet). After that, in December, to France to make *La casa de Bernarda Alba* in French. Then, Cine France[8] wants me to head up their short film department. Grémillon is working there already. I have other prospects in Mexico, but I don't think I'll come back to this continent. I'll leave America to the *americones*.[9] I despise this technological age more every day, the most immoral and anti-spiritual age in history. If there were some forgotten corner of the world where I could get by, I would go there. In Hollywood and in New York I have begun to feel profoundly from the Middle Ages. In all seriousness; but I won't go on because my intention in writing is not to philosophize, but to give you a quick glimpse of my current situation.

Ana María's address is: 153 Córdoba, Mexico City. And Ugarte's: Hamburgo 268. That Eduardo gets odder by the day. Don't forget to send me your address in Madrid so we don't lose touch.

My mother is delighted, because she has now got her hands for me on the 180,000 pesetas, more or less, from Filmófono that you told her about. I sorted everything out in Mexico so that they could transfer it to me via the Portuguese Consulate, but here we are, they've sent me nothing and I don't know what's going on. Of course, I'll do everything possible to get the tax certificate and send it to Alfonso in Spain. I hope that with your help we can get something out of that lot. Thanks in advance.

If you want to write, these are my future contacts: I'm here until the 20th of this month.[10] From the end of August until November, c/o Eduardo Ugarte, Mexico. From December onwards, 48 rue Mazarine, Paris (my mother-in-law's house).

Jeanne sends her best wishes, although she remembers that back in our day she didn't see a lot of you because we kept family out of our *public* lives. The two boys – there are two of them now – are well, growing like weeds. It horrifies me to think of yours, who must be almost grown men and women by now, because they were children in 1934. What a terrifying thought. Give Aurora my love.

And for you my deep friendship,
Luis

Spa Tls, RU/01/04/29; *RUTD* 219–220

[1] English in the original.
[2] Letter from Urgoiti to LB, 5 July 1946 (RU/01/04/28).
[3] As a result of the dispute with Filmófono.
[4] In Rye, Urgoiti is studying new electronic techniques to do with radar and modulated frequencies.
[5] English in the original.
[6] Adaptation co-written by LB and Mauricio Magdaleno based on a novel by Michel Veber.
[7] Original in Spanglish: '*okeyerá*'.
[8] Production and distribution company with links to the French Communist Party; produced documentaries by Lotar and Painlevé between 1945 and 1948.
[9] LB adapts the phrase 'América para los americanos', 'America for the Americans' to 'americones', which translates as 'big americans', and is also a (then) light-hearted, pejorative pun on the Spanish word 'maricones' ('homosexuals').
[10] LB's North Sycamore Avenue address in Hollywood; LB presumably means 20 August, as this letter is dated 30 July.

To Ricardo Urgoiti

Hollywood, 6 August 1946

Dear Ricardo,

I am hugely amazed and, I have to confess, somewhat peeved to find you read reservations and reticence between the lines of my last letter.[1] Either you have read it completely the wrong way or I must, unintentionally, have expressed myself badly. I haven't got a copy of that letter, but I know myself and I know my feelings towards you are absolutely cordial, so I can guarantee that, whether written by me or imagined by you, I meant absolutely no offense in that ill-fated letter. If I quoted your phrase from a few years ago it was only because I found it so convincing at that time, and it seemed a really good way to justify your silence. The proof that I liked it is in the fact I remembered it. I'm going to say it again: I am amazed you read any reservations in my letter.

I see you have set off down the artistic path. That you have started to paint is already a worrying symptom: musician, painter, film-maker … I'm not surprised, and I hope that you will continue, but professionally. No *hobbies*.[2] You could easily trump the local film-makers in Spain and directing would allow you to live well and pursue your other activities. Your 'atomic' tendencies please me less.[3] Everything about working in this lousy technological era makes me sick. If I make my own personal contribution to the 'disposable sub-art form' that is the cinema, it is really in spite of myself and because I've never found, nor do I know how to express myself better in an alternative more long-standing and durable medium. Nuclear fission doesn't shock me any more than steam power for example, and humanity could have got by very well without both. I don't mean I refuse to believe in, or that I am opposed – because that would be madness – to the terrible, prosaic, technological reality of our times: I just want to note that I have no admiration or affinity for it, and that it does not interest me. As far as I'm concerned, the atom has not revealed anything new, it has just confirmed the moral depravity of our age. As an example, and symptom of this, I choose a quote from Churchill[4] (a character as vile as Hitler, but without the aura of paranoia): 'Divine Providence has placed in our hands, in the hands of the Anglo-Saxon nations, this terrible, destructive force. What would our enemies have done had fate placed it in theirs?'[5] This is from a speech he gave the day after the criminal attack on Hiroshima.[6] Such cruel and blasphemous cynicism contains the seeds of the entire 'social' atomic programme we've subsequently seen put in practice. And so on and so forth. I've no more to say on this topic. Men of good faith are working on it out there. But they are the rarely heard minority with negligible influence on the people who wield the guns and the money.

I'd be very grateful if you have time, to hear a few objective and honest lines about what the ardent defenders of the so-called Caudillo are saying about me in Spain. This may be a childish and masochistic interest of mine, but it is genuine. Of course, I'm not going to insist, because I imagine you won't have time to write now, and you might well not want to. You can satisfy my unhealthy curiosity another time.

Wishing you a very good trip, my friend, and until as soon as possible, with my warmest regards,
Luis

PS All the projects I mentioned in another letter, in spite of having signed contracts and options, are still just projects. In the meantime, I'm almost completely broke. I couldn't even afford a trip to New York to see you and sort out a few little things at the same time. I feel I'm incompatible with Hollywood. With Mexico even more so. The best and the only thing in America is New York.

Spa Tlsps, RU/01/04/31; *RUTD* 222

¹　Urgoiti's letter has not survived.
²　English in the original.
³　Reference to Urgoiti's efforts to find work in the scientific and pharmaceutical industries.
⁴　Winston Churchill (1874–1965), British prime minister from 1940 to 1945.
⁵　Comment attributed to Churchill during parliamentary discussion on 15 August 1945.
⁶　The bombing of Hiroshima, ordered by US President Harry Truman, on 6 August 1945.

To Frank Stauffacher[1]

[Los Angeles, August 1946]

Notes on the making of *An Andalusian Dog*[2]

Speaking historically, this film represents a violent reaction against what was then known as 'Vanguard Cinema', which appealed exclusively to the viewer's artistic sensibility and indulged in rational mind-playing games with light and shadow, photographic effects, rhythmical montage and technical resources, while occasionally flaunting a perfectly *'conventional and reasonable'* sense of humour.

An Andalusian Dog situates its director, for the first time, on a purely POETIC-MORAL plane (and by MORAL, I mean the sense that governs our dreams or our parapatric[3] compulsions). The development of the plot eschews, as irrelevant, any notion of a *rational* or *aesthetic* order and any *preoccupation with technique*. As a result, the film is intentionally anti-plastic and anti-artistic and anti-canonical. The plot is the product of a kind of CONSCIOUS psychological automatism that, as such, does not attempt to tell a dream, although it does call on mechanisms analogous to those of dreams.

The film takes its inspiration from poetry, free from the ballast of reason, tradition and morality. Its intention: to provoke an instinctive reaction of attraction or repulsion in the viewer. (Experience tells us that this objective was wholly achieved.)

An Andalusian Dog would not have existed without what came to be known as the Surrealist Movement. The film's 'ideology', its psychic motivation and systematic wielding of the poetic image as a subversive weapon, correspond to those of every truly surrealist work of art. This film makes no attempt to attract or please the viewer; on the contrary, it confronts the viewer, in the sense that he forms part of a society with which surrealism finds itself in direct conflict.

The title of the film is not arbitrary, nor is it the result of a joke; it has a close subconscious relationship with the story. It was selected as the most appropriate of hundreds of other possible titles. And in an intriguing aside, we might note here that it has gone on to obsess some viewers in a way that would not have occurred with an arbitrary title.

The producer-director of the film, Buñuel, wrote the *scénario* in collaboration with the painter, Dalí. Both started with a dream image that, in turn, stimulated others through the process already mentioned, until these took the shape of a continuous form. It should be noted that when an image or idea appeared, the co-writers would immediately reject it if it arose from a memory, their cultural education, or any conscious association with an earlier idea. The only images accepted were those which *moved them deeply* and for which there was no rational explanation.[4] The motivation behind these images was or was intended to be purely irrational: they are as mysterious and inexplicable to the author as to the spectator. *NOTHING*, in the film SYMBOLISES *ANYTHING*. The only way to investigate these symbols might, perhaps, be through psychoanalysis.[5]

[Luis Buñuel]

Spa Tda, AB/573.3; *CUA* 565–66 f

[1] American experimental filmmaker (1917–55); director of Art in Cinema, film society based in San Francisco; Stauffacher asked LB to write a text on *An Andalusian Dog* in August 1946 (ART 29–30).

[2] The final text and the note LB sent Stauffacher have not been preserved; the typed draft with handwritten annotations, reproduced here, was published as 'Luis Buñuel: Notes on the Making of *An Andalusian Dog*', in *Art in Cinema* (San Francisco Museum of Modern Art, 1946), pp. 29–30.

[3] Scientific term meaning 'overlapping' or closely related organisms.

[4] Here, the draft includes the following phrase, crossed out: 'Naturally, in order to achieve this, we completely eschewed all forms of moral or rational self-censorship.'

[5] The draft includes a final handwritten paragraph in Spanish that reproduces, in its entirety, LB's introduction to the script published in *La Révolution surréaliste*, no. 12 (15 December 1929), p. 34: "A successful film": most viewers will think. But what can I do in the face of those who respond passionately to any novelty, even when it insults their most profound beliefs, in the face of a press that is bought or insincere, in the face of a stupid crowd that finds beauty and poetry in something that is, in the end, no more than a desperate, passionate call to crime.

Figure 37 Emigration document issued by the Mexican Consulate in Los Angeles, August 1946.

From Frank Stauffacher

[San Francisco,] 25 August 1946

Dear Luis Buñuel,

Your article arrived today, just after I sent my letter off to you. Thank you very, very much. I read it with the aid of a friend of mine, Amado González – who is going to do the translation – and it sounded very fine indeed.[1]

Yes, we will certainly send you copies of the pamphlet when it comes out, and keep you otherwise informed of the development of the program. Received Henry Miller's[2] *article today also, and of course it is superb. Our disposition toward the pamphlet has brightened considerably since yesterday.*

We wish you good luck and success with your new picture; and again, many thanks...

Sincerely yours,
Frank Stauffacher

Eng CmfL, ACP

[1] Translated eventually by Grace McCann Morley.
[2] American writer (1891–1980), met LB in Paris in the early 1930s; the article is 'The Red Herring and the Diamond-backed Terrapin', in *Art in Cinema*, pp. 4–5.

5

'A Man of Mexican Cinema' (1946–56)

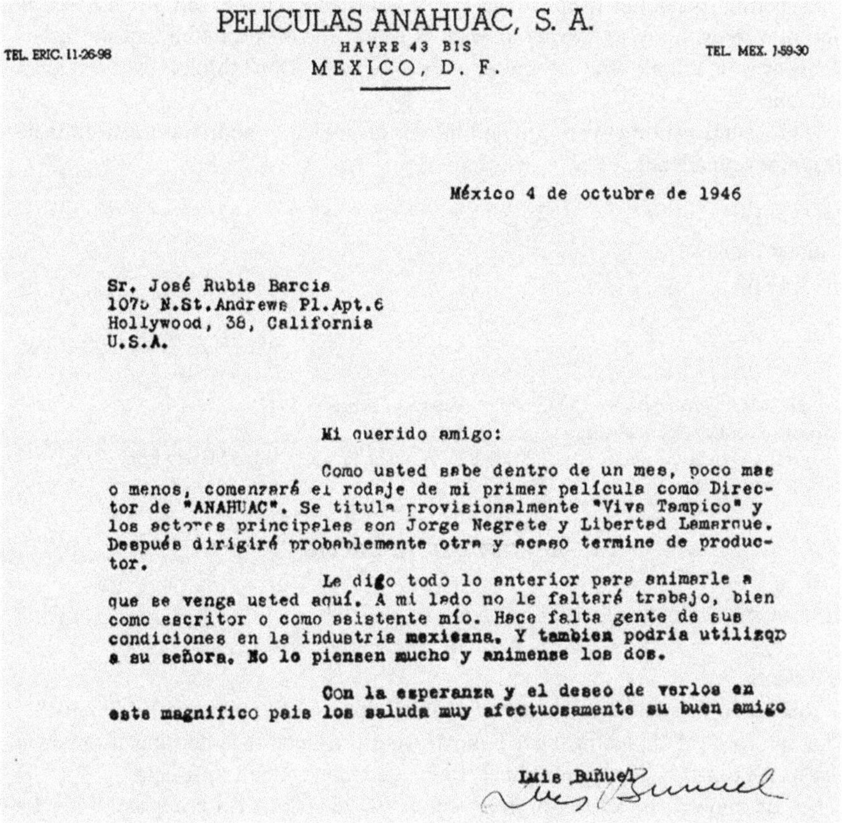

PELICULAS ANAHUAC, S. A.

TEL. ERIC. 11-26-98

HAVRE 43 BIS
MEXICO, D. F.

TEL. MEX. J-59-30

México 4 de octubre de 1946

Sr. José Rubia Barcia
107ט N.St.Andrews Pl.Apt.6
Hollywood, 38, California
U.S.A.

Mi querido amigo:

Como usted sabe dentro de un mes, poco más
o menos, comenzaré el rodaje de mi primer película como Director de "ANAHUAC". Se titula provisionalmente "Viva Tampico" y
los actores principales son Jorge Negrete y Libertad Lamarque.
Después dirigiré probablemente otra y acaso termine de productor.

Le digo todo lo anterior para animarle a
que se venga usted aquí. A mi lado no le faltará trabajo, bien
como escritor o como asistente mío. Hace falta gente de sus
condiciones en la industria mexicana. Y también podría utilizar
a su señora. No lo piensen mucho y anímense los dos.

Con la esperanza y el deseo de verlos en
este magnifico país los saluda muy afectuosamente su buen amigo

Luis Buñuel

Figure 38 Letter from Buñuel to Rubia Barcia, 4 October 1946.

To José Rubia Barcia

José Rubia Barcia
1075 North Saint Andrews Place,
Hollywood 38

Mexico City, 4 October 1946

My dear friend,

As you know, in a month or so I start shooting my first film[1] as an Anahuac[2] director. Its provisional title is *Viva Tampico* and the leading actors are Jorge Negrete and Libertad Lamarque.[3] I'll probably direct another one after that and may even end up producing.

I'm telling you all this to encourage you to come and join me. You would never be short of work with me, as a writer or as an assistant. The Mexican film industry needs people of your calibre. And I could also use your wife.[4] Don't think it over too long, just come.

Waiting and wanting to see you both in this magnificent country, very affectionate greetings, your friend,

Luis Buñuel
Anahuac Films SA
Havre 43 Bis

Spa Tls L, CBC; *CLB* 25–26

---

[1]   *Gran Casino*, filmed between 19 December 1946 and 1 February 1947.
[2]   The name of Danciger's Mexican studios.
[3]   Argentine actress and singer (1908–2000), the 'Queen of Tango', exiled to Mexico from 1945.
[4]   Eva (Evita) López.

To José Rubia Barcia

Mexico City, 11 October 1946

Dear Barcia,

Your letter threw cold water on my financial hopes for the infamous *The Threshold*.[1] What can we do? Still, selling it as a B movie would be better than nothing, if someone buys it! We can only hope that Kohner[2] stays at Republic or San Apapucio.

Let me know if the letter you need will be OK as follows (in synopsis): 'I hereby employ you as my assistant on the next film I make with this studio: on completion, I shall retain your services for successive films and, moreover, will pay your salary out of my own funds, not those of Anahuac or future companies. I guarantee roles for Evita in the aforementioned films, etc.' What I can't do is hire you through Anahuac; I'm sure you'll understand just how risky and potentially inconvenient that would be. If you were here already, I would have employed you as an 'official' writer, then as an assistant. As it is, I've hired Mauricio Magdaleno (who's not at all bad),[3] with a young man called Eduardo Báez as assistant writer, I wouldn't have taken him on had you been here though.

I'm happy with the story. I also managed to sell one by Nino Veber, the friend I found an opening for in my Warner Brothers days, dubbing French scripts. It's a socio-erotic-crime film. Not bad, really good even, in places.

I'm getting on well with Negrete; he's even invited me to lunch at his house on Sunday. He's a big kid and more *macho* than God. The Lamarque woman is much trickier. I haven't met her yet because she has been travelling outside Mexico. We're going to shoot in Tepeyac;[4] the *cameraman* and *art director* are Americans.[5] Dancigers is very easy-going and experienced.

Thanks for taking my brood out riding.

Let me know what you think of my letter-contract.

Love to you and Evita,
Buñuel

Spa Als L, CBC; *CLB* 26–27

[1] *El umbral*, unfilmed script co-written by LB and Rubia.
[2] Paul Kohner (1902–88), US producer and agent of Austrian origin, married to Mexican actress Lupita Tovar.
[3] Magdaleno was the scriptwriter for commercially successful films by Mexican director Emilio 'El Indio' Fernández (1904–86), such as *Flor silvestre* (Wild Flower, 1943) and *María Candelaria* (1944).
[4] Tepeyac Studios, founded in 1946; LB would finally shoot with CLASA Studios (Cinematográfica Latinoamericana, Sociedad Anónima).
[5] Words in italics in English in the original; Jack Draper (1892–1962), director of photography on *Gran Casino*; the art director was, in the end, the Mexican Javier Torres Torija.

To Iris Barry

Mexico City, 27 November 1946

I APPRECIATE YOUR KINDNESS PROPOSING ME FOR SECRETARY OF FILM ARCHIVES[1]. HAVE ACCEPTED, NOW I AM MAKING A NOT TOO BAD FILM HERE. LEAVE FOR FRANCE NEXT MARCH. REMEMBER YOU VERY OFTEN. MY ADDRESS: PELICULAS ANAHUAC, HAVRE, 43BIS, MEXICO CITY. REGARDS,

BUÑUEL

Eng Tel, MoMA/12.04

[1] Barry, who was elected president of the International Federation of Film Archives (FIAF) at their conference in Paris, July 1946, offered LB the post of General Secretary.

To José Rubia Barcia

Mexico City, 6 February 1947

Dear Barcia,

Your letter arrived a few days ago and I had to wait a few more to reply, because I was overwhelmed with work. I'm now at leisure to do so as shooting finished on the 1st of this month. I was getting a bit fed up of that damned Tampico and heaved a sigh of relief after shooting the final scene. In fact, I left the studio with a raging fever and was in bed for three days with the onset of pneumonia. Even today, finally out of bed, I still have stabbing pains in my right side.

I won't say much about the film, as you're already familiar with its fairly mediocre story.[1] I made a few good changes, including a suggestion of yours to do with them not escaping *en masse* from the prison, etc. It certainly won't put me up there with the greats of Mexican cinema, white or Indian,[2] but it has put me on the map as a commercial director. I finished it, although not without great effort and squandered energy, in the thirty-four days they gave me to complete it, managing to stay under budget at the same time.

I've had offers to do other films, particularly with Negrete, who has become fond of me, but for the moment I'm cutting loose and heading off alone to France towards the end of the month at the latest. I'm taking advantage of a free tourist flight that will get me there directly. The main purpose of this trip is to take up my brand-new position as Secretary of the Film Archive[3] and to assess the situation in France for myself. I fear it's not a particularly happy one where cinema is concerned, and I've been told that even what I would earn at Cine France and at the archive wouldn't be enough to put stale bread on the table. I feel duty-bound to make the trip though. I'll probably be back in Mexico by the end of March.

The crisis over here continues with little sign of resolution any time soon. This is not to say though, that all production has stopped. I would say you should come over here at once to stake your claim and wait it out a few months, but I know this would be impossible for a number of understandable reasons. You should wait until I get back and then you could come out at once with your tickets paid. I promise to get you on board as a writer and, for filming, as a dialogue 'arranger'. Our glorious trades union[4] allows no mention of the actual director to prevent a shadow being cast over their wonderful members. But, of course, my title doesn't really matter.

As for your script for *Don Álvaro*,[5] now I know how things work over here I think the only way is to get Armando Calvo[6] to read it. If you want me to, I could arrange an introduction and give him the script. I don't think there are any other suitable actors. Negrete is out of the question, and the Baledones[7] etc., monstrous.

I see you are as ill-informed as ever about dubbing at MGM. I've heard no news that they are planning to come down here and Demetrio, who wrote a few days ago acknowledging payment of my debt, made not the slightest mention of a relocation. I see Godoy's little birds are still spreading rumours.

The general impression among the refugees[8] over here is that there is no sign the situation in Spain is going to improve any time soon. I shall attempt to make it to the Motherland next month under the auspices of the International Film Federation. It seems highly likely I'll be able to spend two weeks there, which would be wonderful. In any case, and if that falls through, I shall go to Biarritz to spend a week with my mother.

As far as I'm concerned, you may do whatever you like with our unfortunate story.[9] Send our very best greetings to Evita's parents. We often reminisce about our splendid banquets and conversations; I always remember Eva with a gastronomical tear and in the warm glow of friendship. Please extend our greetings to the rest of the family of course,

Our warmest regards to you and Evita,
Buñuel
Elba 9F

PS Let me know if I can do anything else for you. You can count on me from 1 April, of course, when I'll be back over here again. I'm leaving my family in Mexico, to Jeanne's great despair. I won't take them to France unless I can do it with $10,000 earned over here, or a guarantee I'll be paid enough over there to live comfortably.

The same day I wrote this letter I took to my bed with a glorious lung infection. To top it all, I was still convalescing from the first illness I gave myself after a bout of over-eating and have now broken out in the most terrible rash. Forgive the delay in sending this unfortunate letter.

Spa Tlsps, CBC; *CLB* 29–31

1   Before filming started, LB sent the script of *Gran Casino* to Rubia in Los Angeles.
2   Pun on nickname, 'el indio', of Mexico's best-known director.
3   FIAF
4   The film-workers' union, Sindicato de Trabajadores de la Producción Cinematográfica (STPC) whose founders included Negrete and the Mexican cinematographer, Gabriel Figueroa (1907–97).
5   *Don Álvaro o la fuerza del sino*, play by Duque de Rivas premiered in 1835; Rubia's unfilmed adaptation is called *Esperándola del cielo*.
6   Armando Calvo Lespier (1919–96), Spanish actor living in Mexico from 1945.
7   Reference to the actor Rafael Baledón (1919–94) and, by extension, to leading actors of commercial Mexican cinema.
8   An estimated 25,000 Spanish refugees arrived in Mexico between 1939 and 1949, in part thanks to the 'open doors' policy of the government of President Lázaro Cárdenas.
9   *El umbral*, also known as *The Great Abyss*, script not filmed during LB's lifetime.

To Iris Barry

Mexico City, 20 March 1947

Dearest Iris,

Your telegram arrived this morning and I'm hurrying to reply. I've been wanting to write to you for a while now, but life has been impossible, and I'm also only just recovering from a bad case of pneumonia. I'm very much afraid – unfortunately! – that as soon as you read this letter you will 'dismiss' me from the post of secretary of the International Federation for which I was so eminently grateful. The reason: it's impossible for me to get to Paris in the next few months. And not only will I lose that position, but another one I was offered a while ago by Cine France, the company where Jean Grémillon works and with whom I was supposed to make some *shorts*[1] and a feature in 1948.

It would be very complicated to explain the reasons I'm obliged to delay my trip but believe me when I say they are pressing and wholly personal. It doesn't even console me to think that I'll have to make another film in Mexico, almost certain to be as trivial as the one I've just made. 'Aztec' films and public taste are truly lamentable and, for now at least, they are without hope of redemption. I'm confused and don't really know what to say to you about the Federation. But I shall do the impossible to retain my position. Would it be possible to move the secretariat over here for a few months? I could pay for a bilingual secretary myself and receive work instructions by post. I would establish an office in my home. Or, alternatively, might a temporary secretary take over Paris? Either way, dear Iris, see what you can do, and be assured of my friendship and gratitude for everything you have already done. Hoping for a resolution and news of your life, all friendship,

Luis
Nilo 52, 2

PS Please see my permanent address above.

Fre Tls, MoMA/12.04; EE 713 f

¹ English in the original.

From Iris Barry

[New York,] 22 March 1947

OPERATION OF INTERNATIONAL FEDERATION SERIOUSLY HANDICAPPED IN YOUR ABSENCE. PLEASE WIRE ME WHEN YOU WILL ARRIVE IN PARIS. REGARDS,

IRIS

Eng Tel, MoMA/12.04

To José Rubia Barcia

Mexico City, 15 May 1947

Dear friend and subordinate, Mr Barcia,
　　As the mountain won't come to me, etc. … You cannot deny that I, this time, am the one showing an interest in maintaining our friendship, the proof of this being the act of writing this letter. But seriously, I'm concerned I've not heard from you or about whether your migratory affairs¹ and those more pertinent to your daily bread are resolved or not. Please write to me at once with a truthful account of your life. For my part, I will then update you on my life and work in this republic because I know you will be interested.
　　I should let you know first of all, that I'm delighted to be living in Mexico. For now, I can breathe freely, or at least so it seems when I compare this lifestyle to elsewhere in the world. My first impression of this country was unpleasant, influenced as I was by

the *Frigidaire*[2] civilization, but my opinion has altered radically since then. Nowadays, Mexico is, in spite of its anarchic tradition, the most stable, peaceful and united country in the world, and this translates into an internal sense of peace that is sorely missing in the sky-scraper society you live in. After nearly a year here, I can confirm that the black legend that hangs over Mexico, the legend of its filth, mortal dangers to human life, and the treacherous nature of its inhabitants, etc., etc., is grossly exaggerated, and even where it's not, it seems paltry to a Spaniard compared with the state of his own country. Lazy and untalented writer that I am, I'm loathe to continue singing Mexico's praises to you: let it suffice to say that I've now resigned from the two positions I held in France and have decided to make my home here voluntarily, I have furnished a 'gorgeous' apartment[3] that is now at the disposal of Mr & Mrs Barcia should they by any chance decide to come to Mexico.

Since finishing the film at the end of February, I've not returned to work. Dancigers offered another one immediately with Libertad Lamarque, but I graciously turned him down.[4] I'll try anything once, but that's enough Lamarque for me. Some fellow called Zacarías is going to do it, an eminent director around these parts. Instead, I'm going to make one with Negrete (who is very amiable) at the end of the year, with a pretty decent script. And until then, although my prospects aren't bad, I have nothing concrete on the horizon.

Gran Casino, the title of the Tampico film – it wasn't called that, because lack of funds precluded any real evocation of time and place[5] – will premiere within the month.[6] My predictions were not wrong. There is nothing in the film I need be ashamed of. A mediocre story, not badly directed, with some technical novelties in *playback*,[7] moderately bad acting, decent cinematography, and that's about all there is to it. And by the way, I made a lot of changes to the version of the script you read. I'm not ashamed of having directed it, because only a film like that would open doors for me to this industry. I finished it exactly on time and within the budget set by the studio, which is *rara avis* around here. And it will be premiered in one of the best theatres,[8] a prerequisite to my joining the union.[9] I'll now have more authority over scripts and although I don't want to delude myself, I think that if I do make another film it will be less trivial than *Gran Casino*. As was to be expected, the *vox populi* and the *populi* press have had quite a go at me.[10] But I find this pleasing rather than annoying, you know my sadomasochistic streak.

My life here is very, very reclusive, although we're always celebrating enormous 'orgies' at home with our four or five good old friends.[11] Tell Evita that if she comes she'll find herself in carefree and youthful company – ours – that holds dances and discussions, even dinners where the guests come dressed as Don Juan. I've no contact with the other refugees. And as for Spain, I no longer think of her, except in the same nostalgic way I sometimes lose myself in reveries about the Middle Ages, a happy era for humanity.

Please tell Evita's mother that we've all become very Mexicanized, to such an extent in fact that even the children won't eat anything unless it comes with *jalapeños* and *tortillas*. Their tolerance for spicy food is a pleasure to see. As it was she who provided our gastronomic introduction to this sort of food, whenever a typical dish arrives at our table we remember her banquets and her extraordinary *poblano* chillies. Please send our warmest greetings to Eva and Señor López and the whole family.

Send me news of your life and work.
A big hug to you both, from your boss,
Luis Buñuel

Spa Tls, CBC; *CLB* 31–33

1   Rubia was on a temporary visa, hoping for permanent residency in the United States.
2   US mass-producer of domestic fridges.
3   On Nilo Street, in Colonia Clavería.
4   *Soledad* (1947), feature directed by Mexican director Miguel Zacarías (1905–2006).
5   Meaning there were insufficient funds to reproduce the port town Tampico during the petrol boom at the beginning of the twentieth century.
6   *Gran Casino* premiered in Mexico City, 12 June 1947.
7   Various musical numbers performed by Lamarque, Negrete and the Calavera Trio.
8   El Cine Palacio, a large, luxurious, expensive cinema as opposed to the cheap local cinemas also known in Spanish as 'de piojitos' (fleapits).
9   The STPC.
10 The film was screened for three weeks to negative reviews by critics, including Efraín Huerta (1914–82) for *Cinema Repórter* and Miguel Ángel Mendoza for *Cartel*.
11 These included Moreno Villa, Pittaluga, Custodio, Ugarte and his wife Pilar Arniches.

Figure 39 Performance of *Don Juan Tenorio* with friends and family, Mexico City, *c*. 1947: standing, Matilde Mantecón, Ernesto García, Ana María Custodio, Ugarte, Concepción de la Torre, Buñuel, Concepción Mantecón; sitting, Pittaluga, Rucar, Rafael Buñuel, Juan Luis Buñuel and Mantecón.

To whom it may concern

[Mexico City, 31 October 1947]

I, Luis Buñuel Portolés, 47 years old, married, film director, born in Calanda, Teruel province, Spaniard, resident of Mexico City, 52 Calle de Nilo and registered accordingly in the National Register of Foreign Nationals, Ledger type RNE 3, number 82214, dated 11 October 1946, hereby declare and swear:

That in the month of March 1935, my mother, Mrs Doña María Portolés Cerezuela, widow and resident of Zaragoza, Spain, lent me, as an investment in my cinematographic projects, the sum of 90,000 pesetas, and that, as I have never returned said amount to my mother, I am currently indebted to my aforementioned mother to the sum of 90,000 pesetas.

As a result, I hereby authorize my brother Alfonso, as legal proxy, to pay our mother the previously indicated amount.[1]

In order fully to satisfy my duties and all relevant and pertinent legal responsibilities, I hereby sign this document in Mexico City, in the presence of Notary Public number 55, Juan Manuel G. de Quevedo, on this day the 31st of October 1947.

Luis Buñuel Portolés[2]

Spa Tls, AB/664

[1] At the conclusion of the legal case with Filmófono, the studio transferred 145,000 pesetas to Alfonso Buñuel, 20 March 1947, 'for his aforementioned brother's contribution to the production of the films *Don Quintin the Bitter, On-guard, Sentry!* and *Who Loves Me?* prior to 31 December' of 1946 (AB/568.62).
[2] Original includes handwritten note by LB's mother: 'As well as the money mentioned here, and in spite of the war, we have also earned 65.000 additional pesetas, a sum which, had it not been for the war, would have been significantly higher.'

To José Rubia Barcia

Mexico City, 12 December 1947

Dear Mr Barcia (*don* José Rubia),

Is Evita suffering from the cold? Are her feet freezing in Sears?[1] I remember just how cold she got at Big Bear Lake,[2] and with the Christmas chills setting in … I remember that Hollywood era with so much nostalgia. I'm sorry, but I did have a wonderful time. It's two years now since you and I were immersed in the search for gory details for the infamous *Umbral*[3] script. I'll say more about that later.

Your letter sounded more optimistic than your previous ones. I think it was absolutely the right thing to accept the teaching position.[4] For all of its shortcomings, it's more desirable and far more dignified than traipsing around the studios looking for work as an artistic director. For that takes qualities which, fortunately, you lack, such as being a little shameless, very sycophantic, more than a bit pushy, something of a backstabber, and a touch illiterate and dim. Above all, your current occupation is the most favourable for you to write *your own things*[5] (which you should publish). I am at your service as your Mexican agent. I will take them personally wherever you wish after reading them myself.

My respectable family and I are getting along just fine and without work since April. If I'm still surviving it is only thanks to my credit with a few friends and with my mother. The sale of *Nazarín*,[6] which I arranged to be paid in Spain, brought in 13,000 pesos here, of which I'm still owed 4,000. What incredible unreliability! I live a very frugal life and hardly see any friends.

Moreno Villa spends a couple of afternoons a week with us. And I occasionally favour Custodio the 'great' critic with my conversation. Juan Larrea, lost as always in his prophetic-theological-poetical dreams, is more difficult to catch up with. He is in New York momentarily. He published a wonderful book over there, in English, called *Guernica*.[7] Ugarte was fired from CLASA because of the crisis. And as for the family, Jeanne dreaming of France and Spain, Juan Luis pining for Hollywood with a genuinely obsessive passion (he's 100 per cent gringo). And the little one, of course, has adapted to life here.

Dubbing has begun, with Azcárraga[8] in charge of one half and Dancigers in charge of the other; in other words, two each that will add up to 15 each if they pass the test. They have sent a supervisor from Metro and two directors, Ramírez and Ortigosa,[9] for whom the union has arranged a special Dubbing Directors branch. I've given two talks on dubbing techniques there, but I'm in no way involved in the work itself. Custodio, whom I recommended to Oscar, is doing a stint as a jobbing writer and seems to be doing OK. Shall I tell you something? If I had to choose between stultifying dubbing work in Mexico and lecturing in Los Angeles, I would definitely choose the latter. No hesitation.

Although need may tempt us to stupid things, I've declined to make more *Gran Casinos*. Although to be honest, I was only offered one option to make a series called *Soledad*, which has just come out. It starts out rather grey and neutral, like the aforementioned film, then turns into a real Salvador or Moraita ...[10] I still have some standards. Now, I shall briefly outline my plans and possibilities:

1) *Nazarín*. Pancho[11] made me wait five months and in the end, he couldn't raise all the money (600,000 pesos). He's passed it on to Ramex.[12] The managing director[13] wants to make it with me. We'll begin in January ... if RKO doesn't slam the door on production over here, which is not impossible. We'll know by the end of the year.

2) *Umbral* Ramex also wants to make this with me, after *Nazarín*, although they'll sign contracts for both at the same time. Noriega loves the story. I think I'll be able to get us $1,500 each. We'll have to wait until the end of the year.

3) With Dancigers. My mother is going to send me 50,000 pesos I will then use to go into co-production with Oscar. We're going to make a really commercial film, *Los sobrinos del capitán Grant*[14] maybe, using a new technique I'm going to introduce over here that will mean I can film the whole thing in seven days.

As you can see, a lot of maybes but no certainties. Not even the loan from my mother. How to get 30,000 pesetas out of Spain these days? Without being a businessman or a *requin industriel*[15] it is very difficult. But we'll give it a go.

To bring this long missive to a close, I'll tell you that, unfortunately, my attempt to sue Warner Brothers has failed.[16] The only plagiarism we could prove was the beginning of the scene. All the rest, the use of slow motion, the climbing hand, etc., etc., I suggested to Florey after I had written the sequence.[17] Ideas that popped up that I would share with him when we were working together.

Regards to all Evita's hospitable and lovely relatives, particularly her parents, and for her and you, very much love,
Buñuel

Spa Tls, CBC; *CLB* 33–36

[1] Chain of department stores established in Chicago in 1886 where Barcia's wife was working.
[2] Lake in the San Bernardino mountains, 160 km east of Los Angeles, where LB and Rubia co-wrote the script below.
[3] Now called *Umbral de sueños* (Threshold of Dreams)
[4] At the University of California, Los Angeles (UCLA).
[5] Rubia went on to write numerous literary and critical works.
[6] Novel by Benito Pérez Galdós (1843–1920), published in 1895; LB films it in 1958.
[7] J. Larrea, *Guernica: Pablo Picasso* (New York: Curt Valentin, 1947).
[8] Emilio Azcárraga Vidaurreta (1895–1972), Mexican industrial of Basque parentage, who founded the Churubusco Studios in 1943.
[9] Carlos David Ortigosa (1915–2007), Mexican announcer and dubbing actor.
[10] Jaime Salvador Valls (1901–76) and Miguel Morayta Martínez (1907–2013), prolific directors of commercial Mexican films, both born in Spain and working in Mexico in the 1940s.
[11] Francisco 'Pancho' Cabrera, Mexican producer and scriptwriter, president of Cabrera Films.
[12] Film company active between 1945 and 1948, a subsidiary of Churubusco and RKO Pictures, the Hollywood studio founded in 1928.
[13] José M. Noriega, Mexican film producer and editor at RKO.
[14] *Les Enfants du capitaine Grant* (1867), Jules Verne novel, much-admired by LB since childhood, after he saw an operetta based on the story at the Circo de Zaragoza theatre.
[15] French in the original (industrial shark).
[16] After seeing *The Beast with Five Fingers* (1945) in Mexico, a Warner's production directed by Florey, LB tried to sue the studio for plagiarizing his text 'Hallucinations about a Dead Hand' (AB/571.5).
[17] LB registered 'Hallucinations about a Dead Hand' with the Screen Writer Guild on 14 November 1945.

To Iris Barry

Mexico City, 22 April 1948

Very dear Iris,

Please don't judge my friendship by the time that has elapsed since I last wrote.

Unfortunately, my pathological terror of correspondence distances me, little by little, from friends I should like to be closer to. However, there is nothing to be done for this illness. I just have to resign myself.

Are you in New York? In Europe? I've no idea, but I would love to have news of you anyway! This letter must suffice, at least to break the ice and, who knows, your reply may begin to consolidate the notion that I should come to New York.

That is why, dear Iris, I would like you to read the script[1] I'm enclosing here with an introduction[2] and give me your sincere impression of it. Depending what you think, I'll tell you my plans in which you play an important role. In my view, the film is fairly exceptional and, still more unusual, original. It will just be a case of polishing it with some surprising gags, some of which you'll see I've added in to give you an idea. You'll also see, as you read through it, that it's not a surrealist film.

I shall wait impatiently for your reply.[3] When I have it, I will write back at far greater length … in spite of my *mail-parapathia*.[4]

Affectionate regards,
Luis

PS The Spanish title is *Illegible, hijo de flauta*, that is, *Illegible, Son of a Flute*. The word 'flauta' in Spanish has an assonant rhyme with 'puta'. But it's very difficult to translate that into English.[5]

Fre Tls, MoMA/12.04

---

[1] *Illegible, hijo de flauta*, co-written with Larrea in 1947, and translated into English as *Illegible, Son of a Flute* (AB/693.2)
[2] Text introducing the script to any potential producer (AB/693.3).
[3] Letter includes a handwritten note by Barry: 'Patience, have courage. I will write. Hugs, Iris'.
[4] In other words that writing letters and being LB are not activities that converge.
[5] In Spanish, the title almost rhymes with 'Son of a whore' or 'Son of a bitch'.

To José Rubia Barcia

Mexico City, 6 July 1948

Dear Barcia,

Your latest letter arrived, to my great joy as always although it has taken me this long to reply, because I've been beset with preoccupations recently. Still, better late than never, and I shall now absolve my sins with these lines.

I always thought finding work at the university was the right thing to do. It may not have been your goal, but until something better comes along, it's the most respectable and least tiresome thing you could do. You may not believe me, but I would swap places if I could. I see you are also still chasing the wicked world of cinema doing things for Godoy and Company.[1] Don't think, as you imply in your letter, that I mock you for doing so: if it brings in a few dollars, I think it's wonderful. Anyway, if things work out well for me here and your migration issues permit, I am convinced we will work together again. You can count on it.

My affairs in this 'beautiful' city are not going well. You wouldn't believe how hard I have to struggle not to fall back on *Gran Casino*-style films. The current crisis, mediocre producers and viewers, and prevailing bad taste are all pushing me towards the heap of run-of-the-mill film-makers. Whenever I come up with an interesting film project, I fall flat on my face. Whereas I've turned down three idiotic films already. So financially speaking, times have been extremely tough. I only get by with help from my family in Spain. But where on earth would I go at this stage?

Succeed or fail, I plan to stay around here. Here is a list of my failures:

Six months with Pancho Cabrera on *Doña Perfecta* and *Nazarín*, I sold him the rights … Failure due to lack of funds.

Noriega is keen to buy our script for *The Threshold* and wants me to make it … Another failure: Ramex ceases production.

I come to an agreement with Rechi[2] to direct *La malquerida* ….[3] He leaves me high and dry and heads off to Los Angeles for two months. When he gets back, he takes on Gavaldón.[4]

Dancigers, with Philip Morris[5] of New York, looks willing to produce a supremely avant-garde story Larrea and I wrote.[6] Not for Mexico, but in English for civilized countries. But when the New York *mister*[7] reads our story, his jaw drops so far, he dislocates it and withdraws the offer to fund.

I think these four are enough to give you an idea. Three days ago, on the other hand, a producer came to my house with Pituka de Foronda,[8] whom I'd never met, to propose I immediately begin filming the Insúa novel *La mujer, el toro y el torero*[9] with Luis Procuna[10] as leading man. It's crazy! Things are bad, bad, bad!

Later on this week, I'll send you two copies of *Illegible, Son of a Flute*, which is the title of a script Juan Larrea and I wrote based on an old book of Juan's that he lost years ago and never published.[11] I'd be really grateful if you could register it at the Screen Writers[12] on Cherokee, and send me the receipt. I'm doing this because the *script*[13] is now wandering the streets of New York with Charles Ford,[14] Iris Barry, etc., and someone (not Iris, of course) might plagiarize it. As you'll see if you read it, it's really unusual, prophetic even … and full of original images. *New Directions Yearbook*[15] wanted to publish it but we turned them down, because that would have made it literature rather than film. I'm sorry for any bother this favour may cause. And I'd be grateful if you could let me know whether registration costs $5 or $10 so I can send you the money.

If you see Kenneth Macgowan,[16] pass on my very warmest wishes. I genuinely admire him; he's one of the most decent people in Hollywood. In my desperation, I nearly wrote to ask him for a place on one of his courses and I almost sent him *Illegible, Son of a Flute* in case, if he liked it, he might be able to do something to help out. But I came to my senses in time.

I often think of you and Evita and of our confabulations, gustation and collaborations with great nostalgia. But this Turkish galley refuses to steer me in your direction.

My very fondest regards,
Luis Buñuel

PS I've insisted Larrea write back to you and he has promised to do it today.

Spa Tlsps, CBC; *CLB* 36–38

---

[1]   Reference to the dubbing company established by actors Federico Godoy and Roberto Ramírez Tafur in Los Angeles.

[2] Santiago Rechi, Mexican producer, who worked on a number of films starring Marlo Moreno, 'Cantinflas' (1911–93), the Mexican comic actor, for Posa Films.

[3] Adaptation of the play by Benavente, premiered in Madrid in 1913.

[4] Roberto Gavaldón (1909–86) Mexican director; the film is, in the end, directed by Emilio Fernández and premiered in Mexico in September 1949.

[5] Tobacco company; New York branch is founded in 1902.

[6] *Illegible, Son of a Flute.*

[7] English in the original, reference to Howard S. Cullman (1891–1972), tobacco magnate with investments in film and theatre.

[8] María 'Pituka' de Foronda and Pinto (1918–99), actress from the Canaries living in Mexico, daughter of the Spanish author Mercedes Pinto (1883–1976), who wrote *Él* (He), the novel LB adapted for the screen in 1952.

[9] Novel by Alberto Álvarez-Insúa (1883–1963), published in Madrid in 1926.

[10] Luis Procuna Montes (1923–95), Mexican bullfighter who starred in the docudrama *¡Torero!* (Bullfighter!), directed by Carlos Velo in 1956.

[11] Originally written by Larrea in Paris 1927–1928, lost in Madrid during the Spanish Civil War.

[12] Screen Writers Guild offices, Cherokee Avenue, Los Angeles.

[13] English in the original.

[14] Charles Henri Ford (1908–2002), US poet and film-maker, who co-edited the surrealist journal *View* in New York from 1940 to 1947.

[15] New Directions, publishing house of US poet James Laughlin, founded in New York in 1936, in order to publish collections of contemporary literature in the form of yearbooks.

[16] In 1947, Dean of the Department of Theatre Arts de UCLA.

To Iris Barry

Mexico City, 7 July 1948

Iris,

I'm beginning to despair at not receiving a response from you to my letter.[1] Although I'm not annoyed even so, because I've ended up responding with silence to friend's letters myself in similar situations and not through lack of friendship, but... I don't really know why. Besides, in your case, I've heard from the outlandish Edward James[2] that you are going through something of a spiritual crisis and would not be in the right frame of mind to write back.

I wanted to come to New York, but it would be an extravagance as I'm still here, after a year, failing every time I come up with an interesting film project. I am, on the other hand, frequently offered rubbish to direct, which I turn down. I should have left Mexico. But where would I go? The future is uncertain. But in spite of everything I've not lost hope.

I would be happy if you liked *Illegible, Son of a Flute*! I'm not sure how successful it is. It's not in fashion, because it's not surrealist or existentialist. It's completely new and prophetic. So we have to face the consequences. The de Noailles no longer exist. Mexico is appalling. But I can't go backwards and leave here. Victory or die trying.

Iris, I remember you with such nostalgia still. Such warmth.

Yours,
Luis

Fre Tls, MoMA/12.04

¹   Of 22 April 1948.
²   British poet (1907–84), patron of the surrealists.

To José Rubia Barcia

Mexico City, 3 August 1948

Dear Barcia,

Many thanks for your speed and *economy* with the literary registration on my behalf.¹ I think it's a good idea to show *Illegible, Son of a Flute* to Macgowan, but not the copy you have. I'm going to enclose a more legible copy of *Illegible, Son of a Flute* with this letter. Do you think I should write a few lines to him as well? I'm not happy with the end of the *scénario*; that is, everything that happens after they find the statue of liberty buried in the desert. Larrea doesn't like it either. But we're not going to make any more changes until there is some real hope of filming it. It would also need enriching with a lot more good gags, some of which I have already. Of course, if a producer can be found, you and I would be working together again. Mr Cullman of New York was keen to make it, but he pulled out at the last minute. I also sent it to Iris Barry, who is very enthusiastic, but can't help for lack of cash. No one else has read it. I shall anxiously await Kenneth's critique and your final opinion.

Everything's going from bad to worse down here. Last week I was supposed to start preparing a film for Dancigers called *El último mono*, by Arniches, but then they devalued the peso and his silent partner, a gringo called Mr Porter, now wants to see what happens before freeing up any dollars. And I think economic disaster is what will happen. Prices are soaring uncontrollably, and the crisis is really beginning to look alarming. I'm even beginning to think I might get out of Mexico. But where to? Venezuela perhaps. Only yesterday I sent a note to Rómulo Gallegos² about setting up a documentary film production company in Venezuela on behalf of an intimate friend of his (Galician, no less).³ All the arrangements will be with Rómulo directly. If that falls through (and let's hope it does because what on earth would I do in Caracas? It's a tropical Valladolid!), I shall have to seriously consider going back to Hollywood. Macgowan's university might be a temporary solution.⁴ I could ask him to find me a one-year contract to teach something spurious, *The advance guard movements and the motion pictures*.⁵ Of course, knowing my terrible luck, I'm sure I wouldn't get that either. Could you look very discreetly, into this possibility for me? Could you try to find out for now if Falkenberg is still there in the editing department. I recommended him to Kenneth and I think he hired him. If Falkenberg is there, I'd write to him to check the waters before writing to Kenneth.

Long may you keep your professorship. This is not the time to dream of empires. A secluded life in Hollywood, even if it were only $100 a week guaranteed, looks like an ascetic ideal to me in this repugnant world.

Very many hugs for Evita (when is she going to take over at Sears?), and many more for you.
L.B.

[PS] Many regards to the Edwins.[6]

I'm also attaching an introduction to *Illegible, Son of a Flute*. I think it's important that Macgowan read it. Read it yourself too and see if you agree with me.

Spa Tlsps, CBC; *CLB* 38–40

[1]   Rubia registered the film script at the Screen Writers Guild on 26 July 1948.
[2]   Rómulo Gallegos Freire (1884–1969), Venezuelan novelist, who founded the Ávila film studio, 1938–1942, president of Venezuela from February to November 1948.
[3]   Possibly Alberto Fernández, 'Mezquita' (1898–1968), trade unionist exiled in Venezuela and, like Rubia Barcia, from Galicia.
[4]   UCLA.
[5]   English in the original.
[6]   Mary and Edwin Rolfe, pseudonym of Solomon Fishman (1909–54), US poet and volunteer in the Lincoln Battalion during the Spanish Civil War, worked as a Hollywood scriptwriter on his return where he met LB in 1944.

To Kenneth Macgowan

Mexico City, 9 August 1948

Dear Kenneth,

I am taking the liberty of writing you these few lines in order to get your opinion on a couple of matters of no small interest to me. So, I take advantage of the friendship you have always shown me.

By my friend, Jose Barcia, I am sending you an original script[1] written by Juan Larrea and myself. Its idea is, I think, something entirely new in movies, and I should like to know if there is any possibility of producing this sort of thing in Hollywood. I am aware that any film company probably would not make it: but is not there some private producer – an actor, for instance – who might be interested in trying out something that leaves the beaten path? By the beaten path in movies, I mean, the realistic interpretation of the world.

To tell the truth, my interest lies not so much in the scenario I am sending you as in the line or direction, which this type of poetic film marks, that is, in the possibilities it opens up. If this particular script were not in itself suitable, other could be made by us.

I am anxious to have your opinion about this script and its possibilities of realisation there.

That what you say will be of great worth to me.

The second matter is this: Is it too late now to make an application to your University for a teaching post in the Cinematographic Department? If there is still time, I should like to make such an application and suggest a series of topics which, I believe, would be of considerable interest.

Here, in Mexico, is wonderful … We continue to make the worst films in the world.

Nevertheless, I am through. I should like to come back to the States, bring my family, take out my final papers and … wait quietly for the next war.

I hope you can find time to send me a line or two in answer to the above questions.
I thank you in advance.

Very sincerely yours
[Luis Buñuel]

Eng Tlu, CBC

¹   *Illegible, Son of a Flute.*

To José Rubia Barcia

Mexico City, 10 August 1948

Dear Barcia,

I wrote to you a few days ago with the *script*¹ of *Illegible, Son of a Flute* for Macgowan. I also said I might send him a few lines myself. In the end I did, and I'm enclosing a copy of my letter to Kenneth here. As you'll see, I'm asking him brazenly for a *job*.² I don't imagine he'll be able to help me though, because the time for accepting new professors is probably already over. Still, there'd be even less chance if I didn't ask. The point is to get out of Mexico … any way possible.

I should hear back from Rómulo Gallegos this week. If he accepts my proposal, I'm sunk: stuffed on Caracas with Venezuelan Savannah for dessert.³ If he doesn't accept, I'm still sunk. As for the great *Illegible, Son of a Flute*, I'm not getting my hopes up. I'll probably end up waiting in Mexico for the dollar to stabilize and making a few pesos with Dancigers to help me get the hell out of here. You'll think I'm joking, but I would take absolutely any kind of *job*⁴ in Hollywood that would let me live obscurely within reach of a gallon of red wine.

Macgowan's address is 10737 Le Conte, Westwood, but I imagine you'll give him the *script*⁵ when you see him at the university.

Very warm regards, thanks, and until next time,
Buñuel

PS Do you think Godoy's production company might be interested in making *Illegible, Son of a Flute*? Although probably not, he and Ramírez being existentialists.
The refugees down here are all itching to skedaddle. It's almost funny.

Spa Tlsps, CBC

¹   English in the original.
²   English in the original.
³   LB's joke 'Caracas a todo pasto y sabana venezolana por postres' is succinctly funny and impossible to translate: 'a todo pasto' means 'at full tilt' (with connotations of 'excess' or 'abundance') and 'pasto' has various associations with food, for example 'meal', etc.; 'sabanas venezolanas' are both a Venezuelan pudding and a reference to the stunning Gran Sabana region in south-eastern Venezuela.
⁴   English in the original.
⁵   English in the original.

To José Rubia Barcia

Mexico City, 5 September 1948

My dear Barcia,

Thank you so much for your lengthy and instructive letter. Kenneth did indeed write back in similar terms to the ones he used in his conversation with you. I don't think he understood *Illegible, Son of a Flute* because, although he calls it a *striking script*,[1] he follows that up immediately with an absolutely standard critique of what he sees as its structural defects. You can't just say of a poetic film like this one, that it lacks a climax, or that the *plot*[2] is underdeveloped or too confusing. You can't judge a naturalist novel and a lyric poem the same way. Still, I'm not about to start arguing cinematic technique with my good friend Macgowan. He thinks there is no chance of it being made in Hollywood anyway. And he's passing me on to that poor man who made that *appalling* film *Dreams That Money Can't Buy*.[3] Said film-maker, Hans Richter, is a German of precious little talent who made a few vanguard films back in 1927 or 1930.[4] I know him well, and the very fact that Macgowan associated that film with *Illegible, Son of a Flute* suggests he regards everything unusual as bizarre in the same way. As for a teaching job, I gather it might be possible next year, as long as I could get some additional income elsewhere. I've taken note, in case something comes up (although not as a Spanish teacher, of course).

I'm finally going to make a film with Dancigers. I'm moving sideways here like a crab. I produced several of Arniches's films, in 1935 and 1936 just for the fun of it and to earn some money.[5] I didn't even put my name to them. And now, 15 years later, it turns out I'm going to be directing *El último mono* by Mr Carlos Arniches 'seriously' and with my name on it. Well, at least as far as light work goes, it's one of the least undignified. They are giving me 18 days to film it. It's going to be a real mess! But I'll fight like mad to add at least a little dignity to the *mise-en-scene* and *script*.[6] I'll be free again in January and if I haven't spent all the money I earn, we'll all go to Los Angeles.

I'm now negotiating with an American company, who want me to film Falla's *Master Peter's Puppet Show*. The terms of the proposal they sent me the day before yesterday are a bit confusing and I've asked for clarification. They talk about sending someone down here to talk things over with me and I've written back saying that I would be more than willing to travel up to them. If they agree (and if they pay my expenses, of course), we'll see each other soon. But if they want to see me and this oh-so-Aztec of lands at the same time, I'll just have to agree. One of the reasons I would really like to come up for a week is to see you, drink co-both (a little neologism)[7] gallons and talk at great length as Evita watches over us with her enigmatic Oriental eyes. And that's that!

I completely agree with you about giving the *script*[8] to Jay Leyda. He's one of the most honourable and intelligent men in American cinema. As well as being one of my best friends in the world. He wrote to me six or seven months ago, and I haven't replied. I hope I'll be able to soon. I'm ashamed … Send my regards if you see him. And to the Edwins as well. What is Rolfe up to? *Working still as writer for Warner's*?[9] I gather from his letters that came to an end.

As for the *dubbing*[10] business you mention, it's impossible. Reasons: I'm not – we're not – businessmen and would surely get our fingers burned. I have only enough money to get me from one day to the next, and that's only when I have some; recently, if it hadn't been for a good friend or two, I would have gone hungry. However, if we can get a bit of capital to start it up, it would be worth thinking about. But where would it come from? They are still doing *dubbing* here and Dancigers is losing money on every film. The union comes up with more obstacles by the day. They're trying to stamp it out. They are ferociously anti*dubbers*. And speaking of Dancigers, he won an Ariel[11] yesterday for best film of 1947.[12] It's pitiful, trying to copy the world's great film producing centres by handing out Ariels and Oscars to the miserable little films they make down here. It's insane. If I didn't have to go to union meetings, I wouldn't have anything to do with the film world here. That's how I keep out of all the mess, envy, sycophancy, machinations, etc., etc.

Who knows if we'll see one another soon, perhaps? Warmest regards to Evita and you, Luis

PS It would be good if you could send me the original[13] for *Cuadernos Americanos*.[14] They are very quick at processing them.

Please hold on to the two copies of the *Illegible, Son of a Flute* script and the 'Introduction'. I may ask you to pass one of them to a certain person soon.

Spa Tlsps, CBC; *CLB* 40–42

---

[1] English in the original.

[2] English in the original.

[3] *Dreams That Money Can Buy* (1947), experimental film by Hans Richter (1888–1976), with Ernst, Ray, Calder, Milhaud and Léger.

[4] Richter made his first film, *Rhytmus 21* in 1921; from 1927 to 1930 he directed eight abstract films and was exiled to New York in 1940.

[5] With Filmófono, *Don Quintin the Bitter* and *On-Guard, Sentry!*

[6] English in the original.

[7] Untranslatable: 'co-sendos': 'sendos' has no direct English translation, but it means 'both' in the sense of 'each of our'.

[8] English in the original (of *Illegible, Son of a Flute*).

[9] Phrase in italics in English in the original.

[10] Barcia's proposal that he and LB set up a dubbing company.

[11] Mexican Academy of Arts' Ariel Awards founded in 1946.

[12] For *La perla* (The Pearl, 1947) dir. Emilio Fernández, co-produced by RKO and Águila Films.

[13] Rubia Barcia's article on the Spanish author and playwright, Ramón María del Valle-Inclán (1866–1936).

[14] Academic journal published at the National Autonomous University of Mexico (UNAM), co-founded in 1942 by writers including Larrea and the exiled Spanish poet León Felipe (1884–1968).

From his mother

Zaragoza, 2 November 1948

Dearest children and much-adored grandchildren, whom I hold so close to my heart,[1] I wrote to you a few days ago but forgot to tell you the most interesting thing and my main reason for writing; when I realized my involuntary forgetfulness, I wanted to write again, but a thousand things this first few days of my return from the summer vacation have prevented me from doing so. It was this: I beg and implore you, in all sincerity, not to send me the 5,000 pesetas you mentioned, because it would make me very unhappy and I would only send it straight back to you. My poor children! Please don't embarrass me! I've been living so far from you for twelve years now, both now and before the war, except for the time when I was lucky enough to live close to you both;[2] you could say we've spent a lifetime apart, without me ever being able to offer anything, before or after you were married, but the most miserly, you might say, of gifts, in comparison with what I have always been able to give all your brothers and sisters; who have had much more, incomparably more. You never wanted an allowance, nor did you accept a single gift for you or for your loved ones; I still remember a hat I once wanted to buy for your wife that you wouldn't accept, insisting that the poor thing took only the 90 or 100 pesetas, I can't remember how much it cost. When your sisters got married I gave them 40,000 pesetas. That was certainly what María spent [and] for the others it was at least 35,000, or perhaps a little more. So, my son, please don't upset me by sending something that would only cause me great pain, and if you can't accept it then give it to those two grandchildren, your darling sons. I believe I am acting in good faith, yet even so you will always be, of all my children, the one who has benefited least; but as this does not bother you in the slightest, that is fine.

Do not leave me too long without news and even if it is only on a postcard, let me know how you all are over there and whether you are happy in your work and your affairs. You could have earned so much more here in Spain! It pains me to think of it! The other day they put on, or premiered, a film by Sáenz de Heredia[3] (your former assistant, I believe?). People like him are doing really well these days, earning shocking amounts.[4] They are having great success here with *Locura de amor*,[5] that is, the story of Mad Juana. It has been very popular and has been on at the same theatre for three weeks now; I don't remember the name of the director. Cinema is really coming along it seems, and if you were here ... imagine! As always, you would have surpassed the others, outshining them in every way. That damned war! It was a disaster for all of us, in terms of money that is, I thank God for sparing our lives, which is an enormous source of happiness of course, when you think of all those poor people who suffered and died. The only thing that pains me now is this long separation, and it weighs on my conscience that I've not yet visited you. Although I don't think I would have been able to make the journey on my own with my little ways and worries, nor would it have been easy for anyone to come with me.

Nor would it put my mind at rest if you came here, on the contrary it would worry me for a number of reasons, so I console myself by praying that God will one day bless me with the joy and satisfaction of embracing you all.[6] That would be plenty, and I am happy to wait for such a fortunate and blessed day. Now my son, it would make me very happy if you found some security for your old age, which seems a long way off now, but time flies and it is very sad not to be comfortable when you are old, it is much more worrying and urgent then, not only for ourselves, but for the dearest loved ones we leave behind, or who came into the world through no fault of their own.

I have been interrupted so many times now that I've forgotten so many of the things I wanted to say. If I don't remember now, I'll tell you later, God willing, in my next letter, because the main purpose of this one was to tell you about the 5,000 pesetas. And once again, I am going to beg you to accept them or, if as usual you don't want anything, that you give them to your sons as a small but very heartfelt gift from their grandmother. Talk to them about me; I know you do already, but I want them to know me well. Tell them how very much I love them. And beautiful, angelic Jeanne, who also knows how much I've always loved her and how much that love has grown, if it were possible for me to feel more affection for her than I do already, it's as if she were my own daughter. I send all four of you a thousand hugs and more kisses besides, from my heart and soul in a letter that is so happy because it is on its way to you all.

Alfonso[7] is still in Madrid, satisfied and content, because he has a new job now, so he is happy and hopeful. I think I told you in my last letter that the bullfighter brothers, the Dominguíns,[8] have asked him to refurbish a hotel and a training-ring for bulls somewhere near Toledo.[9] He's a friend of theirs, the Dominguín bullfighters, so they invited him to spend a few days on their ranch, which he did. And now they have taken him on as their architect and he is very happy, because they are also going to buy a splendid estate for nine million pesetas, apparently; imagine!

Well, my dear son, I'm going to finish for today, because it is clear that I am not going to be left in peace to finish this letter. They have telephoned again from María's house and I am going to go over there; I have been wanting to tell you all this for days and I cannot think of anything more now.

Sending you, Jeanne and the boys thousands of hugs and kisses from your
Mother

[PS] Everyone here tells me to send their love too.

Spa Als, AB/596.1

---

[1]   Letter to LB, his wife and children.
[2]   In Madrid in 1936.
[3]   *Las aguas bajan negras* (1948).
[4]   Heredia became the official Regime director and had great commercial success with the film *Raza* (1941) based on a script written pseudonymously by Franco.
[5]   Directed by Juan de Orduña (1948); based on the life of Queen Juana I of Castile, known as Juana, la Loca (Joanna the Mad).
[6]   They would not meet again until Spring 1955, in Pau, Pyrenean city in southwestern France not far from the border with Spain.
[7]   Alfonso Buñuel, architect working in Madrid.
[8]   'Dominguín', nickname for the famous Spanish bullfighters, the brothers Domingo (1920–75), José (1922–2003) and Luis Miguel González Lucas (1926–96).
[9]   Dominguín family estate near the town of Quismondo.

To José Rubia Barcia

Mexico City, 5 April 1949

Dear Barcia,

Your letter arrived yesterday and I've no choice but to celebrate your wonderful news with enormous congratulations by return post! Bear hugs for Evita and her 'legal spouse' on the soon-to-be happy arrival of the little one I'm already sure will be a boy. And – in all modesty! – I never get this kind of prediction wrong.[1] You'll see. I hope everything goes wonderfully well and that you'll let me know the result.

As soon as you send your article on Valle-Inclán I'll pass it on to Larrea. As you know, *Cuadernos Americanos*'s policy is to publish content related to, or that contributes in some way to promoting the concept of 'America',[2] so it would probably be a good idea, even if you just smuggle in a few lines, to relate your work to that aforementioned and well-worn notion. I'm saying this, because they may have turned down your first article because it was entirely objective and literary with no passing reference even to the dismal 'civilization of corn'. Juan Larrea, America's prophet and a first-rate *heretic*, puts all his tenacious fanaticism, which is no small thing, into guiding the journal in that direction. Send me the article soon, I will read it closely and can guarantee its publication if you adapt it loosely along those guidelines.

I shall now sum up the last year and a half that I have spent completely inactive. Even at this time of cinematic crisis, I was determined not to direct any more stupid films. All my major projects – more than ten of them – failed miserably. It would be painful to recount the hard times I've had. In the end I signed a contract in February, which is what I'm living on now, to make one of my kind of films.[3] It's based entirely on Juvenile Court cases and on files from the Clínica de la conducta.[4] The parts will be played by real Mexican children from the *lumpen-proletariat*, and I'm aiming to shoot it on location. I'm going to make sure it's not like any film on this theme anywhere in the world. It will be more documentary and less literary. I was supposed to start in July, but because of the difficulties associated with the subject, we're going to wait until October and make a Simenon[5] film in the meantime, which actually looks quite interesting. I'm working for Ultramar[6] and Águila Films (a Menasce-Dancigers joint venture). In short, business seems finally about to march ahead … with me leading.

I'm still *completely* isolated from the parties, cabarets, etc. of the sordid little film world down here. My *parties*[7] are always at friends' houses, or better still my own. The guests: León Felipe, Larrea, Imaz,[8] Moreno Villa, Mantecón and the occasional meeting and evening meal with Álvaro Custodio, the great film critic. I also see Gual[9] and the Catalans from the Banco Comercial de la Propiedad,[10] who are all cheerful and easy-going. And that's the extent of my social life.

What are your views on the state of the world? Perhaps better not even to broach a subject we could discuss for hours on end. And when will we be able to do that? I envy your university position and congratulate you on the *Assistant Professor*[11] thing. I don't know if it's my age or just a longing for peace, but I'm strongly attracted to the idea of a fixed job, something like yours, that does not completely rule out doing other things. Still, I shall stay here, tethered to the hard bench of my Mexican film galley.

Warm regards to the Rolfes. Why don't they come to Mexico? And to Jay Leyda. Do you ever see him? I think I heard, or read rather, in one of your letters that you do.

Very fond regards, to Evita's parents first of all, and then to the rest of the clan, and to you both, the friendliest possible wishes from,

L. Buñuel

[PS] Dear Evita,

I'm delighted to hear you'll soon have a baby, but I hope it will be a girl because they are sweeter and better behaved. We are all fine here, but the boys prefer Los Angeles. We eat more chillies and tortillas than the Mexicans and I'm sure my *tamales* and *enchiladas* could now compete with your mother's.

Best wishes to your family and a big hug to you both from,
Jeanne

Spa Tlsps CBC; *CLB* 43–45

1 Elena, Barcia and López's first child (a daughter, despite LB's confident prediction), born September 1949.
2 In this context, Latin America.
3 *The Young and the Damned.*
4 Centre for child psychiatry, linked to the Ministry for Public Education in Mexico City, founded by Dr José Luis Patiño Rojas in 1948.
5 Georges Simenon (1903–89), Belgian writer.
6 Production company directed by Jaime A. Menasce, in business 1948 to 1952, for which LB directed *The Great Madcap, The Young and the Damned* and *Daughter of Deceit.*
7 English in the original.
8 Eugenio Imaz Echeverría (1900–51), philosopher and translator, exiled to Mexico in 1939.
9 Enrique Fernández Gual (1907–73), art critic from Barcelona, exiled to Mexico in 1939.
10 Bank of Commercial Real Estate.
11 English in the original, an academic post Rubia acquired in 1949.

To José Rubia Barcia

Mexico City, 5 September 1949

My dear friend Barcia,

Your most recent letter arrived yesterday, and I'm going to atone for my offensive silence to the previous one replying by return post.

Let's talk about Larrea first: as soon as your essay arrived I passed it on to Juan. He comes for supper with us every Sunday and both then, and on the phone during the week, I've been pushing him for a response to your article. He took at least three weeks to read it. He then said that *Cuadernos* will not publish any articles that long, unless they have exceptional 'American' interest; that they published an essay by Salinas on Valle-Inclán a few years ago,[1] and that only the last 40 pages of what you sent did not repeat, from a different perspective, Salinas's essay. I should say that he only read your article when he saw I was beginning to get annoyed at his lack of concern. And I should add in his defence that Larrea has been paying very little attention to *Cuadernos* over the last two months. He's getting ready for his trip to New York, because he's got a grant,[2] so all his attention and energy is now directed towards the United States. You should decide what to do about his suggestions soon, although I understand how painful the mutilation would be, because the journal will be out on 1 October. Personally, I thought it was excellent, all of it, and I think it should be published as it is. Let me know if I can do anything else to help with its publication.[3] The editors of *Sur* in Buenos Aires are friends of mine. The only thing I think may be a problem for journals like that is the length.

I've also received Rolfe's poem and was touched by its passionate warmth and exuberance.[4] I don't know if they publish *España Nueva*,[5] over here, but I'll find out today and suggest they look at the poem. Altolaguirre is now separated from Conchita[6] and joined in illicit 'nuptials' with Mena.[7] I never see him, but Moreno Villa, who comes over here a lot, sees them often, I'll arrange to meet up with Manolito and discuss your query.[8] I'll write and let you know the outcome. Please send my love to Edwin and his splendid partner.

I'm now starting to put down roots in this loose soil, because where else would I go? I have had a really tough year and a half, but now it's all full speed ahead. I finished a film a month ago,[9] predicted to be a box office success (it's pretty worthless, but decent), and that's vital if I'm to carry on making films. I finished it in nineteen days, it's supposed to be, technically, the best film ever made over here, so I've already got contracts for three others. I'm very enthusiastic about the one I'm going to make now, and if it turns out well, you should get to hear about it. It's about juvenile delinquency, and I based my research for it on around two hundred cases from the Juvenile Courts and a hundred from the Behavioural Clinic, a psychiatric institution in Mexico. The characters are adolescents, Mexico City *lumpen-proletariat*, and the style is a compromise between documentary and fiction – necessary for a commercial film. I'm not having to make any other compromises though, ethical or artistic. As for the other films I'm signed up to and for which I've already received an advance, one is *Doña Perfecta*[10] and the other, with Benito Alazraki,[11] is reasonably interesting.

As you can see, after sowing the seeds these last two years so painfully and through a few major disasters, I'd be a fool to leave Mexico now I can almost touch the fruit. I've now lost the right to immigrate to the US, both my family's and my own. And I've requested Mexican citizenship, which should come through one of these days.[12] My family will still be French, and American through the little one.

I'm shaking with indignation at the Dalí thing,[13] although I should be used to the renegade AVIDA DOLLARS's[14] infamous pirouettes by now. It's an offense to human dignity that will no doubt inspire General Motors to offer him a custom-built Cadillac and a cheque for $10,000 which is, rather than offending human dignity, what the distinguished Catalan is really after.

I trust you'll let me know as soon as there's news of his next trick. Kiss Evita for us and wish her the very best of luck. Jeanne can't stop wondering whether it will be a boy or girl.

Love,
Luis

Spa Tls CBC; *CLB* 45–47

1   P. Salinas, 'Significación del esperpento o Valle-Inclán, hijo pródigo del 98', *Cuadernos Americanos* 6, no. 2 (1947), pp. 218–244.

2   Scholarship from the Guggenhein Foundation to carry out research from 1949 to 1951 on 'The Historical Formation of the Myth of Santiago de Compostela, Patron Saint of Spain'.

3   Eventually published as J. Rubia, 'España and Valle-Inclán: génesis, desarrollo and significado del esperpento', *Universidad de la La Habana* 15, no. 89–90 (Jan–June 1950), pp. 286–364.

4   'Elegy', poem written for the 10th anniversary of the Republican defeat in Madrid.

5   Weekly journal directed by the politician Antoni María Sbert, during his exile in Mexico.

6   Concepción Méndez, former girlfriend of LB.

7   María Luisa Gómez Mena (1907–59), art dealer of Cuban origin, who financed the *Escuela Libre de La Habana* where Rubia worked in 1939.

8   Rubia had asked whether Altolaguirre, director of Mexican publishers *Isla* in 1945, might publish their manuscript of *Threshold of Dreams*.

9   *The Great Madcap,* filmed at the Tepeyac studios between 9 June and 5 July 1949.

10   The film was eventually premiered by Cabrera Films in October 1951, dir. Alejandro Galindo with Mexican actress Dolores del Río (1904–83) as Doña Perfecta.

11   Benito Alazraki Algranti (1921–2007), Mexican scriptwriter and director.

12   LB acquired Mexican citizenship in December 1949.

13   Likely reference to Dalí's triumphant return to Spain with a large Cadillac, celebrated in Barcelona journal *Destino* with an article and front-page photograph of Dalí with his father (*VID* 446).

14   Nickname/anagram for Salvador Dalí, invented by Breton: 'avid for dollars'...

To José Rubia Barcia

Mexico City, 30 January 1950

Dear Barcia,

It's shameful! Really ... the way I've left things with you and Edwin, but in addition to my sloth when it comes to writing letters I've been really busy for months. So, I am now, if only briefly, writing a few lines. We are most delighted with Evita's Galician brush-stroked miniature,[1] whose photos we received, some a while ago and some a few days ago. I imagine you can confirm that she is now a fully-fledged mother. Evita, always in the foreground and a bit blurred in the photos, looks wonderful all the same. We're always thinking back to 'those times' and regretting the way life has removed us from beloved friends and places. But I haven't lost hope we'll meet again. How? I don't know.

I got a friendly and cordial letter from Edwin that I've not replied to and nor will I for lack of love of the epistolary genre. Please send my best wishes and thanks to him and his wife. I have a copy with me here and 100 will be out this week that Jeanne will put in the post.[2] It's all happening now. Send a few lines to let me know when they arrive. I've already told you Larrea and León Felipe really liked the poem and kept a copy each.[3] The rest, my own copy excluded, I still have.

I made a decent little film, *The Great Madcap,* that has turned out to be the most successful comedy this year.[4] I really needed that. It's well-made and entertaining, no more. But on 6 February I start on *The Young and the Damned,* which I hope, if it turns out well, will be exceptional in contemporary international film-making. It's tough, stark, and makes no concessions to the viewer. Realist, but with a hidden vein of powerful, sometimes erotic, poetry. The actors are mostly adolescents from the Mexican *lumpen-proletariat*. The sets could not be uglier. And the whole film is based on legal cases and files from the Behavioural Clinic. I know a lot of the actual people. To sum it up, I'd say that this film is a mixture of elements that have evolved over the last fifteen years from *Land Without Bread* and *The Golden Age*. Figueroa is the cameraman,[5] so he will finally be able to take anti-artistic shots that won't win a single award at the international Autumn Salons.[6] If I'm lucky, it could be good, although I'm concerned the young actors may be a problem. We'll see.

I'll put your essay[7] in one of my dispatches to Edwin. If you have copies when it's published in Cuba, send me one, and if not, I'll still have the original.

I'm writing at the speed of light, because I have to go and see the censors to start preparing things for the film. Forgive any errors and suchlike. Hugs and more hugs to all three.

Luis

[PS] If you see Leyda someday, send him my best. I always remember him fondly. But I didn't reply to his letter either.

                                                Spa Tls CBC; *CLB* 49–50

[1]   Elena Rubia López, daughter (here 'miniature') of Evita and (Galician) José Rubia.
[2]   *Elegía* by Rolfe, translated by Rubia Barcia, limited edition of 500 published by Compañía Editora y Librera, Mexico City in 1949 (AB/1081).
[3]   Letter from LB to Rubia Barcia, 31 October 1949 (*CLB* 48–49).
[4]   Premiere on 25 November 1949.
[5]   English in the original.
[6]   'Salon d'Automne', yearly mid-October exhibition held in Paris on the Champs-Élyseés from 1903 onwards, and, by extension, the Paris Salon and other exhibitions.
[7]   Rubia's original article on Valle-Inclán.

To Lulu Jourdain

Mexico City, 16 May 1950

My dear Lulu,

Your letter arrived a few days ago and as you can see, I am composing myself to write this reply with extraordinary speed. Of course, I did get another from you three months ago wishing me a happy birthday and was as silent as the grave. But you already know that even if I don't reply to your letters I'm always really happy to have your news, because you must be a true friend to persist in a correspondence I so foolishly neglect. That said, I shall now answer your questions.

I think our separation may finally be coming to an end. Although I don't think I'll ever live over there again, I do feel closer to Europe by the day and hope my trips there will be more frequent in future. You could say that since I last saw you, I've done little more than live, or rather, struggle to put bread on the table; but my luck has been changing for nearly a year now and I have some wonderful opportunities workwise. I'm now completely debt-free and have some immediate possibilities to earn enough to afford for a little trip to Europe with my family. What's more, I live well, drink better, and work just the way I like, so, if it wasn't for my old and *dear, dear* Parisian friends and my mother (who has been wonderful), I would have no reason to leave this odious, but irrationally attractive New World.

In addition to all that, as you've already found out, I'm now a Mexican citizen. For my sins.

Now let me tell you something about my life and work. I didn't really start working until about a year ago. I came from the United States with a contract to make a film that was perfect, morally-speaking, but dreary, basically just the best Mexican singer and the best Argentinian tango dancer doing their respective turns as the action happened around them.[1] People were expecting much more from me and whether from disappointment or ill will, they left me, unfortunately, sitting at home doing nothing, completely inert, supine and lifeless (or rather, alive thanks to the generosity of my mother, who has been my cross-continental saviour). But now my outlook has changed so much you could say I'm the most sought-after director in Mexico and I turn down a fair number of films. I made a film that was a big hit over here a year ago, opening doors for me as a 'value-for-money' director.[2] Then, in March, I finished *The Young and the Damned*, a film made with a lot of love, not a single concession to the audience, and for which I am responsible from beginning to end.[3] To give you an idea, it's like *Land Without Bread* with the Mexican *lumpen-proletariat*, real-life characters and not a single invented sequence. It's much closer to real life than the so-called 'neorealist' Italian films.[4] Whether people like it or not, I think it is unique of its kind. All the action is focused on the adolescents.

In June, I'll be starting on another film that's not too bad and I hope to finish by the end of July, because they make films very quickly over here.[5] I've made some in eighteen days; *The Young and the Damned* took four weeks. Ultramar studios have me on an exclusive contract and will pay for a trip to Europe in August. I'm going with the producer to present the film at Venice and prepare for its premiere in Paris.[6] The same studio gave me a Mercury 1950 for making that film, because I've not been able to afford a car since I arrived in Mexico and you really need one here. So, as you can see, business is booming. If you are in Saint Jean de Luz when I'm in Paris in August, I'd love to come and visit you for a few days. I'll be back in France at the beginning of next year, but with Jeanne and the boys.

Jeanne is longing to set foot back on French soil. Although she's adapted well to America and she admits she'd have no particular desire to return if it weren't for family and friends. An aside: the snows of time have now almost completely covered her head. As for me, you can judge from the photo with this letter that was taken a month ago for some official document.

Juan Luis is now 1.83-m tall and a Yankee through and through like all his friends. Rafael is very sweet.

I'll say nothing of old friends, as it's a dismal picture. I see Juanito Vicens once a year and only fleetingly. Ugarte is a changed man. We haven't been in touch for over a year. Sánchez Ventura has changed the most. He hasn't acknowledged me for years now. Never meets up with his old friends. Mantecón is wonderful, as always.

I shall finish now because the unheard-of effort I've put in to writing this has worn me out. I think I can definitely say this time that we will (finally!) meet again this year. Send pictures of your little girl,[7] I have the wonderful photos of you and Hernando that Eli took and that Zizou's niece brought me.

Much love … and see you soon.
Luis

Spa Tls, VL; *LOGD* 641–642 f

[1] Singer, Jorge Negrete, and dancer, Libertad Lamarque, in *Gran Casino*.
[2] *The Great Madcap*.
[3] Filmed at the Tepeyac Studios and exterior locations around Mexico City, 6 February to 9 March 1950.
[4] Post-Second World War Italian film movement known for its focus on working-class characters, outdoor locations and non-professional actors.
[5] Filming of *Susana* at the Churubusco Studios began on 10 July 1950.
[6] *The Young and the Damned* would eventually be presented at Cannes, rather than the Venice Festival.
[7] Nina Viñes, daughter of Hernando and Lulu Viñes, born in 1939.

Figure 40 Filming *Susana*, Buñuel with actors Rosita Quintana and Ernesto Alonso, Mexico, July 1950.

To Lulu Jourdain

Mexico City, 30 August 1950

My dear Lulu,

Your letter of 18 July arrived when I was in the middle of making my most recent film.[1] I finished it a week ago and now 'hasten' to reply. I should say first of all that I am not the slightest worried by the levels of urea in your blood. That will be easy to manage, especially with your sober lifestyle and a few days at a spa. I think you will live long, if always bothered by small ills. I'm the same, although sure to die long before you. A year ago, they told me my gall bladder was shot to pieces. I'm better now though and still drinking like a Cossack. Now I'm full of arthritis, in the form of neuritis, in the optic nerve of both eyes, for example. Everything looks deformed, so much so that if you were to give me a paintbrush right now I'd put El Greco to shame. I have 'sclerosis' in both ears and I'm fairly deaf. So, you see? Compared with me you are young and brimming with health!

Because I didn't finish it on time, this film won't go to Venice, but the producers – I hate these international awards – are going to take it there next year. It will be shown in Paris though this winter. And this of course means that my trip hasn't happened yet; although it will when we present the film in Paris.[2] We'll see each other then, so you and Hernando should begin preparing yourselves to have me so constantly at your side you'll become sick of me and kick me out of your house for being the most troublesome and tenacious visitor ever. It's very likely, although I can't absolutely say for certain, that I shall be knocking on your door in November. I can, though, solemnly swear we will meet this winter. In order to demonstrate that I have no fear of revealing myself with the ravages of time, I'm enclosing two photos taken in the studio a couple of weeks ago. I don't think my personality has changed, I'm still good humoured, stubborn, wilful and at times quite stupid. So, you and Hernando may now prepare to celebrate our reunion with the appropriate passion. The reason I'm still on such good form is that I finally see a chance to work and do something good to recover some part of my fifteen lost years. Very much just between ourselves Lulu, ideologically, I've not changed *at all* since 1936, but I have distanced myself, I suspect forever, from any kind of political activity. I'll tell you more – we'll tell each other more – when we meet.

A few days ago, I received a copy of *Histoire d'un art: Le Cinéma* I ordered from Paris.[3]

It's a magnificent book, surely the best to date on the history of cinema. I'm delighted it's by Sadoul, I feel more affection for him, and more united by our shared memories, every day. Pass on my very warmest regards when you see him. I don't know if he will like my film *The Young and the Damned*, it's relentlessly pessimistic, and the producers cut the opening declaration of faith in, and hope for, a better world to avoid trouble with the censors. I don't think anyone has made a more ferocious film that panders so little to the viewer. In other respects, it's not so unusual. It's a reflection of the moral and economic climate through a plot taken entirely from juvenile court cases and psycho-pedagogic files. It's far more realist than the Italian films, in the style of *Land Without Bread*, but at the same time it has some irrational and cruel elements, the long-lost children of the not yet buried *The Golden Age*. You may not like it either. If it's a commercial success, my producers will let me do whatever I like, and I already have a *scénario* ready that I wrote with Juan Larrea, *Illegible, Son of a Flute* a poetic film about Western man's desperation and dreams of flight. Formally, it's a film without precedent in cinema.

I'm now a Mexican citizen. It's the best passport you can get these days. The country is at peace and developing apace. It would be foolish of me to want to leave for good now that I can work as I like and make a decent living. My life is not exactly ascetic, but certainly isolated from the rest of the world. I don't go out to shows, or meetings, or anything. I sleep on a hard bed and have an almost monastic diet. On the other hand, I drink more than I should. My house is full of friends. Of the old ones, Mantecón is the only one left. Sánchez Ventura hardly speaks to any of us. I see Vicens, briefly, once a year. As for the other refugees, I neither know them … nor want to.

I will bring Piloute[4] a Mexican dress and a silver necklace from Taxco. Then we'll take her photo and put it in some exhibition of children, and your friends will all congratulate you if she wins a prize. Bad jokes aside, lots of kisses to her from me in advance. An enormous hug for Hernando and for both for you from,

Luis

Spa Tls, VL; *LOGD* 643–644 f

¹ *Susana.*
² A private premiere of *The Young and the Damned* was held at Studio 28 in Paris, December 1950.
³ G. Sadoul, *Histoire d'un art: Le Cinéma* (Paris: Flammarion, 1949).
⁴ Nina Viñes.

To Max Aub[1]

Mexico City, 20 September 1950

Dear Max,

The film will be shown on Friday at 8:30, Reforma 503 (4th floor).[2] I'd love to see you there with your family … if you're free.

Best wishes,
Buñuel

[PS] Would you let Magdaleno know if he's already in Mexico? And Revueltas?[3]

Spa Als, MA/15/1

¹ Max Aub Mohrenwitz (1903–72), Spanish author of French-German origin, exiled to Mexico in 1942.
² Private screening of *The Young and the Damned*; Aub collaborated on the script with LB.
³ José Revueltas Sánchez (1914–76), Mexican author, who contributed to the script of Buñuel's *Illusion Travels by Streetcar* (1953).

To Iris Barry and John Abbott

Mexico City, 22 November [1950]

WOULD LIKE TO GO TO NEW YORK IMMEDIATELY, WITH MY PRODUCER OSCAR DANCIGERS, TO SHOW YOU MY NEW FILM THE YOUNG AND THE DAMNED.[1] *THE US CONSUL IS REQUESTING AN OFFICIAL INVITATION FROM YOU. I WOULD BE VERY GRATEFUL IF YOU COULD WIRE ME, INVITING BOTH OF US FOR THIS PURPOSE. I WOULD COVER, OF COURSE, ALL EXPENSES OF THE TRIP.*

BEST WISHES,
LUIS BUÑUEL

Eng Tel, MoMA/12.04; *LBOC* 104 f

[1]   Commercial premiere in Mexico City on 9 November 1950.

To Georges Sadoul

Mexico City, 15 February 1951

Dear Georges,

Your letter only arrived yesterday, in other words a month and a half after you sent it, probably because you put the wrong number on the address.[1]

I saw Sánchez García[2] just after I got back and asked him for a copy of the book, but it hasn't been published yet. As soon as it comes out, he's going to send you one. His address is: 1A, 58 Victoria Street. One of these days I'll send you 19 editions of *Cinevoz*,[3] that is, all the ones you are missing from 17 July 1949. It's no longer being published.

Thank you for the article from *Parallèle 50*.[4] I think Gaillard[5] has really understood my intentions in making the film, and my only regret is that they are not so clear to everyone. The film blends a complete rejection of our debased society with hope for humanity. It's impossible to go any further than that in Mexico. And even then, it was a real achievement to get it past the censors.[6] It's also worth remembering the film was produced by an ultra-commercial studio.

However, I'm not making any excuses. Did you read Simone Dubreuihl's article?[7] She sent me a copy. She also understood the film. In Paris, Thevenot[8] and Jean Lods, Francis Jourdain[9] and Lulu all also talked to me about the film very positively. Jerome has probably told you about our conversation and that I agree with a lot of what he says except the bit about the 'bitterness' of the film having to do with my refugee's perspective. I've convinced him that's not true as neither my habits, nor friends, nor state of mind are those of a refugee. In fact, I'm not a refugee, nor have I ever been one. I don't know where my tendency towards violence and ferocity come from, but I know it's in no way new.

An *abrazo*[10] from,
Buñuel

PS What of Josie Unik?[11] I hope she has recovered. I'm really sorry not to have seen her, after such a long time.

I remember with great fondness those amiable meals at your house with the 'Bohemian crystal'. My best regards to your wife and daughter.

Fre Tlsps, GS/64

[1]   Envelope had Nilo 57, instead of 52.
[2]   José María Sánchez García (1891–1959), Mexican film critic, who published his *Historia del cine mexicano (1896–1929)* in weekly parts in the magazine *Cinema Repórter* between 1951 and 1954.
[3]   Mexican film weekly review published from 1948 to 1950.
[4]   Short-lived French-Czech review published from 1950.
[5]   Possibly the French historian and militant communist Jeanne Gaillard (1909–83).
[6]   The commercial release in October 1950 was initially prohibited by the Mexican government.
[7]   A French critic and translator reviewed *The Young and the Damned* in 'Luis Buñuel casse une fois de plus les vitres avec *Les oubliés*', *Libération*, 28 December 1950.
[8]   Jean Thevenot (1916–83), French journalist
[9]   French painter and designer (1876–1958), father of Lulu Viñes.
[10] Spanish in the original (a hug).
[11] Josie Le Flohic, wife of Pierre Unik; Unik died in unknown circumstances in February 1945, after being sent to the Schmiedeberg concentration camp.

From Octavio Paz[1]

Cannes,[2] 5 April 1951

Dear Luis Buñuel,

Let's fight for *The Young and the Damned*. I am proud to fight for you and your film. I've seen your friends. They are all with you. Prévert sends his warm regards. Picasso his greetings. Intelligent journalists and the young are with you. Thanks to *The Young and the Damned*, something of the heroic epoch has returned. I've organized an 'intimate' gathering a few hours before the screening (Sunday 8th). Prévert, Cocteau, Chagall,[3] Trauner[4] and others will be there (as well as all the journalists and critics with something in their brains, heart, or elsewhere).

Picasso – without us needing to ask – has publicly declared that he will go to the screening of *The Young and the Damned*. If the Jury don't award it a prize (which is not impossible), we are thinking of publishing a pamphlet or joint declaration with the best people. Whatever happens, *The Young and the Damned* will receive an award, but we are aiming at the Grand Prix (the most serious rivals are the Italians, the English and the Russians).[5] Even in the case (which is unlikely, almost impossible) of total defeat, we have already won the popular vote. The press will talk and talk a lot about *The Young and the Damned*. Besides, the Critics Prize is a certainty, if it doesn't win the Grand Prix or Best Director.

I've written something in haste about you.[6] It will be distributed, in French, on the 8th. I think Prévert will then provide a short piece. The copy I'm sending you here (written last night on a useless, although sparkling, Swiss typewriter) *should, I am recommending, be published in* Novedades.[7] *Speak to Benítez*[8] *for me.* It's not much, for someone of your worth, but I had no time to do better.

Warmest regards,
Octavio Paz
Carlton Hotel, Cannes

Als L, AB/572.27–28; *LOGD* 514–515 f

[1]   Octavio Paz Lozano (1914–98), Mexican poet and writer, met LB in Paris in 1937.

[2]   Paz attended the fourth Cannes Festival, 3–20 April 1951, as a delegate of the Mexican government.

[3]   Marc Chagall (1887–1985), Russian-French painter born in Belarus.

[4]   Alexandre Trauner (1906–93), Hungarian art director living in France.

[5]   Films premiered in 1951 competing for the Grand Prix included *Miracolo a Milano*, dir. Vittorio de Sica, *The Browning Version*, dir. Anthony Asquith, and *Kavalier zolotoy zvezdy*, dir. Yuli Raizman.

[6]   'Pourquoi le Mexique présente au Festival de Cannes seulement un film: *Los Olvidados*', 6 pages, April, 1951 (ABR/2015; *LOGD* 516 f); the original has a handwritten note (in Spanish) on the first page: 'Dear Buñuel: I'm sending the text we prepared for journalists before the screening of your film. The translation is by your friend – and mine – Simone Dubreuilh –who sends her best wishes – Yours, Octavio Paz.'

[7]   Mexico City newspaper, whose founders included Emilio Azcárraga and Miguel Alemán Valdés, president of Mexico between 1946 and 1952.

[8]   Fernando Benítez (1912–2000), Mexican journalist and director of *Novedades*.

From Octavio Paz[1]

Cannes, 11 April 1951

Dear Buñuel,

We presented *The Young and the Damned* yesterday. I think we won the battle with the public and the critics. Or rather, your film won the battle. I don't know whether the Jury[2] will award it the Grand Prix. But what is absolutely certain is that everyone (at least up until now) thinks that *The Young and the Damned* is the best film at the Festival. And so we are certain of an award (bearing in mind, of course, last-minute reservations, *surprises* and *permutations*).

I shall now tell you a little of how things went. On 1 April, as soon as I discovered I was going to be an official delegate, I met up with Karol,[3] the film industry delegate (or the delegate of the distributors, I'm still not quite sure). Karol and his wife were completely sceptical. Not only did they not *believe* in your film, I also got the impression they didn't like it. Of course, it was pointless to argue with them. I knew that in a week's time – given the opinions of people they respect – they would change their minds. And that is what happened. Now Karol is proclaiming *The Young and the Damned* will win the Grand Prix.

When I arrived in Cannes on the 3rd, I realized that neither Mexico nor Karol had prepared the screening. There were no pamphlets, no information, nothing. They'd prepared no publicity whatsoever, nor had they tapped into the admiration and friendship people have for you here. My first concern was to mobilize public opinion. Luckily, on the same day, the 3rd, I met up with various friends (journalists and film-makers) who not out of any self-interest, but because of their admiration for your work, dedicated themselves to making *The Young and the Damned* 'the film of the Festival'. Amongst them, I should mention Simone Dubreuilh (your friend), Kyrou[4] (a young friend of Breton's), Frédéric[5] and Langlois[6] (from the Cinémathèque), etc. First of all, they went to see Prévert (who has been wonderful). We secured the help of Cocteau and Chagall. (Picasso, who promised to attend the screening, could not or would not – party politics? His friends were with us anyway.) We also mobilized what Mexican politicians refer to as the Festival 'infantry': journalists, secretaries, etc. Prévert declared it a great film.

Cocteau called the Secretary General several times asking for tickets, etc. And finally, 24 hours in advance, we distributed the text I wrote about you. In short, we stirred up an air of anticipation. Even Karol *woke up* and helped us over the last few days. Danztinguer (is that how you spell it?)[7] turned up at the last minute and – though a little late – was also useful.

The theatre was as full yesterday as it was in your glory days. Something was happening. We distributed our allies strategically. But there was no battle. The film won the public over although – inevitably – there was some incomprehension: the 'sophisticated set' and a few communist groups (I can't be certain of this, but I've been told Sadoul found the film excessively 'negative' and 'unfit for use'). The audience applauded various sequences: the dream, the erotic scene with Jaibo and the mother, the part with the pederast and Pedro, the dialogue between Pedro and his mother, etc. At the end, loud applause. But above all, profound, beautiful emotion. Everyone came out, as we say in Spanish, with their throats dry. There was one moment – when Jaibo wants to put out Pedro's eyes – when some hissed. They were silenced by the applause.

The response could not be more enthusiastic. Prévert declared it the best film he'd seen for a decade. Cocteau quoted Goethe, who declared Beethoven the best musician of his era.[8] 'What about Mozart?',[9] people asked. 'Mozart is not the best, nor the second-best. He is unique; he is in a category apart.' That's what he said of Buñuel. He is not the best, nor the second-best: he is unique, he is in a category apart. Pudovkin[10] *declared it a great film, full of optimism about the value of humanity.** That will confuse the communist journalists. French Radio are inviting all of those personalities on this morning to give their opinion. We'll send them on to you. We'll also send press cuttings. And for now, you can use what I'm telling you for the press (leaving aside, of course, the intimate details, Karol's attitude for example, which are for you alone).

I have to ask a favour: could you add to page five of the article I sent, just after 'major and minor stars', the following: 'We knew that Rodolfo Halffter was a great musician. We didn't realize that music – an art form with infinite power to enchant – could blend in this way with action. Visual imagery, sound and cinematic motion together as one whole. Halffter's music has what it is no exaggeration to call an "interior" quality. That is to say: it does not accompany the drama, nor underline it, nor comment upon it: it emerges from the action, its inevitable response, its necessary complement, unity in motion!'.[11]

I'm asking you to include this paragraph, not only because I think it's fair, but also because I would never forgive myself for forgetting Halffter. Also, could I ask you to have the article copied and sent to Fernando Benítez, editor-in-chief at *Novedades*. It would be good if the article were to appear with a brief note mentioning the success of *The Young and the Damned* and of the opinions transcribed in this letter.

And that's all, apart from these cordial greetings from your friend,**
Octavio Paz

[PS] I'll write with more news soon.[12]

* Chagall made it clear he was in no way surprised: he knew you were a great artist. He also congratulated Figueroa and Halffter.
** Need I say again that I am proud to fight for a film like *The Young and the Damned*?

Spa Als, AB/572.29–34; *LOLB* 53 f

[1] Asterisked notes by Paz.
[2] Presided over by the French writer, André Maurais (1885–1967).
[3] William Karol, Mexican film industry representative in Europe.
[4] Adonis Kyrou (1923–85), Greek-French film critic and director.
[5] Frédéric Rossif (1922–90), French film critic and director born in Montenegro, working with the Cinémathèque from 1948.
[6] Henri Langlois (1914–77), co-founder of the Cinémathèque in 1936 and of FIAF in 1938.
[7] Oscar Dancigers.
[8] Ludwig van Beethoven (1770–1827), composer born in Bonn.
[9] Wolfgang Amadeus Mozart (1756–91), composer born in Salzburg.
[10] Vsevolod Pudovkin (1893–1953), Russian film-maker.
[11] Pittaluga composed the sound track for *The Young and the Damned* but, as he was not a union member, Halffter's name appeared on the credits.
[12] Paz's next letter from Cannes, 16 April 1951 (AB/572.35; *LOGD* 523 f), contained a copy of Prévert's poem.

Figure 41 Celebrating the success of *The Young and the Damned*, Mexico City, 1951: standing, Edward Fitzgerald, Gabriel Figueroa, Oscar Dancigers, Alma Delia Fuentes, Carlos Savage, Roberto Cobo, Alfonso Mejía and José B. Carles; sitting, Luis Buñuel.

From Octavio Paz

Paris, 1 May 1951

Dear Luis Buñuel,

I'm sending some cuttings.[1] There are only a few, just the ones I have to hand, but Dancigers has promised he'll send you all of them. I hope he does. The press and the public are still talking about you and your film. Only yesterday, I got a call from the radio: they wanted the soundtrack – the music – from *The Young and the Damned* to use on one of those 'radiated conversations' they put on over here. I'm not sure who's going to take part in the debate, but I think Péret had been invited, and some others. One of the most *enthusiastic* supporters is Cocteau, who is determined to jump on the bandwagon. Yesterday, I bumped into Miró, who was with Queneau. They both asked whether your film will be screened soon. A Swiss gentleman came to see me yesterday because he wants to distribute the film over there. I told him to go and see your distributor.

Let me explain about the International Critics' Prize: you got a Special Award in combined recognition of your film and your career as a director. The award was created for you to make up for the critics' mistake, or so I've been told by a number of people who were at the debates. The critics usually meet AFTER the Official Jury verdict is announced, with the aim of rectifying possible omissions or injustices. But this time was different. Both juries deliberated at the same time. The 'critics' group needed four rounds of voting because *The Young and the Damned* and *Miracolo a Milano* had the same number of votes and three people insisted on voting for *Fröken Julie*.[3] In the fourth round, *Miracolo a Milano* beat *The Young and the Damned* BY ONE VOTE. When the critics realized that they had coincided with the Jury, and that neither the Grand Prix nor the Special Award had gone to *The Young and the Damned* as expected, they decided to create a Special Prize for you. I should also say that when the awards were being handed out, the only standing ovation from the public was for *The Young and the Damned* (which thrilled Karol, who had not, after all, behaved as badly as his initial attitude led me to expect; quite the opposite in fact). And finally, the *L'Âge du cinéma*[4] has published details of its own awards: Grand Prix, *The Young and the Damned* and *Fröken Julie*. Best Music award: Pittaluga. Of course, these awards are purely platonic.[5]

I'll have the Official Report ready next week.[6] I'll send it along with the Diploma the Jury awarded you and some books. I'll also send some complementary information. I imagine Mr Castillo López[7] will make sure the Ministry pay me what they promised in 'travel expenses'. I'll write to thank him now for nominating me for the post. I'll write to Benítez as well, to let him know I'm very interested in publishing the article[8] in Mexico (it has had quite a lot of success over here and has been cited several times. Friends in high … etc.). I hope we'll meet again soon. One reason I might well be inspired to return would be to learn more about or get involved in the film world with you. I'm not sure whether I could do anything, but it interests me more and more. Are you still considering *Juan Pérez Jolote*?[9]

Warmest regards from your admiring friend,
Octavio Paz
Embassy of the United Mexican States in France

Spa Cmfa L, ABR/1969; *LOGD* 530 f

[1] Two albums of press cuttings on *The Young and the Damned* still exist (ABR/1977, ABR/1978).
[2] Authorized by the Federación Internacional de la Prensa Cinematográfica – FIPRESCI, founded in Brussels in 1930, which distributes prizes at a number of international festivals.
[3] *Fröken Julie* (1951) dir. Alf Sjöberg.
[4] Paris journal inspired by surrealism and co-edited by Kyrou and the film critic Robert Benayoun (1926–96) between 1951 and 1952; their 'prizes' were published in no. 2 (May 1951), p. 39.
[5] 'Platonic' in the sense there is no money attached to them.
[6] Sent by Paz on 23 May 1951.
[7] Jesús Castillo López, at that time the Mexican Government's Director General of Cinematography.
[8] Published as O. Paz, 'El poeta Buñuel', *Novedades*, 3 June 1951, pp. 3–4.
[9] *Juan Pérez Jolote, biografía de un tzotzil* (1948), by Mexican anthropologist Ricardo Pozas Arciniega (1912–94); the Tzotzils are indigenous Mayan inhabitants of central Chiapas, Southern Mexico.

To Juan Larrea

Mexico City, 1 June 1951

Dear Juan,
Here is a letter written in the blink of a shepherd's eye … You may be stunned, but it's true. And if I've decided to write it is, of course, for very practical reasons. And so, to the point.

The day before yesterday Salvatierra came to see me and told me your scholarship is about to run out and that you may return here. Now: your apartment and furniture are about to be passed on to some unknown person and Salvatierra asked me for 2,500 pesos to hold the apartment in case you do come back. As usual, and even though things are going much better for me now, I didn't have the money to hand, so we agreed that he would borrow it in my name from a Venezuelan and that I would pay him back in a month, because I'm about to sign a new contract. I would, of course, be delighted to do that as soon as a bit of cash comes my way. I've moved to a new house and bought all kinds of trinkets and contraptions and, what with the whisky that flows like water in my house, I live very well, but never have any cash in reserve.

I think that whether you stay there or return to Mexico will depend on your visa, won't it? I also think there are many more opportunities to find intellectual work in New York than there are over here. If you write, tell me briefly what your plans are.

Since you left, I've made five films, the best of which is, without a doubt, *The Young and the Damned*. You will have heard that it was awarded two prizes at the Cannes International Film Festival. That has really caused a big stir down here and I'm no longer 'Buñuels, the Catalan director',[1] but 'Buñuel (with no 's'), the great director of the Mexican film industry'.

I haven't lost all hope for *Illegible, Son of a Flute* and think that if you were here, with a few changes and making it a little longer, we could really get it going. Brazil might be the most likely place to try. My old friend Alberto Cavalcanti is working down there as a film director and wants me to join him. At the moment, Brazil's best journal, *Anhembi*,[2] edited by my friend Paulo Duarte has requested a copy of the original, and is willing to publish *Illegible, Son of a Flute*. I think it would be good for us. What do you think? Let me know. For my part, delighted if you would accept.

And what of the great Lucianne?[3] I would love to have one of our joke-spiced conversations again. Although I hope that if we do have to postpone them for a while, it will be because your status as a long-term resident of that city has been resolved, which is, I understand, what you want. Give Lucianne my love. And the little one?[4] Is he speaking English yet? Love to him too.

And more for you,
Luis

PS When I presented *The Young and the Damned* here, Berta León Felipe[5] was outraged and wanted to slap me in the face; León behaved quite correctly but hated the film. Poor old Imaz was the only one who was really enthusiastic about it. If you want to see it (the film) there, tell Lucianne to call Mr Alfred Katz, 550 Fifth Avenue, telephone Plaza 74776, and say that Dancigers and I would like him to let you know when they are holding the first screening.

Spa Tlsps, AF; *ILE* 58 f

[1]   Some of the early articles on LB in the Mexican press identify him, incorrectly, as Catalan (see for example, D. Ruanova, 'A propósito de Buñuels', *Claridades*, October 1950, p. 16).
[2]   Review founded by Paulo Duarte in São Paulo, published between 1950 and 1962.
[3]   Lucianne Larrea Aubry (1930–61), daughter of Larrea and his wife Marguerite Aubry.
[4]   Juan Jaime Larrea Aubry, Larrea's son, born in 1933.
[5]   Berta Gamboa, wife of León Felipe.

From Georges Sadoul

Paris, 10 December 1951

My dear Luis,

I've been wanting to reply for six months now to your letter, as I was considerably moved by it. But at Easter, after finishing my tome of a book,[1] I had an attack of lumbago and, after I recovered from that, an extreme case of fatigue lasted well into the summer. The truth is that I have been dragging myself around for six months now and am only a little improved after my return in November. I had an enormous backlog of work when I arrived back in Paris, where I had practically not set foot since April.

You will know that your film[2] was a monstrous success in Cannes. I saw it again and some of my reservations disappeared. However, the viewers were largely bemused, always, or almost always applauding at quite the wrong moments. For example: an ovation when the cop tells the mother: 'it's the parents' fault, madam'. They thought that statement was a reflection of your own views, but I know it's the opposite, because the character of the mother is truly chilling. On my second viewing, what moved me most was your tenderness towards your characters. But Pudovkin only needed to see *The Young and the Damned* once to understand it and to say as much in places like *Pravda*.[3] I was too under the weather in April to be able to remember now precisely what he said in private, but it was basically that in a festival where the films from capitalist countries were generally dismal and dispiriting, your film (and the Italian films) introduced a sense of condemnation, a cry of rage, or in other words, hope.

You will also have heard that *The Young and the Damned* has been a great success in Paris for two months now. I haven't been to Studio Vendôme yet (the old Opéra cinema, Avenue de l'Opéra), but everyone tells me it is full every night. The cinema had been 'dying' for a long time and they tried to relaunch it with, amongst other things, that repulsive Swedish film, *Fröken Julie* (Grand Prix at Cannes), but with no luck. *The Young and the Damned* is a rejection of society. But what's most important is that everyone tells me that people (high society people) are leaving ashamed. That doesn't mean they understand it all, of course, but at least they've understood the essential. And they're not just going to be entertained by the horror, like the *Grand Guignol*,[4] which is what I feared initially. You may know that at first it was practically sponsored by *Le Figaro* (even more repugnant in 1951, if possible, than in 1930 in the days of Coty[5] and *The Golden Age*); a ploy by the distributor of course. Still, *The Young and the Damned* did not have the impact *Le Figaro* expected, which is crucial.

I was talking about you for hours yesterday with the Lotars,[6] going over so many old and shared memories. They had been interviewed by little Pierre Kast,[7] who wrote an article in *Cahiers du cinéma*[8] (Lulu and Viñes will have sent it to you[9]) full of memories of your friends, and in which you are represented, at the end of the day, as a Rimbaud who removed himself forever to an inaccessible Harar,[10] or like a Gauguin[11] who never wrote from Tahiti. Apart from the tendency to bury you definitively in 'other places', there is little to say about this 'Search for Buñuel'. However, I really disliked the other *Cahiers du cinéma* article: the first one.[12] I wrote a letter correcting Little Kast (in reference to the part where he referred to me without naming me).[13] You'll find a copy of my letter to Kast enclosed, as well as cuttings from my three articles on *The Young and the Damned* published in *L'Humanité*, *Les Lettres françaises*[14] and *L'Écran français*.[15] I expressed some reservations, as you'll see, but it would have been worse if I'd written them the day after Studio 28 and before our (last) meeting on the Champs-Élysées (or even just after it). And I also believe that my reservations have faded (although they haven't yet disappeared altogether).

What irritated me most about Little Kast's article was that he called into question and in the worst possible faith, what I had said about your three films in my *Histoire du cinéma*.[16] Those three pages were difficult for me to write at the time. I made a real effort to put in them, in good faith, what I thought at the time (and what I'm sure you also thought), between 1927 and 1932. At that time, I think I was a witness, rather than an historian. Nevertheless, witnesses are often confused. If you think that at any point in those three pages I betrayed your principles, do please tell me. I could make corrections to future editions, or to the international editions that are underway.

I'm very grateful for the magazines you sent me on Mexican cinema. They will be very useful for the next book I'm preparing (film from 1939 to 1952).[17] But on a personal note, I should like you to keep your promise: to send me the photographs of the Vallée de Chevreuse[18] from 1932. I so much loved the photo you took of poor Norma.[19] I have no other photograph of Pierre Unik and you. If you can, please send me those negatives.

I saw a still from your new film.[20] The Lotars mentioned a letter you sent to the Viñes, they tell me you think it's a very optimistic film. Bravo.

And above all, I would be pleased (and here I think I speak on behalf of all your friends) if the success of *The Young and the Damned* would allow you to return to France. With your wife and children. You must tell your producer that *The Young and the Damned* would not have sold as well nor earned as much had you not come over to prepare its release (it's true). And that its chances of winning the Grand Prix at Cannes would have been much higher if you had been at the Festival (even more true). For all these reasons, they must pay for your travel and an extended stay in Paris at the beginning of 1952, or when the Cannes festival is on.

Until later. Impatiently awaiting your next film. My wife[21] joins me in sending you our warmest regards and best wishes,

Georges Sadoul
3 rue de Bretonvilliers

PS I quoted from your letter in my response to Kast and in the article for *L'Écran français*. Please forgive me, although I'm sure you'll bear me no ill-will for doing so.

I can't find *L'Humanité*, but I think Lulu and Ricardo will send it to you.

Fre Tlsps, AB/572.38–39; *LOGD* 572–573 f

---

[1] Sadoul published the first volume of his monumental *Histoire Générale du cinema* in 1946.

[2] *The Young and the Damned.*

[3] Official Soviet Union Communist Party newspaper founded in 1912; Pudovkin published his response to *The Young and the Damned* in *Literarurnaya Gazeta*, 17 April and 24 May 1951 (*LOGD* 524 f, 538 f).

[4] Genre of Parisian drama 1897 to 1962 specializing in horror.

[5] François Coty (1874–1934), French parfumier, bought the daily newspaper *Le Figaro* in 1922 and founded the Fascist league Solidarité française in 1933.

[6] Eli Lotar and his wife Elisabeth Makovski.

[7] French film critic and director (1920–84).

[8] Film journal founded by French film critics André Bazin (1918–58), Jacques Doniol-Valcroze (1920–89) and Joseph-Maria Lo Duca (1905–2004) in Paris in 1951.

[9] P. Kast, 'À la recherché de Luis Buñuel avec Jean Grémillon, Jean Castanier, Eli Lotar, L. Viñes and Pierre Prévert', *Cahiers du cinéma*, no. 7 (December 1951), pp. 17–23.

[10] Town in Ethiopia where Rimbaud worked as an arms dealer and coffee seller from 1880.

[11] Paul Gauguin (1848–1903), French post-impressionist painter, moved to Tahiti in 1895.

[12] P. Kast, 'Une fonction de constat: notes sur l'œuvre de Buñuel', *Cahiers du cinéma*, no. 7 (1951), pp. 6–16.

[13] Letter from Sadoul to Kast, 5 December 1951, published in 'Correspondance', *Cahiers du cinéma*, no. 8 (January 1952), pp. 75–77.

[14] French journal founded by Jacques Decour and Jean Paulhan in 1941; Sadoul published his review of *The Young and the Damned*, 'Cruauté, tendresse, pitié' in *Les Lettres françaises*, no. 389, 22 November 1951 (*LOGD* 551 f).

[15] French film journal, associated with communism, published from 1943 to 1952; Sadoul published 'Mon ami Buñuel *d'Un chien andalou* à *The Young and the Damned*' in *L'Écran français* no. 335 (12–18 December 1951), p. 12.

[16] Kast referring to the pages Sadoul dedicates to LB in *Histoire d'un art: Le cinéma*.

[17] G. Sadoul, *Histoire générale du cinéma, tome VI: L'Époque contemporaine, 1939–1954*, originally published by Denoël in Paris in 1954.

[18] Some 40 km southeast of Paris.

[19] Nora Sadoul, his first wife, died in 1939.

[20] *Mexican Bus Ride*, filmed by LB in August 1951, produced by Altolaguirre and Mena, based on a script co-written by LB, Altolaguirre and Juan de la Cabada.

[21] Ruta Assia (1904–93), second wife of Sadoul.

To Juan Tomás[1]

[Mexico City, December 1951]

Dear Tomás,

At your request, because I do not normally respond to people who make public comments about my work or about me, I am sending you these lines to reassure you about the ferocious, parapathic[2] compulsions Claude Mauriac[3] attributes to me in his article in *Le Figaro*[4] of 24 November on my film *The Young and the Damned*.

Mauriac feels he has uncovered in the manifest content of the film a whole, terrible, nocturnal world, to which I am myself, naturally, entirely oblivious. The film, according to him, marvellously depicts my Id and my Super-Ego and all the sadomasochistic tendencies that are expressed in 'my passionate nostalgia for purity and in my indulgence, to the point of tedium, in pain'.

I very much regret that I may disappoint such a fine psychoanalyst when I say that there is not a single element of my films that has not been coldly and calculatedly deployed to produce the desired effect. For example, in *The Young and the Damned*, the apparent moments of cruelty and the obsessive elements, such as the repeated use of beatings, the constant interpolation of the hen, etc., etc., were used with 'malice' to enhance the dramatic action meant to convey to the spectator that we do not live in the best of worlds and that our reality is not as stable nor as secure as he might imagine.

Personally, I would not harm a fly, as they say, but if I can make the audience think it is being tortured and that the perpetrator is employed by a society as war-mongering as our own, I should consider the fictitious martyrdom of that fly to have been well worth it.

Very best wishes from,
Luis Buñuel

Spa, Od; *LOGD* 558 f

¹ Mexican journalist working on the Sunday edition, *El redondel* where this letter by LB was published (n.p.).
² LB's Spanish version of the archaic 'parapathy' for 'neurotic'.
³ French writer and journalist (1914–96), film critic for *Le Figaro littéraire*.
⁴ *Le Figaro littéraire*, no. 292 (24 November 1951).

To José Rubia Barcia

Mexico City, 10 March 1952

My dear Barcia,

I'm truly ashamed of my behaviour. My silence in response to your three or four most recent letters deserves all manner of recriminations and insults even. But if you only knew the effort it costs me to write, in spite of my best intentions and the friendship I feel for you both, you would forgive me completely and declare me wholly innocent. My aversion to the typewriter or the fountain pen is bordering on the pathological. But today, finally, and with superhuman effort, I am taking the plunge.

I thought your auspicious open letter¹ was excellent, one of best pieces written on *The Young and the Damned*. The appreciation of the film in some of your paragraphs coincides exactly with some of the reviews in the Paris journals, particularly with Bazin's article in *Esprit*.² So you can imagine how touched I was that the film moved you so deeply and that you understood it so clearly. You asked me, at the beginning, why I did not tell the festival juries to go to hell when they awarded me a prize. In a strange coincidence, two days before receiving your letter, I wrote an article for *The New York Times* in which I responded publicly to that very question.³ I'll send it to you as soon as it arrives, because they are waiting to publish it when *The Young and the Damned*⁴ is on at the Trans-Lux on 52nd Street and Lexington in New York.⁵ The violence with which you underline your suggestion that I should have thrown the trophies at the judges' heads would make your letter unpublishable over here. The Mexican film industry would rise up *en masse* against it. I should say that I love that violence, it's so Spanish and so typical of you. I had thought of giving it to Efraín Huerta at *El Nacional*, but I didn't want to witness the grimace your *ex abrupto* would have brought to his face as a member of the Mexican Academy of Cinematic Arts and Sciences. I suggest you wait for the screening of the film in Los Angeles (the English version I mean),⁶ and get the distributor to publish your letter in an important newspaper over there.⁷ We'll agree on it when the time comes. In the hope it will be published, I've filed your original amongst my very best cuttings. Did you know the film had a five-month run in Paris, the most successful film of the last two years?

I finished another film this summer based on a story by Altolaguirre,⁸ which is the opposite of *The Young and the Damned*. People who have seen the private screenings say it is the most Mexican film ever made in Mexico. It's cheerful and optimistic and fairly original I think, among contemporary films. It's very close to a documentary. It's almost, almost a 'realist farce'. Anyway, you'll see it over there. I hope that in a year I'll be a 'big shot' round here in cinema and that the time will have come for us to do something together. What Mexican cinema needs most is educated writers with imagination and, above all, a modern appreciation of life and art.

The typewriter ribbon has broken and I'm finishing by hand (how terrible!). Your precious little girl is delightful, and I would give I don't know what to have one like her. Of course, I shall have to wait until my next life. Jeanne is also a great admirer of the miniature Evita, who also has a lot of you in her. In the most recent photo, she is starting to look less like her mother and more like her father. Kisses for her and for Evita. And my warmest regards to your in-laws.

Much love,
Buñuel

[PS] Friendship and best wishes to the Rolfes.

Spa Tlsps, CBC; *CLB* 56–58

1   'Open letter' from Barcia to LB, Los Angeles, February 1952, 5 h. (AB/692.2; *LOGD* 576–580 f).
2   French journal founded by Emmanuel Mounier in 1932; LB refers to A. Bazin, 'The Young and the *Damned*', *Esprit* 20, no. 186 (January 1952), pp. 85–89.
3   LB remarks published in English, 'my immediate response was to reject that official honour', in *The Compass*, 30 March 1952, n.p. (ABR/1968).
4   Official title in English of *The Young and the Damned* after its unsubtitled premiere, with the original title, at Cinema 48 in New York.
5   New York film theatre, 586, Lexington Avenue, 1938 to 1965.
6   Rubia saw the Spanish version at the California Cinema in Los Angeles in February 1952.
7   J. Barcia 'Luis Buñuel's *Los olvidados*', *Quarterly of Film, Radio, and Television* 7, no. 4 (Summer 1953), pp. 392–401.
8   *Mexican Bus Ride* co-written by Altolaguirre and Manuel Reachi.

From Michael Redgrave[1]

London, 6 June 1952

Dear Luis Buñuel,

I have heard, through my old friend Basil Wright[2] and through George Pepper,[3] of our proposed film of Robinson Crusoe.[4] *As I have explained to Mr Pepper in a letter of this same date, I am not immediately available, but since I know the film world I realize that it is possible that the project might be delayed even by some months, and I have given him further details of my, I am afraid limited, availability.[5]*

I write to you only to say that few things would give me more pleasure than to be associated with you in such a project, since I have the greatest admiration for what work of yours I have seen. I take this opportunity of offering congratulations that might otherwise have remained in my heart, unknown to you.

Yours sincerely,
Michael Redgrave
Bedford House
Chiswick Mall, London W4

Eng Tls, AB/632.29

¹   British actor (1908–85).
²   British documentary film-maker and film historian (1907–87).
³   US producer, persecuted during the McCarthy era, went into exile in Mexico, where he co-produced
    ¡Torero!, dir. Velo, and LB's *The Young One* (1962), under the pseudonym George P. Werker.
⁴   Novel by English author Daniel Defoe (1660–1731) published in 1719; filmed by LB in 1952.
⁵   Robinson was eventually played by Irish actor, Dan O'Herlihy (1919–2005).

From Hugo Butler¹

[Mexico City,] 3 August [1952]

Dear Luis,

As perhaps you know I saw certain of the material² afternoon of day before yesterday; not everything that has been returned from the North,³ for some of that was being worked up into your rough-cut – but enough to get a feeling of how the picture goes. No need to shout: 'Terrific, Mr Buñuel! Sensational!', or, 'Schary's⁴ chauffeur heard Schary tell his wife he's upping you to a new contract!', or, 'Zanuck⁵ called to ask if you'd be free for Betty Grable's⁶ next!'; enough, perhaps, to say I think you are getting a fine performance from your main performer.⁷

Constructively, as I see Crusoe's conflict with himself being so well and thoroughly explored and dramatized before our eyes, I begin to have certain anxieties for our story of his conflict against nature. Natural, perhaps, that as the shooting has been confined to that one set where most of the conflict with himself takes place, that fear for the other story's success should arise. But precisely because this story of conflict with himself seems to be emerging so strongly do I believe re-examination of the other story necessary. Therefore, at risk of going over ground which you yourself have already crossed and re-crossed, I will be more explicit.

I feel that it is not enough (as the script frequently seems to do) to report Crusoe's triumphs over nature. I feel more strongly than ever that each contest must be completely and fully dramatized. As a member of an audience I would want to sweat with him, strain with him; so that his triumphs are mine and so that I am fully implicated in each struggle. In getting the supplies from the wreck; in lighting the first fire; in saving his gunpowder; growing his first crop and making his bread; in fashioning his clay pots; in his fierce struggle with the ocean current; I would wish the survival of each member of the audience to be in the balance with the survival of Crusoe. Not enough to show (as the script is inclined to do) what happens to Crusoe; more to the point to feel what is occurring; to be short of breath with him; to feel the sweat and dirt with him, and the fear; and to taste the first bite of good bread with him! Most of all, to feel one's heart beat fast with his when he sees, finally, hope of escape from his island prison!

More specifically still: did I sharpen sufficiently his desperate need for, fear of failure, in the making of his first fire? Did I indicate the intensity of eye, the fixedness of purpose, the complete and utter absorption in that crucial task? I think I did not. Similarly, did I dramatize sufficiently his fear of being unable to salvage the supplies of the wreck? Or, to jump ahead, I did not adequately dramatize his difficulty in raising his first crop of grain. It seems he goes from success to success in that venture; no locust *takes his wheat; no birds; no drought; he meets with no set back at all in this venture;* *true, he tells in his journal of losing his first crop;* but we do not see it. *That seed is* *more precious than gold and we never see it in jeopardy. Do worms get half of the* *remaining seed? Mildew? (so that it is a stinking, fermenting mess in his hands). Do* *rains wash it from the earth?*

Something we must have of this nature. One thing; one bitter discouragement which *he overcomes in growing his seed to a crop; one moment when all might have been* *destroyed so that we will taste the first bite of bread with him in relief and delight.*

To jump still further ahead; did I make explicit the two moments of hazard around *which the meeting with Friday[8] must hinge? These two moments are* when it seems Friday will be caught by his pursuers – *and* when it seems Crusoe's life might be lost to the same savages. *Again, I think not. I rather* report *the chase down the sands* *and the fact that the savage aims an arrow at Crusoe. I do not make clear that there is* *danger. And we are rather* handicapped *here; because most people know that Crusoe* *was not killed; and know that Friday escaped from his captors. All the more reason* *for me to have emphasised these moments – to have let there be a moment when –* *Friday skipped and fell in front of his pursuers – and, or,* Crusoe's gun failed to fire. *A moment, in each case, where the decision –as with the growing of the seed – was in* *balance; was in doubt.*

Similarly, and farther ahead again; I report that Crusoe sees the mutineer's longboat – *and knows that this is his chance to leave the island – yet I have not made clear that it may* be his only chance. *I report that Crusoe and Oberzo and the Bos'n[9] follow the mutineers* *to the stockade where they will effect the capture – but at no moment do I bring the* *outcome into doubt. I do not even have the mutineers stop – suddenly – perhaps hearing* *a SOUND behind them; Oberzo falling, or – what? I do not have them stop for one second* *of breathlessness when one could wonder – will they see Crusoe? Will he get off the island?*

So, in these instances at least, when I see how Crusoe's conflict with himself *has been* *dramatized, I fear that his conflict with nature might not be so clearly drawn. And as this* *is the story which most of us recall as Crusoe's story, the main theme, I have run the risk* *of emphasising what you most likely already had in your own planning.*

The other factor, which has to do with both Crusoe's struggle with himself and his *struggle against nature, is the final summation of Crusoe's character as projected by our* *main actor.*

Crusoe, in his wonderful similarity, even symbolization, to and of every man, is beset *with fears, as we know, both as to his ability to control himself and his ability to control* *nature. The fact that, in the end, he has conquered both, is, I feel, the message of hope* *which has made Crusoe the everlasting classic that it remains.*

There is a risk we run with our main actor, I believe, and that is that he will not *emerge, at the end of the picture, as the mature, self-confident, optimistic man who is sure* *of his own values, who, we feel, will conduct himself with surety and triumph in the future.* *Our actor, whose face and physique are neither strong nor robust, may play, despite all* *efforts, the inner, the intellectual and* psychological *Crusoe. We may, because we have* *seen him faced with fears of his own sanity, fears of natural phenomena, have established* *a character which, combined with the lack of robustness of physique, that faintly* turned *down mouth, create a Crusoe who is accompanied by a nimbus of neuroticism. All I can say to this horrific thought is, Marx, God and all prophets forbid!*

The man who leaves that island must be strong, confident, with no tremor of self-reproach or fear for the future. The very picture of an English country gentleman!

Nevertheless, the danger, I believe, exists. And to offset it I believe we must, in the opening exterior scenes of the island, and in his looting of the wreck, digging of his cave, felling of his trees, growing and reaping of his grain, fighting with the savages, paddling and struggling against that ocean current, emerge as a man with no turned down lips, no neuroticism; but as something exemplifying the best of man in his physical heroism; *yes, and inexhaustible competence.*

So much for all that; I trust the wading has not been too tiresome.

To turn to other matters: I saw the sets yesterday as we agreed we should. I thought the set designed as the 'hold' or store-room, magnificent;[10] *I thought the concept of inclining all three sets, inspired; but I have the gravest of reservations about the CABIN SET. The passageway I would say serves well if it be lit in such a low-key manner as to obliterate the details; for they, as with the cabin, are not good. But they can be cured by lighting. But the cabin! Luis, to me, who has spent time on boats and sail-boats, it seems, with all those colours, and the rather delicate architecture, like the boudoir of a French courtesan or, more devastating, like a set designed for one of those Warner Bros. patriotic, colour, two-reelers! It will not give the feeling of a ship inhabited by sailors; but of just what it is, a set. And while I would agree, even admire, that there be in this set some dramatization of the niceties of civilization (the civilization that Crusoe has inhabited up to now) surely it can be done more elegantly, more solidly. Do they not, in this country, have some fine, rich, real wooden panelling, that can be fitted in there. Or, cannot they simulate good panelling; one rich, subdued colour (not brown, there'll be too much of that with the cave, too) but something sober, with a feeling of richness, perhaps trimmed in gilt with a feeling of age; perhaps even more simple, a touch of* heavy silver. *Because I thought that the door-handles in the passageway and the drawer-handles in the cabin were fiercely bad. And no reason. There must be ship's chandlers available where, failing all else, stout articles of bronze can be purchased and, chemically, equipped with a patina of age.*

A couple of other details: in one shot, the one where Friday turns from the chest to say that the gold pieces are 'beautiful' and asks if he can have one, two, three, it seemed to me that his body make-up was too flat, too black; black in the way that minstrel shows, which as you recall, were made up of white men who covered faces and hands in blackened cork, were black. A peculiar, flat black, that throws into too obvious relief the reds and whites of mouths and eyes. Also, point out to the make-up man that the palms of the hands, even of negroes, are not the same colour as the backs of the hands; usually being paler, and pinkish. Better, perhaps, not to make up the palms of the hands but leave them natural. Pepper has, I believe, spoken of the man's make up. I don't concur that it is serious, for I observed that it varied; and that in other shots it was satisfactory; and might even have been no more than the lighting in that one shot ...
On the gold that Crusoe takes from the cabin, it has always seemed to me that it should be a considerable sum. It would be satisfying if, when he leaves the island at the end, we feel he has no economic problems of rehabilitating himself. We can do it with the

soundtrack, indicating plantations in 'the Brazils'; but better to have it backed up with
a considerable *amount of gold.*

That seems about all. I look forward extraordinarily to seeing the footage next week.
I know how hard you are working, and I trust (for the sake of the picture, naturally) that
your stomach is well.

My very best wishes to your wife.
Sincerely,
Señor[11] Boulder

Eng Tlu, HB/3208/7–8

[1] US scriptwriter (1914–68) exiled to Mexico during the McCarthy era.
[2] Rushes of *Robinson Crusoe*; Butler co-wrote the script with LB under the pseudonym Philip Ansel Roll, and filming began on 14 July 1952.
[3] The colour negative had to be sent to Hollywood, as there were no Eastmancolor laboratories in Mexico.
[4] Isadore Schary (1905–80), scriptwriter and executive producer for Metro, co-wrote, with Butler, *Edison, the Man* (1940), for which both were nominated for an Oscar.
[5] Darryl Zanuck (1902–79), US producer and executive at 20th Century Fox.
[6] US actress (1916–73), contracted to 20th Century Fox during the 1940s.
[7] Dan O'Herlihy.
[8] Friday, played by actor Jaime Fernández Reyes, brother of 'Indio' Fernández.
[9] Characters who leave the island with Robinson, played by Felipe de Alba and Chel López.
[10] Set design by Edward Fitzgerald and Pablo Galván.
[11] Spanish in the original.

Figure 42 Buñuel, sitting, with O'Herlihy, standing on the right, filming *Robinson Crusoe*, Mexico, summer 1952.

To José Rubia Barcia

Mexico City, 7 October 1952

My dear friend *don* José,

As always, I was very happy to have news of you in your most recent letter. The photo of Big Bear Lake brought back so many memories; because for me it will always be Big Barcia Lake, we had such good times there, with that discreet and silent little chef listening to our wonderful conversations as she peeled the potatoes for our meals. And indeed, the photo shows the 'gastronomic director' has not changed in the slightest. She's identical. I'm not being flirtatious, because I'm too old now. And your little girl is charming. She looks like both of you. The photo is the image of perfect happiness.

I'm very glad to have news of Kenneth, I have a great deal of admiration for him. Send him my cordial greetings. As for your article,[1] I think it would be infinitely better to publish it in *Quaterly*[2] rather than in a Mexican daily, as you intended. I'll ask for some photos in the office today and add them to this letter.

Mexican Bus Ride premiered here with little box office success, but some critical acclaim.[3] In Paris, on the other hand, it has received a warmer welcome than *The Young and the Damned*. I'm including a cutting that gives an idea of the critics' response. It was awarded the International Critics' Prize at Cannes[4] and the Vanguard Film Grand Prix in Paris. It's been on the bill for nine weeks now and is expected to beat the 18-week screening of *The Young and the Damned*.

I made two films this year: *The Brute*,[5] which could have been very good, but ended up rather mediocre, and *Robinson Crusoe*, which I've just finished in English and Spanish language versions[6] and which, I think, will be of some interest: anti-Hollywood and more for adults than children; I hope they will ban it for children. I've made all my films here in just three or four weeks; *Robinson* took three months to make because, among other reasons, it was filmed in Eastman Color.

I can't believe your migratory status is not yet resolved. I really wish you had come down here with me. I remember Evita was against the idea … as was I, because I was obliged by circumstances to come here. But I've grown to love Mexico as I've got to know it. At the moment, by comparison with the rest of the world, there is an atmosphere of freedom here, there is PEACE, and you can get on with your work without threats or reprisals because you think this way or that.[7] Isn't that marvellous? The country has many drawbacks, but also great virtues. For me personally, which other country would have allowed me to make *The Young and the Damned* and *Mexican Bus Ride*? I've become a Mexican citizen and plan to live here forever. Now, on the basis of advances and bank loans, I'm building myself a house[8] … which will always have a room reserved for you

Much love to you both,
Buñuel

[PS] I'm attaching a few articles in case they are useful for your own.

Spa Tlsps C, CBC; CLB 58–59

[1]   J. Rubia, 'Luis Buñuel's *Los Olvidados*'.

[2]   *Quarterly of Film, Radio, and Television*, founded as *Hollywood Quarterly* in 1945 and renamed *Film Quarterly* from 1958.

[3]   Premiered in Mexico City on 26 June 1952.

[4]   FIPRESCI prize.

[5]   Filmed in March 1952, premiered on 5 February 1953.

[6]   Filmed in both languages for commercial distribution in the United States and Mexico.

[7]   LB was about to start work on *This Strange Passion*, based on the novel by Spanish author, Mercedes Pinto, filmed between November 1952 and January 1953.

[8]   At Cerrada de Félix Cuevas, Colonia del Valle, designed by LB's friend from the Madrid Residencia and fellow exile in Mexican, Spanish architect Arturo Sáenz de la Calzada (1907–2003).

To Robert Favre Le Bret[1]

Robert Favre Le Bret
President of the Cannes International Film Festival
25 rue d'Astorg, Paris VIII

Mexico City, 8 April 1953

Dear Sir,
    After much delay, I have begun the film[2] I mentioned in my previous letter,[3] but I do not expect to complete it until around the 30th of this month.
    It will therefore, much to my regret, be impossible for me to attend this year's Cannes Festival. I am truly sorry.

Thanking you once more for your kind invitation. My most cordial greetings,
Luis Buñuel
Ultramar Films, Reforma 503

Fre Tls, CIN

[1]   French journalist (1904–87), director of the Cannes Film Festival from 1952 to 1972.

[2]   LB's adaptación de *Wuthering Heights*, filmed from 23 March to 23 April 1953.

[3]   Letter from LB to Le Bret, 5 March 1953 (CIN), in response to Le Bret's invitation, 9 February 1953, to LB to be a Festival juror.

From Aurora Bautista[1]

Madrid, 9 April 1953

Dear, greatly admired Luis Buñuel,
    It may seem strange that I should write with no particular and mutual reason for doing so. Nonetheless, I have had cause enough for some time now: the debt of gratitude and admiration owed to you by all film industry professionals, all film aficionados, and above all a Spaniard. I know a number of your friends here in Spain

who have spoken of you, and I follow you through articles and reviews, particularly in *Cahiers du cinéma*. I've also spoken to Alfonso, your brother, on occasion and I saw *The Young and the Damned* in Paris. All of which means I think I now understand and admire you more.[2]

Recently, a project has come up that I felt I had to approach you with. In conversation with Isabel and Concha García Lorca[3] at their house, the idea came up to adapt some of Federico's works for the cinema, particularly the most dramatic ones, *The House of Bernarda Alba, Blood Wedding* and *Yerma*.[4] They've talked to Paco[5] and he agrees. Of course, it is still only a proposal. The direction and the script are the most important things and only you are capable of such an important task.

Do you not think Spain would be the perfect setting for the film? But this is only a suggestion. You would not have to worry about producers. Anyone hearing about it would want to finance it. So, it would be better, until everything is decided, not to discuss our plan too widely. There is just one thing that I want to insist upon and that is that we work to your instructions.

I would be eternally grateful if you would reply to this letter as soon as you are able. I have written it in a great rush and I'm not sure if it is very clear. If you need any details or anything in particular, you can ask me whatever you want.

Affectionate greetings from,
Aurora Bautista
Velázquez 11

[PS] Please let me know if you will be going to Cannes for the upcoming film competition.

Spa Als, AB/625.1–3

[1] Aurora Bautista Zúmel (1925–2012), actress, who became one of the stars of Spanish film of the Franco era after playing the lead role of Queen Juana in *Juana la loca*.
[2] Bautista's father was imprisoned by the Franco regime at the end of the Civil War.
[3] Isabel (1909–2002) and Concepción García Lorca (1903–62), sisters of Federico García Lorca.
[4] Plays written in 1936, 1932 and 1934, respectively.
[5] Francisco García Lorca, brother of the poet.

To José Rubia Barcia

Mexico City, 2 May 1953

My dear friend *don* Pepe,

Many congratulations for the birth, amid the waves of Santa Monica, of your daughter Adelita.[1] Give Evita a hug from me. That's two now! Take care! Two's company but three's a crowd.

You're right: I had to resign from the Museum[2] because I made *The Golden Age*. The Museum wouldn't have accepted if the State Department hadn't put pressure on the Commissioner's Office, which in turn put pressure on the Museum.

I've just flopped at Cannes with a film I thought was good but which, by the looks of things, is not so good after all.[3] It's called *This Strange Passion* and it's about a man delirious with jealousy.

I'm waiting impatiently for your article in *Quaterly*: you can keep the articles I sent you from France.

I'm building a little house where there will always be a room reserved for you and Evita.

Much love,
Buñuel

Spa Als, CBC

[1]   Adela Rubia López.
[2]   Museum of Modern Art, New York.
[3]   *This Strange Passion* screened at the 6th Cannes Festival, 15–29 April 1953, with a jury presided over by Cocteau.

From Georges Sadoul

Paris, 14 May 1953

My dear Luis,

I don't know if you've been told about the muted response your latest film, *This Strange Passion*, received at Cannes. I'm sure you will know that some press announcements implied you would attend the Festival to present the film to the public. I certainly thought you would be there and was expecting you, so I was enormously disappointed.

The Jury, as you know, was chaired by Jean Cocteau. He saw the film before the public. And before the screening he kept saying, in so many words: 'I've witnessed a suicide. Buñuel wrote saying he cared greatly (or somewhat) for *This Strange Passion*. But all I can see is a regrettable, commercial film. Shocking.' I do think, in fact, that he was expressing his sincere opinion and was not motivated by any ill-will. Just as a Bordeaux wine loses its bitterness over time, with age, Cocteau has become a model of benevolence and indulgence. In general, he has been an excellent president of the Cannes' Jury. Except in the case of *This Strange Passion*.

Of course, his comments were reproduced, and a number of critics absented themselves from the Festival on the afternoon the film was screened, because the Mexican gala evening had been set aside for *La red*,[1] that far-fetched, vulgar fabrication by Emilio Fernández. The absences were even more noticeable because *Susana* had been screened six months ago in Paris,[2] with a lot of publicity around your name, and the critics hadn't much appreciated a film that I, personally, enjoyed (unless I'm mistaken?) as a commercial product in that *zarzuela* style you worked in, pseudonymously, some years ago in Madrid.[3] Although I certainly didn't recognize 'my Buñuel', except in one or two images.

Before *This Strange Passion*, they screened a horrible, chauvinistic French film called *Vie passionée de Clémenceau*,[4] the Ministry of War had 'packed the house' with a hundred or so veterans from 1914 to 1918, whose job it was to applaud, loudly, all the vengeful statements, shots of Marshall Foch, and battle scenes.[5] This select audience stayed on to watch your film. So, it was hardly surprising that certain sequences were met with shouts and whistles, just as in the days of *The Golden Age*.

As for me, I barely heard the shouts and whistles. I was 'captivated' from the opening scenes. Transported twenty years back to our youth. Where Cocteau saw a banal commercial film, I saw extraordinary fidelity to the motifs of *The Golden Age* and the rage of an acerbic and destructive humour that destroys, with Arturo de Córdova,[6] all the commercialism of Mexican cinema, attacking it with its own weapons. But what most excited me was the fact that the recuperation (often forcefully highlighted) of the motifs of *The Golden Age* went hand-in-hand with their critique. The abject monster of *This Strange Passion* seemed to me the image, the double, the brother of the hero embodied by Modot, but reviled, destroyed, torn to shreds, rather than, as in *The Golden Age* exalted, glorified and placed on a pedestal. Francisco the sanctimonious, perverse, feudal, the unjust tyrant, both in the bell tower scene and in the encounter with his servant, seemed to me to be turned by your vision into an unprecedented condemnation of all the new incarnations of *Fantômas*[7] or of Maldoror,[8] who tormented some of us in the days of surrealism. To use an (overly solemn) analogy, if *The Golden Age* was your *Maldoror*, I see *This Strange Passion* as your *Poésies* by Isidore Ducasse.[9]

I said all of this (or something similar) in Cannes where, with the exception of five or six critics, *This Strange Passion* was condemned for a surface meaning so poorly understood it might have taken first prize at Catholic central for its 'perfectly edifying' denouement. And so it went on. 48 hours later, André Bazin, who initially shared the general incomprehension, published a defence of your film in the Festival bulletin, *Rendez-vous de Cannes*, published by Cinématographie française.[10] Cocteau was no longer quite so insistent about his earlier opinion, although when I said: 'It is *The Golden Age*' his answer was 'No, it's *The Monetary Age*' (with malice, this time, doubled or tripled). I am, though, convinced that if *This Strange Passion* is screened in Paris, it will definitely attract fans and lengthy eulogies in journals like *Cahiers du cinéma*.[11]

That said, I think your film will be difficult to defend, because it will be misunderstood by mass audiences (of whatever kind) who will only see (at best) its sadism, rather than its critique of sadism. Your intentions (or at least those I attribute to you) will be understood by a hundred initiates at most, that is, by men of our generation and experience, or the subtle aesthetes of Saint Germain des Prés.[12] And to repeat a slogan from *The Golden Age*, 'poetry should be written by everyone'[13] (in other words, for everyone), beginning with cinema. I shall try to explain your film when it premieres in Paris. I doubt these explanations will succeed in convincing anyone beyond a small (and reprehensible) circle of initiates ...

And now for a change of topic. I'm negotiating with Fondo de Cultura Económica[14] and Arnaldo Orfilo Reynal[15] a Mexican edition of my new book *La Vie Charlot*[16] (I sent you a copy in November, did you get it?). However, the editors, who published my little book *El cine*[17] and have just issued a new edition, are not offering very favourable terms. Do you know of any Mexican publisher who might be interested? A serious publishing house, of course, that would be undeterred by competition from Francisco Pina's[18] *Charles Chaplin* (and prepared to produce an initial run of 1,000 copies)?

I would be very grateful if you could write back to me about this soon. And I would also like you to tell me about *This Strange Passion,* and whether I was correct in the intentions I attribute to you. But that can wait for another letter.

When, finally, will you return to France? What does your *Robinson Crusoe* mean for you?

We spoke of you at great length yesterday with Dominique Éluard[19] and Eli Lotar.

Most cordially,
Georges Sadoul

Fre Tls, AB/572.40

---

[1] *La red* (1953); also distributed as *Rossana.*

[2] *Susana* premiered in Paris on 24 November 1952.

[3] Films produced, uncredited, by LB for Filmófono.

[4] Documentary directed by Gilbert Prouteau in 1953 on the life of the French prime minister during the First World War.

[5] Marshall Ferdinand Foch (1851–1929), Commander-in-Chief of the allied forces during the First World War.

[6] Arturo García Rodríguez (1907–73), Mexican actor who played Francisco, the pathologically jealous husband in *This Strange Passion.*

[7] Famous villain in detective fiction by Marcel Allain and Pierre Souvestre, created in 1911 and adapted numerous times for film.

[8] Demonic antihero of *Les Chants de Maldoror* (1869), by Isidore Ducasse, Conde de Lautréamont, much admired by the surrealists.

[9] *Poésies* published by Lautréamont in 1870.

[10] French film journal published 1918 to 1964, with a special bulletin for the Cannes Film Festival.

[11] Bazin, Doniol-Valcroze, Kast and Kyrou were among the critics who included *This Strange Passion* on the list of the ten best films released in 1954, published in *Cahiers du cinéma*, no. 43 (January 1955), p. 5.

[12] Intellectual and artistic district of central Paris after the Second World War.

[13] Declaration by Lautréamont in *Poésies*, adopted by the surrealists.

[14] Mexican publishing house founded by Daniel Cosío Villegas in 1934.

[15] Argentine editor (1897–1998), director of the Fondo de Cultura Económica between 1948 and 1965.

[16] G. Sadoul, *La Vie de Charlot* (Paris: Les éditeurs français réunis, 1952).

[17] *El cine: su historia y su técnica* (Mexico City: Fondo de Cultura Económica, 1950), Spanish edition of *Le Cinéma: Son art, sa technique, son économie* (Paris: La Bibliothèque française, 1948).

[18] Film critic (1900–71), exiled to Mexico where he co-founded the journal *Nuevo Cine*; his biography was *Charles Chaplin, genio de la desventura y la ironía* (Mexico City: Talleres de Juan Pablos, 1952).

[19] Odette Lemort (1914–2000), wife of Éluard from 1951.

To Georges Sadoul

Mexico City, 25 June 1953

My dear Georges,

I'm truly ashamed not to have replied to your letter by return post, but you are already familiar with my horrible laziness when it comes to letter writing. I suppose though, that late is better than never.

Thank you for your very interesting comments about the Cannes Festival and about all the racket the 'revanchists'[1] made against my film, which came as a considerable surprise to me.

I think the Cannes Festival is going from bad to worse, it's become a kind of *Salon d'Automne* of the old days. I can't believe the prizes awarded this year for *Rossana*, for example, or the 'International Award for Good Humour'.

As for *This Strange Passion*, it's not, as Cocteau thought, a film I made 'to make money'. Failure or not, and in spite of some trite sequences, it's a film I had great interest in making.

I'm not sure what people expect of me, but you can't expect a masterpiece given the conditions I work under here in Mexico! When you think that every film I've made down here has been shot in seventeen (*The Brute*, for example) to twenty-three days (*This Strange Passion*).

I would love to find a good story and direct it in France. Here in Mexico, we don't have a single actor or actress of any calibre.

I've discussed your book with a friend of mine who is the head of a publishing house. He's asked me to ask you how much Fondo de Cultura Económica offered for your *Chaplin*. I'm sure they will make you a better one, but they want to find out how much you've been offered, so they don't suggest the same amount.[2]

As soon as I have a little money saved up I will come to Paris; I'm really keen to see old friends and, above all, to have long conversations with you. I hope it will be this winter.

Yours,
Buñuel

Fre Tls, GS/64

---

[1] Revanchism: political policy of regaining lost ground.
[2] Eventually published as *Vida de Chaplin* (Mexico City: Fondo de Cultura, 1955).

From Robert Favre Le Bret

Paris, 19 October 1953

Dear Sir,

You know how sorry I was that you could not attend the Festival last year that reunited so many international film figures, yours was the one true absence.

Once again, I am hoping you may be able to attend the next event,[1] which will take place in Cannes from 25 March to 9 April 1954, and I wanted to ask, as long as Mexico does not enter a film you have directed, whether you would grant us the honour and pleasure of becoming a member of the Jury.

I would be grateful if you would be kind enough to respond to this request as soon as possible, looking forward to hearing from you, I send you my most cordial greetings,

Favre Le Bret

Fre Tlu, CIN

[1]   7th Cannes Film Festival.

To Robert Favre Le Bret

Mexico City, 2 November 1953

Dear Sir,
On my return to Mexico after a few days' absence,[1] I received your letter of 19 October. A copy of it also arrived, thanks to the efforts of Mr Sirol[2] of the French Embassy.

I would be delighted to accept the honour of your invitation to become a member of the Jury of this year's Film Festival at Cannes. From this moment onwards, I shall take appropriate action to ensure I am available on those dates! I shall plan my journey from Mexico to France for around 15 March, in other words, ten days before the Festival.

I look forward to hearing from you, most cordial greetings.
Luis Buñuel
Extremadura 36

Fre Tls, CIN

[1]   LB was filming *Illusion Travels by Streetcar* for CLASA in September and October 1953.
[2]   Jean Sirol, cultural attaché to the French Embassy in Mexico.

To Robert Favre Le Bret

Mexico City, 7 February 1954

Dear Sir,
Everything is arranged and barring unforeseen events I shall be in Paris a few days before the Festival, around 16 March.

I would be grateful if you could clarify the following points:

1)   Could you please let me know who are the other members of the Jury?
2)   Do I cover the cost of the trip and of my accommodation in Cannes?

Looking forward to hearing from you, most cordial greetings.
Luis Buñuel
CLASA Studios, Calzada de Tlalpan

Fre Tls, CIN

From Robert Favre Le Bret

Paris, 11 February 1954

Dear Sir,

I'm replying in haste to your letter of 7 February to supply you with the following information. The Jury is made up of a representative from the Ministry of Foreign Affairs;[1] a representative of the French parliament;[2] an author (probably Marcel Achard[3]); a film-maker (Marc Allégret[4]); a musician (Jacques Ibert[5]); two critics;[6] a representative from the film studios;[7] an actor (probably Noël-Noël[8]); Jean Cocteau; and two overseas delegates, of whom you are one.[9]

If it is not too much trouble, I will reimburse you half the cost of your trip once you are in Paris, unless I can find an alternative arrangement. I shall take care of this immediately and will also send you a return ticket to Mexico with Air France.

We shall, of course, cover the cost of your stay and will take especial care of you. Your friends – and there are many of them – are waiting impatiently for you in France and we would be sorely disappointed if you were unable to make it to Cannes, as your name was publicized some time ago.

Looking forward to hearing from you, most cordial greetings.
Favre Le Bret

Fre Tluf, CIN

[1] In the end, the French politician, Guy Desson (1909–80).
[2] George Lamousse (1909–92), French politician.
[3] French author (1889–1974), substituted by the French scriptwriter Jean Aurenche (1903–92).
[4] Substituted by the French director, Henri Calef (1910–94).
[5] French composer (1890–1962), who worked with Allégret.
[6] Bazin and the French journalist, André Lang (1893–1986).
[7] Jacques-Pierre Frogerais (1893–1980), French producer.
[8] Lucien Éduard Noël (1897–1989), French actor.
[9] LB is the only non-French member of a Jury that also included the historian Philippe Erlanger; trade unionist Georges Raguis; and director of the Centre national de la cinématographie Michel Fourré-Cormeray.

From Amos Vogel[1]

[New York,] 16 March 1954

Dear Mr Buñuel,

You may know that Cinema 16 is America's largest film society and that among our 5,000 members are leading personalities in the fields of the cinema and the arts.

Over the past seven years we have not only presented outstanding documentary, avant-garde and feature film classics of all nations, but have also introduced as speakers such personalities as Norman McLaren,[2] Jean Renoir, Willard Van Dyke,[3] Maya Deren,[4] Dylan Thomas[5] and Arthur Miller.[6]

I am very interested in presenting a special evening during our fall 1954 to spring 1955 season devoted entirely to your work. The program would include representative films of various periods in your life, including possibly An Andalusian Dog, Land Without bread, The Young and the Damned, Él. *However, the most important feature of the evening would be a personal appearance by you – to talk about your films and possibly answer questions from the audience.*

I would certainly be prepared to contribute toward your expense in coming here to the extent of several hundred dollars. Do you think arrangements can be made – or are you possibly already contemplating coming here in conjunction with the release of Robinson Crusoe?[7]

We can discuss further details later on, after I have your agreement in principle.

I should appreciate hearing from you at your early convenience.

Sincerely,
Amos Vogel, Executive Secretary
Cinema 16, 175 Lexington Avenue

Eng Tlu C, AV/I.2/05/13; *BUL* 727–728

---

[1] US film historian born in Vienna (1921–2012), programmer for New York film society Cinema 16 from 1947 to 1963.
[2] Scottish animated film director (1914–87), based in Canada from 1941.
[3] US documentary film-maker (1906–86), director of MoMA Film Library from 1965 to 1974.
[4] US experimental film-maker of Ukranian origin (1917–61).
[5] Welsh poet (1914–53), took part with Deren and Miller in the programme 'Poetry and the Film' organized by Vogel at Cinema 16 on 28 October 1953.
[6] US dramatist and scriptwriter (1915–2005).
[7] Film premiered in the United States in June 1954.

To Jaime García Terrés[1]

[Cannes, April 1954]

My dear friend,
    Your letter arrived yesterday and I'm hurrying to reply. I would be very grateful if you could wait until I get back to send you the corrected and extended version of my lecture notes.[2] I left them in Mexico and, what with the travel preparations, had no time to revise them. The seminar will run for the entire course and I think we might consider publishing them at a later date.[3]
    Over here there is a lot of work to do. More films than ever have been released this year: 36 countries with 40 [films]. And some additional 60 shorts, for which there is

a separate Jury.[4] Some days I've had to watch five films, a foolproof way to deaden the critical faculties.

Nonetheless, I'm very happy to be in France, where I spent so many years in my youth …

Cordially yours, hoping to see you soon.
Luis Buñuel

Spa, Od; *ICO* 92

[1]   Mexican editor and writer (1924–96), director of Difusión cultural at UNAM.
[2]   Delivered by LB at UNAM in 1954.
[3]   Recorded lecture published, uncorrected by LB, in the UNAM journal as LB, 'El cine, instrumento de poesía', *Universidad de México* 13, no. 4 (December 1958), pp. 1–2 and 15; the 1954 Cannes Film Festival took place from 25 March to 9 April.
[4]   Jurors included Tedesco and the Danish film-maker Henning Jensen.

Figure 43 Buñuel, unknown, Cocteau and Aurenche, Cannes, April 1954.

To Janet[1] and Luis Alcoriza[2]

Paris, 9 May 1954

My dearest disciples Luis and Janet,

I assume my favourite will have told you about the series of events that has chained me to this delightful city. I shall be dragging my shackles around her streets until the 22nd of this coming June, at which point I will make my triumphal return to Mexico. I'm counting the days and despairing at how slowly they go by. Although Paris is still a wonderful city, if it were up to me, I would never come back. And I know that I, and not Paris, am to blame for this.

The most interesting part of a letter like the one I'm writing now is the news, and so I shall proceed to tell you as much I can. I won't dwell on Cannes, because that's all in the past now, but I did meet up with almost all my old friends, and many more I knew only by name or reputation. I think my presence was useful up to a point, and that the members of the Jury were fair up to that last moment, which may well have been one of the dirtiest tricks recorded in the annals of any jury, in any part of the world.[3]

Three days ago, after an endless series of events, I signed a contract with Marceau Films[4] to adapt and direct *That is the Dawn*.[5] You will already know [Luis] that I proposed we bring you over, but they turned me down. It's a French-Italian co-production and they're giving me two writers: one French and one Italian.[6] I still haven't given up all hope of adding you to the team, even if I can't get you to France. I'll tell you how and why when we meet. When we finish the adaptation, they'll let me go back to Mexico to fulfil my obligations to CLASA.[7] I have a contract, four million francs, to return to Paris on 2 May 1955 to begin preparation and filming. It's a lofty contract, as long as any Hollywood one. The Technicians' Union,[8] which includes the *metteurs en scène*, has accepted me unanimously, on the basis that they consider me inextricably linked to the French film industry, so I don't need to apply.

I've seen Breton (half an hour at his house) and I met Max Ernst at *Les Deux Magots*[9] yesterday. I also see quite a bit of young Kyrou, whom I'm going to take on as an assistant for the film.[10] Until yesterday, when I began working with the writer,[11] I did nothing but meet up with people, eat like a king and drink like a fascist. It was all getting a bit much. I'm going to be such a fine-dining and imbibing bore. Take care what you put on the table, solid or liquid, when you invite me to dinner! I shall subject every last breadcrumb to a steely critique that will make your sauces tremble.

The response to *This Strange Passion* has been surprising. It has some genuine and passionate supporters: at the Cinémathèque, with the *Journées du Cinéma*[12] crowd, *Cahiers du cinéma, Positif*,[13] Jacques Prévert, Bazin, Simone Dubreuilh, Kyrou and even Sadoul, etc. They've managed to lift the film's Cocteauian curse. Three days ago, UNESCO[14] organized a screening of the film for psychiatrists based in Paris.[15] There were about 50 of them in the screening room: Dr Jacques Lacan,[16] the best-known world specialist in paranoia and director of the Sainte Anne hospital, Paris; Dr Ey,[17] director of the Hospital de Chartres, etc., etc. It would take too long to tell you everything they said and asked after the screening. To sum up: they thought it was a perfect depiction of the syndrome. They were amazed we'd been able to produce such a well-defined characterization. It was the second time Dr Lacan had seen the film. It was such a pleasure for me, the whole event. I'm only sorry you weren't there to share it with me, my number one disciple!

Yesterday, I presented *Land Without Bread* and *The Young and the Damned* to the Renault[18] workers' film club. The discussion with them after the screening was really moving.

I wrote to Orive Alba[19] about my contract and to let him know I'll be working with CLASA from 23 June.[20] Before I left, I gave him *Nazarín* to read. I don't know what he made of it. See if you can think of any other books to suggest to him. I'd like to start working as soon as I get back, because they've only given me an advance of one and a half million[21] from my contract and that's all I'll make until May next year. I'll send most of it to Jeanne to pay the architect[22] and other debts and put bread on the table.

What happened with *The Criminal Life of Archibaldo de la Cruz*? I've heard nothing so do let me know.

I hear you are still working with Gavaldón and, by the looks of it, *very happy*.[23] When do you finish? And what's happening in Mexico with the fall in the peso? And what of our industry? Any news you send will be read with avid interest.

My address: Hotel L'Aiglon, 232 Boulevard Raspail, Paris.

Much love to you both,
Luis

PS My balcony on the fourth floor looks out over Montparnasse Cemetery. I have a *kitchenette*[24] and today I'm going to start cooking my own eggs and steaks. After so many years to be back living the Bohemian bachelors' life in my dear old Paris. You're only as old as you feel!

Spa Als, ALC/01/02; *BRU* 26–27

---

[1] Janet Alcoriza, née Riesenfeld (1918–98), Mexican actress and scriptwriter of Austrian descent, collaborated with LB on the scripts for *The Great Madcap* and *Daughter of Deceit* (1951).

[2] Luis Alcoriza de la Vega (1918–92), scriptwriter and director exiled in Mexico, collaborated with LB on eight films, including *The Young and the Damned* and *This Strange Passion*.

[3] Jury Grand Prix awarded to *Jigokumon* (1953), dir. Teinosuke Kinugasa, and Special Jury Prize to *Monsieur Ripois* (1954), dir. René Clément.

[4] French film company belonging to Edmond Ténoudji (1902–86) and Claude Jaeger (1917–2004), co-producers of LB's *That is the Dawn* (1955), with Italian production company, Laetitia Films.

[5] *Cela s'appelle l'aurore*, novel by French author of Spanish-Algerian descent, Emmanuel Roblès (1914–95), published by Seuil, Paris, 1952.

[6] Script finally written by LB and French writers Jean Ferry (1906–74) and (uncredited) Pierre Laroche (1902–62).

[7] For the premier of *Illusion Travels by Streetcar* in Mexico City, 18 June 1954.

[8] Syndicat national des techniciens et réalisateurs.

[9] Café on Saint Germain des Prés Square in Paris frequented by surrealists.

[10] Eventually, Marcel Camus.

[11] Ferry.

[12] Film festival chaired by Roger Leenhardt and organized by L'Association française pour la diffusion du cinema, Paris, between 1953 and 1960.

[13] French film journal founded by Bernard Chardère in 1952.

[14] Founded in Paris in 1946.

[15] At the UNESCO head office in Paris, event organized by Claude Lévi-Strauss.

[16] French psychiatrist and psychoanalyst (1901–81), whose work would have a major impact on psychoanalytical film theory.

[17] Henri Ey (1900–77), French neurologist and psychiatrist.

[18] Car manufacturers founded by the Renault brothers in 1899.

[19] Armando Orive Alba, Mexican producer of *Illusion Travels by Streetcar* and *The River and Death*.

[20] Filming of LB's next film at the CLASA studios, *The Criminal Life of Archibaldo de la Cruz* starts, in the end, in January 1955.

[21] Francs.

[22] Sáenz de la Calzada.

[23] Alcoriza co-wrote the script of *Sombra verde*, dir. Gavaldón, premiered in 1954.

[24] English in the original.

To Maurice Bessy[1]

Paris, 29 May 1954

Dear Maurice,

This coming Tuesday at 9pm, I shall be screening *Robinson Crusoe* at United Artists, 27 Rue d'Astorg.[2] If you are free and if this children's story is of any interest to you, I'd love to see you, along with the few friends who are coming. I hear Jean's[3] not in Paris. If he gets back, do invite him for me.

Yours,
Buñuel

Fre Asp Od; *RR* 229 f

[1] French film critic and historian (1910–93), director of the journal *Cinémonde*.

[2] Commercial premiere in France on 27 August 1954.

[3] Possible reference to Jean-Placide Mauclaire, from Studio 28, who bought and relaunched *Cinémonde* in 1946.

From André Bazin

Bry-sur-Marne, [May 1954]

Dear Buñuel,

I tried to reach you on the telephone, but to no avail. I left a message at the hotel asking you to call me at Bry-sur-Marne, but perhaps you didn't get it, or weren't able to reach me. The telephone is in my neighbour's house and she sometimes goes out.

I'm sorry I can't get to Paris to meet you and that you will have to come to Bry-sur-Marne if you want to see me, but I hope that Doniol-Valcroze will be able to bring you by car.[1] It is too late now for Thursday, and I'm having lunch with a friend on Friday, but would you like to come for supper on Friday, or at least for an aperitif if you already have dinner plans? As it may be difficult to reach me on the telephone, the easiest thing would be to arrange it with Doniol directly, calling him either at *Cahiers du cinéma*, or at home (IRI 6241). My telephone number is, as you know, Bry-sur-Marne 216, and my address is 53 Avenue de Rigny, Bry-sur-Marne (Seine). Telegrams do work.

Hoping to have the pleasure of shaking you by the hand soon, with fond memories,
André Bazin

Fre Als, AB/691.54

[1] Bazin and Doniol-Valcroze publish interview with LB in *Cahiers du cinéma*, no. 36 (June 1954), pp. 2–14.

To *Positif*

[Paris, May 1954][1]

As a man of Mexican cinema, I like to repeat that, although our film may not be the finished product, it is a work in progress – which may be better – with its roots in the profound sense of death, that is to say, in the Mexican love of life that produces considerable results enhanced by the *ferociously independent spirit* of the Mexican people.

Luis Buñuel

Fre Als, Od; *POS* 3 f

[1] Letter published in a special issue of *Positif* dedicated to Mexican film that includes articles on LB written by Kyrou, Jacques Demeure and others.

To Amos Vogel

[Mexico City,] 24 June 1954

Dear Mr Vogel,
I am very sorry that I have not answered your letter of 16 March, but I have just come back from France where I attended the Cannes Film Festival and did some work on a film in Paris.[1]
Thank you very much for your invitation to attend your special program but I find myself forced not to accept your invitation. Here in Mexico I have two films[2] to make by the end of the winter and in the Spring, I have to return to France and to finish the film that I started this past month.
Thanks again for your invitation.[3]

Sincerely,
Luis Buñuel

[PS] My new address: Cerrada Félix Cuevas 27, México City

Eng Tlsps, AV/I.2/05/13; *BUL* 728

[1] Script of *That is the Dawn* (1956)
[2] *The Criminal Life of Archibaldo de la Cruz* and, possibly, second failed attempt to film *Nazarín*.
[3] On 24 June LB also rejects an invitation to attend a screening of *An Andalusian Dog* and *Mexican Bus Ride* at another New York film club, The Group for Film Study (AB/691.6).

From Miroslava[1]

Mexico City, 1 July 1954

I *formally* pledge to make *any* film with Mr Luis Buñuel, at *no* cost, whatever the size of the role.

Miroslava[2]

Spa Naf, AB/1383.46

[1] Miroslava Šternová (1925–55), Mexican actress, born in Prague.
[2] Played Lavinia in *The Criminal Life of Archibaldo de la Cruz*, committed suicide on 9 March 1955, before the film premiered on 3 April 1954.

From Simone Signoret[1] and Yves Montand[2]

[Paris,] 22 July 1954

Dear Luis,

Barely a day goes by without us mentioning you, which may seem odd given the length of time it has taken to reply to your letter, but it's true. We became so used to you so quickly, it's almost impossible to believe you're now so far away.

It's a shame in a way, that *L'Aurore*[3] won't be made this year, but it's also wonderful to think that it guarantees we'll meet again in a few months' time.

This is the exact opposite of a business letter, so we will not mention Mr Ténoudji's silence,[4] nor of the habitual levity of the charming Claude.[5]

This is just an expression of the friendship we feel for you.

A hug from both of us.
Simone and Yves

Fre Als, AB/632.11

[1] Simone Kaminker (1921–85), French-German actress, starred in LB's *Death in the Garden* (1956).
[2] Ivo Libi (1921–91), French-Italian actor and singer, married Signoret in 1951.
[3] Provisional title of *That is the Dawn*; LB wanted Signoret for Clara, who was eventually played by Lucía Bosé (1931).
[4] Edmond Ténoudji.
[5] Jaeger.

To *PHILM¹* magazine

[Mexico City, July 1954]

Clarification

I must state that the majority of the so-called 'ideas' or statements attributed to me, published in *PHILM* (number 1, June 1954), were never written or formulated by me, particularly those to do with surrealism. Those 'thoughts' have apparently been extracted from old interviews of which I was never aware and for which I feel absolutely no responsibility.

Similarly, I deny having made statements such as '*An Andalusian Dog* was a mistake', '*The Young and the Damned* is also a somewhat irrational film', 'the script is nothing more than a collection of documents', and most of the text entitled '*This Strange Passion* by Buñuel'.

Luis Buñuel

Fre CmfL, ABR/2012.26e

¹   Short-lived journal published in Paris in 1954.

To Amos Vogel

Mexico, 17 September 1954

Dear Mr Vogel,

First, I want to excuse my delay in answering your letter of August 19.¹ I am the first one in criticizing my fault in punctuality. It is perhaps my bad English that prevents me from maintaining a correspondence.

It gives me great pleasure to send you some material on This Strange Passion. *It is a selection of articles recently written in Paris about the film, by some important critics and with whose judgement I generally agree.² I suppose that, out of them, you can take some information for a better explanation of the film.*

The cost of This Strange Passion *was about 100,000 dollars and it took four weeks of filming. I tried to describe objectively a paranoiac character with delirium of interpretation. In the case of* Él *it is a jealous one but with a Spanish or Latin American kind of jealousy.*

The character of Francisco is taken from real life and not from 'imagination'.³ Under a melodramatic form there is a critique of the bourgeoisie and its fundamentals of which each spectator is allowed to interpret in his own fashion or not interpret at all.

I thank you very much for your interest.

Very truly yours,
Luis Buñuel

Eng Tls, AV/I.2/05/13; *BUL* 730

[1] Letter from Vogel to LB asking for information on *This Strange Passion* (AV/I.2/05/13).
[2] LB archived numerous press cuttings on the film (ABR/1982).
[3] Character based in part on LB's brother-in-law, Pedro Galán; LB has joked elsewhere that, of all his characters, this is the one most like himself.

From Vittorio de Sica[1]

[Mexico City, 1954]

To Luis,
yours,
Vittorio[2]

Ita Add, Olu; *ICO* 66 f

[1] Italian actor and director (1901–74).
[2] Dedication on photograph of LB, de Sica and Emilio Fernández.

Figure 44 Buñuel, De Sica and Indio Fernández, 1954.

From Guido Aristarco[1]

Milan, 24 January 1955

Dear Sir,

I have sent, separately, a copy of the first edition of *Bollettino del neorealismo*,[2] which will be published at the same time as no. 51 of *Cinema Nuovo*.

The *Bollettino* will be published henceforth with some regularity and I should be delighted to include in our next edition some of your articles (of no more than half a page of typescript) on topics you judge to be appropriate when you have read the *Bolettino*: projects and filming of neorealist films in Mexico; the influence of neorealism on other films; opinions of critics, actors, technicians and the public on neorealist films screened in Mexico, etc.

I look forward to your reply and thank you in advance for your collaboration with the *Bolletino*, most sincerely yours,

Guido Aristarco
Cinema Nuovo
Via Fatebenefratelli 15

Fre Tls L, AB/691.3

[1] Italian film critic and historian (1918–96), founded *Cinema Nuovo* in 1952.
[2] Including texts by Italian directors Michelangelo Antonioni (1912–2007) and de Sica.

Figure 45 Family gathering at Pau in 1955, after twenty years in exile: Buñuel with his mother, María Portolés, and sisters, Margarita and Conchita Buñuel.

From Amos Vogel

[New York,] 3 February 1955

Dear Luis Buñuel,

Our screening of This Strange Passion *has just taken place and it certainly was one of the most interesting and controversial screenings we have presented at Cinema 16.[1] It was shown to four different audiences. The reaction at all presentations was the same: loud applause and a few hisses.*

There have not been many films in the last few years that have divided our membership as much as This Strange Passion *did. Some of them thought it was an uninteresting, poorly made, melodramatic film. The majority, I am happy to say, disagreed and understood your intentions.*

One of the most laudable comments came from the film historian Jay Leyda who considers This Strange Passion *one of your best works. The many other critics who attended were very favourably impressed or liked the film with reservations.*

I am sure you need not to be told that This Strange Passion *is one of your more controversial films.*

I am also very happy to say that as a direct consequence of our showing, This Strange Passion *was bought by an American distributor (Noel Meadow)[2] for regular theatrical distribution.[3] He will of course subtitle it.*

I am very happy to have been able to show it at Cinema 16 and to thereby have provided an opportunity for interested critics and film people to see it.

At this time, I want to discuss with you the problem of The Golden Age. *I would, needless to say, be very interested to show this film at Cinema 16. What information can you give me? Do you have a print in Mexico? Or are the only remaining prints in Paris and if so, where? I would be personally responsible for the safety of any print sent here and would be very happy to make appropriate financial arrangements. I am sure you will agree that it would be important for the film to be shown here. Cinema 16 is not subject to the usual censorship restrictions and no legal problem would arise in connection with such a showing.[4] The transportation from abroad could, in my opinion, also be arranged without any difficulties.*

Jay Leyda has also drawn my attention to your Goya film. Can you tell me where I can obtain it? Is there a print in America?

I shall appreciate hearing from you at your early convenience.

Very sincerely yours,
[Amos Vogel]

Eng Tlu C, AV/I.2/05/13; *BUL* 730–731

---

[1]   Four screenings at Cinema 16, on 25 and 26 January 1955.
[2]   US publicist and distributor, president of the distribution company, Omnifilms.
[3]   Premiered commercially in the United States as *This Strange Passion*, 3 December 1955.
[4]   As a private film club, Cinema 16 was not subject to the same censorship as commercial cinemas.

Figure 46 Buñuel with crew members filming *That is the Dawn*, Corsica, August 1955.

From Aaron Sloan[1]

New York, 10 January, 1956

Dear Mr Buñuel,

Since my knowledge of French is best when applied to reading, I am answering your letter of December 5 in English.

Your picture opened December 3 at the Trans-Lux 52nd Street Theatre in Manhattan under the title This Strange Passion *to mixed reviews. I am enclosing a representative sample.*

It was of great pleasure for me to work on the picture in its preparatory stages for the American version. It needed extensive cutting, which I supervised; plus, titling. I hope if you ever get a chance to see our version of it, you let me know what you think of the English titles, which I wrote.

So far as the commercial promise in US art theatres for This Strange Passion, I must in all honesty inform you that there is none. The picture flopped irrevocably – completely. Although a couple of New York reviews were highly favourable, the majority were strongly thumbs-down.[2] Moreover, audience word-of-mouth served to compound the critics' bombshells.

At the Trans-Lux in New York, the house suffered one of its worst setbacks in its history during the run of the picture.

If this puzzles you, let it be said that it puzzles me, also. But the above are the facts in the case. Perhaps it should be augured that the taste of the public, so conditioned to pictures with Cinderella-like themes and milk-sop plots, could not appreciate so atmospheric a tale as was presented in This Strange Passion.

I am enclosing various advertising samples, etc., relating to the opening of the picture.[3] Could you, perhaps, send me synopses of your new pictures, including the one you shot in Paris and/or the South of France last summer,[4] and The Criminal Life of Archibaldo de la Cruz?

In closing, may I convey the regards of Jean Cocteau, who said some very nice things about This Strange Passion.

The best to you and your family for the New Year: may it be one of Peace for us all.

Cordially,
Aaron Sloan
Omnifilms, Inc.
229 West 42 Street, New York 36,

Eng Tls L, AB/691.13; BDM 113 f

---

[1] Secretary at Omnifilms.
[2] Including a very negative review by Abe Weiler, 'This Strange Passion, a Mexican Import', The New York Times (5 December 1955), p. 34.
[3] Held at ABR/2048.
[4] That is the Dawn.

From Jean Ferry

Paris, 20 February 1956[1]

My dear Buñuel,
    I have just seen That is the Dawn.[2]
    I'm enclosing a copy of my letter to Monsieur Ténoudji explaining the reasons why I refuse to appear in the credits.
    I hope that the film is a great success.

With my eternal regrets,
Jean Ferry
51 rue Bonaparte

Strictly confidential

Dear Mr Tenoudji,

I have finally, after turning down numerous requests during shooting of the film and after its conclusion, watched *That is the Dawn*.

I hope sincerely that for your sake (and that of for Marchal,[3] who is an admirable man), the film will be a success on all levels, intellectual and financial.

It would be quite unjust, however, if any such success were to be associated with my name. I must confess that none of the ideas for the plot and dialogue attributed to me in the credits, with excessive generosity, would ever have occurred to me, and that I was not consulted nor even aware of their existence before the screening.

As far as dialogue goes, it is not necessarily so very serious, because anyone of my acquaintance will know I write French with a certain degree of ease. No one would ever associate my name with something that seems to have been written in Swiss or Belgian, or some other language that is truly difficult to define, but is certainly not French. Even someone looking for reasons to attack me would not believe I could plumb such depths of mediocrity, if one may speak of depths, that is, when charting such a vacuum.

As for the plot, it was not I who rendered the relationship between Clara and the doctor[4] completely incomprehensible, but a series of mind-boggling cuts. It was not I who had the brilliant idea of indicating the degree of lyrical and ardent passion of the lovers with a heated scene (that I hope will provoke much mirth) where the gentleman takes off his socks and massages his toes, while the woman brings him a fine bowl of steaming soup. I am more than concerned about this, I am beside myself with rage to discover that the wonderful love story between Clara and Valerio we were so deeply moved by has been so crudely dishonoured, sabotaged and ridiculed to the point of ending on the grotesque suggestion of some kind of *ménage à trois*. That decision, so hostile to love and women, plays no small part in freezing the human warmth that permeates the book* and that has been systematically and mercilessly hounded out here ... to be replaced, incidentally, with nothing.

Given its theme, this should have been a romantic, even an excessively romantic film.

And God only knows what faith I had in Buñuel to achieve this. And yet ...

It was not I (who had neither voice nor vote, and you may remember my timid complaints in this respect) who decided to place a volume by Claudel[5] on the policeman's desk (what is achieved by that idiotic provocation?), nor to have him recite parts of Claudel verbatim (my dialogue was stripped right back to nothing because, as far as I can see, there was no space left for it!).

It was not I who came up with the nauseatingly vulgar idea of pushing a dying woman on a cart through a village fiesta (and what a fiesta!). Nor of including an incomprehensible cock-fighting sequence, the purpose of which no one could fathom. Unless it was, of course, to replace one of the love scenes I wrote for Clara and Valerio; or, more deplorably, to suppress certain moments of transition so ineptly that at times one struggles to follow the story.

It was not I who introduced 750 cats into the film; it was not I who... etc., etc.

In short, it is not I who should be applauded if the film is, as I hope and reiterate, a success. Nor should I be criticized by people who share my opinion of it. Those who substituted my work for their own (and I don't know who they all are, as no one had the courtesy to advise of their participation) should take full responsibility.[6] I am aware that my contract agrees to all possible and imaginable alteration to my work. That clause has been applied above and beyond all possible expectation (and misgiving). I am now simply asking to apply the clause that authorizes me to remove my own name from the credits and all publicity.[7]

A scriptwriter is of little account and I hope you will forgive the ridiculous fervour with which I defend myself here, or rather, with which I defend the expectations I had of this film. If I am indifferent to my name being associated with certain projects, by definition less far-reaching, this is not the case with Buñuel, for whom I have always had the highest esteem.

With profound regret, I remain at your disposition.
[Jean Ferry]

PS I am sending a copy of this letter to Mr Jaeger and Mr Buñuel, who have a right to know the reason for my decision, although that said, as far as I am concerned the matter is now closed and you have my word that none of the opinions expressed here to you in confidence, will be communicated by me in public or in private to anyone else.

* And if Mr Roblès expresses his satisfaction, all the better, no?

Fre Tls L, AB/691.9

1   Asterisked note by Ferry.
2   Private screening, as the film premiere was on 9 May 1956.
3   Georges Marchal (1920–97), French actor, lead actor in *That is the Dawn* and *Death in the Garden*, with parts in *Belle de Jour* and *The Milky Way*.
4   The protagonists of the film, Clara (Bosé) and Dr Valerio (Marchal).
5   Paul Claudel (1868–1955), French Catholic poet; LB also places a copy of Dalí's painting *Christ of Saint John of the Cross* (1951) on the wall of the police commissioner's office, a barely veiled criticism of both artists.
6   Laroche, Roblès and LB.
7   Request apparently denied as Ferry's name does appear in the film credits.

New projects and old (1956–61)

Figure 47 Buñuel, between America and Europe, *c.* 1956.

To Juan Larrea

Mexico City, 16 April 1956

Dear Juan,

Both your telegrams have arrived. Of the first, I shall say only that *Pallida mors aequo pulsat pede pauperum tabernas regumque turres.*[1] Of the second, here goes:

The Past: we have been trying for nine years, and in every possible way, to pursue the insane enterprise of *Illegible, Son of a Flute*,[2] offering not only to work for free, but even to put in some of our own miserable money. A resounding failure.

The Present: given the credit I now have, thanks be to God, I am unexpectedly able to revive this project. Barbachano Productions[3] has released two international hits: *Raíces*[4] and *¡Torero!*[5] The illegible Carlos Velo is Barbachano's right-hand man.[6] And the three of us, after an expansive supper, made an unbelievable pact to produce *Illegible, Son of a Flute* as a commercial film.

Bear in mind Juan, that no one else in the world would have taken this on …

1) The film only runs to five reels, an anti-commercial length *par excellence*.[7]
2) It is therefore unmarketable across North and South America, except, should people like it, in little specialized theatres in the United States.
3) It has great potential, though on a smaller scale, in Europe.
4) The final part on the island needs work, and we'll only use a few sections. We all feel it's not nearly as good as the rest.
5) We must expand it to seven reels, condition *sine qua non*.
6) I asked them for the union-agreed minimum of 24,000 pesos for the story or screenplay and, incredibly, they agreed. Half each: although I will, of course, give you the entire sum.
7) As the director, I also requested the minimum fee for four weeks' work, which is 30,000 pesos, and I thought I would give you 10,000 for your return ticket if you should come over. Bear in mind that I charge 125,000 pesos per film in Mexico and $40,000 in France, so you can see the reduction I'm offering, knowing this is a film no one else in the world would make.
8) *If I don't have a letter from you giving me total carte blanche, I won't make the film. That's why I wanted you to come over* and spend 10 days getting everything ready. If we don't make it in June, I won't be able to be involved, because I've signed a contract to start working on a French film in July, *Fever Mounts at El Pao*[8] that I have to film in October. Then, that is, in January 1958, I start on an English film called *The Loved One*[9] with Alec Guinness[10] which I won't finish until April.
9) So, there's no way I could work on *Illegible, Son of a Flute* until the middle of next year, but would Barbachano and Velo still want to make it by then? I don't think so.
10) The only solution as I see it is this: we start working on it, by letter, dialogues, etc.,[11] and *gratis*. When we have it ready and seven rolls long, I'll try and get them

to sign a contract agreeing to make it within 18 months, and to give me a small advance that I would send you. The advance could be about 10,000 pesos.

11) About getting a further $1,000 for the *scénario*, absolutely no chance. I could, though, ask for a share of the profits.

My very best wishes to Lucianne and, of course, to you,
Luis

PS If we don't make *Illegible, Son of a Flute,* we'll have to blame the astral distance we would need to overcome to meet up. You will, though, know that I have been steadfast. I still think the film is very good, although ... it does have its aestheticist, or even, forgive me, Cocteauist moments. At others, it reeks of stale Buñuel. The scenes on the island are all inferior to the rest: instead of raising the film up, it collapses. These are, *grosso modo*, the main shortcomings I see in *Illegible, Son of a Flute.*

Spa Tls, AF; *ILE* 63–64

---

1   'Pale Death, with impartial tread, beats at the poor man's cottage door and at the palaces of kings', line from an ode by Horace quoted by Cervantes in the prologue to *Don Quijote.*
2   *Illegible, Son of a Flute,* or *Illegible, Son of a Trumpet,* according to Larrea's own translation (undated), Filmoteca española, Buñuel Archive, and reproduced in Gabriele Morelli, *Ilegible, hijo de flauta* (Sevilla: Renacimiento, 2007).
3   Manuel Barbachano Ponce (1925–94), independent Mexican producer.
4   *Raíces* (1955), dir. Benito Alazraki, awarded FIPRESCI prize at Cannes in 1955.
5   Awarded Special Mention by the Jury at Venice Festival 1956; nominated for the Oscar for Best Documentary in 1957.
6   Velo and Barbancho co-founded the company, EMA, that produced the weekly film news programme *Tele Revista.*
7   A commercial feature, at no less than seven rolls, lasts longer than seventy-five minutes.
8   *La fiebre sube a El Pao*; Mexican title, *Los ambiciosos*, French-Mexican co-production filmed, eventually, by LB in 1959.
9   Adaptation of novel by Evelyn Waugh, *The Loved One* (1948), that LB is preparing with Hugo Butler.
10   English actor (1914–2000).
11   Larrea has settled in Córdoba, Argentina.

To José Rubia Barcia

Mexico City, 28 October 1956

Dear Barcia,

I was so very pleased to get your letter. It was well over a year since I last heard from you and I acknowledge, to my shame, that I owed you a letter. I find it harder to write every day, although I recognize that writing letters is an effective way of keeping friendships alive.

Jeanne and I really enjoyed the charming photo of your clan. Evita looks beautiful and the girls, who take after you both, are adorable.

You said in your last letter, written a long while ago, that you would be going to Europe. It's such a shame we didn't coincide in Paris, where I've been spending almost half my time for three years now. I've now finished two films in France,[1] and I'm going back next February to make a third, set in Switzerland. My latest films, I'm happy to say – thank God – are just as non-conformist as my first ones. Although I do fare better and have many more friends in Paris, I actually prefer the tomb-like peace I enjoy here. I would travel to North America now and then, but I asked for a visa a year ago and they turned me down.[2] I'll put in another request in a few months … we'll see what happens.

As I said, I'll be going back to France in February and staying there until early July. I think you're planning your trip here with Evita around then. It goes without saying that you are 'obliged' to stay with us. Imagine what a wonderful time we'll have. Whatever happens, just give me a week's notice before you arrive.

Now that it can't be [put off] any longer because you don't have my address, please send the piece you mentioned.[3] I'm very interested to see what course it has now take, or if the same course, how far it has travelled. Letting my fingers wander across the keys makes me pedantic. Really, I only want to know what you're doing for the simple pleasure – and interest – in reading your latest work.

I'll be seeing León Felipe next Monday, that is, the day after tomorrow (I sometimes don't set eyes on him for three years at a time), because they are showing a film[4] neither of us has seen. The director, Carlos Velo, told me León would be at the screening. I'll send you a quick note on Tuesday with that address you wanted because I don't have it with me.

Without more ado, and with warmest regards until Tuesday,
Buñuel

PS León Felipe, Calle Miguel Schultz 73, Mexico City. I got his address from a friend. I'll see León tomorrow and pass on your request.

Spa Tlsps, CBC; *CLB* 68–70

[1]   *That is the Dawn* and *Death in the Garden*, French-Mexican co-productions filmed by LB in Mexico between March and April 1956.
[2]   US government prohibited entry due to LB's former affiliation with the Communist Party.
[3]   Script of *Umbral de sueños*.
[4]   *Torero!*

From Luis García-Abrines[1]

New Haven, February (whatever the day may be) 1957

Dear Distinguished Genius,

It's a while since I wrote, years in fact, and naturally you did not reply. Adolfo Salazar[2] told me you were His Royal Highness, or something like that. I think you will know who I am. My father was a doctor to you and your family.[3] I think he treated your ears. Unsuccessfully, I fear, because I've been told you are quite deaf. When my brother Adolfo[4] finished studying at Stanford and went to Mexico I told him he should look you up and he did just that. And to end this introduction, I should say that I know all the Buñuels except for you and your family. And that's enough of that, for Christ's sake!

I am writing this time to send you an article I've written about you.[5] I'm quite annoyed, because I asked your nephew Leonardo[6] to send me some information, and to write to you to clarify some details and see if I could publish some photographs, etc. And that monster hasn't written to me for months. If there are mistakes in my article you will have to shout at him, not me. You should also shout at the editor[7] of *Yale French Studies,* because he cut out precisely half of it. The background to the article is brief. I am at Yale teaching Spanish Literature and the aforementioned journal asked me to write an article on Spanish film. I told them the only interesting thing about Spain was you and that, if they wanted me to write something, it would be about you and only you. They accepted, and when Leonardo and his wife came to stay for a few days at my house, I discussed it with him and now you know the rest. Please believe me when I say that I wrote the article out of the greatest admiration and respect. If you don't like it, even bearing in mind all the aforementioned extenuating circumstances, please forgive me. My intention was to celebrate Spain, Aragón and Luis Buñuel, in a journal that is well known throughout North American academia.

The anecdotes they have published were told to me by your brother Alfonso and by José Camón.[8] They didn't publish others that Ángel del Río told me,[9] including the one about how you hypnotized him and turned him into a lion. So, I am pretty annoyed about all that too, believe me. One thing I'm quite pleased about is that they haven't cut much of what I said about your mother, Doña María, of whom I am so very fond. She, as you know, regards everyone as good, she simply doesn't understand malice, the result being that she is the only truly good person in the whole of Zaragoza. I'm also sending the article to your mother and to Alfonso.[10] I know he will say it's utter rubbish. I know him well.

Every year here at Yale we screen *Land Without Bread, An Andalusian Dog* and *The Young and the Damned.* We also occasionally screen *This Strange Passion* and *Robinson Crusoe.* Last year I wanted to give a lecture on *The Golden Age.* I wrote to the Museum of Modern Art in New York, but they wrote back saying that they didn't have a copy and that, in any case, it was banned in the United States and had never been screened. I would really like to show it at a private screening for the Faculty here at Yale. Nobody knows about it here, and they bust my balls going on and on about *Le Sang d'un poète.* Can you provide a solution? If it didn't cost too much, I would gladly have a copy made for me, with your permission of course. If you were in New York and had a couple of days free and were interested, you could bring it along and give the lecture yourself. That would be really wonderful. Although, to be clear, I should let you know that Yale doesn't pay much for lectures. I don't think they paid Stravinsky much either when he gave a lecture at Harvard on the poetics of music.[11] They would give you precisely $50, which would just about cover your transport costs. All board and lodgings would be covered by Yale: the department would hold a dinner for you and invite the Faculty; the Dean would hold a small drinks party for you, with all the whole Faculty again; and I would be completely at your disposal naturally, as would my home so that, if you came with your wife or one of your sons, they would be able to stay with me. Let me know what you think.

It would make me very happy if you like the article; and I send my warmest greetings to your wife, your children, and to you from your unconditional friend,

Luis García-Abrines
137 College Street, Yale University
New Haven, Connecticut

[PS] Do you have an address for Mantecón and Millares?[12] I have a palaeography question and I wanted to consult with them before I publish an article on fifteenth-century falconry texts.

Here's a *jota* in your honour, if you haven't heard it already:

Saint Lawrence sat on the pyre
And said to the Jews in ire:
Throw more wood on, you bastards, be bold,
For my balls, they are growing quite cold

Let me know if you'd like more copies and I'll send them. I'm enclosing a programme and supplement for *Don* Adolfo Salazar. I haven't written to him for years. Please ask him to forgive me. I will write. I've had a very Baroja-esque life. I clashed with my family, with society, with politics and with the Church. I left for Paris, where I lived for two years.[13] Then I got married[14] and came to the United States. I'll have to write to him and hope he can forgive me.

Spa Tls, AB/1366

[1] Artist and hispanist (1923–2016), exiled in the United States from 1954, lecturer at Yale University.
[2] Musicologist and composer (1890–1958), exiled in Mexico from 1939.
[3] Adolfo García-Abrines (1886–1968), ear, nose and throat specialist.
[4] Adolfo García-Abrines Calvo, Masters in Engineering from Stanford, California, in 1950.
[5] L. García-Abrines, 'Rebirth of Buñuel', *Yale French Studies*, no. 17 (Summer 1956), pp. 54–66.
[6] Leonardo García Buñuel, son of Pedro García and Conchita Buñuel.
[7] Kenneth Douglas, editor of the special edition on Film, *Yale French Studies*, that included this article by García-Abrines.
[8] José Camón Aznar (1898–1979), art historian.
[9] Historian and hispanist (1901–62), exiled in the United States, lecturer at Columbia University.
[10] Alfonso Buñuel.
[11] Stravinsky gave six lectures at Harvard between 1939 and 1940.
[12] Agustín Millares Carlo (1893–1980), palaeographer, exiled to Mexico in 1939.
[13] From 1952 to 1954.
[14] To Margaret Jounakos, his first wife.

To Juan Larrea

Mexico City, 13 April 1957

BARBACHANO PRODUCTIONS, MEXICO, HAVE DECIDED TO MAKE *ILLEGIBLE, SON OF A FLUTE*. FILMING IN JUNE PAYING YOU $2,000. YOU NEED TO COME IMMEDIATELY FOR TEN DAYS TO REVISE PLOT WITH ME OR GIVE ME PERMISSION TO DO SO. IF COMING, ROUND TRIP WILL BE FUNDED.

REGARDS,
LUIS

Spa Asp, AF; *ILE* 71 f

From Juan Larrea

Córdoba, 14 April 1957

WONDERFUL. TRIP IMPOSSIBLE. I WANT 3,000 PLUS SHARE OF PROFITS. CARTE BLANCHE WITH PROVISOS. I WILL WRITE.[1]

REGARDS TO ALL,
JUAN

Spa Tel, AF; *ILE* 72

[1] Letters from Larrea to LB, 16 and 28 April 1957 (*ILE* 73–79).

To Juan Larrea

Mexico City, 29 April 1957

Dear Juan,

I was very pleased to read your news in the letter that crossed paths with mine to you. I imagine you will have received it by now.

Here is the final result of the negotiations and counter-negotiations. I assure you that this is our best offer and you will have to take my word for this.

As soon as I have your reply to this letter, I will register *Illegible, Son of a Flute* with the Union of Authors and Adaptors of the STPC[1] as a story by Juan Larrea and Luis Buñuel for which the Barbachano company will pay us 12,500 pesos. Larrea will pay 10 per cent on his share (6,250 pesos) and Buñuel, as a union member, only 6 per cent on his share. As I said, I will pass the entire sum over to you. I have managed to get

Barbachano to agree to pay the union subs, and the tax so the 12,500 pesos that is, $1,000, will remain intact.

Then there's adaptation, for which I will be paid a further 12,500 pesos, with Barbachano covering the 6 per cent union subs. And I say, I will be paid because your name can't appear on the adaptation because you're not a union member. It's ridiculous, but that's how it is. I'll get half when I sign the contract and the other half when I submit the adaptation before 1 August. I'll give both sums to you in full. In other words, you will have $1,500 at your disposal.

You can let me know in what form and where I should deposit or send it. It would be best if someone in Córdoba were to pay you in Argentine currency – exchanged at black market rate – and I were to pay someone you choose here in dollars. We will be paid the remaining $500 in August.

All the above depends on whether you accept these conditions or not. I can say in advance though that, whatever your decision, you have my full support.

The screen credits would be as follows: '*Illegible, Son of a Flute.* Story by Juan Larrea and Luis Buñuel. Based on a lost text by Juan Larrea'. And the final credit would say: 'Film adaptation and direction: Luis Buñuel'.

If you accept, I'll get to work straight away, because we have to extend the original *scénario* by about two reels to turn it into a feature, this being the condition *sine qua non*. Of course, you would also need to think about it and send any ideas that occur to you, as well as writing any necessary dialogues, revising mine, etc.

I haven't worked for a year now, but I'm now preparing two films I've signed contracts for: one in French and Spanish versions, the other in English.[2] I start the first on the 15 October and the second in February 1958.[3] So, after 1 August I won't be able to work on *Illegible, Son of a Flute* until we begin filming in April 1958.

I'm enclosing five copies of the contract which, if you accept the terms, you should initial on the first page then sign on the last. Keep a copy for yourself and send me the other four by registered post.

I completely agree we should avoid any allusions to the on-going conflict between embattled, political powers.[4] And if any allusions should arise, as these are such terrible times and we are not going to censor ourselves, we shall take no partisan stance. Anything but grubby political propaganda in such a poetic film.

A big hug for Lucianne and an even bigger one for you,
Luis

[PS] I nearly forgot: five years after the film is released, you would get another $1,000.

This sum comes from the so-called 'small artistic rights' fund which the union charges the studio.

Write this address down: Félix, not Felipe![5]

Spa Tlsps, AF; *ILE* 80–82

---

[1]   Union of Film Production Workers.
[2]   *Fever Mounts at El Pao* and *The Loved One.*
[3]   Both postponed.

⁴ Reference to Larrea's comment in letter to LB, 16 April 1957: 'What would be unacceptable to me would be to find my name associated with something that might wilfully be mis-interpreted as positioning myself in favour of the USSR over the US' (*ILE* 74).
⁵ LB's address in Cerrada Félix Cuevas.

To Juan Larrea

Mexico City, 13 May 1957

Dear Juan,

Your letter arrived about ten days ago, with several sheets of magnificently, illegiblesque ideas, and I'm grateful for both.¹ I, on the other hand, am an abominable sloth when it comes to deciding to write, even when the topic is of such interest to me as this one.

I shall now give you my succinct opinion on the gags and scenarios you sent. I really liked, more than all the others, number one, where the man with the donkey comes across the little group of *Illegible, Son of a Flute* and his friends. It's fresh, original and full of humour. In contrast, my least favourite – banal, facile wit – is the one with the Coca Cola advert. The scenes with the Jehovah's Witnesses and the pillow fight with Don Quixote and Sancho are very good. But given the resources at my disposal, I don't think we can use it. I don't like the penances Carrillo hands out on *The Favourables* (good name for a boat): I find the humour too 'clerical', too 'nice', too scatological ... But I do like it when Napoleon appears. I'd pass on the gypsy episode (superfluous, in my opinion); and on the funnel, which is comical but not funny; but the wooden chest with a monocle and teeth is better and does grab my attention, although it's more literary than cinematic. The slanted horizon, very disturbing and very good. The ending is better than it was, but I'm still not completely satisfied with it yet. As for the music ... I can't stand it when it's used to emphasize or highlight an image, or when it's used as a theme tune for characters or emotions. I am completely against any kind of musical accompaniment or illustration, as you can see from my latest films, which *have no music*. On the other hand, it makes sense when it's part of the film action. For example: someone enters a nightclub where a tango is being played. In this case, Long Live the Tango, because it is part of the film and not some clumsy 'artistic' trick.

I've made a start on the adaptation, and when I have the first 30 pages (it will be nearly 90 pages long) I'll send you a copy to see what you think. I am happy for the story to be accredited exclusively to you, but the adaptation, how can you do it with me if we aren't here together?² Also, filming can't go ahead unless it's registered by the Authors and Adaptors section,³ and they won't accept anyone who has not 'sold and been paid for five scripts, of which *at least three* have been made into films'. An adaptor is a writer familiar with cinematic technique. The only (?) solution to the credits is the one I suggested in my last letter or, if you prefer, this one: 'Story by Juan Larrea, adapted by Buñuel'. So, let me know your thoughts on this soon.

As for the fee, I personally guarantee that you will be paid $3,000, the only thing being that the final $1,000 will come from the Union (without fail) in five years' time. I don't think there's any more I could have done.

I've put my work on hold until we can come to an agreement that is wholly satisfactory to you. If we can't, it would be better to put the whole project temporarily on hold until we find a solution. I hope to hear from you soon.

Warmest regards from,
Luis

[PS] This may be the most accurate and authentic solution. What do you think? 'Story by Juan Larrea. Based on an unpublished book by the same author. Adaptation and direction by Luis Buñuel'. After the film is made, *if it's a success*, you could write the book. It would sell really well ...

Spa Tlsps, AF; *ILE* 83–85

¹   In his letter to LB, 28 April 1957 (*ILE* 76–79), Larrea added eight new, numbered sequences to the script (*ILE* 215–232), with notes on the use of music.
²   Larrea proposed shared credit for the adaptation (*ILE* 79).
³   The STPC.

To Juan Larrea

Mexico City, 7 June 1957

Dear Juan,
       Your latest letter has arrived¹ and I see you definitely agree to the formula for the credits being 'original story by Juan Larrea, based on ...' Good. Everyone's happy.
       At the end of April, I sent you the contracts by registered post, in which both our names appear as the authors. They were signed by me and Barbachano, and there was a space for you to sign. You didn't say whether you received them. If you have them, send them back to me without signing so I can destroy them; if they didn't reach you, let me know anyway so they can be reclaimed from the post office.
       I'm sending new contracts with this letter, naming you as sole author. If you agree with what I say below, sign them and send them back to us at once, because the agreement has to be ready, signed by both parties and paid for, before the collective labour contract between the Production Union and the Association of Producers² expires; in other words, by very early July. If not, the entire project may fall through.
       So that in the future no clouds may 'cast a shadow on our *entente*', I shall now tell you, entirely frankly, my thoughts on the making *Illegible, Son of a Flute* and, to do so, I shall start with a little history.
       After having not thought about our *scénario* for eight or more years, I decided, one day, to read it. I liked it a lot as a spiritual action film, but so many dreadful things had happened in the world since it was written I felt a lot of the scenes and some of the angles no longer made sense. Today, I can honestly say that I would be

incapable of making a film that ends with 'the miraculous growth of wheat sown by two Spaniards on a promised land'. I would suggest that, if that scene is left in, the film needs to end with a profound question mark over the destiny of mankind, and I'm only saying this to come to some sort of compromise with you, because I totally agree with the words you put in the mouth of the Jehovah's Witness: 'WHO CAN DOUBT THAT THESE ARE THE LAST DAYS? WHO IS SO BLIND AS TO IGNORE THE SIGNS RAINING DOWN ON NATIONS? THE END OF THE WORLD IS NIGH.' That is the kind of apocalyptic tone that resonates best with my current beliefs.

During the reading I'm talking about, some of the gags seemed very rusty to me, like the *walkie-talkie* that *Illegible, Son of a Flute* digs up, completely *démodés*.[3] Others, however, still worked just as well. As examples of vanguard film, I would cite: the roast pigeon on the head of the Thinker, the telephone emerging from between the eyebrows, the map of the brain with the little flags.

Examples of stale Buñuel: the shark in the coffin and the monks in the crate.

'Excessive' artistry: the cosmic symphony fishermen.

Political, the Peace movement: the little dove flying out of the suitcase (I'm sure something much better could fly out, something truly portentous. Let's see who can come up with it).

I could maybe give you some more examples, but these are enough to give you a sense of my thoughts. I found the rest really poetic, energetic and relevant.

I'll send you the adaptation, and I should like the ending, if not pessimistic (my position), at least to be inquiring, that might be our compromise. I'm aiming for a completely realistic tone, with no vanguard tricks, using apparently *everyday* images to express the poetic and far from *everyday* theme. At other points, of course, we'll have no choice but to use striking images. Your gag about the man with the donkey is an excellent example of the 'form'. The elements of the scene are commonplace: countryside, some friends walking, a man coming in the opposite direction, a banal conversation ... but the content is mysterious, full of originality and, above all, *humour*.

As I am a very mediocre correspondent, I shall bring this letter to a close. I'm sure what I've said in it will be enough to give you an idea of my vision, which is absolutely essential as I'm going to be making a film based on your work.

I would be grateful if you could reply at once, for the reasons explained. For now, work on the adaptation is mostly on hold.

My warmest regards to both of you,
Luis

[PS] Let me know how you want me to send you the money and where.

Spa Tlsps, AF; *ILE* 88–90

---

[1] Letter from Larrea to LB, 22 May 1957 (*ILE* 86–87).

[2] Asociación de Productores Mexicanos de Películas to which Barbachano belongs.

[3] French in the original.

From James Quinn[1]

London, 8 July 1957

ON BEHALF OF EDINBURGH FILM FESTIVAL[2] I HAVE THE HONOUR TO INVITE YOU TO BE THIS YEAR'S PRESIDENT. FESTIVAL IS FROM 18 AUGUST TO 8 SEPTEMBER AND WE HOPE IT WOULD BE POSSIBLE FOR YOU TO VISIT FESTIVAL BETWEEN THESE DATES.

KINDEST REGARDS[3].
JAMES QUINN

Eng Tel, AB/1426.98

[1] Film producer and exhibitor (1919–2008), director of British Film Institute from 1955 to 1964.
[2] Founded in 1947.
[3] LB did not attend.

To Juan Larrea

Mexico City, 29 July 1957

Dear Juan,

I hope you've received the two cheques; the first is full payment for the story, that is, for the existing screenplay; the second is an advance on the adaptation I'm working on now. But as you hardly 'epistolarize', I don't know if you got them.[1]

I'm enclosing the first 43 pages of my adaptation-*découpage*. I hope that when you check them through that new ideas will come to you and, above all, that you will improve the dialogues. As you'll see, the action only goes up to the conversation between Illegible and Avendaño on the train and yet it already has as many pages as the entire original screenplay. That's because the adaptation needs to have every possible detail about what is happening, step-by-step, as well as new scenes that come up and short dialogues that, without all the detail, it's difficult to foresee.

Nevertheless, I'm really behind schedule and I'm not (or should I say, 'we're not', because I've taken on the responsibility for both of us) making a very good impression. The thing is, I have a lot of work for the other things I'm preparing and that I committed to before setting out on our adventure with *Illegible, Son of a Flute*. So … Help!! Give me a hand with whatever you can!

The fourth part of the story, that is the scenes from the shipwreck to the end, seem weaker each time I look at them. And I'm not talking about the gags, I'm thinking of using almost all of those, even the one with the shark and the monks stuffed in the crate like sardines in a can. I'm talking more about the narrative, what happens. I'm now convinced we should cut Don Quijote and Sancho (although not Illegible and Avendaño), because, as well as the trite and very straightforward symbolism, they have already been done to death, especially in literature. Only Spaniards would get the full sense of what's going on in that fourth part. It needs to be more universal, and less local or national. In a book, you can generalize and universalize a specific theme. But in a film, you get what you see. It may be that our intentions with *Illegible, Son of a Flute* transcend the form. In any case, I MUST ASK YOU TO TRY AND WRITE A NEW VERSION OF THE FINAL PART. I'll try and do the same. I'm not worried about the rest because the narrative works well up to the shipwreck. We just have to find something else for the suitcase, to replace the little dove (of peace?).

From the lush forest of scenarios and gags you sent me I'm only going to use the one about the man leading a donkey, or pig, who meets our heroes, and the one about the submarine and the Coca Cola shout. For one reason or another, I can't use any of the others. The one with the Jehovah's Witnesses for example, is just impossible to film, without a 5-million-dollar budget. The cinematic imagination has to work with the limits of budget and production. So, if you come up with new ideas, try to avoid new sets and crowds, as well as complicated tricks or effects. You'll see what I've come up with when I send you the rest of the adaptation. I hope you will give me your *unbiased*[2] opinion of them, as I have of yours.

Try, Juan, and send me all the ideas and suggestions you can come up with as soon as you can. We really need to keep to our side of the deal.

Very warmest regards to Lucianne and to you,
Luis

[PS] Tell Lucianne I'll give her two *duros*[3] if she can think up something good to go into or come out of suitcase. Two fabulous *machacantes*![4]

I promised to hand in the *découpage* on the 1st of August!!

Spa Tlsps, AF; *ILE* 100 f

[1] Larrea confirmed receipt of both cheques in a letter to Barbachano of 8 July 1957 (*ILE* 96).
[2] English in the original.
[3] 'Duro', commonly used term for the old Spanish 5-peseta coin, now still in use meaning 'coin'.
[4] 'Machacantes' (two silver coins/'duros').

From Juan Larrea

Córdoba, 6 August 1957

Dear Luis,

Your letter with the first part of your adaptation of *Illegible, Son of a Flute* arrived yesterday and your telegram today. What a disappointment! Of all the material we sent you, you only found a use for two details which, *by themselves*, seem really insignificant, one of which in particular, is just a bit of nonsense. It will come as no surprise to you therefore, that our enthusiasm for the search for novelties currently stands at the unenviable position of less than zero.

However, that is not important. What is, on the other hand, and fundamentally so for me, is that you dispensed with the Jehovah's Witnesses scene because, so you say, you do not have a $5 million budget. Lucianne swears blind that with modern laboratory techniques and in the style of a commercially imperfect film with which some of the other effects are conceived, the shooting of that particular adventure does not pose an insurmountable obstacle. I don't know and don't care to know. What I do know is that in my letter to you of 22 May I expressed my concern at the notion that scene (the one you thought was 'very good') might be cut as I could not imagine the film without it, and I begged you to reassure me in that respect. This was my measured way of letting you know that this was a condition of the *sine qua non* kind. As you did not reply to this point and as silence, as they say, implies consent, I was persuaded, as I explained on 14 June, to return the signed contract to you so as not to waste any more of your time and to spare you any further trouble, but warning you that I was doing so on the assumption that you would include that scene, which I consider, for many reasons, to be indispensable, critical.

The contract is now signed of course, and the law is completely on your side, but in my view the rules that apply to you and me are those that govern behaviour between friends, and I am speaking to you now in that belief. If that scene is cut I would prefer to abandon the film.

And I would prefer that to be the case to such a degree that I am returning the $1,500. That money was almost vital to us but, as you know from your own experience, some things matter more than money. I believe you will understand that this is not about being fanciful or stubborn. *Illegible, Son of a Flute* has become essential to my life, as something both prophetic of our times and those that will follow. For me that scene – perfectly realized – is so important, in terms of its universality, truth and transcendence that, in my view, its absence justifies the failure to make the film in 1948 and the failure to make it in 1957. To cut it out is to behead the story, to strip it of its fundamental purpose. It may seem excessive or even ridiculous to you, but that is how it is. And so, I implore you in the strongest possible terms that if you cannot find a technical solution to these obstacles, that you honour our friendship and ignore the contract I sent to you under the circumstances I have explained.

In general, we liked your adaptation, although not, for example, the sequence with the hussar which, with its forced French *fin-de-siècle*[1] effect, seemed to me to leave a lot to be desired. Also, I think it is a grave error, not to say an act of contempt, that you have taken the idea of the noisy, but invisible city from the Jehovah's Witness scene, with all its expressive and pertinent grandeur, and moved it to the train station scene, where it is just a pointless bauble. It is a bit like the footprint in the sand that was completely incongruous in your *Robinson Crusoe*. Some of the dialogues also seem a little weak to me.

Lucianne really thought she had hit the nail on the head with the content of the suitcase. Although that does not really say much, of course.

I am sorry if this causes you any embarrassment Luis, but, as they say in these unstable lands: no way! I am surely the more annoyed and disadvantaged party. None of which means I am any less grateful for the willingness you have shown towards us, nor that I neglect to send you, as always, my most cordial regards,

Juan

Spa Cmfa, AB/572.21; *CLB* 175–177

[1] 'End of the (nineteenth) century', French in the original.

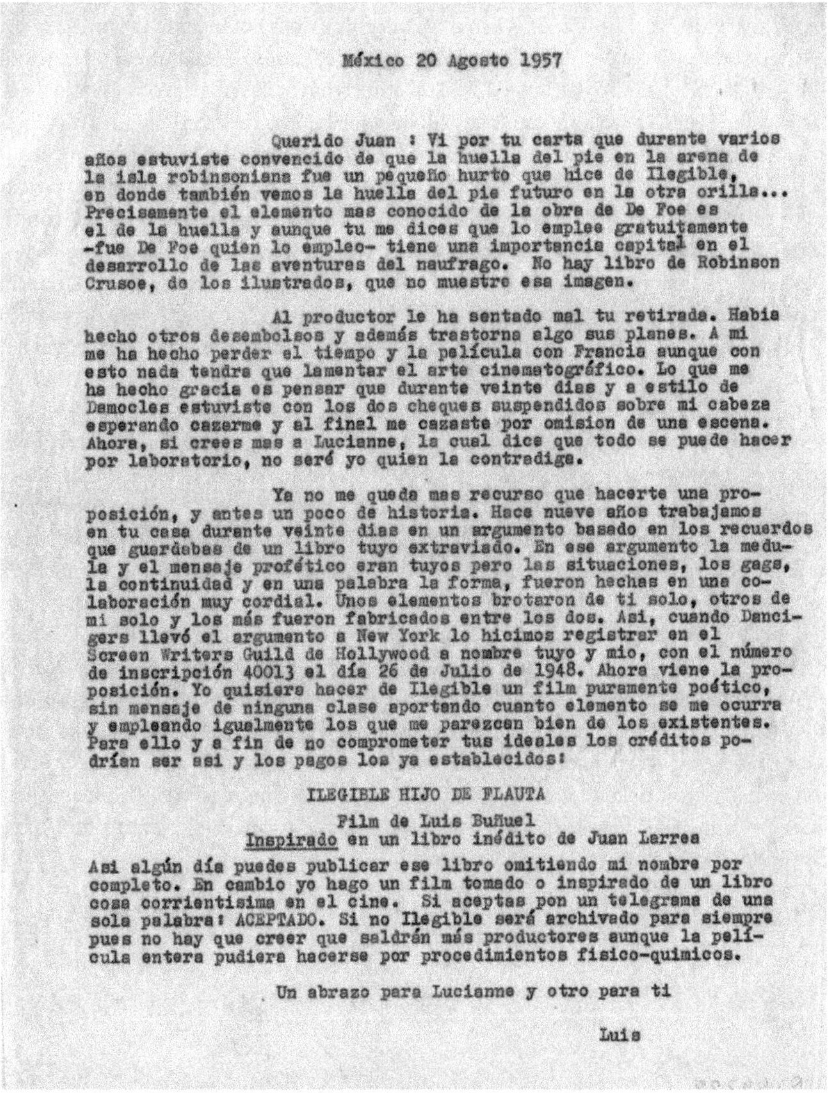

México 20 Agosto 1957

Querido Juan : Vi por tu carta que durante varios
años estuviste convencido de que la huella del pie en la arena de
la isla robinsoniana fue un pequeño hurto que hice de Ilegible,
en donde también vemos la huella del pie futuro en la otra orilla...
Precisamente el elemento mas conocido de la obra de De Foe es
el de la huella y aunque tu me dices que lo emplee gratuitamente
—fue De Foe quien lo empleo— tiene una importancia capital en el
desarrollo de las aventuras del naufrago. No hay libro de Robinson
Crusoe, de los ilustrados, que no muestre esa imagen.

Al productor le ha sentado mal tu retirada. Había
hecho otros desembolsos y además trastorna algo sus planes. A mi
me ha hecho perder el tiempo y la película con Francia aunque con
esto nada tendrá que lamentar el arte cinematográfico. Lo que me
ha hecho gracia es pensar que durante veinte días y a estilo de
Damocles estuviste con los dos cheques suspendidos sobre mi cabeza
esperando cazarme y al final me cazaste por omision de una escena.
Ahora, si crees mas a Lucianne, la cual dice que todo se puede hacer
por laboratorio, no seré yo quien la contradiga.

Ya no me queda mas recurso que hacerte una pro-
posición, y antes un poco de historia. Hace nueve años trabajamos
en tu casa durante veinte dias en un argumento basado en los recuerdos
que guardabas de un libro tuyo extraviado. En ese argumento la medu-
la y el mensaje profético eran tuyos pero las situaciones, los gags,
la continuidad y en una palabra la forma, fueron hechas en una colaboración muy cordial. Unos elementos brotaron de ti solo, otros de
mi solo y los más fueron fabricados entre los dos. Asi, cuando Dancigers llevó el argumento a New York lo hicimos registrar en el
Screen Writers Guild de Hollywood a nombre tuyo y mio, con el número
de inscripción 40013 el día 26 de Julio de 1948. Ahora viene la pro-
posición. Yo quisiera hacer de Ilegible un film puramente poético,
sin mensaje de ninguna clase aportando cuanto elemento se me ocurra
y empleando igualmente los que me parezcan bien de los existentes.
Para ello y a fin de no comprometer tus ideales los créditos po-
drían ser asi y los pagos los ya establecidos:

ILEGIBLE HIJO DE FLAUTA

Film de Luis Buñuel
Inspirado en un libro inédito de Juan Larrea

Asi algún día puedes publicar ese libro omitiendo mi nombre por
completo. En cambio yo hago un film tomado o inspirado de un libro
cosa corrientisima en el cine. Si aceptas pon un telegrama de una
sola palabra: ACEPTADO. Si no Ilegible será archivado para siempre
pues no hay que creer que saldrán más productores aunque la película entera pudiera hacerse por procedimientos fisico-quimicos.

Un abrazo para Lucianne y otro para ti

Luis

Figure 48 Letter Buñuel to Larrea, 20 August 1957.

To Juan Larrea

Mexico City, 20 August 1957

Dear Juan,

From your letter I see that you have been convinced for some years now that I pilfered the footprint in the sands of the Robinsonian island from *Illegible, Son of a Flute*, which also has the imprint of a future foot on the far shore …[1] In fact, the footprint is the best-known thing in Defoe's work, and although you may think I used it gratuitously (it was actually Defoe who used it), it is central to the development of the story of the castaway. There is no illustrated edition of *Robinson Crusoe* that does not include that image.

The producer[2] has not taken kindly to your departure. He had already incurred other costs and it has also disrupted his plans somewhat. It has made me waste my time and lose the French film, although that will be no great loss to the art of cinema. What I find funny is the thought of you holding those two cheques suspended over my head for three weeks like the proverbial sword of Damocles, waiting to catch me out, and that in the end, it was over the omission of just one scene. If you want to believe Lucianne's view that it can all be done in a laboratory, I am certainly not going to contradict her.

My only remaining option is to make a proposition and, before so doing, retrace the past. Nine years ago, we worked together for three weeks at your house on a story based on what you remembered of a lost book of yours. The backbone and the prophetic message of that story were yours, but the situations, the gags, the coherence, in a word, the form was the result of a most cordial collaboration. Some elements were yours alone, others mine alone, and the rest we came up with together. So, when Dancigers took the story to New York, we had it registered[3] at the Screen Writers Guild of Hollywood on 26 July 1948 in your name and mine, registration number 40013. Here comes my proposition: I should like to make *Illegible, Son of a Flute* a purely poetic film, with no message of any kind, adding any elements I feel appropriate, and using as much of the existing detail as I see fit. In order to do so without compromising your ideals, the credits could read as follows and the payments could remain as already agreed: 'Illegible, Son of a Flute. Film by Luis Buñuel. *Inspired* by an unpublished book by Juan Larrea.'

You can publish the book one day with no reference to my name. While I, on the other hand, can make a film based on, or inspired by a book, as happens all the time in cinema. If you accept, just send a one-word telegram: *Agreed*. If you don't, *Illegible, Son of a Flute* will be filed away forever, because there is no reason to think another producer will come forward, even if it were possible to make the entire film bio-chemically (or 'by physico-chemical means').

My regards to you,
Luis

Tls, AB/572.22; *CLB* 177–178

[1]	Of the river Hades, or death.
[2]	Barbachano.
[3]	Via Rubia Barcia.

From Alec Guinness

Steep Marsh, 3 October 1957

Dear Mr Buñuel
I am most distressed at the temporary collapse of The Loved One *. I shall hope that something can be done about it in the future, but I'm afraid that under the circumstances I must start looking for solid work this month. I have written at great length to Mr Preminger[1] so won't cover the same ground, but basically my feeling is that a first-class cast won't be found under the present circumstances, and although I know you would do wonders I feel it is a picture which needs sophisticated acting. I am most sad at missing the opportunity of being directed by you (at least for the present) – I was the envy of so many actors here when it looked as if it was going ahead.*

If the two films I have to do by contract in 1958 were commercial propositions I would think again about it, but as I'm only receiving a percentage on them it would mean that I would earn no money at all in 1958[2] if I did Loved One *on a* pari-passu[3] *basis and be in acute difficulties with our tax authorities. I'm so very sorry – and do hope a year's time may improve the situation.*

Yours sincerely,
Alec Guinness
Kettlebrook Meadows

Steep Marsh
Nr. Petersfield

Eng Als, AB/632.10

---

[1] Inwald 'Ingo' Preminger (1911–2006), US producer of Austro-Hungarian descent, brother of film-maker Otto Preminger.
[2] In 1958, Guinness wrote the script for and starred in *The Horse's Mouth*, dir. Ronald Neame.
[3] French in original 'On an equal footing'/'At the same rate'. 'Side by side'.

From Alejo Carpentier[1]

Mexico City, January 1958

For Luis Buñuel,
    Whose work has accompanied and enriched my life, from my adolescence, from the heroic days of *The Golden Age*.

With all my admiration and affection,
Alejo Carpentier

Spa Ad (A. Carpentier, *El acoso*, Editorial Losada, Buenos Aires, 1956), AB/149

---

[1] Cuban writer (1904–80), who lived in Paris 1927 to 1939 where he met LB.

From Jacques Ledoux[1]

Brussels, 7 March 1958

DEAR BUÑUEL,
WE INSIST YOU ATTEND, AS JURY MEMBER, EXPERIMENTAL CINEMA
FESTIVAL FOR ONE WEEK FROM 20 TO 27 APRIL.[2] WE WILL COVER TRAVEL
AND ACCOMMODATION COSTS AND WOULD CERTAINLY BE DELIGHTED
TO SEE YOU AGAIN.[3]

LEDOUX

Fre Tel, AB/1426.100

---

[1] Belgian historian (1921–88), head conservator at the Brussels Cinémáthèque from 1948.
[2] International Festival of Experimental Film, Knokke-le-Zoute, also known as EXPRMNTL, second
     edition held in April 1958.
[3] LB did not attend.

To the editor of the *Novedades* newspaper

Mexico City, 9 April 1958

Dear friend del Río,
   It's never too late to correct mistakes, and so, with these lines, I am setting myself
the task of *undoing*[1] one whose elaboration in no way calls into question the good faith
of any party. I leave entirely to your discretion the exclusive right to publish this letter
and shall now proceed directly to a succinct account of the facts.
   Some weeks ago, *Novedades*, followed by other weeklies and magazines, published
the news that *The Criminal Life of Archibaldo de la Cruz*, a Mexican film I directed
in 1954, had received the distinction of being judged the best film screened in Paris
in 1957. This award was based on voting by twenty-four of the most distinguished
Parisian writers on cinema in a survey organized by the learned magazine *Cahiers du
cinéma*, in its issue number 79 of January of this year.[2]
   Each writer was asked to provide the names, in his opinion, of the ten best films of
the year. The film with the highest overall number of mentions according to that survey
was *The Criminal Life of Archibaldo de la Cruz*, followed, in order of importance, by
films such *A King in New York*,[3] *The Girl Can't Help It*,[4] *The Wrong Man*,[5] *Nights of
Cabiria*,[6] *Twelve Angry Men*,[7] *A Face in the Crowd*,[8] *The Bridge on the River Kwai*,[9] etc.
In other words, the reports in the Mexican press were limited to an objective statement
of the facts and were not, and are not, mistaken.
   But in issue number 80 of the aforementioned magazine, corresponding to
February of this year, that I happen to have seen today, the calculation has been
arrived at differently.[10] It is no longer the film with the most votes that heads a list now
derived from only ten of the critics; so that even if the other fourteen critics had not
considered a film worthy of mention, it might still, according to the new calculations,

be considered the best. It is interesting to note, for example, that while Henri Agel[11] lists the films in alphabetical order, François Truffaut[12] does not indicate any order of preference.

As a result, according to these criteria, *The Criminal Life of Archibaldo de la Cruz* is ranked 5 out of the ten best films with 74 points, preceded in order of importance by *A King in New York*, with 84 points, and between that film and *The Criminal Life of Archibaldo de la Cruz* the following three films: *The Girl Can't Help It, Nights of Cabiria* and *The Wrong Man*. The five films mentioned above then follow the Mexican film.

Of course, it is not for me to lecture anyone on the scrutiny of votes and I fully accept the *Cahiers du cinema* verdict.

I want to take this opportunity to express my heartfelt thanks to PECIME,[13] and to its president and my dear friend Tort in particular,[14] for the tribute they were preparing for me[15] that will now not take place as it would be 'a little' inappropriate. If this misunderstanding has left anyone in something of an undignified position, it is me, alone, and not the Mexican film critics, who were simply using this Festival to express their goodwill, generosity and, through my film, their genuine affection for Mexican cinema.

SIC TRANSIT GLORIA![16]

Your affectionate friend,
Luis Buñuel

[PS] With copy for J. M. Tort, President of PECIME.

Spa Od; *NOV* np (ABR/2016.72)

---

[1] 'Desfacer' in the original, old Spanish.

[2] 'Les dix meilleurs films de l'année', *Cahiers du cinéma*, no. 79 (January 1958), p. 3; signatories include Bazin, Braunberger, Doniol-Valcroze, Kast, Mauriac and Sadoul.

[3] *A King in New York* (1957), dir. Charles Chaplin; LB translated for Mexican press the 'French' titles.

[4] *The Girl Can't Help It* (1957), dir. Frank Tashlin.

[5] *The Wrong Man* (1957), dir. Alfred Hitchcock (1899–1980).

[6] *Le Notti di Cabiria* (1957), dir. Federico Fellini (1920–93).

[7] *Twelve Angry Men* (1957), dir. Sidney Lumet (1924–2011).

[8] *A Face in the Crowd* (1957), dir. Elia Kazan.

[9] *The Bridge on the River Kwai* (1957), dir. David Lean.

[10] 'Les dix meilleurs films de l'année', *Cahiers du cinéma*, no. 80 (February 1958), p. 48.

[11] French film critic and historian (1911–2008).

[12] French film-maker (1932–84), wrote for *Cahiers du cinéma* in his youth.

[13] Periodistas Cinematográficos de Mexico, association founded by Efraín Huerta in 1945.

[14] Juan Manuel Tort, Mexican film critic.

[15] March 1957, PECIME organized a 'semana de Luis Buñuel' (Week of LB) (ABR/2016.76).

[16] 'Thus passes the glory of the world', traditionally voiced at inaugural ceremonies by in-coming Pope.

Figure 49 Marga López, Rabal, Figueroa, Buñuel and others, photographed by Manuel Álvarez Bravo during filming of *Nazarín*, summer 1958. Courtesy of the Archivo de la Fundación Televisa, División Fílmica.

To José Rubia Barcia

Mexico City, 24 September 1958

My dear Barcia,

I read your letter blushing from head to toe. And that head is now lowered in shame. You are right: my anti-epistolary attitude is bad for friendship. Please don't think I don't struggle with that particular failing, but it always defeats me. That said, my fond memories, my loyalty to our close friendship, and my affection for *Dómine Palmeta*,[1] are stronger by the day and I shall prove that if one day, and I hope it will be soon, it suits you to come and spend some time with us. From now onwards, I shall always endeavour to reply to your letters, even if it is only to acknowledge their receipt.

I think *Nazarín* has turned out well.[2] I had complete freedom in making it. And, as usual, I didn't worry about whether people would like it or not. I have kept the personalities or characters as Galdós described them, but the focus, the underlying direction and meaning of the priest's vicissitudes[3] have been Buñuelized and updated.

I didn't attempt to paraphrase the gospels, because that strikes me as a trite gimmick, and *démodé*.[4] At the end it is DOUBT, rather than the Holy Spirit, that descends upon Nazarín. The film was made in five weeks, so compared with the big films made in the US it will seem rather poorly produced. I would love to know what you think of it because when I am making a film, I really only think about the effect it might have on my true friends.

I shall write to García Formentí[5] today asking him to let me read your book.[6] You may not believe it, but the completely isolated life I lead means I have no contact with anyone except Altolaguirre (who, very much between you and me, has gone a bit mad), and I only see him once a year. But I'll drop in on him with the book and see if he will publish it. That task, at least, I can promise to fulfil.

My son Juan Luis has graduated from Oberlin College and is now working as an assistant director. He's gone to spend three months in Paris, his birthplace. The fascists may get their hooks in him. My other son, Rafael, finishes *high school*[7] this year and I'll send him off to some *college*[8] over there next year. Jeanne is very well, busy with the tasks typical of her sex.

Send me the photo of you, Evita and the girls and give all three of them a hug from me.

And a very big hug for you from,
Luis Buñuel

Spa Tls, CBC; *CLB* 70–71

---

[1] Allusion to the politically satirical anonymous pamphlet *La república de los canallas, ó Aventuras and descalabros del dómine Palmeta* (Buenos Aires: Impr. del Plata, 1868).
[2] LB filmed *Nazarín* with Barbachano Productions in July and August 1958.
[3] In LB's version, Father Nazario, played by Francisco Rabal (1926–2001), devotes his wandering life to others with only randomly helpful acts of self-mortification.
[4] French in the original.
[5] Arturo García Formentí, Mexican writer and lawyer.
[6] Manuscript of *Umbral de sueños*.
[7] English in the original.
[8] English in the original.

To Paulette [Dorisse][1]

Mexico City, 1 December 1958

My dear Paulette,

I sent two copies of the adaptation of *Fever Mounts at El Pao*[2] to Mr Borderie[3] last week, and I am hoping that by the time you receive this letter, one copy will have reached you. Luckily, filming is still three and a half months away,[4] which will give me time to introduce new improvements, as well as the changes that are likely to emerge from your notes. I am happy with the work in general. Despite what you may think, the adaptation was very, very difficult.

On a close reading, the novel is a tangled web of intrigue, melodrama and *déjà vu*.[5] The whole first part – all that drama of jealousy and betrayal – has been cut. And I can tell you now that Vázquez's[6] victory over the slaves needs to be made more interesting. But for now, that's all we've come up with. Also, in the novel, Vázquez's character is torn between love and ambition: in the adaptation, as well as those two forces of opposition there is another equally strong one: his character's innate honesty.

Goldblatt[7] will soon finish his first draft of the dialogues that, as you will see, are marked on the adaptation. As soon as he's finished, he will leave for Paris and I would prefer the final editing to be carried out under his supervision: by Gérard, Borderie and yourself.[8]

Juan Luis will be back soon and will leave for Spain around 15 December to meet my mother and my siblings. Could I ask you again, please, to deposit 100,000 francs for him? You have been such a wonderful help to him, another great debt I owe to your friendship.

Warmest, warmest wishes,
[Luis Buñuel]

Fre Tluf C, CIN

[1]   French agent at CIMURA, with clients including LB, Simone Signoret and Gérard Philipe.
[2]   Film script based on the novel by French author, Henry Castillou (1921–94).
[3]   Raymond Borderie (1897–1982), French producer of *Fever Mounts at El Pao*.
[4]   Started 11 May 1959.
[5]   French in the original.
[6]   Ramón Vázquez, male lead played by Philipe.
[7]   Goldblatt credited under pseudonym Charles Dorat.
[8]   French scriptwriter, Louis Sapin, also worked on the dialogues.

To Robert Favre Le Bret

Mexico City, 16 March 1959

Dear friend,

First of all, I want to thank you for your interest in my latest film, *Nazarín*. The reason Mexico chose to present *The Soldiers of Sancho Villa*[1] at the Festival[2] is because it has a more local, more Mexican focus, unlike mine which has no songs, no revolutionaries and no big Mexican stars.

I made *Nazarín* with love. The superficial, too superficial viewer will see the film as a return to Christianity, and so it will provoke my old friends. People who have seen it here say it is my best film. I don't know.

A copy left last Saturday for Paris, where it is awaiting subtitles. Mr Font, the representative of the producer Manuel Barbachano (*Roots, Bullfighter!*), will get it to you as soon as the subtitles are finished. That is, by 25 March at the latest. If the film is going to be screened at the Festival, we'll send you a better-quality copy because that one has a few minor defects.

My best wishes,
Luis Buñuel

Fre Tls, CIN

[1] *La cucaracha* (*The Soldiers of Pancho Villa*, 1958) dir. Ismael Rodríguez, high-budget feature, set at the beginning of the Mexican Revolution, starring María Félix (1914–2002) and Emilio Fernández.
[2] 12th Cannes Festival, May 1959.

To Robert Favre Le Bret

Mexico City, April 1959

HOPE YOU HAVE SEEN THE SUBTITLED COPY OF *NAZARÍN*. THE COPY FOR THE FESTIVAL WITH AMENDED SUBTITLES WILL BE WITH YOU ON 22 APRIL.

VERY CORDIAL REGARDS,
BUÑUEL

Fre Tel, CIN

To Robert Favre Le Bret

Mexico City, 24 April 1959

THEY ARE SAYING OVER HERE THAT *NAZARÍN* HAS BEEN REJECTED FOR THE FESTIVAL.[1] GRATEFUL IF YOU COULD CONFIRM OR CORRECT.

AGAIN, CORDIAL REGARDS,
BUÑUEL

Fre Tel, CIN

[1] The Mexican Cultural Delegation to Cannes boycotted *Nazarín* in favour of Mexico's official entry, *La cucaracha*, in competition for the Palme d'Or.

From Robert Favre Le Bret

Paris, 24 April 1959

NAZARÍN UNAMIMOUSLY INVITED BY FESTIVAL COUNCIL. WILL BE SCREENED 11 MAY. HOPE YOU WILL BE THERE.[1]

VERY CORDIAL REGARDS,
FAVRE LE BRET

Fre Tel C, CIN

[1] LB did not attend.

From Emilio Fernández

Cannes, 12 May [1959]

Luis Buñuel
Hotel Las Hamacas, Acapulco

IF YOU WEREN'T DEAF YOU WOULD HAVE HEARD THE UNIVERSAL APPLAUSE FOR *NAZARÍN* FROM OVER THERE.[1]
I CONGRATULATE MYSELF ON BEING YOUR FRIEND

EMILIO FERNANDEZ

Spa Tel, ABR/2039.46

[1]   After screening at Cannes.

From Manuel Barbachano

Cannes, 15 May [1959]

JURY AWARDED *NAZARÍN* INTERNATIONAL GRAND PRIX.[1] OVERJOYED, SENDING ADMIRATION AND AFFECTION,

MANOLO

Spa Tel, ABR/2039.28

[1]   *Nazarín* was awarded the International Prize at Cannes, *La cucaracha* was unsuccessful.

From María Luisa Elío[1] and Jomi García Ascot[2]

Mexico City, 15 May [1959]

MANY CONGRATULATIONS.
HUGE HUGS.
MARÍA LUISA AND JOMI

Spa Tel, ABR/2039.49

[1]   Writer and scriptwriter (1926–2009), exiled to Mexico after the Civil War.
[2]   Film critic and director (1927–86), Elío's husband, worked on newsreels produced by Barbachano and Velo.

From Julio Bracho[1]

Mexico City, 15 May [1959]

Luis Buñuel & Gabriel Figueroa
    Hotel Las Hamacas, Acapulco

MANY CONGRATULATIONS ON YOUR TRIUMPH, WHICH IS ALSO MEXICAN CINEMA'S,
    JULIO BRACHO

Spa Tel, ABR/2039.31

[1]   Mexican film director (1909–1978).

From Jean Rouverol[1] and Hugo Butler

Mexico City, 16 May [1959]

ALL OUR CONGRATULATIONS ON UTTERLY WELL-DESERVED SUCCESS, JEAN AND HUGO BUTLER[2]

Spa Tel, ABR/2039.9

[1] US actress (1916–2017), married to Hugo Butler.
[2] Butler and LB worked together on the script of *The Young One* that year, filmed between January and February 1960.

From Marga López[1]

Mexico City, 16 May [1959]

SO PROUD AGAIN TO HAVE TAKEN PART IN *NAZARÍN*.
MOST SINCERE CONGRATULATIONS,
MARGA LOPEZ

Spa Tel, ABR/2039.3

[1] Mexican actress of Argentine descent (1924–2005), played Beatriz in *Nazarín*.

From Rafael Corkidi[1]

Mexico City, 16 May [1959]

THANK YOU AND THANK YOU AGAIN FOR MAKING MEXICAN CINEMA AN ART FORM. RAFAEL CORKIDI, UNITED PRODUCERS SA

Spa Tel, ABR/2039.24

[1] Mexican film-maker and director of photography (1930–2013).

From Juan Antonio Bardem,[1] Aurora Bautista, Luis Miguel and Domingo Dominguín, Ricardo Muñoz Suay,[2] Francisco Rabal and Fernando Rey[3]

Pontevedra, 17 May [1959]

SO EXCITED. SEND BROTHERLY CONGRATULATIONS AND UNCONDITIONAL FRIENDLY ALLEGIANCE.
BARDEL, RABAL, RICARDO, FERNANDO REY, AURORA BAUTISTA, DOMINGUINES

Spa Tel, ABR/2039.39

[1] Film director (1922–2002), associate of Spanish production company Unión Industrial Cinematográfica (UNINCI) active from 1949 to 1962.
[2] Film producer (1917–97) attached to UNINCI, co-produced *Viridiana*.
[3] Fernando Casado Arambillet (1917–94), actor in *Viridiana*, *Tristana*, *The Discreet Charm of the Bourgeoisie* and *That Obscure Object of Desire*.

From Roberto Gavaldón

Mexico City, 19 May [1959]

SENDING SINCERE BEST WISHES ON SUCCESS OF YOUR FILM *NAZARÍN*.
ROBERTO GAVALDÓN

Spa Tel, ABR/2039.16

From Mary Meerson[1] and Henri Langlois

Paris, 21 May 1959

Luis Buñuel
Tepeyac Studios, Mexico City

THRILLED WITH YOUR GREAT SUCCESS AT CANNES. WOULD LIKE TO
INFORM YOU COPY OF *THE CRIMINAL LIFE OF ARCHIBALDO DE LA CRUZ* WE
LENT TO MAGE'S[2] COMPANY WAS NEVER RETURNED. KEIGEL[3] PROMISED TO
GET IT BACK FOR US, BUT THE ISSUE WAS LEFT UNRESOLVED WHEN HE DIED.
IMPLORE YOU TO INTERCEDE TO RECOVER COPY, WE HOPE IT IS STILL IN
GOOD CONDITION. WILL MEET YOUR REPRESENTATIVE[4] IN PARIS NEXT WEEK.

WARM REGARDS,
MARY AND HENRI LANGLOIS

Fre Tel, AB/1523.1–2

[1] French-Russian dancer (1900–93), partner of Langlois from 1940, programmer for Cinémathèque.
[2] Jacques Mage, owner of the distribution chain Cinéphone and distributor in France of *Death in the Garden*.
[3] Léonide Keigel (1904–57), co-founder of *Cahiers du cinéma*, brother-in-law of Mage.
[4] Paulette Dorisse.

From Claude Jaeger

Paris, 28 May [1959]

Dear Luis,
    I am meeting Margot. She's late, so I'm taking the opportunity to write to you. In
fact, I've been waiting for a peaceful moment since Cannes to send you a few words:
just to say that I've seen *Nazarín* and that it is a magnificent film. A lot of people in
Cannes were puzzled, although the reception overall was favourable (I hope that this
will, at the very least, help you with your work).
    I don't know whether it's because I know you well or because I'm so clever, but I
found what I would call a perfect sense of clarity and *evidence* (in the positive meaning
of the word) in the film. Sensitive and unrelenting. In short, I liked it immensely and

want to see it again soon. The most interesting and undoubtedly the *newest* film at the Festival. And what a relief: finally, a retort to the insufferable Fellini.

A lot work, and rarely entertaining, of course. The family is doing well.

With appreciation and warmest regards,

Claude J.
Procinex[1], 62 Foch Avenue

Fre Als L, AB/691.48

[1] French film and production and distribution company.

Figure 50 Figueroa, unknown, Félix, Russian Ambassador to Mexico, Philipe and Buñuel, during filming of *Fever Mounts at El Pao*, Mexico City, June 1959.

To José Francisco Aranda[1]

Mexico City, 6 July 1959

Dear Aranda,

Juan Luis gave me your letter to read and I'm replying now, if only briefly. I ask you to forgive me in advance if these lines seem excessively succinct and curt: I am a terrible correspondent.

I read your article in *Cinéma 57*.[2] I'm very grateful for your interest in me and your very good intentions in writing, but I have to say it is full of inaccuracies, doubtless due to erroneous sources of information. You attribute to me thoughts I've never expressed, like *'Il faut aimer l'histoire et la simplicité chronologique,*[3] etc.' (page 16). My mother is not from a wealthy family nor of noble extraction. The photo *Buñuel in 1927, lors d'une retraite*[4] is actually Buñuel dressed as a monk because I was, amongst many other things, an extra in Epstein's *Mauprat*. Those are not Aragonese peasants wandering through a salon in *The Golden Age*. I have not, from 1935 to 1937, or ever, been a member of the Communist Party. My grades at the Jesuit school were sometimes good, sometimes bad, and I was never an emperor or a prince, although I did win some minor prizes. My friendship with the priest in Las Hurdes is very exaggerated. My reading of the Holy Scriptures is not complete, but fragmentary and brief, I wouldn't be able to quote a single paragraph. I should love to know which scenes from my films contain phrases from the Old Testament, unless they are in *Robinson Crusoe* where the responsibility is Defoe's, not mine.

I've never taken up the habit of eating raw meat in imitation of primitive tribes. I don't understand the bit about using classical music as a form of self-flagellation and I really don't know what that means. Epstein and 'la Dulac'[5] never invited me to take part in *Filmed Songs,*[6] and I don't even know the film. I did take part, wholeheartedly, in the 'wild surrealist revolution'. I did not write, nor was I involved in, *Our Natacha.*[7] Everything attributed to me in relation to *Spain 1936*[8] is inaccurate. As the cultural attaché of the Republican Embassy in Paris, I did have a responsibility for films shot in Spain and even organized the editing of a documentary whose title I don't remember.[9] But nothing beyond that. I had nothing to do with *The Spanish Earth*[10] or *The Heart of Spain.*[11] Etc., etc.

In the above declarations, you will have noticed I make no comment on your personal evaluations of me or of my films. I'm simply pointing out the factual errors.

It goes without saying that if I am in France, I will let you know so that we can meet up.

Very cordially yours,
Buñuel

[PS] Juan Luis is going to Paris at the end of the week.

Warning! Don't trust anything my sister Conchita tells you, at times her imagination borders on the delirious.

Spa Tlsps, ARA/09/07–2

---

[1] Film critic and historian (1925–89), dedicated the majority of his book on avant-garde Spanish film to LB.
[2] F. Aranda, 'Buñuel Espagnol', *Cinéma 57*, no. 23 (December 1957), pp. 15–31.
[3] 'You have to love straightforward chronology of the plot', in French in the original.
[4] 'Buñuel, on a retreat in 1927', in French in original.
[5] Germaine Dulac (1882–1942), French film-maker.
[6] *Les Chansons filmées*, generic name for short films illustrating popular songs, produced in France between the First and Second World Wars.
[7] Feature directed by Benito Perojo in 1936, with Ana María Custodio as Natacha.
[8] *España leal in armas,* also known as *Espagne 1936*, left-wing Spanish Civil War propaganda film.
[9] LB supervised editing of two documentaries, *Espagne 1936* (1937) and *Espagne 1937* (1938).
[10] Left-wing Spanish Civil War propaganda film, dir. Ivens.
[11] Documentary, dir. Herbert Kline and other members of the cooperative Frontier Films, on the Civil War.

To José Rubia Barcia

Mexico City, 6 July 1959

My dear Barcia,

I have been tied up for two months now making a film,[1] but I finished with all that complication a few days ago and can now dedicate some time to write back to my friends, something I don't always do, unfortunately.

I've called Altolaguirre twice now with no success, he sometimes turns into the invisible man for months. I don't know what's happened to your book,[2] although I suppose you are in touch with him. As I said, I gave Manolo one of the copies I had – I kept the better quality one – and the drawings, which are excellent by the way.[3] Let me know if you want me to send you that copy by registered airmail and how the editing is going. Although I may be in touch with Manolo before then.

It may not be too long before we meet. I'm using a lawyer in New York to help me get a visa, which, as I mentioned, they've refused me a few times now. Things are going well and may be resolved by the end of the month.[4] If so, I may travel to Los Angeles in September because I'm going to make a film with Guinness, *The Loved One*, that involves some location shooting up there. Only the thought of seeing you again makes that trip attractive. What a wonderful time we'll have in endless conversation over a glass of good *bourbon*. I would even accept a small banquet fashioned by Evita's own and inimitable hands. And meet your two daughters, whom I've watched grow up in the photos you've both sent me. Just as Evita looks like you, the girls look like both you and Evita.

My *hereu*[5] Juan Luis is an assistant director and he's leaving this week for his birthplace, Paris, with the money made on my latest film.[6] The little one, Rafael, finished *high school*[7] this year and is going to study in the United States. I've no idea what he's going to do or where he's going to study. He's written to three or four universities and is waiting to hear whether he's been accepted or not. Do you think he could go to your university?[8] He wants to study Arts, Humanities and Modern Languages, so who knows? I definitely want him to live in a student residence or something like that. Anything rather than on his own in a private house. If you have time, I'd appreciate your advice.

Nazarín has been the most successful film of my career. It won the International Prize at Cannes this year and is breaking box office records over here. ¡*Rara avis*!

Much love to you all,
Luis Buñuel

[PS] If I do make *The Loved One*,[9] and contracts are about to be signed, I'll publish your book myself.

Spa Tlsps, CBC; *CLB* 73–74

---

1. Shooting of *Fever Mounts at El Pao* finished on 28 June 1959.
2. Manuscript of *Umbral de sueños*.
3. By surrealist painter, Eugenio Fernández Granell (1912–2001), exiled in New York.

4 LB acquires a visa and travels to New York on 22 September 1959 to work on pre-production towards *The Young One*.
5 'Heir', Catalan in the original.
6 As Assistant Director on *Fever Mounts at El Pao*.
7 English in the original.
8 UCLA.
9 Project eventually cancelled.

Figure 51 Muñoz Suay, Buñuel, Rucar and Bardem, Mexico City, summer 1959.

To José Rubia Barcia

Mexico City, 27 July 1959

Dear Barcia,

A few words to let you know that after writing my previous letter,[1] I discovered it was already too late to apply for entry to the *colleges*.[2] So rather than bothering you, I'm going to accept the place that I mentioned Rafael was offered at the University of New Mexico. He can spend his first year there and then we'll see.[3]

Now for some bad news. Manolito[4] went to Spain with María Luisa to present an – 'absurd'[5] – film he made at the San Sebastián Film Festival.[6] It was the Fray Luis[7] version of the *Song of Songs* with a black woman in the lead role.[8] On his way back to Madrid, two days ago, he crashed his car.[9] María Luisa was killed and he was seriously injured, and is now being operated on in Burgos by two surgeons from Madrid. I now understand why no one answered when I called his home to ask about your book. No further comment!

A big hug for you and for Evita,
Luis

PS I received a call tonight with the news that Manolo has died. The news has really upset me. Poor Manolito!

Spa Als, CBC; *CLB* 75–76

1   In letter from LB to Rubia, 23 July 1959, CBC (*CLB* 74–75).
2   English in the original.
3   Rafael Buñuel graduated with a degree in Performing Arts from UCLA.
4   Altolaguirre.
5   LB uses inverted commas, not in a pejorative sense, but to indicate that this was an ambitious project of Altolaguirre's to make a film version of the *Song of Songs* with an Afro-Cuban actress in the lead.
6   At the 7th edition, 11–20 July 1959.
7   Fray Luis de León (1527–91), Spanish mystic and poet, imprisoned for producing an unauthorized translation into the vernacular of the biblical *Song of Songs* on which Altolaguirre based his adaptation.
8   Isolina Herrera, Cuban actress.
9   At Cubo de Bureba, near Burgos, 23 July 1959.

To Elena Garro[1]

[Mexico City, July 1959]

My distinguished friend,

Jeanne has just told me what is going on[2] and *I am truly sorry*. I am enclosing 150 pesos so that you can go to Cuernavaca. I am sorry I can't see you now, because we have to go out, but I would prefer to talk to Octavio beforehand anyway to find out what has happened because, as I know from painful personal experience, it is better not to interfere in situations like yours without knowing the full facts.

Hoping and wishing with all my heart that your differences may be resolved, I am very cordially yours,

Buñuel

Spa Als, EG/1/25

1   Mexican writer (1916–98), first wife of Octavio Paz.
2   Her marriage to Paz was dissolved on 15 July 1959.

From François Truffaut

Paris, 25 August 1959[1]

Dear Sir,

First, allow me to express my profound admiration for *Nazarín*, a film of such magnificent simplicity, logic, intelligence and beauty.[2]

Unfortunately, I also see it as my duty to pester you: in October we will publish issue no.100 of *Cahiers du cinéma*. This is an important occasion for us and we would be sorry if your name were not to appear on an index that will include many of *Cahiers'* film-maker friends: Renoir, Becker, Bresson,[3] McLaren, Cocteau, Tati,[4] etc. Doniol-

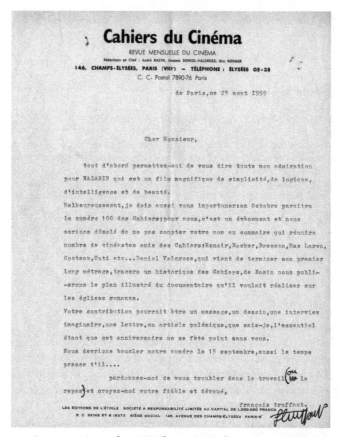

Figure 52 Letter from Truffaut to Buñuel, 25 August 1959.

Valcroze, who has just made his first feature,[5] will write a historical review of *Cahiers*;[6] and we will publish the illustrated script of the documentary Bazin wanted to make about Roman churches.[7]

Your contribution could be a message, a drawing, an imaginary interview, a letter, a polemic, anything; the main thing is that we should not celebrate this anniversary without you.[8]

We need to finalize submissions on 15 September, so time is short ...

Forgive me for interrupting your work (or rest) and be assured of my loyalty and devotion,

François Truffaut
Cahiers du cinema
146 Champs-Élysées

Fre Tls L, AB/632.34

[1] On *Cahiers du Cinéma* letterhead.
[2] Truffaut saw *Nazarín* at Cannes, where he was awarded Best Director for his first feature, *Les Quatre cents coups* (1959).

³   Robert Bresson (1901–99), French film-maker.
⁴   Jacques Tati (1907–82), French film-maker.
⁵   *L'Eau à la bouche* (1959), produced by Braunberger.
⁶   J. Doniol-Valcroze, 'L'histoire des *Cahiers*', *Cahiers du cinéma*, no. 100 (October 1959), pp. 62–68.
⁷   A. Bazin, 'Les églises romanes de Saintonge', *Cahiers du cinéma*, no. 100, pp. 55–60.
⁸   LB, Bresson, McLaren and Tati did not contribute; those who did included Becker, Cocteau, Renoir and Ingmar Bergman (1918–2011).

To Anne Philipe[1]

Mexico City, 26 November 1959

TERRIBLY SADDENED BY THE NEWS.[2]
OUR HEARTS ARE WITH YOU,
OSCAR DANCIGERS AND LUIS BUÑUEL

Fre Tel, AGP/221-B23

¹   Nicole Navaux (1917–90), Belgian actress, married Gérard Philipe in 1951.
²   Gérard Philipe died of liver cancer on 25 November 1959, aged 36, shortly after completing *Fever Mounts at El Pao*.

From Alfredo Guevara[1]

Havana, 11 December 1959

Distinguished and admired friend,
     On Monday we begin our first film, *Historias de la revolución*.[2] It will be directed by Jomi[3] and Gutiérrez Alea. Martelli[4] will be director of photography.
     This is the birth of our cinema. And I am writing these lines to you out of the fondness and admiration we feel for you. Our cinema is inspired by you, by Buñuel, Chaplin, Eisenstein, Zavattini … We've not yet chosen our path. The time is not right yet. We are knocking on every door. Seeking out lessons everywhere. Retracing every path. Along yours, we will find our own; following your footsteps, or perhaps going in the opposite direction. But whatever our final direction, we hope to receive the necessary help, inspiration and collaboration from you all.

With fondness and admiration,
Alfredo Guevara,
Instituto Cubano del Arte e Industria Cinematográficos
Calle 23 – 1155

Spa Tls L, AB/691.16; *TIE* 64

¹   Director and co-founder of the Cuban Institute of Film Art and Industry (ICAIC) in March 1959, after the Cuban Revolution.
²   ICAIC's first feature, dir. Tomás Gutiérrez Alea (1928–96).

³   García Ascot, whose episodes 'Un día de trabajo' (A Work Day) and 'Los novios' (The Lovers) would
    be included in the feature *Cuba 58* (1962), co-dir. Jorge Fraga.
⁴   Otello Martelli (1902–2000), Italian director of photography, worked on *La dolce vita* (1960) with Fellini.

To Alfredo Guevara

Mexico City, 27 December 1959

My dear friend,

Thank you for your letter, so full of enthusiasm and promise for the cinema of the
new Cuba. You can imagine the magnitude of my hopes for your resounding success; you
are in a splendid position from which to make wonderful cinema. Make the most of this
moment while you are in charge, because no one can predict the future. Make as much
progress along your path as you can before the 'sinister vulture' of commercial film begins
to stretch out its wings. Look into the mirror of Mexico and you'll see what that 'sinister
bird' has reduced her cinema to. Whatever you achieve today may well guide tomorrow.

How can I help? I'm not sure. But you can count on me for whatever you need.

Warmest regards,
Luis Buñuel

Spa Tls C, ASV; *NCL* 68

To Robert Hughes[1]

Mexico City, 1959

Questionnaire for the yearly publication Film: Book 1 (The Audience and the
Filmmaker)[2]

    *Q1. What specific difficulties have you experienced which have been caused by
interpretations of the 'audience' by producers, distributors, censors, etc?*

    *A1. Except during my first three films, all made before 1932, and produced with
absolute independence –An Andalusian Dog, The Golden Age and Land Without
Bread – I have always felt the pressure more or less heavily exerted by the producer.
But one might deduce from your questions that the producers and distributors are to
blame by their special interpretation of public taste for the limitations imposed on the
filmmaker. In my opinion, the real responsibility for the spiritual stagnation of cinema
lies with the amorphous mass, routinary and conformist, that makes up the audience.
The producer limits himself merely to throwing to the beasts the food they demand of
him. A businessman neither better nor worse than the others of his time, the producer
has no scruples. He is capable of leaping from one ideological plane to another, even if
the systems are morally and artistically antagonistic, so long as he is guaranteed prestige
and economic success. For the moment it is impossible to foresee any moral elevation of
human society. For this reason, there does not appear even a glimmer of the spiritual
improvement of the audience. One might even predict the contrary. Filmmakers will*

continue dragging the heavy chains of servility put upon them by the industry and the producers, who, as faithful representatives of the public, will continue their tyrannical repression of the artists' freedom.

Q2. What do you consider one of the most encouraging developments in film in recent years?

Q3. What do you consider one of the most discouraging developments?

A2 & 3. To my way of thinking there is not one indication in the film production of recent years, either 'capitalist' or 'communist' that encourages any hope of the spiritual improvement of cinema – unless it be in its technical aspect, where the progress of both is unquestionable.

Q4. What film or films would you make if you were free from the non-artistic limitations of sponsorship, censorship, etc.?

A4. If it were possible for me, I would make films which, apart from entertaining the audience, would convey to them the absolute certainty that they DO NOT LIVE IN THE BEST OF ALL POSSIBLE WORLDS. And in doing this I believe that my intentions would be highly constructive. Movies today, including the so-called neo-realist, are dedicated to a task contrary to this. How is it possible to hope for an improvement in the audience – and consequently in the producers – when every day we are told in these films, even in the most insipid comedies, that our social institutions, our concepts of Country, Religion, Love, etc., etc., are, while perhaps imperfect, UNIQUE AND NECESSARY? The true 'opium of the audience' is conformity; and the entire, gigantic film world is dedicated to the propagation of this comfortable feeling, wrapped though it is at times in the insidious disguise of art.

Eng, Od; *FB* 40–41

---

[1]   Critic and documentary film director, co-edited books on film for New York publishers Grove Press from 1959.

[2]   LB's responses translated by J. O. Scrymgeour and published in R. Hughes (ed.), *Film: Book 1. The Audience and the Film-maker* (New York: Grove Press, 1959), pp. 40–41.

From Robert Hughes

New York [1959]

Dear Señor Buñuel
    Finally.
    And again, thank you for your reply – it was certainly the most pungent and candid of the lot.[1]

I'd love to have your reaction to the book. Sincerely
Robert Hughes
Grove Press
795 Broadway, New York 3, New York

[PS] Also, should I send a review copy to Cinevoz? *Any other Mexican publication? Or would you rather I didn't?*

Eng Tls, AB/1376

---

¹ Directors who responded to the questionnaire include Lindsay Anderson, Clément, Dreyer, Kazan, Lean, Satyajit Ray and Renoir.

From Georges Sadoul

Paris, 5 February 1960

Dear Luis,

It has been a long time since we last wrote, but I'm sure my silence does not stop you believing in my long and loyal friendship. Several of our mutual friends have told me you will come to France around the time of the Cannes Film Festival. My wife and I would love to welcome you to our home and spend some relaxed time with you.

Anne Philippe came to dinner last week, the first time we'd seen her since the death of poor Gérard, we had so much to talk about that we didn't have a chance to ask her about you, we were also afraid of stirring up sad, recent memories. We were genuinely relieved to discover that Gérard's death was not related to any kind of amoebic infection. The doctors were mistaken, thinking there was an amoebic connection, when it was in fact cancer; so, no one can now claim he died prematurely because he went to make a film in Mexico, where he was supposed to have contracted a terrible illness.

From what I've heard, you didn't much like *Fever Mounts at El Pao*; it is true that it shares certain of the defects of other big-budget international co-productions. I'm not personally a great fan of that film.¹ As for *Nazarín*, I'm convinced it is a masterpiece, although you may well know that I haven't yet finalized my opinion of the film. The day I saw it at Cannes I was so exhausted I had to pinch myself to stay awake, so I understood very little, except for how beautiful it was.

By the way, I've been asked to speak to you about the film's premiere in Paris.² The Art House Film Theatre, which is supported by the association of cinema critics,³ is keen to have your film on its programme in early March. It's not a particularly important theatre, but it has a group of loyal supporters and its programmes are always of the highest quality. I imagine the decision depends less on you than on your Mexican producer, but should your French distributors find themselves presented with similar financial offers, I think the Art House Film Theatre would be a good choice.

I have to go to Argentina in March, and will spend some time in Brazil, but apparently it will be impossible for me to return via Mexico. I hope I'll be able to get to the Acapulco Festival one year, and then be able to visit you at your home in Mexico.⁴

Our most loyal and sincere friendship,
Georges Sadoul

PS I've just discovered in a note from Nancy Cunard that it appears our poor old friend Juan Vicens has died in China. Can it be true? I don't want to believe it. I saw him in

Moscow with his wife[5] at the end of 1956, but only very briefly unfortunately. Let me know whether this terrible news is true or not![6]

Fre Tlsps, AB/572.41

1 Premiered in Paris, 6 January 1960.
2 *Nazarín* was not commercially released in France until November 1960.
3 Possibly, the French film critics' union, founded in 1946.
4 Sadoul visited LB's home in Mexico in December 1960, after serving on Jury at the Festival of Acapulco, but LB was in Madrid.
5 María Luisa González, exiled in Paris, then Moscow.
6 Vicens died of a heart attack in Peking in 1959.

From Henry Castillou

[Paris,] 18 February 1960

Dear Mr Buñuel,

I have waited a few weeks to write this letter after the premiere of *Fever Mounts at El Pao* in Paris, because I wanted to allow some time for my first impressions to settle and to free myself from the opinions I hear or read wherever I go. Also, as I had never seen my characters come to life on the screen before, I felt, at first, a strange kind of awe which I think paralyzed all my critical powers ... I have just seen the film for the fourth time. I liked it as much as the first time, and I have been better able to appreciate its qualities.

You have handled the subject matter in an extremely sober, classical way, almost always suggesting rather than emphasizing it. In my opinion, that was the best style in this case. You've avoided all picturesque clichés, and shown none of the uprising, which would have taken up time and detracted from the central drama.

The 'subtle' setting, as a backdrop to political life in South America, is admirable.[1] Far from common in cinema! I really liked the pastor's arrival at the official tribunal on the day of the national festival. Not at all forced. A simple image that says a great deal ...

One reader, Captain Rostain,[2] a Navy Commander at Bordeaux, who lived in Venezuela for several years, sent me a copy of a long letter that he had sent to the cinema critic at *Le Figaro Littéraire*. Amongst other things, he says:

'The dirty intrigue around Inés[3] represents exactly the kind of pressure exerted on certain people by Pérez Jiménez's[4] Chief-of-Police and his boss, the Minister of the Interior ...[5] I would even add that Gual's[6] blackmail is nothing compared to the real stories I have been told. Cárdenas's arrest and García's[7] faked escape were all part of the daily tragedy of three years ago, although deaths in prison were usually blamed on "indigestion" ... Some of my Latin American associates recognized very lifelike characters in the film, often to be found sitting in offices or on the streets. It was clever to make Gérard Philipe half-French, a good way of reflecting his character's uncertainty ...'

I think I understand, more or less, the difficulties that you may have faced. I wanted you to be able to do exactly as you wished, even if that meant distancing yourself further still from my novel. But I repeat, in all sincerity, that I found the film, exactly as it is, very interesting and I liked it a lot. I hope to be able to discuss it with you, and better express my gratitude on a trip I'm am planning to make to Mexico in a few months' time.

With great admiration,
Henry Castillou

Fre Als, AB/691.15

¹ Castillou's novel and LB's adaptation were located in an imaginary Central American country.
² Louis Rostain (1906–84), French sailor.
³ Inés Rojas, character played by María Félix.
⁴ Marcos Pérez Jiménez (1914–2001), president of Venezuela between1953 and 1958; involved in military coup that removed legally elected Venezuelan President Rómulo Gallegos in 1948.
⁵ Laureano Vallenilla Lanz (1912–73), Interior Minister during Pérez Jiménez's presidency.
⁶ Alejandro Gual, character played by Jean Servais.
⁷ Lieutenant García and the teacher, Juan Cárdenas, played by Raúl Dantés and Domingo Soler, respectively.

To Francisco Rabal

Cannes, 8 May 1960

Dear nephew,¹
    Many thanks for your highly effective intervention.² The consulate in Paris did indeed advise me that the visa was ready. But another telegram arrived the following day saying exactly the opposite, as it seems certain 'formalities' had not been attended to. They say they will let me know when everything has been resolved. No idea whether this will take a day or a month. What I do know is that if I have no visa by the 15th, I'm going back to Mexico. Either way, your actions, interest, seriousness and INFLUENCE accelerated a process that no one, not Rodrigáñez,³ Pepín or Dominguins, had managed to move forward a single centimetre before you became involved.
    Give Ricardo, whose telegram I have received, a very big hug from me. I hope I'll be able to give him one in person very soon.
    Many kisses for my niece and my small grandchildren,⁴ and *idem* to you.

Your uncle,
Luis
Hotel Mont Fleury

[PS] I see my hopes of sitting with you at the card table in Doña Salvadora's⁵ house beginning to fade.
    My film⁶ was screened at the gala session yesterday. Great success.

Spa Als, FR; *QUE* 27–28

¹ LB and Rabal refer to one another affectionately and respectively, as 'uncle' and 'nephew'.
² To obtain entry visa for Spain.

³ Eduardo Rodrígañez, engineer and agronomist, friend of LB.
⁴ Asunción Balaguer Golobart (born 1925), actress and wife of Rabal, and their children, Teresa (1952) and Benito (1954).
⁵ Possible reference to Doña Julia, owner of Rabal's favourite Madrid bar.
⁶ *The Young One* screened as part of the official selection at Cannes in 1960.

Figure 53 Buñuel photographed by Luc Fournol, Paris, *c.* 1960.

To Francisco Rabal

Cannes, 10 May 1960

Dear Paco

I do not believe there has ever been a more active, helpful and *influential* nephew than you. Three days ago, the Consulate informed me that this time they were serious, and I now have the visa that will prevent them condemning me to the *garrote vil*¹ in Spain. And all thanks to you.

Cesáreo,² whom I'd not met in person before, gave me your card yesterday when I went to greet those two wonderful boys, Portabella and Saura, after the screening of *The Deliquents*.³

It was Juan Luis who spoke to you on the phone today because I couldn't hear a thing. I'm leaving for Paris on the 15th, I'll collect my visa there on the 16th and leave on the 17th for that unknown land – certainly and sadly not the one I once knew – known as Spain. I'll stop off in Barcelona to see my sister⁴ then I'll spend eight to ten days in Zaragoza, and you'll find me in Madrid around 1 June. I'll let you have precise details of my arrival.

I would really like to see the cynical-sentimental Ricardo in Paris on Monday 16, when I'll be there. Send a telegram to CIMURA, to let me know where he is staying, so they can give me the address.

Many, many hugs from,
Luis B.

Spa Als, FR; *BVMC* f

---

[1] Strangulation device used in Spain to execute prisoners from 1820, abolished after the transition to democracy in 1978; last recorded use for the execution of a political prisoner, the anarchist, Salvador Puig Antich, on 2 May 1974.
[2] Césareo Gónzalez Rodríguez (1903–68), producer, founder of Suevia Films in 1940.
[3] *Los golfos* (1960), first feature directed by Carlos Saura Atarés, produced by Films 59, company founded by producer and director Pere Portabella i Ràfols (born 1929).
[4] Conchita.

To Pierre Braunberger

Madrid, 13 June 1960

My dear Pierre,
    Please set aside half an hour of your time this Saturday at 11am when I'll be coming to your office to see you with the following programme:

    1) Possibility of making a film with you.
    2) Settling our accounts.
    3) Whether there is still any kind of contract between us?
    4) Say my goodbyes, because I leave for Mexico on the 21st.

Regards,
Buñuel

[PS] I can be contacted at CIMURA.

Fre Als, PB

From Amos Vogel

New York, 20 June 1960

Dear Mr Buñuel,
    I wanted to let you know of the success of our Nazarín[1] screening. While I was not in New York at the time – I lectured in Western Europe and served as a judge at two film festivals – I was told by my associates here that the audience followed the film with the closest

attention – much more so than is usual even for this critical and vocal audience – and then accorded the film a large round of applause. What is even more significant is the fact that the ending of the film – as intended by you – made it impossible for them to 'put the film out of their minds' but instead compelled them to keep on thinking about it and your intentions. This was further fostered by the program notes we presented, a copy of which is enclosed.[2]

I understand that there were even more critics and film specialists at this screening than usual, as might have been expected given the very special nature and reputation of the film. People like Herman Weinberg,[3] Arthur Knight,[4] Kenneth Tynan[5] (the theatre critic of The New Yorker[6]*), Dr. Siegfried Kracauer,[7] Marc Blitzstein[8] William Everson,[9] Lionel Rogosin,[10] Shirley Clarke,[11] Ed Harrison[12] (the well-known distributor), Archer Winsten[13] attended this screening. I understand there were many others, but since I myself was not present, I cannot give you any further information.*

I am very pleased with the success of this presentation, and also very happy to have once again been able to introduce a previously unknown film by you to America.

So far, I have not been contacted by any commercial distributor regarding the film. It is of course possible that they have contacted Barbachano directly, but I have a feeling that there is a great deal of resistance to the film by the distributors and exhibitors here due to their essential conservative and commercial attitude. To put it differently, there is neither sex nor sadism in Nazarín, *while there is possibly more intellectual content than they consider suitable for their peacefully sleeping movie audiences. Perhaps you don't agree with me on this, but in any case, this is my opinion.*

I have just had a phone call from Richard Griffith at the Museum of Modern Art asking whether he can borrow our print of Nazarín *for his forthcoming series of your film in December. I informed him that of course I had no objections, but that the permission would have to come either from you or Mr Barbachano. I am holding the print until I hear from either you or him.*

As to The Criminal Life of Archibaldo de la Cruz, *I wanted to let you know that we have not yet received the subtitled print, and I am wondering how it is progressing. This is now becoming a more serious matter, since my programming deadlines for next season (October 1960 till May 1961)[14] occur on July 20th. It is imperative that the subtitled print be in my hands before July 20th, since otherwise I would be taking too much of a risk in announcing a film for our new schedule which is not yet in my hands.*

On the other hand, if you were to personally assure me that the subtitled print would reach us no later than, say, August, I would be willing to take the risk.

My plan is to show the film on one of our first programs of the new season. I am sure that it will be a very successful and significant presentation.

While I have written to the producer about the film,[15] I have received no reply. I would therefore appreciate your checking into this matter and advising me as to the present status of the film.

There is an additional reason for bringing this matter to a successful conclusion: Dick Griffith informed me of his interest in including Archibaldo *in the cycle to be presented at the Museum, and he was very happy to hear that a subtitled version would be available, since he realizes that this particular film cannot be shown without subtitles.*

If at all possible, please try to write me at your earliest convenience as regards Archibaldo.

I also would like to continue discussing with you the possibility of showing The Golden
Age *and also the possibility of a personal appearance by you at Cinema 16 in the fall or
winter. Do you have any plans to come to New York at that time?*

With best personal regards.
Very sincerely yours,
Amos Vogel
Executive Secretary

Eng Tls L, AB/2013; *BUL* 733–735

[1] In Cinema 16.
[2] In the file on 'Nazarín' (AV/II.1/35/F24).
[3] US film critic (1908–83), *Cahiers du cinéma* correspondent in New York.
[4] US film critic (1916–91), deputy director of MoMA between 1940 and 1941.
[5] English theatre critic and writer (1927–80).
[6] Journal founded by Harold Ross (1892–1951) in New York in 1925.
[7] German sociologist and film theorist (1889–1966), exiled in New York between 1941 and 1943.
[8] US composer (1905–64).
[9] British film historian (1929–96), based in New York from 1950.
[10] US film-maker (1924–2000).
[11] US experimental film director (1919–97).
[12] US distributor, who distributed films by Kurosawa and Ray in the United States.
[13] US film critic (1911–97), associated with *The New York Post.*
[14] At Cinema 16.
[15] Roberto Figueroa or Alfonso Patiño Gómez, producers of *The Criminal Life of Archibaldo de la Cruz.*

From Jean Gaborit and Jacques Maréchal[1]

Paris, 29 June 1960

Dear Maestro,

We hope you had a good return journey.

Please let us express once again[2] what a great honour it was to meet you and what
wonderful memories we cherish of our conversations.

As we promised in Paris, we are sending you four copies of a draft contract for the
acquisition of *The Young and the Damned* from Mr Menasce's company;[3] we believe
Mr Arditti will be able to sign on behalf of the company. You could draw up the final
contract on Mr Menasce's company letterhead.

We have drawn up a straightforward contract, as a straight sale is the best option.

Afterwards, we would be willing to sign a similar contract with you for both films.[4]
We could revise the contract with Ms Dorisse, reviewing the percentage in your favour.

We would be very grateful if you could let us know very soon if Mr Arditti accepts
the proposed contract and whether he will be able to sign. We could screen the film
immediately, together with *An Andalusian Dog*, if Ms Peillon agrees.[5]

When we know what revisions have to be made to the complete version of *Land
Without Bread*, we will be able to tell you how much we can pay you in commission.

We think we have resolved the *Tristan and Isolde* issue through an intermediary at a specialist record club.[6]

Hoping to hear from you soon, and that you have every faith in the seriousness of our commitment,

Jean Gaborit and Jacques Maréchal
Les Grands Films Classiques, 22 Rue de L'Échiquier

PS Please send all correspondence by registered mail to Jean Gaborit, 9 Rue du Général Niox, Paris XVI.

Fre Tls L, AB/568.19

[1] French film distributors, founders of Les Grands Film Classiques in 1956 for restoration and screening of full-length versions of classic films.
[2] Letter from J. Gaborit to LB, 19 June 1960 (AB/568.16).
[3] Draft of contract transferring rights to *The Young and the Damned* from Ultramar Films to LB for five years (AB/568.20).
[4] *An Andalusian Dog* and *The Young and the Damned*.
[5] Employee of Pierre Braunberger.
[6] Following LB's instructions, Les Grands Film Classiques made a sound copy of *An Andalusian Dog* in 1960, at 24 frames per second, with music by Wagner and Argentine tangos recorded in the 1950s.

To Gustavo Alatriste[1]

Gustavo Alatriste

377 Insurgentes Sur, Mexico City
Mexico City, 10 August 1960

Dear Gustavo,

As of today, we have come to the following agreement:

1) I shall write a film script at your request and on your instruction for a film you will produce. The provisional title of this film is *Viridiana*. You agree to pay me ONE HUNDRED THOUSAND PESOS (100,000) for this work.
2) You are contracting my services from this point onwards as the director of the aforementioned film and agree to pay me ONE HUNDRED AND FIFTY THOUSAND PESOS (150,000), if the film is shot in Mexico, or TWO HUNDRED AND FIFTY THOUSAND PESOS (250,000) if the film is shot in Spain.

If I should go to Spain, you agree to pay for the return ticket, and $15 daily maintenance.

Please sign below to indicate your agreement,

Luis Buñuel
In agreement:
Gustavo Alatriste

Tls, ACMEC; *UNI* 448 f

[1] Mexican producer (1922–2006), who produced *Viridiana*, *The Exterminating Angel* and *Simon of the Desert*.

To José Rubia Barcia

Mexico City, 8 September 1960[1]

My dear Barcia,

Full of remorse and with a supreme effort of will, I am finally replying to your letter of 7 August. If it wasn't for your annual letter, you would indeed never hear from me directly, although that would not mean I would cease to have the same great friendship for you as always.

I was deeply moved by my trip to Spain. I met wonderful groups of young 'nonconformists'.[2] I have hopes for the revival of Spain. I plan to go back and if it wasn't for my 'advanced' age, I would go back and live there.

I've asked my book dealer for *La novela del indio Tupinamba*.[3] If you let me know, I will pass the original copy of your book[4] that I have looked after so carefully, to De Andrea at once. As for the book you are going to publish in English on Valle Inclán, I am assuming that it is the same wonderful essay on him you sent me some years ago.[5]

I've now crossed, although with the usual bother of the consulate waiting rooms, the golden threshold. You cannot imagine how much I want to get to Hollywood, just to see you and your family and to relive the old days. I'm sure it won't be long now before I put this plan into action. I was about to sign a contract to make a film with Harold Hecht,[6] but nothing came of it. I would actually prefer to go as a tourist and spend a week or so in Los Angeles. Jeanne and I found the girls delightful, although I did feel a certain 'melancholic sorrow' to see reflected in them how the years have passed for me. I'm now in my 60s. Still smoking and drinking like a barbarian Cossack. But getting by OK.

The last film I made here that got the Jury Special Mention at the Cannes Festival, is called *The Young One*.[7] It's made with American actors and in English. It addresses issues of race and sex, with the rape by a white man of a girl.

Columbia is going to distribute it. It stars Zachary Scott.[8] The other actors, four in total, I found in New York, on Broadway.[9]

I'm now preparing a film for November (you can see I'm getting some wonderful opportunities here in Mexico) about the life of an 'enlightened' novice,[10] who, if not wholly Molino-ist,[11] is at least rather Galician-ist, thanks to her countryman Prisciliano.[12] This will all sound a bit mad, but it will make more sense when you see the film.

Exhausted by the gigantic effort involved in writing this letter, I shall sign off with huge hugs that I ask you to distribute, equally, between Evita and the two girls,

Buñuel

Spa Tls L, CBC; *CLB* 77–79

[1]   'French Line' letterhead.
[2]   Saura and Portabella, among others.
[3]   Surrealist novel by Granell, published by Costa-Amic in Mexico City in 1959.
[4]   *Umbral de sueños.*

⁵ Barcia's new book, *A Bibliography and Iconography of Valle Inclán* (Los Angeles: University of California Press, 1960).
⁶ US producer (1907–85), associate of actor Burt Lancaster between 1954 and 1959.
⁷ *The Young One* received a 'Special Mention' Jury award.
⁸ US actor (1914–65).
⁹ Bernie Hamilton, Key Meersman, Crahan Denton and Mexican actor, Claudio Brook (1927–95).
¹⁰ *Viridiana*.
¹¹ 'Molinosismo', contemplative, mystical order founded by priest Miguel de Molinos (1628–96).
¹² Galician Bishop (340–385), one of the first Christians sentenced to death for heresy.

To Susan Franklin[1]

Mexico, 19 September 1960

Dear Mrs Franklin,

I received your letter² of September 1, and I apologize not to have answered you sooner.

I am sorry that I cannot give permission to Mr Aranda for the publication of the scenario made by me in collaboration with Mr Larrea. Neither for the scenario nor for the theoretical explanation that precedes the story. The reason is that Mr Larrea do[es] not agree that the whole thing be published. It looks like that he is preparing a book about the same subject, but of a philosophical stand point.

I do not know if I can be of any help for the preparation of the series of my films. In any case the Paris Cinematheque has many of them. Mr Amos Vogel has a subtitled English copy of The Criminal Life of Archibaldo de la Cruz *and he has my request to lend it to you. I think he has also* Nazarín.

My warm regards to Mr Griffith and please do to absolve me for my poor English.

Yours sincerely
Luis Buñuel

Eng Tls, MoMA/12.04

¹ Deputy Director, MoMA.
² Letter from Susan Franklin to LB (MoMA 12.04).

To Pere Portabella

Mexico City, 8 October 1960[1]

My dear Portabella,

I'm a terrible 'epistolary', so I'll get straight to the point for the sake of brevity. But before getting down to this, I wanted to say what wonderful memories I have of you and Elena,² of those meetings and trips to Cuenca, La Companza, etc., that we may soon be able to repeat far more often …

In Madrid, I made a verbal agreement to be formalized on my return to Mexico, with Gustavo Alatriste, the Mexican industrialist and husband of Silvia Pinal,³ who has had nothing up until now to do with the cinema. He's given me absolute *freedom* to make a film. I began work on 1 July and will have the whole script finished by the end of this month. Alatriste is coming on the 10th, the day after tomorrow, to Madrid. We were going to shoot the film in Mexico at the end of November, but at the last minute he decided to make it in Spain, beginning in January. I told him that, if he wants to go into co-production, he should speak to you, and in case he does, I've enclosed a synopsis of the film. It is called *Viridiana*. It's an original story and an inevitable continuum along my old lines. It's full of ideas but could seem a bit soft in terms of form and it is, as far as possible, a commercial film. The most important thing, the details, are not in the synopsis. I have great faith in the character of timid Don Jaime[4] and in the behaviour and reactions of the beggars, particularly the witch's Sabbath at the end.

Alatriste will also see Muñoz Suay. He'll try and see you at the Plaza. He is staying with Silvia Pinal at the Torre de Madrid, Plaza de España. I've recommended you particularly warmly to him. If you do arrange something, you would be the real producer because he knows nothing about film. He has been extremely good to me. But he'll give you a detailed *Who's Who* before coming to any arrangement.[5]

Give my very best to the remarkable Saura, I think of him often. I read the wonderful review of *The Deliquents*[6] in *Positif.*

Much love to Elena and you
from, Luis Buñuel

Spa Als L, PP; *CUA* 570–571 f

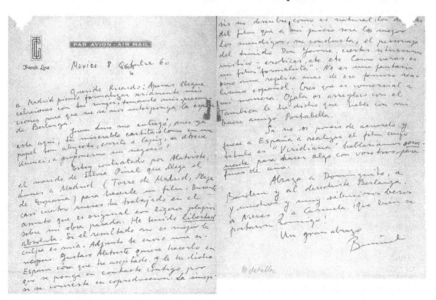

Figure 54 Letter from Buñuel to Muñoz Suay, 8 October 1960.

---

1   'French Line (*à bord*)' letterhead.
2   Wife of Portabella.
3   Mexican actress (born 1931), starred in three films directed by LB and produced by her husband Alastriste.
4   Played by Fernando Rey.

⁵ English in the original.
⁶ Robert Benayoun, 'Los Golfos', *Positif*, no. 35 (July 1960), p. 31.

To Ricardo Muñoz Suay

Mexico City, 8 October 1960[1]

Dear Ricardo,

As soon as I get to Madrid I am seriously planning to formalize my relationship with your wife,[2] taking precautions to make sure Berlanga's wife[3] doesn't come between us.

Juan Luis is here now, and he passed on your miserable little letter. A business proposal from UNINCI on such a wretched piece of paper and in pencil, what a cheek?!

I have a contract with Alatriste (Silvia Pinal's husband), who is arriving in Madrid on Monday, to make a film. I've been working on the story for nearly four months, which is original, with some light plagiarizing of my earlier works.[4] I've had *complete freedom*. If the result is no better, it will be my fault. I am enclosing the synopsis. Gustavo Alatriste wants to make it in Spain and I've agreed. And I've told him to get in touch with you if it turns into a co-production. Of course, the synopsis doesn't give away all the details that I think will be the film's best features. The beggars, their behaviour, the character of timid Don Jaime, certain mystical-erotic scenes, etc., etc. As you will see, it is a 'formalist' film. It's another version of the famous Spanish realism, rather than a fantasy. I think it's my version of commercial. I hope you can arrange something with him. I've also told him to speak to my good friend Portabella.

If you don't come to an arrangement with him and I go to Spain to make the film, which is called *Viridiana*, we'll talk *seriously* about making something together at the end of the year.

Give Dominguito a hug from me,[5] and one for Bardem and the right-wing Berlanga. And many, very silent kisses to Nieves and Carmela. They were so good to me!

Much
love,
Buñuel

Spa Als L, RMS; *CUA* 568–569 f

¹ 'French Line' headed letterpaper.
² Nieves Arrazola (born 1916).
³ Luis García Berlanga (1921–2010), film director attached to UNINCI, husband of María Jesús Manrique (1921–2010).
⁴ *Viridiana* loosely based on the novel *Halma* (1895) by Galdós.
⁵ Domingo Dominguín.

To UNINCI

Madrid, 25 November 1960

LUIS BUÑUEL PORTOLÉS and JULIO ALEJANDRO DE CASTRO,[1] authors of
the story and dialogues of *Viridiana*, HEREBY DECLARE THAT: on 25 November
1960, they have ceded all rights to the aforementioned story and dialogues to the
production company UNIÓN INDUSTRIAL CINEMATOGRÁFICA SA (UNINCI
SA), for the production of a film of the same name.[2]

Madrid, 25 November 1960
Luis Buñuel and Julio Alejandro

Spa Tls, AMEC; *UNI* 452 f

[1]   Poet and scriptwriter (1906–95), exiled in the Philippines and Mexico, worked with LB on five film
    scripts, including *Nazarín* and *Viridiana*.
[2]   Filmed in Madrid, February and March 1961.

To José Francisco Aranda

[Madrid, 1960][1]

Questions to Luis Buñuel for the book Luis Buñuel: Critical Biography *by José Francisco
Aranda.*[2]

1. *May I publish your 1938 'Autobiography'*[3] *held at the Museum of Modern Art in
   New York, which the Museum has sent with their permission.*
      I can't imagine it's of any interest, but you can publish it. I wrote it because they
   asked for it in America when I applied for a job.
2. *Whether I can expand it with information gathered from various family members,
   friends, critics, intellectuals, etc., and whether I should put those in after your own or
   alongside your own (indicating their origin).*
      You can expand it but do make sure that your sources are authentic and
   verified.
3. *Whether you or he*[4] *could send me the biography from 1939 to 1959 on, let's say, 4
   sheets of paper such as these.*
      Juan Luis will be able to tell you, because he lived it with me. He's also more
   sensible and objective than my dear sister Conchita.[5]
4. *Whether you remember any journals, and if so in which issues, you published any
   poetry, literary articles (I've got everything on cinema).*
      In *La Gaceta Literaria, Horizonte,*[6] *Le Surréalisme au service de la révolution.*[7]
5. *Whether you worked for Epstein paid or unpaid; whether, as has been suggested,
   you had any influence, in* The Fall of the House of Usher, *on the shots of the guitar
   strings that break, the editing of the alternating shots of the toads and the baby owl.*
      I worked for free, I had no influence over that film.

6. *Whether you had any input* into The Siren of the Tropics *(furniture, guns on the wall, directorial details, etc.).*

   No input.

7. *What did you do on* Les Chansons filmées *and on which you worked? The soundtrack?*

   I don't know that film and so had no input.

8. *Whether you produced anything in Spain for Latin America (other than* Juan Simón's daughter, Don Quintín the Sourpuss, Sentry, Keep Watch! *and* Who loves Me?*)*

   No.

9. *How much should I say about* España leal in armas *and whether you can give me any information or photos?*

   I had no role, other than as an embassy attaché, in that film.

10. *A brief note on* The Vatican of Pius XII *from March of Time.*

    I only translated the English.

11. *Whether you took part, if only indirectly or as part of a team, in any New York documentaries.*

    No. But I did edit lots of versions of films that had already been made.

12. *Whether I can transcribe, fully or partially,* Goya and the Duquesa de Alba.[8]

    No, because I think it's dreadful. I only wrote it to see if I could sell it to Paramount.

13. *I need a good photo of* The Great Casino, The Great Madcap, The Brute, Susana, Illusion Travels by Streetcar, The River and Death, *and* Republic of Sin.

    Juan Luis will bring you what he can, but it won't be easy.

14. *I need a photo, details, story and any Mexican reviews of* The Daughter of Deceit, *about which I have no information whatsoever.*

    That film was a Mexican *remake*[9] of *Don Quintin the Bitter.*

15. *If there is a copy of* A Woman without Love, *which two writers have mentioned as yours (wrongly, I think).*

    That's a film I made in two weeks of no interest at all.

16. *Anything else that might occur to you. I would like written authorization from Luis Buñuel. If you like, I can send you the book before it goes to the editors. I'd love to have a few words from him.*

    I'd be very grateful if, for the sake of objectivity and accuracy, you would send me a draft. I'll limit myself to agreeing details or facts about my life if they are accurate and correcting them if they aren't.[10]

[Luis Buñuel]

Spa Alu, ARA/09/07/03

---

[1] Questions typed by Aranda and addressed to Juan Luis, with handwritten answers by LB.

[2] F. Aranda, *Luis Buñuel: Biografía crítica* (Barcelona: Lumen, 1969).

[3] 'Autobiography' dated July 1939 (MoMA/12.05).

4 Aranda gave the questionnaire to Juan Luis Buñuel ('you') to pass on to his father ('he').
5 Published article 'Mon frère Luis', *Positif*, no. 42 (November 1961), pp. 19–25.
6 Art journal edited by Juan Chabás, Pedro Garfias and José Rivas Panedas in Madrid in 1922 and 1923, in which LB published 'Instrumentación', *Horizonte*, no. 2 (30 November 1922), p. 4, and 'Suburbios', *Horizonte*, no. 4 (January 1923), p. 9.
7 LB published 'Une Girafe' in *Le Surréalisme au service de la révolution*, no. 6 (16 May 1933), pp. 4–36.
8 'The Duchess of Alba and Goya' (MoMA/12.06), new undated version in English of the 1926 script, 23 h.
9 English in the original.
10 LB revised and added notes to Aranda's book, publication delayed until 1969.

Figure 55 Buñuel during filming of *Viridiana*, Madrid, February 1961.

To Jean Giono[1]

Jean Giono
Avenue Bretteville, Neuilly sur Seine

Madrid, 19 March 1961

WOULD BE DELIGHTED TO MAKE *THE HUSSAR*.[2]
THANK YOU,
BUÑUEL

Fre Tel, JG

1 French writer (1895–1970)
2 *Le hussard sur le toit* (Paris: Gallimard, 1951); Giono had sent a dedicated copy to LB in 1951 (AB/ 150).

To Katia Acín Monrás[1]

Madrid, 1 April 1961

My dear friend Katia,

As I'm not back in Mexico until June and have access to some money over here, I am taking the liberty of enclosing a cheque from the Banco Español de Crédito (number 350612) for the sum of 60,000 pesetas, as an advance on the sum I intend to send you and your sister[2] as soon as I can check and adjust my accounts in Mexico. It goes without saying that this, and any other money I send, is to be shared equally between you and your sister. I am sure that in doing so, I am fulfilling the wishes of your dear parents, were they still alive.[3] I would be grateful if you could confirm receipt of this letter.

I was delighted to meet you. Do please send my best regards to your husband[4] and to your sister.

Yours, most cordially,
Luis Buñuel
Torre de Madrid 17–8[5]

Spa Tda, AB/1401.15; *FA* f

[1] Artist (1923–2004), daughter of Ramón Acín.
[2] Sol Acín Monrás (1925–98).
[3] Acín and his wife Concha Monrás, assassinated by Nationalists in August 1936.
[4] Federico García Bragado, lawyer.
[5] Includes handwritten note by Buñuel: 'I sent another 25,000 pesetas on the 24th of December 1962, through my brother-in-law Vicente Mercadal.'

From Sol Acín Monrás

Huesca, 4 April 1961

Dear friend,

I am acknowledging receipt of your letter and cheque and, most importantly, sending our thanks for your wonderful gesture and for the on-going friendship you feel for my parents that is so clear in every line of your letter.

I am spending a few days in Huesca, but my usual address is Barcelona (Calle Viladomat 226, 2o, 1a). If you are ever there, I would be delighted to meet you in person, if it were of no inconvenience to you and you were to let me know where I might find you. It would be like having a momentary connection with a world we've only been able to imagine, but which nonetheless remains very real.

Thank you once again.
Cordially yours,

Sol Acín
38 General Franco, Huesca

Spa Als, AB/1401.17

To Domingo [Dominguín]

Paris, 2 May 1961

Dear Domingo,

Quintana[1] brought me the publicity material[2] for Cannes yesterday, and I was very disappointed. It's not easy to throw together something so stupid and tasteless, and yet so pretentious at the same time. Here is my brief critique of said material:

1) What a horrible poster of the living dead! What a garish blend of colours! That alone is an insult to the film. I hope you burn it and scatter its ashes.

2) Silvia and Alatriste will be offended and for good reason. I was there when you promised her name would appear at the top of the list of actors. This was a reasonable request because, all other considerations aside, she is undoubtedly the protagonist of the film. You've not only failed to keep that promise, but you've not even added her name to that dreadful photo of her on one of the back covers.[3]

3) The photographs are all extremely poor quality, the sepia-tinted ones are the worst. They look like pumpkins!

4) My handsome figure appears on the front cover. 'What wonderful publicity my dear friends have provided for me!' was my immediate hope, only to be immediately dashed when I find myself described as the executive producer of 'nefarious' films. I can't decide whether this cutting remark is an attack on objectivity or my own back.

5) Less said the better about the translation into English. But, for Christ's sake ...! Let's hope no English-speaker reads it. The literal translation into English of titles of my films sold to English-speaking countries is, however, an extraordinary lapse. And what translations! Why didn't someone ask me for the English titles of those films?

6) Shamelessly vacuous publicity for the countless producers who have taken advantage of the arrival of *Viridiana*, UNINCI, Films 59, Argentina, etc. Many of their films are lost to history, in many cases without trace. Why spend two whole pages on each one: *Sonatas*,[4] *Los golfos, El cochecito*[5] etc.? Three pages on *Viridiana* and eight on out-of-date material. It's provincial and pretentious. Laughable!

7) Anarchic, confused profusion of pamphlets. Just one, discrete, intelligent and up-to-date one, would have been enough.

8) Whose idea was it to get the production company to write its own critique of *Viridiana*? What's left for the critics?

9) Another grave insult to Silvia. Her biography mentions her triumph at Cannes with the Tulio Demicheli film.[6] Did you not know that in the history of the Cannes Festival this film is by far the most heckled, mocked and derided? I was there at the screening. A cruel joke on Silvia! Because its failure was not her fault of course.

And I could go on at length about this stuff you've pulled together, but I can't be bothered. I'm going to ask only one thing, seriously: burn it all. It's petulant, shabby, inaccurate, provincial, and the colours and typography are dreadful. It would be better for the film to arrive with no word and be condemned for what's in it, than beforehand, for what's been said about it.

Anxiously awaiting your agreement and confirmation of your arrival. You should send apologies to Alatriste, Quintana tells me you were foolish enough to send him copies.

Best wishes,
Luis Buñuel

Spa Tls, RMS; *UNI* 489–491

[1]   Gustavo Quintana, head of production, *Viridiana*.
[2]   Publicity material for presentation of *Viridiana* at Cannes in 1961.
[3]   Trilugal pressbook for *Viridiana* (ARA/16/10).
[4]   Feature co-produced by UNINCI and Barbachano Productions in 1959, dir. Bardem and starring María Félix, Aurora Bautista, Fernando Rey and Francisco Rabal.
[5]   *El cochecito* (1960), produced by Films 59, dir. Marco Ferreri.
[6]   Argentine film-maker (1914–92), director of *Un extraño en la escalera* in 1955, starring Silvia Pinal and Arturo de Córdova, presented at Cannes that year.

From Robert Favre Le Bret

Paris, 6 June 1961

My dear friend,
    Nothing could have made me happier than to see you emerge victorious from the votes that awarded you the Grand Prix at the International Film Festival.[1]
    Your name had already appeared several times over the years on the list of winners at Cannes, but I was hoping you would get the top prize one day. And finally, that day has come, and it is so well deserved!
    The announcement of the award met with unanimous and positive approval, which is rare indeed … As well as the intrinsic value of the film, your loyalty to the medium has won you that Palme d'Or.
    I should, however, express two regrets. The first being that your health prevented you from coming to Cannes, where I should very much have liked to congratulate you in person. The second, that measures have been taken against the Director General of Spanish Cinematography and Theatre, Muñoz Fontán,[2] arbitrary measures that have surprised and saddened me at the same time.

I hope to have the pleasure of seeing you again in the near future, whether in France or in Mexico.

With admiration and friendship,
Favre Le Bret

PS I didn't write earlier, because I only got your address from your son today.

Fre Tls, AB/1426.103

[1] *Viridiana* screened at Cannes on 17 May 1961 and was awarded joint *Palme d'Or* the following day with *Une aussi longue absence* (The Long Absence, 1961), dir. Henri Colpi; Jury members, presided over by Giono, included Pedro Armendáriz, Mauriac and Italian critic Luigi Chiarini (1900–75).
[2] José María Muñoz Fontán, sacked by Franco when *Viridiana* was declared to be blasphemous by the Vatican press ('Ribalta dei fatti', *L'Osservatore Romano*, 21 May 1961, p. 2).

To José Rubia Barcia

Mexico City, 19 June 1961

My dear Don José,

Your 'annual' letter has arrived, and I am hurrying to reply. I shall start by bringing you up to date with my life. I spent six months in Spain where I made a film called *Viridiana*. Last May, it won the Grand Prix at the Cannes Festival. *L'Osservatore Romano* called it 'sinful and sacrilegious'. As a result, Franco sacked the Director General of Cinematography, the President of UniEspaña[1] and the Censor-in-Chief. It has caused an uproar in Paris like *The Golden Age*.

People says[2] it's my best film. Who knows?! I did make it with complete and utter freedom though, both from the producer and the authorities, which is incredible. My name and the film title are banned in Spain.[3]

I found your book[4] waiting for me when I got back from Paris three weeks ago. I've re-read it and I'm even more impressed than when I read the manuscript some, three, I think, years ago. It's very well presented[5] and edited. I wouldn't be surprised, of course, if that kind of book doesn't reach the masses and never becomes a *bestseller*. Bollocks to *bestsellers*. I congratulate you on its publication. The important thing is that it is out.

I'm delighted you are finally coming to Mexico mid-August. Your room upstairs is already waiting. Bed, board and great conversation, even a glass or two! What more could you want?! It will be so good to see you again. I hope you won't find me too aged. I'll be fairly busy, so the only thing I won't be able to do is to accompany you on trips to Mexico, if you make any. I mean, trips around the republic. But at home, your wish is my command.

Multiple kisses to Evita and the girls, and a hug for you,
Buñuel

Spa Desc, CBC; *CLB* 79–80

¹ Jorge Tussell, president of UniEspaña, government organization under Franco for the promotion of Spanish film abroad.
² English in the original.
³ *Viridiana* was not premiered in Spain until 9 April 1977.
⁴ *Umbral de sueños*, eventually published by Orbe Publications in Los Angeles in 1961.
⁵ The book has, in the form of an epigraph, an Alexandrine sonnet by Jorge Guillén.

To Zachary Scott

Mexico, 20 June 1961

Dear Zachary,
I have been in Europe for seven months and came back to Mexico only fifteen days ago. Between the correspondence that heaped during my absence I find your very kind letter. But I am a very bad correspondent and especially now that my 'secretary' Juan Luis is absent. He has remained in Paris.

Thanks a lot, to you and Ruth[1] for your cable about the Golden Palm of Viridiana *that I shot in Madrid. I had a total freedom not only from my Mexican producer Mr Alatriste, who is not at all related with motion pictures, but from the Spanish authorities. Unbelievable!*

You know that I shall be very happy if we meet again in a film, for instance, in Under the Volcano.[2] *But I am under contract with the same Mr Alatriste for another film.[3] I shall not be free until February 1962. I imagine that you will not be able to wait until then. But if it does not mind, my only condition would be that the whole film be made in Mexico. As for the treatment, it could be made during the remaining of the year. I have not a special name of writer to give to you. It is obvious that I would revise, add, suppress, etc., the treatment afterwards, without interference of the author.*

When shall I see you both again? I have a very pleasant memory of our last meeting in Cannes.

My fondest wishes to Ruth.
Cordially yours,
Luis Buñuel

Eng Tls, ZSA

1 Ruth Ford (1911–2009), US actress, Scott's second wife.
2 Film adaptation of *Under the Volcano* (London: Jonathan Cape, 1947), novel by English writer Malcolm Lowry (1909-57).
3 *The Exterminating Angel*

From Vinicio Beretta[1]

Locarno, 4 August 1961

My dear Don Luis,

Now that the XIV International Film Festival[2] has ended, it gives me great pleasure to tell you that the screening of your film outside the competition was an enormous success.

At the very last minute, I was confronted, personally, with a series of difficult obstacles raised by the Spanish authorities: both in Madrid (from the General Board of Cinematography[3]), and in Bern (from the Spanish Embassy in Switzerland), they bombarded me with telegrams and phone calls in an attempt to prevent us screening your film which, the Spaniards claimed, was 'smuggled' out of Spain.[4] Naturally, I refused to accede to Francoist desires:[5] that would have been impossible due to my sincere affection for you, my admiration for your work, and the fact that I believe *Viridiana* to be a genuine masterpiece.

I hope to be back in Mexico in November and I would love to meet up you again, of course.

With most affectionate regards, Yours,
Vinicio Beretta
Festival Internazionale del Film

Fre Tls L, AB/1426.102

[1] Film critic (1920–72), director of the Locarno International Film Festival between 1960 and 1966.
[2] Founded in Locarno, Switzerland, in 1946.
[3] Dirección General de Cinematografía, directed at that time by the Falangist journalist Jesús Suevos.
[4] To justify its prohibition, Nationalist authorities claimed the copy of *Viridiana* was smuggled out of Spain (the board of censors only saw an unfinished copy, which was only edited for sound in Paris a few days before being screened at Cannes).
[5] Letter from Beretta to the Spanish Ambassador to Switzerland, 24 July 1961 (*UNI* 581).

From Álvaro Mutis[1]

Mexico City, 18 August 1961

My dear Luis,

I wanted to put down in writing the impression made on me by *Viridiana*, firstly, because words spoken with the all the emotion and enthusiasm of mutual friendship always sound so banal, and secondly because it pains me to think that the grim routine that stifles so much in life might also swallow up, along with so many other treasures, this opportunity to tell you what your film means to me.

The first thing that surprised me about *Viridiana* was the story itself. Until now, I had always been bothered by a certain awkwardness and artificiality in film narratives, the way 'what happens' comes up against the limitations of this medium that are so much more evident than those of other art forms. There was always a kind of orthopaedic

Figure 56 With members of the Nuevo Cine group in Mexico City, 1961; standing, unknown, García Ascot, José Luis González de León, Buñuel, Gabriel Ramírez, Armando Bartra and unknown; bending, de la Colina, Elizondo and García Riera.

adjustment of the story to the rigid mould of a system of expression of dubious efficacy. Then suddenly, last night, I witnessed the miracle of 'knowing', participating in facts, feelings, settings and symbols that could only have been transmitted to me in this unique form, and with the same endlessly vital efficiency of a Goya, or of the episode with the lions in *Don Quijote*, of Sanseverina's love.[2] For the first time, cinema has managed fully to communicate to me a whole world, specific, ever- lasting and created with that *duende*[3] some still call genius.

How odd – and how appropriate! – that the first film to provide all this for me should be a Spanish film, and Spanish in its very essence, rather than in dubious local colour or heroic anecdotes; Spanish like the Archpriest of Hita,[4] like Quevedo, like Larra,[5] like Goya, again, and also like Saint Teresa[6] or Saint Ignatious.[7] In short, I have seen the rebirth of a voice that was lost twenty years ago to criminals, lies, sanctimoniousness, and the humiliating and bitter shadow of exile. The voice of Spain that is so vital to us now that we are reduced more each day to a senseless and circumscribed servitude.

I believe the primary virtue of *Viridiana*, beyond overcoming the limitations that made cinema a suspect craft, lies in being so quintessentially Spanish.

Luis, *Viridiana* is so important, so transcendental for the world and for Spain that the silence that might fall on it and the obstacles that might be put in the way of its exhibition, rather than discouraging us, show us that cinema, thanks to you, is beginning to see the end of that painful process all true and lasting art has to suffer before becoming a legacy for all mankind and the evidence of our passage through this world.

It is not order exactly, nor much less clarity that have helped me this time to communicate my thoughts on *Viridiana* to you. These lines are just a heartfelt testament of my admiration for you and your work. Only today, some of those of us who were there last night at the screening of your film[8] were saying that knowing we are your friends and remembering that you share with us this slice of human life, is one of the few consolations left to us in this ugly age of artificial satellites and other such lamentable devices.

A huge hug from your dear friend,
Álvaro Mutis
Tele Journal, 48 Córdoba

Spa Tls L, AB/2054.21

1. Colombian writer (1923–2013), based in Mexico from 1956.
2. Duchess Gina Sanseverina, character in Stendhal's novel, *La Chartreuse de Parme* (1839).
3. Spanish term for a kind of 'inner demon' of creative inspiration made famous by Lorca's lecture delivered in Argentina in 1933 on the 'Theory and Play of the *Duende*'.
4. Medieval poet, Juan Ruiz, known as the Archpriest of Hita (1283–1351), author of one of Spain's most highly regarded collections of poetry, *El Libro del buen amor* (The Book of Good Love).
5. Mariano José de Larra (1809–37), Spanish journalist and writer.
6. Santa Teresa de Jesús (1515–82), famous Spanish mystic and author.
7. San Ignacio de Loyola (1491–1556), soldier and religious leader, founded the Catholic order the Society of Jesus.
8. Possibly at a private view organized by Alatriste; *Viridiana* was not premiered in Mexico until 1963.

From José Bergamín

Madrid, 1 September 1961

Dear friend Luis,

I found your letter when I got back from spending August in Galicia, travelling through the towns of the Rías Bajas, spending a few days in Pontevedra then on to Santiago. I didn't know any of the places, not León nor Zamora, which I discovered on that trip. It was a really hot summer with fiery suns, very Galician. I was really excited about Zamora, most of all. And as always, Toro and Tordesillas … And always that contrast between the marvellous and the horrific that is so Spanish.

I think the review you sent me of *Viridiana* is wonderful. Accurate in all depth and detail. The best I've read on *Viridiana*, which I haven't yet seen, although I do hope to soon (unofficially, of course).[1] Here, as you know, utter silence has been decreed while the crooked official administration goes on spinning its flimsy web for every idiotic and ambitious fly to fall into.

As I've spoken to almost no one about this, or anything else, while I was away from Madrid, there's not much I can tell you. My impression is that the extraordinary 'Viridianesque' *faena*[2] preceded a sudden and fatal *coup de grace*. Have they not yet sent you the ears and tail? I hope you will soon be back in spite of everything and to spite totalitarianism.

As for my title,[3] do with it what you wish (and if the $300 wasn't a joke, so much the better!). It's yours anyway. I'd love to see it up in lights already.

To all our living, dead and dying friends a big hug, and another to you from,
Pepe

[PS] Send my love to Jeanne.

If you see Sánchez Ventura, tell him I'll write, and that I've seen a lot of his son over here; he's a wonderful boy.

Spa Tlsps, AB/600; VIR 547 f

[1] Clandestine copies of *Viridiana* in Spain included the copy belonging to José Fernández Aguayo (1911–99), its director of photography.

[2] Bergamín was playing with the double meaning of 'faena' as both a 'dirty trick' and the preliminary steps of a bullfighter towards the final 'estocada' or, as used here, 'coup de grace', in French (killing of the bull); at a bullfight, the judge may then award the bullfighter one ear, two ears or the ears and tail according to the level of skill demonstrated.

[3] 'The Exterminating Angel', LB offered Bergamín US$300 for the rights to this title (that Bergamín had taken from the biblical Book of Revelations).

To Francisco Rabal

Mexico City, 6 September 1961

My dear nephew, favourite among my numerous nephews,

Your postcards arrive regularly, and they always make me very happy as, among other reasons, you are the only person who sends me news from time to time. May they continue, and may you not forget me. But I am now going to ask you for more than a few simple lines.

After the major scandal caused by some girlfriend and a chap called Jorge,[1] I've tried to get in touch with the producers, who have behaved like pigs. Since I left Domingo in Paris, he's not sent a single line. I'm ready to do whatever I can to help them, but to do that I need to know what's going on and how I may be useful.[2] So I'm giving up in the face of their rude silence. They have also treated Juan Luis very badly. They left him in the lurch after insisting he put himself at their and Alatriste's disposal. Not only have they not paid him what they promised, they've not replied to a single one of his letters or telegrams.[3]

I'd be really grateful if you could tell me as much as you can about what the situation is in Spain: what's going on officially and with our friends Domingo, Juan Antonio, etc. Also, tell me if you think that little film has once again closed to me the door to our beloved Spain. As a tourist even, because I do realize that as a director there's no chance.

I'm preparing a film I can really have some fun with.[4] I have in mind for you the role of a certain elegant colonel. I'll let you know about filming well in advance. Gustavo's producing. I'm working on the script now.

Give your lot a big kiss from me: Asunción, tough little Rabalito, and my small leading lady.[5] And a hug to Damián.[6] How is your father getting on?

Much love,
Luis

Spa Tls, FR; BVMC f

1   Reference to Rabal's character in *Viridiana*, and the character, Viridiana.
2   Concerning commercial release of *Viridiana* following court case between UNINCI and Alatriste.
3   UNINCI dissolved after prohibition of *Viridiana*.
4   *The Exterminating Angel.*
5   Teresa Rabal, who played the child, Rita, in *Viridiana*.
6   Damián Rabal (1920–91), agent and brother of the actor.

7

From *The Exterminating Angel* to *Simon of the Desert* (1961–6)

To José Rubia Barcia

Mexico City, 2 October 1961

My dear *don* Pepe,

I thought Rafael was only going stay with you for a few days, but I gather from your last letter that in fact he spent quite a while at your house. I'm so sorry if he put you to any trouble, but, as there's nothing I can do about that now, please accept our sincere thanks to you and Evita, from this dwelling *de senectute*.[1]

López Fandos[2] is in Argentina and will be there until the end of November. Anyway, I passed on to Alatriste what you said in your letter about distribution, etc., and the journal and *Viridiana*.[3] So it's up to him now. As for you, you could rein in the kindness a bit having done what you promised and forget about this Mexican business. The mess over the film is getting worse. It's now banned in France,[4] and some producers over here also tried, unsuccessfully, to get the government to ban it. Alatriste's solicitor left yesterday for New York, Paris and Madrid to try and sort it all out. It will be distributed in the US by Kinsley,[5] if they let him that is.[6] And now another owner has popped up declaring he's the film's only legal representative.[7] It all looks to me like some scheme hatched up by the Spanish authorities to get that castrated copy[8] I made for Spain out on general release. But enough of all that mess.

If you see Rafael, please tell him it's really important he gets the grades he needs for UCLA this first semester. He'll probably get carried away with the novelty of it all over there, girls and young people generally, and think he's in Capua[9] rather than Los Angeles.

I went by Espresate's Madero bookshop[10] yesterday and asked if *Umbral de sueños* had arrived and when it was going on sale. He's not received anything yet. What's your publisher up to? It's certainly not a book for the masses, but with decent distribution it could still sell reasonably well. Carlos Fuentes[11] won't be here until November and Paz, who's leaving the embassy in Paris, will be back here at some point. I want to hand them your book myself, but until they arrive I could let Espresate display them in the shop window. What do you think?

Until I hear from you, I'm going to give them to him anyway; there'll always be time to get them back.

Huge hugs for the whole Barcia family,
Buñuel

PS Gustavo Alatriste's address: Libros y Revistas, 108 Mier y Pesado, Mexico City 12.

Spa Tlsps, CBC; *CLB* 84–85

¹ Latin in the original: allusion to Cicero's 44 BCE essay 'On Old Age'.
² Blas López Fandos (1912–65), Spanish producer in exile in Mexico.
³ Information from Rubia to Alatriste about the possibility of selling the film in the United States.
⁴ After pressure put on the French government by the Spanish authorities to ban *Viridiana* in France, the film premiered on 4 April 1962 at the Studio des Ursulines.
⁵ Edward Kingsley (1914–62), US distributor, president of Kingsley-International Pictures, a subsidiary of Columbia Pictures.
⁶ *Viridiana* premiered in the United States in March 1962.
⁷ Joaquín Martí Domingo, Mexican living in Barcelona, associate member of UNINCI.
⁸ Cut to avoid censorship in Spain.
⁹ City of Imperial Rome.
¹⁰ Tomás Espresate Pons (1904–94), politician exiled to Mexico in 1942, founded the Madero bookshop with Enrique Naval in 1951.
¹¹ Mexican writer (1928–2012).

To Domingo Dominguín

Mexico City, 3 October 1961[1]

Dear Domingo,

A few words at top speed to warn you about something important: if, in all this mess about the film belonging to both Alatriste and UNINCI, you felt the need to use the document signing my rights to the story to UNINCI, under no circumstances do so, because Alatriste has a document demonstrating the opposite. You'll remember my intention, when I asked you for it, was to reassure him I wasn't trying to sell the film twice over. So, I gave him the document. But now I've suddenly realized this wretched mess could be used against you. Be careful!

I hope the copy Marti[2] is marketing is not the one I made for Spain.[3] For all our sakes and for the sake of our friendship.

You've left me completely out of all this, without even considering I might well have made a useful mediator and, with no word from you since I left Paris, all my information has come from just the one side (Alatriste's), this suggests to me an utter contempt for friendship that I do hope will not make this messy situation worse.

I felt I should warn you before it's too late, although I don't really believe you would take such dangerous steps to try to prove *total* ownership of the film.

I have nothing else to say.

Regards,
Luis

PS I sent you two letters a while ago. I then tried to reach you through Rabal, but to no effect on your insulting silence.

Tda, AB/1401.5; *LBAR* 426–427

[1] Draft with handwritten corrections including, crossed-out: 'I'm sending this letter in the same envelope as one to Ana María, so she can pass it on, just in case'.
[2] Joaquín Martí.
[3] UNINCI's negative of *Viridiana* was being marketed internationally by Martí and Dominguín despite a co-producer's contract reserving this right to Alatriste.

To Zachary Scott

Mexico City, 7 December 1961

My dear friend,

I've been meaning to reply to your kind letter of 21 November for a couple of weeks now. But I wanted to do it in English, so I kept putting it off for another day. Today though, I decided to write back 'in whatever language' because if I didn't it might be months before you got it. Forgive me: you can practise your Spanish reading these lines.

There's been a union dispute going on here between Mexican producers and technicians for months now, which is why I still haven't started the film that should have been on sets[1] from mid-November. If everything works out as we expect, I'll start shooting in Churubusco on 15 January. That means I won't be free until mid-April.

I've had several proposals from France in recent months, and one of them is very interesting.[2] I'm just waiting to read Harvey Breit's[3] treatment of *Under the Volcano* before accepting. If I think I can make a good film out of it, I'll put off going to France until Autumn 1962, but if not, I'll be in France in May.

Once we've agreed on the treatment, we could set a date to start filming.

I don't think, given the current situation in the Mexican film industry, that any producer here would take on your project as a co-production.

Until I've read Breit's treatment, or *script*,[4] I don't think you need to come over, although I would of course be delighted to see you for that or for any other reason.

Juan Luis is in Cambodia (Indochina) as assistant on an Anglo-French production.[5] He'll be back in Paris on 3 January.

I'd need to see the *script*[6] to estimate the cost of filming *Under the Volcano*. But even without considering the cost of the book and the salaries of the director and the actors, you would need to budget for at least one and a half million pesos.

My warmest regards to you and Ruth,
Luis Buñuel

Spa Tls, ZSA

[1] English in the original (on set); *The Exterminating Angel* eventually filmed at Churubusco Studios from 29 January to 9 March 1962.
[2] Possible reference to *Diary of a Chambermaid*.
[3] US journalist and playwright (1909–68), editor of Lowry's correspondence.
[4] English in the original.
[5] *Ton Ombre est la mienne* (1961), dir. André Michel, filmed in Angkor Wat.
[6] English in the original.

To Robert Favre Le Bret

Mexico City, 19 March 1962

Dear friend,

Thank you again for the very kind invitation to take part in the Jury at the Festival this year, but it will have to wait until next year when, if all goes well, I should be delighted to come to Cannes, I like it there a lot.

I think my film, *The Exterminating Angel,* is fairly unusual and worthy of a Festival like yours.[1] It will arrive with an official certificate to say it is 100% Mexican. Unfortunately, I cannot be there to present it myself, but Silvia Pinal, Gustavo Alatriste and my son Juan Luis will represent me.

Could I suggest you put the Alatristes up at the Carlton? They belong to that kind of *glitzy* crowd. Although I'm also sure that, like last year,[2] they'll be happy with whatever hotel you choose.

I promise the film will be in Cannes before 10 May. If it is at all possible, Alatriste would like the screening to take place four or five days before the end of the Festival.

Most cordially,
Luis Buñuel

Fre Tls, CIN

[1] *The Exterminating Angel* was screened at the official selection for 15th Cannes Film Festival in May 1962.
[2] For the screening of *Viridiana*.

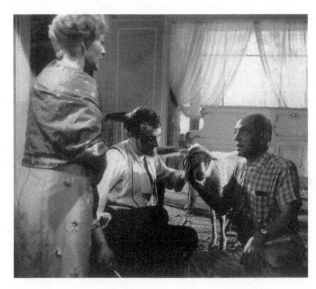

Figure 57 Pinal, Enrique Rambal and Buñuel, filming *The Exterminating Angel*, Mexico City, March 1962.

To Ricardo Muñoz Suay

Mexico City, 8 April 1962

Dear Ricardo,

Just when you're least expecting it, a letter from me arrives. My conscience was plaguing me for not having replied to your letter from Paris congratulating me on 22 February.[1]

I'm so sorry you've broken off your commercial and personal relationship with Domingo.[2] According to Juan Luis, Domingo cut you off because I said you were useless, an idiot, etc. That is precisely the way rows like this start. I won't deign to prolong this one: if the three of us meet again someday, I'll get it out in the open. But even if what Domingo claims I said were true, it would be very shabby to bring it into a row between friends. And speaking of Domingo, I had a letter from Mr Gilbert Samson, the owner of the Hotel Aiglon, just yesterday saying that, a month ago, our friend asked him for 150,000 francs, on top of the 100,000 francs he already owes in room bills.[3] He promised to pay it back in two or three days and has not been heard of since, he's not answering any letters asking for the money or telephone calls, because Mr Samson tried to call Madrid. That seems a really low trick to me. I feel quite embarrassed. There's no point in writing to Domingo, he never replies. If only he would write back to Samson and tell him he'll pay off his debts as soon as the situation is sorted out. What can we do?

Despite my friendship with Domingo, or rather because of it, I find it outrageous. I also think he's blaming Juan Luis for everything that happened with Alatriste. Juan will end up the bad guy in this story. I'll also set that straight one day. Thirty Domingos couldn't compare to one Juan Luis when it comes to honour. As soon as money and self-interest come into the equation, friendships dissolve.

I'd really like to know what you're doing, what you're working on and who with. You say Nieves still has work editing, but nothing about yourself. I have that natural slight concern that won't go until I hear what you're up to.

I'm presenting a film at Cannes made with far greater freedom than *Viridiana*. It's called *The Exterminating Angel*. The *scénario* and the dialogues are all mine and it's based on something I wrote five years ago with Alcoriza called *Los Náufragos de la calle de la Providencia*.[4] I don't know if it's good or just OK, but it's definitely unprecedented. It's ten reels, eight take place in a seven-metre-square room with twenty-one people, and no-one goes in or out. 'What a bore!', you'll be thinking. And you may be right.

Hugs to Nieves and kisses for the little Muñoz Suays.

As I don't think you are useless or idiotic (what nonsense!), I send another hug to you. If you chance to see or speak to Domingo, you can show him this letter. I'd give anything to be able to reach him myself: to have a chat and get this all off my chest.

Luis

Spa Tls, RMS

1 LB's birthday.
2 At UNINCI.
3 Letter from Samson to LB, 6 April 1962 (AB/1401.1).
4 Literally, The Castaways on Providence Street.

To Emmanuel Roblès

Mexico City, 14 May 1962

My dear friend,

Many thanks for your kind letter of [6] April. How embarrassing! It's taken me over a month to write back. But I do know I'm a terrible correspondent.

I feel very well-rewarded by the way you and some other friends responded to *Viridiana*, and proud to have made it. When I make a film, you could say I never think about the general public, just the handful of friends whose judgement I value most.

My dear friend Roblès, what I wouldn't give to film your wonderful *Montserrat*.[1] I've often wondered whether you could pay Fox back for the vile trick they played on you[2] by plagiarizing yourself, changing the place and maybe the time; whether you could come up with a script on exactly the same ethical dilemma.

Do please give it some thought.

I'm presenting another film at Cannes this year that I think may be a flop, but I'm pleased with it, relatively that is.

Very warmest regards from your friend,
Luis

Spa Tls, ER

[1]   Play written by Roblès in 1948 about a Spanish official sent to Venezuela to capture Simón Bolívar at the beginning of the nineteenth century.
[2]   20th Century Fox bought the rights to the novel (and the film adaptation by Lillian Hellman), but did not make the film.

From Gustavo Alatriste

Cannes, 23 May 1962

INTERNATIONAL FILM CRITICS' PRIZE AND AUTHORS' PRIZE.[1] I'M ORGANIZING A TEDEUM[2] AND HAVE INVITED THE POPE.

REGARDS,
ALATRISTE

Spa Tel, ABR/2050.160

[1]   *The Exterminating Angel* was awarded the FIPRESCI Prize and the Screenwriters' Guild at the Cannes Festival.
[2]   'Te Deum'; early Christian hymn of praise to God.

To Pierre Braunberger

Mexico City, 3 June 1962

My dear Pierre,

Please forgive the overly official letter I sent you. I just copied a 'business' template because I don't much like writing. Let's speak now as friends.

I have no recollection of our agreement on 20 November 1950, when, according to your letter, I ceded all distribution rights to *Land Without Bread ad infinitum* and, more importantly, to *An Andalusian Dog*. Could you, urgently, send me a copy of that document so I can see what I need to do to honour our agreement. It's very odd that I've never had a copy of that agreement. Or perhaps I did, I don't remember. Either way, I need that photocopy urgently.

The urgency comes from the fact that on my last visit to Spain, I finally met the two daughters of Ramón Acín, my friend who was executed on the first day of the Civil War[1] and who lent me the money to make *Land Without Bread*. I worked out what the film made between 1937 and 1961 and gave Acín's daughters the sum total of my earnings.

I now have an opportunity to sell the film and make my friends THREE TIMES MORE than what you've paid me over almost twenty years distribution which, to be honest, hasn't added up to much. I'm sure you'll see why I want to make a little more for my friends, whose financial situation is far from buoyant.[2]

Of course, all things being equal, I'd rather go with you than Gaborit: but before getting into any details, I'd like to see a copy of our written agreement.

One more thing: I'd like you to take back the copy the Société du Cinéma Panthéon deposited at the Centre National de la Cinématographie on 18 August 1945, the one that lists the Société as producer and scriptwriter. I'm sure this happened after Liberation to comply with some sort of legal requirement and because we weren't in touch, but I feel it is now time to correct that.

With all friendship,
Luis Buñuel

Fre Tls, PB

[1] Acín was shot on 6 August 1936.
[2] In a letter to LB, 8 June 1962, Braunberger gave up distribution rights to *An Andalusian Dog*, but asked to keep rights to *Tierra sin pan* (AB/568.35); LB agreed.

To Francisco Rabal

Mexico City, 23 July 1962

Dear most splendid nephew,

You're always so friendly and attentive, and I'm always so slippery and bad-mannered, failing to respond to your letters. Well, that's all over and I'm launching myself into this reply. With the same bold courage as I wrote to Fernando Rey a month ago. I thought you were in France because I read you were making a film over there. I mentioned my nephew a lot, of course, in my letter to Fernando, but you know how he loves to hear colleagues criticized, so I did have to pick on you to satisfy his sadistic tendencies. Please don't read that letter!

You wouldn't believe how often I think of our cinematic adventures and how much I'd like to renew them. I've asked Fernando to look into my situation in Spain and let me know. Theoretically, I have two wonderful opportunities for you and for him. Over here in Mexico too, when I'm looking for projects, I'm always trying to fit you in (a starring role, of course, not one of those bit parts I usually give to Fernando). It's such a shame! I'd really love to work in Spain again, but … I've had a few offers from France and England, but I can't decide, because of my poor hearing and how seriously they take film-making over there. So different from the friendly flippant way we work together!

I'm delighted to see you're so in fashion everywhere, Italy, Argentina, Spain, France …[1] We should sing you the International! I'd rather meet you in Spain, of course, even if it were just as two friends with no work. Alatriste is planning a co-production of *Divinas palabras*[2] in Spain. He thinks there's a chance the 'authorities' will accept it, but I think it's unlikely. It would be a great project for me. Wonderful parts for you and Fernando. We'll see what happens.

You didn't say what you think about the UNINCI-Alatriste mess. I'd really love to know, because so far, all my information has come from Gustavo. I've had not a word from that pig Domingo since I left him in Paris over a year ago. *Viridiana* has been an amazing success commercially, but between the thieving agents, producers' cuts, lawyers and all the mess, I'm not sure what it will make in the end. In France it's only predicted to cover just over production costs.

What film are you on now working in Paris, which director?[3] Send word, however brief.

I want to get to Madrid some way or other in October for a couple of months. But it depends if I'm well and if this bloody ear doesn't get worse, which looks unlikely.

Much love,
Luis

Spa Tls, FR; *BVMC* f

---

[1] In 1962, Rabal is starring in *L'Eclisse* (The Eclipse), directed by Michelangelo Antonioni in Italy, and in *Setenta veces siete* (The Female), directed by Leopoldo Torre Nilsson in Argentina.
[2] Famous Spanish play by Valle-Inclán published in 1919.
[3] With Georges Lampin in the film *Mathias Sandorf,* premiered in 1963.

To Zachary Scott

Mexico City, 8 August, 1962

My dear Zachary,

I suppose that you have returned from your long stay in Italy. I envy your immersion in humanism in the magnificent Italy.

I get, from diverse and varied sources, news that the work on the screen play of Under the Volcano *continues. My actual producer, Gustavo Alatriste* (Viridiana *and* The Exterminating Angel*) had dinner with Harry Breit (in Madrid) who spoke to them of your project.*

I am greatly interested in reading the treatment so far because this is the starting point for our working together again. I hold very dear memories of our Young One. *I hope that with the* Under the Volcano *we will be able to renew our friendship.*

For the moment, while waiting for news concerning the Under the Volcano, *I am preparing another film which, if at all possible, I will do in Spain during the beginning of 1963.*[1]

Figueroa has founded his own production house here in Mexico.

The mortal crisis of the awful Mexican cinema continues. Very few films are being shot. Juan Luis is now in Mexico … for the moment.

Then I await news from you. Give Ruth a strong abrazo[2] *for me.*

Yours sincerely,
Luis Buñuel

Eng Tls, ZSA

---

[1] Possibly, *Divinas palabras,* an unrealized project of LB's.
[2] Spanish in the original (hug).

To Zachary Scott

Mexico City, 15 August 62

Dear Zachary,

I received your letter of August 5th which must have crossed ways with my letter sent to you on that same date.

I'll answer briefly the questions you ask me. I think it more convenient that you send me Harvey Breit's screenplay the moment it is finished. In that way I can study it calmly. Immediately after we can see what dates you both could come down here to discuss the treatment.

The use of my time is as follows: there is a possibility that I may go to Spain for the months of October and November. After that, I'll come back to Mexico to start a film[1] around the first of February. I should be free during the beginning of April.

If your project of the Under the Volcano *becomes a fact, we could perhaps agree to film it in June of 1963. I have several offers to do films in Europe but I rather it be the* Under the Volcano.

Best wishes to Ruth and yourself,
Luis Buñuel

Eng Tls, ZSA

[1]   Possibly, *Simon of the Desert*, filming postponed until November 1964.

To Emmanuel Roblès

Mexico City, 17 August 1962

Dear friend,

Your letter from Paris arrived three days ago, and the postcard you sent from Sofia came yesterday.[1] Thank you.

I was surprised to hear Juan J. Ortega[2] was interested in a film adaption of your work. But it's greatly to his credit, because up until now, artistically, he's made very poor-quality films.

He's one of the most insipid Mexican producer-directors. Even if he did agree to me directing *Montserrat*, I'd be very reluctant to put myself in his hands. Your work deserves a far more financially sound production company.

I was talking to my producer, Gustavo Alatriste (*Viridiana* and *The Exterminating Angel*), yesterday about your project and Ortega's proposal. He's very interested in the possibility of producing *Montserrat* himself, and he wouldn't interfere with the adaptation and filming. He also told me he would take on all responsibility for any conflict with Fox. How? I don't know. In the meantime, if I were you, I would stall any business decisions over intellectual property, author's rights, etc. He will write to you. Alatriste is an exceptional producer and he's behaved very professionally towards me. He does, however, like an adventure and can take risks. Also, I'd like to stay out of any arrangement you come to with him.

I'm hoping to get to Paris at the end of September. Even if it was only to spend a good while together and revive our old friendship the trip would be worth it.

My most cordial regards,
Luis Buñuel

Spa Tls, ER

¹ The letter from E. Roblès to LB, 1 June 1962 (AB/585), saying he might re-adapt *Montserrat*; the card from Sofia has not survived.
² Juan José Ortega (1904–96), Mexican commercial film producer and director.

To Francisco Rabal

Mexico City, 3 September 1962

My dear uncle Paco,¹
You'll forgive me for addressing you in the familiar, but I feel the age difference between us is not sufficient to warrant an 'usted'.²

I finally have my visa – with all pomp and ceremony – to go to Spain at the end of this month, or maybe earlier. I'm not going over with any prospect of making a film, because I'm already contracted to Alatriste for the next one.³ I'll be there for two or three months writing my 'story' (no idea what it's about yet), although if the *Divine Words* project comes through I'll stay on much longer. At the moment, the Valle-Inclán thing is at the 'we'll see' phase. They want $20,000 for the book, which seems absurd to me. Outside Spain, no one, except Spanish teachers, has heard of Valle-Inclán.

Yesterday, Alatriste told me not to consider any film project or propose one myself, unless your name is on it as the 'leading man'. And he's right. Whether it's a Polish, French, Italian or Yank film, that's the role I see you in. The same way that for some of the old man roles I – only sometimes – see Fernando Rey.

In Hollywood, at Warner Brothers, I got to know the Italian producer Dario Sabatello.⁴ He has a production company in Rome now, called Produzione DS. He's determined to make a film with me. Do you know him? If you have any information, let me know. Trade secret.

Hugs and many of them from your nephew,
Luis

[PS] I'm sure we'll meet up in Madrid. Once I'm in Spain, it'll take a corkscrew to get me out.

Spa Tlsps, FR; *BVMC* f

¹ Reversing their usual affectionate greetings to one another as 'uncle' and 'nephew' here, LB calls Rabal (over twenty years younger) 'uncle'; a joke on seniority that continues in the comment in the first line about using the familiar 'tú', instead of the more formal 'usted'.
² See above.
³ *Simon of the Desert.*
⁴ Italian producer (1911–92) who worked on dubbing for Warner Brothers in the mid-1940s.

To Dalton Trumbo[1]

Mexico City, 4 October 1962

Dear Mr Trumbo,

I have just received, brought by Mr José Bolaños,[2] your admirable Johnny Got his Gun[3] *which I had already read when living in New York City some twenty years ago. I shall re-read it with much interest for it seems to me that it is as important now as it was then.*

I am leaving for Madrid this coming Sunday from where I shall visit Paris and Rome to attend some affairs concerning the cinema. My address, for the next month, will be:

Torre de Madrid, Plaza de España, Madrid

Bolaños tells me that you are planning a trip to Europe. It would be very pleasant if we were to meet over there. If you are going to Rome, please send me your address and, if at all possible, I shall try to co-ordinate my trip with yours.

I have asked Rafael to deliver this letter to you[4] and to extend my best wishes.

Please give my salutations to your wife.[5]

Sincerely,
Luis Buñuel

Eng Tlsps, DT/72/05

[1]   US author and scriptwriter (1905–76).
[2]   Mexican scriptwriter and director (1935–94).
[3]   *Johnny Got His Gun*, Trumbo's anti-war novel published by J. B. Lippincott in Philadelphia in 1939.
[4]   In Los Angeles.
[5]   Cleo Beth Fincher (1916–2009).

From Dalton Trumbo

[Honolulu,] 10 October 1962

Sr Luis Buñuel
Torre de Madrid, Plaza de España

Dear Mr Buñuel:

After ten years, we are in touch again![1] I remember very well the evening we met at the Pepper's house, with you and the Hugo Butlers.

I don't know whether or not you are prone to compliments, but in any event, I think I should tell you that Fred Zinnemann,[2] with whom I am now working on Hawaii,[3] *admires your work extravagantly and speaks of you with the deepest respect.*

I don't know whether there is anything in Johnny Got his Gun *or not. Certainly, if Jose Bolanos had not brought the matter up, I should never had thought of it.*

My schedule is rather over-extended these days, but if you should have any ideas about filming the book, I would consider it an honour to be associated with you and the project.

I thought I might be in Rome late this year, but it appears now that I shall have to remain here on Hawaii.

Cordially,
Dalton Trumbo

Eng CmfL, DT/72/05

---

¹ After being imprisoned during the McCarthy era, Trumbo moved into exile in Mexico at the end of 1951.
² US film-maker (1907–97), of Austrian descent.
³ Working on the script for film *Hawaii* (1966), directed, in the end, by George Roy Hill.

To Luis Alcoriza

Madrid, 26 November 1962

Dear Luis,

A promise made is a debt unpaid. I have a chance to make any film I like over here on a very *ad hoc* basis with the producers.¹ They'll pay me enough to hire you. So, I propose the following:

1) You get a visa for Spain. I'm sure you'll get one, because over here they don't give a damn about your part in the La Paz thing.
2) I'll pay your economy class round-trip.
3) I'll pay a daily allowance, so you can lunch, dine and sleep in the manner that befits you.
4) 30,000 pesos to spend TWO MONTHS adapting something very interesting with me.

In other words, you would be in Spain for TWO MONTHS. Juan Luis told me your film² has been put back until March, which is why I think this project would suit you. I should say again that I would be paying you; not the producers. Too costly for them. Let me know if you agree and I'll confirm details, or retract, which is not up to me, but to the circumstances. I need a telegram with your answer, so I can act fast.

Please don't mention this letter to anyone. Except Janet, give her a hug from me.

Luis

[PS] If all goes well, it would be good if you could be here by 15 December *at the latest*. I'm sure you would get a contract for a *good* film once you were over here.

Alatriste *has quitted*.³ It's also likely I'll be back in Mexico very soon.

Spa Tlsps, ALC/01/04; *BRU* 28

---

¹ Associates of Época Films, production company formed by the critic Eduardo Ducay Berdejo (1926–2016), the poet Joaquín Gurruchaga (1910–2000), and the scriptwriter Leonardo Martín Méndez (1920–73).
² Possibly *Amor y sexo* filmed by Alcoriza in 1963.
³ English in the original.

To Francisco Rabal

Madrid, 28 November 1962

My dear nephew Paco,

Your letter arrived, and I am somewhat displeased to see you take issue with such a worthy actor, who does his best despite being Galician, old and all that.[1] The next time I see him I shall, without wishing to spread tittle-tattle, read him your letter.

At the moment I'm hovering, undecided. I may go back to Mexico, but it's equally likely I'll stay here or even end up in Paris. I think I'll come to a decision sometime between now and 5 December.

Alatriste decided, after much toing and froing, to back out of the co-production. I'm really sorry, because it's quite tricky for me to make a film with a Spanish company. There are two production companies, however, who want me to make a film with them, on whatever I want, one after the other. They're both reliable and extraordinarily friendly people, one lot in particular. I'm not sure what to do. I don't like the idea of being away from Mexico for so long, it could be a year. I'm not ambitious like you; I just want to get back to my monastic Mexican retreat. But over there, unless it's with Gustavo, I don't see much hope making a decent film. The best thing would be for all my friends to pay me a little monthly subscription, so I could retire from the filthy film business.

I'd be so sorry to leave without seeing you. But it would be very difficult – unless I decide to stay and work here – for me to wait until 20 December to see you in Madrid. I know I've felt your absence, I mean I've missed you, on this trip. I've only had one good meal, with my nephew Damián at the Mesón de Fuencarral. Before I leave, come what may, I shall visit your wife and children.

Until soon, perhaps, and until then, much love,
Luis Buñuel

Spa Tls, FR; *BVMC* f

---

1   Bantering, as in the previous letter, about an imaginary 'rivalry' between LB's two favourite actors, Rabal and Rey.

From Julio Cortázar[1]

Paris, 30 November 1962

Dear Buñuel,

Yes, *dear* Buñuel: dear for all that you are and for all that you've done and still do to wrench this stupid world from its carapace of daily, rotten habits. I never thought I would be fortunate enough to write to you, personally, to tell you, first and foremost, what your films have meant for those Argentines of my generation who chanced upon the pure marvel of *The Golden Age* in their youth and felt not all was lost as long as there were poets like you, rebels like you. I remember that when I arrived in Paris for the first time, twelve years ago, *The Young and the Damned* had just premiered there. It made such an impression on me that the very same night I wrote a review for *Sur*,[2] even though I'm quite bad at writing reviews and don't have the critical sense to write them well. And this year, a few months ago, I was at a private screening of *The Exterminating Angel* which had the same fabulous effect on me as *The Golden Age*, like an escape from all the conventional and no more than intelligent films you see these days. I am such an admirer of Bergman, Resnais[3] and Truffaut, but the films you make always have that dizzying rift in reality, that glimpse of the beyond that is really the only thing poets care about. And for that, you are one of the few reasons I'm glad to have lived at this time. And I say this, without mincing my words, because I know you will understand.

You can imagine how delighted I am at the possibility that one of my stories might provide the theme for part of your next film.[4] Even more so, when it might be accompanied by *Aura*,[5] which I find remarkable and by the equally remarkable *Gradiva*.[6] I know that in your hands, my maenades[7] would take the final leap they could not in my story, held back by literary considerations I no longer believe in and that should, anyway, be broken, as you have broken so many stupid taboos sustained by a hypocrisy we know all too well.

I am loath to mention money after everything I've just said, but bitter pills should be swallowed fast, and I hope that in the future we'll be able to meet up or write and talk of other things. I suggest $4,000, and I'm doing so on the basis of payments for two Argentine film adaptations of stories of mine (*La cifra impar*,[8] which has just premiered in Buenos Aires, and *El persiguidor*,[9] which is being filmed and should be finished around now).

I'm sending this to your address in Spain, although you put your Mexican address at the bottom of your letter, because I think I understood you would be in Madrid a while longer. I do hope you will be able to come to Paris soon, as you mentioned in your letter. I'm shy and socially inept, but I think that, with you, I would feel such a close friend at once that the idea of meeting you here and discussing so many things makes me very happy.[10]

Thank you for everything and warmest regards from your friend,
Julio Cortázar
Place du Général Beuret

Spa Tls, AB/611; *LOGD* 91 f

[1]   Argentinian writer (1914–84), based in Paris from 1951.
[2]   J. Cortázar, 'Los olvidados', *Sur*, no. 209–210 (March–April 1952), pp. 170–172.
[3]   Alain Resnais (1922–2014), French film-maker.
[4]   Cortázar's short story 'Las ménades', published in the collection *Final de juego* (Mexico City: Los Presentes, 1956); LB is planning to adapt it as one episode in a three-episode Época Films feature.
[5]   Short novel by Carlos Fuentes (Mexico City: Editorial Era, 1962).
[6]   Novel by German author, Wilhelm Jensen (1837–1911), serialized in Viennese newspaper *Neue freie Presse* (New Free Press) in June and July 1902, much admired by Freud.
[7]   Greek: female member of Dionysian orgiastic cult ('frenzied woman').

⁸ Directed by Manuel Antín, based on Cortázar's story 'Cartas de mamá' from the book *Las armas secretas* (Buenos Aires: Editorial Sudamericana, 1959) and premiered on 15 November 1962.

⁹ Directed by Osias Wilenski, based on Cortázar's story by the same name, also published in *Las armas secretas*; premiere postponed until 1965.

¹⁰ Cortázar and LB met in a cafe in Paris in December 1962.

To Carlos Fuentes

Madrid, [November 1962]

Carlos Fuentes
Segunda Cerrada Frontera 14
San Ángel, Mexico City

WONDERFUL OPPORTUNITY TO FILM *AURA*. WOULD BE GRATEFUL IF YOU COULD WIRE HOW MUCH YOU WOULD ASK IN PRINCIPLE FOR RIGHTS TO THE STORY.¹

REGARDS,
BUÑUEL

Spa Tel, CF/93/17

¹ Fuentes asked for US$5,000 (CF/93/17).

To Carlos Fuentes

Madrid, 11 December 1962

AURA WILL FORM PART OF A TRILOGY WITH *MAENADES* AND *GRADIVA*. I HAVE TOTAL FREEDOM. CONFIDENTIALLY, CORTÁZAR IS ASKING $4,000. WE COULD MAYBE WRITE THE ADAPTATION TOGETHER. REPLY SOONEST.

REGARDS,
BUÑUEL

Spa Tel, CF/93/17

Figure 58 Étoiles de Cristal winners, Académie du Cinéma, Paris, 18 December 1962: Truffaut, Buñuel (International Prize for *Viridiana*), Moreau and Albert Finney.

To Juan Larrea

Mexico City, 1 January 1963

My dear Juan,

I got the telegram with your address in Spain when I arrived home yesterday.

I'll keep this very brief. Because this letter would go on for ever if I started telling you all about my life and everything that's happened since we last met. So, to the point.

I am going to adapt three or four stories for the screen. One may be *Gradiva*, another *Aura*, by Carlos Fuentes, and a third 'The Maenades' by Julio Cortázar, with a possible fourth story of mine. One of those may also be replaced by another that's still up in the air. Anything's possible. But what is for sure. I'd like to make *Illegible, Son of the Flute*. At only three reels it would be ideal, it wouldn't have to be 'padded out'.

So, I'm asking your permission under the following terms. We will not correspond by letter again until the film is finished. I will try to honour your ideas. If, however, there were some deviations, I would include *Illegible, Son of the Flute* with the other stories under the following credit: 'Title: *Leandro Villalobos*. Film inspired by *Illegible, Son of the Flute* by Juan Larrea. Adaptation by Luis Buñuel'.

That would safeguard the integrity of your work, because everyone knows the author is not responsible for the adaptation. I want to make the film, because it still has such cinematic possibilities. If you agree and if *Illegible, Son of the Flute* is included in my film, I could get you 1,000 dollars.

I think that's enough for now. I'd like your reply with a 'yes' or 'no' by telegram, so that I can get started, or give up on the idea. Although you could always expand on your thoughts later in a letter.

If I don't hear from you before the 10th of this month, I'll assume it's a no.[1]

Buñuel

[PS] Theoretically, the film will be made in Spain, Italy, Mexico …

Another possible credit: '*Illegible, Son of the Flute*. Story by Juan Larrea. Adaptation by L. Buñuel'.

Spa Tlsps, AF; *ILE* 115–116

---

[1]   Larrea accepts in principle (*ILE* 117).

To Guillermo de Torre

Mexico City, 4 January 1963

Dear friend Guillermo,

I have here, from Madrid, the lines you wrote to me a few days after my 'unfortunate' telephone conversation with you.

I never answer the telephone, and when I did that time, the thing I always fear will happen happened. I can't hear names and whoever is calling thinks I'll get them if they shout loud enough. A hopeless task. All that happens is that I get anxious, unable to associate ideas, almost obnubilated.[1] To me, your name sounded like Yerma de Sorra (I turn the 't's into 's's and vice versa). When you explained that we met in Toledo, with Chueca,[2] I said I remembered. That wasn't true. I couldn't link you with Yerma de Sorra. Luckily, as I'm sure you will appreciate, I only get that comatose on the telephone.

I'm so sorry that, not having seen one another for so many years and with so much to discuss, we couldn't meet up. But you say you'll be staying in Madrid for a few months and I have to go back on about 15 March. So, all is not lost. I'll send you a letter as soon as I arrive. We'll talk at great length and you'll find your interlocutor is not that dimwit who picked up the phone.

My most cordial greetings,
Luis Buñuel

Spa Tls, BNE/Mss/22820/48

---

[1]   From Latin: covered in clouds, or fog.
[2]   Fernando Chueca Goitia (1911–2004), architect.

To Eduardo Ducay

Mexico City, 16 January 1963

Dear friend Ducay,

I sent you all a telegram yesterday to let you know your long-awaited letter had finally arrived, and only a trifling nine days late. That's how correspondence gets to

Mexico at the moment. Even letters from New York from my son Juan Luis arrive eight days late, and that's only a four-hour flight. An anomaly caused by the vast pile of Christmas cards blocking up the post offices.

I started on the adaptation of *Aura* yesterday, which meant I had a telephone conversation with Carlos Fuentes, and that brought up something unexpected that may ruin all our plans for the story. Carlos told me that the edition of the novella due to be published in Spain has been vetoed by the censor as sacrilegious and immoral. I thanked him for being so noble and passing that along. That being the case, I think there's no point in us considering *Aura*, so the notion of filming three stories collapses, because the idea of a new trilogy with *Gradiva*, 'The Girl'[1] and 'The Maenades' feels like a ludicrous mismatch to me.

That doesn't mean you shouldn't check with the Ministry of Information if you want to. A pointless task though, the author is hardly going to lie[2] just for the sake of it. Especially when he's more than happy for us to carry on with the project.

Carlos and I also think – a bit late in the day – that *Gradiva* and *Aura* together might be a bit repetitive. In both there is the same 'psychic' atmosphere, that is, a lonely, young dreamer, falls in love with the ghost of a very beautiful, distant woman.

Things to consider

The date for deciding the subject of the film has passed, but if you agree we could make one more attempt to save the partnership.

I've just re-read a story called *Tristana*[3] by Galdós I have always liked a lot. There's a lot in it that would make an interesting film. It would cost about as much as *The Eternal Husband*.[4] The rights shouldn't be more than 100,000 pesetas. The cast could be appealing. Fernando Rey as the old man and your own exclusive Rocío Dúrcal[5] as the female lead. The rest are minor roles. We could set it today or in the 1930s. Read it and wire me your thoughts with a 'yes' or a 'no' to save time.

Don't worry about the details or take the events and characters in the book as given. As with *Nazarín*, I could adapt it to today's tastes. For example, I'm thinking of completely changing the character of the painter. The scenes in the *atelier*[6] are really dated.

If this new direction doesn't appeal to you, I still think there's another possibility: three comic tales: 'The Girl', 'The Maenades' and a new one I would write.

And if none of these interests you, I'll wait to hear your ideas.

I'll say no more about *The Eternal Husband*. Jealousy is almost impossible as a theme, and the betrayed husband even worse. I could maybe have a go at it, but it's likely my adaptation would have precious little to do with the original.

Most cordial greetings from your friend,
Buñuel

Spa Tls, ED

---

[1] Story about the kidnapping of a girl co-written by LB and Alcoriza in 1958.
[2] Meaning Fuentes has no reason to lie about the likelihood of his own work being censored.
[3] Published by La Guirnalda in Madrid in 1892.

⁴   *Vechny muzh*, novel by Dostoyevsky published in the magazine *Zarya* in Saint Petersburg, 1870.
⁵   Spanish actress and singer (1944–2006), under contract to Época Films.
⁶   French in the original (studio).

Figure 59 Buñuel, Alatriste, Rucar, Fernández and Pinal at baptism of Viridiana Alatriste
Pinal, Mexico City, January 1963.

To Leonardo Martín

Mexico City, 21 January 1963

Dear friend Leonardo,
   'What's done is done'. And in this case, what's done is *Tristana*.¹ There are many obstacles still to overcome, but it's worth it. I'm taking the liberty of indicating some things to consider as follows.
   Adaptation
   As with all my adaptations, I can never say whether the result will remain close to the book or lead me down unsuspected avenues.
   I think it's out of the question to move the action, characters and events to the present day. Everything would be out of date because in the eighty years since Galdós wrote the book, our customs, even our way of expressing emotions, have completely changed. The action would need to be set in Segovia, for example, or in Toledo.² Time has barely passed there. And it would be easy to conjure up the atmosphere, and the Garridos and Tristanas³ of the 1920s, in a way that only a 'super-production' could manage in Madrid at the moment.

It would be better, if you don't mind me trespassing on your territory here, just to take out an option on the book. There would always be time to go back later and pay the full amount when we've seen the adaptation.

As time is short, I'm going to take on someone to do the adaptation with me. It's Julio Alejandro, with whom I worked on the first version of *Viridiana*. Would you agree to me offering him 100,000 pesetas, with me contributing half?

Actors

Fernando Rey is perfect for the role of Don Lope Garrido. I've taken the risk of suggesting Durcal, and it was a risk, because I've only seen a photo of her, but she is about the same age as Tristana and she's pretty. You'll know better than I whether she can carry it off, as an actress, and what she's like to direct, how natural her voice is, etc., etc. Of course, as soon as I get to Madrid I'll watch a couple of her films. If she isn't right for the part, you could start thinking of a substitute, and a foreigner, if possible, so we can make it a co-production. It's really important that Tristana (and I mean the character) is exceptional. The censors would be more lenient with a co-production don't you think? The other characters would be easy enough to find over there.

By about the end of February I'll be able to give you an idea of the general direction of the film. It would be wonderful if one of you could come over here to exchange ideas. Of course, I won't be going to Spain until the end of March, by which time it will be finished, unless there are any unexpected obstacles.

That's all for the moment. Most cordially,
Luis Buñuel

Spa Tls, ED

---

1   Impossible to replicate the pun on Tristana's 'chest' in these first two sentences; the original Spanish phrase is 'a lo hecho, pecho' ('a lo hecho' [to what has been done] 'pecho' [breast/chest]) meaning, figuratively, to shield oneself, in this case, the 'breastplate' is *Tristana*.

2   The novel is set in Chamberí, Madrid.

3   Tristana Reluz and don Lope Garrido, central characters in the novel.

To José Bolaños

José Bolaños
404 Suderman, Mexico City

Mexico City, 5 February 1963

Esteemed friend,

Further to our conversation yesterday, it is my pleasure to confirm the conclusions we came to, those being, in principle, that I agree to make a film produced by you and based on Dalton Trumbo's wonderful novel, *Johnny Got His Gun*. The other preconditions stipulated were as follows:

1) The *screenplay*[1] to be planned and written by Mr Dalton Trumbo.

2) Of paramount importance to me is to have it on record that the 'case' of Joe, the protagonist doesn't appeal to me so much for his memories of the happy times in his life, as for his terrible, internal struggle to make contact with his fellow men, the gradual discovery of his utter mutilation,[2] the agony of adapting to a new way of living, his titanic struggle to distinguish his waking life from his dreams, his frenetic way of communicating with those around him and, finally, his last, heart-breaking contact with the outside world.

3) I soon have to make a film in Europe that I will finish towards the end of July.[3] Then I will be preparing a course I have to give at the University of Harvard, which will be over by February 1964. From that date, I will be available to begin preparing and filming *Johnny Got His Gun*.

4) We shall decide on the final terms of the contract in due course.

5) I reserve the right to accept any interesting proposals that may come up before we have reached a definitive agreement and signed the corresponding contract.

6) At that time, on signing said contract, you will pay me the sum of 10,000 dollars advance on my salary.

Without more ado, I remain your affectionate friend,
Luis Buñuel

Spa Tls, DT/72/05

[1] English in the original.
[2] Wounded by shrapnel in the First World War, Johnny has lost his arms and legs, and his ability to speak, smell, see and hear.
[3] Filming of *Diary of a Chambermaid* was finally postponed until October 1963.

To Leonardo Martín

Mexico City, 8 February 1963

Dear friend Leonardo,

Your letter arrived, with the final approval for *Tristana*. I have been working on it continuously now for three weeks and, as expected, I have found all paths blocked by the thorny emotions and tastes of a stale era only the 'wordsmithery' of a genius like Galdós could make palatable. Working with Julio Alejandro has helped, because thanks to his implacable presence I have to 'think', come what may, for seven hours a day. Incidentally, you can pay the 50,000 pesetas you agreed to give Alicia whenever you find it convenient. Julio will give me receipts for his 100,000-peseta salary, that is, for 20,000 pesos.

Please let me know if it would be very disruptive to you if I were two weeks late with the treatment for the dialogues. That is, if I were to send it to you on 15 April, rather than 31 March, which means we would start in the studio between 20 and 30 May. Preparation will be easy. I did warn you that I tend to let arranged deadlines slip past only at the treatment phase. Finding inspiration is elusive, there's a lot of mulling over and then when it finally comes, it sometimes says the silliest things.

And now for something very important. Have you heard about the ENORMOUS scandal over *Viridiana* in Italy? Approved by the censor, it premiered in Rome on 18 January. Great critical and box office success. The Attorney General, *dottore* Spagnuolo,[1] sees it in Milan and immediately bans it as 'an attack on State religion', availing himself, they say, of new legislation on censorship. From that moment, entire pages in papers and illustrated magazines devoted to the issue: Milan critics organize a public protest; directors and writers protest on their part, De Seta,[2] Dino Risi,[3] Lattuada,[4] Monicelli,[5] Moravia,[6] etc. The socialist newspaper *Avanti!*[7] gives it a centre-page spread, publishing all the dialogues from the film and taking advantage of the occasion to lash out at the Spanish government in my name. *Il Corriere della Sera*,[8] on the other hand (and I'm grateful) quotes me saying that I don't try to 'play politics' in my films and that I don't use film as a pulpit to preach or spread propaganda about anything or anyone. An important Italian producer[9] wrote to me saying: 'The *Viridiana* affair is on everyone's lips. All the intellectuals and the entire left protesting for all they're worth and, as a result, you've become the most up-to-date symbol of the endless battle between progressives and reactionaries.'[10] And then he says he wants to sign me up as soon as I finish working with you.

I'm only telling you all this to let you know, in case it affects our project. It may be worth checking the waters at the Dirección General de Cine?[11] I'll wait to hear from you.

Fond regards, your friend,
Buñuel

Spa/Ita Tls, ED

[1] Carmelo Spagnuolo, magistrate, censor, and Attorney General of Milan.
[2] Vittorio de Seta (1923–2011), Italian director and documentary film-maker.
[3] Italian director (1916–2008).
[4] Alberto Lattuada (1914–2005), Italian film-maker.
[5] Mario Monicelli (1915–2010), Italian film-maker.
[6] Alberto Moravia (1907–90), Italian novelist.
[7] Founded in Rome in 1896, official newspaper of the Italian Socialist Party.
[8] Founded in Milan in 1876.
[9] Possibly, Sabatello.
[10] Quotation in Italian in the original.
[11] Spanish Directorate-General of Cinema.

To Juan Larrea

Mexico City, 12 February 1963

Dear Juan,

Jeanne and I were dreadfully upset by your letter,[1] which arrived this morning. Neither we nor our mutual acquaintances (yours and ours) were aware of your terribly painful tragedy.[2] I put your interest in Lucianne's name appearing alongside your own in the credits of *Illegible, Son of the Flute* down simply to the love of a father for his daughter. And, oddly, it was only in your third letter that you broke this disastrous news. I imagine that was because you took it for granted we would know already. Another feat by that vile creature the aeroplane. I would discuss this devastating event with you at length, but I'm a dreadful letter-writer. I just want you to know that when we heard your news we felt most wholly and compassionately for you. Very warm wishes from both of us, dear Juan. You are not *of this world*.

We didn't go ahead with *Illegible, Son of the Flute* because the other stories fell through, one because of the censors and another for financial reasons. But don't think I've completely given up on it. I will get back to it one of these days. And I can guarantee that the film won't run to more than three or four reels, *maximum*.

I'm attempting a second Spanish venture taking on any ecclesiastical censorship they care to impose. I hope to emerge, *à l'instar*[3] *Viridiana*, unscathed.

When shall we meet up again? At the moment, I think it would be difficult and life is moving on. Let's not lose hope. More warmest wishes from Jeanne and me,

Luis

[PS] Juan Luis suddenly got married to an American woman in New York a few days ago.[4] He's a future film director and Rafael is studying theatre and film at the University of Los Angeles, California.

Spa Tlsps, AF; ILE 125–125

[1] Letter from Larrea to LB, 5 February 1963 (AB/643).
[2] Lucianne Larrea and her husband died in a plane crash in Brazil, 23 November 1961.
[3] French in the original (as with).
[4] Joyce Sherman Buñuel (1941), US film-maker and first wife of Juan Luis Buñuel.

To Robert G. Gardner

México City, 2 March 1963

Dear Bob Gardner,

I received your letter of February 25th,[1] *containing the official invitation to visit Harvard this fall as a visiting artist. I consider this a great honour and wish to take this opportunity to thank the University and you personally.*

But at the last moment, some problems have arisen which may prevent me from accepting your invitation. I will try to explain.

I have two signed contracts in Europe, executed some months ago. One is for a picture in Spain which will terminate in August of this year.[2] *The second is a French production,* Memoirs of a Chambermaid[3] *by Octave Mirbeau, preparation and production of which should occupy me from September 1963 to July 1964.*

When you first told me of the possibility of the Harvard invitation, I wrote the French producer[4] *asking that he postpone my contract until March 1964. He replied that he would try to do so. But four days ago, I received a letter from him in which he stated that contracts with actors, studios, etc. made it imperative that I commence work in October 1963.*

Nevertheless, I am writing them again, insisting that my request be granted, and that they adjust their schedule accordingly. Therefore, in ten days I should be able to wire you definitely whether or not I can come to Cambridge. Can you please wait until then?

Should the French producer grant my request, I accept the salary and conditions stated in your letter such as presenting various of my films, working with the students on the film etc. And I most grateful for the invitation extended to my wife and son.

Until soon and with kindest personal regards. Sincerely,
Luis Buñuel

Eng CmfL, AB/1426.121

1   AB/1426.120.
2   *Tristana* with Época Films.
3   *Le Journal d'une femme de chambre*, novel by French writer Octave Mirbeau (1848–1917), published by Fasquelle in Paris in 1900.
4   Serge Silberman (1917–2003), French producer of Polish descent, co-produced *Diary of a Chambermaid* with Michel Safra and Henri Baum.

To Francisco Rabal

Mexico City, 18 March 1963

My dear nephew Paco,

Your letter moved your decrepit old uncle, it was so warm and so affectionate. At our age (Fernando Rey's and mine I mean), things we once considered a sign of weakness in our youth, now, as the grave draws near (Fernando Rey's and mine I mean) make us weep with gratitude. It would be an arch-delight to stay with you and the family, but my work in Madrid forces me to stay at the Torre again. I'll take one apartment for me and, as they are small, another one above to receive certain young ladies who, as you well know, are always bothering me. What is there to say? I clearly wasn't born to be a monk!

It goes without saying that I would be delighted if my dearest niece, your wife, were to invite me to eat at your house and would prepare something worthy of me, gastronomically speaking; that is, something to suit a Spanish mule driver: Arganda wine, salted onions, Manchego cheese and bread. Have the children changed much? And my little leading lady? And the handsome little stocky fellow? Give them all a hug from me. I'd also really like to see my nephew Damián, we've become closer and closer since *Viridiana*. And give María Asunción a special hug from me.

I am indeed going to make *Tristana*. It's quite an adventure. It took me months to decide. The fact is I have no real interest in almost anything. What tempted me in this case was the idea of making a film that was perfectly reactionary *in form*. So that even a tribunal of bishops could watch it and not find a single thing to cut. So that one reverend would even be driven to shout: 'Stop the film! We are quite reactionary enough already.' Of course, I would be delighted if you were in it, but unfortunately the part of the painter is not worthy of you. If I could only 'pad it out' a bit! We'll see. As for the role of Don Lope, I'll offer it to Fernando, but he may already be too old. We'll see!

I'll be in Madrid at the very beginning of April. I'll be going, as I said, to the Torre. Obviously, I'll call you at once.

Much love,
L. Buñuel

Spa Tls, FR; *BVMC* f

To Pierre Lherminier[1]

[Mexico City,] March 1963

I met Armand Tallier[2] in 1927, when I went to his office at Studio des Ursulines to ask for his help organizing a screening – with discussion – of vanguard films at the Society of Conferences and Courses in Madrid. Thanks to him, I was able to introduce Spain to *Entr'acte, Nothing but Time, Ménilmontant*,[3] the dream sequence from *The Whirlpool of Fate*, etc. That was the first time that the members of the Society of Conferences, Madrid's intellectual elite, realized film could be a serious art form and not just frivolous entertainment.

It was Tallier who presented *An Andalusian Dog* at the Ursulines with *The Mysteries of the Château of Dice*.[4]

Back then, he was always the first person we thought of when we wanted to plan any kind of cinematic escapade.

[Luis Buñuel]

Fre, Od; *ARM 29*

---

[1] French film editor and historian, director of the film section of publishing house, Éditions Seghers.
[2] French actor (1887–1958), co-founder of the Studio des Ursulines film theatre, in 1925.
[3] Film (named after an area in Paris) directed by Dimitri Kirsanov in 1926.
[4] *Les Mystères du Château du Dé,* experimental short, produced by the de Noailles and directed by Man Ray in 1929, premiered with *An Andalusian Dog* on 6 June 1929.

From Isaías Gluzman[1]

Ein Dor,[2] [April 1963]

My dear Sir,

I must begin by saying how astounded we all were by your so swift and gracious reply, we hadn't for a moment imagined you would find the time to reply.[3] We thank you for this extreme kindness from the bottom of our hearts, both for sending the book by Ado Kyrou,[4] and – in particular – for your thoughts on *Viridiana*.

We were a little surprised by your comment that '*Viridiana* has no political agenda.'[5] We were all convinced that scenes like the one with the beggars' supper were essentially designed to convey a clearly delineated and partisan moral message. Although of course, viewers do tend to interpret an artist's work in ways that do not necessarily correspond with the author's own intentions.

I should say that the best critics in our country wrote the most thoughtful eulogies about *Viridiana*, even journalists who do not normally write about cinema felt obliged to dedicate their daily column to your film. The very best critic in the country, Leev Bar-Nof,[6] wrote in *Davar*:[7] 'One of the most unique and authentic works of art in the history of cinema.' Uri Keisari, in *Maariv*:[8] 'Run and see *Viridiana* now, because it's one of those films that cinema only produces every ten or fifteen years.'

As for your thoughts on the possibility of improving humankind, I should say that this might be a unique opportunity for you to get to know a place like the one where I live: a *kibbutz*. I imagine you have already heard of *kibbutzim*, where we pursue a collective way of life, without the circulation of money, because society meets the needs of the individual. Unlike collectivization in communist countries, in a *kibbutz* you can enter or leave freely and there are no 'bosses' because the most important positions are rotated every year or two. It is the most democratic society in the world and even the representatives of three of the workers parties, who mostly live in *kibbutzim*, live under exactly the same conditions as everyone else.

Of course, the *kibbutz* is now on the defensive against attacks from bourgeois society that harass us and attempt to strangle us economically and socially. In spite of this (and despite the fact that communist countries still insist it is an impossible 'utopia'), the *kibbutz* continues to survive and to symbolize just what 'a new man in the spiritual sense' might be.

But I'm sure I have bothered and wearied you enough already. If I have mentioned the *kibbutz*, it is not just because of your words about 'spiritual change', but also to invite you, should you ever visit Israel, to come and get to know our *kibbutz* (we are advocates of the revolutionary socialist Mapam party[9]).

Until then, we eagerly await the arrival of *The Exterminating Angel* over here, we have read such fascinating reviews of it in French newspapers. We do not understand why it has not yet come to Israel (perhaps you could give the distributors a nudge?).

Mr Buñuel, I thank you once again, most sincerely for your letter and the book, and I do hope you will be able to visit us one day.

We also hope that you will continue to make works as magisterial as *Viridiana*. After watching all the Bergman, Antonioni, Resnais, etc., with all their quest for new styles, it was marvellously refreshing to enjoy a work that says so much, so simply and in such a short space of time.

If you were interested in any critical reviews from Israel, I would be very happy to send them to you, although they would, of course, be in Hebrew.

With my very best wishes,
Isaías Gluzman
Ein Dor, Lower Galilee, Israel

Spa Als, AB/691.26–27

[1] Israeli film specialist of Latin American descent.
[2] Kibbutz founded in 1948 in Lower Galilee, Israel.
[3] LB's letter responding to I. Gluzman's letter to LB, 3 March 1963 (691.1), has not been preserved in the Gluzman family archives.
[4] A. Kyrou, *Luis Buñuel* (Paris: Éditions Seghers, 1962).
[5] In his first letter, Gluzman says: 'Some of us (we are Marxists) think that you are advocating world revolution in *Viridiana*, because the parable about the dog indicates there are thousands of others enslaved and that bourgeois 'philanthropy' is nothing more than hypocrisy. The other position is that your work is essentially anarchist and that you do not believe Man is capable of building a better world. Would it be very impertinent of me to ask you to clarify?' (AB/691.1).
[6] Israeli film critic.
[7] Hebrew newspaper founded in Tel Aviv in 1925, during the British Mandate of Palestine.
[8] Israeli newspaper co-founded by journalists including Uri Keisavi and Azriel Carlebach in Tel Aviv in 1948.
[9] Marzist-Zionist party founded in Israel in 1948.

To Gabriel Figueroa

Madrid, 23 May 1963[1]

Dear Gaby,

I promised to write as soon as I had a clear sense of my future plans and I can now tell you, briefly, the following:

1) In spite of the ENORMOUS freedom everyone enjoys in this country, I have been forbidden to make *Tristana*[2] as you may already have heard. I'm sure *Doña* Carmen[3] would not cut a single preposition in Mexico. But here, they have slit my syntax from ear to ear. Perhaps because their grammar is better than Mexicans'.

2) I had a contract with France to write and direct Mirbeau's *The Diary of a Chambermaid*, starting from 1 September. Given the Spanish ban, I've managed to bring the French film forward and will now start on 1 June. I'll be completely finished by January 1964.

3) I'm going to sign up with the Spanish producers of *Tristana* to make the film with them in Mexico from next February, maybe in San Luis, Queretaro, or Guanajuato.* I should finish in May or June 1964. Naturally, I will need a good director of photography. I'd be grateful if you could recommend one.[4]

4) After that, I have another with Globe Films in Italy. Everything is ready, but I won't sign up for that one until the end of the year, because Mexico is 'calling' me and I'm starting to crave some quiet; and film, when I'm not working with you lot, is monstrous trouble. I'm under quite a lot of pressure from the Italians and my agent, but I think I can stall until December … when I'll be quite fed up with my tourist life over here.

Because of all this, although plans may change at the last minute of course, I can't commit to CLASA[5] at the moment. Could you please explain this to our dear friend Dolores, and also send her my best wishes.

Love to the great Felipe and dear Gachupín Lafuente. And for you, your wife, and small brood, my most particular and cordial love.

Buñuel

[PS] LONG LIVE MEXICO! Paris is magnificent, but … Mexico is great!

* I want *Tristana* to be a co-production and so do the producers (who are excellent people). They will get in touch with CLASA.

Spa Tlsps, GF; *TURIA*

---

¹ Asterisked note by LB.
² French censors stopped production after examining the script.
³ Possibly, María del Carmen Millán (1914–82), Mexican academic.
⁴ A joke: LB clearly hopes to work with Figueroa.
⁵ Figueroa was made Secretary of the Board of Production at CLASA in 1959.

To Carlos Fuentes

Madrid, 22 August 1963

My dear Carlos,

Your letter arrived yesterday, and I was not surprised to hear that you're in Europe: my network of spies had already told me. What a trip you two are having! And what a 'culture vulture' Rita[1] will be when she gets back to Mexico. I'm sure you won't visit anywhere or see anything as cool as Mexico though.

I see they've finally published your article in *Show*.[2] My plans, in a couple of words, are: to make *Diary of a Chambermaid* between now and January with *Doña* Juana Moreau[3] (needs must …), and then go back to Mexico and forget cinema for a few months. There are two 'firm' contracts[4] waiting for me, but I think I can avoid them. I'm seriously thinking about retiring, or at most making a film every couple of years with Alatriste in Mexico. I find the idea of contemplating, rather than being involved in life more attractive by the day. You can live so intensely when completely idle, and time is so uselessly wasted on work: our work may be intellectual, but we do not live fully in ourselves, as a certain hetaera from Avila once said.[5] *À BAS LE TRAVAIL!*[6]

I don't think the Spanish censors would even let me film *Little Red Riding Hood*. In fact, I'm sure they wouldn't. They'd see Little Red Riding Hood as a symbol for Spain; Franco as the Big Bad Wolf, and grandma as the Common Market.[7]

How wonderful that we'll be able to meet up in Paris! I'd be grateful if you would send a *pneumatique* as soon as you arrive, to Hotel Aiglon, 232 Boulevard Raspail (I wouldn't even answer the phone to my own father) and I'll get in touch with you at once, if you give me the address. I'll be there from 5 September to early January – wonderful!

Very cordial hugs much very, as they say in Mexico,[8] to Rita and you.
Buñuel

Spa Tls, CF/93/17

[1] Rita Macedo Guzmán (1925–93), Mexican actress with roles in *The Criminal Life of Archibaldo de la Cruz*, *Nazarín* and *The Exterminating Angel*, first wife of Fuentes.
[2] C. Fuentes, 'Luis Buñuel: The Macabre Maker of Movie-Making', *Show* 3, no. 11 (November 1963), pp. 81, 134–135.
[3] Jeanne Moreau (1928–2017), French actress, who stars as the protagonist, Célestine.
[4] *Johnny got his Gun* and *Under the Volcano*.
[5] Light-hearted reference to the famous poem, 'Vivo sin vivir en mí', by Spanish mystic Saint Teresa (1515–82) lamenting the pain of living unable to 'live in the self', or rather, having to live life yearning for death/union with God.
[6] 'Down with work!', French in the original, slogan adopted by Paul Lafargue (son-in-law of Marx) in his book *La Droit à la paresse* (1880), much-admired by the surrealists.
[7] Central American Common Market founded in 1960.
[8] 'Abrazos muy cordiales, mucho muy' in the original.

To Carlos Fuentes

Paris, 4 October 1963

Dear Carlos,

Your Turkish letter has arrived. What a cultural jaunt you're concocting. You are only missing far China, old Cipangu,[1] and Khitai,[2] although better not to set foot now in counter- revolutionary countries like Spain, China, etc.

I am waiting impatiently for you to arrive. But we work here on Saturdays as well, and all day. So, I'd be grateful if you could make sure we arrange to meet on a Sunday. You are all invited to lunch and long conversation, although I retire to my lair at around 6. Since I got to Paris I've only been out to dinner once, at my old friend Louis Aragon's house, an important person, if such a thing exists.

I also hope you'll come to the scene of the crime any day of the week, it's three-quarters of an hour from Paris,[3] and I'll introduce you to the *morruda femme de chambre*.[4]

A big hug for Rita and you.
Buñuel
Hotel Aiglon

[PS] Alberti is wandering around Paris.

Spa Tlsps, CF/93/17

[1] European name for Japan during the Middle Ages.
[2] Kara-kitai, empire in Central Asia conquered by Mongols in 1218.
[3] *Diary of a Chambermaid* was partly filmed in Mennecy, south-east of Paris, from 21 October 1963.
[4] 'Morruda' ('full-lipped' and/or 'a liking for sweets') left in the original as the play on Moreau's surname, does not translate in English.

Figure 60 Buñuel, next to camera, with son Juan Luis Buñuel, standing under megaphone, and crew members, *Diary of a Chambermaid*, Mennecy, October 1963.

To Dalton Trumbo

Dalton Trumbo
13 Piazza San Salvatore
Roma, Italia

Paris, 14 October 1963

Dear Trumbo,

I received your telegram informing me that you are delaying your trip to Paris because you are ill.[1] I hope this letter will find you completely recovered.

Regarding other matters, I prefer to warn you that in spite of Bolaños' good intention of uniting us in a film, one shouldn't place too much confidence in his ability to realize such a project. It would be prudent if you didn't come to Paris before the first of November at which time I will know with all certainty if Bolaños can carry out his idea. I will write or telegraph you at that time.

I trust that this letter will remain entirely confidential between you and me. Yours,
Luis Buñuel

Eng Tls, DT/72/05

[1] Telegram from Trumbo to LB, 12 October 1963 (DT/72/05).

To Zachary Scott

Paris, 29 October 1963

Dear Zachary,

I was very grateful for your last two letters which I received through Juan Luis. Everything you told me regarding Mr Houseman[1] seems very good and I am confident that he would be an ideal producer for Under the Volcano.

Jeanne Moreau spoke to me about the letter you wrote to her some time ago. She would love to work with us. However, I think it would be wise to assure her participation as soon as you can because she is very solicited by producers and directors.

Finally, as adaptors of the film, I propose Hugo Butler and Carlos Fuentes, who has an enormous cinematographic sense, is a great writer and a young man of exceptional merits. I won't give you his curriculum vitae now, but I will send it whenever you like. Without a doubt, he is the most universal Mexican today. As far as I'm concerned, his collaboration is almost indispensable to this project. He believes that Lowry's book is the best contemporary novel on auto-destruction. Lastly, he also worked on the script adaptation of Oscar Lewis' The Sanchez Family,[2] in collaboration with Abby Mann.[3]

I am leading a rather reclusive existence. I neither see nor receive anybody. But then, I am working very hard. The actual filming[4] should be over in December and I am longing to return to Mexico where I should arrive sometime in the middle of January. That would be the time to arrange something definite about this business. If that is not possible, I will begin work, in February, for Alatriste,[5] my producer on Viridiana *and* The Exterminating Angel.

I embrace Ruth and yourself very warmly.
Luis Buñuel

P.S. Carlos Fuentes is in Europe, but he will return to Mexico around the tenth of November. His address is:
  Segunda Cerrada de Frontera 14
  San Angel
  Mexico City

Eng Tls, ZSA

---

[1] John Houseman (1902–88), Anglo-American producer born in Bucharest.
[2] US anthropologist (1914–70), author of *The Children of Sánchez: Autobiography of a Mexican Family* (New York: Random House, 1961).
[3] US scriptwriter and producer (1927–2008).
[4] Of *Diary of a Chambermaid*.
[5] *Simon of the Desert*, filmed, eventually, in November and December 1964.

To Carlos Fuentes

Paris, 12 November 1963

Dear Carlos,

Show finally arrived. I thought your article was *very good*, in spite of its sensationalist, decorative touches. You and Rita, look very handsome in your garden

If *Under the Volcano* goes ahead, rest assured you'll be working on the adaptation. It's the least I can do.

Another thing. To be able to make my *sketch* film we've come up with – I've proposed to Época Films – the following: I'll film 'The Maenades' in Spain; they'll suggest Alain Resnais film *Aura* here; and Fellini, *Gradiva* in Italy. Reason: 'The Maenades' is probably the only thing I would be allowed to film in Spain, and even that's not certain. You can let me know later whether, if it goes ahead, you agree. I'll speak to Resnais myself and give him the text. Let me know if there's a French translation.

A hug for Rita, another for you and a half for the Fuentecita.[1]

Luis Buñuel

Spa Als, CF/93/17

[1] Play on words: 'Fuentecita' ('little fountain/spring/source'), for Fuentes's daughter, Cecilia Fuentes Macedo, born in 1962.

From François Truffaut

Paris, 15 November 1963[1]

Dear Monsieur Buñuel,

Two years ago, a lady sent me a handwritten *scénario* in a notebook. It was an old story, based on a real case of incest in Andorra.

It was a fairly candid and melodramatic piece of work, which gave it a certain sense of beauty and power. Remembering that you based *This Strange Passion* on a somewhat affected and insipid novel by a woman[2] and finding a certain Mexican tone in this script by Mrs Pauline Charles, I took the liberty of giving her your address in Mexico.

I also advised this lady to prepare a typed version of her *scénario*, because a manuscript is so easily lost. She had it typed especially for you and has written to me again this morning asking me if you received the *scénario*, and if you had, what you thought of it and whether you might return it because it is the only typed copy she has.

I hope I haven't caused too much trouble with all this.

I'm also enclosing a copy of the lady's letter, because it is very congenial and, that way, you will be able to reply to her directly.[3]

I've heard excellent reports of your filming from Jeanne Moreau and I'm very sorry I wasn't able to pay you all a visit. I should very much like to talk with you when you finish and, following on from the conversation we had a few months ago on the terrace of that café in Saint Philippe du Roule, would be very keen to hear your views on Jeanne's acting.

With my most cordial greetings,
[François Truffaut]

Fre Tluf, FT; *FTC* 251

[1] Handwritten annotation with LB's address, c/o Speva Films, 35 rue de Ponthieu, Paris.
[2] M. Pinto, *Él* (Montevideo: Editorial de la Casa del Estudiante, 1926).
[3] Letter from P. Charles to F. Truffaut, 15 November 1963 (FT).

To François Truffaut

Paris, 24 November 1963

My dear Truffaut,

I have written to Mrs Pauline Charles. She will have to wait until I get back to Mexico for me to read and return her *scénario*.

I'm looking forward to finishing my film, so we can meet again, this time with a good meal in front of us and with my chambermaid Jeanne Moreau. She's the most enchanting woman and an exceptional actress. You were right.[1]

See you soon.

Cordially,
Buñuel

Fre Als C, FT

[1] Truffaut directed Moreau in *Jules et Jim* (1962).

From Richard Griffith

Mr Luis Buñuel
c/o Twentieth Century-Fox France Inc.
33 Champs-Elysees
Paris 8

New York, 2 December 1963[1]

Dear Luis,

I write you at the request of David O. Selznick.

Mrs Selznick, who as you know is Jennifer Jones,[2] has long been an admirer of your work, and knows of your admiration for Portrait of Jenny.[3] *She was talking about you with Henry Miller recently, and Miller suggested that the two of you might enjoy the experience of working together, if you have a story or a part that is suitable. I know Miss Jones' salary may be a bit steep for you under ordinary circumstances, but I am authorized to say that adjustments could well be made if you have something that interests her and which you think is right for her.*

I am also asked to say that this is not a suggestion that Mr Selznick produce one of your pictures or provide financial backing. He simply asked me to find out if I could whether it would interest you to work with Miss Jones – a suggestion which, I rather gather, she is shy of making to you directly.

Do let me know what you think of this, or, if you prefer to get in touch with the Selznicks directly, their California address and phone numbers are: 9335 Washington Boulevard, Culver City, Upton 0-2931.

I hope all goes well with the new Diary of a Chambermaid.[4] *How I look forward to seeing what you will make of that ancient but still relevant and tonic tale.*

Cordially,
Richard Griffith, Curator
Film Library, The Museum of Modern Art

Eng Tls L, AB/634

[1]   Carbon copy sent to Selznick.
[2]   US actress (1919–2009).
[3]   *Portrait of Jenny* (1948), by German-US director William Dieterle, produced by Selznick, starring Jones.
[4]   Jean Renoir adapted and directed Mirbeau's novel for the US version of *Diary of a Chambermaid* (1946).

To Richard Griffith

Zaragoza, 29 December 1963

Dear Richard,
I received your letter of the 2nd of December through 20th Century Fox but was unable to answer you before because I was in the middle of shooting.

You would be doing me a great service if, when you have the chance to see Jennifer Jones, you would assure her of the great admiration I have for her. In my judgment, and for my taste, her interpretation of 'Jenny' is, by far, the best in cinema history, and as for the film itself, The Portrait of Jenny I have always held it amongst the five best films that the cinema has ever offered us.[1]

As for the possibility of our working together, I think that it would present many difficulties. For several years now, I have had total and absolute liberty in choosing my themes, in writing the scénarios, in selecting the actors, in directing the film, and finally in editing it. I have the notion that under these conditions, there would not be anybody in Hollywood who would be interested in signing a contract with me. Aside from this, I would demand an astronomical salary, perhaps a sum which far exceeds that which Hollywood usually pays to its best directors.

I hope that I will be able to visit you if I pass by New York. It has been so many years since we last saw each other.

Cordially,
Luis Buñuel
CI-MU-RA
2 Rue Paul Cézanne
Paris VIII

Eng Tls, MoMA/12.04; *EE* 780 f

[1]   Included on LB's list of the ten best films, *Sight and Sound*, vol. 22, no. 1 (July–Sept 1952), p. 18.

To Richard Griffith

Paris, 11 January 1964

Dear Richard,

I received your reply[1] to the letter I sent you from Spain. Thank you.

Do please pass on solicitous greetings to Mrs Jones and tell her that if I come across a story that might interest her, I will let her know at once. It would be a pleasure to work with someone I admire so much. But it will be difficult this year, 1964, because I have already signed a contract to write and direct a film.[2]

My son Juan Luis is in New York at the moment. I've asked for the address. He'll come and see you to organize the retrospective of my films with you.[3] I'm also planning to go to New York around 15 February.[4] We can speak then.

I'm so pleased about the 'triumphant' return of Iris.[5] I have very good memories of my time at the Museum.

Affectionately,
Buñuel

Fre Als, MoMA/12.04

[1] Letter from Griffith to LB, 3 January 1964 (MoMA/12.04).
[2] *Simon of the Desert.*
[3] Griffith was planning a retrospective on LB at the MoMA, after the cancellation of the museum's planned film series in 1960.
[4] LB travelled to New York on 21 February 1964.
[5] September 1963, event at MoMA to celebrate return of Barry to New York after years abroad.

To Ivor Montagu

Paris, 12 January 1964

Dear friend,

Thanks for your letter.[1] So long without news from you!

You can do whatever you like with the photos of my film and with the film itself.[2] No need to ask my permission.

When will we see each other again? If I'm in London for any reason, I'll let you know so that we can meet up.

Until then, I send you most cordial greetings,
Luis Buñuel

Fre Als, IM/379

[1] Letter from Ivor Montagu to LB, 17 December 1963 (IM/379), requesting permission to reproduce two shots from *Land Without Bread* in his book *Film World* (Harmondsworth: Penguin, 1964).
[2] Reference to the copy deposited by Montagu at the British Film Institute in 1939.

To Oscar Lewis

Paris, 6 February 1964

My esteemed friend Lewis,

   Your letter arrived here in Paris, where I've been now for six months. Having finished my film,[1] I'm returning to Mexico at the end of the month.

   I'm so disappointed that I can't take advantage of this opportunity[2] to buy the rights to the book; or rather, that my producer can't, because I don't have that kind of money. I still think, as I always have, that right now it's completely ridiculous to attempt to make that film in Mexico. Who knows whether that will be the case in the near future … But at the moment no producer (they always like to play it safe) would want to take on that project.

   You know how much I admire the book, and that it would be the highpoint of my career to make the film. So, you will understand how frustrating it is to have to side-line myself from the project.

   They are making a good job of publicizing the French translation over here.[3] There was an article in today's *Le Figaro* by Claude Mauriac. I've also seen it described as the best foreign book of 1963. Well-deserved.

Very cordially yours,
Luis Buñuel

Spa Als, OL

---

[1] *Diary of a Chambermaid.*
[2] Reference to the fact that the timeframe specified in the rights to the adaptation of *Los hijos de Sánchez* (The Sons of Sánchez), bought by Abby Mann, has run out.
[3] By Céline Zins, published in Paris by Gallimard, in 1963.

To Ruth and Zachary Scott

[Paris,] 11 February 1964

Dear Ruth and Zachary:

   If you want to take lunch with me dans un bon bistrot[1] *I shall wait for you in my hotel next Thursday 13, at noon. If you cannot come, please let me know where I can find you at the same time.*

Yours, abrazos,[2]
Buñuel

Eng/Fre Als, ZSA

---

[1] French in the original (in a good bistro).
[2] Spanish in the original (hugs).

To Francisco Rabal

Paris, 13 February 1964

Dear Paco,

Great happiness at your postcard, as I see – from the fact that you can write again – that you can now use your 'oar' …[1] I'd be very grateful if, when you finally get the all-clear, you would write to me in Mexico to let me know how you are feeling physically and mentally … and what plans you have in mind.

I'm delivering a copy of my film[2] on Tuesday for the premier. It will be shown from 4 March at the Colisée and the Marivaux.[3] The far right may protest.[4] Not my problem! I'll be in Mexico! My producers can sort it out.

I'll be home on Friday 21 February. I'm a touch neurasthenic. Eleven months alone in my hotel. I don't see anyone these days.

Much love to all yours and to María Asunción in particular.

Another big hug for you from,

YOUR UNCLE,
Luis

Spa Als, FR; *BVMC* f

[1] Rabal damaged his arm in a car accident in December 1963.
[2] *Diary of a Chambermaid.*
[3] Paris film theatres.
[4] The film attacks the French anti-Semitic right and, in the final sequence, far-right members of a fascist demonstration at Cherbourg shout '¡Viva Chiappe!' (Long live, Chiappe!), a reference to Jean Chiappe, the Prefect of Police responsible for banning *The Golden Age.*

To Pierre Braunberger

Mexico City, 7 March 1964

My dear Pierre,

Three or four days ago the copy of *Land Without Bread* left for 95 Champs-Élysées, Paris.[1] This is the information:

'Air France, BII aircraft, flight number 0570363277. Box with three reels of film, master copy of *Land Without Bread*, 850m of film, insured at $200, with $27.04 freight to pay'.

Fortunately, I put one of my friends in charge of sending the copy; if I hadn't I would never have been capable of doing it myself. I really hate that kind of procedure: stamp from the Film Directorate, export licence, packaging, courier agents, etc., etc. Dreadful! But it's done. I hope you won't be as shocking as I was and take five months to pay the rest of the 1,500 francs; that is, exactly the same length of time it has taken me to send you the film. Although, in fitting symmetry, you have every right to delay payment.

Finally, I'm back in my convent after ten months in hotels in Europe, in relative solitude, and so far from my friends. I'm a slave to my deafness.

Please send most affectionate best wishes to your wife and daughter Nicole, I have wonderful memories of them.[2]

All best,
Luis Buñuel

[PS] The copy I have sent you is excellent, and it's the only complete copy there is. The first reel has sound in French; the other two have no sound.

Fre Tlsps, PB

---

[1] Braunberger had ordered a complete, restored copy.
[2] Braunberger and his wife coincided with LB in Madrid in July 1963.

From Oscar Lewenstein[1]

London, 26 March 1964

Dear Don Luis,

Please forgive me for not having written to you sooner, but we have only just had confirmation from United Artists that they are prepared to go ahead with the picture[2] providing that:

(1) We replace Zachary Scott with an English star, and
(2) the budget does not exceed $500,000.

As far as the first point is concerned, Zachary himself has very sweetly agreed to allow the film to proceed without him playing the part of the Consul,[3] providing that you are agreeable to this. I do hope you will be. Tony[4] and I feel that there are a number of English actors who could play the part and particularly we would suggest Paul Scofield[5] should he be available. We think he would be absolutely wonderful. As for Zachary, we have suggested that he might be connected with the film as an Associate Producer and possible play the part of the film director. Do you think this is a good idea?

As far as the second point is concerned, it would only be possible to do the film within this budget if you were able to shoot it in seven weeks which you said you thought would be possible, and providing that you, Jeanne Moreau and everyone else would take smaller fees than were originally suggested, i.e. it would not be possible to pay you a fee of $80,000. Most probably the best we could do would be something like half that, plus a percentage of the profits of the film.

I am going to Paris tomorrow and will discuss the matter fully with Madame Dorisse, but I hope so much that you will be able to consider this sympathetically.

Apart from the above, I understand that we have another problem and that is that you have now undertaken another film[6] and would not be free to shoot Under the Volcano *until sometime around February or March. Jeanne Moreau, I believe, is only free until the end of January and then not until September or October of next year. Whilst I am in Paris I will see Jeanne and Micheline Rozan[7] and go into this more thoroughly, but I would like your views on it.*

Lastly, I had a note some time ago from Madame Dorisse saying that you wanted us to commission a script, rather than have you yourself work upon the screen play at this stage. Is this correct, and if so do you think it would be a good idea to get Harvey Breit to do a first draft screenplay, since we are already committed to paying him anyway? Or would you prefer us to approach Carlos Fuentes at this stage?

I shall be staying in Paris at the Hotel St. Regis, Place de la Concorde, Telephone No. Elysees 4190, and I shall be there until the morning of Thursday, 2nd April. It would be nice to hear from you whilst I am still there about your reaction to all this.

Again, please forgive all the delays. Tony and I and all our colleagues are most happy that we have been able to persuade United Artists to go ahead with this project. We very much want to work with you on it, and hope that despite all the difficulties it can go ahead.

With all good wishes, Yours sincerely,
Oscar Lewenstein
Woodfall Film Presentations Ltd[8]
11a Curzon Street, London W

Eng Tls L, AB/1404.30

1 British film and theatre producer (1917–97).
2 *Under the Volcano.*
3 British consul, Geoffrey Firmin, protagonist of the novel.
4 Tony Richardson (1928–91), British film-maker, published his interview with LB 'The Films of Luis Buñuel' in *Sight and Sound* 23, no. 3 (January–March 1954), pp. 125–130.
5 English actor (1922–2008).
6 *Simon of the Desert.*
7 French theatrical agent and producer.
8 The letterhead indicates that Woodfall's associates are (in addition to Lewenstein and Richardson), John Osborne, Oscar Beuselinck and James Isherwood.

To Oscar Lewenstein

Mexico, 30 March 1964[1]

Dear Mr Lewenstein,
I have just received your letter of the 26 March. In Paris we had agreed, in principle, on certain terms and now I find, through no fault of your own, that these have been changed.
First: I think that Zachary Scott is the actor indicated for the role of the Consul.
Second: I had asked 80,000 dollars for doing the film. Here in Mexico, for a local Mexican Spanish speaking film – The Exterminating Angel – I get 50,000 dollars. Therefore, I do not think that for an international production I should be expected to accept $40,000.
We had agreed that I would receive a letter from you by 1 March to settle our agreements.

I did not receive the letter and have since signed with another producer. I will therefore be occupied till the end of November.

In any case, I was very pleased to have met you and keep a fond memory of our reunion. I am sorry that things have turned out this way and hope that we can meet again in more productive circumstances.

Yours sincerely,
LB

P.S. Please give my best regards to Tony Richardson.

Eng Tls, ZSA

---

[1] Carbon copy sent to Zachary Scott and Paulette Dorisse.

To Dalton Trumbo

Dalton Trumbo
6231 Annan Trail, Los Angeles

Mexico City, 13 April 1964

IF POSSIBLE, I SHOULD LIKE TO SEE YOU SOON AS IT IS EASIER FOR YOU TO MAKE TRIP, OUR MEETING COULD BE HELD HERE. I AM NOW IN POSITION TO TALK IN EARNEST ABOUT JOHNNY GOT HIS GUN. I KEEP A VERY PLEASANT MEMORY OF YOUR WIFE AND YOUR LAST STAY HERE. VIVAN LOS GRINGOS[1]

REGARDS,
LUIS BUÑUEL

Eng Tel, DT/72/05

---

[1] Spanish in the original (long live the *gringos*).

From Dalton Trumbo

Los Angeles, 15 April 1964

WILL ARRIVE MEXICO CITY FRIDAY FOR TWO DAY WORKING SPREE.[1] *QUE VIVA MEXICO.*[2]

DALTON TRUMBO

Eng Tel, DT/72/05

---

[1] Trumbo arrived in Mexico City on 17 April to discuss the adaptation of his novel with LB.
[2] Spanish in the original (long live Mexico).

To Ruth Ford Scott

Mexico City, 21 April 1964

Dear Ruth,

If I could make me understood with my miserable English I should try to convey to you my gratitude for all you have made for Rafael, who, by the way, he has momentarily retired, with a broken ankle. Impossible to be best introduced in the NY theatre ambiance. Now, it is up to him.

Please tell Zachary that the Volcano *has to be made with him as the Consul or it will not be made … by me.*

Till soon, perhaps, with all my best regards
Luis Buñuel

PS This letter has not been supervised by Juan Luis.

Eng Als, ZS/LMC2740

To Pierre Braunberger

Mexico City, 21 April 1964

My dear Pierre,

Writing a letter. What a pain!

If I were in Paris, I would be happy to feature in a film about surrealism,[1] but it would be difficult to take part from Mexico. Also, I don't have any documents from that time that might be of some use to you and the others. That said, if you think of any way I can help out, just ask. Send Brunius sincere and friendly regards.

I don't agree with the laboratory.[2] The copy I sent you is definitely better quality than the one you are using. It's the first one taken from the original negative whereas yours is a duplicate, or even a duplicate of a duplicate. Also, mine is *complete*.

As for the money you still have to pay me, I can wait three months before claiming it. I blame myself for the four-month delay sending you the material, although it was unavoidable as the copy was in Mexico and I couldn't really get anyone to inspect the enormous pile of reels, because my wife had no idea where it was.

Best,
Luis Buñuel

Fre Tls, PB

---

[1] In a letter dated 19 March 1964, Braunberger and Brunius ask LB to contribute to the making of the documentary *Le Surréalisme* (AB/568.45–47).
[2] Reference to the copy of *Land Without Bread*.

To Francisco Rabal

Mexico City, 21 April 1964

Dear little nephew Paco,

If I had your facility for throwing together a letter, I would not be so out of step with you on this epistolary terrain. You can't imagine how happy it makes me to get your news and how unhappy it makes me to have to send you mine. But, with enormous effort, I am setting myself to write you fifteen or twenty lines.

I'm very anxious to hear whether you are out of the sling by now and, most importantly, how your arm is. As soon as you can move it freely, send word to put my mind at rest.

It was very annoying you thought I was plagiarizing you with the snail scene.[1] I was about to write you an irate letter, but then I thought: 'If this suggestion of Paco's bothers me so much, then it must be true. If it weren't, I would simply find it funny.' So, I now confess and state for the record, that any snail-business[2] that appears, or that may appear in my films is the property of: Paco Rabal.

I am completely idle. Long may it last. My next film will almost definitely be in English, made here and in the United States. When are we going to work together again, Paco? What fun we had!

I'd be very grateful if you could give me your final thoughts on Saura's film.[3] I'm hoping for a positive report.

Many kisses for María Inmaculada and the children, not forgetting a hug for good old Damián. And for you, the constant and familiar affection of your kind uncle,

Buñuel

Spa Tls, FR; *BVMC* f

---

[1] Reference to the sequence with the snail in *Nazarín*.
[2] 'Caracolada' in the original, meaning 'escargot' or 'snails cooked in sauce'.
[3] *Llanto por un bandido* (1964), starring Rabal, with LB in a cameo role as an executioner, was shot in Summer, 1963.

Figure 61 At the restaurant El Correo Español, Mexico City, *c.* 1964: Isaac, Alcoriza, Alfredo and Arturo Ripstein, Sigfrido García, Jorge Bustos, Savage, García Riera and Buñuel.

To Oscar Lewis

Mexico, 29 May 1964[1]

Dear friend Lewis,

Unluckily I wasn't home either of the two times you phoned. In any case, I wouldn't have been able to talk with you because I don't hear the telephone voice well. I think we can communicate better by letter or cablegram.

Your book[2] is admirable and in some aspects superior, if that is possible, to The Children of Sánchez. *But as to making a film of it in Mexico, it is impossible, or even more so, than the other. I don't believe you should nourish any hopes about that. Of course, by limiting the film to the more positive aspects of the book – or those which would be so regarded by the gentlemen of the government – it would be easy enough to carry out this project. However, I am not willing, in this or any other similar matter, to make any kind of compromise. The film should reflect the same objective, complete, vital images as regards politics, society, etc., that is presented in the book. That is something we can't even dream about at present. Better to wait for a more favourable time ... if it ever comes.*

I congratulate you warmly on the achievement reflected in Pedro Martínez.

Very cordially yours,
Buñuel

Eng CmfL, OL

[1] The only existing copy of this letter has apparently been translated from a Spanish original now missing.
[2] *Pedro Martínez: A Mexican Peasant and his Family* (New York: Random House, 1964).

From Jeanne Moreau

[Midi, June 1964]

I haven't written to you for a long time, for the simple reason that I had to spend eight days in Paris. First of all, to dub that horrible American film, *The Train*,[1] and then to meet people I'm going to work with and sign a contract for *Mata Hari, Agente H-21*.[2] I'll be filming, directed by my ex-husband,[3] from 17 August in a deserted Paris, because there is no studio filming at all. I will have finished the film by the time you come to Paris in October; I'll be waiting for you and we'll be able to spend a few days in south of France with Anna[4] if you still want to.

I never grow tired of my good health. The house is beautiful. I have two German shepherds; my little white cat, who has grown a lot; my brother came; my son[5] has just arrived; and my sister[6] and mother[7] will be here in a few days' time. I like having everyone close by, I may be turning into a very boring woman, but everything seems extraordinary to me. I'm never depressed now, I'm nearly always in a good mood, and I am sleeping, which is very unusual for me, without pills. As I'm getting more sociable every day, I've accepted another invitation from my Italian friend, the one I was in Tripoli with, and I'll be in Venice from 12 to 23 July, living a worldly life of luxury.

We'll swim every day and there'll be endless changing of outfits. I will probably tire of it after a week and be delighted to get back home.

I was so happy to get your letter, and even more so to know that you are reading mine.

Your replies may be short, but it doesn't matter; it's like a long conversation, full of silences; besides, I talk a lot and you little. That's just the way it is. I think of you often. I saw Jean-Claude Carrière[8] when I was in Paris. He's working with Louis Malle[9] on our Mexican film.[10] I don't know anything about the story yet, but they seem really happy with it, which is the main thing.

Anna took a picture of me, which I'm sending: my hair has grown, and I've put on weight.

From a note that Juan Luis sent me, I discovered he was putting on an exhibition, that is really exciting, as was finding out that he knows how to make peppered rabbit. *Very important.*

Work hard. I send you much love.

Yours,
Jeanne

Fre Als, AB/648.11–12

[1]   *The Train*, dir. John Frankenheimer, premiered in Paris in September 1964.
[2]   *Mata Hari, agent H 21*, dir. Jean-Louis Richard (1927–2012), based on a script by Richard and Truffaut, in 1964.
[3]   Richard, Moreau's husband between 1949 and 1951.
[4]   Anna Pradella, personal assistant to Moreau.
[5]   Jérôme Richard (born 1949).
[6]   Michelle Moreau.
[7]   Katherine Buckley, British ballerina living in France.
[8]   French scriptwriter (born 1931), worked with LB on nine features, including *Diary of a Chambermaid* and *Belle de Jour.*
[9]   French director (1932–95).
[10] *¡Viva María!*, filmed in Mexico in 1965, directed by Malle based on a script co-written with Carrière, produced by Dancigers, and starring Moreau and Brigitte Bardot (born 1934).
[11] His first exhibition, of copper sculptures, at the Galería Diana, Mexico City, in 1964.

From Dino de Laurentiis[1]

Rome, 24 July 1964

PLEASE CONSIDER THIS TELEGRAM STRICTLY CONFIDENTIAL. I AM ABOUT TO BEGIN WORK, AFTER SOME PRELIMINARY ORGANIZATION, ON A CONTEMPORARY EPISODIC FILM IN THREE PARTS, EACH STARRING SORAYA.[2] THE FIRST TWO DIRECTORS ARE MAURO BOLOGNINI[3] AND MICHELANGELO ANTONIONI. FOR THE THIRD I THOUGHT OF YOU. PLEASE WIRE AT ONCE IF YOU ARE INTERESTED AND AVAILABLE. WE CAN ALSO SEND YOU THE PLOT BUT ARE OPEN TO CONSIDERING AN ORIGINAL IDEA OF YOUR OWN.[4]

CORDIAL GREETINGS,
DINO DE LAURENTIIS

Ita Tel, AB/639.2–3

¹   Italian producer (1919–2010).
²   Princess Soraya of Iran (1932–2001), separated from the Shah of Iran in 1959, occasional actress.
³   Italian director (1922–2001).
⁴   The film is made as *I tre volti* (1965); third part directed in the end by Franco Indovina.

From Pierre Braunberger

Paris, 17 September 1964

My dear Luis,

I don't know where you are in the world at the moment, perhaps Mexico, where I am sending this letter.

I have wanted to make a film of *La Celestina*¹ for a long time now. Jaime Camino,² a young Spanish producer (a great friend of Jacques Doniol Valcroze), wants to co-produce with me.

In the brief conversation you and I had you said period films worry you. I've spoken to Jean Renoir, who is very enthusiastic, but fears he is too old now for a production on that scale. His idea was to set the story in a different period. Would you like me to send you Renoir's notes on this?

Think it over seriously. It's an important project.

Write soon.

Your friend,
Pierre Braunberger

Fre Tlsps, AB/1404.1

¹   *La Celestina*, or *The Comedy of Calisto and Melibea*, major work of Spanish literature, late medieval novel in dialogue attributed to Fernando de Rojas and published *c*. 1500.
²   Film director and writer (1936–2015).

To José Rubia Barcia

Mexico City, 21 September 1964

My dear *don* Pepe,

What a man and a genius you are … which is why I'm writing back after receiving your annual letter. Of course, if you'd given me some warning about your operation, I would have asked after your health much more often. As the little tumour thing is now over, my sympathies for the crippling cost of this sort of thing in America. If you have time, send word, if only on a postcard, of your complete recovery. I too had a small, benign tumour on my tonsils. They took it out and that was that.

As you were making your way back to Los Angeles from Europe, I was arriving in Paris to make the Mirbeau film, *Diary of a Chambermaid*, with Jeanne Moreau, which I finished last February. I've been here since then. I'm now going to make a *sketch* in four-reels about Saint Simeon the Stylite[1] for the singular Alatriste del Sur production company.[2] And if possible, I'll be back in Spain on holiday for a couple of months at the end of the year. Then I'll come back here to work on the film Dalton Trumbo is writing at the moment based on his book *Johnny got his Gun*, which will probably be made in your adoptive country, which means we would see a lot of each other… if filming goes ahead.

Rafael is in New York, writing, *soi-dissant*,[3] for the theatre. Juan Luis is here and will be going to Paris, when he's finished his military service, with his distinguished wife. Jeanne, as always 'loving Mexico'.

I'm very grateful for your invitation, or rather your work on an invitation for me to come over for the film conference. I think I mentioned that I turned down a similar offer from Harvard, the thing is that, if I have to leave Mexico at my advanced age, I'd prefer it was to see Spain before I die, if only one last time.

That cutting about diseases of the ear was very interesting, but it only confirmed what I already knew: that everything is curable except problems with the auditory nerve, which is precisely what is wrong with my ears.

Give Evita a big hug, and kisses for my two little nieces. And a warm embrace for you from

Luis

Tls, CBC; *JGG* 10

[1] Christian saint and ascetic (390–459), who chose to live the last thirty-seven years of his life on top of a pillar in the Syrian desert near Aleppo.
[2] Reference to the fact that Alatriste functioned independently from the film industry (he made his fortune selling furniture) and 'del Sur' (from the south), in reference to Mexico.
[3] French in the original ('supposedly' or 'so he says').

To Pierre Braunberger

Mexico City, 29 September 1964

My dear Pierre,

Thank you for your letter, and particularly for the offer to direct *La Celestina*. I'm very sorry to have to say no, and not just because 'the period' intimidates me, but for exactly the same reason as Renoir: I'm intimidated by my age. I feel lazy, and I only want to go back to Europe on holiday, rather than to work. I've practically retired from film-making, except in Mexico where I feel at home and work 'as a family'. Although either way, I don't think I will be making films much longer. Apart from that, I think it's a very good idea to make *La Celestina*.

Although I do think it is best left to its own period rather than moved to our own.

On another note: the seven- or eight-month delayed, at my request to *punish myself for my sins*, payment of the final 1,500 francs for *Land Without Bread* is now over. So, could you begin to think about how payment might be made through CIMURA? I saw a copy of the version I sent you, I'd kept as a memento. The photography is EXCELLENT.

Yours,
Luis Buñuel

Tls, PB; *PBP* 202 f

Figure 62 Filming *Simon of the Desert*, Mexico, November 1964.

To Francisco Rabal

Mexico City, 11 January 1965

Dear Paco,
Your letter arrived from Oxford and I was unpleasantly surprised to hear they were going to operate again on that arm I thought was completely cured.[1] But from what you say, I gather you're on the final stretch now and that this latest operation is just to make sure there won't be any more setbacks. I hope so. A year of doctors and casts is more than enough!

No one over here was right for the part of Saint Simeon (a bearded, skeletal old man), so we were considering Fernando, or Fernán Gómez,[2] but at the last minute, among all the auditions we found one that would do by a chap called Claudio Brook, a Mexican actor (he played the protestant priest in *The Young One*).[3] I finished the film in five reels, which was – Good Lord! – strangely satisfying, although I may take it up to the more normal hour and a half. We'll see.[4]

This year, I'm not sure when, I want to spend a couple of months in Spain! I'm semi- retired from the cinema, but I may, it's by no means certain, take up an offer from Silberman,[5] who wants to return to the scene of the crime with me. Your letter says your film will premiere on the 14th of this month. I wish you great success, that would please me far more than if it were my own.

Big hugs for María Asunción and the children and an even bigger one for you from your

uncle Luis

Spa Tls, FR; *BVMC* f

---

[1] January 1965, Rabal's arm is treated by Dr Josep Trueta at the Nuffield Orthopaedic Centre, University of Oxford.
[2] Fernando Fernán Gómez (1921–2007), actor and film director.
[3] Also the butler, Julio, in *The Exterminating Angel*.
[4] *Simon of the Desert* was planned by Alatriste and LB as one episode in a three-part film (the other parts to be directed by Fellini and Jules Dassin) hence its final 43-minute length.
[5] They would work together again on *The Milky Way*.
[6] Possibly the film *Marie Chantal contre Dr. Kha* (1965), dir. Claude Chabrol, starring Rabal.

From Giancarlo Zagni[1]

Rome, 31 January 1965

Dear Buñuel,

I hope your film about the Stylite saint is finished and that it will be a great film, like all your others.[2] I can't wait to see it.

I'll be finishing my black comedy next week[3] and it should be in cinemas at the end of February.

I'd love to know what you think of *La Coda di Pandora*,[4] because I have a producer ready to make the film if it's directed by you. The English are also interested and are going to do a stage adaptation.[5] I think you could make a marvellous film out of it. If you would prefer to shoot it in Mexico, I could organize that.

As soon as you can, thanking you in advance for your thoughts.

Very best wishes from Alida,[6] and I send mine, also, to Mrs Jeanne.

Very best wishes,
Giancarlo
3 Via Apollo Pizio, Rome

PS Your film with Moreau is also a big hit in Italy![7]

Spa Tls, AB/1404.25

---

[1] Italian director and scriptwriter (1926–2013), taught at UNAM in 1963.
[2] *Simon of the Desert* premiered at the Venice Festival, 27 August 1965.
[3] His section for *Umorismo in nero* (1965), three-part film also co-directed by Claude Autant- Lara and José María Forqué, premiered in April 1965.
[4] Play by Guglielmo Biraghi.
[5] Premiered in the UK with the title *The forty cats, or Pandora's tail: A Play in two parts*.
[6] Baronesa Alida Valli (1921–2006), Italian actress, Zagni's partner.
[7] *Diary of a Chambermaid* premiered in Italy on September 1964.

To Robert Favre Le Bret

Mexico City, 31 March 1965

Dear friend,

Thank you for your kind letter and for your interest in my participation in the next Cannes Festival.[1] However, unfortunately, the film[2] I'm finishing at the moment has only five reels and will become part of a feature when another director, we don't yet know who it will be, completes the other half.[3]

I'm taking this opportunity to recommend very highly to you a Mexican film made by my old partner Luis Alcoriza, two and a quarter hours long, called *Tarahumara*.[4] It's definitely good enough to aspire to the Palme d'Or. The producer, Mr Matouk,[5] wants to send it to Moscow,[6] but if you were to request it he would be delighted to send it to you. Mexico has nothing for Cannes this year.

I'll be in Europe for the Festival, and if *Always Further On* is screened, I'd be very happy to receive an invitation from you to 'do some festival politicking in support of *Always Further On*'.

Very cordially,
Buñuel

Fre Tls, CIN

---

[1] 18th Cannes Film Festival celebrated in May 1965; members of the jury included Aub, Ténoudji and Ledoux.
[2] *Simon of the Desert*.
[3] Never produced.
[4] *Tarahumara* (1964), written and directed by Alcoriza.
[5] Antonio Matouk (1920–2003), Mexican producer.
[6] *Tarahumara* did not compete at the 4th Moscow Film Festival.

From Luis Alcoriza

Paris, 30 May 1965

Dear Luis,

Friends in high places are worth their weight in gold, and yours must really have counted at Cannes. Del Río[1] said as much, and her wise words turned out to be prophetic: They gave me the Critics' Prize![2] Thank you, Luis! I'll never forget this gift from you! I'm imagining the headline in *Novedades*: 'Big *enchilada* Buñuel gets pupil prize, backed by Festival mafia'.

According to Max Aub, they were officially going to give me Best Script, but as they were about to vote, Favre Le Bret came in and told the Jury that the film had already won the FIPRESCI prize. That, according to Max, is why the Jury chose the English film *The Hill*[3] instead. I don't know if it's true. You must have been surprised to get my telegram from Paris, but I do sometimes behave like a lunatic. The same afternoon I heard about the awards I sent you one that will probably never reach you. You won't believe me, but it was like this. I wrote it in my own little hand and sent it to the Torre de Madrid in: Paris, France! As I was travelling separately from the others the next day on the aeroplane, I had time to think and I realized my stupid mistake. I can only excuse myself by saying I was overcome with excitement – the whole delegation was going crazy – and a bit drunk, which somewhat stunted my faculties.

Naturally, and now I'm not joking, I owe the award to you for practically forcing me to come and adding prestige to the film.

The kindness and friendship you have shown are truly worthy of the person you are, I don't know what else to say. I'm going to [book] a plane ticket tomorrow for the 3rd. I'll send a telegram with the result and my arrival date. See you soon.

Warm regards,
Luis

Spa Als, AB/618

---

[1] Possibly, Dolores del Río.
[2] *Tarahumara* won the Premio FIPRESCI at Cannes.
[3] *The Hill* (1965), dir. Sidney Lumet, Anglo-American co-production, won the Prize for Best Script at Cannes.

Figure 63 Acapulco, *c.* 1965: standing, left to right, Walter Achugar, Michel, Novais Teixeira, Arturo Ripstein and Isaac; sitting, Alcoriza, Buñuel, Ladislav Kachtik, García Márquez, Matouk and Gloria Marín.

To Ricardo Muñoz Suay

Mexico City, 27 June 1965

Dear Ricardo,

Back on the high plains of the New World, I'm up to my toupee in work and all manner of frenetic activity.[1] The worst thing is I'm completely out of my depth and can't concentrate enough to write a single sensible line. My poor imagination is always fleeing back to Madrid, and I'm far more interested in remembering friends than in the dirty tricks my characters are supposed to be up to.

How are you? How are your children and your wife? That marvellous creature, prodigious in kindness, and unrivalled maker of indescribable paellas and stews. May God bless you all! Speaking of God, I'm so miserable and helpless so far away from you that I've not even been to Communion[2] since I got back.

I had a really lovely card from Amparo and Alfredo.[3] They were passing through Hollywood and lamenting that their brief stay meant it was impossible for them to come and see me. Charming! He says you told him about *Divinas palabras* and that he thinks it's a wonderful idea. I do too, but what I'd like to know is whether you're going to work on getting the rights, which would mean I would start thinking of it as something for the near future (starting at the beginning of next year, for example), or whether it's more of a long-term project. I'd be really grateful if you could give me a clear answer on this, as you well know what it would mean to me, for so many reasons, to make that film in Spain. I don't want to get my hopes up for nothing.

I'll be leaping back over the ocean on 18 June to be on the jury at the Locarno Festival.[4] I'm going to try my best to get to Madrid for a few days, or at least to Barcelona, although it won't be easy because of the commitments I have over here and the fact that I'm already behind on my work. The delay has also hit my already pretty empty pockets hard, which[5] makes things even more difficult. That said, I'm so hungry for a decent paella at times … you never know what may happen.

Send fraternal regards to Saura, Regueiro,[6] Manuel and that young Basque with the unpronounceable name.[7] Such a shame to have to leave such a wonderful crowd when we were only just getting to know one another!

I was very touched by your love of religious artefacts. You are, underneath it all, a good man. And if at times – very few – you blaspheme (a Spanish vice, after all), I think the fact of pronouncing God's name – even if it is to offend him – will secure you remission.

See you soon. Lots of kisses to Nieves, and for you a big hug, just one, though not a Dominguin-ish[8] one,

Luis

Spa Tls, RMS; *CUA* 595 f

[1] General reference to work, rather than to one specific film.
[2] Joke: LB is clearly not a practising Catholic.
[3] Actress Amparo Soler Leal (1933–2013) and her husband, producer Alfredo Matas Salinas (1920–96).
[4] LB did not attend the Locarno Festival; he was, in the end, in El Escorial, Spain, working on the script for *The Monk* with Carrière.
[5] Untranslatable pun omitted here on 'peso' (weight) and 'pesos' (Mexican currency); in Spanish, a 'razón de peso' is an *obvious* reason, LB's 'a razón de pesos' in the plural indicates the reason is not only obvious but has obvious financial implications.
[6] Francisco Regueiro (1934), director and scriptwriter.
[7] Possibly the producer Elías Querejeta (1934–2013), who worked for UNINCI, or the director Antxon Eceiza (1935–2011), both young directors associated with the movement known as Spanish 'New Cinema'.
[8] Reference to the falling-out between LB and Domingo Dominguín over *Viridiana*.

From Salvador Dalí

Roses, [July 1965]

DEAR LUIS,
  I LIKE *AN ANDALUSIAN DOG* MORE AND MORE. WOULD YOU LIKE TO MAKE SEQUEL TOGETHER, SAME LENGTH, BASED ON IDEA THAT WILL MAKE YOU WEEP FOR JOY? ONLY FIVE DAYS SHOOTING. COME THIS WEEKEND TO CADAQUÉS OR I WILL COME TO MADRID.

BEST,
DALÍ

Fre Tel, AB/562; BMS 216

To Salvador Dalí

Madrid, 3 July 1965

I got your extraordinary telegram, but that's all water under the bridge now.[1]

Buñuel

Spa Tel, FSD/3579

---

[1] LB's laconic reply is the Spanish refrain: 'agua pasada no mueve molinos', literally, 'water gone by won't move windmills'.

To Ricardo Muñoz Suay

El Escorial, 26 July 1965

Dear Ricardo,
I got your letter and am sending my strict instructions. You are invited to lunch, with Nieves of course, next Sunday. I'll be waiting for you at the Torre, Apartment 20 – 3 at 1pm, or perhaps 1:30, but no later. If you want, you could also let Villegas López[1] know; I was interested in his interpretation of *The Exterminating Angel*.[2] Also, I'm very familiar with his name and his articles because he's of our era. If you don't think it's a good idea for him to lunch with us, you could ask him to come to Torre de Madrid on Sunday at 6pm.
Write to me at the Torre with your acceptance (or rejection?). I arrive in Madrid on Saturday. Whatever you say in your letter, I'll agree to, because I don't make telephone calls, and I don't pick up if it rings.
Of course, if Nieves is still not quite well, I'd prefer you didn't move the invitation to your house. Would you prefer to meet for supper? If so, Sunday at 8 at the aforementioned. You know my horror at the Spanish habit of eating so late.

Warm regards,
Luis

Spa Tls, RMS

---

[1] Manuel Villegas López (1906–80), film critic, who worked on *Nuestro cinema* edited by Piqueras, exiled to Argentina between 1939 and 1953.
[2] M. Villegas, 'Prólogo', in L. Buñuel, *The Exterminating Angel* (Barcelona: Aymá, 1964), pp. 7–14.

From Luigi Chiarini[1]

Venice, 23 August 1965

CONFIRM SCREENING OF *SIMON OF THE DESERT* EVENING OF 27 AUGUST, WARMLY INVITE YOU TO ATTEND AGAIN AS OUR SPECIAL GUEST OF HONOUR.[2]

CORDIALLY,
CHIARINI,
DIRECTOR, VENICE FILM FESTIVAL

Ita Tel, BIE/200

[1]   Italian film critic (1900–75), director of the Venice Film Festival between 1963 and 1968.
[2]   *Simon of the Desert* screened in competition at the 26th Venice Festival.

To Luigi Chiarini

[Madrid,] 24 August 1965

IMPOSSIBLE FOR ME TO ACCEPT YOUR KIND INVITATION FOR REASONS EXPLAINED IN MY LETTER.[1] SINCERE THANKS AGAIN.

CORDIALLY,
BUÑUEL

Spa Tel, BIE/200

[1]   Not preserved.

From Luis and Janet Alcoriza

Mexico City, 7 September 1965
VERITABLE TRIUMPH, VENERABLE *MAESTRO*.[1]
CONGRATULATIONS AND WARM REGARDS,
ALCORIZAS

Spa Tel, AB/1524.4

[1]   *Simon of the Desert* won the Special Jury Prize in Venice; Jay Leyda was one of the Jury members.

To Janet and Luis Alcoriza

Madrid, 8 September 1965

My dearest Jeannette and de la Vega[1]
    I was delighted to get your telegram and I accept, touched by the label 'maestro', but you can keep your 'venerable' for your *rabbi*.[2] Let it be known, Luis, I shall always have my *souvenir from Constantinople* in the shape of a microscopic stitch. *Sans blague!*[3]

Over here, I've been insulted behind my back and to my face over the blessed *Simon of the Desert*. I've just cut out the umpteenth article from *Informaciones*[4] saying, as you'll see, I have nothing to do with Spain. I, who love Spain so much.

I didn't answer Luis's two letters because there was nothing to say. I was happy to have them, to hear about your trip and your disappointment as a jury member, but I had nothing to say, because I was just over here making slow and languid progress on the adaptation. I had a wonderful month in El Escorial, which I hardly knew and now love. I went to work there to be less accessible to the five or six friends I see regularly, and that Luis knows well.

I'll be in Mexico from around the 22nd. I'm going to stop off for a few days in New York to see the boys. I'm very much looking forward to being back in our beautiful Mexico,[5] so proud of my Mexican passport. I'll be back in Paris in early January next year to prepare and film *The Monk,* although there's little of the original left in the adaptation.

They attack me, but the Spanish press occasionally praises Luis. I kept two or three articles about the Cannes Festival for you, but they've mysteriously disappeared. The *Shark Hunters*[6] also went down very well. They're not all anti-Semites those Falangists at *Informaciones*.

I imagine Gustavo is puffed-up and super-megalomaniacal with all his awards. Good for him! I hope Luis will inherit my number-one-son mantle and that God is good to him. What I do find absolutely unbelievable is the way he abandoned his *Simon in the Desert* at the Festival, completely and utterly, when he knew I wasn't going to be there. I hope that good old Servando[7] will represent our lovely Mexico at the Festival. I'd love to meet up for a bit of our usual bragging.

A theoretical hug for now in place of the real one I shall give you both soon. Even Jeanne doesn't know when I arrive, but certainly not before the week of the 20th.

Goodbye,
Luis

[PS] I am planning to sign my contract with Sarita Matouk[8] as soon as I arrive. Send my best wishes, and to Matouk as well. When do you start *Sortilegio?*[9]

I can't find the cutting from *Informaciones*. It was good. I'm sorry!

Spa Tlsps, ALC/01/01; *BRU* 28–29

---

[1] Full surname: Alcoriza de la Vega.
[2] French in the original.
[3] French in the original (I'm not kidding).
[4] Evening paper published in Madrid between 1922 and 1983, with noticeably pro-Nazi and anti-Jewish sympathies during the war period.
[5] 'Lindo' (pretty) in the original in reference to the refrain 'México lindo y querido' (Beautiful and beloved Mexico) in a mariachi/ranchero song popularized by Negrete.
[6] *Tiburoneros,* feature produced by Matouk and directed by Alcoriza in 1962.
[7] Servando González (1923–2008), Mexican film director.
[8] Sara Matouk, head of production, and sister of Matouk.
[9] Meaning 'spell' or 'enchantment', a provisional title perhaps for Alcoriza's section called 'Divertimento' for the feature-length *Juego peligroso* (1967), co-directed by Alcoriza and Arturo Ripstein (born 1943).

To Ricardo Muñoz Suay

Mexico City, 11 October 1965

Dear Ricardo,

You may now put a song in your heart, because I've finally 'condescended' to reply to a letter. And it's only because yours was so warm and detailed that I've no option but to sacrifice myself and write back.

At the moment, I can't send you any of the things you asked for, *namely*,[1] *scripts*,[2] photos, etc., etc. Once the film[3] is finished …. To hell with it. You should approach your future boss Alatriste and may God go with you.

I knew a bit about the awards you told me all about. I saw Saura, but I don't think he liked the film at all. He hardly said anything about what went on in Venice.

Alcoriza is copying Nieves in these tropical climes, making green rice like yours. But he hasn't invited me over yet. He just told me it was excellent.

If everything goes smoothly, I'll leave for Europe around December and, if so, I'll spend Christmas between Madrid and Calanda. Obviously, we'll exchange invitations to dine on tripe, or grilled sardines, etc.

I'm still basking somewhat over here in a warm and gelatinous pool of total sloth. I never leave the house and only meet up to have lunch with a friend once a week. With the script[4] finished, there's nothing to do but wait. I'm regretting now that I didn't get on with preparing the film, which was postponed at my request until January.

Kisses for Nieves and a hug for you,
Luis

Spa Tls, RMS

[1]   English in the original.
[2]   English in the original.
[3]   *Simon of the Desert.*
[4]   *The Monk.*

To Emmanuel Roblès

Mexico City, 15 October 1965

Dear friend Roblès,

I got back from five months in Europe a couple of weeks ago and found your latest book[1] waiting for me, which I read at once. I liked it as much as I do all your work, although this one, and *Montserrat*, seem to me even better. Reading *Plaidoyer pour un rebelle* raised troubling questions for my conscience and, just as when I read *Monserrat*, it made me revise certain of my ideas that I thought were set in stone. *Mer libre* has the kind of hero, admirable and odious at the same time, that it is extremely difficult to forget. Wonderful – both plays! They'd both make magnificent films.

I'm really grateful you thought of me to adapt *Montserrat* for the television. I'm sorry I can't accept, because I'm committed to work in Paris, where I'm going at the beginning of next year to make what may be my last film: *The Monk*. I'll be in Paris until June, and I hope that you'll put aside a date for us right now to have a long and friendly meal over a couple of bottles of Beaujolais. *The Monk* may be my farewell to cinema, because I'm thinking of withdrawing from all the fuss and bother of film-making. I should also say that making films for television doesn't really appeal. I think it might ruin *Montserrat*.

Most cordially,
Luis Buñuel

Spa Tls, ER

¹   Containing two plays, *Plaidoyer pour un rebelle* and *Mer libre* (Paris: Seuil, 1965).

To Gustavo Durán

Mexico City, 2 November 1965

Dear Gustavo,
   I'll admit it's a disgrace that I haven't replied to any of your laconic missives, always containing an article, from places like Katanga, London or Athens, etc. But, as the years go by, my idleness and the great difficulty I've always had with correspondence are getting worse.
   Like you, I thought Pablo de La Fuente's¹ book (which I got a year ago) was wonderful. But I'm now too semi-retired from cinema, and too semi-fed-up with it to make it into a film. I'm going back to Paris now – in January – to make what may be my last film, *The Monk*: the gothic novel by Matthew Lewis, as I'm sure you know.
   I've had news of you and yours from time to time, but not from you of course. Demetrio and Mercedes fill me in if I happen to be in New York. How is the very good and kind Bontë?² I imagine she's with you. If so, give her a kiss from me. As for your daughters,³ I only know the middle one, the one I met at your house in New York. She got married, didn't she? And I heard the eldest is now completely recovered.

Warmest regards, Gustavo, from your very old friend,
Buñuel

Spa Tls, GD

¹   Writer (1906–76), living in exile in Chile, author of *Los esfuerzos inútiles* (Santiago de Chile: Nuevo Extremo, [1949]), a signed copy of which LB had in his library (AB/1384).
²   Bontë Crompton (1914–2002), wife of Durán.
³   Cheli, Lucy and Jane Durán.

To Jean Claude Carrière

Jean Claude Carrière
2 La Bruyère Square, Paris IX
Mexico City, 6 November 1965

Dear Jean Claude,

I was very happy to have news of you, Auguste[1] and Iris,[2] who, according to you, still remembers Monsieur 'Bunuene'. I want to see all three of you again, and so, this very instant, I invite myself to supper at your house any night of the first two weeks in January. What a cheek!

I'm not sure about your notes on the feudal script.[3] I don't, for example, agree with you that much would be gained by knowing that the Prior[4] was abandoned as a boy, or that Talamour is the son of the 'duke' of Talamour.

I do, however, think we need to add a new scene at the beginning to show the extent of Ambrosio's proud (what a word!) piety, to make his fall from grace more striking, and I think we need to extend his seduction by Matilda. At the moment, he falls at the first sight of her breasts.

I also wanted to say that, unbeknownst to us, we have announced the coming of the Antichrist in this film. For the following reasons:

'According to Scriptures (Saint John, Saint Paul, Saint Ambrosio,[5] the Bible, etc., etc.), at the End of Days the Beast of the Apocalypse that Saint John identifies with the hermeneutic number, 666, in other words as the Antichrist, will come down to earth for three and a half years. That satanic creature will take on the role of Pope and will work miracles and prodigious acts. Pico della Mirandola[6] predicted his arrival in 1990, in other words, in just a few years' time.'

All of this is in the script.

1) Is it not true that the atomic age is widely considered to be the end of the human race? And 1990 is just around the corner!
2) Is it not true that Ambrosio is a creature inspired and guided by Satan?
3) Is it not true that he becomes the Pope?

I think, as it stands, the film is one hundred per cent Catholic. We should change the title to: *Ambrosio or the Antichrist, Pope 666*, etc. What do you think? Or just: *The Antichrist*. If you see Serge, who no longer writes to me, discuss this new idea with him. Of course, we'd have to keep the ending with the Pope and his blessings.

Juan Luis and Joyce should have arrived by now and will surely have called you. If you see them, do give them some advice about buying the apartment.

Send my regards to the Malles.[7] I can't wait to hear about the premier of *¡Viva María!*[8]

Yours,
LB

[PS] I've just received a letter from Silberman dated 20 October! I'm going to reply at once.

Fre Tlsps, JCC

---

[1]　Auguste Bouy, French actress and painter, first wife of Carrière.
[2]　Iris, daughter of Carrière and Bouy.
[3]　*The Monk.*
[4]　The Prior Ambrosio, one of the main characters in the script, together with Talamour and Matilda.

[5] Early Christians: Paul of Tarsus, John the Apostle, and Ambrose of Milan.
[6] Giovanni Pico (1463–94), humanist, born in Mirandola, condemned as a heretic.
[7] Louis Malle and first wife, French actress Anne-Marie Deschodt (1938–2014), who featured in *The Discreet Charm of the Bourgeoisie* and *The Phantom of Liberty*.
[8] Comic feature starring Bardot and Moreau as circus singers, dancers and central American revolutionaries.

To Oscar Lewis

Mexico City, 15 November 1965

Dear friend Oscar Lewis,

I'm so sorry I couldn't accept the invitation to work on your book, both for the pleasure it would have given me to work with Hugo Butler and for the great admiration I have always felt for *The Children of Sánchez*.

Here in Mexico, there are two writers who would be *most elegant* co-adaptors: one is Luis Alcoriza, whom I've already mentioned to you, and who has several offers of work as a director. But it would all depend on the conditions and fee for the adaptation. Another writer, very well-regarded, is Gabriel García Márquez, he has written several *remarkable* books and is an excellent adaptor. You can write to him *care of*[1] Luis Buñuel at my house, because I don't have his current address. To Alcoriza, at home: 205 Monte Albán, Colonia Narvarte.

I'm going back to Europe in December for six months to make the film I wrote this summer in Madrid.[2] If between now and June, work has still not begun on *The Children of Sánchez* I'd be delighted to co-adapt it with Hugo, although not with anyone else.

I'm looking forward with great interest to the launch of your Puerto Rican book.[3] Very affectionately

Luis Buñuel

Spa Tls, OL

[1] English in the original.
[2] *The Monk*.
[3] *La Vida: A Puerto Rican Family in the Culture of Poverty – San Juan and New York* (New York: Random House, 1966).

To Oscar Lewis

Mexico City, 13 December 1965

Esteemed friend Oscar Lewis,

I'm very grateful for the chance to see a preview of your two wonderful chapters on *The Ríos Family*.[1] I was really moved to read those excerpts of the lives of Felicita and little Gaby.[2] I thought it might be difficult after *The Children of Sánchez* to come up with distinct characters and different situations in such a similar setting. The language is so rich. I can't think of another book that highlights so acutely, and without any need for comment, the abject in society, its injustice, and hence, the infinite injustice of God. I can't wait for the book to come out, and I'm sure it will be a sensation.[3] To me, it already is.

I'm going to Europe at the end of the month to make my new film based on Lewis's gothic novel *The Monk*. It's an Anglo-French co-production. I really am sorry I couldn't work on the adaptation of *The Children of Sánchez* with my friend Hugo. But rest assured – if by next June it is still pending – I would take it on with great pleasure.

Warm regards from your friend,
Buñuel

Spa Tls, OL

¹ Provisional title of *La Vida*....
² Members of the Ríos family.
³ Lewis went on to receive the National Book Award in 1967.

To Francisco Rabal

Mexico City, 13 December 1965

My dear nephew,

Your letter arrived with the address you promised to send me,¹ so I can now write back.

I'm really sorry to hear about Damián,² although if it's any consolation, on my recent visit to the ear specialist I was told that there's the most revolting infection in my right sinus and I have both a polyp and an enormous cyst. As it doesn't hurt though, I've no intention of having an operation. Let's hope that, at worst, Damián turns out to have something like that.

I was in Acapulco for the Festival Review;³ practically forced by the film people over here. And I had a dreadful time, because I picked up some terrible typhoid-like infection. My temperature only went down a couple of days ago. Still, I won the FIPRESCI⁴ Bazin award for the third time. Down with prizes! I can't stand them anymore. They're worse than fleas and stick like lice – or worse.

As for Friar Lewis, things are looking very, very difficult I have to say. It's an Anglo-French co-production and at the moment the English have two competitors, by the grace of Sam Spiegel⁵ that is, as he has them both under contract: Omar Sharif⁶ and Peter O'Toole.⁷ Jeanne Moreau for the French. It's not that you wouldn't be good as the monk, although you're a bit over-qualified as an actor. It's just that you (a Spaniard), one of the two English (I've turned down Laurence Olivier⁸) and a French woman, as well as a young Italian girl, would be an abominable pot-pourri. We'll have time to discuss it in Paris, because when I get there they'll all still be waiting for their contracts. We should film in France. I hardly need to say how much you mean to me, as well as a friend, as someone I love working with and whom I admire greatly as an actor. Enough: we'll see.
Luis

[PS] Let's meet up in Paris on 6 January, Epiphany, although I'll be there a few days before.

Spa Tlsps, FR; *BVMC* f

1   Paris address of Muñoz Suay.
2   Suffering from bronchitis.
3   LB attended the 8th Reseña Mundial de los Festivales Cinematográficos the Acapulco film festival celebrated from 21 November to 1 December 1965.
4   The 'André Bazin Gold Medal' for *Simon of the Desert, Nazarín* and *The Exterminating Angel*.
5   US producer of polish descent (1901–85), producer of films including *Lawrence of Arabia* (1962).
6   Egyptian actor (1932–2015).
7   Anglo-Irish actor (1932–2013).
8   English actor (1907–89).

From François Truffaut

London, 4 January 1966

Dear Sir [Buñuel],

I asked Jeanne[1] for your address, so I could write to you (with some considerable delay) after we met at Cannes last year. I am touched by the kindness you've shown me each time we've met. I suppose I feel the link with André Bazin through you, because he was there the first time we met.[2] The other person we have in common is Jeanne, who is having a rather bad time of it at home in the South of France at the moment after a romantic set-back. A letter from you would really cheer her up right now.

Five days to go before filming starts on my new film, *Fahrenheit 451*,[3] and I've begun to feel horribly afraid. I can't imagine you trembling at the thought of filming, but that may just be my own lack of imagination. Either way, I hope to have that wisdom, your kind of wisdom, one day. I would so much like to see you this year.

Your true friend,
François Truffaut

Fre Als, AB/607

1   Moreau.
2   To whom Truffaut dedicated *The 400 Blows*.
3   Based on the novel of the same name by Ray Bradbury and filmed at Pinewood Studios, London.

From Carlos Saura

[Madrid, January 1966]

Dear Luis:

I have no news of you, nor have I sent any. How are you? I'd love to see you, truly, I often think of how much I have come to admire you – which now has nothing to do with the fact you make films like a God – and I really want us to have a meal again at some tavern in Madrid, Toledo, or wherever, to carry on our interrupted conversation.

I haven't written to Alcoriza either, and as I'm feeling sentimental today, could you please pass on to him from me all the kinds of things you say to a friend so briefly met, but with whom you share so much in common. I saw his film *The Shark Hunters* and liked it a lot, particularly the sincerity and honesty, rare qualities in the film world.

How is *The Monk* going? When do you start? Are you coming to Spain?

My film *La caza*[1] turned out quite well, I like it, it's a bit German, and not very funny, just enough to appeal to my friends and annoy the government. Also, it looks as if it's going to sell ... I should have liked to dedicate it to you, as you wanted, but I would almost prefer to do so with the next one, *Peppermint Frappé*,[2] I mentioned that one to you once, although you won't remember. The only link with you in this film is that a girl appears in a couple of hallucinations (a bit like your niece) playing the drum. As for the rest, I try from a distance, good manners not precluding courage, to live up to my label as 'most favoured disciple of Mr Buñuel' although in fact I'm beginning to tire of it.

I've been doing target practice with a. 22 carbine. What a useless weapon compared with your Colts from the Cuban war![3] I'll take you on whenever you get here: I'm a pretty bad shot, but I'll improve with my maestro.

Well, Luis, these lines are just to remind you that we love you and miss you over here. Come over soon, we need you. All that radioactive strontium in Almería[4] will finish off your Spanish friends, so I think you should say goodbye before that happens.

A big hug. I know I owe you a tape of the drums of Calanda. It's all ready for you. If you want me to send it, you only have to say. That's emotional blackmail to get you to write.

Carlos

[PS] I assume you'll be coming to Calanda for Easter! We'll be waiting for you. Adela[5] sends you a kiss. Women!

Spa Tlsps, AB/632.5

[1] *La caza* (1966), the first of Saura's many collaborations with the producer Elías Querejeta, premiered in Barcelona, 9 November 1966.
[2] Premiered in Madrid, 9 October 1967.
[3] Colt revolvers, part of LB's collection, a hobby inherited from his father who owned a gun shop in Havana until the outbreak of the Spanish-US war in Cuba in 1898.
[4] Reference to the nuclear bombs dropped in an accidental collision between two North American bombers near Palomares, Almeria, 17 January 1966.
[5] Adela Medrano, journalist and Saura's partner, who adds a handwritten note: 'Love and kisses, Adela'.

To Ricardo Muñoz Suay

Mexico City, 7 March 1966

Dear Ricardo,

I got your letter, which I was naturally expecting, as you appear to regard my birthday as more memorable than Jesus Christ's himself. Thank you, dear Ricardo.

There's no *script*[1] for *Simon of the Desert*, but to please you I'm going to make some copies of my own working script. If I can get it done, I'll send you one with a few photographs. I must warn you they're almost all terrible. It's the most meagre production.

I really liked what you said about Saura's film[2] and I'm surprised you need to see it again to offer an opinion on its content. What squeamish prudence! I'm sure it's good in every way.

I'm so happy there's finally a decent, even a good, film in Spain to wipe out *Los Tarantos*,[3] *Del rosa al amarillo*,[4] *Los pianos mecánicos*,[5] etc.

I might be going to Spain soon. After what happened with the falling-out over *The Monk*, I'm owed a fortune, although my agent does think I'll get something.[6] For the moment, I can't do anything with the adaptation until the legal audit is finished.

I sent your letter to Juan Luis in Paris. His address is: 11 Rue Roli, Paris XIV. I bought him the apartment in the end, so that he would inherit something in life and not have to wish for his father's death, as you and I did with ours.

Very cordially yours,
Luis

Spa Tls, RMS

[1] 'Script' in English in original; two copies now preserved (AB/1479 and AB/1480).
[2] *The Hunt.*
[3] *Los Tarantos* (1963), Romeo and Juliet inspired Flamenco musical directed by Francisco Rovira-Beleta, nominated for Best Foreign Film at the Academy Awards.
[4] *Del rosa al amarillo* (1963), comic feature directed by Manuel Summers.
[5] *Los pianos mecánicos* (1965), French-Spanish co-production directed by Juan Antonio Bardem, presented at the Cannes Film Festival in 1965.
[6] Filming of *The Monk* was cancelled, apparently due to a rift between co-producers.

To Francisco Rabal

Mexico City, 4 April 1966

Dear Paco,

Your letter made me very happy and I'm only writing back to say how anxious I am to see your impression of me *d'apres*[1] French television.[2] What strikes me as very bad faith, according to your version, is the bit about the braying,[3] which if I remember correctly, was such a sore point for Sancho.[4]

I was thinking of turning up to do a bit of drumming myself, but I decided against it, so that Juan Luis would have more freedom and be spared the irritation of having to listen to all my advice.[5] I'm thinking of going to Spain this spring anyway. I have in mind to suggest a very vague film project over there. My version of Quijote maybe, with you as Sancho and Fernando as the Ill-favoured Knight. Or Buzzati's wonderful[6] *Un caso clínico*,[7] which would be great for you. Of course, I'm probably just dreaming, who knows? But, what I do know for sure is that the only place I really want to make films now – relatively speaking, that is – is Spain.

I'm really glad Damián is better. Send him a big hug from me. And the same to María Asunción with kisses.

I'm so happy to hear from Juan Luis that you two often meet up at your house or at his. He told me about the ferocious stew made by a miserable – very appealing – Portuguese chap called Novais.[8] I think there were a few upset stomachs!

The incredible film of *The Monk* I was going to make, has now been irrevocably ditched.

All the more so now, after the wretched banning of *La Religieuse*,[9] which is like some First Communion film compared to *The Monk*. As soon as I arrive in France (if I go), I'll get someone to screen it for me. I have every faith in Rivette … and you.

YOU'RE TRAVELLING TOO MUCH! Enough globetrotting …

Hugs from your
UNCLE

Spa Cmfa, FR; *BVMC* f

[1] French in the original ('according on' or here 'on').
[2] Reference to Rabal imitating LB's Aragonese accent in the documentary *Luis Buñuel* (1964), directed by Robert Valey for the series 'Cinéastes de notre temps', produced by Janine Bazin for French television.
[3] In the documentary, filmed in Toledo, a donkey braying in the background interrupts an interview between Valey and LB; LB, amused, suggests viewers will think it been added in as a symbolic (and pejorative) reference to their discussion.
[4] In *Don Quijote*.
[5] During the filming of the documentary on LB's hometown, *Calanda* (1966), by Juan Luis Buñuel.
[6] Italian writer (1906–72)
[7] Play (1953), based on a story by Buzzati 'Sette piani' (1937).
[8] Joaquim Novais Teixeira (1899–1972), Portuguese journalist and film critic.
[9] *La Religieuse* (1966), dir. Jacques Rivette (1928–2016), featuring Rabal, and banned by the government of President Charles de Gaulle (1890–1970) on 31 March 1966.

To Oscar Lewis

Mexico City, 5 April 1966

My esteemed friend,

I've received your very interesting and instructive letter. Alatriste did indeed say he was going to call you to see whether you would, in principle, allow him to produce and me to direct one or other of your five families. I did ask him to wait until I was sure I could take on the work. I really don't like to bother people until I'm sure I'll be able to fulfil a commitment. He, however, is very business-like.

At the moment, Mr Alatriste is only interested in making films that are *sketches*,[1] and he wanted me to direct three, with three of your families, which isn't something I like the sound of. *Item:*[2] I have projects coming up very soon in Europe that I'm resisting, because I have more or less retired from film-making. But I'm almost certain to be travelling to Europe this Spring to come to some final decision over there.

I should say though, that I would be very interested to make a film – feature-length – of your wonderful 'Gutiérrez Family',[3] but that would depend on a set of circumstances it would take too long to explain in a letter. If an opportunity comes up though, I would get in touch with you directly.

If I were ten years younger, I would put myself forward at once to make a film based on your new book about Puerto Rico.[4] But I'm definitely ruling myself out, because I just don't have the energy to work over there for several months.

The Mexican government is getting more and more stubborn about defending its 'national honour'. I don't think there would be any objection to your 'Gutiérrez Family', though.

The Mexican bookshop windows are overflowing with copies of *The Sons of Sánchez* and *Five Families*. Thanks to the revolting Morlet and Lavin.[5]

I'm very keen to see your book about Puerto Rico. I'm sure it will have social as well as literary repercussions.

Very cordially yours,
Luis Buñuel

Spa Tls, OL

---

1   English in the original.
2   Latin in original ('also' or 'in the same manner').
3   One of the families portrayed by Lewis in *Antropología de la pobreza: Cinco familias* (1959).
4   *La Vida*.
5   Ironic reference to the fact that the objections of the censors, Morlet and Lavin, to Lewis's work helped with its publicity and distribution.

From Carlos Fuentes

Paris, 16 April 1966

Very dear Luis,

A few lines, to tell you how excited I was to go and see *The Golden Age* at the Palais de Chaillot[1] a few days ago. There wasn't enough room for everyone; there were three long queues four people deep: tall, young and all there to demonstrate that they could, and would, be intellectually free and ethically responsible spectators, and that they wouldn't be treated like morons or children. Yes, that screening of your great film, Luis, became a tacit, enthusiastic and ironic demonstration in favour of artistic freedom just as the Gaullist censors were banning *The Nun*. But also, importantly: those young people identified completely with *The Golden Age*, with the imagery and meaning, the wonderful currency of Buñuel's art; your films are now finding their new and true audience: these young people, for whom surrealism's great insight – that playfulness and ethics together can be explosive, revolutionary – has now become today's direct answer to the failure of life and art. They are setting themselves apart from the kind of art that is either just about form, pure, gratuitous style; or just about ideology, committed and ideological morality in the very worst sense of the words. I'm going to write something about this for *Siempre;!*[2] *The Golden Age* impressed me more than ever. I have been watching signs of the *révolte*[3] going on throughout this trip, in the United States with popular singers like Bob Dylan[4] and Joan Baez,[5] writers like Norman Mailer[6] and cartoonists like Feiffer,[7] in German theatre with Peter Weiss's

Marat/Sade,[8] in the whole *anti-establishment*[9] movement in England, in Bellocchio's[10] new Italian cinema, and suddenly, after watching *The Golden Age* again, I've become aware of a real sense of unity, power and the potential for non-conformism right now: a potential way of living that is complete and revolutionary, that won't degenerate into different approaches (playful or ethical), but that binds them in a kind of total humanity, a continual moving-forward of experience and conscience. I was moved, Luis, and I wanted to write to you as soon as possible to tell you, and to thank you, just as those young people who crowded into the Cinémathèque were thanking you.

I talked about you a lot with Octavio Paz when he was in Rome; and now, in Paris, with Vargas Llosa,[11] Cortázar, Rodríguez Monegal,[12] Gironella;[13] we're always discussing you and your work that we increasingly believe is the great point of reference for, and development of, writers and painters of Spanish descent. I'm going to Madrid with Gironella sometime in the middle of May; we want to write a book together[14] about the deaths of the kings: Felipe II[15] and Carlos the Cursed.[16] As for me, I've handed in my new novel, *Cambio de piel*, to be translated in New York,[17] and I'm now finishing *Zona sagrada*,[18] it's a novel about metamorphosis, about a film star and her son (who are really Circe and Telegonus, Ulysses's forgotten son[19]). I based it on the María-Quique[20] relationship, but very different of course, and much elaborated; it's not at all biographical.

Filming of *Aura* in Rome has finished.[21] I haven't seen the results yet, and I imagine they've had to make a lot of changes to stretch it to an hour and a half. The sets were wonderful though, as were Damiano Damiani's intentions. Bini,[22] the producer, is both intelligent and willing to take risks (he produced Pasolini's[23] films, *Il vangelo secondo Matteo*, etc.), he's also interested in doing something with Mexico.

I was sad to read in *Le Monde*[24] that production has stopped on *The Monk*. I can understand it, looking at the disgraceful treatment of *La Religieuse*. What can be done? If you want me to talk to Bini, let me know. Of course, there is the Vatican, but Bini managed to make and release *La mandragola*[25] without cuts; he might be interested in filming it in Mexico, etc.

I found a beautiful little flat on the Rue du Cherche-Midi, on the corner of the Rue de l'Abbé Grégoire, near the Boulevard Raspail. I find it very easy to work in this city, stimulated by the theatres, exhibitions, and a daily film at the Rue Champollion, where people are now queuing up to see *The Young One*.

Rita and Cecilia send kisses; I send friendship, admiration, and affectionate best wishes to Jeanne, and the hope we shall meet again soon at La Closerie[26] over a good Negroni.[27]

Your friend,
Carlos Fuentes

Spa Tls, AB/632.6

[1] Home of the Cinémathèque from 1963.
[2] Mexican weekly founded by José Pagés in 1953.
[3] French in the original.
[4] US singer (1941), received the Nobel Prize for Literature in 2016.
[5] US singer and activist (1941).
[6] US writer (1923–2007).
[7] Jules Feiffer (1929), satirical US artist.

8   German film-maker, writer and painter (1915–82), based in Sweden, wrote the play *Marat/Sade* in 1963.

9   'Anti-establishment' in English in the original, to refer to various UK countercultural, anti-war and feminist groups.

10 Marco Bellocchio (born 1939) Italian film-maker.

11 Mario Vargas Llosa (born 1936), Peruvian writer, received the Nobel Prize for Literature in 2010.

12 Emir Rodríguez Monegal (1921–85), Uruguayan literary critic.

13 Alberto Gironella (1929–99), Mexican painter.

14 *Terra Nostra* by Fuentes, illustrated with lithographs by Gironella, whose publication by Joaquín Mortiz in Mexico City was delayed until 1975.

15 Spanish monarch (1527–98), King of Spain from 1556 until his death in 1598.

16 Carlos II of Spain (1661–1700), nicknamed 'the Bewitched', king from 1665 until his death in 1700.

17 *Cambio de piel*, published by Joaquín Mortiz in Mexico City in 1966, and as *A Change of Skin* (translated by Sam Hileman) (New York: Farrar, Straus and Giroux, 1967).

18 *Zona sagrada* (Mexico City: Siglo XXI, 1967).

19 According to classical myth, Telegono is the child of Circe and Ulysses, King of Ithaca.

20 María Félix and her son Enrique.

21 Film adaptation called *La strega in amore* (The Witch, 1966), dir. Damiano Damiani (1922–2013).

22 Alfredo Bini (1926–2010), Italian producer.

23 Pier Paolo Pasolini (1922–75), Italian film-maker and writer; Bini produced a number of his films including *Accattone* (Vagabond, 1961), *Mamma Roma* (1963) and *Il Vangelo secondo Matteo* (The Gospel According to Matthew, 1964).

24 French newspaper founded by Hubert Beuve-Méry in Paris in 1944.

25 *La Mandragola* (1965), film produced by Bini and directed by Lattuada based on the sixteenth-century play of the same name written by Machiavelli.

26 La Closerie des Lilas, Parisian café frequented by artists in the boulevard du Montparnasse.

27 Cocktail: gin, vermouth and Campari.

To Jean Claude Carrière

Mexico City, 22 April 1966

My dear Jean Claude,

I was delighted to receive the letter you sent three months ago, as I am all your letters. I didn't reply because there was nothing to say after all. So ... forgive me.

I've had an offer from Robert Hakim,[1] via CIMURA, that – incredibly – I've all but accepted. Between you and me it's a ridiculous story but tempting. I made it a *sine qua non* condition that I write the adaptation in El Escorial with you, if you agree. It's *Belle de Jour* by Kessel.[2] A swarm of prostitutes with outrageous Super-ego/Id conflicts.[3] It would be interesting to see what we could make of it. Oh, and not a bit of humour, all the better to cleanse ourselves of *The Monk*.

Paulette will be in touch, because I've written to her. Read the book first. It's completely the opposite of modern cinema: a very, very well-planned story, so artificial it's really tempting.

A friendly hug from me to Auguste and my little niece, your daughter; and for you, my warmest regards,

Luis

PS I've done nothing, whatsoever, for eight months. Idleness is wonderful. It never gets boring.

Fre Tlsps, JCC

---

¹ French producer of Egyptian descent (1907–92), co-director of Paris Film Productions with his brother, Raymond (1909–80).

² Joseph Kessel (1898–1979), French author of *Belle de Jour* (Paris: Gallimard, 1928).

³ According to Freudian psychoanalysis.

8

International recognition (1966–70)

To Francisco Rabal

Paris, 30 August 1966

Dear nephew Paco,

Your agent[1] tells me you are accepting the role of Hyppolite[2] and I'm glad, because that means we'll be working together, although less glad, on the other hand, because I think you could and should do better things. So, let it be noted: you have been forewarned. Still no luck finding someone to play Marcel.[3] So few people have what I'm looking for.

I'd be grateful if you could bring me two 40-capsule bottles of Rastinon (Hoechst) when you come to Paris. It's for my hypoglycaemia and I can't get it here. In Madrid, you can get it in any pharmacy.

We start filming around 10 October.
A big hug from your
UNCLE

Spa Als, FR; *BVMC* f

[1] His sister, Lola Rabal.
[2] In *Belle de jour*.
[3] Played by French actor Pierre Clémenti (1942–99).

To Carlos Fuentes

Carlos Fuentes
71 Rue du Cherche Midi

Paris, 18 September [1966]

Dear Carlos,

Delighted with your first award for best script.[1] What a triumph! If you have a copy, send it to me at once. I hope (seriously) you're going to invite me out on some of those 50,000 *pesitos*.[2]

If you want to phone Oscar,[3] you could say the three of us might meet next Saturday at 7:30 to eat at La Closerie perhaps, or wherever you both prefer (an aperitif in La Closerie and dinner somewhere else maybe).

To watch the report on TV, any time on Saturday afternoon would be best for me. I look forward to hearing from you.

Congratulations and warm regards,
Buñuel

Spa Pmf, CF/93/17

---

[1] Fuentes and Gabriel García Márquez co-wrote the screenplay for *Tiempo de morir* (1966); a Mexican western directed by Auturo Ripstein (born 1943) awarded the Silver Goddess for best film at the annual ceremony held by the Asociación de Periodistas Cinematográficos de México (PECIME).
[2] Diminutive form of Mexican 'peso' to emphasize the joke.
[3] Lewis.

To Jay Leyda

Paris, 24 October 1966

My dear Jay,
I'm in Paris making a film.[1] I'll be here until January.

As for *Espagne 1937*, I was only the producer and supervisor. It was Dreyfus (who is now a director and whose real name is Jean Paul Le Chanois[2]) who did the editing and put the film together. I gave him the material shot in Spain by two Soviet cameramen, one of whom was Karmen.[3]

I can't remember how many reels it was altogether.[4] Perhaps I chose the background music,[5] which was paid for by the Republican government.[6] We had very little money. That's really all I can tell you about that film.

I'd love to have a 16mm copy.

When will we meet again? It's been so long since I've shaken your hand!

Yours,
Buñuel

[PS] Pierre Unik and I did the voice-over for the film (I think!).

Fre Als C, JL/83/03/07

---

[1] *Belle de jour*, filming started on 10 October 1966.
[2] French film-maker (1909–85), director of *Espagne 1936* (1937), which LB is confusing here with *Espagne 1937* (1938).
[3] Roman Karmen (1906–78), Russian documentary film-maker; Boris Makaseiev also contributed to *Espagne 1936*.

⁴ Thirty-five-minute documentary.
⁵ Including *Els Segadors* (official national anthem of Catalonia), the *Internationale* (French left-wing anthem and official anthem of the Second International, 1889–1916, in France) and *Himno de Riego* (national anthem of the Second Republic in Spain).
⁶ *Espagne 1936,* co-produced by Cineliberté and the Ministry of Propaganda during the Second Republic in Valencia.

To Georges Sadoul

Paris, 24 October 1966

My very dear Georges,

I was so glad to get your letter and will certainly, as agreed, pay you a visit.[1] I've kept the letter, because the itinerary is so detailed.

I'm going to leave it a few days, because I spend Sundays alone in my room to give my terrible hearing a rest from the daily racket.

Also, I'm too old now to get through a 10-hour working day without having to sit down, fed up with some leading lady's miniskirt or annoyed at having to choose between a 35 or a 40mm lens. *They both can go to hell.*[2] So I'll warn you when I'm coming. It'll be as soon as I finish the film though (so still another six weeks away).

Give Ruta a very affectionate hug from me, and my unconditional friendship for you as always.

Luis Buñuel

Fre Als, GS/64

[1] To Sadoul's country house.
[2] English in the original.

To Jean-Claude Carrière

Paris, 10 November 1966

Jean-Claude,

On Sunday afternoon, I have to see the General Secretary of the Mexican Union. So, if it's not inconvenient, I'd prefer it if you came to my house at 10am. Then we can eat at midday with the Barros' and Conchita[1] and Auguste at the Gare de Lyon, where *I'll be filming the scene with the Duke.*[2]

I have some ideas that will make you weep for joy.[3] Here's one below.
LB

Extract:[4]
Duke: Are you going to take the train?
Séverine (*smiling*): No, sir, but I often come to this restaurant in my thoughts.

Duke: Good Lord, you scamp![5] I see you prefer prams to trains.
(Wonderful! So refined and so slick).

Fre Ans, JCC

[1]   José Luis Barros Malvar (1923–2001), surgeon, and his wife.
[2]   Character from *Belle de jour* played by Georges Marchal.
[3]   LB is alluding to Dalí's telegram of July 1953.
[4]   Dialogue between the duke and Séverine in *Belle de Jour*.
[5]   LB uses 'pícara', from the Spanish word for the endearingly, amoral (female) protagonist of an
      episodic, *picaresque novel*.

Figure 64 Piccoli, Deneuve and Buñuel filming *Belle de jour*, Paris, November 1966.

To Francisco Rabal

Paris, 15 December 1966

Dear little nephew Paco,
    The day before yesterday, I got back from the south[1] with the film completely
finished.
    I'll start editing today. But the purpose of this letter is not to tell you what I'm doing,
but to tell you (brace yourself …) that they've asked me to dub your entire part with
a more suitable voice because no one can make out a word of your French. Of course,
the flamenco and the *Tenorio*[2] would still be your voice. They've even asked me to do
the dubbing. I'm warning you in case you want to cancel your trip to Paris and spend
Christmas and the New Year with your family instead.

I shall await your response, which I imagine will be furious, by return post. People can be as rude to you as they like, and you don't take the slightest offence, but … a word against your French.

Someone else with a 'beautiful voice' who could also do your dubbing would be Carrière. Hugs and kisses for my niece and grandchildren, and a big hug for you from your uncle

Luis

Spa Tls, FR; *BVMC* f

---

[1] Of France, with *Belle de jour*.
[2] Rabal's character sings a song from Cartagena (famous Roman port city in south-eastern Spain) and recites a paragraph from Zorillla's mid-nineteenth-century *Don Juan Tenorio*.

To Carlos Fuentes

Madrid, [1966]

ENJOYED READING ABOUT YOUR ADVENTURES WITH CLAUDIA CARDINALE,[1] I SENT THE MANUSCRIPT TO CORTÁZAR. I GOT THE BOOK ON MADNESS.[2] THANK YOU.

REGARDS,
BUÑUEL

Spa Tel, CF/93/17

---

[1] Italian actress (1938).
[2] Michel Foucault, *Folie et déraison: Histoire de la folie a l'âge classique* (Paris: Union Générale d'Éditions, 1964), dedicated to LB by Fuentes (AB/741).

To Georges Sadoul

Paris, 7 January 196[7]

My dear Georges,

I only finished work, finally, yesterday. But I'm going to Spain and won't be back until around 26 January. Then I'll have to finish post-production and after that, around 5 February, I'll be going back to Mexico. So, I'll write towards the end of this month to organize that lunch we planned with Ruta.

Hugs to you both.
Luis

Fre Pas, GS/83B5

Figure 65 Buñuel and Sadoul, Droue sur Drouette, 5 February 1967.

From Catherine Deneuve[1]

[Paris, January 1967]

Don Luis,

First of all, Happy New Year, but I also wanted to say farewell; I'm sorry I had to say good-bye so abruptly in the studio, although I find it easier to say it in a letter anyway. I am happy and proud to have worked with you. Although I may at times have disagreed with you or disappointed you, I hope you feel no bitterness towards me. I have complete confidence in you and none in myself. At times, it's even difficult to distinguish between the two, but I want you know how much I respect you. Perhaps one day, in Mexico.

Cordially yours,
Catherine

Fre Als, AB/635

---

[1]   French actress (1943) who played Séverine in *Belle de jour*.

To Oscar Lewis

Mexico City, 7 February 1967

My dear friend,

Ridiculous! I was waiting for my son Juan Luis to finish reading *La vida*, which he stole before I got back to Mexico, before replying to your letter. But as he is working every day and reads so slowly, I asked him to return it, which he did yesterday. I'm going to start reading today, but I didn't want to delay replying any longer, especially after that telephone call from Díez-Canedo.[1]

I got here two weeks ago and Barbachano, with his thousands of different projects including two films, is not here.[2] I wanted to remind you anyway, of our conversation in Paris: 'For the moment, I'm not thinking of making any more films.' And I say 'for the moment' because I may change my mind. I think it is time for me to retire. You know how much I admire the quality and focus of your work. But I still think, given the current state of cinema here, it would take an intervention on the part of some kind of a 'patron'. The setting, the rawness, the candour, etc., etc., rule out professional actors, or at least *stars*,[3] and that on its own is a serious obstacle to any film adaptation. A small minority apart, no one wants to get involved in the *desperation* of 'life' or, because of that, to finance that kind of film.

If my *pathetic* predilection for the life you show us does make me take on a film adaptation one day, it would have to be on a very modest budget, and we'd have to find that patron. At the moment, Barbachano only produces the most *commercial* and *hackneyed* features.

So, Lewis my friend: if the moment comes, I'll be the first to contact you. For now, though, I'm just waiting to see what my very limited future has in store.

I'll stop now, because I'm going to start reading *La vida*.

Yours, with true friendship and admiration,
L. Buñuel

Spa Tls, OL

[1] Joaquín Díez-Canedo (1917–99), exiled to Mexico in 1940, editor of the publishing house Joaquín Mortiz.
[2] Barbachano is producing an adaptation of Juan Rulfo's *Pedro Páramo*, directed by Velo.
[3] English in the original.

From Ado Kyrou

Paris, 24 March 1967

My dear Luis,

Thank you for your letter. I thought you'd already left, it was all so busy. I haven't been able to see your film yet,[1] and I'm very impatient because the photos and what I've heard about it have really whetted my appetite.

Losfeld[2] told me that if the books haven't arrived yet, it's because your instructions (apparently you told him it wasn't urgent) said not to bother sending them by airmail. But he assures me it shouldn't take long and that you'll also get the new edition of my *Amour-Erotisme et Cinéma*.[3]

And now, something I wanted to ask you: How is *The Monk* going? Have you finally decided not to direct it? And before I say anything else, I want to make it quite clear that I hope you'll change your mind and direct *The Monk*.

But in case you do decide not to do it and if, obviously, you haven't sold your *scénario* yet, I have a proposition for you.

As well as comics, Losfeld now wants to publish graphic novels (completely different from the ones currently on the market, obviously), and he'd also like to get into films, taking part in production and reserving the right to market stills taken from the film as an illustrated novel. He's also found a partner, who has made a very considerable offer. Not enough to make a film of course, but, with his advance payments from the Centre du cinéma[4] and other interested producers, he has solid financial backing.

Losfeld is interested in *The Monk* and we agreed to ask what you think before looking for another project that would only be less interesting. I forgot to say, although you will probably have already guessed, that I would be directing.

If you think this all seems feasible (and I hope it doesn't, because I would really prefer you to direct *The Monk*), write and let me know what your financial, and other terms would be.

That's all for now then.

Regards to your family. My wife and children say hullo.
I hope to hear from you soon.

Your friend,
Ado Kyrou

Fre Als, AB/1383.45

---

[1] Private viewing; *Belle de jour* premiered commercially on 24 May 1967.
[2] Éric Losfeld (1922–79), Belgian editor, owner of Éditions Arcanes and Le Terrain Vague, promoter of *Positif*.
[3] A. Kyrou, *Amour-Érotisme et Cinéma* (Paris: Le Terrain Vague, 1957), reissued by Losfeld in 1966 (AB/961).
[4] National film centre founded by the French government in 1946.

From José Fernández Aguayo

Madrid, 6 April 1967

Very esteemed *don* Luis,

I have no luck when it comes to seeing you and spending time with you when you're in Madrid; the last time I went to see you in February, the concierge at the hotel told me you'd left that morning for Paris.

Rabal, whom I was asking about you, gave me your address. He also told me you couldn't go ahead with the script you gave me to read, because the rights had been bought in Italy.

Don Luis, some friends and I have a production company, Alpe Films,[1] with which we've made eight films, including the last three films by Pedro Mario Herrero.[2]

We would very much like and are keen to make a film with you in Spain on any script of your choice that it might be possible to make over here. Censorship is not as bad here now as when we made *Viridiana*. So, if this sounds good to you, you could write and give me all the details you think we would need and we would be ready to start in June, if that suits.

Hoping you are well and that you will be with us here soon, at your service as always.

Warmest regards from your friend,
José Fernández Aguayo
139 Calle Jorge Juan

Spa Tls, AB/1404.34

[1] Madrid production company.
[2] Spanish director (1928–2005), whose films *La barrera* (The Barrier, 1966) and *Club de solteros* (Batchelors' Club, 1967) were produced by Alpe.

To Luigi Chiarini

Mexico City, 11 May 1967

Dear friend,

Paris Film Productions have sent word from the Hakimß brothers that you have asked to see my latest film, *Belle de Jour*. Thank you: I'm touched by your interest and would be delighted to know if the film meets with the requirements and 'politics' of your Festival.[1] Unusually for me, I'm quite pleased with *Belle de jour*, I had quite a lot of freedom to express myself. I'd be pleased if my friends were also 'quite satisfied'. As the director, I've asked the producers to show the film, should it be accepted, without cuts of any kind, that is, to screen the full version of *Belle de Jour*.

With all friendship,
Luis Buñuel

Fre Tls, BIE/229

[1] Chiarini invited LB to the Venice Festival on 7 March 1967 (AB/691.42).

From Jean-Claude Carrière

Paris, [25 May 1967]

Dear Luis,

Last night was the premier[1] so off we went, Auguste and I, our hearts pounding. I want to give you as accurate a report as possible. I'll say at once that it was a great success, although I imagine you are indifferent to that.

1) The cuts.[2] Unfortunately there were some. First, the bloodstain. We see Pallas[3] put the towel away and turn to go back to the bed. The bloodstain is 'perceptible'. This creates slightly odd continuity, very 'new wave', between Pallas on the stairs watching the Mongol leave[4] and Pallas in the bedroom putting the towel away.

Major cuts have been made to the castle scene though: the Grünewald[5] painting, the mass (a shame for me[6]) and, inexplicably, the short scene where the butler[7] puts Séverine in the coffin and tells her what to do ('close your eyes', etc.). That's all. It doesn't change the 'meaning' of the story, and in terms of continuity it actually works very well. They've cut the fireplace scene, the scene where the butler dresses Séverine, and the walking down the corridor sequence. The point where the Duke comes in with his camera and everything that follows.

Those are the only cuts. And to be honest, I feel quite relaxed about them. As I hadn't heard from the Hakims in months, I was afraid there would be far more.

2) Public reception. Fantastic. Watching it with a few hundred people, *it doesn't feel like the same film*. For example, there was a lot of laughter. The scene with the professor,[8] carried along by a laughing audience, is extraordinary. Then suddenly, they stop laughing and their stomachs drop when he falls down on all fours and says: 'I love you.' Another scene they laughed at lot at was the second bit of the sequence with Piccoli[9] and Séverine, when he finds her in the brothel. They didn't stop laughing from 'what I liked about you was your virtue...' up to the chocolates for Pierre.[10] And at the end, when we see Séverine from behind in the arm- chair, some people spoke out aloud, calling Husson an absolute bastard. Which just goes to show how well the audience responds to Séverine and takes her side.

On the way out, I heard someone saying: 'I couldn't take my eyes off the screen, I don't know why.'

There were other laughs, too, when Clémenti shudders with horror at Severine's birthmark. A shocked 'Oh!' when Clémenti arrives at Séverine's apartment at the end. Different reactions at every turn. You get the sense that, at a certain point, the viewers take off with no clear idea where they are any longer, watching it like a dream.

Auguste told me: 'The woman next to me was floating ten centimetres above her seat. She was flying without even noticing.'

Everyone was there last night. First, all the actors. On the first row of the balcony, between Sorel and Clémenti, *there was a seat left empty, completely by chance, throughout the entire film*. But I knew you were sitting there the whole time, incognito.

The Hakims were there too, radiant. The film really has had a staggering opening: the three rooms were full the first day for the first session. It's been sold in the US for $500,000 to that American distributor[11] who made a fortune with *Un Homme et une femme*;[12] for $80,000 in Japan, etc. Everyone says it's making a fortune.

It's been selected for Venice.[13] Don't worry about the producers. There's no point.

Jean Sorel's wife[14] watched the film surreptitiously at the first session in the afternoon at the Bretagne.[15] Then she came back to watch it again in the evening. Juliette Gréco[16] was 'fascinated'. Some women were weeping by the end. The quality of the copy was very good. The duel scene, relatively dark, is magnificent.

3) My reaction, of little importance. Once again, I came away feeling utterly battered. It has a powerful effect on me. This time I felt I saw a perfectly real, realist, nucleus: the brothel. And around that nucleus, 'progressively unreal' circles. There's no clear divide between fantasy and reality, just a series of degrees, shades. The characters of Sorel and Clémenti (who never takes part in the fantasy sequences) have a certain unreal quality. They're intermediaries of a sort. The sequence with the Duke is not definitely imaginary either. It could have happened. What's wonderful is that it's not clear.

It made me think a lot of Breton's famous comment in the *Second Manifesto*:[17] 'Everything leads us to believe that there is a point at which life and death, the real and the imaginary ... are no longer perceived as contradictions.' I think that, by circling around that point in the final sequence, you've managed to *reveal* it.

The reviews aren't out yet, but that doesn't matter at all. We already know it'll get good press and it won't teach you anything new. Better it was bad and instructive.

After the screening, people couldn't bring themselves to leave. They stayed over an hour discussing the film and most were dazed. Auguste and I came home together. We drank a bottle of Beaujolais, then more alcohol with cheese, and raised our brimming glasses to you. We were happy, very much in love, and a bit drunk.

It was very late when we eventually went to bed. I asked Auguste to put on black stockings, a pink corset and a lace bra, but she doesn't have any. So, I just said: 'lie down'. I would like us to conceive a child tonight.

I didn't miss you, because I know you don't like those kinds of events. But I reminded myself I really should catch a plane to Mexico every now and again, just to give you a hug.

(Incidentally, *Belle de jour* is being shown with a very good documentary about Hector Guimard,[18] the famous 'style nouille'[19] architect and interior designer. It goes very well with the film.)

Luis, everyone over here says you've never been on better form, a lot of them think *Belle de jour* is your best work (others hate it, which is also important).

Someone said that in ten years' time, you would make the film to end all films.

Luis, even when you can't hear anything, when you can't see anything, when you can't drive any more, and when the doctors put you on milk and mineral water, YOU HAVE TO MAKE FILMS!

Make them in Patagonian, in Javanese or in Mongolian; make them in Honolulu or in Stalingrad; make them with Lollobrigida,[20] Cardinal Spellman[21] and Johnson's daughter,[22] hire Steinbeck[23] to write the dialogues, sign up anyone and everyone, put a camera in front of a blank white wall and film that wall for two hours, do whatever, but do something! MAKE FILMS!

Make ten, twenty, films non-stop, it doesn't really matter whether you want to or not, even when you're trapped in a wheelchair, you have to make films. Even when you're dead, you'll have to carry on making them.

Although I'm beginning to think you'll never die. Unless you decide to of course.

And finally, in all this news we are accustomed to think of as good news (there's always a silver lining after all), I have to tell you, so we don't lose the benefit of feeling cursed, that La Cascade restaurant was completely destroyed in a fire a few days ago.

That's all,
Sending my best wishes,
Jean-Claude

[PS] *Le Figaro* has summed up the film as: 'THE FALL OF A HIGH-CLASS WOMAN'. Marvellous.

Fre Als, ABR/2047.2

---

[1] Of *Belle de jour* in Paris.
[2] Ordered by censors.
[3] Brothel servant in *Belle de jour*, played by French actress Marguerite Dupuy, known as Muni (1929–99).
[4] Character played by actor Iska Khan.
[5] *Crucifixion* by German painter Matthias Grünewald (1445–1528), in the Duke's castle in *Belle de jour*.
[6] Carrière's cameo as a priest, in the castle sequence, was cut by censors.
[7] Played by Bernard Musson.
[8] Masochistic brothel client, played by François Maistre.
[9] Michel Piccoli plays Henri Husson, louche friend of the couple, who introduces the notion of the brothel (and middle-class wives working in them) to Séverine.
[10] Séverine's husband, French actor Jean Sorel (born 1934).
[11] Allied Artists Pictures, production and distribution company founded by Walter Mirisch in 1946.
[12] Commercially successful French feature directed by Claude Lelouch in 1966.
[13] *Belle de jour* screened at the 28th Venice Festival held from 26 August to 8 September 1967.
[14] Italian actress Anna Maria Ferrero (born 1934).
[15] Film theatre in Montparnasse.
[16] French actress and singer (born 1927).
[17] *Second Surrealist Manifesto*.
[18] French architect (1867–1942).
[19] French reference to art nouveau or modernist style, usually used by detractors.
[20] Italian actress (born 1927).
[21] US bishop (1888–1967), lifelong archbishop of New York from 1939.
[22] Lyndon B. Johnson (1908–73), US president from 1963 to 1969.
[23] John Steinbeck (1902–68), US writer, winner of the Nobel Prize for Literature in 1962.

To Jean-Claude Carrière

Mexico City, 29 May 1967

My dear Jean-Claude,

Many thanks for your letter, your enthusiasm and unique friendship almost moved me. You also gave a wonderful account of the film premiere. Delightful love scene with Auguste in which frustration – no pink corset, no black stockings – is offset by the compulsive urge to procreate.

Between ourselves, strictly between you and me: I think those cuts were 'suggested' – God forgive me – to the censors by the Hakims. Why? Because they're exactly the same ones the Colisée asked them to make. We'll talk about this again someday. For me, the Duke's scene without those frames seems a bit frivolous.

You say nothing of the great Catherine. Was she at the screening?

I've been thinking a lot, a lot, particularly since reading your letter, about making *The Monk definitively* my final film. But the thought of leaving my wife, abandoning my home in this absurd country, the fear of a thousand illnesses looming over me, my deafness, etc., etc. all prevent me deciding. If I do decide though, we'd have to work on the script for at least a month or two, and I wouldn't do anything unless I was sure you wanted to work on it with me. 'I have some ideas about *The Monk* that'll make you weep for joy' (Dalí).

I live a completely idle life, wallowing in the most stultifying sloth. At times I do get bored.

Kiss Auguste and Iris for me. And for you, all my friendship.
Luis

Fre Tls, JCC

To Francisco Rabal

Mexico City, 29 May 1967

My dear nephew Paco,

I got your letter with the articles about your TNP[1] project. I think it's a wonderful idea and wish you all success. Let me know what happens. As for directing the *Tenorio*, I have to say I wouldn't be the least interested.[2] Anyone could do it as well or better than I could. Really. It would just be a repeat of the *Tenorio*s I saw as a child. Apart from which, I have absolutely no inclination to spend a month in a Madrid theatre. Although if you put it on in October, that wouldn't stop me coming to Madrid to see you at the premiere.[3] I could maybe make a few suggestions during final rehearsals. We'll see.

Belle de jour has premiered in Paris. It seems it was a success. They sold it the following day to the United States – to the distributor of *Un Homme et une femme* – for half a million dollars, and to Japan for 80,000. A pretty good deal, of which I won't, thank God, see a penny.

I'm inundated with requests to go and work in Paris, but for the moment I'm staying at home, wrapped in my cocoon of vulgar sloth. Doing nothing. Old age, nephew, old, old age.

Give your wife and children kisses from me, and for you a big hug from, your uncle

Spa Tls, FR; *BVMC* f

¹ Teatro nacional popular; Rabal was hoping to establish a Spanish equivalent to the French Théâtre National Populaire, founded in Paris by Firmin Gémier in 1920.
² LB directed *Don Juan Tenorio* (and played the part of Don Diego) at the Manolo Fábregas Theatre Centre in Mexico City, from 30 October to 7 November 1954.
³ Rabal starred in a TV adaptation of *Don Juan Tenorio* directed by Gustavo Pérez Puig in 1966.

From Jean-Claude Carrière

Paris, 7 June [1967]

Dear Luis,

We've just spent a week in the Midi (we took Iris after she had her tonsils out …) and so I didn't see your letter until we got back, and it made me *weep for joy*. I've said it before and I'll say it again: if you do make *The Monk* I'd be happy to help out as an assistant, intern, sound engineer, or whatever you like. I surrender myself to you, bound hand and foot. In fact, we saw several extraordinary castles in Avignon. Although, thinking about it, why not make the film in Mexico? It might be difficult to get the long shots of the castle, but there's sure to be a way around that.

You asked if I would agree to work on the script again. Truly, that's the most absurd question I've ever heard. The only problem is as follows: your decision (if you have made one) throws cold water on my plans, because I've just signed a contract to write another film¹ (if only I'd known…). In theory, I'll be busy until the end of July, although I think we'll have finished by the 15th. It's with Jacques Deray, you know him well.² It won't be filmed until next year. For the moment, it's just a case of coming up with a first draft, the story is already in place.

I think we should finish it in about five or six weeks.

There's nothing after that. I was supposed to go back to Brazil, but I cancelled. It was only to help out a bit at the start of shooting.³ Nothing essential.

In other words, after about 20 or 25 July, I'm all yours in Madrid or Mexico, as you wish.

I'm sorry for the delay. If I hadn't signed anything I'd be getting on a plane right now.

Now let's discuss *Belle de jour,* which is already history. Huge commercial success: 38,000 tickets sold the first week.

The Hakims are calling it a 'raging' success!

Opinions are about 70 per cent favourable and 30 per cent very hostile, there's no in-between.⁴ Firstly, some of the bourgeois press is up in arms. *Aurore*⁵ notes that you've always had 'perverse tendencies' and recommends families don't see the film. *Le Figaro* finds it fairly childish and says it 'makes you smile' (?).[6] *Le Monde* published a single moderate review, suggesting, correctly, that the scenes with Pierre and Séverine are 'very banal', although conceding that the film has 'two or three beautiful sequences'.[7] Critics who watched the film at private screenings, missing out on the reactions and laughter of the general public, seem not to have understood the humour, they've taken everything at face value, finding the Clémenti character 'caricature-esque' etc.

Those who saw the film with the general public, on the other hand, love it. *Paris Match*[8] gives it the highest rating (two stars) and hyperbolic praise. As does *L'Express*,[9] which quotes J. Kessel confessing he was left 'speechless' and saying it's a masterpiece. *L'Observateur*[10] was also very much in favour: 'One of the most freely expressed, most beautiful films Buñuel has made', they highlight the surrealist and revolutionary aspects and quote extensively from de Sade.

However, as *L'Observateur* has really taken against me, I've no idea why, they note that I squeezed a couple of 'indecent jokes' into the film just to make '25 million' (!). Not that I care at all.

The two best reviews appeared in *Candide*.[11] They say it's an enormously important film and Aubriant[12] talks at great length, very acceptably, about the humour.

One curious detail: he interprets the ending as the proof that it's all a dream within a dream. When Pierre gets up out of his chair, it proves that nothing has happened. But he does implicitly recognize there are other ways of reading it.

There were other reviews, but as I was in the Midi, I didn't see them all. Friends of mine who've seen the film, and who are worthy of seeing it, love it. Most of all the women. Some leave traumatized and come to me for explanations. The men sometimes seem offended by the distasteful role they play in the film. At the end of one public screening, a man stood up all red in the face and shouted out loud: That's right! They're all the same!'

Anyway, I get all kinds of phone calls from people with questions like: 'What's in the little black box?',[13] or 'What's false? What's real?'. It's very difficult to respond to that second one. According to their imaginative capacity, each spectator sees more or less reality, more or less fantasy. The Duke's scene could be true or false. The scene with the Mongol too. And some see the whole film as 'Buñuel dreaming about the fate of the heroine in a Kessel soap opera.' So, you see the subtle interpretative knots they get tied up in. There are three, even four, levels of interpretation. I wonder what will happen when the film is shown in the provinces. And what I wouldn't give to have a prostitute's view of it.

Definitely though, it works. I didn't say a word about your letter to Silberman or anyone else. I am still very excited. At your service, sir.

Warm regards,
Jean-Claude

[PS] We also had a letter from Joyce this morning. She doesn't seem over-the-moon in Durango, but I think she's fine.

Fre Als, ABR/2047.3

¹ *La Piscine* (1969), directed by Jacques Deray and co-adapted by Carrière based on a story by Jean Emmanuel Conil.
² Deray worked as assistant director with LB on *That is the Dawn*.
³ *Pour un amour lointain* (1968), dir. Edmond Séchan, script by Carrière.
⁴ Numerous press clippings on *Belle de jour* held at AB/1984 and AB/2047.
⁵ French newspaper printed from 1944 to 1985.
⁶ Claude Mauriac reviewed the film for *Le Figaro littéraire*, no. 1103 (5–11 June 1967).
⁷ Possibly review by Jean de Baroncelli published in *Le Monde* (28 May 1967).
⁸ French weekly founded in 1949.
⁹ French weekly founded in 1953; review of *Belle de jour* signed by Pierre Billard published 29 May 1967.
¹⁰ French weekly founded in 1964.
¹¹ French weekly founded in 1961.
¹² Michel Aubriant (1919–71), French film critic.
¹³ The buzzing box the Mongol client opens and shows Séverine at the brothel – viewers are not shown what is inside.

To Luigi Chiarini

Mexico City, 13 June 1967

Dear friend,

I'm grateful for your kind invitation to the next Festival and I will do whatever I can to get there, although I do find long journeys very daunting. Either way, I hope you will allow me to give you a definite answer towards the beginning of August. It all depends on my health, which is fine at the moment.

I'm glad the film has been formally accepted to the Festival. As everyone knows, it's the only festival that interests me, for its rigorous selection and seriousness. I see *Belle de jour* as a comedy and I would be delighted if someone, or a few people, saw it that way in Venice. As for me taking part in 'Cinéastes de notre temps',¹ if you think that would interest the Venice Festival, I can only say yes.

Best wishes,
Luis Buñuel

Fre Tls, BIE/229

¹ TV documentary series profiling film directors from 1964 to 1972.

To Jean-Claude Carrière

Mexico City, 16 June 1967

My dear Jean-Claude,

Your latest letter, like the first one, *filled me* with information about the film. I had no idea what happened in those two weeks after the premiere. I've had about fifteen reviews from the Hakims.¹ With no comment. As for the half a million dollars from the United States, I think it's *wishful thinking of yours*.²

Chiarini has invited me to Venice.[3] If you were going, I would go. And afterwards we could work on some stale script. In Madrid, of course. Meanwhile, Mr Carlos Fuentes has been appointed to the Venice jury. Yet again, of course, I conspired to bring this about and as my wishes are commands… *voilà*! We should now try to get Louis Malle on the Jury as well. And Auguste, if possible.

Regards to Jacques Deray. As soon as you are free, we'll see what we can do with *The Monk*.

Warmest regards,
Luis

Fre Tls, JCC

[1] In AB/1984 and AB/2047.
[2] In italics and English in the original.
[3] Venice Film Festival.

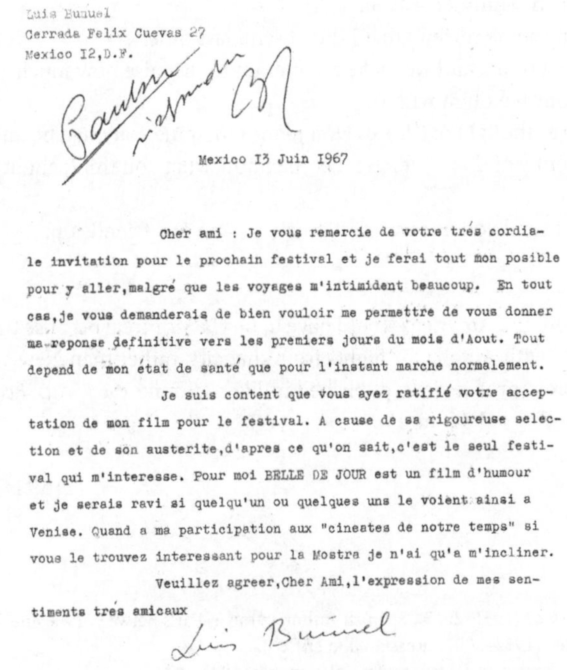

Luis Buñuel
Cerrada Felix Cuevas 27
Mexico 12,D.F.

Mexico 13 Juin 1967

Cher ami : Je vous remercie de votre très cordiale invitation pour le prochain festival et je ferai tout mon posible pour y aller,malgré que les voyages m'intimident beaucoup. En tout cas,je vous demanderais de bien vouloir me permettre de vous donner ma reponse definitive vers les premiers jours du mois d'Aout. Tout depend de mon état de santé que pour l'instant marche normalement.

Je suis content que vous ayez ratifié votre acceptation de mon film pour le festival. A cause de sa rigoureuse selection et de son austerite,d'apres ce qu'on sait,c'est le seul festival qui m'interesse. Pour moi BELLE DE JOUR est un film d'humour et je serais ravi si quelqu'un ou quelques uns le voient ainsi a Venise. Quand a ma participation aux "cineastes de notre temps" si vous le trouvez interessant pour la Mostra je n'ai qu'a m'incliner.

Veuillez agreer,Cher Ami,l'expression de mes sentiments très amicaux

Luis Buñuel

Figure 66 Letter from Buñuel to Chiarini, 13 June 1967.

From Robert Hakim

Paris, 21 June 1967

My dear Luis,

We were very pleased to receive your letter of 16 June.

I wanted to let you know that I really think Mr Chiarini will do everything he can to ensure you get the Golden Lion, and he is prepared to pay for your return trip from Montreal to Venice, and I, of course, would be delighted to cover the cost of your return trip from Mexico to Montreal. All your expenses in Venice would be paid.

I believe this offer bodes well, and I don't have to tell you how happy we would be to see you again over here, so I'm really hoping you will make the trip.

The Members of the Jury this year, as well as your friend Carlos Fuentes (whom I remember well), will be: Alberto Moravia, as President; Juan Goytisolo,[1] from Spain; Yurenev,[2] from the Soviet Union; Erwin Leiser,[3] from Germany; Susan Sontag,[4] from the United States; and Violette Morin,[5] from France.

Obviously, as you say, if Raymond and Jean-Claude were there as well it would be a mere formality!

The film starts its fifth week of exclusive screenings today and the box office is good, particularly for the summer season.

I'm enclosing some reviews that I didn't send last time.[6]

I think of you often, and we make no attempt to disguise how much we would love you to make your next film with us.

Have you ever thought of a life of Don Juan? I imagine you must be interested in the life and philosophy of that character. Let me know what you think about it.

Raymond and I send you our warmest greetings and our friendship.
Robert

PS Your trip from the Americas would have to be via Montreal because the Festival has an arrangement with Alitalia for flights from that city, rather than New York.

I am enclosing three reviews published in *Elle*,[7] 15 June 1967, *Aux Écoutes*, 31 May 1967, and *Paris-Presse*,[8] 8 June 1967.

Fre Tls L, AB/2047.8

---

[1] Juan Goytisolo Gay (1931–2017), Spanish author, living in Paris between 1956 and 1968.
[2] Rostilav Yurenev (1912–2002), Russian film critic.
[3] German film historian and documentary film-maker (1923–96).
[4] US writer (1933–2004).
[5] Violette Chapellaubeau (born 1917), French journalist, married to Edgar Morin.
[6] In AB/1984 and AB/2047.
[7] French women's weekly founded in 1945.
[8] Paris daily, 1944 to 1970.

To Luigi Chiarini

Mexico City, 27 June 1967

Dear friend,

Just a few lines to thank you, sincerely, for your offer regarding my trip to Venice. I must, however, sadly decline for the following reasons: the journey via Montreal is too long, over 24 hours travel (with a 10-hour stopover in Montreal). I would also like to spend a few days in Madrid before attending the Festival. So, if I were to make the trip, depending on my health, which is excellent at the moment, I would cover my own travel costs. That way, my trip would be wholly non-partisan and justifiable, because I would love to see you.

Hoping to see you again very soon, cordial greetings,
Luis Buñuel

Fre Cmf; BIE/229

To Ruth Ford Scott

Mexico City, 10 July 1967

My dear friend Ruth,

I have the letter you wrote to Juan on 14 June and am hurrying to reply.

First of all, a thousand pardons for not sharing with you my distress and sincere pain at the death of your husband, my great friend Zachary.[1] Unfortunately, that's how I am, incapable of expressing my emotions, out of excessive shyness perhaps, just when all others rush in to convey their condolences and sorrow. Please know that I cherish an indelible memory of the wonderful man and extraordinary friend that Zachary was to me.

As for *Under the Volcano*, I don't think I will ever make it, because I am all but retired from my trade. And I say 'all but' because I still have a project in Europe[2] that I am trying to turn down, as I have on two or three other occasions. After all, I'm 67 now and don't have my old enthusiasm for making films. Also, I've always thought, as I've mentioned to Lewenstein, that *for me* that would be the most difficult novel to adapt for cinema. As difficult, or more so than adapting the novels of Kafka.[3] An example: *The Trial* that bad film by Welles.[4]

Dear Ruth, if I am ever in New York I'll let you know. I would be absolutely delighted to see you again.

My warm regards and friendship,
Luis Buñuel

PS I don't think that my last film, *Belle de jour*, is quite as extraordinary as Monsieur Giroux[5] claims.

Fre Tlsps, ZS/LMC2740

[1] Zachary Scott died of a brain tumour, aged 51, on 3 October 1965.
[2] A second attempt to film *The Monk*.
[3] Franz Kafka (1883–1924), writer born in Prague, author of *Der Prozess* (The Trial, 1925).
[4] Orson Welles (1915–85), US film-maker and actor, directed *The Trial* in 1962.
[5] Possibly the US writer Robert Giroux (1914–2008).

To Carlos Fuentes

Mexico City, 11 July 1967

My dear Carlos,

I've not yet completely decided whether to embark on the ARDUOUS adventure the journey to Venice would be for me, so GOD HELP ME. Ceremonies horrify me, the dinners with strangers, the journalists and above all, the drag of sitting through all those film screenings. But I am, on the other hand, very keen to see you again, with the chubby one[1] and your Rita, from whom, after a swift greeting, I would drag you away to go to Harry's Bar.[2] Although I don't believe the Martini you mention can be any better than the ones they serve in Plaza bar in New York.[3] Also, if I do go, it would be out of respect for Chiarini who has treated me with truly *touchante*[4] cordiality. He offered to cover my travel to the Festival, which I turned down, thanking him a lot, because the journey had to be via Montreal, where I would have had to wait for ten hours. Can you imagine? What on earth would I do with all that time in Montreal? If I go, I'll pay my own way.

As for *Belle de jour*, I'm annoyed because the censors have made some drastic cuts. To start with, they've cut all the religious part out of the sequence with the necrophiliac Duke, turning it into something vacuous and insipid. Eroticism without religion, particularly Christianity, is like a feast with no salt.

Send my best regards to Goytisolo. There'll be a fat cheque for you, and one for him if I get the Gold Lion. And for Rita, a magnificent solitaire. So ... onwards. Absolute discretion.

Until very soon perhaps. A big hug,
Luis

Spa Tls, CF/93/17

[1] Cecilia Fuentes Macedo.
[2] Venice bar founded by Giuseppe Cipriani in 1931, famous for dry Martinis.
[3] Hotel Plaza built in 1907 at the corner of Fifth Avene and Central Park South.
[4] Galicism (from '*touchant*'), in place of the Spanish 'conmovedora' (moving).

To Serge Silberman

Mexico City, 20 July 1967

My dear Serge,

Really, in all the time I've known you, you never been so worryingly silent. It's months since I've heard from you. How are you? And the family? And business?[1] I do hope you have five minutes to reply to these pressing questions. I would also like to know if you'll be in Paris this August. I'll certainly pass through on my way to Venice, where I've been invited all-expenses-paid. Although I'm still not sure if I'll go.

I do nothing here. I read. I get bored. I'm not working. I'm floating. My health, as always. Preserved with gin and tobacco.

They say my film *Belle de jour* is a 'commercial success'. A bad sign. As for you, I suspect you're not overly enthusiastic. Why do I suspect that? I don't know, but I don't blame you.

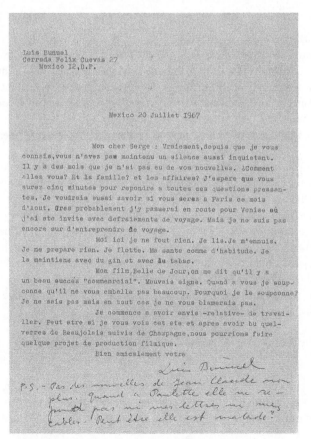

Figure 67 Letter from Buñuel to Silberman, 20 July 1967.

I'm beginning to take a – relative – interest in work. Maybe, if I see you this summer, and we drink a few glasses of Beaujolais followed by champagne, we might come up with some cinematic plan.[2]

With friendship,
Luis Buñuel

PS I've not heard from Jean-Claude either. And as for Paulette, she doesn't reply to my letters or telegrams. Maybe she's ill?

Fre Tlsps, RS

---

1   Silberman founded Greenwich Film Productions in 1966.
2   LB directed *The Milky Way*, produced by Silberman, in 1968.

To Ado Kyrou

Mexico City, 20 July 1967

My dear Ado,
    Many thanks for your *Amour-Erotisme et Cinéma*, which arrived a few days ago. Even though I'd read the first edition, this one overwhelmed me and I 'devoured' it like a completely new book. I really like the tone, so passionate and violent, and at times so tender and sincere. This book and *Manuel du petit spectateur*[1] are my favourites. And that's not to mention *Cartes postales* …[2] Thanks again.
    The Monk is still waiting. But I'll have to decide soon. Whatever happens, I'll keep you informed.[3]
    I assume you've seen *Belle de jour*. And I'm sure you will already know it was mutilated by the censors. For example, the scene with the necrophiliac Duke has been stripped of all religious content: the Requiem mass, the Grünewald Christ, the butler's advice to Séverine when she is in the coffin, etc. They've made it all very superficial. They've made other cuts too. I would really have preferred them to ban the film altogether. As you say, they should suppress all the 'positive' elements in Christian films the way they suppress all the 'negative' elements in atheist films. Perhaps we're only allowed to make films in the style of that idiot Hitchcock.
    Give your wife a hug from me and don't forget the little Kyrous. I hope to come to Europe soon and see you all.

Very cordially yours,
Buñuel

PS What are you doing at the moment? Greece must be over for you.[4] Shit, shit.
    I've had two Martinis and I'm not sure what I've said about you in this letter; it's a shame, forgive me.

Fre Tlsps C, JCC

[1] A. Kyrou, *Manuel du parfait petit spectateur* n.p. [Paris, 1958] (AB/854).

[2] A. Kyrou, *L'Âge d'or de la carte postale* (Paris: Balland/Le Terrain Vague, 1966).

[3] Kyrou directed an adaptation of *The Monk* in 1972, based on LB and Carrière's script.

[4] Allusion to the extreme right coup in April 1967 that brought in the Regime of the Colonels.

To Francisco Rabal

Mexico City, 29 July 1967

My dear little nephew Paco,

As I do, at times, get solemnly bored in my idleness, I write to my friends, for which I offer you all my congratulations.

I got your letter, articles and 'interviuados',[1] and I can see you still profess the same admiration and loyalty for your uncle, for which I am ever in your debt. Thank you, Paco. I've been re-reading all the theatrical *Don Juans,* from the first: Tirso[2] (horrible), Molière[3] (acceptable in parts), Goldoni[4] (mediocre), Dumas[5] (well, that one is the inspiration for Zorrilla, premiered six years before Don José's version), Rostand[6] (foul), Pushkin[7] (insipid).

Don't you think, from a cultural perspective, it might be good for the TNP to stage Dumas's version before Zorilla's *Tenorio,* to show how one writer can be inspired by and outshine another, as Zorilla did with Dumas? Just throwing out a hook to see if you bite. The Argentine *Editorial Futuro* has published all those *Don Juans* in a single edition called *Don Juan en el drama,*[8] with a prologue by Jacinto Grau[9] (touch wood though because they say he's a jinx).

I've been invited to Venice, but I don't know if I'll go. As they are paying for the travel, I may decide to spend three months in Spain, so I'd be able to come and see your *Tenorio.* (Beware catatonic-epileptic spasms when you recite the bit that goes 'I called on God but was not heard …!')

La Putain du jour,[10] you took part in, is becoming fabulously successful financially. Bad news: I got it wrong. I think it's been sold in the United States for a million dollars. In Paris, they covered costs with the premiere. I'm sure they're exaggerating, IT'S NOT THAT GOOD.

If you see Fernando, give him a big hug from me, even though he stood me up so badly the day before I left Madrid. If I do go to Madrid, I shall demand a detailed explanation. I never forget a snub.

Kisses to my niece, your wife, and to my little grand-nephews, and for you, whatever you want from the uncle of yours that I am,
Luis

Spa Tls, FR; *BVMC* f

[1] Spanglish, combining English 'interviewees' with Spanish 'entrevistados'.

[2] Tirso de Molina, pseudonym of Fray Gabriel Téllez (1579–1648), poet and dramatist, and assumed author of *El burlador de Sevilla* (1616), the first version of the myth of Don Juan.

[3] The French dramatist, Jean-Baptiste Poquelin (Molière) (1622–73), published his version of *Don Juan* in 1665.

[4] Carlo Goldoni (1707–93), Venetian dramatist, whose *Don Giovanni Tenorio* was published in 1735.

[5] Alexandre Dumas (1802–70), French novelist and dramatist, whose *Don Juan de Marana* premiered in 1836, eight years before the Spanish dramatist Zorrilla published his *Don Juan Tenorio*.

[6] Edmond Rostand (1868–1918), French dramatist, whose *La Dernière nuit de Don Juan* was published in 1921.

[7] Alexander Pushkin (1799–1837), Russian writer, whose *Kamenny gost* (1830) recreates the life of Don Juan.

[8] *Don Juan en el drama* (Buenos Aires: Editorial Futuro, 1944).

[9] Jacinto Grau (1877–1958), dramatist, exiled to Argentina, where he wrote the preface for *Don Juan en el drama* and *Don Juan en el tiempo y en el espacio* (Buenos Aires: Raigal, 1953).

[10] French in the original (whore of the day), joking reference to *Belle de jour*.

To the magazine *Nuestro Cine*[1]

Mexico City, 8 August 1967

Mr Carlos Rodríguez Sanz,[2] Mr Manuel Pérez Estremera,[3] Mr Vicente Molina Foix,[4] and Mr Augusto Martínez Torres.[5]

Dear friends,

I would be very grateful if you would publish this letter in the next edition of *Nuestro Cine*.[6] My aim is to clarify, conclude and even to correct altogether some of the declarations in the interview you conducted with me that was published recently in *Nuestro Cine*[7].

If I remember correctly, I objected to our conversation being recorded and to notes being taken, as it was my wish and intention that our dialogue remain there, between us, and if I agreed to the meeting it was only out of good will towards you all, as I have an aversion to expressing myself in public.

I assume, meeting up after the interview, that you drafted the text you have published from memory and, I am sure, in good faith. In this case though, the mountain gave birth not to a small mouse, but to an enormous Lycosidae.[8]

It is not the same thing to comment, blurt out ideas, venture judgements, rant in a relatively tongue-in-cheek way around a café table or with a group of friends, as it is to publish that chat verbatim, and here, I refer exclusively to the language, to the style, which in this case seems pedestrian, parochial, vernacular and low-grade. That verbiage, if it really was perpetrated as published, is frankly displeasing.

All the more so when that *flat-footed style* comes incrusted with opinions and ideas that represent the exact opposite of what one actually thinks, in such cases, the outrage is almost unbearable. In an intimate and friendly conversation, a gesture can soften or correct what is said, a wink of an eye or a smile can completely alter the meaning of a sentence. The absence of these has no doubt contributed to this distortion of my views. I shall now correct or clarify some of the notions set out in that interview with which I do not agree:

1) You have me say: 'I'm an Arts and Philosophy graduate, specializing in History, from the University of Madrid, but I wasn't able to study much because of my family.' I really don't understand how I could have said any such thing, because when I was studying my father was already dead, which made me practically the head of the family, and I didn't really pull my weight. If I didn't study enough it was because I loved wasting time – or saving it – with my coterie in those days: Pepín Bello, Federico García Lorca, Alberti, Dalí, Vicens, etc.

2) A comment from you: 'Buñuel insists on the lack of wine being a problem. He has a few bottles, but they are already packed for the trip to Paris.' It is true that I regretted not being able to toast you because my bottles were empty, but from that to taking bottles to *the City of Lights* …[9] If I were going to the Sahara, perhaps …

3) About Kessel's novel *Belle de jour* I spoke very harshly: 'I don't like it at all, but I agreed to make the film …'. Here, there must be some omission on my part. Something fundamental in that novel interested me a great deal, had that not been the case, I would not have adapted it for the cinema. It was the passionate conflict between the protagonist's conscience, her sense of duty, and her masochistic compulsions, as I think is made clear in the film.

4) A comment of yours referring to *Belle de jour*: '… the censors cut a line or two …'. Had it only been a line! They cut essential images and mutilated an entire scene, the one with the necrophiliac Duke, removing the religious element altogether; an unfortunate decision that neutralizes, or near-neutralizes the whole sequence. Eroticism with no Christianity is half-baked eroticism.

5) I declare in another passage – did I really? – that my two producers for *The Monk* 'had come to blows', in other words, had a fist fight. It did not come to that, because what I actually said was that they had gone their separate ways, were no longer working together.

6) You asked me what recent Mexican cinema most interested me, and I replied (really?): 'Paco Michel has done something very cute, he's adapted a story by Carlos Fuentes.' Manuel (not Paco) Michel has made an interesting experimental film[10] based on a story he wrote himself. There is a difference!

7) 'The Mexican Government is very open to all countries.' What I may have meant to say was that 'Mexico's foreign policy is exemplary and genuinely democratic.' And I concluded: 'In all ways Mexico is the most free of all the South American countries.' And there was I, thinking that, geographically speaking, that country was part of the northern hemisphere of the American continent …

8) 'Well, yes, I am very fond of animals … It's just a shame you can't make money out of it.' If I said that, I should be committed to an asylum, because such dyslogia[11] is a symptom of serious mental disorder.

9) About Alcoriza's films: *Tarahumara* seems better to me than *Tiburones*, and 'Divertimento',[12] the latest one, more finished and more accomplished than the earlier ones, because the end-result matches the original intention.

10) 'Carlos Fuentes is making his way in the footsteps of Cortázar.' If that were the case, he would do better to forget literature and devote himself to some other

activity. But there's no smoke without fire ... What I may have said is that in one
of his most recent books Carlos was following a tendency I call *cosmopolitan*, that
may have come from Cortázar's novel *Rayuela*,[13] which is not my favourite of all
that stupendous writer's works. I'm not the person to illuminate Carlos Fuentes's
path, it is already clearly mapped out as that of one of the great American writers.

11) And, lastly, could I ask you to compare what I say about my producer Gustavo
Alatriste with what I am purported to say in that infamous interview. Gustavo
Alatriste is a friend who makes a lot of money and who is, amongst many other things,
passionate about film. He is the best producer I have had, because he has given me the
pleasure of absolute freedom, both in the choice of story and in the film-making. For
his company (that he alone runs) I have made three films based on original stories:
Viridiana, The Exterminating Angel and *Simon of the Desert*. I did, indeed, come across
serious difficulties with the latter, mostly due to the technical shortcomings of the
studios. Gustavo Alatriste has never reneged on his financial commitments to me, nor
to any of the staff or crew who worked on those three productions. If, one day when
we were on location, the caterer threatened to refuse us food (a threat he did not carry
out in the end), it was because he wanted to be paid up-front for the food for our staff.
Neither the producer, nor the production manager were there when this happened.
The film is five short reels. I told Alatriste that I would make it ten if he wanted, as long
as he did not show it, as he did, at the 1965 Venice Film Festival. I would have liked
to conclude the film with the death of the ancient Simon at the top of a twenty-metre
column. But the film had already lost its virginity in Venice.

And I close with apologies for how long and perhaps ungainly this letter has become.

Cordially,
Buñuel

Spa, Od; NUE 8–9

[1] Madrid film journal founded by José Ángel Ezcurra, printed from 1961 to 1971; published Saura's article 'Buñuel', *Nuestro cine*, no. 16 (January 1963), pp. 15–17.
[2] Film-maker and writer (1942–85).
[3] Critic and film programmer (born 1944).
[4] Writer and film critic (born 1946).
[5] Critic and film producer (born 1942).
[6] 'Carta de Luis Buñuel', *Nuestro cine*, no. 65 (September 1967), pp. 8–9.
[7] Interview at the Torre de Madrid in January 1967, published as 'Entrevista con Buñuel', *Nuestro cine*, no. 63 (July 1967), pp. 11–18.
[8] Reference to Aesop's fable 'The Mountain in Labour' where a mountain labours to produce only a tiny mouse: a cautionary tale about empty threats or promising much and delivering little; the spider (former entomologist) LB swaps for the mouse, commonly known as a 'wolfspider'.
[9] Paris, known as *la Ville lumière*.
[10] The section 'Tarde de agosto' directed by Mexican filmmaker Manuel Michel (1928–1983) in *Viento distante* (1965) dir. Salomón Laitner, Manuel Michel, Sergio Vejar.
[11] Difficulty expressing oneself due to impairment of powers of reasoning.
[12] Alcoriza's section of the feature *Juego peligroso*, also containing 'HO' by Mexican film-maker Arturo Ripstein (1943–).
[13] J. Cortázar, *Rayuela* (Buenos Aires: Editorial Sudamericana, 1963).

To Carlos Fuentes

Mexico City, 9 August 1967

My dear Carlos,

I still haven't decided whether to go to the Festival.[1] My producers will pay for the travel, and friends and collaborators keep writing to ask me to join them. If I do go in the end, it will only be for three or four days and then, to get the most out of the trip, to spend three or four months in Spain. Unfortunately, as you're a Jury member, I wouldn't be able to spend time with you for fear of being labelled a bootlicker, or of being accused of trying to *blackmail* you. My Spanish friends are travelling there *en masse*. I think Carlos Saura is showing his latest film that I'm sure will be very good.[2]

Everything is still the same over here, or at least I think it is, I lead a quasi-monastic life. The latest news was the assassination of King Lopitos of Acapulco.[3] An extraordinary subject for a Mexican film. Or an indigenous novel. 50,000 tenant farmers, his subjects, have sworn to avenge his death one way or another. Blood may flow all the way down to Caleta.[4] La Laja[5] is at boiling point. The attack was definitely politically motivated, because the aforesaid King was the governor of the official governors.

I've met a young writer, Pedro Miret,[6] whose parents were Catalan refugees, and I've read a book of his called *Esta noche... vienen rojos and azules*[7] which I found extraordinary, and poetic. In terms of language, the style is nothing special, but I was captivated by the content.[8] You could place him up there with Kafka, Buzzati, the Chirico[9] of *Hebdomeros*, irrational surrealism ... If I do go to Venice, I'll bring you a copy to see if you have the completely opposite reaction.

Some young Spaniards have published a conversation they had with me in Madrid (a reconstructed conversation, because they didn't even take notes)[10] in which, amongst a thousand other banal points expressed in pedestrian language, they have me say: 'Carlos Fuentes is making his way in the footsteps of Cortázar.' Can you imagine? I wouldn't have bothered to correct it, but as there were a dozen more twisted and absurd statements in it, I've sent a long letter of correction for them to publish in the next edition.

I'm very much looking forward to reading your new book as, from your letter, it sounds similar to, or written in the same spirit as *Aura*. (Not, fortunately, Cortázar.) When is it out? I imagine it's already well underway.

Your contumacy[11] in remaining such a long time in that insignificant little city,[12] has made you a traitor to the homeland of Juárez. Whatever you concoct over there you could just as easily cogitate (what an ugly little word) in Catemaco,[13] or by the river Papaloapan,[14] so much more powerful, pristine and suggestive than those miserable, malodorous little canals of the Venetian republic. But I suppose it's up to you ...

Hugs and kisses for Rita and the ex-chubby child. I hope I will see her and see you all soon.[15] Another big hug for you.
Luis

Spa Tls, CF/93/17

[1] Venice.
[2] *Peppermint frappé*, eventually presented at the Berlinale (Berlin International Film Festival) in 1968, rather than at Venice.
[3] Alfredo López Cisneros (1923–66), Mexican popular leader, assassinated on 4 August 1967.
[4] Acapulco beach.
[5] Area of Acapulco with local groups led by King Lopitos.
[6] Pedro Fernández Miret (1932–88), writer and scriptwriter, exiled to Mexico in 1939.
[7] By P. Fernández Miret (Buenos Aires: Hermes 1964).
[8] LB wrote some preliminary words to the second edition (Buenos Aires: Sudamericana, 1972).
[9] Giorgio de Chirico (1888–1978), Italian painter and writer (1888–1978), *Hebdomeros* was published in Paris by Éditions du Carrefour in 1929.
[10] Interview published in *Nuevo cine.*
[11] Stubborn refusal to obey authority/court order.
[12] Venice.
[13] Municipal of Veracruz, México.
[14] River in Veracruz.
[15] LB attended the screening of *Belle de jour* at the Venice Festival with actors Clémenti, Deneuve and Sorel.

To Adelio Ferrero[1] and Ricardo Muñoz Suay

Venice, [8] September 1967
Questions to Luis Buñuel for the Milanese journal Cinema Nuovo *by Adelio Ferrero and Ricardo Muñoz Suay, September 1967*[2]

1) *We heard you say once, that the most important men of this century are Freud, Einstein,*[3] *Lenin*[4] *and Breton. Could you tell us a bit more about why?*
   All four have pointed towards and illuminated our path through life, they have enriched our understanding of ourselves, opened up a marvellous and poetic world, a new understanding of the universe, or, in a revolutionary sense, have led us towards a different kind of society that *may be* less unjust than our own.

2) *How present is Spain in your ideological and cultural make-up?*
   As the earth that feeds and makes a tree grow. Although, culturally speaking, I owe a lot to France, because of my surrealist experience.

3) *Eroticism and Catholicism are frequently joined in your films. What relationship do you see between two elements so apparently opposed?*
   Eroticism without Catholicism is only half the eroticism, because it lacks the sense of sin. I think it was Saint Thomas[5] who said that, even for married couples in the Christian church, copulation was a venial sin.

4) *Are you satisfied with* Belle de jour? *What made you choose Kessel's novel?*
   What interested me in the novel was the conflict between the conscience of the heroine and her masochistic compulsions. I am *never* satisfied with my films.

5) *And* Simon of the Desert? *We saw the film in Venice and liked it a lot. What have you done with the film. Do you intend to complete it?*

I wanted to make it into a ten-reel film, but as my producer had already taken it to Venice, I abandoned that idea. Like other films I've made for Alatriste, the general public will get to see *Simon of the Desert* in ten or twelve years' time.

6) *What do you think of the 'new waves' in cinema today? Do they seem so 'new' to you?*
Except for Godard,[6] I don't see anything new in the new waves. To my mind, the most human, the most vigorous new wave is happening in Brazil.

7) *Have you seen* The War is Over?[7] *What do you think of the film?*
I haven't seen the film. I will one day. I rarely go to the cinema.

Spa Alu, RMS; *CUA* 596–597 f

---

[1] Italian film critic, (1935–77), worked on the journal *Cinema nuovo*, edited by Aristarco.
[2] Questions typewritten on original document with handwritten replies from LB.
[3] Albert Einstein (1879–1955), German physicist.
[4] Vladimir Ilich Uliánov, 'Lenin' (1870–1924), Russian politician leader of the Soviet Union from 1922 until his death.
[5] Thomas Aquinas (1225–74), Catholic theologian born in Roccasecca, central Italy.
[6] Jean-Luc Godard (born 1930), French-Swiss film-maker, screened *La Chinoise* at the Venice Festival in 1967.
[7] *La guerre est finie* (1966), directed by Resnais, scripted by Jorge Semprún, the story of a Spanish communist (played by Yves Montand) exiled to France.

Figure 68 Moravia, Leiser and Buñuel with the Golden Lion, Venice Film Festival, 8 September 1967.

From Salvador Dalí

Cadaqués, 14 September 1967[1]

GREETINGS,
DALÍ

Spa Tel, AB/577.5; *LAT* 151

[1] *Belle de jour* awarded Gold Lion at Venice on 8 September 1967.

From Rafael Alberti

Venice, 16 September 1967

CONGRATULATIONS FROM THE CHICKEN AND THE COMMANDANT,[1]
RAFAEL ALBERTI

Spa Tel, AB/632.4

[1] Reference to an 'anaglyph' (minimalist poem made up of three nouns, one of which had to be 'chicken' and the third of which had to have no relation to the first) that Alberti wrote at the Residencia: 'El pin, el pan, el pun, la gallina y el comandante' in R. Alberti, *Con la luz primera* (Mexico City: Edaf, 2002), p. 568.

From José Donoso[1]

Madrid, 26 September 1967

Dear Mr Buñuel,

A few lines to offer my greetings and warm congratulations on your triumph at Venice.

Our mutual friend Carlos Fuentes planned to introduce us a few years ago in Mexico, but we were unable to meet up. I feel I am within my rights to send you these lines though, because I know that you read and had good things to say about some of my novels (*Coronación*,[2] *El lugar sin límites*,[3] *Ese domingo*[4]), which made me very happy.

My wife[5] and I are living in Madrid – probably for just over a year – and have just moved into a little flat at 3 Calle de la Escalinata, in the heart of old Madrid. I imagine the whole of Spain is seeking you out right now, but if you do find yourself with a moment to spare, nothing would please me more than to pass by and say hello or invite you to share a bottle of wine with me, my wife and my dog. My telephone is 247–8671 and I rarely leave home before 2pm.

Once again, warmest congratulations and regards,
José Donoso

Spa Tls, AB/632.21

1   Chilean writer (1924–96).
2   *Coronación* (Santiago de Chile: Nascimento, 1957).
3   *El lugar sin límites* (Mexico City: Joaquín Mortiz, 1966).
4   *Este domingo* (Santiago de Chile: Zig-Zag, 1966).
5   María Esther Serrano (1926–97), Chilean painter.

To José Donoso

Madrid, 14 October 1967

Dear Donoso,

Thank-you for your book,[1] it has, alongside its other qualities, an extraordinary atmosphere and succulent eroticism. I hope we will be able to discuss it soon.

I've been coming and going, here and there. On Monday I'm going to a mountain village in Andalusia. I'll be in touch when I get back to arrange a meeting.

Very cordial greetings,
Buñuel

Spa Als, JD/62/03

1   *El lugar sin límites.*

To Augusto Martínez Torres

Madrid, 9 November [1967]

Note: This will be the last time I talk to you all – or anyone else – about cinema. Thank-you for sending me the article.[1]

Yours,
[Buñuel]

Spa Ans, Od; *BSD* 74 f

1   Augusto M. Torres, 'Echoes d'une conversation: Luis Buñuel et Glauber Rocha', *Cinéma* 68, no. 123 (February 1968), 48–53.

To Carlos Fuentes

Madrid, 13 November 1967

Dear Carlos,

I was very pleased to get your letter. I thought you were at Lake Maggiore. How is Oxford? I assume your plans haven't changed. And Rita and the child? Are they going to Mexico soon? If so, I'll see them there because I plan to leave here (Madrid is loathsome) at the end of the week. I'll go to Paris for eight or ten days to meet my granddaughter.[1] By early December I'll be with the little Indians. What a relief!

Over here, José Donoso visited once, over a month ago, then García Márquez. The former plans to spend a year in Spain and the latter, who was on his way to Barcelona, for a couple of years. I showed them *Cambio de piel*[2] in Italian, which I still haven't been able to get into despite knowing the language. I am taking great care of it, because of its two impressive dedications,[3] but as far as reading goes, I'm waiting for an edition in a language more accessible to me.

I am frankly moved by your expression of friendship towards me. I mean the book you're writing on my films,[4] etc. Under no circumstances will I accept that you 'submit' the book to me before publication. Whatever next?! I shall consider myself very honoured by whatever you say, and I'm sure it will add to my understanding of myself. Speaking in all seriousness.

Here is the recipe for Bugnuellonnnni:[5] half an ounce of English gin, a quarter of Carpano and a quarter of sweet Martini. It's a mild plagiarism of and improvement on the Negroni. My firearms, which I have in their dozens, are important calibres. The handguns: a .38 Special, a .357 Magnum, the famous .45 owned by any self-respecting Mexican, and, lastly, the most powerful of the handguns is a .44 Magnum, the one the US police so amiably use to stop getaway vehicles. A single bullet can go straight through the driver and knock out the engine.

Daggers in the shape of a crucifix were sold in Albacete and all over Spain. They were banned because of *Viridiana*.[6] The La Closerie affair was in 1926 or 1927. (A banquet for Madame Rachilde,[7] a lot of big-shot intellectuals and a few surrealists.) When she asked them to say something at the end of the meal, I think it was Péret who stood up and slapped her. There was an almighty fuss and La Closerie was closed for several months. I wasn't a member of the group at that point; and, anyway, I thought that the surrealists were a bunch of *yéyés* back then,[8] but I do remember the restaurant being closed. I don't think Aragón was there, but if you're interested I could ask one of the survivors.

Sontag's[9] book arrived, and I wrote to thank the publisher and praise the author (the least I could do), but I turned down the invitation to adapt it for cinema. If I go back to film-making (and I doubt I will) it would have to be something big: a fine swansong or a sepulchral silence. Besides, unless you're on the Jury, I'm not going to any festivals.

Lots of kisses for Rita and my ex-chubby one. And a very big hug for you,
Luis

PS I've heard nothing whatsoever about Raymond Durgnat's book[10] or the English reviews of the valetudinarian *Belle de jour*.

My address in Paris from 20 to 30 November is, as always, Hotel Aiglon, 232 Boulevard Raspail. After that, the address in Mexico.

Spa Tls, CF/93/17

1 Juliette Buñuel, daughter of Juan Luis and Joyce, born in 1967.
2 C. Fuentes, *Cambio di pelle* (Madrid: Feltrinelli, 1967).
3 Copy Fuentes gave to LB (AB/1057).
4 From October to December 1967, Fuentes was working on the manuscript of *Luis Buñuel o la mirada de la medusa* (CF/143/1), intended for publication with Gallimard in Paris and Joaquín Mortiz in Mexico City.
5 The 'Buñueloni' in response to questions sent by Fuentes for his book on LB, on 1 November 1967 (AB/615).
6 There is a detailed close-up of the knife/crucifix used in the film.
7 Pseudonym of Marguerite Vallete-Eymery (1860–1953), French writer.
8 '*Yéyés*' widely used in 1960s continental Europe (from the English 'yeah, yeah') associated with bands like the Beatles, and singer songwriters like Serge Gainsbourg and Françoise Hardy.
9 Possible reference to the novel *Death Kit* (New York: Farrar, Straus & Giroux, 1967).
10 R. Durgnat, *Luis Buñuel* (London: Studio Vista, 1967).

To Pilar Bayona

Madrid, 14 November 1967

My dear Pilar,

Thank you so much for remembering me, and what a wonderful photographer you've become! I wish I could have been there with you in Calanda. This time, as always, I was only in Zaragoza for a few days and had no time to do anything. I'll be leaving for Paris in the next few days and from there to Mexico. When shall we meet up? Without fail, on my next trip to Europe this April. Give Carmencita[1] a hug for me, and more for you, dear, admirable Pilar.

Luis Buñuel

Spa Als, PBA

1 Carmen Bayona, sister of Pilar, born in 1909.

To Jean-Claude Carrière

Mexico City, 29 January 1968

My dear Jean-Claude,

I was very excited to get your letter as always. Ah! What a wonderful friend you would be if it weren't for your inhuman diets!

If I had picked out your room, as requested, you would now owe me $1,000. Such optimism! No signs of life from Serge and the fateful date will arrive in two days' time: '31 January'. I'm assuming he can't go ahead with the film.[1] No matter: it's fairly stupid, after all, the film. Who on earth would be interested in the *homousios* or *homooúsios*;[2] that is, whether a pederast is consubstantial[3] or just similar, but different?

My idleness has now reached the outer edges of Nirvana. I've read a little about the *Dominus canis*,[4] in a relaxed and very unfocussed way, and a long history of the Church that I'd already skimmed even more light-heartedly, years ago. I've come across truly hilarious things in the Gospels. But I'm keeping them to myself.

A big secret: the Hakims made me read a book so I could give them my 'opinion' on it, called *L'Arbre de noël* by Michel Bataille.[5] I'd like you to read it too. I'll wait to hear what you think, before I say what I think. Just remember that you and I could make gold from minute flecks of iron pyrite.

I shall await news from Serge, anyway, even if it is, as I imagine it will be, bad news.

Give our dear friend Auguste and her little 'Sosias',[6] your good daughter, a big hug from me

Yours,
Buñuel

Fre Tls, JCC

---

[1] *The Milky Way*, co-written by LB and Carrière at the Cazorla Parador, Autumn 1967.
[2] Greek: the 'Godhead', theological concept of the 'Three-in-One' (Father, Son and Holy Ghost) that awards divine status to Christ and that is argued over, incongruously, by different characters in *The Milky Way*.
[3] 'Consubstantiation': Catholic belief that the blood and body of Christ are in the bread and wine of Holy Communion (also discussed by characters in *The Milky Way*).
[4] Latin: 'Master', or 'Lord's Dog', alluding to the Dominican order of the Catholic Church founded by Domingo de Guzmán in 1216.
[5] French writer (1926–2008), author of *L'Arbre de Noël* (Paris: Julliard, 1967).
[6] Meaning 'clone', or 'dead-ringer' from *Amphitryon*, a comedy by Plautus (*c.* 254–184 BCE) in which the characters of the master and his slave, Sosias, are cloned.

To Jean-Claude Carrière

Mexico City, 31 January 1968

Dear Jean-Claude,

This morning – today was the fateful date – I received a telegram from Silberman agreeing to make *The* more-or-less *Milky Way* according – he says – to our protocol of last 22 November. I've never received nor read that protocol. Or at least, as far as I remember. I asked him to send it by return post, but in principle and PRACTICALLY QUAKING IN MY BOOTS, I am accepting his offer.

I hadn't written to you until yesterday because I assumed there was nothing going on. And because I'd replied in a very vague way to the Hakims' proposal about a book by Michel Bataille.

If everything works out in the end, would you prefer to come here or for me to go to France?[1] Or for us to go to Cazorla again, buying a brand-new Peugeot beforehand that you alone would drive? Or we could go to San José Purúa[2] over here? Let me know. As for me, my only worry is that I'll kick the bucket during pre-production – never during the adaptation – or perhaps during production. Not much we can do about that. If I followed your regime, I'd be there at your funeral. But seriously, I'd be delighted to make *The Milky Way* if it wasn't for the FEAR of not being able to finish the film. We alcoholics, diabetics, emphysematics, arthritics, etc. have cause to be concerned ... and the producers who hire us are pendejos.[3]

Anyway, I'm confident that the less well-versed we are in Theology or the study of Synoptics[4] or Acts,[5] the more interesting things we'll find. A cocktail at the right time is worth more than any book. I haven't read the provisional script again; I'm too afraid.

Cordially,
Luis

Fre Tls, JCC

[1] To work on a second version of the script of *The Milky Way*.
[2] Spa in remote area of State of Michoacán.
[3] Spanish in the original (idiots).
[4] The 'synoptic' evangelists: Matthew, Mark, Luke.
[5] Acts of the Apostles, fifth book of the New Testament.

To Richard Gallon[1]

Mexico City, 5 February 1968

Dear Sir,

Your letter has arrived with the copies of the contract.[2] I agree to the financial arrangements, but I find all the rest too complicated.

An Andalusian Dog, The Golden Age and *Nazarín* have all been published in other languages; I would have to revise their respective contracts with the help of a solicitor. But all the relevant documents are in Paris. We would have to wait for my next trip to France to finalize our contract. It would also be very difficult for me to provide you with copies of the films.

I propose, if you agree, that you have the three films translated and that, instead of contacting me, you contact the respective publishers. Here are their addresses: for *An Andalusian Dog* and *The Golden Age*, *L'Avant-Scène* magazine,[3] 27 Rue Saint André des Arts, Paris VI, France. For *Nazarín,* Suhrkamp Verlag publishing house,[4] P.O. Box 2446, Frankfurt am Main 6, Germany.

Those editions were very carefully produced, and I entirely agree with their version of the texts.

If I don't hear from you, I'll write again from Paris.

I'll keep a copy of your contract.

Most cordial greetings,
Luis Buñuel

Fre Tls, GP

[1] Editor of Grove Press in New York.
[2] To publish English translations of the scripts of *An Andalusian Dog, The Golden Age* and *Nazarín.*

³　*L'Avant-Scène Cinéma*, French journal founded in 1961, specializing in film scripts, published LB's two surrealist films in the double issue, 27–28 (June-July 1963).
⁴　German publishing house founded by Peter Suhrkamp in Frankfurt in 1950.

To Serge Silberman

Mexico City, [5] February 1968

My dear Serge,

The famous protocol has arrived. I didn't even realize it was a protocol. Agreed. Thanks.

If you want me to go to Europe rather than have Jean-Claude come here, I'm willing. This would save you a return trip Paris–Mexico. We could work at the Cazorla or the Civitate Christiana,[1] in Assisi, Italy, or in the Dominican convent of Our Lady of France,[2] Spain. We have a lot of work to do on the script. It needs to be a real action film ... about Faith and Reason (for those who have any).

I'm sure I signed the telegram. It was sent by the PTT.[3] Why wouldn't I sign it?

I look forward to receiving the contract you mention.

With all friendship,
Luis Buñuel

PS Although we are fond of Tenoudji and he of us, bear in mind he's a faithful follower of the Torah, etc. I'm counting on you to ensure I have the freedom to express myself with no theological or ideological pressure from any side. You know me well enough to know I'm not a dictator who thinks he's infallible ... But I do remember the visit Tenoudji paid to my hotel when I was about to start *Diary of a Chambermaid* ...

Fre Tls, RS

¹　Association founded by Giovanni Rosi in 1939, based in Assisi, where Pasolini began preparations for *Il Vangelo secondo Matteo* (1964).
²　At the top of the Peña de Francia, Salamanca province, around 30 km north of Las Hurdes.
³　French postal service established in 1921.

To José Rubia Barcia

Mexico City, 6 February 1968

My dear *don* Pepe,

I have just received your scholarly essay with a few lines attached.[1] It's been a very long time since I last wrote. I've had news of you from time to time and I was very happy to hear from you, but my laziness when it comes to answering letters is truly deplorable. And is the sole reason for my silence.

I'm sure we must have been in Europe at the same time. I was in Venice shortly before or after you were in Italy. We may well have coincided in Spain and France as well. What a shame. I would love to have seen you all.

There's not much to say about my family. Jeanne, consumed, as always, by the labours of her …[2] etc. Juan Luis and his wife Joyce live in Paris and have a five-month-old girl. Rafael is still in New York working as an as-yet-unpublished playwright. It appears his debut will be in the next couple of months in a theatre *off* Broadway.[3] And as for their father, he made a film in France that had – unusually – huge commercial success. It is called *Belle de jour*. I'm sure you'll see it over there. It hasn't reached the United States yet. Now I may – almost certainly – be going back to Paris to make one of my 'action' films, about religious heresy, from the gnostics, via your countryman Priscillian, to the Jansenists and then up to many contemporary heterodoxies.[4]

I'm sure if I bumped into your daughters in the street I wouldn't know or recognize them. If you have any recent photos, please send some. I hope and wish you would all come down here, if only for a few days. I would even pay for your flights. It's the least I can do. After all, it's only three hours from here to Los Angeles. Go on, just let me know and we can arrange the best time for your visit.

Warmest regards to Evita. The same to you,
Buñuel

Spa Tls, CBC; CLB 91

[1] Rubia sent LB, in his letter of 26 October 1966, a piece he had written on *La casa de Bernarda Alba* for a 'Homage to Ángel del Río' (*CLB* 89–90).
[2] Truncated mock reference to conservative Spanish (Franco Regime-style) discourse on the 'fairer sex'.…
[3] Rafael Buñuel premiered both works together, *Seventeen Boxes* and *Let There Be Light*, at La Mama Experimental Theatre Club, New York, 24 April 1968.
[4] *The Milky Way*.

To Jean-Claude Carrière

Mexico City, 8 February 1968

Jean-Claude,

Agreed, you're coming to Mexico! I'll book the room for you from 20 February. Don't come any earlier for reasons I'll explain in person.

Bring me two little packets of herring, and liquorice for Jeanne. I'd also like two packets of pipe tobacco, French tobacco. I think it's called Saint Jacques? It's very well known anyway. Gold packet.

Don't bring any books. I have all we need here … in my head.

Of course, I'll come and meet you at the airport … in the Mustang, which I won't let you touch, not even the steering wheel, at any point during your stay.

Have you read Guitton's[1] *Le Christ écartelé*? And the *Apologeticus* by the *Emperor* Tertullian?[2] I have.

That's all for now. What's wrong with Auguste? Do let me know.

Yours,
LB

Fre Als, JCC

¹ Jean Guitton (1901–99), French theologian, author of *Le Christ écartelé* (Paris: la Librairie académique Perrin, 1963).
² Carthaginian theologian, defender of Christianity (155–240), author of *Apologeticum* (197).

To *Cahiers du cinéma*

Cahiers du cinéma
65 Champs-Élysées, Paris

Mexico City [February 1968]

AS A SYMBOL OF MY SUPPORT FOR LANGLOIS[1], TRUE CREATOR AND INSTIGATOR OF THE CINÉMATHÈQUE FRANÇAISE, I WITHDRAW PERMISSION FOR MY FILMS TO BE SCREENED AT SAID INSTITUTION.[2]

LUIS BUÑUEL

Fre Tel, CCF/23-B12

¹ Dismissed, by the French Minister of Culture and the writer André Malraux (1901–76), from his post as Director of the Paris Cinémathèque at the beginning of 1968.
² Permission also withdrawn by others including Chaplin, Fellini, Godard, Hitchcock, Truffaut and Welles until Langlois was reinstated on 22 April 1968.

To Serge Silberman

San José Purúa, 17 March 1968

My dear Serge,

We[1] have been here for two weeks and will return to Mexico City tomorrow. The script[2] is nearly finished. It still needs some final revisions, but you will definitely have it in Paris before 1 April. The dialogues are finished, there are some new scenes, others, cut, and it's 120 pages in all. I'll be able to draw up the technical script from the manuscript in a couple of hours. As usual, I will only number scenes to help with the work plan.

Of course, I am completely happy to hear what you have to say, and, above all, to make sure the film doesn't become too expensive. You may be surprised at the number of characters (80, I think), but only about fifteen (there's no star) are important. We'll discuss that in more detail, as well as the endless location changes, which will, in the end, be quite straightforward.

I'm happy with our work.

I've reserved my suite at the Aiglon for April 15, so you can read, re-read, think about, show it to the relevant people, make copies, etc. I think two weeks will be enough for all those steps and procedures. If there are no unexpected surprises, we could begin filming, as agreed, two months after April 15, in other words, on June 15.

I don't know if I'll stay here in Mexico until April 15 or go to Spain. I'll let you know so we don't lose contact, and if necessary I could come to Paris earlier. Jean-Claude is planning to spend a few days in New York. He'll be leaving here before the end of the month.

Very cordially yours,
Luis

Fre Tls, RS

[1]   LB and Carrière.
[2]   Of *The Milky Way*.

To Francisco Rabal

Paris, 25 April 1968

Dear Paco,

I was also very sorry our meeting was cancelled, mostly because of what happened to you. An unexpected and very unpleasant surprise. Reliable sources tell me just how painful renal colic can be. I'm amazed you had the strength to write me those lines. You should have just sent word. I assume you are well again. When you write, tell me what preventative measures your doctor has prescribed.

I imagine your illness meant you couldn't go to Valladolid[1] but, according to a letter from a Jesuit[2] and a telegram from the director of the Festival,[3] they will be screening your film *Nazarín* on the 25th, today. As long as they cut out everything but your acting, it should all be fine.[4]

I'm getting ready to start shooting on about 15 June if everything is ready by then.[5] As I mentioned in Madrid, there's almost no chance of you working on it, not because you would have difficulty working in France, but because I can't adapt any of the bit-parts to suit you the way I could with Hippolytus of Murcia. And if you enjoy working with me, I enjoy working with you even more. Quite apart from the laughs, there is, of course, your striking screen presence. I'm taking advantage of the fact Fernando can't hear us to praise you, because you know how jealous he gets. Speaking of Fernando: not a soul in Calanda had heard of him, which made him devilishly bad-tempered. I, on the hand, had to sign so many autographs I got quite fed up.

Big hugs for my niece and my grand-nephews, and an enormous hug for you from your Uncle Luis

Spa Tls, FR; *BVMC* f

[1]   To the 13th Semana Internacional de Cine (SEMINICI), Valladolid, from 21–28 April.
[2]   Possibly, Manuel Alcalá, Jesuit Father and author of *Buñuel: Cine e ideología* (Madrid: Cuadernos para el Diálogo, 1973).
[3]   Antolín de Santiago Juárez, provincial delegate of the Spanish Ministry of Information and Tourism.

⁴ LB's usual bantering with Rabal; *Nazarín* was awarded Special Jury Mention and Cinestudio journal prize.
⁵ Filming of *The Milky Way* began 20 August 1968.

To Robert Benayoun

Paris, 7 May 1968

Dear Benayoun,

Indeed, I do find interviews on TV or anywhere else a far too unpleasant prospect, so ... I would on the other hand, be delighted to have lunch with you and Kyrou. The only free moment I have is on Thursday 9 May at 1:00. Come to my hotel. Do let Kyrou know. If you can't make it, send a message and we'll meet up when you get back from Cannes¹ with Ado.

Yours,
Buñuel

Fre Asp, JCC

¹ The Cannes Film Festival was cancelled shortly after opening, 10 May, marking a show of solidarity with May '68 protests.

To Carlos Fuentes

Paris, 7 July 1968

Dear Carlos,

Your letter¹ arrived two days ago, the day after I got back to Paris from Madrid.

I didn't want to get back to work until the elections were over, the result was just as I expected.² I have no wish to work and would far rather dedicate myself to more or less frivolous meditation than to an activity that is beginning to feel idiotic to me: searching for little camera angles, suggesting nonsense bits of verbal-mime to the actors. But what can I do ...?

Apart from all the running about preparing the film,³ I live a completely secluded life. I don't see anyone except my children, whom I visit two or three times a week. I go to bed early to avoid smoking and drinking too much. I can really feel the 70-year threshold approaching.

When you come over, I'll need you to concede your Sundays so we can lunch together, because the rest of the week I'm busy from 9 in the morning to 7 or 8 at night.

The Hakims are determined to get me to direct *Under the Volcano* for them, whatever it takes. I've refused to write the adaptation, because I think it's impossible, but I've told them that if they can get it to me all neatly seasoned and spiced, I may do it. I also told them you're a big fan of the book and that you didn't think the adaptation would be too difficult. They're going to phone you or write. In spite of my admiration for your great gifts in any literary, cinematic or even political sphere, I'm still reserving the right to turn down the adaptation. The conversion of the book to screen would have to be at least as important for film as the book is for literature.

Warmest regards,
Luis

[PS] I wrote this letter three days ago. Please forgive its many mistakes and the delay.

Spa Tlsps, CF/93/17

1   Letter from Fuentes to LB, 29 June 1968 (CF/93/17).
2   French elections on 23 and 30 June 1968 returned absolute majority for the Gaullist Union for the Defence of the Republic.
3   *The Milky Way*.

From Max Aub

Mexico City, 18 July 1968

Dear Luis,

To write to you after 60 years, I'd have to think it was important. The night before last, I was having dinner with Antonio Ruano,[1] who works for Aguilar, and he suggested I write a *great* book about you. At first, I was a bit bemused, but later, talking it through, I realized it wasn't such an absurd idea after all.

Clearly, only Sadoul could have written a 'great' book about you. Who else? And then I began to imagine, not exactly what Aguilar is after, which is a huge book with hundreds of photos and analysis of your films, but a serious kind of *Jusep Torres Campalans*[2] taking in the history of our entire generation. By the following evening, I was already seeing how it might come together, with your childhood and youth, the *Residencia*, Dalí and Federico, and up to your departure for Paris being the first part. Surrealism, and the two films, the second part. Your transformation: Las Hurdes, the Second Republic, the third. The Civil War. Exile. Mexico.

Now, I clearly wouldn't be able to write this book unless I work with you. I mean, talking, telling you the things I know – things I couldn't print without your permission – and the things I don't know that you'd have to tell me. I'm not thinking we'd sit down face to face for the ten, fifteen, or however many sessions it would take; rather that we'd chat after, or before dinner, over some red or white wine, in Mexico, in Paris, or in Madrid (because they've now given me a visa).

I said all this – more or less – to the people at Aguilar before waiting to hear from you. I'm writing a lot of books at once as usual, but nothing urgent. I quite like the idea of this book: our era, film, the history we've shared, in Spain, France, or Mexico, then back to Paris and Madrid.

I spoke to Jeanne, I know how busy you are these days. Send me a couple of lines to say 'yes' or 'no'. If you accept, I'm happy to meet wherever you like, and I don't mind whether it's a Bourdeaux or a Beaujolais…

The same love as always,
Max
Euclides Flat 5, 3rd Floor

Spa Tls, AB/647.2

¹ Editor (1930–2009), head of the Mexican branch of the Madrid-based publishing house, Editorial
   Aguilar, founded in 1923.
² M. Aub, *Jusep Torres Campalans* (Mexico City: Tezontle, 1958), fictionalized biography of Catalan
   painter, Torres Campalans, whose exhibitions Aub organized in Mexico City and New York.

To Max Aub

Paris, 25 July 1968

Dear Max,

I accept your proposal, but I should warn you I won't be available until the last day of filming,¹ that is, until more or less October 25. We could meet up then: in Paris, until 20 November, or in Mexico from 1 December. We'll talk and, most of all, we'll drink. I start filming on 20 August.

Warm regards,
Luis

PS I'm beginning to get a bit fed up with this film work.

Spa Als, MA/15/3

¹ Of *The Milky Way*.

Figure 69 Christian Matras, behind camera, and Buñuel filming *The Milky Way*, France, September 1968. Courtesy of Royal Books, Baltimore.

To Max Aub

Paris, 30 September 1968

Dear Max,

The film will be finished at the end of October. So, we could chat – not too much of course – at the beginning of November. I might go to Spain while the editor[1] organizes what should only be a week's work for me. Anyway, those are the gaps in my schedule.

Warm regards,
LB

PS I calculate the last turn of the crank will be on 22 October at 5:30pm. But I have to go to Santiago[2] for a couple of days to visit Priscillian.

Spa Als, MA/15/5

[1] Louisette Hautecoeur, French editor of three features by LB, including *Belle de jour* and *The Milky Way*.
[2] Santiago de Compostela, final destiny of the pilgrim protagonists in *The Milky Way*.

To Max Aub

Paris, 6 October 1968

Dear Max,

It looks as if I'll be in Santiago from October 20–25, for the two or three days clandestine filming we have to do in Spain.[1] Then I'll be back in Paris until 10 November. While they're sorting out post-production, I'll go back to Spain for a week's holiday.

You haven't commented on events in Mexico.[2] I see its immediate future LADEN with menace.

Warm regards,
Luis

Spa Als, MA/15/6

[1] LB did not apply to Franco authorities for permission.
[2] On 2 October 1968, 400 people were assassinated by the army at Tlatelolco Square on presidential orders in an attempt to end Mexican student protests.

To Carlos Fuentes

Paris, 14 October 1968

Dear Carlos,

You've caught me on the last week of filming,[1] working day and night, as weather permits. It would be very difficult for us to meet before this Sunday at 5pm in my hotel.

The following Monday, the 20th, I leave for Spain (to finish the clandestine filming). However, next Saturday, I'll be filming all day at the Saint Maurice studios in Joinville. If you could come, I'd be delighted. Write to say which you choose.

Warm regards,
Luis

PS Filming in the studio from midday to 7:30pm.

Spa Als, CF/93/17

[1] Of *The Milky Way*.

To Serge Silberman

Mexico City, 12 February 1969

My dear Serge,

I may well be deaf, but you're as dumb as a fish. For a month and a half since I last saw you that is,[1] not a single word. Given your pro-activity, your punctuality, your seriousness with regard to all cinematic and personal affairs, that's surprising.

If you have a moment, I'd be pleased if you would answer the following questions that are very much on my mind:

1) What happened with the censors?
2) What happened with the special effects?
3) When and how are you planning to screen the film?
4) I know you screened it for quite a few people … carefully selected; what was the general response? And I know you didn't attend the Delluc Prize Ceremony.[2]

If, as well as these questions, you can give me any other news, I'd be very grateful.

I'm still here, in this blossoming country, calm as a bowl of milk, living my life of shocking sloth. For the moment, I'm not even thinking about cinema. I'll await your visit in March to see if I can rouse myself to take up my dazzling life as a film director again. And your gift of *The Milky Way* in 16mm!

I remember very fondly those good times, work and friendship, with you over all those months. As well as an excellent friend, you are an ideal secretary. And formidably shrewd: as demonstrated by our terrible experience in Brussels.

Warmest regards,
Buñuel

Fre Tls, RS

[1] LB went back to Mexico in December 1968 after finishing *The Milky Way*.
[2] The Louis Delluc Prize, awarded in December to the best French film of the year; awarded to *Baisers volés* (Truffaut 1968).

To Serge Silberman

Mexico, 9 March 1969

My dear Serge,

My last letter crossed with your long and detailed one. You are unstoppable, yet in spite of all your activities, you found the energy to write several pages crammed with words. First of all, I want to say you can be overly reticent at times. If you'd written asking me to delay signing with Braunberger, I would have done so at once.[1] I spoke to Alatriste yesterday, he's also on our side. I'm assuming Braunberger accepted your proposal. That said, and although you are far more experienced than I when it comes to these things, I don't see why making two films at the same time would necessarily be detrimental to both sides. Braunberger may have been thinking about capitalizing on the publicity *The Milky Way* should attract. Anyway, I'm on your side.

I thought the *ABC*[2] supplement would come out in Milan on the same day as the premiere there. But in the end, all the fuss helped the film pass the censors!

This time I am interested in the press and public response to the film. Did the Atheists' League pay, or the Vatican? I hope you have great success.

One of these days I'll finally get around to sorting through my old papers to find the contract selling *An Andalusian Dog* to Grands Films Classiques, which was handled by Mrs Peillon for her usual cut.

You invited me to the premiere, and I send most cordial thanks, but I hate travelling (even more so just two months after my long stay in Europe). Barbachano invited me to go to New York on the 20th of this month, to put me up in a suite in the Plaza, etc. Why? Apparently, the cardinal of New York[3] wants to give me a prize for directing *Nazarín*. Of course, I declined, and reserved the right to decline the award too.

That's all for now. Warmest regards,
Luis

PS I hope you've now got my letter asking whether you could subscribe[4] me under the name 'Buñuel' to some kind of press agency.

Fre Tlsps, RS

---

[1] Possible reference to the marketing, in France, of *Simon of the Desert*, which premiered in Paris on 15 March 1969.
[2] Milan weekly, printed from 1960 and 1978.
[3] Terence Cooke (1921–83), archbishop of New York from 1968 until his death.
[4] Take out a subscription for LB so that a Paris agency would send on copies of all press references to 'Buñuel'.

From Louis Aragon, Miguel Ángel Asturias *et al.*

[Paris, March 1969]

YOUR FRIENDS SALUTE YOU ON THE PREMIERE OF *THE MILKY WAY* IN PARIS.[1] THEY ADORE YOUR FILMS. AND THEY ADORE YOU. GRANT THEM THE PLEASURE OF YOUR COMPANY ON THE 13 MARCH AT THE CINÉMA BONAPARTE.[2]

LOUIS ARAGON, MIGUEL ÁNGEL ASTURIAS,[3] ROBERT BENAYOUL, YVONNE BABY,[4] JOSE BERGAMÍN, MAURICE BESSY, PIERRE BILLARD, GEORGES CHARENSOL, LO DUCA,[5] ADO KYROU, JEANNE MOREAU, SAMUEL LACHIZE,[6] HENRI LANGLOIS, LOUIS MALLE, RUTA SADOUL, FRANCOIS TRUFFAUT, LUCE VIGO[7]

Fre Tel, AB/692.20

[1] 13 March 1969.
[2] 430-seat Paris cinema.
[3] Guatemalan writer (1899–1974), received the Nobel Prize for Literature in 1967.
[4] French journalist (1929), daughter of Ruta Assia (Sadoul) with her first husband, Jean Baby; interviewed LB for *Le Monde* in 1961, 1965 and 1972.
[5] Joseph-Maria Lo Duca (1905–2004), French-Italian film critic and co-founder of *Cahiers du cinéma*.
[6] French film critic (1925–2006).
[7] Film critic (1931–2017), daughter of Jean Vigo.

To Francisco Rabal

Mexico City, 14 April 1969

My dear and much-admired nephew Paco,

A couple of lines just to ask a favour. I think they're putting *Nazarín* on at the Goya[1] over there. I'd be very grateful if you would go and see it, then write and tell me if there were any cuts and if so, from the censors or that lousy Pelimex?[2] Is the laughing Christ[3] still in it? And the scene with railway workers? Etc. How's the copy? If any of these things are awry, protest in the very first interview you give. I'm delighted for you that they're showing the film over there at last.

It won't be long before I can hug you myself. Sending a few now in advance. A thousand hugs from your *oncle*,[4]

Luis
[PS] Write to me!

Spa Als, FR; *BVMC* f

[1] Madrid cinema.
[2] Mexican distribution company.
[3] Shot of painting of Christ laughing, removed from the censored copy.
[4] French in the original (uncle).

From Francisco Rabal

Madrid, April 1969

Dear Uncle,

Simon of the Desert and *The Milky Way* were screened last night at the Week of Values[1] in Valladolid… etc.

So off we went, Damián, my sister-in-law, María Asunción, Doctor Barros (formidable!), Gloria, Saura, Chaplin[2] and a load of friends. Your nephew Pedro[3] and his wife too. Such expectation, so many youngsters, huge excitement for us all.

How can I convey the full range and quantity of our impressions? Both films were furiously applauded and there was the occasional isolated and timid protest, sometimes fanatical, drowned out by the impact and beauty of your work and the appreciative applause. None of this would have been possible two years ago.

I asked the journalists I met to send copies of their reviews, and I'll send them on to you at once.

I loved the ending of *The Milky Way* and so many other things I'll tell you about – and others I'll ask you about – when you come. Let this letter be advance warning of my renewed admiration and fondness for you. Hugs to your family from mine, and a huge hug from your proud – and proud to be your – nephew,

Paco

Spa Als, AB/647.3; *BDM* 191–192 f

[1] Between 1960 and 1972, SEMINCI held a *Semana Internacional de Cine Religioso y de Valores Humanos;* this one held on 20–27 April 1969.
[2] Geraldine Chaplin (born 1944), Anglo-American actress, daughter of Charles Chaplin, and partner of Saura from 1967 to 1979.
[3] Pedro Christian García Buñuel (1940–2008), Conchita's son.

To Francisco Rabal

Mexico City, 2 May 1969

Dear Paco,

A thousand thanks at least, for the articles you sent and for your notes on Valladolid. You're the only one who has kept me informed. I'd have liked a few more details on the catcalls and the viewers who walked out, but you've done more than enough with your summary of events.

The *Tristana* project is still completely up in the air, but with or without *Tristana*, I'm still planning to go to Madrid in October for two months.

A huge hug from your uncle,
Luis

[PS] You deserve a much longer letter but I'm in a hurry. Sorry.

Spa Als, FR; *BVMC* f

To Pierre Braunberger

Mexico City, 3 May 1969

My dear Pierre,

As usual, just a few words, because neither us is fond of the epistolary genre.

I'd very much like to have one or two reviews of *Simon of the Desert*, because I have no idea how the public reacted to the film.

Although I wouldn't take them as gospel, they might at least give me some idea. And if you have any comments of your own to add, all the better.

Warm regards,
Luis Buñuel

PS Many thanks for the telegram about *The Milky Way*. It was a great pleasure to read.

Fre Tlsps, PB

To Ricardo Muñoz Suay

Mexico City, 3 May 1969

Dear Ricardo,

I see from your letter that both you and Nieves have been ill.[1] It seems to have been more a shock than anything else, but you should take care of yourself: not too much, of course! Several friends have had the same thing and they are as fit as fiddles. These days it's a challenge to find anyone completely immune to the thousand and one diseases of our scummy century. The only good advice, I feel, is not to take your work too seriously. If you get to the studio and the set's not ready and Sarita Montiel[2] hasn't shown up … 'Action!' Let them both go to hell, while you relax. Stress is the worst thing.

La Séquestrée de Poitiers, the book I mean, was one of the many (or should I say the few) books that the surrealists liked, but as far as I know they never wrote about or commented on it. The interesting thing about the book or the case it describes, is how, in a world supposedly run on reason, utterly irrational things can suddenly occur that undermine or change that assumption. Hitler, for example. That a 'satanic' madman could enthral millions in the country of reason and philosophy is another example. I won't go on though because I'm anti-epistolic.

I'd like to hear what you and Nieves think of *The Lacteal Way*. I've heard nothing about what happened at Valladolid.

Of course, if *Tristana* goes ahead (who knows?), I'd like you to be there and not to lose your temper even if Fernando Rey can't remember his lines. Relax!

Hugs for Nieves and hugs for you,
Luis

Spa Tls, RMS

¹ Letter from Suay to LB, 28 April 1969 (RMS), in which he mentions his coronary problems and his wife Nieves' influenza.
² María Antonia Abad Fernández (1928–2013), actress.

Figure 70 Buñuel, Roces and Mantecón, Mexico City, *c.* 1969.

To Eduardo Ducay

Mexico City, 20 May 1969

Dear Ducay,

I think one of my letters must have gone astray, because in your letter which has just arrived, of 17 May, you ask me again what I think of Deneuve as *Tristana*. On 9 May, when I returned the bank certificate to you, I also sent another letter with my thoughts on that. I'll repeat more or less what I said then:

1) Catherine's ultra-Nordic look is no good for a character supposedly born in Salamanca, or even in Madrid, etc. Unless, for example, the plot makes it clear that her Swedish parents moved to Toledo and she was born and raised there.
2) No one would believe Deneuve was a little *virgin* orphan girl despoiled by the wicked Don Lope.
3) She's one of those actresses who, no matter the role, will always be Catherine Deneuve and not the character.
4) She's burning herself out making one film after the next.
5) As a star, she's has pretentions and is not easy to direct.

6) Her fee is astronomical and, to be honest, if the film is mediocre, her presence won't save it. And if it turns out well, by not hiring her you'd have saved the $500,000 she might well cost.

Apart from this, she'd be perfect for the second half of the film, from the amputation onwards.[1]

I'm still thinking about the script,[2] which I think is a bit short.[3] But if we add anything new, I promise it won't shock the censors.

Julio says that he doesn't want to charge you anything for the little bit of work I gave him, but don't say anything; let him tell you himself.

I wouldn't mind if filming began at the beginning of September, with a month and a half of preparation beforehand.

Regards,
Buñuel

Spa Tls, ED

---

[1] Tristana, played by Deneuve, has her leg amputated.
[2] English in the original.
[3] Co-written by LB and Julio Alejandro.

To Francisco Rabal

Mexico City, 30 June 1969

My dear nephew Paco,

A thousand thanks for your letter-report on Valladolid. And for the cuttings and the interviews in which you bring my illustrious name so brilliantly to light.[1] We'll discuss this and many other things soon. I can't wait to see you.

As for *Tristana*, everything is still very much up in the air. The Época Films people are high-flying paranoid obsessives. Or intrepid adventurers, you might say, they've no idea what they're getting themselves into filming with me: prohibitions and director's heart attacks, not to mention deafness, deranged prostates, emphysemas, etc.

I had word yesterday of the death of my poor mother.[2] A release for her and for those of us who watched her sink into total and irreversible amnesia. She was the best mother in the world, but she died, spiritually, over ten years ago.[3]

A big hug from,
YOUR UNCLE

PS When I see the heavens on a starlit night my soul cries out: 'I believe in your divine will, oh little God of mine.' Death to the atheists!

Spa Als, FR; *BVMC* f

1   Press cuttings held in AB/2056.
2   María Portolés died June 1969 (AB/659.1).
3   Suffering from Alzheimers.

To Eduardo Ducay and Joaquín Gurruchaga

San José Purúa Spa, Michoacán, 20 July 1969

My dear and *fearless* producers,

The only news I've had since Eduardo left is 1) Deneuve has been hired; 2) that filming of *Tristana* has been blocked, although it was approved by the censors.[1] I'm now waiting to see if I'll be allowed to make a foreign film in Spain.

I sent you a telegram the day before yesterday announcing my arrival, with Iberia, on the morning of 30 July. I asked if you could book me an apartment *high* up in the Torre, either 1 or 2, as both have views over the Sierra or the Casa de Campo.[2]

If parts of the film are going to be shot in France, *I would like* to take on Pierre Lary as another first assistant, he's worked with me for years. We can discuss it when I arrive.

Don't print the *scripts*[3] until I arrive, because I've come up with some new scenes I think are interesting, *especially* a new and 'extraordinary' ending. I've definitely finished with the storyline though.

After three or four days in Madrid talking to you, I'll be taking three days to go to Zaragoza. My mother died, and I'm the eldest son. I need to go and see what's going on.

I'd have liked some detail on the decisions of the censors, the ban, etc, but you are both 'hermetic', if you'll forgive the insult.

What happened with Silberman?[4]

The Italian actor's[5] voice wasn't so good, although, with everyone speaking in Spanish, one in French, another in Italian, locations shot in Portugal – which should be avoided – and studios in France, it's going to be a mule of a film, I mean, a bit hybrid and hair-brained. It's a shame! And although you don't seem worried, I AM!

I'll wait to hear your thoughts on this letter.

See you soon. Warm regards,
Buñuel

Spa Als L, ED

1   The script.
2   The Sierra del Guadarrama, and the Casa de Campo, a public park to the West of Madrid.
3   English in the original.
4   After standing down as a potential co-producer of *Tristana* with Época Films.
5   Franco Nero (born 1941), who plays the painter, Horacio.

To Antonio Gálvez[1]

[Mexico City, July 1969]

My dear friend Gálvez,

I did get your letter[2] and I now find myself, shamefully, writing back a month later. I share your dread of epistolary literature, particularly when it involves writing a paragraph or more on your extraordinary photographic character study. I've tried a few times to write back summing up my thoughts on your work, but so far, I've only managed a few horribly literary little paragraphs. I don't despair of coming up with a solution and, when that finally 'blossoms', I'll send it at once. In the meantime, though, forget about me, I deserve it.

I'm now taking advantage to ask if you would mind me reproducing the photo you took of me superimposed over a brick wall with the Pope to the right below.[3] It's for a new art cinema opening here in Mexico called the Buñuel Auditorium, they want to blow up a copy of it for the entrance. My Mexican producer, Alatriste, owns it and insists on naming it after me, which doesn't best please me. But as he wants a picture of me for the foyer, I'd prefer it were that photograph, which I think is the best one anyone has taken of me.

I'm going to Paris and Madrid around October. Until then, my warmest regards,
Buñuel

[PS] I read your interview in *Índice*.[4] Very interesting. Thank you.

Spa Tlsps, AG; *BREL* 24 f

[1]   Artist and photographer (born 1921), living in Paris from 1965 to 1992.
[2]   Asking LB if he would write an introduction to Gálvez's book of photographs, *Luis Buñuel* (Paris: Le Terrain Vague, 1970).
[3]   Photomontage by Galvés, alluding to the fantasy sequence where the Pope is shot in *The Milky Way*.
[4]   Journal founded in1945 and directed by Juan Fernández Figueroa from 1951 to 1976.

To Ernesto Laura[1]

Madrid [19 August 1969]

VERY GRATEFUL FOR YOUR KIND INVITATION.[2] IF I'M FREE, I WOULD BE DELIGHTED TO COME TO VENICE.

KIND REGARDS,
BUÑUEL

Spa Tel, BIE/256

[1]   Italian film critic (born 1932), director of the Venice Film Festival in 1969 and 1970.
[2]   Inviting LB to Venice to receive a lifetime achievement award, 18 August 1969 (AB/1418.1).

To Ernesto Laura

Mexico City, 29 August 1969

Dear Mr Laura,

First of all, I want to thank you for your very kind letter, which I found deeply moving. I thought I would be able to convey my thanks in person, but my plans to travel to Venice have changed, unfortunately.

I have been suffering for two days now from an unpleasant nervous tension that has had a particularly bad effect on my hearing. For the moment, I have lost almost all auditory function. The doctor says a few days of treatment should begin to correct this, relatively-speaking, that is, as I've had trouble with my hearing for some time now: under these conditions, it would be unwise of me to take on the meetings, conversations, interviews, etc., to which you have so kindly invited me. So, it is with sincere and deep regret that I find myself having to cancel my trip to Venice.

I have been in contact with Dolores del Río, who will be in Venice with Gaby Figueroa from 4 September, staying at the Gritti Palace,[1] and she will be kind enough to accept the award in my name.

I would be eternally grateful if you can forgive me this 'desertion', due solely to forces beyond my control.

With my thanks and best wishes,
Luis Buñuel

PS If by chance I were suddenly to feel better, I would catch the first flight to Venice, but not without sending you advance warning by telegram.

Fre Tls, BIE/256

[1]   Venetian hotel in Santa Maria del Giglio.

To Carlos Fuentes

Madrid, 8 September 1969

My dear Carlos,

You may well not believe this, but until yesterday, when I got back from Venice, I had not laid hands on your manuscript (*typuscript*[1]) and your letter.[2] Apart from any delay caused by the Mexican post, I was in Portugal[3] for ten days, and then a further five days in Venice. I won't be able to read it until tomorrow, when things calm down. So, briefly, being allergic to letter writing, I'm sending my first impressions. I'm really curious to see what you've made of an inverse adaptation, from a *scénario* to a short novel that is, and both by the same author.

Today, no less, we'll find out whether I'm banned from filming over here or not. So far, I've not been allowed to do any shooting, neither as a Spanish production nor a foreign one, not even with a provisional licence to film.[4]

I graciously declined an invitation to go to Venice to collect my trophy and they had to send that big Swiss pirate Beretta, who practically dragged me there by the ears. You were on my mind a lot in that wonderful city. I didn't see a single journalist and I didn't have to make a single public comment. I spent all my time with my sister at the Cipriani[5] and I only saw Muñoz Suay.

I was very sorry not to see you before I left Mexico, but I didn't know where to get your address in Cuernavaca. Not that I would have got there to see you, because when I'm in Mexico, I never leave Félix Cuevas.

Speak soon, by letter, a big hug,
Luis

Spa Tls, CF/93/17

[1] 'Typerito' in the original, neologism/contraction of the Spanish 'manuscrito mecanografiado'.
[2] Letter from Fuentes to LB, 9 August 1969 (CF/93/17), accompanying the original text of the short novel *Cumpleaños* that he wrote in Cuernavaca, based on the film script of *Birthdays*.
[3] In search of exterior locations for *Tristana*.
[4] *Tristana* received official permission after a closed meeting between LB and the Minister for Information and Tourism, Manuel Fraga Iribarne, sometime between July 1962 and October 1969.
[5] Harry's Bar.

Figure 71 Ducay, Buñuel, Zapata and Sabatello during production of *Tristana*, Toledo, 1969.

To Eduardo Ducay and Joaquín Gurruchaga

Madrid, 10 September 1969

Dear friends Joaquín and Eduardo,

I am inclined to honour my promise to make *Tristana*, but you should know that, if you insist, it will be with no great enthusiasm. I really don't think I can face the eleven or more weeks of filming, not counting the month and a bit for preparation. I never could, even when I was young. I'm always completely exhausted by the eighth week. Travelling all over the place, eating in different hotels, etc., are a surefire *K.O.*[1] for me.

In case you do decide not to go ahead with this adventure, I'm enclosing a cheque for $25,000 to cover what I've received so far of my total salary, a decision I take freely and of my own accord. I'm also prepared to offer Fernando Rey 100,000 pesetas and any other not too onerous payments in compensation.

Either way, I shall be here in Spain for a month or so, although I won't be working on the film. I would be grateful if you could send me your final decision today if at all possible. And if you do decide to go ahead, that you will accept any responsibility for what may happen.[2]

I am very grateful to you for your truly cordial and amicable behaviour towards me. And although my contract was with you, I extend these lines to Mr Zapata. I am equally grateful to him for everything.

Yours, most cordially,
Luis Buñuel

Spa Tls, ED

[1] Anglicism in the original (from 'knockout').
[2] *Tristana* filmed in Madrid and Toledo from 27 October 1969.

Figure 72 Buñuel and Rey during break in filming *Tristana*, Toledo, 1969.

To Jean-Claude Carrière

Madrid, 23 October 1969

My dear Jean-Claude,

I shall be delighted to see you with or without news.[1] Although, as you well know, when I'm filming, physical limitations and lack of energy make me quite incapable of doing anything not work-related. But I'll be at your service between takes. Thanks to my deafness, I have my lunch apart from the others, supper alone, then bed at 8:30.

I start filming this Monday. I'll be in Toledo for the whole of November, then in the studio for the whole of December.[2]

I have lots of things that I want to discuss with you too.

Pierre Lary is here, as well as Catherine Deneuve, and Truffaut, who'll be visiting her from time to time. They could stand in to keep you company, if you were missing me.

Hugs from me to Auguste and little Iris.

Yours,
Luis

Fre Als, JCC

[1] To filming of *Tristana*.
[2] Verona de Colmenar Viejo Studios.

To Jean-Claude Carrière

Madrid, 9 November 1969

My dear Jean-Claude,

Delighted the translation of *Tristana* is in your hands.[1] And even more so to be seeing you soon, although I would have preferred to meet when I finish. You know I'm a bit of a hermit when I'm filming: old-age! And we have so much to discuss.

Catherine, marvellously docile, charming, etc. Like a different woman.

My warmest regards,
Luis

[PS] I am *delighted* you like *Tristana*. Excuse this laconic note. My pen is sticking to the paper.

Fre Als, JCC

[1] Translation of script for dubbing into French.

From the students of the Madrid Escuela Oficial de Cine[1]

[Madrid, March 1970]

In light of your decision not to visit the EOC after reading the pamphlet 'Buñuel at the EOC',[2] we want to express our gratitude to you for taking that stance under the present circumstances. It goes a long way towards mitigating the references to and assumptions made about you in the aforesaid pamphlet.[3]

We had thought of reissuing you an invitation, this time in the name of all students at the EOC, rather than as an initiative 'handled' by Management, but we came to the conclusion that it would be better not to, given the sad situation in which the EOC currently finds itself.

At the moment, the School is run by a Lieutenant Colonel who is on active duty in the mornings and who functions as a censor and head-teacher in the afternoon.[4] We don't need to explain to you the significance of this, nor the blackly comic scenarios it produces ('Freedom of expression? Your speeches about freedom of expression make me laugh!'; 'Can't you make films about anything but sex, politics and religion?' and 'I'm neither authorizing nor banning your script.' etc., etc.). Other senior executives include the current 'Head of Practical Film-making', a Cuban exile; and the School Secretary, a man who takes daily communion, a hypocrite and a censor in his spare time, etc., etc.

The censorship we are subject to is even more harsh – if that were possible – than the official system outside the School, it would be an overstatement to describe our education as non-existent, while the bureaucracy is like the worst fantasies of Mihura.[5] All the casual labourers at the School were sacked recently as part of financial restructuring ordered by the Ministry of Finance,[6] which has, of course, robbed them of salaries they depended on to survive.

For this and many other reasons, we feel this is not an opportune moment for a person of your prestige and stature to be used to benefit the current management.

In light of the fact also that a very small number of students, led by people not attached to the EOC, has established itself as your 'exclusive' and 'altruistic' defence, sending you a letter of apology that the majority of students were not permitted to read or sign, for 'strange' and 'biased' reasons, we have found it opportune to send you this open letter on behalf of the entire student body to reiterate our sincere thanks.

[Unsigned]

PS As we have not had time to collect all the signatures, we would like you to know we are sending this letter now, and that it will be followed in a few days' time by another copy with the signatures of the majority of the student body.

Spa Tlu, AB/1402.21

1 The official government Instituto de Investigaciones y Experiencias Cinematográficas and film school created in 1947, and re-named the Escuela Oficial de Cine (EOC) from 1962 until it closed in 1976.
2 'Buñuel en la EOC. *Cella s'appelle…* la sumisión': pamphlet referencing LB's title *That is the Dawn*, distributed anonymously by a group of students at the EOC criticizing LB for filming *Tristana* in Spain while the Franco regime was still in power (AB/1402.22).

³ LB cancelled a visit to the EOC as a result of this pamphlet.
⁴ Possibly, Félix Martialay Martín-Sánchez (1925–2009), Falangist film critic, tutor at the Escuela Oficial de Periodismo.
⁵ Miguel Mihura Santos (1905–77), pro-Franco comic dramatist.
⁶ Occupied by the economist Alberto Monreal Luque from 1969 to 1973.

From César Santos Fontenla[1]

Madrid, 11 March 1970

Dear friend,

This morning I finally got to see a copy of the famous 'paperlet'[2] about the Film School I first heard about last Sunday morning. No need to say how deranged and deplorable it all seems to me. The 'reply'[3] is very good, as long as it's not just some silly game cooked up by some other 'anonymous' source. It's high time this infantile nonsense stopped. Whatever happens, all the friends I've discussed this with are on your side and prepared to state that in public.

Warmest regards and deepest admiration.
Santos

PS I'm still waiting for you to offer me a role as Head Esquire of Hare Gobblers. Even if it's a non-speaking, purely cosmetic part, of course! Hope to see you soon.

Spa Als, AB/1402.23

¹ Film critic (1931–2001), who contributed to the Spanish journals *Cinema universitario, Nuestro Cine* and *Triunfo* author of *Luis Buñuel: es peligroso asomarse al interior* (Madrid: Jaguar, 2000), with prologue by Francisco Rabal.
² 'Papela' in the original, neologism made up of 'papel' (paper) and the final 'a' of 'panfleta' (pamphlet), the EOC pamphlet condemning LB.
³ See (above) letter from students of the EOC to LB.

From Catherine Deneuve

Paris, 21 March [1970]

My dear *don* Luis,

I found it impossible to express my feelings about *Tristana* to you the other day; everything prevented me, the airport, the people, the surprise of bumping into you there; and the fact your letter had already made me so very happy.

I understood and appreciated what a powerful story it was from the first day of filming and from start to finish was never disappointed; what's more, my first viewing of the film has left me astounded. Your vision has given Don Lope and Tristana a depth and truth I've rarely encountered. I watched, every day, how precisely you directed

Fernando, your attention and precision. It was so impressive, and I have now seen it all reflected in the film.

I have to do the French dubbing in a week's time, and I shall strive to do my very best, because, in spite of everything, it is still frustrating to hear someone else speak my lines.[1] Although I was prepared, it was still something of a shock. I know that for you the Spanish version IS the film, but I hope the French version won't disappoint you, should you see it someday.

Jean-Claude Carrière will be supervising the text; I think he is close enough to you to convey the real sense of the Spanish.

I shall finish here, my dear *Don* Luis. I enjoyed watching the film even more than making it, and I am happy and proud to have worked with you again. Until soon, perhaps.

Cordially,
Catherine

Fre Als L, AB/636.1

---

[1] Deneuve was dubbed in the Spanish version of the film premiered at the Amaya Cinema, Madrid, 29 March 1970.

From Carlo Ponti[1]

Rome, 21 April 1970

DEAR MR BUÑUEL,
I AM NEGOTIATING WITH FRANCISCO GARCIA LORCA ACQUISITION RIGHTS TO LA CASA DE BERNARDA ALBA OF WHICH I INTEND PRODUCING PICTURE AND WOULD APPRECIATE YOUR ADVISING ME WHETHER YOU WOULD BE INTERESTED AND AVAILABLE DIRECT SAID PICTURE. PLEASE CABLE ME AT FOLLOWING ADDRESS: CHAMPION ROMA, ALSO GIVING ME YOUR TELEPHONE NUMBER.

BEST REGARDS,
CARLO PONTI

Eng Tel, AB/647.1

---

[1] Italian producer (1912–2007).

To Eduardo Ducay

Mexico City, 29 April 1970

Dear Eduardo,
Many thanks for all the cuttings.[1] They've given me a good idea of what's going on with the film in Spain. And your updates about the response from the audience completed the report. I'm very happy for you. You had more faith in the outcome than

I did. I thought, and I still do, that such a 'disagreeable' film would never be a success. It's a mystery.

I loved Begoña Ducay's drawing.[2] Such a shame to give a Basque name to such a lovely little girl. But the name does not the woman make, and I hope and trust her Aragonese blood will overcome that folly.[3] Send her kisses from me. I remember seeing her at the studio, but I didn't realize she'd seen me filming. Her drawing is better than a work photo and I'm going to keep it.[4]

I finally heard, first from Favre Le Bret and then from you, about the solution to screening the film at Cannes.[5] So, everything is sorted out and infamy will not be mine. When you write, could you tell me about that Cannes-ian screening? Will it be the Spanish copy?[6] Who did the French subtitles? If they're not done well, it could ruin the film. It's very presumptuous of Catherine, given the small percentage her character has of the dialogue, to have wanted the ENTIRE film dubbed into French.

I'm still completely *dolce far niente* over here, and ready to remain so until the end of days.

My warm regards to the wonderful Joaquín. And most affectionate greetings to Mercedes.

More warm regards for you,
Buñuel

[PS] Are either of you going to Cannes? We could at least try to get them to give *Tristana* the Luis Buñuel prize.[7] Speak to Muñoz Suay, he has clout.

Spa Tlsps, ED

[1] Held in ABR/2043.
[2] Daughter of Eduardo Ducay, who drew LB as he was directing *Tristana*.
[3] Both LB and Ducay are from Aragon, northern Spain.
[4] Held in ABR/2043.
[5] *Tristana* screened out of competition at the Cannes Film Festival on 4 May 1970.
[6] Copy screened at Cannes in Spanish with subtitles.
[7] Prize created by Suay and awarded at both the Cannes and Venice Film Festivals from 1965.

From Juan Luis Buñuel

Paris, 29 April 1970

Dear both,

We went to see *Tristana* last night. Invitees: Jean Gabin, Coco Chanel… and Salvador Dalí, who came in with his moustache, Gala, and a very pretty girl. *Tout Paris*[1] was there. Silberman, Lary, Novais, and Jean-Claude too… The Barcelona copy was bad; you can see everything much better now and the sound is perfect. The dubbing we were concerned about was fine after the first five minutes. Rey was well dubbed. The audience laughed a lot, there was some frightened screaming at Rey's head,[2] and at the end (the death of Don Lope) there were a lot of 'Oh, nos'.

Lots of applause at the end. Great excitement and lots of comments.

Gabin: 'I liked it, but I would have cut the scene with the false leg on the bed'.[3] Everyone says it's a miracle Gabin came, because he never goes out.

Dalí. A journalist asked him: 'What do you think of the film, Monsieur Dalí?' Dalí: 'Buñuel likes Toledo a lot.'

Jean-Claude and Novais were very happy. They liked it a lot. Everyone is saying it's Deneuve's best work. It's true, she's amazing. Novais says it's better than *The Milky Way*.

Silberman, a bit envious. I liked it better the second time, except the scene with Tristana and Nero and her confession.

But I think the dubbing works well. And that's what everyone was worried about. Once you get used to it …

In short, it was a success and there was much applause. Old Lotte Eisner[4] from the Cinémathèque hugged me and told me that the film was 'brilliant, as always'. I don't think she understood a word.

Well, that's all for now. I'll write again from Cannes.[5]

Hugs,
Juan Luis

PS René Solís called me this morning from Mexico to congratulate me on my PECIME prize for *Chontalpa*.[6] He must be mad or drunk to call me from Mexico for that.

Spa Als, AB/1383.6

[1] French in the original.
[2] Sequence (Tristana's fantasy) with don Lope's severed head hanging from the church bell tower.
[3] Tristana's prosthesis, after one of her legs is amputated due to a tumour.
[4] Franco-German film historian (1896–1983), who worked at the Cinémathèque française.
[5] Letter sent by J. L. Buñuel to LB from Cannes, 6 May 1970 (AB/1526.1–2).
[6] *Plan Chontalpa* (1969), documentary short by Demetrio Bilbatua, produced by Juan Luis Buñuel in Mexico.

To Jean-Claude Carrière

Mexico City, 5 May 1970

My dear Jean-Claude,

I was so excited to get your letter,[1] especially after our long silence since the last time I saw you in Paris, in January.

You are always the first person to write to me after the screening of one of my 'modest' films in Paris. Your letter was a very good and comprehensive critical-review of *Tristana*. I only wonder whether your extraordinary sense of friendship urges you towards an overly sentimental and subjective critique. There is one thing in your critique I absolutely refuse to accept. You say that the only thing about the film that puzzled you, and that you maybe didn't like, was the 'retrocurrent' ending.[2] This is

PRECISELY the best bit of the entire film. So much the worse for you. One day you'll come to appreciate the philosophical depth of that sublime conclusion.

I was very amused by Iris's *Triste-Ana*.[3] Give her a kiss from me. And another to my favourite actress, her mother.

I would love to see you again. I really miss your company and working with you. I have wonderful memories of those long work sessions we've shared for a good few years now. Come over with Silberman. Who knows, perhaps we could start again. Tell Serge, first of all, to send me *The Plumed Serpent*.[4] I also sometimes wonder about a film all about the PLAGUE. But an original one. Not Defoe, or Giono, or Camus, etc. It could be called THE FEAR that destroys all human bonds, positive emotions, even love, perhaps. But for the moment it's just a few very vague ideas.

If I don't go ahead with the latest film, I'll come to Europe in October and will go at once to see you act in your film.[5] I'm so curious. The book was good, and from what you tell me the film is too. When is the premiere?[6]

Warmest regards,
Luis

[PS] Could you please phone Dorfman[7] – I don't know his address – and ask him to send some reviews of the film so I can get a sense of *the ambiance*. Thanks in advance.

Fre Tlsps, JCC

[1]   Letter from Carrière to LB, 29 April [1970] (AB/646.12).
[2]   Not clear whether the neologism 'retrocurrent' is LB's or Carriere's, but the film ends with a flashback through various key moments to the beginning of the film.
[3]   Triste-Ana (Sad-Ana), a play on Tristana's name.
[4]   *The Plumed Serpent*, D. H. Lawrence (London: Secker, 1926), set in Mexico.
[5]   *L'Alliance* (1971), dir. Christian de Chalonge, based on a co-adaptacion by Carrière of the novel by the same name published in 1962, and in which he plays Hughes.
[6]   *L'Alliance* premiered in Paris on 15 January 1971.
[7]   Robert Dorfman (1912–99), French producer, co-producer of *Tristana* with Época Films.

From Fernando Rey

Cannes, 6 May [1970]

Dear Luis,

I should have written this letter from Madrid with more time, but I can't resist the temptation to send a few lines to let you know *what happened* last night with *Tristana*. As you know, the film premiered in Paris to *very good* reviews. But the 11am screening yesterday was far more successful than the one in the capital. The critics who saw the French version are now saying the Spanish version is far better and that it's a shame that one wasn't used for the premiere. The evening show was just as successful. A very important Swedish critic told me it's your best film, and he's seen it twice. That's the general view of the critics. So, I can honestly say that once again, *and quite rightly,* that you've triumphed at the Festival.

The press conference that only your son Juan Luis and I attended was very interesting and incredibly busy. Everything was made *very clear* and it was very interesting.

If it's been a resounding success in Spain, as you will know it has by now, the response in France and at Cannes has surpassed all expectations in my view, even without taking the effect of your name into account. Your friend, Miguel Ángel Asturias, has also been to see it twice, the two different versions, and is really impressed. Last night (*and this is important*) Juan Luis and I spoke to the buyers for South America and Mexico and they told us the distributors, including the Mexican one, Borges[1] (I think), have asked for THE FRENCH VERSION! It's insane! Juan Luis and I don't understand it. What can we do? It *makes no sense*!

I'm going to Madrid tomorrow, I'm 'between jobs', but hoping the future will sort itself out. I've gone down well with the public. I'll write from Spain.

A hug from your grateful FRIEND,
Fernando
Hotel Martínez

[1] Hiram García Borja, then Mexican Director General of Film.

Spa Als L, AB/632.26

From Louis Malle

[Paris, May 1970]

Dear Luis,

Please don't be too annoyed by this fan letter: I saw *Tristana* last night and was moved. Your friends don't really know how to describe it: it is at once gentle and ferocious, brilliant and indifferent, pessimistic and generous, iconic and rebellious, with a deep overall sense of ambiguity and contradiction. I came out of the cinema exhausted and excited, with no strength nor desire to examine my emotions. I don't know what to think of the characters, except that they are among the most alive, the most authentic I've seen in cinema. Forgive me: your film is unforgettable without presuming, without forcing the tone. The location, the era, the social milieu it describes … but I also think it's one of your most intimate, most personal films. The audience is left bemused (and how much so!) by the film's sobriety, by the dry narrative and the ellipses (which are wonderful!). You felt they wanted the answers to the sequential enigmas that make up the film; they need to be told: there is nothing to explain here! The reviewers have not understood it either: they are eulogies, but banal ones with the usual clichés, except a few (like the one by Astruc[1] in this week's *Paris Match*). Now that you've gone back to being a cursed film-maker, I hope you will be back at work again soon.

Very fond regards,
Louis Malle
22 rue d'Artois

PS It's also one of your funniest films!

Fre Als, AB/609

¹ Alexandre Astruc (1923–2016), French critic and film-maker.

To Jean-Claude Carrière

Mexico City, 29 May 1970

My dear Jean-Claude,
    Do whatever you like with the publication of *The Monk*.¹ I only hope that by the end
of the script it's clear that Ambrosio is the Anti-Pope. I'm sure you'll appreciate that my
reason for not going ahead with the film, or at least the main reason, is genuine panic
at the thought of all the special effects.
    I shall be delighted to see you over here with the great Serge, that formidable
Parisian producer. But I should warn you that flights, particularly returns to Paris, will
be very difficult to come by. And accommodation here, the same. You could stay with
me, despite the absolute lack of any real comfort at my lovely home. At the moment,
we have no domestic help, although that will be sorted out by then. Give me a week's
notice. I'll look for a hotel, and if I don't find anything, you can stay with me. Down
with football!²
    Louis Malle sent me a letter I found very touching. I may well write back. In the
meantime, send him my warmest regards.
    The success of *Tristana* in Spain has been extraordinary. The censors have not cut
anything. People are even starting to say I've been recuperated by the *establishment*.³
I've even, like *Don* Lope, got a few friends who are priests. I may have to make it clear
that I'm still the man I always have been, *mordieu!*⁴
    When am I going to get to see *L'Alliance*, where you are everything script-writer,
adaptor, author, actor, etc., etc.? I'm intending to get to Europe in October whatever
happens. You can imagine how keen I am to see that film.
    As for the film about the plague, I've given it no more thought. It was just a whim
after a few *dry martinis*.⁵

Warmest regards,
Luis

[PS] Dorfman has sent me some articles. My *flashback*⁶ in *Tristana* was also a whim.

Fre Tlsps, JCC

[1] Script published as L. Buñuel and J. C. Carrière, *Le Moine* (Paris: Éric Losfeld, 1971).
[2] Allusion to the Football World Cup, held in Mexico between 31 May and 21 June 1970.
[3] English in the original.
[4] Medieval French in the original (my God).
[5] English in the original.
[6] English in the original.

To Eduardo Ducay

Mexico City, 28 May 1970

Dear Eduardo,

I got your letter with some very tasteful articles on the film compiled by *Cuadernos para el Diálogo*,[1] which I've never read. What annoys me most – and it's not just them – is that they think my aim in *Tristana* was to 'criticize 19th-century Spanish liberalism'.[2] Talk about politically tone-deaf! I couldn't give a damn about that. And if I've given up scandal, for which they reprimand me, facile and direct scandal, it's because I don't find that kind of subversion useful now. The article seems completely reactionary to me. I'm an abomination when I cause a scandal, and when I don't, I've sold out to the *establishment*.

I'd be delighted if you could visit, but I must warn you that you'll have difficulty finding flights and accommodation, because of the World Cup. If you do decide to come over, my advice would be to wait until after 1 July and, whatever you do decide, to let me know in advance.

Looking at the books you've suggested for adaptation, the only one I might be interested in is *Crónica del Alba*,[3] I've not read the first volume though, because I bought the second and third volumes in Madrid, but they didn't have the one you recommend. I'll see if I can get it over here.

I am still blissfully happy watching the days go by, completely idle. I do read a lot though – I know excessive reading is more dangerous than any drug – looking serenely for something I might adapt. Nothing has clicked yet.

That's all for now. Warmest regards,
Luis

[PS] I'm still waiting for the letter Joaquín promised me at the end of your last letter.

Spa Tls, ED

[1] Including M. Bilbatúa, 'Tristana', *Cuadernos para el Diálogo*, no. 79 (April 1970), pp. 47–48.
[2] According to Bilbatúa, *Tristana* symbolizes 'the failure of our bourgeoisie to bring about a revolution' (p. 48).
[3] A series of nine novels by Ramón J. Sender, published in Mexico and the United States between 1942 and 1965; LB seems to be referring to the three-volume edition published in Barcelona by Aymá in 1965.

To Louis Malle

Mexico City, 4 June 1970

My dear Louis,

Your letter left me confused, stupefied and, I have to admit, moved … and grateful. I didn't think you would like *Tristana*. The only real satisfaction I get in the end, from making a film, is if my friends enjoy it. I've kept your letter as a wonderful memory of 'my career', which is, I really think this time, coming to an end. Although I would like to end it with a good *churro*.[1] But, for the moment I have no good ideas, or any real desire to work, despite the *dry martinis*[2] I drink every day for inspiration.

Jean-Claude, our new leading-lady, writes often and keeps me informed about you all. I think he may even pay a visit with an ultra-commercial producer known as 'the man in silver' (Silverman[3]). They'll almost certainly return to Paris without me. But I'm thinking of going to Madrid and Paris in October for three or four months. That will be the time to visit your mansion[4] and chat at length in front of a roaring fire of twelfth-century logs, raising an enormous glass of Hippocras (Picon-lemon-beer).[5]

Warmest regards,
Luis

Fre Tls, LMA/1960/B232

[1] 'Churro', used commonly for films in Mexico to mean a 'flop', the opposite of what Aranda describes as LB's 'anti-churros'.
[2] English in the original.
[3] Spanish in the original ('hombre de plata'), play on the English translation of Serge Silberman's surname.
[4] Malle bought a sixteenth-century castle near Cahors, France in 1968.
[5] Drink made with wine, sugar and cinnamon, or with other ingredients including beer or Picon bitter.

To Dalton Trumbo

Dalton Trumbo
8710 St Ives Drive
Los Angeles, California

Mexico City, 5 July 1970

I KNOW YOU ARE SHOOTING NOW JOHNNY GOT HIS GUN,[1] *THE MOST MOVING BOOK EVER WRITTEN. I VIOLENTLY WISH THE FILM CAN BE AS GOOD AS THE SUBJECT DESERVES AGAIN.*

BEST WISHES,
BUÑUEL

Eng Tel, DT/72/05

[1] Trumbo began filming *Johnny got his Gun* in California, Summer 1970.

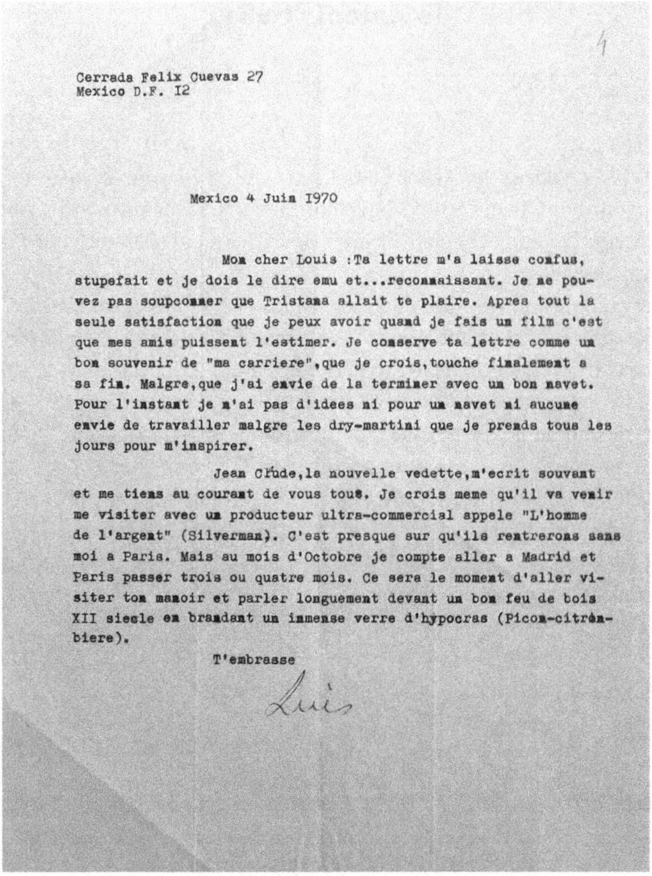

Figure 73 Letter from Buñuel to Malle, 4 June 1970.

From Dalton Trumbo

Los Angeles, 7 July 1970

DEAR LUIS,
I WILL NEVER BE ABLE TO DO JOHNNY AS WELL AS YOU WOULD HAVE
DONE IT, BUT YOUR GOOD WISHES WILL HELP ME MORE THAN YOU'LL
EVER KNOW.

SALUD,[1]
DALTON

Eng Tel C, DT/72/05

---

[1]   Spanish in the original.

To Antonio Gálvez

Mexico City, 7 July 1970

My dear Gálvez,

A *thousand apologies* for the fact that, according to your editor,[1] the delay in publishing your book is my fault. I have not the faintest idea what to write. A poem about the breeze stroking the hair of my beloved? An essay about you? I'm an anti-essayist born and bred.

Ramblings about contemporary politics? Or how about Marcuse?[2] Absurd. A serious and sensible discussion of photography as a form of artistic expression? Horrific. Etc. So, what then? If I were one of those writers who can describe an ant so it sounds like a cathedral, I would send you my lucubrations[3] at once, but sadly I'm not.

I think you should go ahead and publish without my contribution. If, and I'm not making any promises here, something worthy of the book should occur to me (Oh sweet miracle!) in the next week or next three months, I would rush to send it to you. Seriously.

Warmest regards from your friend,
Luis Buñuel

PS Mr Losfeld can publish this letter for you, if he dares.[4]

Spa Tlsps, AG; *BREL* 25 f

[1] Éric Losfeld.
[2] Herbert Marcuse (1898–1979), US-German philosopher popular with students in the 1960s.
[3] 'Lucubraciones' in the original: archaic term for pedantic writing.
[4] Published in translation as the preface to Gálvez's book *Luis Buñuel*.

To José Francisco Aranda

Mexico City, 22 July 1970

My dear Aranda,

What alarmed me, reading your letter, was that you don't have the copies of Unamuno's letters.[1] I'm sure that when I left Madrid, I either sent them to you or left them for Conchita to give to you. In fact, I remember telling her not to publish them for reasons it would take too long to explain. I suppose this loss, if loss it is, is not so important though, because they were photocopies, weren't they? Keep me posted.

I am so happy *for you* that your book[2] has been a success and that they want to translate it.[3] Two or three more have come out since, one of which is longer and in Japanese.[4] Olé!

I'm leaving for a ten-day holiday tomorrow, if you can call it that for someone on perpetual holiday. When I get back, I'll send you a couple of splendid photos by Mary

Ellen,[5] a famous Yankee photographer. And for my 'ingenious' caption, you could use the statement 'issued' in *The Milky Way*: 'My hatred for science and horror of technology may one day move me closer to that absurd belief in God'.[6]

Warm regards from your biographical subject,
Luis

[PS] Over and above and in spite of the ineffable Leyda, I think my excrplay[7] on Goya is utter rubbish.

Spa Tls, ARA/09/07-4

[1] Letters that Aranda gave to LB in the hope he might publish them in Mexico.
[2] *Luis Buñuel: Biografía crítica*.
[3] Aranda's biography of LB was published in English in 1975 and in Dutch in 1977.
[4] Possible reference to the translation of Kyrou's book published by Sanichi Shobo in Tokyo in 1970.
[5] Mary Ellen Mark (1940–2015), US photographer, attends the filming of *Tristana*; also photographed LB at home in Mexico in 1971.
[6] Comment from one of the characters in *The Milky Way*.
[7] 'Excreargumento' in the Spanish original, combining 'excrement' with 'argumento' (plot/screenplay).

To Eduardo Ducay

Mexico City, 2 October 1970

Dear Eduardo,

Thank-you for your congratulations *about Tristana*,[1] which I warmly return to you, its distinguished producers. I suppose you will have seen the articles in *The New York Times*,[2] for which I shall now transfer the $5,000 I promised. They don't say a word about Deneuve; I wasn't going to pay for her publicity too. I'll have no one outshine me.

The Filmófono films are flammable, because at that time I don't think there was any inflammable material.[3] Anyway, they're there if there's any chance of shipping them.

I leave for New York on the 8th. I'll be spending two whole days there visiting my son. Then on the 12th, Columbus Day,[4] I'll be in Madrid, but I'm not sure what time so I'll see you at the Torre de Madrid rather than the airport. We could have supper that day or the day after, although I would prefer lunch to supper if we do it on the 13th. Leave a message for me at the Torre. I'd be grateful if you don't tell anyone I'm coming.

L'Avant-Scène have asked for the script of *Tristana* but I don't have one. Do you have any left?[5]

In the end, Juan Luis's deal with United Artists fell through. But Paramount have offered him a $5,000 option until December. It seems Bulgaria are interested in a co-production. And so time moves on.

Warm regards,
Luis

Spa Tls, ED

1. English in the original; *Tristana* premiered at the New York Film Festival on 20 September 1970.
2. Vincent Canby's review of *Tristana*, *The New York Times*, 21 September 1970 (the reference to $5,000 is, of course, a joke.)
3. Cellulose acetate film began to be used instead of flammable nitrocellulose from the late 1940s onwards.
4. Columbus Day or, as LB calls it in the original, 'día de la raza' (Day of the Race), national holiday to celebrate the arrival of Columbus in America in 1492.
5. French script of *Tristana* published in *L'Avant-Scène Cinéma*, no. 110 (January 1971).

To Serge Silberman

Madrid, 16 December 1970

My dear Serge,

Thank you for your telegram and letter. Would you like to have lunch with me next Tuesday, the 22nd? If so, I'll come to your office at 12:30. If not, leave a message at the Aiglon about when we should meet.

Best wishes,
Buñuel

PS My decision not to work again is irrevocable. Down with *The Discreet Charm of the Bourgeiosie!*[1]

Fre Ans, RS

1. LB and Carrière co-wrote the first version of the script for *The Discreet Charm* between October and December 1970.

9

'A lot of dynamite in here...' (1970–8)

From Robert [Benayoun]

Paris, 29 December 1970

My dear Luis,

I have just finished reading *The Discreet Charm of the Bourgeoisie*. It's a very poised and provocative *scénario*, and the narrative development reminded me of some books by Chesterton,[1] where the very story itself is called into question. The bishop is wonderful. You and Jean-Claude clearly take great delight in surprising one another. As always with your work, I laughed a lot at the humour, but here the depiction of the characters is also very serious. I think it's one of the most challenging scripts you've come up with since *The Golden Age* and *The Exterminating Angel*, and in such a deceptively serene way. There's a lot of dynamite in here. It's magnificent.

To sum up, I really hope that one day you will really want to make it.

Very affectionate greetings, until we meet again,
Robert

Fre Als, AB/1402.18

[1]   G. K. Chesterton (1874–1936), English writer.

To Max Aub

Madrid, 13 January 1971

Dear Max,

I normally receive, and greet, your laconic missives in respectful silence. But I'm breaking that silence this time, even though I'll be back in Mexico by the end of the month.

I have a copy of the Buñuelesque Album.[1] Not very well printed by that crazy Losfeld and ditto Gálvez. I think they are going to improve on that. But either way, too much Buñuel.

Enough!

I've arranged for someone to take photographs of the countryside near Calanda. Although I don't think they'll get here before I leave.

I've heroically resisted signing any contracts. In spite of having written (well, Carrière has written) the most intimate and funny script I think I've ever come up with. Silberman wanted to start filming at the end of March. I said no. I prefer writing scripts to filming them. This one's called *The Discreet Charm of the Bourgeoisie*. As for Ripstein's project with *Deseada*,[2] we'll discuss it, but I doubt I'll accept. I think I'm definitely, sincerely, intending to retire. I would have to be very bored to return to my old ways.

My warm regards to your patient and splendid wife. Likewise, to you,
Luis

[PS] What was it you found in *The Brute*? It can't have been that much of a revelation.

Spa Tlsps, MA/15/11

[1]   *Luis Buñuel*, by Gálvez.
[2]   Aub mentions in a letter to LB of 4 January 1971 that the Mexican producer Alfredo Ripstein (1916–2007) has proposed a film version of Max Aub's play *Deseada* (Mexico City: Tezontle, 1950), to be adapted by Julio Alejandro and directed by LB (MA/15/10).

To José Donoso

Madrid, 27 January 1971

Dear Donoso,

I only started reading *El obsceno pájaro de la noche*[1] ten days ago because I've been travelling non-stop the last few weeks. I finished it two days ago.

I think it's exceptional; a masterpiece. I'm really impressed. I can't stop thinking about the mute boy, Mother Benita, or Peta Ponce.[2] The savage atmosphere, the obsessive reiteration, the changing characters, the 'purely surrealist' narrative, irrational associations, immense creative freedom and disdain for the distinction between good and evil, beauty and ugliness, etc., etc., left me flabbergasted.

I'm flying to Mexico this afternoon, so I'll have to stop 'cogitating'. Most enthusiastic regards,
[Luis Buñuel]

[PS] Carlos Fuentes and Barbachano have wired saying they want to make *El lugar sin límites* with me in Mexico. I think I've retired from film-making, but I won't say anything until I've spoken to them. It's all Carlos's idea.

Warmest regards to your wife – whom I found extraordinarily charming – and likewise to you,
Luis Buñuel

Spa Als, JD/64/06

[1]   J. Donoso, *El obsceno pájaro de la noche* (Barcelona: Seix Barral, 1970).
[2]   Characters in the novel.

To Pierre Braunberger

Mexico City, 20 February 1971

My dear Pierre,

I lost our contract after signing it.[1] I thought I had the US and Mexican film clubs. Reading the copy of the contract you sent me, I see I was mistaken.

So, I owe you $1,000. That's the amount Anthology Cinema in the United States paid a few months ago for the film.

As soon as it arrived, I sent the money straight on to Ramón Acín's daughters: he was, as you know, the real producer of the film. In fact, that's what I've done with all the money you've sent me from commercial screenings of the film.

I got the same amount for that sale – and the film can only be screened at Anthology – as I got from you for the global rights to the film. I think I deserve a commission.

I'm such a fine businessman: this deal will cost me $2,000. So be it.

If I go to Paris in Spring, I can pay you back in person. Otherwise, I'll send you the money.

Looking forward to hearing from you. Cordially,
Luis Buñuel

PS I'm not making any more films. 71 years old the day after tomorrow.

Fre Tlsps, PB

[1]   For distribution rights to *Land Without Bread*.

To Eduardo Ducay

Mexico City, 1 March 1971

Dear Eduardo,

I was passing the Diplomático[1] recently and thought: 'It's such a pity my two henchmen aren't staying in there, so I could invite them to lunch.' And I am now, with great pleasure, taking the leap from that thought to these few lines.

More or less a month ago, I accepted an invitation to join the American Academy of Motion Picture Arts and Sciences.[2] I also thought: 'When I'm a member I'll be out of the whole Oscar thing.' I was wrong.[3]

This is the nomination: 'Award for Best Foreign Language Film, *Tristana* (Spain). Production by Forbes Films Ltd, United Cineworld, Época Films, Talia Film SA, Les Films Corona and Selenia Cinematografica.'[4]

My name isn't on it, so I won't be needing to make a public protest if the wretched little statue does go to that film. I won't be attending the ceremony, of course.[5] But as the trophy might be useful to you, I'm letting you know so that if need be, you can send an Época representative to Hollywood. Perhaps Fernando Rey? Or Sabatello might well be up for it!

Over here, there's a real renaissance in Mexico's frail film industry. New production companies and young directors turning up en masse. The government is promoting film. I've had some offers, but I'm staying out of it. Keeping up my mind-numbing *dolce far niente*.[6] For how long? *Chi lo sa*.[7]

Warmest regards and greetings to Mercedes. More likewise, to you and Joaquín,
Luis

Spa Tls, ED

1. Hotel Diplomático on Insurgentes Sur, near LB's house where Ducay and Gurruchaga stayed on their first visit to Mexico City.
2. US Academy responsible for Oscar awards founded in Los Angeles in 1927.
3. *Tristana* nominated for 'Best Foreign Language Film' in 1971.
4. Companies involved in the film's international production and distribution.
5. Held in Los Angeles, 15 April 1971.
6. Italian in the original ('doing [sweet] nothing' or 'living in the moment').
7. Italian in the original (Who knows?).

To Eduardo Ducay

Época Films
79 Princesa, Madrid 8

Mexico City, 6 March 1971

Dear Eduardo,
 A telegram has just arrived from Hollywood that I am transcribing for you here:

CONGRATULATIONS. YOUR FILM *TRISTANA* IS AMONG THE FIVE NOMINEES FOR THE BEST FOREIGN LANGUAGE FILM AWARD. THE ACADEMY HAS RESERVED FLIGHTS AND ACCOMMODATION FOR A REPRESENTATIVE OF THE FILM TO ATTEND THE CEREMONY AND THE GOVERNOR'S BALL AS A GUEST OF THE ACADEMY. SINCERELY HOPE YOU WILL BE ABLE TO ATTEND. VERY INTERESTING PROGRAM OF EVENTS DEVISED FOR OUR FOREIGN VISITORS. ARRIVAL IN LOS ANGELES 12 APRIL. RETURN FLIGHT FRIDAY 16. WE REGRET THAT THE ACADEMY CAN COVER FLIGHTS AND ACCOMMODATION FOR ONE REPRESENTATIVE FOR EACH FOREIGN LANGUAGE FILM ONLY. SHOULD YOUR COMPANY WISH TO DO SO, THEY ARE WELCOME TO FUND COST OF ADDITIONAL GUESTS. LET US KNOW AND WE WILL RESERVE ROOMS AND SEATS ON THE SAME FLIGHT AS YOUR OWN. TICKET WILL ARRIVE BY AIRMAIL. PLEASE WIRE IMMEDIATELY IF YOU ARE ABLE TO ATTEND. ADDRESS: AMPASHOLLY (HOLLYWOOD, CALIFORNIA). BEST WISHES.

Signed: Daniel Taradash,[1] President of the Motion Pictures Academy. I sent back the following:

VERY GRATEFUL FOR YOUR KIND INVITATION TO ATTEND THE ACADEMY
AWARDS. SORRY I AM UNABLE TO ACCEPT, AS *RELUCTANT*[2] TO TAKE PART
IN ANY FORM OF PUBLIC CELEBRATION. I WILL CONTACT ÉPOCA FILMS TO
SEE IF THEY CAN SEND A REPRESENTATIVE AND, IF POSSIBLE, *TRISTANA*'S
LEADING MAN, FERNANDO REY.[3] THANKS AGAIN.
BEST WISHES,[4] LUIS BUÑUEL.

Your decision.
Regards,
Luis

Spa Tls, ED

[1]   US scriptwriter (1913–2003), and President of the Academy from 1970 to 1973.
[2]   English in the original.
[3]   Rey attended in place of LB.
[4]   English in the original.

To José Rubia Barcia

Mexico City, 27 March 1971

My dear Don Pepe,
    I didn't answer to your extremely kind and friendly letter,[1] because until yesterday I
couldn't decide whether to come to the city with the sole purpose of visiting you. Today,
finally, I've decided to postpone our meeting for a few more months perhaps. There are
a number of reasons for this, and some may well be influenced by my extreme aversion
to travel. I also, very reluctantly, have to travel to France in a month's time thanks to
an almighty mix-up with the French Tax Office. As the Cannes Festival is funding my
trip, I'll take the opportunity to meet with one of my production company's lawyers
and let him sort out that irritating business. Of course, when I come and see you, it
will be by plane; road or rail is out of the question. As for Jeanne, you won't see her
by any of these methods, unless you should take one of them to come to spend your
holidays with us.
    My travel plans – once I'd made up my mind to go – took me to the US Consulate
where I found tourists gathered in their dozens. I asked to see the consul, but after two
hours waiting, I left cursing him, *inwardly*, of course. I can't stand waiting-rooms, not
even to see a doctor. As a Member of the Academy of Motion Pictures, Arts and Sciences,
and as *Tristana* has been nominated for one of those despicable little statues this year,
and as I have an official all-expenses-paid invite to the odious Oscars, I'd intended to use
those arguments – albeit with some shame – for the appointed son of consul so-and-so.
As I left the Consulate, I saved myself the humiliation. No need to tell you I'd never have
dreamt of attending that cinematic calamity, of course, *vanitas vanitatum*.[2]
    Dear Evita and Don Pepe, we must meet up this year without fail. A big hug for you
both, but not for your daughters because it would probably annoy their boyfriends.

Luis

[PS] A few months ago, Mexican television wanted to buy the story you and I wrote in your city. I haven't heard from them since.

Spa Tlsps, CBC; *CLB* 96–97

¹   Letter from Rubia to LB, 1 March 1971 (AB/572.56), inviting him to Los Angeles.
²   From the phrase: 'Vanitas vanitatum dixit Ecclesiastes omnia vanitas' (vanity of vanities says the Preacher, all is vanity), Old Testament, Book of Ecclesiastes (1:2).

From Dalton Trumbo

Beverly Hills, 31 March 1971

DEAR LUIS,
  I TOOK JOHNNY GOT HIS GUN *TO PARIS WHERE IT WAS UNANIMOUSLY ACCEPTED FOR CRITICS WEEK. FAVRE LE BRET SAID IT WAS POWERFUL BUT NOT THE KIND OF FILM HE THOUGHT PEOPLE WOULD WANT TO SEE IN THE FESTIVAL.¹ SEVERAL PEOPLE IN EUROPE ARE URGING HIM TO RECONSIDER AND ALLOW IT TO ENTER IN COMPETITION. I AM TOLD THE DEADLINE FOR ENTRANCE IS 48 HOURS HENCE. IF YOU CAN FIND AN HONORABLE WAY TO CABLE HIM ABOUT ACCEPTING THE FILM BEFORE YOU HAVE SEEN IT, I AM TOLD IT WOULD HELP US GREATLY. IF NOT, I UNDERSTAND. IN THE MEANWHILE, YOU WILL SEE IT THE FIRST OF THE WEEK.*

SALUD²,
DALTON

Eng Tel, AB/638.1; *JGG* 16 f

¹   24th Cannes Festival, 12 to 27 May 1971.
²   Spanish in the original.

To Robert Favre Le Bret

Mexico City, 6 April 1971

DEAR FRIEND,
  MAY I DRAW YOUR ATTENTION TO DALTON TRUMBO'S TENDER AND HEARTBREAKING FILM *JOHNNY GOT HIS GUN*. WOULD IT BE POSSIBLE TO SHOW IT AT THE FESTIVAL? PEOPLE SHOULD SEE THIS WONDERFUL, IMPORTANT CONTEMPORARY FILM.

SEE YOU SOON, VERY AFFECTIONATELY,
YOUR FRIEND,
LUIS BUÑUEL

Fre Tel C, DT/72/05

From Robert Favre Le Bret

Paris, 8 April 1971

I WILL CERTAINLY SHOW THE FILM *JOHNNY GOT HIS GUN* AT CANNES, EITHER IN CRITICS' WEEK OR IN THE MAIN COMPETITION IF I CAN FIND SPACE. A PLEASURE TO HEAR FROM YOU AGAIN,

IN FRIENDSHIP,
FAVRE LE BRET

Fre Tel C, DT/72/05

To Dalton Trumbo

Mexico City, 8 April 1971

Dear Dalton,

Yesterday, I sent you by airmail a copy of the telegram I sent to Favre Le Bret about *Johnny Got his Gun*. I hope you will let me know if your film is accepted for the Cannes Festival in the end.[1] If not, you could show it at the 'Directors' Fortnight'[2] in Cannes? Their programmes can be more interesting than the official festival and the people who go are real film-makers.

I really liked *Johnny Got his Gun*; I found it almost as heart-breaking as the book. It has moments of such intense emotion, like the scene where they use Morse code to communicate with the injured man, or the nurse kissing Johnny's forehead, the first love scene with the young man and his girlfriend, etc. I was *unpleasantly* surprised though, by the scene where the nurse masturbates her patient. I think it *taints* the immense purity and tenderness of the film. The actor you chose to play Johnny is wonderful: his innocent gaze and ineffable youth definitely highlight his inexorable fate.

Most of my friends who saw the film liked it very much, including Carlos Fuentes. If they had any slight criticisms it was for some of the *flashbacks*, like the dream sequences, which they didn't quite get. Others found the film a little too long. But these criticisms really don't matter. What matters is that they were all impressed.

I hope to see you at Cannes.
Warm regards,
Luis Buñuel

Spa Tls, DT/72/05

---

[1] *Johnny Got His Gun* was screened in the official selection and won the Grand Jury Prize.
[2] Screenings running parallel with the official selection from 1969.

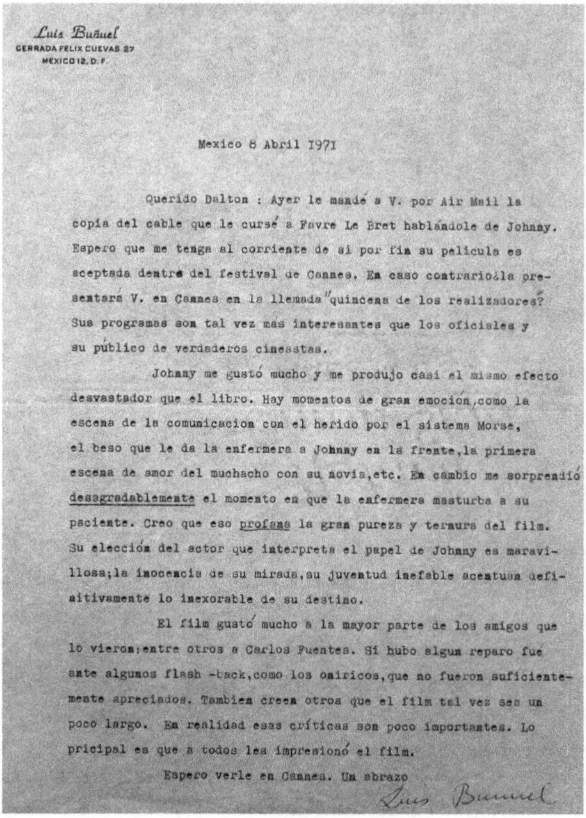

Luis Buñuel
CERRADA FELIX CUEVAS 27
MEXICO 12, D. F.

Mexico 8 Abril 1971

Querido Dalton : Ayer le mandé a V. por Air Mail la copia del cable que le cursé a Favre Le Bret hablándole de Johnny. Espero que me tenga al corriente de si por fin su película es aceptada dentro del festival de Cannes. En caso contrario¿la presentará V. en Cannes en la llamada "quincena de los realizadores"? Sus programas son tal vez mas interesantes que los oficiales y su público de verdaderos cineastas.

Johnny me gustó mucho y me produjo casi el mismo efecto devastador que el libro. Hay momentos de gran emoción,como la escena de la comunicación con el herido por el sistema Morse, el beso que le da la enfermera a Johnny en la frente,la primera escena de amor del muchacho con su novia,etc. En cambio me sorprendió desagradablemente el momento en que la enfermera masturba a su paciente. Creo que eso profana la gran pureza y ternura del film. Su elección del actor que interpreta el papel de Johnny es maravillosa;la inocencia de su mirada,su juventud inefable acentúan definitivamente lo inexorable de su destino.

El film gustó mucho a la mayor parte de los amigos que lo vieron;entre otros a Carlos Fuentes. Si hubo algún reparo fue ante algunos flash -back,como los oníricos,que no fueron suficientemente apreciados. También creen otros que el film tal vez sea un poco largo. En realidad esas críticas son poco importantes. Lo principal es que a todos les impresionó el film.

Espero verle en Cannes. Un abrazo
Luis Buñuel

Figure 74 Letter from Buñuel to Trumbo, 8 April 1971.

To José Donoso

Mexico City, 14 April 1971

Dear friend Donoso,

Thank-you for your letter to which, as is my custom, I am replying late thanks to my darned laziness.

I haven't had any news, or a letter, from those young Chileans you mentioned. But as soon as I do, I will give them my full attention. You already know what a fan I am of *El lugar sin límites* and that I was prepared to get involved, despite my reluctance to work, when the Spaniards[1] put a total ban on making the film. I signed up to make a film in Europe[2] over a year ago now, but I'm still reluctant to see it through. I'm hoping to get out of it completely in a few days, because the producer[3] is coming to Mexico to see me. The problem is I'm just NOT INTERESTED in cinema. I see myself as retired, although if I get too bored one day, nothing but failing health will prevent me going back.

I heard from family in Spain that you were planning to go to Calanda for the drums.[4] Did you ever get there?

I'll be in Europe next month. I think I'll be able to visit you as promised. I'll let you know.

Warmest regards to María Pilar and you from,
Luis Buñuel

[PS] Wonderful to hear you've nearly finished your new book. No need to tell you how impatient I am to see it published.[5]

Spa Tls, JD/64/06

[1]   Spanish government Board of Censors.
[2]   *The Discreet Charm of the Bourgeoisie.*
[3]   Silberman.
[4]   In 1971, Donoso bought a house in Calaceite, Teruel, 50 km from Calanda.
[5]   *Cuentos* (Barcelona: Seix Barral, 1971).

To Serge Silberman

Mexico City, 24 April 1971

My dear Serge,

I'm writing these lines, still savouring the memory of your recent visit, to tell you about my definitive travel plans to France.

I leave Mexico on 8 May and fly nonstop to Nice arriving on the evening of the 9th. The next Air France flight leaves Mexico on 11 May, which would arrive too late to get to Cannes, where I've been invited by Favre.

You were right, and as my legs are beginning to trouble me, I would prefer to stay in a hotel on La Croisette.[1] Would you be kind enough to mention this to Favre Le Bret, without asking, *by Jove*,[2] for an imperial suite. A bed and a four-legged bidet would do for me.

Another thing. I won't have any French money. Could you please bring 2,000 francs that I'll repay with a cheque from my French CIC[3] account.

One final thing. If I'm not in excellent health and Herculean strength, I'll cancel the trip. Although I would of course warn you in plenty of time.

Your attentive FRIEND,
Luis

PS I've written to Favre to let him know the ticket has arrived and that I'll be in Cannes on 9 May. I also mentioned staying on La Croisette to him.

Fre Tlsps, RS

[1]   Famous pedestrianized walkway by the beach in Cannes, with the Palais where the Festival is held.
[2]   English in the original.
[3]   Crédit Industriel et Commercial, French bank founded in 1859.

To Eduardo Ducay

Mexico City, 5 May 1971

Dear Eduardo,

Your letter from the Antarctic finally arrived. I thought you'd been eaten by sabre-toothed penguins.

I may come to Zaragoza from Cannes, which means I'll be in Spain from about 20 May.

I'll keep you posted. I'll stop in Paris on my way back to Mexico.

I'd be grateful if you could ring and find out whether the medal the Círculo de Bellas Artes has so *graciously* offered me is *REAL* gold.[1] If so, I'll have it. If not, out with the trash. Also, Zapata wrote months ago saying the Union had an ENORMOUS pile of cash for the director of *Tristana*.[2] Do you think I should claim it? If so, I shall pocket it and throw a party in Seville, to which you are invited. If you think I shouldn't, I'll leave it and have a simple supper at Bajamar's[3] to keep me right with you and yours.

I imagine you'll be getting the letter from Buzatti about making *Sette piani* and *Un amore* with me.[4] *Rien à faire.*[5]

I had a telegram from a Mr José Frade[6] three days ago, I don't know him but he's proposing I make Galdós's *Tormento*.[7] He said, amongst other things: 'We agree to your conditions in advance.' I've never had such a friendly telegram! I replied the usual about stopping work and retirement, etc. But if I go to Madrid, I'll pay him a visit.

Best wishes to Mercedes and hugs for the little ones, and you,
Luis

[PS] What's the CEC?[8] The awards you mention, are they also gold? I only accept gold, platinum, or German marks.

Spa Tlsps, ED

---

[1] *Tristana* was awarded Gold Medal for Best Picture in 1970 by the Spanish cultural Círculo de Bellas Artes.
[2] El Sindicato Nacional del Espectáculo español awarded LB Best Director in 1970.
[3] Seafood restaurant in the famous shopping street in central Madrid, the Gran Vía, now nicknamed the Spanish Broadway.
[4] *Setti piani* first appeared in a collection of short stories by Buzzati, *I sette messaggere* (1942). *Un amore* was published in Milan by Mondadori in 1963.
[5] French in the original (Nothing to do/It's a no go).
[6] José Frade Almohalla (born 1938), film producer and distributor.
[7] Novel published by Galdós in 1884.
[8] Círculo de Escritores Cinematográficos founded in Madrid in 1945.

To Serge Silberman

Madrid, 26 May 1971

My dear Serge,

The Last Temptation[1] seems 'stately' to me, a work of great talent, an extraordinary reworking of the Gospels, deeply moving, etc., etc. It's based on the dialogues, so it's theatrical despite some brief interludes of swift exterior action. I would discuss it with you at length except that, like you, I hate writing letters. If I don't send the script by airmail, I'll bring it in person.[2] I still don't know when I'll get the train to Paris. I'll be staying here in Madrid for a week or so. At La Torre, of course.

Affectionately yours,
Luis Buñuel

[PS] Is it possible to get The Last Temptation in French?[3]

Fre Als, RS

[1] English in the original, referring to the novel by Greek writer, Nikos Kazantzakis (1883–1957), O teleftéos pirasmós (Athens: Difros, 1955), translated as The Last Temptation of Christ (New York: Simon & Schuster, 1960).
[2] LB was contracted by Sidney Lumet to revise a script based on Kazantzakis's novel.
[3] La dernière tentation (Paris: Plon, 1970) (AB/28).

From Serge Silberman

Paris, 31 May 1971

My dear Luis,

I finally got back from Cannes on Saturday 29 May.

Although it is Whit Monday today (I have decided to celebrate all the religious and national holidays the world has to offer), I'm in my office, where I found your letter of 26 May.

If my calculations are correct, you will be in Paris on the 5 or 6 of June. I hope it will be around then, because I have to go to New York on 8 June, and from New York to Montreal on 10 June, then back again to New York around 16 June returning to Paris on 18 June.

When you arrive in Paris, you'll find Kazantzakis's book (The Last Temptation) in French.

I should like to meet up and talk before I leave for New York. We might even decide you could join me for a few days in New York around 16 June.

I should also like to set a date with you to start shooting the film.[1] That would make me happy, relaxed, and encourage me to carry on with this awful job.

As for the award winners at Cannes, I am more than delighted.

I loved Losey's film, The Go-Between.[2] I think you would like it too.

I hated *Death in Venice*,[3] which was awarded a consolation and farewell prize.
I was delighted about *Johnny got his Gun* (what a shame you didn't make that film!).
Very happy about *Joe Hill*[4] and *Sacco and Vanzetti*.[5]
The fact that you were at Cannes was a blessing for all of us, especially me.
I hope to see you soon.

Affectionately yours,
[Serge]

Fre Tluf, RS

[1] *Discreet Charm of the Bourgeoisie.*
[2] *The Go-Between* (1971) won the Palme d'Or that year at Cannes.
[3] *Morte a Venezia* (1971), dir. Luchino Visconti, won 25th Birthday Award at the 1971 Cannes Film Festival.
[4] *Joe Hill* (1971), dir. Bo Widerberg, awarded joint Grand Jury Prize with Trumbo's film.
[5] *Sacco e Vanzetti* (1971), dir. Giuliano Montaldo, Best Actor for Riccardo Cucciolla as Nicola Sacco.

To Eduardo Ducay

Mexico City, 12 July 1971

Dear Eduardo,

I got your letter, and Joaquín's arrived today to confirm it. I hope you've read mine about a medical check-up I had to postpone because my doctor is out of the country.

You can come to Mexico if you like, and you will be warmly welcome, but I want you know in advance that I DEFINITELY do not want to travel to Europe for work, and I'm not even sure I'd want to go on holiday. My mind is made up whatever excellent terms you offer in relation to creative freedom, budget and fee. I assume this will come as no surprise to you. I'm not acting on a whim or attempting to make you beg. I just don't have the enthusiasm or strength for the work involved in film production … especially so far from home.

Right now, I've accepted a project to revise an adaptation for the American director Sidney Lumet. The initial treatment is based on Kazantzakis's book, *The Last Temptation*. This will keep me occupied until the end of August. I've not yet started, because the director needs to come over, so we can agree terms.

Naturally, I will let Zapata know, because I was liaising with him over my fee, etc.

That's all for now, warmest regards,
Luis

Spa Tls, ED

From Antonis Samarakis[1]

Athens, 25 July 1971

Dear Luis Buñuel, great friend,

I cannot find the words to express my joy and delight. I have just received your letter of 12 July,[2] and I am so happy! I am fully conscious of the honour bestowed on me by Luis Buñuel. I am deeply moved to know that you liked *Tò láthos*.[3]

Yes, I have received a lot of offers to make a film adaptation of *Tò láthos*.[4] They have come from various countries: France, Italy, Sweden, Denmark, United States, Japan, etc. I have reached a tentative arrangement with a French producer, who has a six-month option. That option began on 1 April. But I've not yet signed a contract, not even for the option.

I am sending you separately today the French translation of my novel *Sima kindinou*[5] with some brief notes. *Sima kindinou* was published in Greece and is now on its sixth edition. It has also come out in translation in a number of other countries. And if I may be so bold, it has had great success in all of these. The novel will soon be published in French. The translation I am sending you is not the best quality. However, I would be delighted if you would read it.

I hope I will have the pleasure of receiving another letter from you. Forgive me, I am not feeling well this afternoon and must stop writing now.

With my utmost appreciation, esteem and eternal friendship,
Antonis
53 Taygetou Ippolytou

Fre Tls, AB/1402.12

---

[1] Greek writer (1919–2003).
[2] Letter from LB (responding to an initial letter from Samarakis dated 30 April 1971), (AB/1042.11), not preserved in the Samarakis archives in Athens.
[3] A. Samarakis, *Tò láthos* (Athens: Estia, 1965).
[4] The novel won the Grand prix de littérature policière in France in 1970.
[5] A. Samarakis, *Sima kindinou* (Athens: Mpolari, 1959).

To José Donoso

Mexico City, 15 August 1971

Dear Pepe,

The English translation[1] you sent of *El lugar sin límites* arrived in good time. I was intending to show it to a French producer who was supposed to be here in the city from 2 August. He still hasn't arrived. I also spoke to the local production company, Marco Polo,[2] whose executive producer read the book in Spanish. I've not had a reply. In any case, the agreement was to wait for the Frenchman, so that they could discuss it with him. I'm expecting him to arrive any day now.

Have patience and don't remove my portrait[3] from your bookshelf just yet. As soon as I have news from the producers, good or bad, I'll let you know.

A big hug for the three Donosos.
Buñuel

Spa Tls, JD/64/06

[1] Typed.
[2] Cinematográfica Marco Polo, Mexican production company co-owned by brothers Leopoldo and Marco Silva from 1971 to 1975.
[3] Of LB.

To Joaquín Gurruchaga

Mexico City, 15 August 1971

Dear Joaquín,

From your last letter I assume you are now in San Sebastián. I'm sending this letter to Madrid, as requested.

Out of sheer laziness, my eternal companion, I postponed the medical check-ups I wanted to have done. But I finally took the plunge and am now in the hands of dentists, cardiologists, analysts, etc. This Calvary is not yet complete, but the signs are good. A bit senile, of course, but not as bad as I thought. I'll let you know my test results, in which I hope to scrape a shameful 'pass'.

I've decided to go back – or not to go back – to film-making and I'll give you my answer before 1 September. I may ask you to come over here and see me; if so, it would for a definite agreement.

In my last, now distant, letter from Eduardo, he was talking about a joint arrangement with Cine Técnica[1] and Época. I assume that doesn't rule out Zapata. Can you enlighten me. I don't think it would be appropriate for me to exclude him, as my latest proposal with you came from him.

I also need to come to a decision for or against my project with Silberman. Carrière has been here for two weeks. I have reshaped, corrected, expanded and perfected *The Discreet Charm of the Bourgeoisie*, which I'm now really pleased with. Silberman is in Canada and will be coming to visit in the next few days. Even if I do get back into filming, Paris is out of the question.[2]

That's all for now,

Warmest regards to Conchita[3] and you,
Luis

PS My arrangement with Sidney Lumet over the script of *The Last Temptation* fell through at the last minute. I was disappointed because, from a purely 'business' side, it was a great deal.

Congratulations to you and Conchita on María Luisa's[4] wedding. We're internationalizing you both!

Spa Tlsps, ED

1   Spanish producer.
2   Finally filmed in Paris from May to July 1972.
3   Conchita Zamacona, his wife.
4   María Luisa Gurruchaga Zamacona, daughter of Joaquín Gurruchaga.

To Eduardo Ducay

Mexico City, 25 August 1971

Dear Eduardo,

Your telegram has just arrived. Before you come over, I hope you will read the long letter I sent to Joaquín. I also sent you a new version of 'the discreet bourgeoisie' three days ago by registered post.[1] I think it's much better than the one you have at the moment. You should read that too before you set off.

This time, if you do finally come over, I should warn you we'll be eating out. My house is full. We are: *ménage*[2] Jeanne and Luis, sons Juan Luis and Rafael, daughter-in-law Joyce, granddaughter, Rafael's girlfriend. And four in the kitchen. Between you and me: it's awful. And it's going to be a while.

Regards,
Luis

PS The Diplomático, marvellous. Honestly. I saw the rooms and the suites a few days ago. Suite: 175 pesos = $15.

Spa Als, ED

1   For a potential co-production with Silberman of *The Discreet Charm of the Bourgeoisie*.
2   'Household', French in original.

To José Donoso

Mexico City, 26 August 1971

Dear Pepe,

The translation of *El lugar sin límites* from Brandt and Brandt arrived the day before yesterday,[1] but it has handwritten corrections, I imagine from the translator,[2] that make it almost impossible to read, especially for a producer with no time to decipher it. In other words, neither this one nor the one you sent me is any use to me. Never mind. I'll keep them for you and just wait patiently for the book to come out.[3]

Serge Silberman got here on 24, rather than 4 August as he'd originally thought. He was only here for a day. He took *El lugar sin límites* away with him in Spanish. I don't think his understanding of the language will be sufficient, because, as he speaks eight or ten languages, he doesn't really have an in-depth knowledge of any of them. He told me though, that even without reading it he is interested in a co-production with Mexico. I've had an option with him now for two years to make a film of mine called *The Discreet Charm of the Bourgeoisie*, but I've been putting him off up until now to avoid having to spend eight months in a hotel in Paris.

The Mexican production company Marco Polo is also willing to co-produce *El lugar sin límites* over here with France.

So now I'm the only missing link. I'll decide as soon as I can get out of the two options that, I repeat, I've had for the last two years: one with Silberman, and the other with Época Films to make an original film called *Mater Purissima*.[4] Ducay and Gurruchaga will be coming over in a few days to try and convince me.

In short: I'm not sure, I may go for one of those two options first of all, or neither and make *El lugar sin límites* instead or, I may just sit back and do nothing, the perfect picture of utter laziness.

Even though nothing is finalized as yet, at least you can see I am still taking a serious interest in your book, how could I not! Let's see what comes of so much prevarication. Ah, if I were only 50 again, a mere youngster, I'd have only to forge gloriously ahead.

Multiple hugs,
Luis

                                                                    Spa Tls, JD/64/06

[1]   Literary agency founded by Carl Brandt in 1913.
[2]   Suzanne Jill Levine.
[3]   J. Donoso, *Hell Has No Limits* (New York: E. P. Dutton, 1972).
[4]   About his childhood with the Jesuits.

To Jonas Mekas

Mexico, 9 September 1971

Dear Jonas Mekas,

There is a small problem concerning the copy of Land Without Bread *that I let you have in May 1970. Let me explain it briefly:*

In 1963 I sold my rights to this film to Mr Pierre Braunberger of Paris. Nevertheless, I was convinced that I had the right to lend or give a copy of this film to cultural organizations for non-commercial *purposes.*

When I came to an agreement with you at Anthology Cinema concerning the use of Land Without Bread, *I wrote to Mr Braunberger about this. He answered saying that he had sold his rights to the United States to a New York company, MacGraw Hill, which could now legally intervene invalidating the rights I gave you to project* Land Without Bread.

I want to avoid all possible legal complications that might arise because I have no lawyer and I understand nothing about this legal mumble jumble. Therefore, I propose the following:

Before you go ahead with the proposed projection of Land Without Bread *on the 17th of this month, contact MacGraw Hill and offer them the thousand dollars that you gave me. I will then immediately send these thousand dollars back to you. In case MacGraw Hill refuses your offer, cancel the projection of the film and I will return the money to you anyway, plus any costs you have already incurred concerning the copy.*

In order to compensate for your not projecting the film, I could intervene so that Anthology Cinema would obtain a copy of The Golden Age, *it being understood that your organization pay only the costs of the copy. Furthermore, I will also return the thousand dollars you paid me.*

I expect there should be no problem, and attentively await your reply.

Sincerely yours,
Luis Buñuel[1]

Eng Tls, AB/647.9–10

---

[1]   Mekas wrote a letter subsequently to LB, dated 22 September 1971 (AB/647.8), explaining that the problem was resolved as he, Mekas, had paid McGraw Hill directly and that LB could keep the $1,000 Mekas had sent him.

To Eduardo Ducay and Joaquín Gurruchuga

Mexico City, 14 September 1971

Eduardo Ducay and Joaquín Gurruchuga
Hotel Diplomático, Mexico City

I hereby commit to direct, on behalf of yourselves and Mr Serge Silberman, the *scénario* entitled *The Discreet Charm of the Bourgeoisie* jointly authored by Jean-Claude Carrière and myself, on the assumption that the three of you will reach an agreement on the terms of the co-production.

Filming will take place in Spain, in French or Spanish, as you decide.

Should the aforesaid agreement over co-production prove impossible to reach, and as I do not, for personal reasons, wish to film in Paris, I would agree to make the film in Spain with you (Cine Técnica and Época Films) as sole producers, although not without prior consultation with Mr Silberman.

One very important condition for me is that – whatever the final agreement over production – work on the film starts, at the very latest, before 30 October 1971.

I remain, in anticipation of a resolution to this matter, your friend,
Luis Buñuel

Spa Tls, ED

From Joseph Losey

[Mexico City,] 17 September 1971

Dear Buñuel,

It has been more than thirty-five years since we met. Perhaps you will remember coming to my house in New York on several occasions, having been sent to me by our mutual friend, Joris Ivens. I still see Joris, and it is strange that with him and our many other mutual friends, from poor George Pepper[1] to Jeanne Moreau, that we never seem to have encountered each other in the intervening years.

As you perhaps have seen, I am here shooting locations of a picture about the assassination of Trotsky,[2] and I understand that you are now in Mexico. It would be pleasant to greet you, if you have a few minutes. If you feel like it, do drop me a note or give me a ring, and perhaps we can have a brief drink one evening after shooting. I am scheduled to leave on 29 September.

Sincerely yours,
Joseph Losey

Eng Tlts C, JLC/Buñuel

[1] Pepper died of lung cancer in 1969.
[2] *The Assassination of Trotsky* (1972), dir. Losey.

To Joseph Losey

Mexico, 20 September 1971

Dear Losey,

Very glad to see you again after so many years by gone.

As I told your secretary I shall be happy if your wife and you can come tomorrow Tuesday to lunch with us at home. One o'clock or half past one will be O.K.

As you are going to see Romy,[1] please let her know that I hope she will also came with you as promised.

Till tomorrow.
Sincerely,
Luis Buñuel

Eng Tls, JLC/Buñuel

[1] Romy Schneider (1938–82), Austrian actress who acted in *The Assassination of Trotsky*.

From Joseph Losey

[Mexico City,] 22 September 1971

Dear Luis,

It was a very warm and good meeting with you after all these years, and delightful to meet your attractive family. I am sorry my own immediate problems intruded to such an extent,[1] but am most grateful to you and Fuentes for your intervention. I hope I won't have to call on either of you for more help. Actually, I believe that thanks to your assistance, the crisis can now be coped with.

Patricia[2] very much regrets not having met you and your wife, and we hope there will perhaps be an hour for a drink before we leave; but if not, we must surely meet in Paris or Rome or London, once we return after Christmas. My permanent address and telephone number in London are: 29 Royal Avenue, London S. W. 3, 730–6393. My Rome address, until after Christmas, is: 19 Via della Vetrina, telephone 655–293.

Many thanks and kindest regard to your wife and son,
[Joseph Losey]

P.S. The little boy in The Go-Between *is named Dominic Guard,[3] and his address is 12 Pleydell Avenue, London W. 6. He will be absolutely delighted to have a note from you.*

Eng Tluf C, JLC/Buñuel

[1]   Concerning permission to shoot in Mexico.
[2]   Patricia Mohan (born 1930), third wife of Losey.
[3]   English actor (born 1956).

Figure 75 Fuentes, Schneider, Buñuel, Losey and Ramón Xirau during production of *The Assassination of Trotsky* in Mexico City, September 1971.

From Marcos Aguinis[1]

Rio Cuarto, 23 September 1971

Much appreciated and admired Luis Buñuel,

Thank you for your letter of 26 August[2] and for your kind words of praise about *La cruz invertida*.[3] The 71 years you mention by no means reflect your mental brilliance, as you demonstrate in your recent films. I am still postponing my response to another director, trusting that you will come to a positive decision and resolve to go ahead. The symbolism in *La cruz invertida*, especially in chapters 1, 35 and 78, is rich material for your talent.

I therefore await your reply. As a doctor I can assure you that creative work (with the accompanying dose of sacrifice, pain and anguish) far from damaging only revitalizes true genius. As is your case.

Very affectionate greetings from,
Marcos Aguinis
Avenida Italia 1262

Spa Tls, AB/1383.15

[1] Argentinian writer and doctor (born 1935).
[2] In response to a letter from Aguinis to LB, 3 August 1971 (AB/2054.12).
[3] M. Aguinis, *La cruz invertida* (Barcelona: Planeta, 1970); copy held in the Buñuel Archives (7th edition, May 1971), with handwritten dedication by the author: 'In homage to the implacable and magnificent Buñuel, this work: a naked shout, compromised and derailed by love' (AB/349).

To José Donoso

Mexico City, 28 September 1971

Dear Pepe,

Towards the end of October, I shall be travelling to Spain and France in search of a few winter months, my favourite season. I may, while I'm there, fulfil my obligation to make an original film I've had ready now for nearly two years. I'm still not sure. Silberman is pushing me, and I continue to resist. One way or another I'll be back in Mexico in March.

Marco Polo is determined to make *El lugar sin límites* here in Mexico, with me, that is. I've accepted, provisionally. That would be when I get back. So, do please let me know how much you want for the film rights to your novel. I have proposed, and they have agreed, to ask you for a six or seven-month option on the book. So, tell me as well how much you want to charge them. They will write to you as soon as I let them know your decision. To give you an idea what they normally pay around here I can say that they paid Carlos Fuentes $7,000 for the rights to one of his short novels.[1] It's the same company.

Hugs for all three from,
Luis

PS Despite the above, you should still take my portrait off your bookshelf regardless. Depending on the outcome, you can put it back, or throw it on the fire.

Spa Tlsps, JD/64/06

¹ Short story 'La muñeca reina', published in *Cantar de ciegos* (Mexico City: Joaquín Mortiz, 1964), adaptation produced by Marco Polo and directed by the Mexican film-maker, Sergio Olhovich (born 1941) in 1972.

To Eduardo Ducay

Mexico City, 1 October 1971

Dear Eduardo,

The two letters in one envelope have arrived, one of them being a copy of the letter you sent to Silberman. It's all fine except that Serge's workload may delay his arrangement with you. Preparations should, however, begin at the end of this month as agreed. For me, 'time is money' is the imperative. I'm going to reserve an Iberia flight for the 20th of this month. I will confirm the exact date. I'll pay for my ticket here and we can sort out the money over there.

I'm very glad it looks as if Fernando may be available. Romy Schneider is available over here and is desperate to do something in the film, even if it's only a walk-on part. I can't think of a more amiable or more cordial star. She has, of course, offered to drop everything to make *Mater Purissima*, which Carlos Fuentes discussed with her. But that's another story altogether.

No signs of life from Julio since we saw him here. So much the better. It seems he wasn't interested in doing the job in stages. For the moment, the only thing I've decided on is 'the discreet bourgeoisie'.

Did you get an envelope with cuttings – about *Tristana* – from Buenos Aires?

Warm regards to Joaquín, and to you,
Luis

Spa Tls, ED

To Eduardo Ducay

Mexico City, 4 October 1971

Dear Eduardo,

I've booked and paid for a ticket on an Iberia flight on 21 October. This means we can start preparations a few days after that.¹ Serge, despite sending a telegram from Paris to say he'd received my letter and would write to me from New York, has not done so. I fear his many current preoccupations mean he's not really interested in 'getting stuck into' the bourgeoisie. Either way, if he's not come to some arrangement with you between now and the 15th or 20th, I would assume that means he's not interested in the project for whatever reason. In that case, I am at your disposal, and would not for a moment consider setting aside *The Discreet Charm of the Bourgeoisie* project to think about *Mater Purissima*.

If Silberman does pull out, what will you do? Naturally, I would not want to interfere in the least in your co-production arrangements, as long as the only people authorized to communicate and work with me are you and Joaquín.

I'll be ready to sign a contract with Época and Cine Técnica as soon as I arrive in Madrid. I won't write to you again unless something comes up. See you in Madrid on the 21st.

Warm regards,
Luis

[PS] I haven't heard anything from Julio. It's for the best, really, because I have no wish to hoard films. If *absolutely necessary*, I can bring my trip to Madrid forward. Let me know.

Spa Tlsps, ED

¹ For filming *The Discreet Charm of the Bourgeoisie*.

From José Donoso

Calaceite, 4 October 1971

Dear Luis,

Your letter arrived yesterday. I am happy, as you can imagine, about your plan to film *El lugar sin límites*. And that Marco Polo is interested, which I imagine reflects your own interest. In the meantime, and just in case, I have asked the maid to give your portrait a bit of a dust.

As for the rights, as long as you make the film, I would be prepared to accept whatever they offer. Nevertheless, I'm sure you will secure the best possible deal for me with the producers. I think that asking 10,000 for the novel and about 1,000 (discountable from the 10,000) for the option wouldn't be too much but of course, between me, myself and I, I would happily accept less because I'm so keen to see what you would do with my poor Manuela.¹ Write to me as soon as you hear anything and ask them to write to me as well.

As always, there has been discreet contact with the Zaragozan Buñuels. Leonardo García was briefly considering buying a house here in Calaceite, but then he disappeared. We met the formidable Alicia playing poker in the ruins of the Calanda mansion with a series of Indian ghosts.² Pedro has taken some magisterial photos of me with my daughter.

I should say that I'm expecting delivery of six tons of firewood today. It's for the bonfire on which I shall burn your portrait if you don't make the film: I'll send you the ashes. I'll also be sending you psychiatrists' bills for myself, my wife and Pilarcita; we will be having regular sessions with them while we wait for you to finish the film in

Spain. I can't wait to see you back here soon. I shall have partridges ready, and some sensational wines I've discovered recently (they are the verger's which will no doubt interest you). Write soon. I am happy (for how long I don't know), and for now, we send you three big hugs from María Pilar, Pilarcita and me,

José Donoso

Spa Tls, AB/632.23

¹ Transvestite character in the novel.
² Reference both to the fact that LB claimed to have seen the ghost of his father at the family home in Calanda just after he died, and to returning Spanish ('indianos') emigrants to the Americas.

To Eduardo Ducay

Mexico City, 16 October 1971

I ENVY YOU THE BENEFITS OF *TRISTANA'S* GREAT SUCCESS IN LONDON WITH PUBLIC AND PRESS. NO NEWS OF OUR PROJECT. DELAYING MY TRIP TO MADRID.

REGARDS,
LUIS

Spa Tel, ED

To José Donoso

Mexico City, 27 October 1971

Dear Pepe,
    Marco Polo will write offering you $1,000 for a six-month option on *El lugar sin límites*. Of course, until I sign they won't take any further steps, and for the moment I'm holding back for reasons of ... old age. Between now and March, who knows where I'll be.
    I'm going to Europe in November. We'll see each other there. I mean, in Calaceite. Big hugs to the little Pilaricas, and you,

Luis

PS Slow and steady wins the race. Don't write here again in case I leave before your letter arrives.

Spa Als, JD/64/06

To Serge Silberman

Mexico City, 10 November 1971

My dear Serge,

Your letter of 4 November arrived today. But it's the first since you last left Mexico.

I'm going to postpone my trip to Madrid. I'll be there around 19 November and I'll contact you by letter or telegram. I hope Irène[1] is recovering from the operation and that it went well. From what you said, it didn't sound too serious, which is a relief.

I'm becoming less impressed with *The Discreet Charm of the Bourgeoisie*. If it goes ahead, it will, in any case, need reworking. As I'm sure you'll agree. A script is never perfect. It just has to be as far from imperfect as possible. For the moment, I'm still floating, undecided.

Hope to see you soon.
Yours,
Luis

Fre Tls, RS

[1]   French producer, wife of Silberman.

To Jean-Claude Carrière

Jean-Claude Carrière
904 North Bedford Dr.
90210 Beverly Hills, California

Mexico City, 11 November 1971

Dear Juanito Claudio,

I'm writing to you in the language of Cervantes, so you won't forget it.

What are you doing in Los Angeles? Did you succeed in your ambition to join the film industry in that legendary city? I'm not best pleased with your new-found affection for American imperialism. You will have to provide a very good explanation for such reactionary behaviour.

I leave for Madrid on 16 November. As usual, you will be able to reach me at Torre de Madrid: write to me there. You say you'll be in Paris from 5 or 10 December. I'm sure we will meet up.

Serge wrote yesterday to say he is still willing to make the sweet charm of the bourgeoisie, but as sole and exclusive producer.[1] I still haven't decided. Either way, we would need to put in about ten days work on the *script*.[2] I'm less pleased with it by the day, and if I don't start filming at once I'll end up hating it. I have some new ideas that will make you weep for joy when you hear them. I hope we'll be able to spend a couple of weeks together from 10 December.

Warmest regards from your disciple and admirer,
Luis

Spa Tls, JCC

---

¹ *The Discreet Charm of the Bourgeoisie* was eventually produced solely by Silberman, without Época Films or Cine Técnica.
² English in the original.

To Maurice Bessy

Mexico City, 16 February 1972

IMMENSELY GRATEFUL AND VERY HONOURED BY YOUR PROPOSAL THAT I CHAIR THE JURY. UNFORTUNATELY, I HAVE TO DECLINE YOUR OFFER BECAUSE THE PRESIDENCY WOULD BE FOR ME AN ONEROUS AND WORLDLY TASK BEYOND MY CAPABILITIES.

AFFECTIONATELY YOURS,
LUIS BUÑUEL

Fre Tls, AB/1426.81

To Serge Silberman

Mexico City, 18 February 1972

My dear Serge,
    I sent you a telegram thanking you for your long and thoughtful letter. I agree with almost all your points. I do think it was rather absurd of me to attempt to make a wholly French film in Mexico. My fears about spending six months in Paris no doubt caused my delirium. I am also grateful that, out of friendship and a wish to please me, you've agreed to start negotiating with the Silvas. But this is all water under the bridge now and need not be mentioned again.
    It seems you have undertaken certain obligations in relation to the film. If they bind you, financially or morally, to distributors, etc., you only have to say, and I'll come to your office to sign the contract, with a few modifications, and get to work.
    Otherwise, I have no objection to making the film, although I'll remind you again of the following:

1) I am concerned that I won't be able to cope with the stress and fatigue of eight weeks of work.
2) I am not as convinced as you and Jean-Claude of the merits of the script.
    Although that happens with all my work. If I do go ahead though, it will be with no lack of enthusiasm and good will.

If you decide I should go to Paris, I'd prefer to arrange the ticket with my agency over here, because they take care of visas and all the other annoying bureaucracy. Pay me in Paris exactly what I would need for Air France, because I assume they will be able to transfer the money to your account.

And to finish this letter, which is as boring as the minutiae above, I'll tell you what I'm sure you already know. Maurice sent me an official telegram inviting me to chair the Jury at Cannes. I sent sincere thanks but turned it down because of the day-to-day obligations of the presidency. I would, though, have agreed to be a member of the Jury if you'd been one too.

Awaiting your 'orders', your friend.
Luis

Fre Tls, RS

To Serge Silberman

Mexico City, 1 March 1972

My dear Serge,

I imagine you received my telegram saying I would be in the office on 13 March awaiting your instructions. I explained the reasons for the delay briefly in that telegram. I'll give you the full detail in Paris.

Could you tell Ully[1] that, if he does start work on the script, he should use the latest version Jean-Claude sent in December, not one of the earlier versions with the list of actors that you sent me. I think it would be a good idea to make a few copies of the latest version, although it's not the definitive one, because I still mean to work on the script with Jean-Claude. There won't be any very significant changes though.

My medical check-up uncovered one very serious ailment: the 72 years I recently turned last 22 February. The rest is OK.

With all my friendship, and delighted that we'll be meeting again soon,
Luis

[PS] I've reserved a suite in the Aiglon. Don't come to meet me at Orly (please).

Fre Tlsps, RS

---

[1] Ulrich Pickard, head of production at Greenwich Film Productions.

To José Donoso

Paris, 3 April 1972

Dear Pepe,

It's a couple of weeks since I arrived in Paris. I got your last letter, but as I was still unsure what I was doing, I didn't reply. I can now though, because I have come to a decision. As I mentioned, Greenwich Film Productions have been wanting for a couple of years now to make a film with me based on an original script of mine called *The Discreet Charm of the Bourgeoisie*.

Silberman came to Mexico five times to persuade me. I turned him down four times, but on the fifth I gave in, more out of weakness than any real desire to make a film, especially over here in Paris: I'm in a hotel until August(!) when I'll return to Mexico. My health and enthusiasm will then dictate whether, from September, I shall be able to give serious thought to filming your book.[1] I've told the people at Marco Polo and they are going to wait until I get back. For now, you can throw my portrait on that heap of firewood you are warming yourself with.

I'll go to see Barrault[2] or invite him to my office. They tell me that 'wonderful' Spanish actor, Antonio Vico, I auditioned not so long ago in Madrid, died a couple of months ago.[3]

That's all I wanted to tell you for now. Time will tell the rest. Hugs for Pilar and kisses for the little one. More hugs for you,

Luis

Spa Tls, JD/65/04

[1] *El lugar sin límites.*
[2] Jean Louis Barrault (1910–94), French actor and director.
[3] Vico died in Madrid, 20 March 1972.

To Carlos Fuentes

Paris, 18 April 1972

Dear Carlos,

Delighted to hear from you.[1] The copy of *Tiempo mexicano*[2] you sent to me in Madrid in January, arrived two days ago. That's the fault of the Torre de Madrid, not the post office. Reading it makes me feel ultra-American.[3] Stupendous. Full of admiration for your skills and knowledge (I am, that is, not the book). After the stress of my daily labours[4] reading it is an oasis for me, although the book is certainly not. Congratulations to the author.

I would love to see you over here. I am at your service, although my cloistered life precludes certain excesses. I get up at 6:30 and go to bed by 9pm at the latest. I have to see so many people and the nervous tension by the end of the day is most unpleasant. Bloody deafness.

I start shooting on 15 May.

Gavin[5] wrote to me. I can find no dignified way to include him in this ultra-French film with only one foreign part: Fernando Rey, as the ambassador of the Republic of Miranda.

Hope to see you soon, and my very warmest regards
Carlos.
Luis

Spa Tls, CF/93/17

[1] Letter from Fuentes to LB, 8 April 1972 (CF/93/17).
[2] C. Fuentes, *Tiempo mexicano* (Mexico: Joaquín Mortiz, 1971) (AB/1054).

³ 'Me estoy ultra-americanizando': becoming even more assimilated into Latin American culture.
⁴ Preproduction on *The Discreet Charm of the Bourgeoisie,* filming of which, over forty-four days, began 23 May 1972.
⁵ John Gavin (born 1931), US actor, who played Pedro Páramo in the film directed by Velo.

To José Donoso

Paris, 24 April 1972

Dear Pepe,

Just a few lines to say that if I'm 'in good shape' this September (I've already written this to you) I shall throw myself into *El lugar sin límites*. But without Barrault! I've seen some sequences of a film he's in. He is nothing (absolutely nothing) like Manuela. An aberration on my part that I even considered him for that all-important role. I was remembering 30 years ago when I saw him in Cervantes' *Numancia*.[1] He was, and still is, a wonderful actor and mime artist. But his diction, features and expressions of *long-term actor* do not correspond in any way to Manuela. In my view, at least.

That's the problem with this film, finding a wonderful[2] Manuela.

Warm regards,
Luis

Spa Als, JD/65/04

¹ Barrault staged Cervantes's tragedy *El cerco de Numancia* (1585) in Paris in 1937.
² 'Estupenda' ('wonderful', feminine) in other words, a male actor good enough to play the role of a transvestite.

To José Donoso

Paris, 29 April [1972]

Dear Pepe,

This is a lot of correspondence for such a dreadful letter-writer as the undersigned. Although Barrault did not, in the sequences I saw, look right for Manuela, I wanted to make sure by seeing him in person. He came to visit me here at the hotel[1] yesterday at my invitation, and I got a much better impression of him. Or is it just that I have so much admiration for him as an actor? I gave him the translation of your book that arrived a couple of days ago – typed – and asked him to take his time reading it, because there's no hurry and he's very busy. He said that as it's for me, etc., etc., he would have no objection to travelling to Mexico, and that he won't be free to work over there until next March. It was a very friendly exchange.

This is a first step. Let's hope more will follow ...

I think that unless it's a few short lines, I won't write again until I finish the film.[2]

Warm regards,
Luis

[PS] I'd rather keep this quiet for the moment. When Barrault gets back to me with a decision after reading *El lugar sin límites*, I'll let you know.[3]

Spa Tlsps, JD/65/04

1   Aiglon.
2   Filming of *The Discreet Charm of the Bourgeoisie* finished at the beginning of July 1972.
3   The film version of *El lugar sin límites* (1979) was eventually directed by Arturo Ripstein based on a script co-written by Donoso and Pacheco, with Roberto Cobo playing Manuela.

From Jean Louis Barrault

Chambourcy, 4 July 1972

Dear friend,

I've realized that ever since our last meeting I can't stop thinking about your fascinating proposal.

This is the result: I'm just too keen to work with you. So, I accept the role of Manuela. Am I or am I not an actor? If I am an actor, and if *you* think I'm right for the role, there is absolutely no reason not to do it. I was just panicking.

I am therefore handing myself over to you with *total* confidence and taking the plunge. No more hesitation.

Especially as over and above all this there is my admiration and friendship for you. Let's connect the era of *Numancia* with the future months that are ours to share.

I love to construct 'memories'. This should become *one* of those. I would also love it if Jeanne Moreau, whom I admire so much, were to take part in the adventure. With my consent and my affection,

J. L. Barrault

Fre Als, AB/647.19

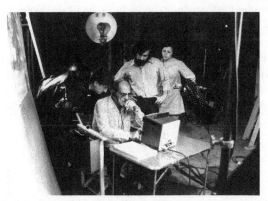

Figure 76 Buñuel, in front of monitor, filming *The Discreet Charm of the Bourgeoisie*, Paris, July 1972.

To Ricardo Muñoz Suay

Paris, 1 September 1972

Dear Ricardo,

I'm about ready for the off. When 'thou doth read' these lines, I may already have taken flight for my homeland. I am so sorry not to have seen you, but my trip to Mexico cannot wait. I am sick and tired of all the commitments, meetings, etc., and you could say that I'm escaping all the chaos.

I knew about my 'debt' to the Treasury. Zapata's lawyers have power of attorney and are dealing with it.

My film[1] will premiere in Paris, in eleven cinemas, on 15 September. I don't think it will get through the Spanish and French censors (who are seeing it this Friday), but who knows.[2]

Warmest regards to Nieves and you,
L. Buñuel

Spa Als, RMS

[1]   *The Discreet Charm of the Bourgeoisie.*
[2]   Premiered in Spain on 21 April 1973, without cuts.

To Serge Silberman

Mexico City, 29 September 1972

My dear Serge,

My special envoy, Ully Picard, will tell you that:

1) I shall travel to New York if your marvellous contact in the State Department and the Department of Justice requests a visa from the United States' Consulate in Mexico allowing me to stay in New York for the duration of the Festival.[1] I already have a *waiver.*[2] That should make it easier to get the permit.
2) If I don't get the visa, I'll wait for you here and we can go to Purúa together when you arrive from New York.
3) Please bring me two packets of genuine Gitanes.[3]
4) I am very happy, more for you than for me that the film is working out better than expected.

Yours,
Luis

Fre Als, RS

¹ *The Discreet Charm of the Bourgeoisie* premiered at the 10th New York Film Festival on 13 October 1972.
² English in the original.
³ French cigarettes sold from 1910.

To José Rubia Barcia

Mexico City, 9 November 1972

My dear *don* Pepe,

Frankly, if you'd been on one of those sabbatical years you have so *often*, I wouldn't have come over, because I'm less sociable and less in favour of international 'shin digs'¹ every day. Although, I wouldn't have minded having another look at that city, I remember so bitter-sweetly.

I am truly grateful for the invitation to stay with you, but as I am an invited guest and will have to socialize – as little as possible – I would prefer to grin and bear it in a hotel. My producer² is going to meet me there and we'll be staying at the Beverly Wilshire Hotel. Jeanne doesn't want to come so I'm making Rafael keep me company, he's been here in Mexico for a year now and is married to a French girl.³ He's also very keen to see you.

I arrive the morning of the 15th on Western Airlines, flight 604, but there will probably be some unknown annoying official waiting for me at the airport. The best thing would probably be for you to come to the hotel at 5pm, so we can have our first meeting 'face to face' and in private.

Although I'm still drinking and smoking as much as ever, I lead a very sedate life. I always go to bed at 8:30 and likewise get up at 6:00. I never stay up late. Except over in Los Angeles where, exceptionally, I shall visit you at your home at whatever time you wish. I would prefer, at least sometimes, to visit you in the evenings. I would of course be delighted to meet any of your friends who will be my friends, at your house.

Longing to give you both a hug, from your very old friend who can still get about without a wheelchair,

Luis

PS I don't know where Leonardo lives. If you want to get in touch with him, we could all have lunch together on Saturday the 17th. I'll be over there for about a week.

Spa Tlsps, CBC; *CLB* 97–98

¹ LB was invited to Los Angeles and attended the screening of *The Discreet Charm of the Bourgeoisie* at the 2nd Filmex Festival, 19 November 1972.
² Silberman.
³ Dominique Buñuel.

To Serge Silberman

Mexico City, [November] 1972

ENORMOUSLY GRATEFUL FOR YOUR TELEGRAM. I ARRIVE IN LOS ANGELES ON 15 NOVEMBER. I HAVE VISA AND PLANE TICKETS. HAVE ASKED THE FESTIVAL TO RESERVE ROOMS FOR ME AT THE BEVERLY WILSHIRE. SEE YOU SOON.

REGARDS,
BUÑUEL[1]

Fre Tel, RS

---

[1] LB attended a dinner organized in his honour at the home of the film-maker George Cukor in Los Angeles in November 1972; guests included John Ford, Hitchcock, Rouben Mamoulian, Robert Mulligan, George Stevens, Billy Wilder, Robert Wise and William Wyler.

From Carlos Saura

Madrid, 10 November 1972

Dear Luis,

It's been such a long since I've had any news of you, I think it must be since you went back to Mexico just before Christmas 1971, in other words almost a year ago now. In all that time, I've been about to write to you so often, and maybe even did, I can't remember, but in the end, I decided to wait to see you in person. Unfortunately, that didn't work out, because when you were in Paris making *The Discreet Charm of the Bourgeoisie*, I was in Madrid working on my latest film, *Ana y los lobos*,[1] which, after endless ups and downs of all kinds, I have finally completed, although we are still waiting for the go-ahead from the censor to screen it in Spain.[2] We'll see …

I was finally able to see *The Discreet Charm of the Bourgeoisie* a couple of days ago, in Geneva. And that is mainly why I'm writing. First, to say it is a wonderful film, possibly one of your best, if not your very best. Wonderful, Luis. I haven't enjoyed myself so much for a long time. Not since *The Milky Way*, I think. This time, Luis, I think you have found the perfect balance between a whole series of things that, although they crop up in your other films, come together here to form a unified whole. And, most of all, it is your most naked film, in the sense that it is the most personal, or if you like, the film in which you reveal the most of yourself. And not only because there are so many allusions to your friends and yourself, but also because the memories (I imagine from childhood) have such strength and presence, and are inserted so boldly into the narrative that you have automatically taken that extremely difficult leap (to which I believe a good few of us are committed) from immediate reality to that other plane of imaginative, dreamt, or hallucinated reality. That marvellous leap where the lucid reality of traditional narrative turns to nightmare.

I don't know, Luis, there are so many things I'd like to discuss with you. I hate writing. I find it really laborious and prefer not to do it. Although I do find it less difficult to write to you, if I'm honest.

I was a bit worried by the systemic presence of death in the film. Most of the dream-realities end in, or are interrupted by, death, generally violent deaths, even suicidal in some cases. I don't recall such an, almost obsessive, presence of death in any of your other films.

In your case it soothes me to remember though that, as Octavio Paz said: 'the fascination with death is not so much a trait of adulthood or of old age, but of youth.'[3]

Luis, an enormous hug. Best wishes to your wife. I hope to see you very soon,
Saura

[PS] and Gerarda.[4]

Spa Tls, AB/632.17

[1] Produced by Querejeta and premiered 20 May 1973 at the Cannes Film Festival.
[2] *Ana y los lobos* premiered in Spain, June 1973.
[3] In Paz's essay 'Conquista y colonia', published in the book-length essay *El laberinto de la soledad* (Mexico: Cuadernos Americanos, 1950).
[4] Postscript by Geraldine Chaplin.

Figure 77 Meal in honour of Buñuel at Cukor's home in Hollywood, 20 November 1972; standing, Mulligan, Wyler, Cukor, Wise, Carrière, Silberman, Charles Champlin and Rafael Buñuel; sitting, Wilder, Stevens, Buñuel, Hitchcock and Mamoulian.

To Serge Silberman

Mexico City, 25 November 1972

My dear Serge,

Splendid journey, just 2 hours 45 minutes.[1] We are very grateful for your incomparable hospitality, your dedication to us and your generosity. Squirrels are lazy and inept in comparison with you. Your public persona, on the other hand, is less commendable. I laughed a lot when Rafael told me you reminded him of Groucho Marx,[2] and that Gui, so elegant and urbane, was like a modern-day Adolphe Menjou. Groucho and Menjou: what a couple! Thank you again for everything.

Over here, the film has had an unprecedented success. More than a thousand people, most of them students, were left outside the cinema. More tickets sold than *The Godfather*.[3] The press is predicting huge commercial success. As usual, the audience laughed a lot. It's sold more tickets than all the other French films of course. The screening was quite good by all accounts, although for the first one at 4pm the projectionist changed the reel just as the sergeant was about to tell the colonel he wanted to tell him about a dream, so there was an abrupt and inexplicable jump to the street of the dead.

That's all I have to tell you.

Sending you affectionate regards,
Luis

PS For my part, I don't intend to allow the Spanish censors to make a single cut.

Fre Tlsps, RS

[1]   From Los Angeles to Mexico City.
[2]   US comic actor and film-maker (1890–1977).
[3]   *The Godfather* (1972), dir. Francis Ford Coppola.

To José Donoso

Mexico City, 29 November 1972

Dear Pepe,

Your letter arrived ten days after you sent it. Delighted to *sponsor* you for the scholarship.[1] Delighted and honoured.

I hope to get over there before long and we shall talk at great length, but my permanent address is the Mexican one. They forward my letters on to wherever I may be.

Salomón Laiter is a young director from over here, a bit crazy, but *very talented* judging from a film of his[2] I've seen and recommended to Cannes for the Festival. He's young.

Warmest regards to María Pilar and *ditto* to you,
Luis

Spa Als, JD/65/04

---

¹ Donoso was awarded a grant by the Guggenheim Foundation in 1973.
² Possibly, *Las puertas del paraíso* (1971), based on a short story by Elena Garro.

From Fritz Lang[1]

Beverly Hills, December 1972

To Luis Buñuel,[2]
Profoundly happy *Les trois lumières*[3] were able to illuminate your path!

With all most sincere admiration,
Fritz Lang

Fre Da, Od; *AUG* 354 f

---

¹ Austro-German film-maker (1890–1976), exiled to the United States in 1934.
² Dedication, handwritten by Lang, on a photograph of the director, who met LB in Los Angeles in November 1972.
³ French title of Lang's film *Der müde Tod* (1921), a film LB discovered in the 1920s and often cited as having inspired his decision to become a film-maker.

To the Museum of Modern Art, New York

12 February 1973

TO WHOM IT MAY CONCERN
I give permission to The Museum of Modern Art in New York to collect and preserve my films including The Golden Age *upon the understanding that they will be shown only on the Museum premises.*

Luis Buñuel

Eng Tls, MoMA/12.04; *EE* 838 f

To whom it may concern

At La Barraca,[1] 27 February 1973

I hereby certify that I shall make no more films, and in particular, no film called *The Phantom of Liberty.*[2]

LB

Spa Ans, SS; *CUA* 608 f

---

¹ Madrid restaurant, founded in 1935.
² Title of film, in English in the original, directed by LB in 1974.

To Serge Silberman

Madrid, 1 March 1973

Dear Serge,

Just a couple of lines. I have found a wonderful, truly exceptional place to entertain you. Complete solitude, great comfort, in an old Benedictine convent 1,200 m above sea level. Perfect solitude.

The address is:

Luis Buñuel
Hotel Santa María del Paular
Rascafría, Spain
Telephone: Rascafría (Madrid) 64

We're[1] going on Monday 5th.
I don't know if you can phone from Paris. You should try anyway, as you love talking on the telephone so much.

Very affectionately,
Luis

Fre Ans, RS

[1] LB and Carrière, to work on the script for *The Phantom of Liberty*.

From Gustavo Alatriste

[Mexico City,] 18 March 1973

LUIS BUÑUEL
HOTEL SANTA MARÍA DEL PAULAR, RASCAFRÍA

DEAR *DON* LUIS,

I OFFER YOU THE SUM OF 500,000 DOLLARS (TAX FREE), PAYABLE IN THE COUNTRY OF YOUR CHOICE TO MAKE THE FILM WE DISCUSSED. IF YOU ACCEPT I SHALL FLY TO SPAIN TO SIGN ON A NAPKIN.

WARMEST REGARDS,
ALATRISTE

Spa Tel, AB/622

To [Rafael] Buñuel

Buñuel
6006 Romaine Street
Hollywood, California

[Madrid, March 1973]

Buy a dinner jacket and a dress for Dominique to go with Serge next Tuesday to the Oscars.[1] *He'll be in the Wilshire[2]* from Sunday 25th.

Luis

[PS] Write to me, from today, at Torre de Madrid. Kisses.

Spa Ans, RS

---

[1] *The Discreet Charm of the Bourgeoisie* nominated for Best Foreign Film at the Oscars of 27 March 1973.
[2] English in the original.

From Gordon Stulberg[1]

Beverly Hills, 9 April 1973

Dear Mr Buñuel,

Now that the excitement of the Awards has died down, may I take this occasion to express the profound gratitude and admiration of the entire company and myself and my family with respect to the recognition you so richly deserved.[2]

It was equally delightful and perhaps much more satisfying that the nomination and the award has engendered a series of retrospectives and re-releases of your films so that many hundreds of thousands of people who might otherwise have been denied the privilege, may have the opportunity of seeing more of your works.

I hope this note finds you in the very best of health. We all look forward to seeing you again in the near future.

With every best wish.
Cordially,
Gordon Stulberg
Twentieth Century-Fox Film Corporation

Eng Tls L, AB/1426.40

---

[1] US producer (1923–2000) and President of 20th Century Fox (distributors of *The Discreet Charm of the Bourgeoisie* in the United States) from 1971 to 1974.
[2] *The Discreet Charm of the Bourgeoisie* won the award, received by Silberman.

From Federico Fellini

Rome, 3 May [1973]

Dearest Luigi,[1]

I saw *The Discreet Charm of the Bourgeoisie* last night.[2] To say how much I enjoyed your film, how much it delighted and fascinated me suddenly seems too obvious, quite insufficient to convey the feelings and the deep, personal emotion that have made me hasten to write to you at once.

The vitality, superb quality, dispassionate and disturbing fantasy, humour – so cruel and so human – the provocative and omnipresent creative freedom of your latest film, at one point opened my eyes to the incarnation of a nourishing and protective divinity, whose creativity withstands the mortifications and blows of time. And at that precise moment, I felt a sense of great consolation, reassuring confidence, and a confused and lively gratitude towards you.

That is what I wanted to tell you, dearest maestro. Most affectionate greetings and wishing you good luck and great work,

Yours,
Federico Fellini
Via Margutta 110

Ita Als, AB/632.7; *BDM* 215–216 f

1   Luis, italianized in Fellini's letter.
2   Premiered in Italy on 11 April 1973.

Figure 78 Buñuel in disguise, holding Oscar awarded to *The Discreet Charm of the Bourgeoisie*, 1973.

To Francisco Rabal

Madrid, 5 May 1973

Dear Paco,

I am truly sorry I won't be able to come to your house on Sunday. It is my last day here and I have to spend five or six hours with Max Aub's son-in-law[1] before I leave, so I can go through and approve a number of things in the book Max wrote about me that the aforesaid son-in-law is putting together.[2] I could see you tonight, but I don't feel well.

I think your script[3] will struggle with the censors. It's well written, very visual, and it all depends how it is filmed. As it is at the moment, it looks like a 'populist' melodrama to me. Fairly innocent. There may be a few too many songs. As you said yourself. In short: the main thing is that you 'feel it' from the heart and that way it will always be very humane. My dear nephew: what a megodrama you've written!!

Hug María Asunción, Teresa and Benito for me. I would have loved to see them.

Hugs to you from
your UNCLE,
Luis

PS I'm not in the mood, nor well enough to go to Cannes.

Spa Als, FR; *BVMC* f

[1] Federico Álvarez Arregui (born 1927), editor and translator, who took over the book on LB after Aub's death on 22 July 1972.
[2] M. Aub, *Luis Buñuel*, ed. and prologue by F. Álvarez (Madrid: Aguilar, 1985).
[3] Unpublished script by Rabal based on his childhood in the mining seaport of Águilas, Murcia, south-eastern province of Spain.

To Serge Silberman

Mexico City, 10 June 1973

My dear Serge,

I sent a telegram answering yours and announcing this letter. It was over a month since I'd heard from you.

I'm happy to hear you'll soon be here, but not under the conditions you propose, only meeting once a day, not wiring me on your arrival, etc. Let's do what we always do and go to San José where, in spite of the 'immense luxury', we shall enjoy the utmost peace. Before you arrive, I shall go over there one day to make sure it's still possible to stay there.

I've decided, finally, not to let myself be gutted by our favourite actor, José Luis Barros.[1] I am feeling reasonably well, and the diet has worked. I'm still drinking as much as ever. Of course!

The Discreet Charm of the Bourgeoisie is going into its sixth week in a 3,000-seat cinema, the most expensive in Mexico ($1.25). It's a long way from the centre. I've no idea why anyone would go all the way over there. I don't know how the film's doing in Europe. But you can tell me when you get here.

I can't remember if I sent you the number you asked for, of my account in Paris. To make sure, I'm including it here.[2]

I don't have an account now with Banque Transatlantique.[3] You also mentioned Jacqueline has some tax-related documents for me. If I need to file them, bring them over.

No one writes to me, not even my 'faithful' Jean-Claude. What is he up to?

Warmest regards,
Luis

[PS] Send a telegram as soon as you arrive. If it's not too late, I'll come and meet you. I never leave home now after 7pm.

Fre Tlsps, RS

[1] Joke: Barros, LB's doctor, appears briefly with LB, Silberman and Bergamín, in *The Phantom of Liberty*.
[2] LB includes the account number, omitted here.
[3] French bank founded in 1881.

From Serge Silberman

Paris, 6 July 1973

Dearest Luis,

Firstly, please forgive me for not writing by hand. But I think you will understand my writing more easily this way.

See what you've reduced me to! Working and doing my own typing.

Despite what I said in my telegram, I've not been able to write until today. I did get your telegram meanwhile. It confirms my fears. That is, you seem very stressed.

Let's talk seriously now. I would never oblige you by force.[1] I've never done that, not psychologically … nor physically. No human has that right over another. What's more, it's not in my nature. I have a genuine fear of meddling in other peoples' affairs. I'd never let anyone do that to me.

Now that I've spoken about me, let's speak a bit about you. I may have no right to do this, but I'm assuming the right as I consider myself, honestly and sincerely, your friend.

1) Try to forget that I'm a film producer.
2) I don't care about the film, even less so now. I really don't care! And I said as much to Gustavo Alatriste, who came to visit me in Paris a few days ago. And I said the same thing the day before yesterday to José Luis Barros when he phoned me from Madrid.

3) The only thing I care about now is your health and, and most of all, your well-being.

4) I think it is completely unreasonable not to see one or two specialists and not to trust them, especially when you have a very good surgeon to hand, who is also, and above all, a friend.[2]

5) I think it's unreasonable to refuse, in a fit of pique or depression or on principle, or maybe even to prove to yourself and your friends that you can still be stubborn, that you are still reckless (or perhaps just, plainly and simply, to annoy them and spite your own nose …); to refuse – as I say – to recover as soon as possible and restore yourself to your formidable former state, mentally, in the first instance, and then physically, or vice versa if that's possible.

6) I think you are behaving like a child. Or a bit like a prima donna. Or perhaps it's just your contrary nature, with a touch of supposed humour, tainted black.

7) I hope it is not just laziness!

8) I assure you that before long, we will all be laughing about this and teasing you a bit about your behaviour. Because you are actually in fine physical shape (in spite of the little niggles). It is your spirits, mainly, that are not doing so well.

9) I say (I SHOUT): BE CAREFUL… Don't retreat into your shell or shut yourself up voluntarily in a prison of your own making.

10) If you do decide once and for all to stay in Mexico until mid or late September, I suggest I send Jean-Claude over there in August.

11) Jean-Claude's visit, even revising the final version of the script, would not commit you to anything.

12) I, on the other hand, do commit myself to accept your decision over the dates (should there be any dates).

13) I am, therefore, putting in this same envelope a letter of commitment on my part.

14) I apologize for the tone and shape of my previous telegram. I think that we get anxious mostly (exclusively perhaps) for our friends, with our friends, and because of our friends.

15) As for Jean-Claude, please don't refuse his visit. I've had problems because he planned to work with you from the end of June. So, when I got back from Mexico, he had to change everything around, which wasn't easy, to free himself up from everything else so as to be able to work with you from the end of July to the end of August, or early September.

16) This would also allow me to get to Mexico for a week in August, as I too get bored.

17) I met up with Gustavo Alatriste and his wife[3] in Paris. I had lunch with them at Fouquet's[4] (on the terrace, very nice). He used all his charm on me. He said he was fond of me because of you. He's very intelligent, and despite his talent for business, he can be very human at times. He has called me three times from Madrid since then. He's leaving for Mexico today. I was very touched, because he seems to adore you.

18) In any event, and if it won't annoy you, I shall come to Mexico for two or three days or perhaps a little longer, from Los Angeles, where I have to be. But I

wouldn't do this without making sure beforehand that this will not cause you any stress. If not, it would be a pleasure for me.

[Serge]

PS Re. the letter from Greenwich Film Productions of 28 June 1973).[5] In relation to shooting dates, we'll sign by mutual agreement according to the state of your health and your decision. If possible, we could specify before the end of 1973 or perhaps early 1974.[6]

In terms of the author's rights, experience has taught us that 20 years is too little time.

We'd need to extend this, although as you are interested in 10 % of the profits,[7] this would probably not be a problem for you.

Fre Tluf, RS

[1] To film *The Phantom of Liberty*.
[2] Barros.
[3] Sonia Infante (born 1944), Mexican actress.
[4] Restaurant on the Champs Élysées, Paris, founded by Louis Fouquet in 1899.
[5] With regard to filming *The Phantom of Liberty*.
[6] Filming began in Paris on 4 February 1974.
[7] At the box office.

To Jean-Claude Carrière

Mexico City, 11 July 1973

My dear Juan Claudio,

I am so ashamed of my epistolary abulia; it's taken me so many days to reply to your so cordial, informative, funny and, above all, 'millenarian' letter. I agree that soon (the second millennium is ending), the end of the world will come with or without the Pope and with or without Christ. I won't see it, but you will meet the consequences. I also agree with you that it will be a wonderful spectacle, but as I will already be safe and sound 'lost among the shadows'. On to other things!

Serge's enthusiasm led you to believe I was coming to Paris ready to seek out actors, locations, choose sets and all the other wretched minutiae of our profession. Nothing further from my true intentions. I currently have no wish to go back to my old ways. I don't feel ill, certainly a lot better than in Paular and, if not happy, I am at least content with my current state of domestic eutrapelia.[1] If I felt under no obligation to make the film, I would be quite happy to start working with you right now on *The Phantom*,[2] or something else, until it was completely ready. It's a miserable twist of fate that something written in peaceful seclusion means you then have to spend six months or more travelling here and there, surrounded by people and stress. The best thing would be for Serge to buy the *script*[3] from us then make the film with one of the countless directors wandering about out there. But that's unthinkable.

I may come to Europe, depending on my health, around October, but on holiday. I hope before then, I can get my hands on your book,[4] which I am very keen to read. Could you not take advantage of some acquaintance travelling to Mexico and send it to me? Or give me the name of the publisher and the title so that I can order it from here.

If you can arrange for us to finish the *script*,[5] which I haven't read again, with no obligation on my part to film it, I'm at your disposal right now.

You said Auguste and Iris were preparing to go on holiday, but just in case they are still with you, pass on hugs and kisses from me.

And for you whatever you like from your aged and apathetic friend,
Luis

Spa Tls, JCC

[1] 'Wittiness', Greek, according to Aristotle, a conversational virtue.
[2] Provisional title of *The Phantom of Liberty*.
[3] English in the *original*.
[4] J-C. Carrière, *Le pari* (Paris: Laffont, 1973) (AB/523).
[5] English in the original.

To Serge Silberman

Mexico City, 17 July 1973

My dear Serge,

First of all, thank-you for the advance on profits from *The Discreet Charm of the Bourgeoisie*. I've already written to the Transatlantique asking them to transfer the 45,000 francs to the CIC. Following Jacqueline's instructions, I've left the rest, so the account doesn't go into the red.

I got your long letter with the contract attached, and I accept without further discussion, if I manage to make the film, although at the moment the thought of such a prospect horrifies me. I have no desire to work and still less to leave my home and live in a hotel for several months. Please consider this a very serious decision.

As for my health, it is sorting itself out more or less. I certainly don't need eminent international experts to examine me anyway. There are some very good specialists here in Mexico too. And above all, staying at home is the best remedy there is.

I told you not to send Jean-Claude over. I would have preferred to wait until the Autumn, because by then I'll know where I stand with a lot of things that I won't go into now. You say I'm stubborn, but you … In any event, do whatever you like. I'm not making any promises, even if, right in the middle of our joint efforts, work has to stop, and 'poor' Jean-Claude has to return to Paris empty-handed.

You may not believe me, but I am perfectly content with my current state of inactivity and, trust me, have no need to ruminate on my more-or-less imaginary illnesses.

As for the wonderful bottles you are saving for me, Rodolfo[1] says you could send them to me 'care of' him without an import licence. As soon as the courier confirms their arrival at customs, I am to let Rodolfo know and he will make sure they get to my house without the import duty. He also took the opportunity to say that President Echevarría[2] is sending me a case of bottles from his *stock*.[3] I'm not joking.

I will be truly delighted to see you in Mexico again.

With much affection,
Luis

Fre Tls, RS

---

[1]   Mexican actor, Rodolfo Echeverría Álvarez (1926–2004), listed as Rodolfo Landa in *The Criminal Life of Archibaldo de la Cruz*, is director of the Banco Nacional Cinematográfico of Mexico from 1970.
[2]   Luis Echeverría Álvarez (born 1922), Mexican politician and President of Mexico from 1970 to 1976, brother of Rodolfo Echeverría.
[3]   English in the original.

To Carmen Sampietro[1]

[Mexico City, 25 October 1973][2]

When you were still very young, you were the first person who got me to respond emotionally to music. I remember you had the piano scores for various operas: *Carmen, Faust*,[3] etc. Farewell to those days! But *not yet* to this life.

Your faithful,
Luis

Spa Ans, *LL; PAS* 7

---

[1]   Childhood friend of LB, with whom he also shared some of his earliest film-viewing experiences.
[2]   Text written on the back of a photograph of LB, with handwritten dedication: 'To Carmen Sampietro, my unforgettable childhood friend. Your friend always, LB'.
[3]   Opera by Charles Gounod premiered in 1859.

To Giorgio Tinazzi[1]

Mexico City, [December 1973]

I have received the copy of *Avanti!* with your article[2] on me and some old poems (1927) I thought were lost. I'm truly grateful.

I hope one day to have the pleasure of meeting you in person.

Your friend,
L. Buñuel

Spa Als, GT

---

[1]   Italian film-maker (1939–), author of *Il cinema de Luis Buñuel* (Palermo: Palumbo, 1973) (AB/774).
[2]   Tinazzi's article held with cuttings in ABR/1999.

To Francisco Rabal

Paris, 21 January 1974

Dear Paco,

I was also very sorry not to see you in Madrid during the brief time I was there. The second time I tried to get in touch no one answered the phone at your house. It was Juan Luis who called. I thought you must all be in Águilas.

I am *very sorry* I can't find a way to add you or Fernando to the cast of my film.[1] Lawyers, doctors, Napoleonic soldiers, gendarmes, prefects of police, etc., all very French. And no important roles for them either. Silberman regrets your absence as much as I do. I've wracked my brains trying to come up with a way to 'get you both in' but haven't come up with anything.

If I remain in good health, and if I make another film in Spain, I've sketched out an idea for you and Fernando, him as a Jew and you as a Palestinian. I've mentioned it in passing to your Galician colleague.[2]

Very sad not to be with you, sending hugs.

Your uncle,
Luis

Spa Als, FR; *BVMC* f

[1] *The Phantom of Liberty.*
[2] Fernando Rey.

To José Donoso

Paris, 24 February 1974

Dear Pepe,

I got your letter. Dancigers is a good friend of mine and is to be trusted. Which doesn't mean the script of your *El obsceno párajo de la noche*[1] might not turn out *too political.* That's not the best direction for the film to go in. But you have a say as the author. It depends what contract you've signed.

Until I finish my film[2] (in April), I'm completely isolated from all social and even friendly contact. When I am free, I'll see what I can do for your friend, although I don't think, what with my isolated life cut off from film people, it will be much.

Kisses for Pilar and your little girl, and a big hug for you from,
Luis

Spa Als, JD/67/02

[1] For an unrealized adaptation of the novel.
[2] *The Phantom of Liberty.*

Figure 79 Vitti, Silberman and Buñuel during filming of *The Phantom of Liberty*, Paris, February 1974.

To Carlos Fuentes

Paris, 3 March 1974

My dear Carlos,

My 74 years thank you for your birthday wishes, and for my part I also accept them with a sad smile of farewell.

I see your migration[1] issues are completely resolved and wonder if Don Luis E.[2] had something to do with that. Mine are in the process of being sorted out by Mr Moskovitz,[3] Saltzman[4] and Silberman's lawyer in New York. It turns out the State Department had a pretty sizable file on me.[5] I may get an ordinary visa this month without the famous *Exemption*[6] 28 C d, etc. If so, I'll go to New York in June[7] via Mexico, and will descend upon your home in Virigina[8] to have fun with all the *zorras*[9] that, according to you, surround you on all sides.

And you, still working on your book![10] I now see you have more trouble writing a novel than I do writing a letter! I'm waiting impatiently for you to get to the final full stop.

There are 70 actors in this film *The Phantom of Liberty*, all with very small parts. When you see it, you'll realize why it just wasn't possible to get María Casares[11] in.

I'm happy to try and help García Riera[12] in any way I can. You just have to let me know how. Television and advertising horrify me, although I am grateful for your new attempt to take up your cudgels 'on my behalf'.[13] I really don't think I deserve so much of your attention. I'm embarrassed.

I've been filming for four weeks now with a good few more to go. This *Phantom of Liberty* may be more popular than the one about the bourgeoisie. But I don't want to get my hopes up.

Have you read the monstrous book *Comment devenir Dalí?*[14] Unbelievable!

Kisses for Silvia[15] and the baby[16] and, what the hell, kisses for you too!
Luis

Spa Tls, CF/93/17

[1] US government had previously denied Fuentes a visa in 1962 and 1969.
[2] Luís Echeverría.
[3] Irving Moskovitz (1913–96), US lawyer.
[4] Harry Saltzman (1915–94), Canadian producer based in the UK.
[5] Ninety-two-page FBI file on LB's activities from 1941 to 1971.
[6] English in the original.
[7] LB did not travel to New York until October 1974.
[8] In 1974, Fuentes was living near the capital in the State of Virginia, funded by a grant from the Woodrow Wilson International Center for Scholars, Washington.
[9] Joke with black humour and sexual innuendo on LB's part, as 'zorras' (vixens), a prerogative also commonly used to mean 'prostitutes'.
[10] *Terra nostra* (Mexico City: Joaquín Mortiz, 1975).
[11] Actress (1922–96), exiled to France in 1939.
[12] Film critic and historian (1931–2002), who arrived in Mexico in 1944.
[13] Fuentes intended to report on LB for Mexican TV Channel 13.
[14] S. Dalí, *Les aveux inavouables de Salvador Dalí (The Unspeakable Confessions of Salvador Dalí)* (Paris: Laffont, 1973) (AB/299).
[15] Silvia Lemus (born 1945), journalist and second wife of Fuentes.
[16] Natalia Fuentes Lemus (1974–2005).

To [Joaquín Aranda][1]

Paris, 4 March 1974

I imagine your friends' notion[2] is not based on any objective interest in an anthology of my 'literary work', but rather on a certain sympathy for my films. I really don't think my 'writings' have any merit on their own, although they might round off a biography. They've been published here and there already and some of them are in the book by Max Aub that is about to be published. So, although I'm grateful for their interest, I must decline their request out of embarrassment firstly, and secondly, to save them from a flop.

Warm regards from,
Luis

Spa Als, Od; *ELB* 6 f

[1] Journalist and film critic (1931–2006), married to one of LB's nieces (daughter of his brother Leonardo).
[2] To publish a collection of literary texts written by LB in his youth.

To Luis Alcoriza

Paris, 31 March 1974

Dear Luis,

I've been meaning to write to you for a while and you may have felt the same way, because every time I take a trip to Europe we exchange a few brief letters. Let's offer mutual forgiveness.

I've been filming for eight weeks,[1] five days a week, and still have another two to go. I haven't even had a cold, although I'm sick of the bloody camera. I'm pleased with some bits of the film and dissatisfied and annoyed with most of it. I'm in the doldrums, because I have no enthusiasm, and I need it to get the project going. Our 'dear' public will have 'the last word'.

I've heard something about your film[2] from Jeanne, who was there for some of Jeannette's (is that how you write it?) physiognomic transformation. Amongst other things, she told me you could have murdered Pancho Córdova,[3] because you had to do one take 21 times. Still, I imagine the film will be good thanks to your interest and abilities as a *metteur en scène*.[4] How did the 50 vultures go? When I get back to Mexico at the beginning of June the editing will be done, and I'd really like to see it, even if the sound mixing isn't finished.

You know my thoughts on Jodorowsky.[5] His film *La montaña sagrada*,[6] in terms of filming and production quality is fantastic. By comparison, Fellini looks like a modest director of little technical skill. Of course, I could do without all that Zen and Buddha;[7] but as a director he's extraordinary. Over here, the press claim I inspired him, but I know I don't hold a candle to him. By my calculations, the film must have cost about four million dollars. How did he manage to convince a producer[8] to let him handle that much money? Genius! What a shrewd businessman!

As you know, my film[9] is made up of twelve 'episodes' you might call them, linked by some anecdotal character who joins the end of one to the next, providing a kind of overall continuity. One of those episodes is the idea about the kidnapping of a girl, it lasts about five minutes; two scenes, one at a school and the other at the police station. Our treatment[10] didn't fit in a two or three-reel film, because it was too long and when the disappearing trick had been used once, to repeat it would have been an annoying tautology. Obviously, we didn't use it, which is why I think I should pay you for any hypothetical sale we might have made. If you agree, I'd like to give you 50,000 pesos compensation. Or more, if you think that's only fair. Let me know and I'll pay you whenever you like. This is a personal offer of course, nothing to do with the producer.

I was also thinking of making a film with you that I would just produce, nothing else. But we can discuss that later. We'd have to forget that joke about what a tyrant I'd be to the director of course. I could put up some of the capital with ... Alatriste?

Marciano de la Fuente,[11] a Spanish producer, came here to see me and told me you were definitely going to Spain to make *Misericordia*[12] by Galdós. That could be a stupendous film. It was one of my favourite projects back in the day. When you write back, let me know when you're going to Spain. I'm thinking of going before I return to Mexico.

Tired out by all this writing, I leave you. Kisses for Janet.

Warm regards,
Luis

Spa Tls, ALC/01/03; *BRU* 29–30

¹ *The Phantom of Liberty.*
² *Presagio* (1974), dir. Alcoriza, based on a script co-written with García Márquez.
³ Mexican actor and director (1916–90), played Father Angel in *Presagio.*
⁴ French in the original.
⁵ Alejandro Jodorowsky (born 1929), Franco-Chilean film-maker, lived in Mexico from 1960 to 1974.
⁶ Surrealist film directed, written and acted by Jodorowsky in 1973.
⁷ Reference to the seven superior beings the protagonist encounters.
⁸ ABCKO, US film and musical production company, founded by Allen Klein in 1961.
⁹ *The Phantom of Liberty.*
¹⁰ 'La niña' co-written by LB and Luis Alcoriza.
¹¹ Spanish producer (1925–), Subdirector General de Cinematografía between 1973 and 1977.
¹² Published by Galdós in 1897.

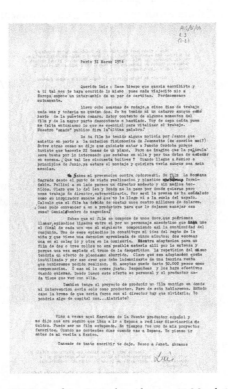

Figure 80 Letter from Buñuel to Alcoriza, 31 March 1974.

To Alexander Calder

Paris, 29 April 1974

My dear Sandy/Alex,

You are wrong about me. You are a dear friend to me, and I remember the kindness and friendship you showed me in New York. If we didn't meet up often in Mexico, it wasn't just my fault. You've been incredibly busy and I, to tell the truth, rather anti-social.

Hope to see you soon and raise a glass of red wine to your good health.

My regards,
Luis

Fre Als, AC

To whom it may concern

[Paris,] May 1974

I swear by God that I shall never again succumb to the infectious extroversion of our age: I shall never collaborate with any technological instrument such as cinema.

Goodbye,
LB

Spa Ans, SS; *CUA* 609 f

From Luis Alcoriza

Mexico City, 24 June 1974

I have received from Luis Buñuel the sum of $2,000 towards my contribution to a treatment (without dialogues) prepared in 1958 based on an original idea of his to do with the kidnapping of a girl; not used, as the concept was used by Buñuel in his latest film.

Luis Alcoriza

Spa Tls, AB/1532

To Gabriel Figueroa

Mexico City, 5 July 1974

Dear Gaby,

I have received the attached letter (this is a copy).[1] If I decide to go to the *meeting*,[2] would you like to accompany me in the capacity of *favourite photographer*? I'm just sounding you out before replying to those gentlemen. At the moment, I don't feel particularly inclined to accept.

Warm regards,
Buñuel

Spa Als, GF

1   Letter from Forslund to LB, 20 June 1974 (AB/1426.60).
2   English in the original.

From Serge Silberman

[Paris,] 5 July 1974

DEAR LUIS,
   I KEPT SILENT ON PURPOSE TO GIVE YOU A FEW DAYS' PEACE. I PUT ON A SINGLE SCREENING FOR THE ACTORS, CARRIÈRE, THE DISTRIBUTOR AND THE CINEMA OWNERS. THEY ALL LOVE THE FILM. THEY THINK IT IS A MASTERPIECE, YOUR BEST FILM. AM SO HAPPY FOR YOU. ARE YOU STILL HAPPY TO ADD A SECOND SUBTITLE TO THE BEGINNING OF THE FILM, AFTER 'DOWN WITH FREEDOM!', THE ONE ABOUT 'DEATH TO THE FRENCH!'?[1] AM PERSONALLY IN FAVOUR OF DOING SO. PLEASE REPLY URGENTLY. PLEASE ALSO PAY $1,000 TO HENRY NOEL DUPUY,[2] ADMINISTRACIÓN DE CORREOS 9, DORMITORIO 0, NORTE MÉXICO 9. MY RESPONSIBILITY AND WILL REPAY YOU AT ONCE. WILL SEND PERSONAL LETTER TO YOU TODAY. EVERYONE SENDS WARMEST REGARDS.

AFFECTIONATELY,
SERGE

Fre Tel C, RS

1   This credit (A bas la liberté) appears in the film trailer.
2   Nephew of Muni sentenced to three and a half years in prison in Mexico on 4 April 1973.

To Serge Silberman

Mexico City, 8 July 1974

My dear Serge,
   Your telegram only arrived on Saturday night and I didn't send mine until today, Monday. The subtitle 'Death to the French!' is very appropriate.

I'm glad your guests enjoyed the film. I imagine Jean-Claude will write to me about it as well, he usually does.

My journey[1] was fine, despite being taken under the mild effects of alcohol. There was no one sitting next to me although first class was almost full.

I will give Henry Noel the $1,000 in instalments, because it might be stolen by the guards, the governor, or other inmates. He has been sentenced to THREE AND A HALF YEARS. I haven't seen him, but a Franco-Mexican family who have a son in the same prison, go to visit him – their boy – twice a week and will pass on the money. I gave them 1,000 pesos yesterday. He's very happy in prison. He wrote[2] to say that several Mexican companies, even MGL, want to buy his script *Le Lézard méxicain*.[3] Can you imagine! His cell has a TV and A BAR! He's writing a lot and is delighted. In Mexico, you can visit prisoners in their cells, and during the day the inmates can wander wherever they want. I shall go along one day and visit that dear disciple, because I am his 'dear, very dear master'. I think Muni may be unaware of the little detail of the THREE AND A HALF YEARS.

Looking forward to the letter you mention in your telegram, I am at your service my very dear GODFATHER, your humble servant,

Luis

Fre Tls, RS

[1] From Paris to Mexico City, after post-production on *The Phantom of Liberty*.
[2] Letters from Dupuy to LB held at the Filmoteca Española.
[3] French in the original (Mexican lizard).

To Bengt Forslund

[Mexico City, August 1974][1]

Dear Mr Forslund,

In your letter of 20 June 1974, you mention a weekend devoted to a seminary for directors beginning January 1974. I assume you meant January 1975.

If I'm in Europe at that time and my health permits, I'd be delighted to participate.

However, at this time it is difficult to make such a long-range commitment since my plans are still uncertain.

Nevertheless, as soon as I have a clearer idea of my schedule, I shall let you know.

Thanking you for your considerate invitation, I remain,

Sincerely yours,
LB

PS If I attend the seminary, my photographer, M. G. Figueroa will be happy to join me. He has already accepted.

Eng Tda, AB/1426.64

[1] Handwritten letter (presumably dictated, as not in LB's handwriting).

From Fernando Rey

Marseille, 9 September [1974]

Dear Luis,

I am reading reviews – which I'm sure you'll soon be getting – of your film.[1] They're extraordinary, and comprehensible. This time, they don't try to analyse the film intellectually, they just launch into eulogies like someone raving about coming out of the sea after a long swim, and nothing else.

Hurrah for your fecundity and I'm glad those Martinis at the Parador – first discovered on our secret (?) trip – were so useful to you ... I know you hate these parenthetical *asides*, and I'm already on my second!

I was in Madrid for 24 hours for the dubbing of Juan's film.[2] It's good enough to be one of yours. *Seriously!* I think Juan should get over his complex and just *be your clear disciple and successor.* He's the only one who could do it and should do it. This is worthy of a long dissertation and I have no time; when we see each other next ... I'm only here until 5 October, then to Paris and then Madrid.

A MILLION HUGS
Fernando Rey
Le Grand Hotel Noailles

Spa Als L, AB/632.25

[1] Cuttings on *The Phantom of Liberty* held in ABR/2040.
[2] *La femme aux bottes rouges* (1974), dir. Juan Luis Buñuel.

From Carlos Fuentes

[Virginia,] 11 September 1974

My dear Luis,

Your congratulatory telegram gave us almost as much joy as the birth of our daughter. To you and Jeanne, our very profound thanks for such a kind gesture. Distinguishing features of the little one: Natalia, nine pounds, hair the colour of midnight, skin like a camellia. If she inherits her mother's blue eyes, you should put her under contract right now for the film you'll be making in 1994 (if cinema still exists, if the world still exists and George Orwell's[1] prophecies have not come true).

I hope you'll be able to send me a few lines about *The Phantom of Liberty*. Over here, they've just started a Buñuel season in the American Film Institute at the Kennedy Center[2] and I'm sending a cutting about it from *The Washington Post*[3] (the paper that brought down a president![4]).

Yesterday, I got to the 1033rd page of the draft of the *El Escorial* novel.[5] I can see the light at the end of the tunnel after seven years' labour, and I'll be back in Mexico in January with the finished draft. I really want you to read it before I hand it over to the printer and into unknown hands. After all (and I say this in the prologue), this vast tome was inspired by conversations I had with you and Gironella in the café at the *Gare de Lyon*. I'm very satisfied with what I've written: the novel is a true ghost of the eternal Spain, royal courts with tormented kings, mad queens, idiotic princes, flatulent dwarves, flagellants, heretics, inquisitors, scheming secretaries, monks racked with doubt, howling nuns, rebellious fantasists, hawks and Spanish bulldogs, and partial reincarnations of Don Juan, Quijote and Celestina, who never get to fulfil their destiny or write their books. You'll forgive me if the most 'positive' character, or at least the most likeable member of that witches' sabbath, is an Aragonese student and native of Calanda called Ludovico who is blind by choice: having decided to shut his eyes and keep them shut until the world changes.

Silvia and the children send kisses to you and Jeanne; and I send a hug full of my old and unwavering friendship from,

[Carlos Fuentes]

Spa Tluf, CF 93/17

1. Reference to British writer George Orwell's (1903–50) famously apocalyptic novel *1984* (London: Secker & Warburg, 1949).
2. Founded in Washington in 1971, location for a number of film cycles organized by the American Film Institute, founded in Los Angeles in 1967.
3. US daily founded in 1877.
4. Richard Nixon resigned from his position as US President in August 1974 following the 'Watergate' scandal broken by *The Washington Post*.
5. *Terra nostra*.

From Penelope Gilliatt[1]

Luis Buñuel
The Pierre Hotel, New York

New York, 10 October 1974

Dear Mr Buñuel,

I would love to meet with you in order to write an article similar to the one I wrote on Mr Renoir that I attach here[2] (I've written many others, but this is perhaps closest to the one I would like to write on you.) For the last ten or fifteen years, I've been a great admirer of your character, your exquisite, witty and subtle sense of humour and, of course, your films. I am not interested, not by a long stretch of the imagination, in hunting down icons ... I've written a film myself (*Sunday Bloody Sunday*[3]), as well as two novels and numerous stories,[4] which has made me averse to theory.

Would it be possible to join you as an observer (and friend, I hope) during your time here? Not while you are being interviewed by other people, but when you want to chat, take a walk, 'kill time' (as they say here in New York, although I assure you it's neither dangerous nor true), etc., etc. Of course, I will be going to the premiere of your latest film.[5] What a celebration.

My home number is 595 5888 and you will always be welcome,

Penelope Gilliatt
The New Yorker

25 West 43rd Street

[PS] For six months a year I write reviews for *The New Yorker*: film reviews, that is. I am English (I worked at *The Observer*[6] for seven years) and something of a red-head, which makes me easy to recognize; I'm an old friend of David Robinson[7] from London. You are, above all, magnificent.[8]

Fre Tls L, AB/1402.8

1 English film critic and scriptwriter (1932–93), wife of John Osborne from 1963 to 1968.
2 P. Gilliatt, 'Le Meneur de Jeu', *The New Yorker*, 23 August 1969, 34–61.
3 Directed by John Schlesinger in 1971.
4 The novels, *One by One* (1965) and *State of Change* (1967); collection of short stories, *Nobody's Business* (1972); all published by Secker & Warburg.
5 *The Phantom of Liberty* premiered at the 12th New York Film Festival on 13 October 1974.
6 British weekly founded in 1791.
7 English film critic (born 1930), translator into English of J. F. Aranda's biography of LB.
8 Published as P. Gilliatt, 'Long Live the Living: A Profile on Luis Buñuel', *The New Yorker*, 5 December 1977, 53–72.

From Amos Vogel

New York, [October 1974]

Dear Luis,

Two years ago[1] you kindly gave me permission to use stills from your early films in this book – here it is[2] – and perhaps it is the kind of book you might agree is necessary in our day and age…

If so, if you agree it is, would you perhaps be willing to give me a brief quote – a sentence or so – that we could use in our advertising? Random House is my American publisher. You could send it to the above address. Of course, if you have a 'policy' of not doing this kind of thing, I shall completely understand.

Amos
15 Washington Place

Eng Als, AB/1402.6; *BUL 736*

1 Letter from Vogel to LB, October 1972 (AB/1543).
2 A. Vogel, *Film as a Subversive Art* (New York: Random House, 1974).

To Amos Vogel

New York, 15 October 1974[1]

Dear friend,
　　Many thanks for the book, which looks really interesting. I'm leaving for Mexico, where I'll have time to read it. Although I'm a dreadful correspondent, I will try to send you a few words when I've read it.

I'm sorry I didn't get to see you, but I've been quite *snowed-under*.

Yours sincerely,
Buñuel

Fre Als L, AV/92/03; *BUL 737*

[1]   'Pierre Hotel' letterhead.

To Bengt Forslund

[Mexico City, 22 October 1974]

Most esteemed Mr Forslund,
    I sent you a telegram[1] yesterday saying: 'I RECEIVED YOUR LETTER[2] ONLY YESTERDAY. I AM REPLYING TO LET YOU KNOW IN ADVANCE THAT PURELY FOR HEALTH REASONS I WILL NOT SADLY BE ABLE TO ATTEND THE SEMINAR'; I feel I should now provide you with more detail about the reasons that prevent me attending the seminar: my hearing problems have got worse recently and they are accompanied by some very unpleasant complications of the inner ear. In other words, I find myself completely incapacitated for any kind of social interaction. I would find it extremely stressful to attend meeting under these circumstances. I must therefore decline.
    Please believe how difficult this decision has been for me, to forgo meeting the supporters of your film archive and Bergman, for whom I feel genuine sympathy and admiration, and not to be able to travel to Sweden, a country I adore. It is a real shame.
    If we are to be substituted by another film-maker and director of photography, and you feel Mr Figueroa's presence would no longer be appropriate, I think it would be best if you let him know this when you are able.

Yours sincerely,
[Luis Buñuel]

Fre Tda, AB/1426.59

[1]   A draft in Spanish of this telegram exists (AB/1426.58).
[2]   From Forslund, 2 October 1974 (AB/1426.62).

From Serge Silberman

[Paris,] 24 October 1974

DEAR LUIS,
    THE FRENCH POSTAL SERVICE IS ON TOTAL STRIKE. *THE PHANTOM OF LIBERTY* IN ITS SIXTH WEEK OF SCREENING HAS SOLD MORE THAN 300,000

TICKETS AND IS EXPECTED TO GET TO 450,000 OR EVEN 500,000 BEFORE EXCLUSIVE RIGHTS END. PENELOPE GILLIAT, A FRIEND OF VICENTE CANBY, WHOM WE HAD LUNCH WITH IN NEW YORK, CALLED TO LET ME KNOW SHE WILL BE TRAVELLING TO MEXICO WITH *THE NEW YORKER*, NOT CONNECTED TO YOU. SHE WOULD LIKE TO SHAKE YOUR HAND IN MEXICO AND GREET YOU. CANBY ALSO BEGS ME TO ASK IF YOU WOULD INVITE HER FOR A DRINK AT YOUR HOUSE. I SUGGEST DINNER, SO JEANNE COULD HELP YOU OUT WITH THE CONVERSATION SHOULD IT GO ON FOR A WHILE. UNTIL VERY SOON.

AFFECTIONATELY,
YOUR SERGE

Fre Tel C, RS

To Serge Silberman

Mexico City, 28 December 1974

My dear Serge,

I was happy to hear your voice, although with some difficulty, on Christmas night. You must have called at three in the morning. I congratulate you on being in such good shape you could manage to stay awake until that inconvenient hour.

If I do overcome my fear of future illness, I should like to travel to Europe between 10 and 20 January. And if I'm still in one piece, I would like to stay until May because Spring over here is awful.

I got the wonderful review you sent me from *L'Ami du 20e*.[1] 'That old anarchist ...' Incidentally, I've had no news about the film and haven't received a single press cutting, except the ones you sent me after the premiere. I read in the *Heraldo*[2] here today that *Time*[3] (the New York magazine) rated *The Phantom of Liberty* among the ten best films of the year, together with *Amarcord*,[4] etc. What an honour!

I had a note today from the Beverly Wilshire asking for the $222 still owing from my stay at the hotel. I sent a cheque straight away and a telegram apologizing. I'm assuming, as I gave you the money for the bill, it must be the difference between the discount they offer you and the price I should have paid not having the right to that offer. I'm attaching the note, so you can take a look and let me know if you agree.

Alatriste is coming to see me today and I'm going to ask if he's sent that cheque for one and a half million dollars he promised to Paul Kohner to finance a film with Bergman. I haven't seen him since our lunches at the Plaza.

Looking forward to hearing your news if you have any, and wishing you a wonderful start to the new year,

Luis

PS How is the film going? If by any chance, my son Rafael needs money, would you be so good as to give him an advance and I'll pay you back in due course.

Fre Tlsps, RS

¹ Catholic newspaper founded in Paris XX in 1945.
² *Heraldo de México*, daily paper published in Mexico City between 1965 and 2003.
³ Weekly founded in New York in 1923.
⁴ Semi-autobiographical film directed by Fellini in 1973.

From Luis Echeverría

Los Pinos,¹ 22 February 1975

Very esteemed maestro,

I did not want to let the day on which you celebrate 75 years of fecund life go by without sending my warm best wishes.

I do so with admiration and respect for a man who has, like every true artist, left behind him a bountiful harvest to enrich and ennoble his peers. This is particularly true in your case, as your aesthetic sensibility has invariably accompanied, one could even say has been committed to, a clear and critical examination of society. In this way, your service to freedom and the realm of human possibilities has repaid society many times over for all that it has inspired and evoked in you.

It is years now since you chose to live in Mexico and to exercise your citizenship to the full. Here, you have doubtless found inspiration and detail for the creation of many of your films.

Our country, which has waged a long struggle for sovereignty as a nation, as well as for its cultural survival, and that is now determined to build a society that not only respects, but also encourages and nourishes free thought and deeds, will always value, in every way, the vital source of inspiration and reflection that is your work.

I wish you, with great affection, many more years of service to your contemporaries and your countrymen.

L. Echeverría

Spa Tls L, AB/640.1

¹ Official residence of the Mexican President indicated by printed letterhead.

To Luis Echeverría

Mexico City, 22 February 1975

Mr President,

I thank you most sincerely for your letter of congratulations on my 75th birthday (a door thrown wide open, almost, to the Abyss), for your words of encouragement, for your generosity when speaking of my work and, most of all, for your humanity. I am utterly sceptical about the immediate future for human society and have taken refuge for a long time now in my last bastion, the cult of friendship, and your letter reflects that sentiment I so much appreciate.

I am also proud that you associate my name, although my contribution has been infinitesimal, to the survival of Mexican culture 'that is now' – in your words – 'determined to build a society that that not only respects, but also encourages and nourishes[1] thought and deeds'

It only remains for me humbly to ask, Mr President, that you accept my faithful and steadfast friendship,

Luis Buñuel

Spa Ad C, AB/640.3

[1] Quote missing 'free' (consciously or unconsciously?).

Figure 81 Cortázar, Fuentes, Buñuel, Echevarría and, in the background, Jodorowsky, at celebrations for Buñuel's birthday organized by the painter Gironella, at Galería GDA, Mexico City, February 1975.

To Francisco Rabal

Francisco Rabal
Hotel Castellana (room 706),
57 Paseo de la Castellana, Madrid

Madrid, 6 May 1975

Dear nephew Paco,

I received the two photographs which, although rather blurred, allowed me to perceive a disturbing landscape.

I am sorry I have to cancel our meeting on Wednesday. I've managed to get a ticket for tomorrow (the original reservation was for Friday), because I need to get home. I'm looking forward to some solitude and peace. I don't know when I'll be back.

I'd be grateful if you could send me that unbelievable magazine, *Europeo*,[1] because I don't know how or when I'd be able to get hold of it. The only thing I stand by, privately and in public, is what they say I said about you.[2] If you don't want the trouble of such a generous favour, send me the date and address of the magazine.

A big hug from your uncle,
Luis

Spa Als, FR; *QUE* npf

[1]   Weekly founded in Madrid in 1963, which published declarations by LB.
[2]   That Rabal is his favourite actor and more talented than Marlon Brando.

To whom it may concern

[Madrid,] May 1975

For the love of God: I shall make no more little films.
Yours,
LB

Spa Ans, SS; *CUA* 609 f

To Giorgio Tinazzi

Mexico City, 11 June 1975

Dear Mr Tinazzi,

After three months away, I am back in Mexico and have found your letter. Please forgive this long-delayed reply. I have to confess also to being hopelessly lazy when it comes to answering letters from friends.

I really enjoyed your book, although my weak understanding of Italian prevented me going into enough depth to be sure I understood it all precisely. I'm taking advantage of this opportunity though, to thank you for your interest in my work.

As for my Mexican films, it would be best if most of them just disappeared. The only ones of any interest are *The Young and the Damned, Robinson Crusoe, Susana, This Strange Passion, The Criminal Life of Archibaldo de la Cruz, The Exterminating Angel, Nazarín, Simon of the Desert* and *The Young One*. I only made the others because I needed to earn a living. They were all made in three weeks with few technical resources.

I hope to meet you in person someday,

Cordially yours,
Luis Buñuel

Fre Tls, GT

To José Donoso

Mexico City, 21 July 1975

Dear Pepe,

Your letter arrived and in view of my objectionable laziness when it comes to correspondence, I am responding too quickly.

I spent a couple of hours, invited by Figueroa, at the filming of *Coronatione*,[1] and I am adding that E to avoid the consonant. It's directed by the same film-maker who made Fuentes's film *Muñeca reina*.[2] He's very discreet. I can't tell you much about it, because I only saw them shoot one scene where Carmen Montejo[3] gives a rousing monologue, five minutes of screen time.

The male lead is Ernesto Alonso,[4] who worked with me on *The Criminal Life of Archibaldo de la Cruz*. The set was good: a mansion, well known in Mexico City dating back to Don Porfirio.[5] To conclude: how it will turn out remains a mystery.

Princeton[6] is a wonderful university I visited a number of times, because the head of the Spanish section was a good friend of mine.[7] As was Américo Castro,[8] who taught there for a few years.

I will be delighted to see you all in September, if I'm not already in Europe.

Affectionate hugs to Pilar and a kiss for the little one.

For you, whatever you like from,
Luis

[PS] Regards to Losey if you see him.

Spa Tls, JD/68/02

---

[1] Directed by Sergio Olhovich in 1975, based on the novel of the same title by Donoso; the joke about the added 'e' is a reference to the view that words that ending a consonant sound bad in Spanish.

[2] Directed by Olovich based on an original short story by Fuentes published in the collection *Cantar de ciegos* (1964).

[3] Cuban-Mexican actress (1925–2013).

[4] Mexican actor (1917–2007), played Archibaldo de la Cruz in *The Criminal Life of Archibaldo de la Cruz*.

[5] Porfirio Díaz (1830–1915), Mexican general and President of Mexico between 1884 and 1911.

[6] US university founded in 1746, where Donoso was teaching classes on creative writing in 1975.

[7] LB visited Princeton at the beginning of the 1940s.

[8] Américo Castro Quesada (1885–1972), linguist and historian, professor at Princeton University between 1940 and 1953.

To Charles de Noailles

Mexico City, 22 July 1975

My dear Charles,

I've been away from Mexico for a while and found your letter when I got back on 12 June. Please forgive this delayed reply.

It would take too long to explain everything that has happened[1] in a letter, especially for someone like me who has so little talent for writing. So, instead of providing the answers to everything in your letter, this reply is going to be very concise. I plan to travel to Paris in October and it would be wonderful to see you again and discuss the troublesome ghost of *The Golden Age* in more detail.

I should let you know first that any screenings at film archives around the world are not free of charge. The audience has to buy a ticket, as they would do in any public cinema, the only difference is that the money does not go to the people who run the archives, but towards the costs, which are fairly high, of running those institutions. I think that's the case with Anthology Film Archives in New York, which is run by Mr Mekas, who is very well known in the New York film world and is the editor of *Film Culture*,[2] which has been the best film journal for years now. I don't think the Bleecker Street[3] copy would have been lent out by Anthology Film Archives for commercial screenings. I'm sure it wouldn't. There are, though, a lot of pirate copies, here in Mexico I know at least three people who have a 16mm copy! The Dominican priest Julián Pablo, Mr Alatriste and a student called Carrillo. Alatriste and Father Julián got their copies from him. I've no idea how Carrillo got his hands on a 16mm negative. What I do know is that, for now at least, the film has not been shown commercially.

I have had requests to screen *The Golden Age* from different film archives and cultural institutions. I have replied saying that there is no objection on my part, but that the owner, Mr de Noailles, is absolutely opposed to all commercial exploitation of the film. The most recent requests were from the Museum of Modern Art in New York and from the Max Ernst exhibition at the Grand Palais in Paris.[4]

[Luis]

Fre Tda, AB/569.21

---

[1]   Relating to the commercial exploitation of pirate copies of *The Golden Age*.
[2]   Journal founded by Mekas in New York, published between 1954 and 1996.
[3]   Bleecker Street Cinema, Greenwich Village, New York.
[4]   Between 16 May and 18 August 1975.

To Eduardo Ducay

Mexico City, 18 September 1975

Dear Eduardo,

Your letter arrived just before I left for Beverly Hills (Los Angeles), and I was there for ten days. I took it with me so I could write back to you from there, but not only did I not do so, I also managed to lose the letter. I loathe myself when something like that happens, because I'm usually very careful and organized. I went to see my younger son who is living up there.

As always, Autumn will push me towards Europe in search of golden leaves, cold skies and dear friends. That is, if socio-political-terrorist events don't get in the way. The whole world makes me sick, and things are just as bad over here. But if I don't go and you do decide to come over, I'd be delighted. I have indescribable memories of your previous visits. What a shame dismal old age prevents me from renewing our 'professional' relationship and returning to Spain to work on a new Gurruchaga-Ducay ... (NOT Sabatello!) production.

I'm glad business is going well for you. It is important for financial peace of mind.

My life is delightfully monotonous. I've been asked, almost officially, to make a film over here. But I'm resisting. Silberman has asked too. And even though he's treated me so well, I'm also putting him off. One of the problems with old age is the lack of enthusiasm. Nothing interests me. Except my sterile leisure.

Hugs to Mercedes, your brood, and you,
Luis

Spa Tls, ED

From Pedro Ángel Palou Pérez[1]

Puebla, 16 October 1975

Distinguished and genteel friend,

With cordial greetings, I am writing to let you know that the formal inauguration of the Film Archive of this institution[2] will take place on Thursday 13 November at 7:30pm. The Archive will be named LUIS BUÑUEL in your honour, and we hereby confirm the invitation extended to you by our Film Coordinator, Mr Fernando Osorio,[3] to visit the aforementioned Film Archive.

Hoping to have the pleasure of your gracious company, may I take this opportunity to reiterate to you my heartfelt admiration and distinguished regards,

Pedro Ángel Palou, General Director
Casa de la Cultura, Oriente 5

Spa Tls L, AB/1426.69

¹   Mexican writer (born 1932).
²   La Casa de la Cultura, Puebla, México.
³   Fernando Osorio Alarcón (born 1953), founder of the Mexican Cinemateca.

To Pedro Ángel Palou Pérez y Fernando Osorio Alarcón

Mexico City, [October 1975]

[Dear Sirs,]

I am grateful for the kindness you have shown towards my work in cinema by naming the Cinemateca after me, although I would have preferred it to be after someone else, or even, had it been possible, a name that did not refer to any individual in particular. What matters though, is your important work, especially if your archive appreciates film not as a sacred cow or museum piece, but as something living, and liberating, that serves to disrupt the conventional workings of thought and culture. Of course, 'culture' is a word I cannot write without blushing.

I send you my regards and wish the new Cinemateca success for many centuries to come.

Luis Buñuel

Spa, Od; *ZZZ* 52

To Amos Vogel

Mexico City, 13 November 1975

Dear Amos Vogel,

I've just got back from the country and found your telegram. It's difficult to compress my overall response to your book¹ into a few lines, especially in English. Still, here, thinking in Spanish then translating, literally into my horrendous English, is what you requested. If you do use these lines, please have them translated into correct English:

*I have gone through the intense garden of your book with the inducement of a fruit long-time forbidden. To my judgement it takes an outstanding place, if not unique in the already extensive cinematographical bibliography. Its pictorial enlightenment accompanied by your commentary makes this work an invaluable album for the cineaste.*²

Very affectionately yours,
Luis Buñuel

Fre/Eng (in italics) Als, AV/106/06, *BUL 737–738*

¹   *Film as a subversive art.*
²   Used as promotional material by Random House on back-cover of US editions.

From Muni

[Paris, 1975]

Dear *maestro*, my *maestro*,
   I am enveloped. Your friends are with me.[1]
   I would love to be with you. Say a brief prayer, dear *maestro*, that my wish comes true.

I hold you close, so close to my little heart,[2]
Muni

Fre Pau Di, AB/1403.06

[1] Postcard with collage by Gironella on the back that includes image of LB in bishop's mitre.
[2] Includes drawing of a small heart by Muni.

To Manuel de Muga[1]

[Mexico City, 1975]

In remembrance of Joan Prats[2]
   I never met Joan Prats. I first heard of him in 1930, through the Dalí of those days and Hurtado[3] (from *Mirador*). They told me he wanted to give me a hat. It was his reward for my film, damned back in those days, *The Golden Age*. The gift of the hat was the start of our friendship. From that moment on we were always in contact ... through friends: José Luis Sert, Miró, Hurtado, many others, and my sister Margarita and brother Alfonso. When would we meet in person? 'Tell him that this year I'm going to go and meet him and collect my hat.' People had stopped wearing them for quite a while by then. And in that way nearly half a century went by.
   Three years ago, I was in Barcelona and went to the shop to see him. Joan was there serving a customer. It must have been him. Why did I not go in? Fear perhaps, of effusive greetings in front of a stranger? Or perhaps some deeper compulsion? The client didn't leave. 'I'll come back tomorrow.' But the next day a telegram arrived, and I had to go to Paris. Then, his death.
   The image I have of Joan through our mutual friends is so lifelike that his death is like losing one of my very closest companions. And I'm left without that wonderful hat of friendship. Just its ghostly memory.

Luis Buñuel

Spa Olu; *HJP* sp

[1] Editor (1916–2006), founder of publishing house, Ediciones Polígrafa, in Barcelona in 1968.
[2] Art promoter and patron (1891–1970), close friend of Miró.
[3] Amadeu de Hurtado (1875–1950), lawyer and politician, founded the weekly *Mirador* in Barcelona, published between 1929 and 1938.

To José Luis Borau[1]

Madrid, 16 March 1976

To José Luis Borau,
   With my great admiration for *Furtivos*[2] and hoping to meet you soon.
Cordial greetings from

L. Buñuel

Spa Da, Olu; *CUA* 547 f

---

[1]   Film-maker (1929–2012).
[2]   Co-written, produced and directed by Borau in 1975.

From Patricia and Richard Gillan[1]

London, 25 May 1976

Dear Mr Buñuel,
   My wife and I have written a book called *Sexual Therapy Today*[2] that will soon be published in England, the United States and some other European countries. I am enclosing a copy with this letter. It would be an honour for us if you would allow us to dedicate this book to you.[3] For we have always been great admirers of your films, especially those more concerned with the erotic such as, for example, *Belle de jour*, etc.
   In our work within the area of sexual therapy, we have often suggested our patients watch your films in order to enrich their fantasy lives and develop their sensuality. We have had marvellous results, and this has made us feel a little closer to you, even to the extent that one could say that through your films you have become our 'co-therapist' for part of the treatment. We hope you will enjoy the book and that you will write to let us know what you think. We take our leave of you, thanking you in advance for your time.

With our appreciation,
Patricia and Richard Gillan
Institute of Psychiatry,
Maudsley Hospital
Denmark Hill,
London SE5 8AF

Spa Tls L, AB/1402.59

---

[1]   British therapists associated with the Institute for Psychiatry at the Maudsley Hospital, London.
[2]   Patricia and Richard Gillan, *Sex Therapy Today* (London: Open Books, 1976).
[3]   The dedication reads: 'We would like to pay tribute to the films which have helped to enrich our own fantasies and sex lives and those of others. We are particularly indebted to Buñuel, Borowczyk, Leopold Torre-Nilsson, Makevejev, Ken Russell, von Sternberg, Pasolini, Nagisa Oshima, Bertolucci, Fellini and Falcon Stuart.'

To Paul de Angelis[1]

Zaragoza, [June 1976]

Here are some lines as requested.[2] I'm very conscious that I have no gift for this kind of thing. Still, if you publish them, please be good enough to correct my French.

'In *Le Cornet acoustique*[3] the body of a perfidious abbess, who died in mortal sin, gives off a scent of holiness ... The representatives of abominable governments, who drag us towards utter debacle, freeze to death in front of their microphones ... And so on and so forth. Reading this book frees us from the miserable social and political reality of our days and, through the dark humour of her delirious fantasy, Leonora reveals to us the secret magic of her paintings.'

[Luis Buñuel]

Fre Tda, AB/1402.62

[1]   US editor of the St. Martin's Press founded in London in 1952.
[2]   Letter from Angelis to LB, 25 June 1976 (AB/1402.61), asking for promotional comment for *The Hearing Trumpet* (London: St. Martin Press, 1976), novel by the English born Mexican surrealist painter Leonora Carrington (1917–2011).
[3]   LB uses the French title of the novel (Paris: Flammarion, 1974).

From Charles de Noailles

Paris, 29 June 1976

Dear Luis,

Your letter of 9 June has arrived, and it made the crossing in 15 days, which is not too bad for correspondence between Mexico and France.

I am in complete agreement with you on everything that concerns the future of the film. I have absolutely no intention of handing *The Golden Age* over to anybody. What I want is to find an agent who will screen the film under the usual conditions, in the United States or somewhere else, for a limited amount of time established by prior agreement.

I am sorry to say that this is going far from well. I've not yet been able to get the registry at the National Centre of Cinematography in Rue Lubeck to issue a formal acknowledgement of the film's existence in France. They sent me a form to sign, I signed it and sent it back last April, since then, nothing.

When the holidays were over, my lawyer wrote to them on my instructions. Without that formal acknowledgement, I can do absolutely nothing. I did not, at first, appreciate the powerful inertia that comes over cinematographic circles in response to requests made of them.

I shall, of course, keep you informed as to my progress. The original copy is still with Henri Langlois and it will continue to be available to the Cinémathèque.

I would be delighted if you enact your plan to come to Europe this year. At our age and above all at mine,[1] so few old friends remain that we would always love to be able to shake them by the hand.

Most cordial greetings,
Charles

Fre, Ou, *BMS* 334

[1] De Noailles was 84 years old.

To Tom Luddy[1]

Mexico City, 12 July 1976

Dear Mr Luddy,

First of all, I must thank you for your kind letter and also apologize for not having been able to meet you here for health reasons during your recent visit to Mexico.

Please believe me when I say how very grateful I was for all the information you sent me on Telluride,[2] both on film and on the wonderful surroundings of the festival. Unfortunately, I am unable to accept your invitation for the following reasons: I never travel unless it is absolutely unavoidable; my hearing problems, especially in English, would prevent me communicating with the various people I would need to meet; and I shall leave it at that, so you don't have to carry on reading about my troubles.

If you come back to Mexico, I would be delighted to meet you and talk at great length.

Cordially,
Luis Buñuel

Fre Tls, TFF 36

[1] Film critic and US film producer (born 1943).
[2] Film Festival, Colorado, United States.

To Jean-Claude Carrière

Mexico City, 11 August 1976

Dear Jean-Claude,

Better to send a few lines in response to your two latest letters than maintain a sullen silence on both. As you know, I am practically word-blind.

Congratulations on taking possession of your labyrinthine manor[1] and I accept your invitation the next time I am in Paris, to an out-door lunch in your garden which, if you allow me, I am going to christen La Chênaie,[2] in honour of its leafiness, shadiness and excellent oxygenation.

Serge, who is still stubbornly trying to get me to work, has sent me a long, rigorous, exhaustive and dictatorial contract with your signature at the bottom, to begin, from

15 September, rewriting, preparing and making that oh-so-familiar film.[3] I have not followed your lead and, instead of signing in my turn, have held on to the document.

This is a summary of my response:

I agree to finish and improve on the script,[4] which I calculate will take a month. Working with you, of course. We would have to start here in Mexico from 15 September. Or, if you both prefer, I could come to Paris from 15 October. If you are not free, I could happily wait, for months if need be, until you are … unless I am ambushed beforehand by the chap with the scythe, also known as Parcae or Moirai.[5]

When we have finished, and we are all three happy with it, the decision whether to proceed would be mine. I would need to feel confident in my physical strength and health, because the stress and effort required to make a film are tremendous. And that's without even mentioning the possible illnesses that might afflict a valetudinarian such as this one.

I think the script as it is, from the beginning to the point when Don Mateo[6] goes to Conchita's[7] house for the first time, is really badly put together, in that classic and *démodé*[8] Hollywood *boy meets girl*[9] way of immediately introducing the audience to the protagonists, and I won't go on because I'm no film critic. I have some ideas that I would be 'proud' to share with you and that 'will make you weep for joy'.

Between the two of us. Do not commit yourself to working with me if the conditions our friend Serge offers don't seem favourable. I imagine he will be wanting to protect himself against the insecurity of not having me tied down. And, what's more, I can only work enjoyably with you.

Hugs and kisses for Auguste and Iris, and likewise for you,
Luis

Spa Tls, JC

1. Carrière moved to a new house in rue Victor Massé, Paris, in 1976.
2. French in the original (Holm Oak).
3. *That Obscure Object of Desire*.
4. First version of the script co-written by LB and Carrière, based on the novel *La Femme et le pantin* published by French author Pierre Louÿs in 1898.
5. Personifications of the three Fates representing death in Greek (*Moirai*) and Roman (*Parcae*) mythology.
6. Character in *That Obscure Object of Desire* played by Fernando Rey and alternately described in Spanish and French as Mateo or Matthieu (Matthew).
7. Character in the film played by two actresses, French, Caroline Bouquet, and Spanish, Ángela Molina.
8. French in the original.
9. English in the original.

To Jean-Claude Carrière

[Paris, October 1976]

Dear Jean-Claude,

Here's an outline of the way the dialogue might go.[1] Please correct or make any changes necessary. *Thanks,*[2]

[Luis]

Dialogue in the cabaret between Don Mateo and D (still to be translated³)
D. – Don Mateo?
M. – Yes, I am he. May I help you?
D. – Conchita has told me all about you.
M. – Well … delighted to meet you. Please, sit down. Would you like a drink?
D. – That would be very nice.
(*The waiter is serving another table. Mateo waits until he has finished to call him over*).
M. – So you are a friend of Conchita's.
D. – A soulmate. She's a little star.
M. – Quite.
D. (*She studies Don Mateo's face*) – But you're not as old as she claimed!
M. – Really! She says I'm very old?
D. – More or less. She also says you're a very good man, though rather innocent …
M. – I'm glad. Incidentally, what's this about a visit to the doctor?
D. – Are you interested? If you'd like to see her, I'll go with you.
M. – Let's.
(*They get up and leave*).

Fre/Spa Tls, JCC

¹ For *That Obscure Object of Desire*, filmed in Paris, Lausanne, Madrid and Seville between February and June 1977.
² English in the original.
³ Into French as LB wrote this short dialogue in Spanish.

Figure 82 Bouquet, Molina and Buñuel during filming of *That Obscure Object of Desire*, spring 1977.

From Howard Gotlieb[1]

Boston, 8 April 1977

Dear Mr Buñuel,

I am writing to you once again relative to the matter which I raised in an earlier letter to you of 21 April 1971. We remain most interested in becoming the repository of your papers.

As I wrote before, your work is much admired here, and it is our feeling that the materials relating to your career, and to your life, should be carefully preserved. The Twentieth Century Archives in our new library offers such preservation and attracts an increasing body of scholars.

We very much wish a Luis Buñuel Collection to be a part of the research centre we have created here, and I do hope that you will consider this proposal.[2]

Sincerely yours,
Howard B. Gotlieb
Director of Special Collections
Mugar Memorial Library
Boston University
771 Commonwealth Avenue
Boston, Massachusetts 02215

Eng Tls L, AB/1404.15

[1] US librarian (1926–2005), archivist at Boston University, founded in 1839.
[2] LB left part of his archive to the Lausanne Cinemathèque suisse (letter from Freddy Buache to LB, 23 August 1977, AB/1404.16); on the film-maker's death the rest of his archive was acquired by the Spanish government.

To Denise Tual

[Paris,] 15 July 1977

To my dear Denise,
    who changed the course of my life by getting me out of Hollywood in 1945.

Today, I thank you,
Luis

Fre Add, Olu; *TEM* 144 [b]

From Luis Gasca[1]

San Sebastián, 9 August 1977

Dear Don Luis,
    On behalf of San Sebastián and the Basque people, it is my great honour to invite you to spend a few days with us during the XXV International San Sebastián Film

Festival.[2] The festival closes with a screening of your film, *That Obscure Object of Desire*,[3] on 21 September and we would be delighted if you could be with us to receive our affection, admiration and friendship.[4]

Mr Silberman has suggested the most comfortable way for you to travel would be to fly from Mexico to Paris and then, accompanied by Mr Silberman, travel by Pullman,[5] or on the overnight express from Paris–Hendaye.

We will send you the tickets for this trip in a separate letter as a personal invitation, independent of any delegation, and I take this opportunity to send you my warmest regards, admiration and esteem,

Luis Gasca, Director
International Film Festival, San Sebastián

Spa Tls L, AB/1426.44

[1] Editor (born 1933) and director of the San Sebastian Film Festival in 1977.
[2] 10–21 September 1977.
[3] Released commercially in Paris on 17 August 1977.
[4] LB attended the Festival, where he was awarded an honorary Concha de Oro,
[5] George Pullman, US industrialist who designed and manufactured the Pullman sleeping car.

Figure 83 Buñuel photographed by Jack Garofalo, at his home in Cerrada Félix Cuevas, Mexico City, August 1977.

To Gustavo Alatriste

[Madrid,] 30 August 1977

I have received from Mr Gustavo Alatriste the sum of $25,000 in payment towards the film adaptation of *La casa de Bernarda Alba*, in accordance with the letter of agreement dated 30 August.[1]

Luis Buñuel

Spa CmfL, AB/1382.13

¹   Letter from Alatriste to LB, 30 August 1977(AB/1382.10), in which he agreed to pay LB US$100,000
    to adapt Lorca's play, and US$400,000 to direct it in early 1978.

To Ricardo Muñoz Suay

Madrid, 19 October 1977

Dear Ricardo,
    Viscount Charles de Noailles has every *possible* right to do whatever he pleases with
the corpse of *The Golden Age*, according to the document I signed for him two years
ago. I won't be writing to him, of course, because I owe him several letters and wouldn't
know how to explain myself. I don't care whether he burns the film or gives it away. I'm
sick of getting bogged down with film issues.

I won't be leaving here before 27 October. I hope I'll see you around. Regards,
Luis

Spa Als, RMS; *CAC* 194

From Serge Silberman

Paris, 20 December [1977]

DEAR LUIS,
    I'VE JUST RECEIVED THE FOLLOWING TELEX:
    'THE NATIONAL SOCIETY OF FILM CRITICS[1] HAS VOTED LUIS BUÑUEL
BEST DIRECTOR OF THE YEAR. THE NATIONAL FILM BOARD[2] HAS VOTED
THAT OBSCURE OBJECT OF DESIRE BEST FILM OF THE YEAR WITH BUÑUEL
AS BEST DIRECTOR.
    AFFECTIONATELY, GUY'

WARM REGARDS,
SERGE

Fre/Eng Tel, ABR/2054.4

¹   Founded in New York in 1966 by Hollis Alpert, Pauline Kael, Richard Schickel and others.
²   National Board of Review of Motion Pictures, founded in New York in 1909.

From Gustavo Alatriste

[Mexico City,] 12 January 1978

Dear *don* Luis,

   Following our conversation, you agree to work with me as writing consultant and advisor on issues I may wish to consult with you regarding cinema production.

   This agreement may be annulled by either party with fifteen days' notice.

   Your fee for this consultancy will be 50,000 pesos per month from January 1978.

Regards,
Gustavo

Spa Als, AB/1382.14

From Frank Capra[1]

Los Angeles, 4 February 1978

LUIS BUÑUEL
7950 SUNSET BOULEVARD, HOLLYWOOD

   DUE TO A MISFORTUNE (INFLUENZA), I SHALL NOT HAVE THE HONOUR OF CONVEYING MY RESPECTS AGAIN TO OUR BELOVED GIANT.[2]

HEALTH AND LOVE,
FRANK CAPRA
LA QUINTA, CALIFORNIA 92253

Spa Tel, AB/632.14

[1]   US-Italian film-maker (1897–1991).
[2]   At a meeting regarding LB's visit to Los Angeles in February 1978.

From José Rubia Barcia

Los Angeles, 26 February 1978

My dear *don* Luis,

   We loved your visit here. As you know, it is always a pleasure to have you with us. I hope Jeanne will be inspired to come occasionally as well.

   I am sending you two *masterful* photographs as a memento.

   I am also sending you a copy of my old paper on *The House of Bernarda Alba*, so that we can disagree on a more solid footing when we meet again. I think I articulate my errors better in writing. When speaking, particularly with a certain degree of wit, they are more easily hidden.

I have told the head of the Film Department, Professor Hawkins,[1] that you may agree to attend, and even answer a couple of questions after the screening of *An Andalucian Dog* and *The Golden Age* during our series of events to commemorate the Generation of '27.[2] He was delighted, touched and excited by the idea, he even asked if I might not be aware that your son Rafael had studied with them. He insisted he would find out himself whether copies of the films could be found, and an appropriate venue. I let him speak before warning him nothing was decided yet. Let me know please if you will agree to come. I will give my talk on 'Vicente Aleixandre and the Generation of 27' on 26 April, Aleixandre's birthday.[3] The films could be shown together on the night of the 27th (of course, this all depends on whether we can get copies and find a suitable venue). The symposium will take place on the 29th and 30th. I've also just written to Juan Larrea, whom I already know will be coming to Chicago in the first week of April, in the hope that he can be persuaded to come down here too. I'm having a little trouble accessing sufficient funds. Although I do hope to be able to cover any costs that arise. I mentioned that, in your case, and if you agree, the university would at least have to pay the return airfare and a minimum of three nights' accommodation in a hotel of your choice. Send me a couple of lines with your decision, more than anything so that they don't begin to think I'm making all this up.

I'm also sending a copy of an initial project I've drawn up that I'm working on.

Eva and our dear Elena and Adela send you and Jeanne their love and best wishes, and I add warm regards of my own to you both,

Don Pepe

Spa Tls, AB/1426.154

---

[1]   Richard Hawkins (1923–2015), US academic, UCLA professor from 1953 to 1991.
[2]   At UCLA.
[3]   Vicente Aleixandre y Merlo (1898–1984), poet, received the Nobel Prize for Literature in 1977.

From Howard W. Koch[1]

Beverly Hills, 1 March 1978

Dear Mr Buñuel,

I am very happy to inform you officially that you have been nominated for an Academy Award for your adapted screenplay of That Obscure Object of Desire.[2]

The Academy, of course, is very hopeful that you will attend the 50th Annual Awards Presentation on Monday, April 3, 1978 at the Dorothy Chandler Pavilion of the Los Angeles Music Centre.

You will soon receive further information and later a formal invitation to the Awards Program.[3]

Sincerely,
Howard W. Koch
President

Academy of Motion Picture Arts and Sciences
Beverly Hills, California

Eng Tls L Od; *BDM* 228 f

[1] US director and producer (1916–2001), President of the Academy between 1977 and 1979.
[2] With Carrière.
[3] LB did not attend; the Oscar for Best Screen Adaptation went to Alvin Sargent for *Julia* (1977).

10

The last Buñuel (1978–83)

To Eduardo Ducay

Mexico City, 17 April 1978

Dear Eduardo,

Your letter arrived along with the programme[1] for that mildewed and mummified corpse formerly known as *The Golden Age*. Who would have thought fifty years ago that viewers would now watch it with an untroubled digestion and a smile on their faces. Maybe they will react the same way, and far sooner, to the Baader-Meinhof gang.[2]

I would be delighted to see you again in this god-forsaken place. Try to come at the end of May, when the rainy season starts. Right now, Mexico City is a pile of dust and toxic heat. I haven't been over this year because, frankly, what's going on in Spain[3] right now doesn't much appeal. Speaking as a tourist that is.

Opthalmologically, I'm worse now than when I visited the doctor in Madrid. As well as being deaf, I shall soon also be using two pairs of glasses like Goya. It makes me quite isolated and my only comfort is the dry martini that transports me momentarily back to my youth. I'm having a very good time, doing nothing, no more thoughts about *traveling*,[4] or damned camera angles.

Give the wonderful Joaquín a hug from me, and for your family, with you and Mercedes at the head, whatever you would have of me, with great affection,

Luis

Spa Tls, ED

---

[1] Designed by Iván Zulueta, for marketing the film *The Golden Age* in Spain in June 1978, by distributors José Esteban Alenda Distribución.
[2] German far left terrorist group, active from 1970 to 1998, named after key members Andreas Baader (1943–77) and Ulrike Meinhof (1934–76).
[3] Reference to the upheavals of the transition to democracy in Spain, following the death of Franco in November 1975 and the first general elections of 1977, won by the right-wing coalition party the Unión Centro Democrático (UCD).
[4] English in the original (missing the second 'l') for travelling or dolly shot.

To Eduardo Ducay

Mexico City, 9 June 1978

Dear Eduardo,

I am very sorry that you and Joaquín have had to cancel your trip to Mexico for the reasons explained in your letter. I live such a quiet life that the days you would have been here would have been a real pleasure.

There's no smoke ... Sure enough, after nearly a year negotiating with Silberman, I've agreed to write an original script for him,[1] but *with no* obligation on my part or his to film it. It could be made by another director or sold to make back what he will have paid me, which is a fair amount. I'm happy with that arrangement, because my inactivity was beginning to bother me. If only I had the energy to make another film. Along with my other aches and pains, my sight is very bad at the moment. I only feel youthful, strong and optimistic for fifteen minutes after ingesting a decent Martini.

I'm also under a certain amount of pressure from the official Mexican film industry to make a film and have been for a while now. It would be more comfortable to work here rather than abroad, but alongside other reasons, I have no 'Mexican' ideas and the technical resources for film production over here are pretty poor.

I have no plans to leave Mexico at the moment and, although Spain is a rather unattractive place for a tourist at this difficult historical moment, I think I'll go over there at the end of the summer.

Love to Mercedes and a big hug for you, your faithful servant,
Luis

Spa Tls, ED

---

[1] *Agón o una ceremonia suntuosa*, co-written by LB and Carrière in 1978, never filmed, published posthumously as *Agón* (Teruel: Instituto de Estudios Turolenses, 1995).

To Charles de Noailles

[Mexico City, August 1978]

My dear Charles,

I am about to disrupt your peace with what is for me an important question about *The Golden Age*.

I was looking through my correspondence and I found a letter addressed to you, dated 7 July 1978, with a document entitled 'Transfer of Copyright' forwarded to me by your lawyers. There is a clause that says: 'Mr Buñuel will receive ten per cent of the net total from such and such a date, etc., etc. from Viscount de Noailles for commercial screenings of the film, etc., etc.'.

I wanted to say that, I WAIVE, from now on any sum in terms of profit that I might be owed from sales of *The Golden Age*.

If you think we should make this waiver official, you could ask your lawyer to draw up the appropriate document for me to sign at once.

I have decided to do this because of the horror of having to declare any yearly earnings to the consulate, to take account of all the yearly sums, fill out documents, and all the other associated annoyances.

I would be very grateful if you could reply to this letter. I will, in any event, send back at once any cheque I might receive from you.

I'm sending a copy of this letter to your Paris address. Since that letter where I spoke so openly to you, I've had no news of you. My health is not good now.

With all friendship,
[Luis Buñuel]

Fre Tluf; AB/568.34

From Elena Poniatowska[1]

[Mexico City, 1978]

For Luis and Jeanne,

I'm sending a copy of this little love story about the relationship between a Russian-French painter[2] and that monster Diego Rivera[3] (she's called Angelina Belov), with much affection and admiration …

Elena

[PS] And a violet.[4]

Spa Ad (E. Poniatowska, *Querido Diego, te abraza Quiela* (Dear Diego, Love Quiela) (Mexico City: Biblioteca Era, 1978), AB/168

---

[1] Mexican writer (born 1932).
[2] Angelina Petrovna Belova (Angelina Beloff) (1879–1969), Mexican painter of Russian origin, married to Diego Ribera from 1913 to 1916.
[3] Mexican painter and muralist (1886–1957); married Belova when they both lived in Paris in 1913, left her on returning to Mexico in 1916.
[4] Dried violet placed in the book by Poniatowska.

To Jean-Claude Carrière

Mexico City, 12 February 1979

My dear Jean-Claude,

I imagine Serge will have spoken to you about the long telegram I sent him a few days ago, when I got out of hospital after being shut in for three days on liquid feed with a drip in my arm and a nasogastric tube. I've been recovering slowly at home since then on an extremely strict diet. I weighed 69 kilos before the attack and barely 65 now. This slip in my health was caused by an infection after a nasty gall bladder attack.

They are going to scan my gall bladder in a few days, because it doesn't show up on normal X-rays. The doctor has warned me they may have to operate. Dreadful! A laborious operation at 79 years old. I don't know if I'll agree to that.

As you can imagine, I don't know whether, and I think it's unlikely, I'll be in a fit state to start work on 15 March as we planned. And even if I am, no question of going to San José, because no hotel or restaurant would be able to provide the diet they've got me on. Thanks to Jeanne, who is looking after me, I'm getting better and almost in no pain now.

It would be best if you forget about me and carry on without me. My mental state also leaves a lot to be desired. Along with other unpleasant things, I have absolutely no concentration.

I have a profound and genuine desire not to go back to work and not to leave Mexico, I mean, not to leave my house.

I'll find out about the operation sometime between the 17th and the 20th and will write to Serge then, he may not have received the long telegram I sent him on the 5th of this month. By the way, how is Serge? I'd like to know. I haven't had any news from him since I was last over there.

Much love,
Luis

Spa Tls, JCC

To Serge Silberman

[Mexico City,] 26 February 1979

Dear Serge,

First things first, my thanks to you and Ully for your best wishes on my birthday, although it would have been more correct to send condolences for my almost 80 years. The day before, a telex from Ully arrived with the unpleasant surprise that you had to have further surgery to do a bone graft on your leg, but that you were recovering well. I hope to hear good news soon. That accident really was very unfortunate.

I wrote you a long letter before this one that I tore up because it was an unbearable litany of all my physical ailments. I'll now sum up the essential.

I spoke to my doctor yesterday and he said they would wait two weeks for me to recover a bit more before scanning my gall bladder. I weighed 69 kilos when I was in Paris and now only 63. They will probably have to operate, but I am reluctant to let them rummage around in my insides, even though my intestines and the area around my liver are in a lamentable state. I'd prefer just to carry on with my strict diet.

To summarise the torn-up letter: I've decided not to work again whatever happens, and not to leave home any more. I'm going to wait at least a few months to see what results from this current indisposition. You can imagine just how much I regret this situation. To see you again, I'm going to have to wait and hope that one of your Los Angeles trips will bring you down this way for a few days.

As for the second payment for my latest script,[1] I don't want it now that you're not going to be able to make the film. After long and 'painful' reflection, I think what you've already given me for my work is sufficient.

With all friendship,
[Luis]

Fre Tlsps, RS

[1]   *Agón.*

To Jean-Claude Carrière

Mexico City, 1 March 1979

My dear Jean-Claude,
   A miracle! Your letter of 19 February took only 8 days to arrive. Reading it, I was so embarrassed, I was touched, I wanted to hide under my office desk! No one has ever spoken to me with such tenderness, warmth and friendship as you do in those lines. At first, I thought it was your usual 'carrieresque' humour, but then I realized you were being sincere and that you meant it seriously. To conclude: words cannot express the immense pleasure you have given me. For my part, you know how long I've regarded you as a brother and how much and in how many ways I admire you. And that's quite enough of all that!
   I wrote to Serge three days ago telling him I'd decided to stop all work of any kind and not return to Europe or even leave my 'home'. I finished by adding that I wanted to let some months go by, as many as I need, to see what would become of the endless ailments I shall save myself the trouble of describing to you here. Has Serge mentioned it to you? Maybe he hasn't got it yet. I hope that, as we are friends, he will understand the way I feel and won't put any more pressure on me. Ully sent a telegram about his bone graft. But he said it had gone very well and that he hoped I would go with him to Cannes ('Oh vain hope'[1]).
   You shouldn't come over here yet to play nursemaid to a pitiful old hypochondriac. Let's let some time pass. That will tell.

With all my friendship and a big hug,
Luis

Spa Tls, JCC

[1]   Allusion to the Golden Age Spanish mystic, San Juan de la Cruz, on the dangers of lamenting what has been lost.

To Marcel Oms

Mexico City, 17 April 1979

Dear Marcel Oms,

Your letter took nineteen days to arrive. That is not so unusual, although letters from Europe normally arrive in ten to twelve days. Anyway, the telegram you and Borde[1] sent had already arrived before that. I sent a telegram to Silberman at once and wrote to him soon afterwards. He's the only person with authority over films by Greenwich Film Productions. I imagine everything is sorted out by now.

I have now definitely retired from all film-related activity and I am happy. Retirement, voluntary retirement that is, feels good.

If possible, I'd like to have a programme from the surrealist festival I hear you may be organizing one of these days.[2]

My sincere friendship to you and Borde,
Luis Buñuel

Fre Tls, Od; *CAC* 200 f

[1] Raymond Borde (1920–2004), French film critic.
[2] At Cinémathèque de Tolouse, towards the end of 1979.

To Carlos Fuentes

Mexico City, 7 May 1979

My dear Carlos,

Despite my agraphia,[1] and with superhuman effort, I'm taking up the *typewriter*[2] to thank you for dedicating your upcoming book *Sueños y fantasmas*[3] to my shameful upcoming 80 years. As usual, I've used the same phrase 'upcoming' twice in one sentence. My language is that limited. Seriously, I really want to read it. When will it be out?[4] I hope you will send me a copy at once. You will remember how much I liked your first ghost, *Aura*.

I got back to Mexico in February. I was having gall bladder attacks. They wanted to operate. I refused. I'm still utterly idle. I don't want to go back to work on anything. I wrote so to Silberman. And the worst thing is I have no projects of any kind. I may go to Paris in October if I'm strong enough. So, it's unlikely I'll come to see you in Princeton, which holds such fond memories, it of me and I of it. I hope you will visit this corrupt little country soon, so you can marvel at the great Genghis Hank's[5] arterial roadway and so that I can invite you to a banquet worthy of you both.

Give Silvia and the girls a kiss from me, and a big hug for you,
Luis

Spa Tls, CF/93/17; *CAC* 200 fCF/93/17

1   LB uses the term 'agrafia' (neurological impairment resulting in difficulty writing) to refer to his lack of enthusiasm for writing letters. Used less commonly in English than Spanish, the adjective 'ágrafo', that recurs so much more frequently in these late letters, has been translated as 'word-blind'.

2   English in the original.

3   Provisional title of Fuentes's novel *Una familia lejana* dedicated to LB on his 80th birthday.

4   C. Fuentes, *Una familia lejana* (Mexico City: Era, 1980) (AB/1049).

5   Carlos Hank González (1927–2001), Mexican politician, nicknamed 'Gengis Hank' (after the Mongolian emperor c. 1162–1227) for over-seeing the new road system that cut a swathe through Mexico City.

Figure 84 Forman and Buñuel, Mexico City, 1979.

To Jean-Claude Carrière

Mexico City, 18 July 1979

My dear Jean-Claude,

I got the letter you wrote soon after you got back to Paris from New York and before leaving for Quiberon.[1] As always, so full of such concrete information about our friends and you.

Serge sent a long handwritten letter all about the terrible time he's had recently. And you told me about the bomb the tax office dropped on him concerning the modest sum of three million dollars in back taxes. How could this have happened to him, surrounded as he is by brilliant accountants and tax experts? Serge also mentioned you and I might do him an enormous favour that you'd already agreed to and that you might come to Mexico to explain. I was wondering: could you explain before crossing the ocean? Either way, I'd be delighted to see you over here for whatever reason.

As you are such a globetrotter, are you going to Montreal in August? Mr Losique[2] has invited me, he wants to dedicate the Festival[3] to me, and – get this! – even wants to give me the keys to the city! He swears no one will bother me and that I won't have to talk to a single journalist. I won't go, of course. I've detached myself from all human vanities. That still seem very attractive to you. Hence your great elation at the Palme d'Or.[4] You had more success with my films, with a Golden Lion at Venice and an Oscar at that cinematographic Mecca.

Je suis plus que jamais,[5] I'm more determined than ever not to work again. I'm not interested. I loathe cinema. I'm having a splendid time alone, I never get bored (a bit sometimes), half an hour's exercise every day and the rest in my study reading and meditating on the afterlife, where I hope to enjoy the ineffable sight of our Maker.

I'd be grateful if when you see Serge, you could convince him of my wish for peace and solitude, although I am able to relinquish the latter whenever I like. And that I do not want to work regardless.

I'd be very happy to see Milos[6] and you to discuss the Pope or whatever. Incidentally: I must tell you about my interview with the Soviet delegation, who came to see me about the Moscow Festival. You and Milos came up among the other topics of conversation … I'll tell you all about it.

A kiss for Augusta, two for Iris, and three hugs for you.

See you soon, no?

Luis

[PS] With my permission, Jeanne sends you a chaste kiss.

Spa Tlsps, JCC

[1] French coastal town in Brittany.
[2] Serge Losique (born 1931), Canadian film critic born in Yugoslavia.
[3] Montreal World Film Festival founded by Losique in 1977.
[4] For *Die Blechtrommel* (1979), dir. Volker Schlöndorff, based on the novel by Günter Grass adapted by Schlöndorff, Carrière and Franz Seitz.
[5] French in the original (I am more than ever).
[6] Milos Forman (born 1932), Czech film-maker, directed *Taking Off* (1971) based on a script co-written with Carrière.

To Robert Benayoun

Mexico City, 24 September 1979

My dear Robert,

Your script arrived safely and I'm glad I read it. If we could speak, we would spend a long time discussing it, but unfortunately I'm word-blind and my laziness and the difficulty I have expressing myself in writing force me to be overly concise:

1) I think the story is extraordinarily original. There are some truly funny situations. I did wonder whether, when the audience has adapted, or got used to the mismatch in the characters' ages, they might just see the film as a series of scenes going no-where, that is, a series of *sketchs*.[1]

2) The first half is very interesting.
3) As for giving you ideas, I would love to, but I find this kind of script very complicated and, given my present levels of inertia, impossible.

But, this very subjective disquisition aside, a film only counts when it is screened, because a good *scénario* can turn into a mediocre film and vice versa. What I want now is for you to be able to make it.

Very affectionately yours,
Luis

Fre Tls, JCC

¹ English in the original, missing 'e' ('sketches').

To Virginia Higginbotham[1]

Mexico City, 22 October 1979

Dear Miss Virginia,

I am sincerely grateful to you for sending me your book[2] and I'm impressed by your extensive and well-informed study of my work, although there is, at times, the odd mistake in the biographical section. For example, I have never joined a party; I have always been politically independent and continue to be so, although it is true that during our Civil War I worked very closely with the CP as it was the only one fighting first and foremost to win the war rather than, as was the case with others, to wage a revolution while Franco's forces were advancing inexorably on. But that's just a small biographical error of no real significance.

I hope, if you come to Mexico one day, to have the pleasure of meeting you in person.

Until then, my very best regards,
Luis Buñuel

Spa Tls C, ABR/1990–19

¹ US hispanist, lecturer at the University of Texas, Austin.
² V. Higginbotham, *Luis Buñuel* (Boston: Twayne Publishers, 1979).

To Jean-Claude Carrière

Mexico City, 23 October 1979

Very dear Jean-Claude,

I got the letter you sent via Juan Luis. He was with us for two weeks then he flew to Maine[1] three days ago to spend a couple of weeks at his friend Charles's ranch, where wolves roam, beavers toil, and the odd whale swims in the sea.

As always, I was very happy to get your long letter with so much information of interest to me: the Festival at Biarritz,[2] news of our friends, your projects and adventures, etc. Juan Luis described your current state of chrematistic[3] opulence as comparable only to that of an Arab Sheikh. And all thanks to your fiduciary role in *The Tin Drum* and your work with Milos, and other such like. Don't forget me in your will. Envious, like the good Spaniard that I am, I can only forgive your financial success if I share in it … and even then …

I quite like your idea of us working together again on three *sketchs*,[4] one by me and the two by other *metteurs*.[5] Although I think it might be difficult to find a producer: as you know, that kind of film nearly always has little or no success. Another hurdle: finding enough sufficiently interesting ideas. And as for the producer, I wouldn't work with anyone but Serge. Completely withdrawn from the 'vain world's uproar', I 'follow, free from strife the hidden path, of yore chosen by the few who conned true wisdom's lore'.[6] I can't remember if that's Calderón,[7] Fray Luis, or me.

Considering my decrepitude, my health is not all that bad. I never go out and avoid muscular atrophy by exercising half an hour a day. As for smoking and drinking, as always, I am unwavering in my affections. For the hellish short time we are on this mortal coil …

A shower of kisses, from Jeanne as well, to be distributed among the women in your care. And a hug for you that I only wish could be Herculean,

Luis

Spa Tls, JCC

1   Northern state in New England.
2   First Latin American Film Festival in Biarritz held at the end of September 1979.
3   From the Greek, meaning related to, or occupied in the gaining of wealth.
4   As previously in English in the original without the 'e'.
5   French in the original (directors).
6   Lines from the poem 'Vida retirada' by Fray Luis de León.
7   Pedro Calderón de la Barca (1600–81), Spanish Golden Age writer.

To Francisco Rabal

Mexico City, 23 October 1979

My dear little nephew Paco,
    Your news always arrives on the postcards you send from the various places you act in. I am grateful, although I don't write back. Writing and answering letters is a kind of forced labour for me, I try to avoid it whenever I can.

Have you finished *Fortunata*[1] yet? What part did you play?[2] The priest? I'm now completely retired on the fatal cusp of 80 winters. I never go out. My health, decrepitude apart, is not bad, thanks to the smoking and boozing.

When are we going to meet? For the first time in many years, I won't be going to Europe this autumn and winter. To Spain no chance. I'm a bit sick of the political situation there. The only party I sympathize with at the moment is the one that says, 'We were better off against Franco'.[3]

Kisses for María Asunción and a big hug for you. Your uncle,
Luis

[PS] And lots of love from your aunt Jeanne.

Spa Als, FR; *BVMC* f

1 *Fortunata y Jacinta*, TV adaptation of the novel published by Galdós in 1887, directed by Mario Camus in 1979.
2 Rabal played Fortunata's uncle.
3 Phrase popularized by the left-wing Spanish humourist, writer and journalist, Manuel Vázquez Montalbán (1939–2003).

To Carmen Bayona

Carmen Bayona
5 Paseo de las Damas, Zaragoza

Mexico City, 15 December 1979

TOTALLY STUNNED BY THE NEWS OF THE DEATH OF MY VERY DEAR FRIEND PILAR.[1] MY DEEPEST SYMPATHIES AND MOST TENDER REGARDS TO YOU,

LUIS BUÑUEL

Spa Tel, PBA

1 Pilar Bayona died after being hit by a car in Zaragoza, 13 December 1979.

To Eduardo Ducay

Mexico City, 11 February 1980

Dear Eduardo,
I was very happy to get your letter. I'm a poor and lazy writer, so I'll make this short.

1) Pay no attention to anything the filthy press says. In spite of the pressure I'm subjected to, I DON'T INTEND TO MAKE ANY MORE FILMS. I'll be 80 in a few days. It's high time I shut up.
2) I've read *Extramuros*.[1] A wonderful novel, and a magnificent writer I hadn't come across. If you see him, congratulate him for me.
3) Spain has no appeal for me right now. I prefer to stay here. I'm with the band shouting 'We were better off against Franco.' Still, if I have the energy I may go to Madrid for a couple of weeks in May to see old friends like you.

My warmest regards to your family, and likewise to you,
Luis

PS I hardly ever leave home, which stokes my fierce pessimism about the state of society and the world today.

Spa Als, ED

---

[1] *Extramuros* (Barcelona: Vergara, 1978); novel by Spanish writer Jesús Fernández Santos (1926–88) about a fake miracle in a Spanish convent.

To Eduardo Ducay

Eduardo Ducay
29 Durango, El Plantío, Madrid
Zaragoza, 7 April 1980

I WILL BE IN TOWN FOR TWO DAYS. IF YOU CAN, WE SHOULD EAT AT LHARDY'S,[1] THE TWO COUPLES, MINE AND BARROS'S. RESERVE THE JAPANESE ROOM FOR US NEXT THURSDAY AT 8:30. PLEASE BE DISCREET.

REGARDS,
LUIS

Spa Tel, ED

---

[1] Famous Madrid restaurant established by Emilio Huguenin Lhardy in 1838.

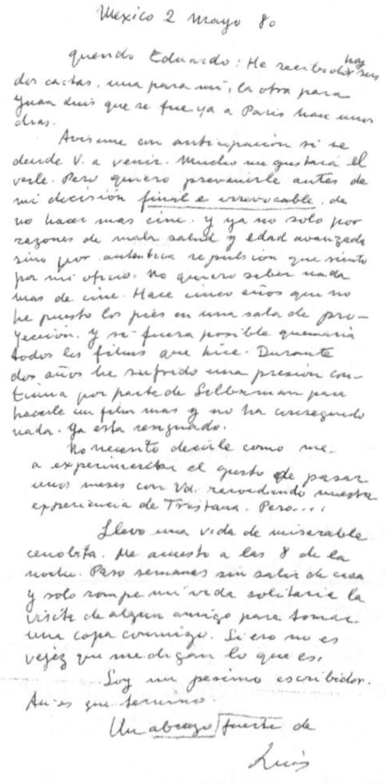

Figure 85 Letter from Buñuel to Ducay, 2 May 1980.

To Eduardo Ducay

Mexico City, 2 May 1980

Dear Eduardo,

Your two letters arrived today: one for me and the other for Juan Luis, who left for Paris a few days ago.

Let me know in advance if you do decide to come. I would really like to see you. But I have to warn you about my *final and irrevocable* decision not to make any more films, it's not now just because of my great age and poor health, but also on account of the genuine sense of revulsion I feel for my profession. I have no interest in film now. It's been five years since I set foot in a cinema. And if I could, I would burn all the films I've made. Silberman has been trying to persuade me, continuously, for two years now to make one more film for him and has got no-where. He's given up finally.

You don't need me to tell you how painful it is to think I'll never be able spend a few months with you again, reliving our experiences with *Tristana*. But …

I live like a dreary monk. I go to bed at 8 o'clock. I spend weeks without going out and only a visit from some friend or other to share a glass of wine interrupts my solitary existence. If that's not old age, I don't know what is.

I'm a dreadful letter-writer.

So, I'll leave it here.

Warmest regards from,
Luis

Spa Als, ED

To Jean-Claude Carrière

Mexico City, 5 June 1980

Very dear Jean-Claude,

Your letter momentarily interrupted my solitude with all that information about friends, lunches, your projects, etc., etc., but I was envious, we obsolete old folk hate young folk like you, so healthy and full of hope.

I have little, or more accurately, nothing of interest to tell you. My health is not bad, but I'm spiritually battered. I stick to my old habits and my only entertainment is drinking and smoking in moderation and reading, although with visual difficulty and to no great end.

I haven't heard from Serge since April. How times have changed! I used to get a telex or letter from him almost every week. Of course, we were working on the same things, so we had more to talk about. He's now utterly absorbed in his various activities,[1] which is incompatible with my complete isolation from the VANITIES OF THIS WORLD. If you see him, encourage him to write and tell me how his leg is.

When you see Denise Tual please ask her to send me her memoirs,[2] or at least tell me the title and publisher. Reading it would bring back happy memories of that part of my life.

I wish you all the success you had with the premiere of your *Aide-Memoire*.[3] Tell me how it goes.

Writing is easy for you. Send a few lines to me now and again, because your letters always bring lively and interesting news.

I read a very complimentary article in the AFP[4] about Juan Luis's TV mini-series.[5] It seems to have been a success. I'm very pleased.

The only thing I didn't like in your letter was a display of that amorality for which I, a Spaniard cut from the old cloth, have always chastised you. Your lines refer to some young girl maybe, or maybe not losing her virginity. Unbelievable, Jean-Claude … and I shall say no more.

When will I leave this beautiful country again? I don't know. It may be too late. To be honest, at the moment travelling does not appeal to me at all.

Multiple kisses for Augusta and Iris, and the same for you,
Luis

Spa Tls, JCC

---

[1] Silberman produced *Diva* (1981), dir. Jean-Jacques Beineix.
[2] D. Tual, *Le Temps dévoré* (París: Fayard, 1980).
[3] Play by Carrière, premiered at the Théâtre de l'Atelier in 1968, then at the Théâtre Saint Georges in Paris in 1980.
[4] Agence France-Presse founded in 1944.
[5] *Fantômas*; TV mini-series in four episodes co-directed by Juan Luis Buñuel and Claude Chabrol for French, German and Swiss TV in 1980.

From Virginia Higginbotham

Austin, 15 July 1980

Most distinguished Mr Buñuel,

Thank-you for the letter you sent last October informing me of an error in my book (*Luis Buñuel*, Boston: Twayne Publishers, 1979). The source for your association with the CP was the English version of Francisco Aranda's critical biography.[1] I am enclosing the photocopied page. There is no reference to it in the Spanish version of Aranda's book.

A North American critic, Andrew Sarris[2] of Columbia University in New York, has now mentioned my book in an article[3] solely in order to cite this reference to Buñuel's association with the CP. I am also enclosing a copy of this article.

I am writing to ask your permission to quote from your letter of 22 October 1979, where you explain that: 'I have never belonged to a party … although it is true that during our Civil War I worked very closely with the CP, as it was the only one that was fighting first and foremost to win the war …'.

With your permission, I shall quote that phrase when I write to Professor Sarris and the *Village Voice* to clarify this. I should very much like to correct mistake that, once made, appears to have acquired a life of its own.

I hope you are well and that there is another Buñuel film on the way.

Yours sincerely,
Virginia Higginbotham

PS This autumn I will be teaching a university course here[4] called: 'Buñuel and Saura'.

Spa Tls, AB/2053.7

[1]   J. F. Aranda, *Luis Buñuel: A Critical Biography* (London: Secker & Warburg, 1975).
[2]   US film critic (1928–2012).
[3]   A. Sarris, 'Films in Focus: Buñuel at the Beginning', *The Village Voice*, 5 May 1980, p. 39.
[4]   University of Texas, Austin.

To José Rivera[1]

Mexico City, 23 December 1980

Dear Pepe,

I am enclosing authorization for you to collect my medal from the Town Hall.[2] It's been over nine weeks now since the operation and my health is not good.

Cystoscopy and ablation, followed by three weeks of phlebitis and now, really high glucose levels. I'm just not getting better, and I don't think I can improve. My vision – dreadful; even with glasses, reading and writing is almost impossible. I've decided only to reply to letters from family, and only very briefly. I've made my bed and must now lie on it … I will soon be 81 …

Love to Alicia and the little ones, and to you,
Luis

[PS] Show this letter to Conchita.

Spa Tls, CBC

[1]   Husband of Alicia Galán Buñuel, nephew-in-law of LB.
[2]   Medalla de Oro from the Zaragoza Town Hall, awarded to LB by Mayor Ramón Sáinz de Baranda, 21 April 1980 (AB/1426.27).

To Jean-Claude Carrière

Mexico City, 19 January 1981

My dear and favourite disciple,

As always, great happiness at the arrival of your two most recent letters, and this reply from me is mainly to the second one.

I'm in no fit state to travel and still less for tributes. What would I do in Cannes[1] – even though I love it – with all these years on my back? Greet dozens of people and waves of journalists, etc.? I'd rather stay in my monastic cell and allow the time I have left, that I neither think nor hope will be long, slip sweetly by. Thank Jacob[2] and Favre Le Bret on my behalf for the invitation, I am sadly unable to accept.

As for my biography,[3] I don't think it's a bad idea in principle, and it would mean we could spend about a month together. You could come to Mexico whenever you like, and we could go up to San José; because I could do with getting some oxygen in my lungs before we start. But we'd need to set up some kind of contract with Laffont beforehand,[4] the main clause being that whatever you write would have to be approved by me. I'm very much afraid of your excessive and inventive imagination. *Je connais mes moutons.*[5] So I accept, in principle, and you can come whenever suits you.

I got the lovely little letter from Iris. Give her a kiss from me, another for Auguste and, for you, my greetings, although cold and correct ones, for fear that you'll invent things for that biography of yours.

Luis

PS I've completely recovered from the operation and am smoking and drinking much more than before.

It would be good if Laffont would pay for the stay at San José.

Spa Tlsps, JCC

[1] At the homage to LB planned by the Cannes Film Festival, 1981.
[2] Gilles Jacob (born 1930), French film critic and director of the Cannes Film Festival from 1977 to 2001.
[3] Carrière suggested producing a book on LB's life based around a series of conversations with the director.
[4] Robert Laffont (1916–2010), French editor, founder of publishers, Laffont, in 1941.
[5] French in the original (I know my sheep), words attributed to Christ: 'I am the good shepherd, I know my sheep and my sheep know me' (John 10:27).

To Giorgio Tinazzi

Mexico City, 17 April 1981

Dear Mr Tinazzi,

Thank you for your letter.[1] I haven't seen the interview you mention in *Positif*, but I'm happy to give you the translation rights you ask for.[2] I would be grateful if you would send me a copy of the original in French.

Best wishes,
Luis Buñuel

PS I was delighted to receive a copy of the book[3] you wrote on my work published by Marsilio. Thank you again.

After three years, I'm now completely retired from all film activity.

Yours,

Fre Tlsps, GT

1 Letter from Tinazzi to LB, 29 March 1981 (AB/1374).
2 Reference to an extract that Tinazzi wanted to translate and publish in Italian from LB's conversations with José de la Colina and Tomás Pérez Turrent published in *Positif*, no. 238 (January 1981), pp. 2–7.
3 Reissue of Tinazzi's book on LB with Venetian publishers Marsilio.

From Íñigo Cavero[1]

Madrid, [1] May 1981

MOST DISTINGUISHED MR *DON* LUIS BUÑUEL PORTOLÉS,
 IT GIVES ME GREAT PLEASURE TO INFORM YOU THAT HIS MAJESTY THE KING,[2] ON THE INSTIGATION OF THIS MINISTRY AND AFTER DELIBERATION BY THE COUNCIL OF MINISTERS IN RECOGNITION OF YOUR ACHIEVEMENTS, HAS SEEN FIT TO AWARD YOU THE GOLD MEDAL OF MERIT IN FINE ARTS. WITH MY CONGRATULATIONS AND VERY BEST WISHES,

ÍÑIGO CAVERO LATAILLADE, MINISTER OF CULTURE

Spa Tel, AB/1426.3

1 Politician (1929–2002), Minister of Culture, Spain, 1980 to 1981.
2 Juan Carlos I (1938), King of Spain, 1975 to 2014.

To Íñigo Cavero

Mexico City, 12 May 1981

Dear Sir Minister of Culture,
 I am profoundly grateful for the honour bestowed upon me by the Ministry, particularly as it comes from my beloved Spain.

Yours faithfully,
Luis Buñuel

Spa Ans, AB/1426.10

To Claudio Isaac[1]

Mexico City, 6 July [1981]

Dear Claudio,
 I have read your *script*[2] and like it very much. I have faith in your talent, and that this will make a good film. The only thing I don't like is the title. But that can easily be changed for the better. I suggest you take it to Doña Margarita.[3] If she likes it, it's a done deal, I mean, the film will get made. Let me know how things go.

Warm regards,
Luis Buñuel

Spa Als, CI; MED 38 f

[1]   Mexican film-maker (born 1957), son of Alberto Isaac and author of *Luis Buñuel: A mediodía* (Mexico City: Conaculta, 2002), in which he notes that LB said: 'I don't want to go overboard with the praise; so to make it sound more realistic, I'm going to say I don't like the title' (p. 36).

[2]   English in the original, referring to *El día que murió Pedro Infante*, directed by Isaac in 1982.

[3]   Margarita López Portillo (1914–2006), Mexican writer, director of the Comisión de Radio, Televisión y Cinematografía, and sister of José López Portillo, Mexican president, 1976 to 1982.

To Jean-Claude Carrière

Mexico City, 3 October 1981

My dear J-Cl,

I wrote a – relatively – long letter to you yesterday, but I forgot something important: to congratulate you on your 50 youthful years, and to regret that we were not able to celebrate together over a glass of wine. I envy you. I was as strong as an ox at that age, and now ... well, you can see how life goes by and 'how cometh Death in stealthy surprise ... How fain is memory to measure each latter day inferior to those of old'.[1]

No news of Serge. For two months now. If you have any, please let me know in your next letter.

I've looked through the memoirs.[2] Cutting out the section on my films (that was of no interest whatsoever) will make it very short. I imagine it would be good for commercial reasons to make it more 'baroque', as the publisher suggests, in other words, more scandalous, but you should just tell them I'm not Dalí, although if I wanted, I could be and more besides. If it wasn't for your sake, for all the friendly interest you've put into writing these memoirs, I'd stop the whole thing right now. Well, if we do carry on, I'll do my best to avoid falling into banal and foolish tales.

Write to me.

With love,
Luis

PS The great Louis Malle came to see me a week ago. I had a wonderful time. He drinks like a fish.

Spa Tlsps, JCC

[1]   Line from *Coplas por la muerte de su padre* (1476), by Spanish poet Jorge Manrique.

[2]   The conversations LB had with Carrière from which Carrière drafted LB's 'autobiography', *Mon Dernier soupir*.

To Agustín Sánchez Vidal

Mexico City, 5 November 1981

My dear friend,

It is a great pleasure to reply to your letter of 24 October of 1980!! Somewhat late, but better late than never! Blame my idleness as a writer, my poor sight and my infamous agraphia. I thought your letter was wonderful and I have filed it among my papers.

Joaquín has written from time to time and he's told me about the prologue (30 pages long!) you've written for the book.[1] I'm sure it will be the only bit worth reading of my poetic-surrealist-critical-arbitrary ramblings. I think Joaquín's friendship and affection for me clouded his editorial judgement.

Incidentally: the Madrid Complutense[2] published a book recently with a foreword from the Rector[3] and my name in the title.[4] There's a short story (if you can call it that?) of mine in there called 'The Pleasant Orders of Saint Huesca'. It's my favourite of my little spawn. Do you have it?

I have very fond memories of you and Joaquín coming to stay in this country, whose 'fascism was only tempered by its corruption'.

Warm regards from,
Luis Buñuel

Spa Als, ASV

[1] A. Sánchez Vidal (ed.), *Luis Buñuel: Obra literaria* (Zaragoza: Ediciones de Heraldo de Aragón, 1982).
[2] The Complutense University awarded LB doctor *honoris causa*, January 1981.
[3] Francisco Bustelo García (1933), Rector of the Complutense from 1981 to 1983.
[4] Antonio Lara (ed.), *La imaginación en libertad: Homenaje a Luis Buñuel* (Madrid: Universidad Complutense, 1981).

To Gustavo Alatriste

Mexico City, 18 November 1981

Dear Gustavo,

I'm writing to let you know that Claudio Isaac, son of our mutual friend Alberto, will be coming to see you. He's a very intelligent young man and a good film-maker. He wants to talk to you about a project he's very interested in. I'd be grateful if you would see him.

Fond regards,
Luis Buñuel

PS I read Claudio's script[1] and I think it has potential for a film.

Spa Als, CI; *MED* 37 f

[1] *El día que murió Pedro Infante.*

Figure 86 Saura and Buñuel, Madrid, 1980. Courtesy of Antonio García-Rayo, Madrid.

To Eduardo Ducay

Mexico City, 29 December 1981

Dear Eduardo,

I got your very affectionate letter that, rather than making me happy, made me sad. You painted such a bright picture of the fun we would have if I came to see you in Madrid, our lunches over wine and martinis, our long and 'fecund' conversations, etc., etc., and it all only served to highlight my repugnant old age, my nostalgia, and my isolation. For me, just going from my house to the Diplomático[1] is a Sunday outing, and I have to take food for a break along the way, as if I were going up into the mountains. I was comforted, on the other hand, to hear you may have to make a business trip to this shocking megalopolis. I very much hope you do. I would really love to see you over here.

I barely remember the cinema now. I sometimes ask myself if I ever was a film-maker or whether it was some second cousin of mine.

I shall soon be 82 years old, a propitious moment to find out whether or not (horrible question!) there is an afterlife. If there is, I fear I'm going down.[2] My health is OK, but my sight is worse. It's a struggle to read or write, although I have a reasonable field of vision.

What of your family? I hope all is well and wish you all the best for the new year, although I think it may well be a bad one for humanity. My pessimism is absolute.

Give my actor-surgeon[3] a big hug from me, and another to Joaquín, even though he's Basque. And for you, my most affectionate regards,

Luis

PS The mysterious hotel whose name Barros wouldn't tell us is called, I think, Empireo, between the Prado Museum and the Retiro. But I would rather, if I do go to Madrid, stay at the Plaza, although I have been told a room there now costs *un œuf*[4] (!!!)

Spa Als, ED

[1]   Hotel in central Mexico City.
[2]   To Hell.
[3]   Barros.
[4]   French in the original (an egg), from the Spanish phrase 'costar un huevo' (to cost an arm and a leg).

To William Sloan[1]

Mr William Sloan
Museum of Modern Art, New York

Mexico City, 6 February 1982

Dear Mr Sloan,
    The Triumph of the Will *of Leni Riefensthal and* The Conquest of Poland *– I don't remember the name of the author*[2] *– were about 12 reels each one. Iris Barry asked me to make with both films a single one of about 12 reels. During the last war this work was sent to the American Consulates of this continent on behalf of anti-Nazi propaganda. I have never heard about my work since 1948.*
    I'm sorry not to be more explicit and so laconic but my sight is bad and have some difficulty in writing. More than that: my nearly forgotten English is awful.

Cordially yours,
Buñuel

Eng Als, MoMA/12.08

[1]   US librarian, born in Canada, Chief Cataloguer at the MoMA from 1980.
[2]   Fritz Hippler.

To his son Juan Luis

[Mexico City,] 2 March 1982

Dear Juan Luis,
    I see from your letter that you've received the $50,000 I transferred via a bank in New York.
    You don't owe me anything. It's a gift given freely. I'm old now and have almost no expenses: you are still young and have two children,[1] and I know that it will be useful to have a little money to hand for any unforeseen events, in case you were out of work for example, or had bills to pay for any unexpected illnesses the children, you, or your wife might have.

I'll write again when I have more time,
[Luis]

Fre Alu, AB/1536

¹ Juliette (born 1967) and Diego Buñuel (born 1975).

To Jean-Claude Carrière

Mexico City, 12 March 1982

My dear Jean-Claude,

I shall be brief but, as always, intelligent.

Two parcels of the memoirs¹, 14 copies in all, arrived here yesterday. The printing, the format, etc., all very good; the title on the other hand, in letters far smaller than my name, which is scandalously large, made me blush. I do hope that annoying exhibitionism can be avoided in the foreign-language editions.

The French, very good. Don't tell anyone you wrote it.²

I think you should thank Laffont, then ask him to do me a favour. I would like him to send three copies to Zaragoza to: Joaquín Aranda, Heraldo de Aragón, 28 Independencia, Zaragoza, Spain. Joaquín will keep a copy and give the others to Conchita and her son, Pedro Cristian. It's the last favour I shall ask of our publisher. I've heard he sent two copies to someone over here a couple of days ago, who works in television and is an expert in 'communicology'. I'd also like Juan Luis and the Viñes to have a copy. Talk to my son. I assume the tome hasn't arrived in bookshops yet.

Exhausted, I'll sign off now,

Love,
Luis

Spa Als, JCC

¹ The dedications included the following: 'Jean-Claude Carrière helped me write this book based on a faithful account of our extensive conversations,' p. 7.
² Laffont published *Mon Dernier soupir* in Paris, March 1982.

Figure 87 Cover of French edition of *My Last Breath*, published by Robert Laffont, Paris, March 1982.

To José Rubia Barcia

Mexico City, 14 April 1982

My dear friend *don* Pepe,

Thank you for your letter, with the letter from your friend Rodríguez Puértolas enclosed.[1] I am so sorry I won't be able to accept his invitation to the tribute in Galicia, but I no longer travel. I scarcely leave the house. From time to time one or two good friends come to see me, and the days go by up here on my Stylite pillar. It's been more than two years since I even left the house for Zócalo.[2] I've turned down dozens of invitations, including *five honoris causa*, the most recent from Harvard[3] and the Complutense; one of those prizes given out by King *Don* Juan Carlos, may God preserve him; others from the television in England and Austria, etc. Forgive the showing off, but as well as making me blush, it's a way of explaining why I won't be accepting Puértolas's invitation this time. At my time of life … I have a genuine horror of these tributes. The only thing I do now is raise a glass or two with a friend.

Although I can barely read now (I have to use a special neon magnifying glass and powerful lamps), I'm waiting impatiently for your new book.[4] For my part, I'm sending a copy of mine, *Mon Dernier soupir*, published by Laffont in Paris a month ago. It will come out in Spanish in May, published by Plaza y Janés in Barcelona. It's a series of memories and reflections by a repulsive old man bidding farewell to the world.

Even when I'm typing, I can hardly make out what I'm saying. So, I'll end here, with congratulations to those who may well already be happy grandparents. Give my love to the mother. And for you both, the now ancient but unwavering affection of

Luis

PS I have absolutely no interest in hearing about film now. It's been years since I've set foot in a cinema and I *never* watch television.

When I post this letter, I'll also send you my book by registered airmail. I sent Rafael a copy a few days ago.

Spa Tlsps, CBC; *CLB* 100–101

---

[1] Julio Rodríguez Puértolas (born 1936), literary critic and historian.
[2] Central square in Mexico City.
[3] Letter from Derek Bok to LB, 2 February 1980 (AB/1426.25), informing LB that Harvard University has awarded him the title Doctor of Arts.
[4] J. Rubia Barcia, *Cantigas de bendizer: A aza enraizada* (Sada: Edicións do Castro, 1981) (AB/923), bilingual edition, Galician-Castilian.

From Francisco Rabal

Madrid, 14 May 1982

Dear uncle,

Although it's been a while since I wrote you a long letter (I've sent postcards), do not think I have forgotten you, I get regular news of you through our mutual friends, most recently from Juan Estelrich,[1] who told me you were in good shape and fine humour, and that you sent your always affectionate greetings to this nephew of yours. A few days ago, the Madrid *ABC* published a preview in two parts of your memoirs, *Mi último suspiro*. I was really touched by your fond memories of me and laughed at the jokes you played on Fernando and other friends. I can't wait to read the whole thing in Spanish, which Plaza and Janés have announced will be out soon. I was thinking of sending you copies of the *ABC* with you on the front cover, but I only have one copy and I imagine someone will already have sent you them. If not, let me know and I will.

I also read a few days ago that Juan Luis was in Madrid as a jury member for a Fantasy Film Festival. As there was no sign of him, I went looking and we managed to coincide. He was overwhelmed with endless screenings, talks etc. I spent an afternoon with him and then didn't see him again, but we were very happy to meet up, and he seemed to be on great form.

I finished an action film last Saturday, co-produced by the Americans and in 3D for a change.[2] Before that I was in *La colmena*[3] by Camilo José Cela.[4] There are not many films, or many good films, being made in Spain. It's all dominated by the multinationals, but I get by, and with the children provided for and financially independent Asunción and I have no real problems. I've just been asked to do a stage production of *King Lear*[5] and I think I'll take it. It would be on at open-air theatres around Spain in summer and then, from October, in Madrid.

My daughter Teresa is having great success with a children's musical[6] and they've bought a huge marquee for 2,000 people that they can put up wherever they like, in local squares or parks all over the place, and it's making a lot of money. She's going to make a film now, splitting the finance with a distributor.[7] She didn't have children and adopted a new-born baby, who's now two.[8] My son Benito is still working as an assistant director and hoping to be able to direct independently soon, he has no shortage of work. From him, I have two other grandchildren: Paquito, seven years old, and a girl of nine months.[9]

María Asunción is very well and very happy, because I've been leading a peaceful and austere life for a while now. That's right, uncle, I very seldom go out at night, hardly ever drink, and my life is generally healthy, sensible and very calm. I'm telling you this because I know you've sometimes worried about my other more 'fun-loving' life. Although reports on that were somewhat exaggerated …

Damián is still working as an actors' agent, doing quite well. His health is also good, although he should stop smoking. I should too, of course, but I'm just the same in that respect, smoking away.

So, uncle, I've told you, broadly-speaking, my most important news, so you are not missing out, and although I know you are now a reluctant letter-writer, I would be very pleased to get a few lines with your news and news of Aunt Juana, to whom I send much love.

With love from Asunción and my lot, and a big hug from your nephew,
Paco

Spa Als, AB/647.4

---

[1] Assistant director (born 1927), Head of Production on *Tristana*.
[2] *El tesoro de las cuatro coronas* (1982), Spanish-US co-production, dir. Ferdinando Baldi.
[3] Feature directed by Mario Camus in 1982.
[4] Writer (1916–2002), received the Nobel Prize for Literature in 1989, author of the *La colmena* (Buenos Aires: Emecé, 1951), on which the film by Camus is based.
[5] To be directed by Miguel Narros at the Roman theatre in Sagunto, Valencia, Spain.
[6] *El Circo de Teresa Rabal.*
[7] *Loca por el circo* (1982), directed by Luis María Delgado, co-produced by Starfilm and distributed by Filmayer.
[8] Luis Eduardo Rodrigo Rabal, adoptive son of Eduardo Rodrigo and Teresa Rabal.
[9] Francisco Liberto Rabal (born 1975) and Candela Rabal (born 1981), son and daughter of Benito Rabal and Silvia Cerezales.

To Emilio Sanz de Soto[1]

Mexico City, 23 May 1982

My dear Emilio,

First of all, I'm offended that you begin your long and impressive letter[2] by reminding me 'who you are'. If it were a joke I'd let it pass, but … I have very, very fond memories of you and much admiration for your vast knowledge and incredible erudition. I regard you, no matter what, as one of my best friends, and that's that.

Your letter is, without doubt, the most interesting and extraordinary one I've ever received. I could spend hours talking to you, but you are faced with an anti-writer, with total agraphia, blind as a bat, and deaf to boot, although that defect has little to do with letter-writing. I have become a dreadful old man. I no longer travel and scarcely leave home. And only now and again does an old friend come around to have a drink and talk a while.

You have AMAZED me with your incredibly wide and detailed knowledge about so many things. For example: that you knew who Tom Kilpatrick was and could even give me the titles of the films he wrote scripts for. I was a very close friend of his, and I still couldn't recall, for my memoirs, the title of a film he made when I was in Hollywood. You provided me with it in your letter: *Doctor Cyclops*.[3]

What I would give to spend a few hours chatting with you, but I think it would be difficult.

Forgive the brevity, but I've run out of energy for writing. Generally, I don't reply to letters.

I shall file your letter with my books.

My very warmest regards,
Luis

[PS] I realize that my oft-remembered and dear friend Corpus Barga's[4] book is admirably well written, but I've only read fragments, because I found it supremely boring. Ginorella has been angry with me ever since he discovered what I think of it. He's a borderline insane Hispanophile, Hispanist, Hispanophrenic, but I'm fond of him and I do admire him as a painter.

Send whatever greetings you like on my part to the wonderful José Hernández.[5]

Spa Als, SS; *CUA* 630–631 f

[1]   Film historian and artistic director (1924–2007), collaborated with Saura.
[2]   Nine-page letter from Sanz de Soto to LB, 23 April 1982 (AB/1382).
[3]   *Doctor Cyclops* (1940), dir. Ernest B. Shoedsack based on a script by Kilpatrick.
[4]   *Los pasos contados* series of memoirs by Barga, published by Edhasa, Barcelona, between 1963 and 1973.
[5]   Painter (1944–2013).

To Francisco Rabal

Mexico City, 25 May 1982

Paco, my dear nephew,

As I'm half-blind and almost never answer my correspondence now, I'll be very brief.

Thank you for your letter, which provides, with such appealing garrulousness, a close account of your loved ones. It was a while since I'd had news of them, but I see all is well. Of you, I hear regularly through your postcards or friends who have seen you and tell me about you. It's good that without giving up drinking, you are now enjoying it, like me, in moderation. People who don't smoke or drink are generally assholes. Forgive my language.

I don't leave home for anything now. Occasionally some friend or other will come and see me. The rest of the time I spend thinking about nonsense, or about our filthy human society and where it is taking us. Then I have a martini immediately, to forget.

It's a shame I have no energy to make films now. I'll die without making another one with you. The ones I did make have left me with very pleasant memories of true friendship.

A huge hug from your uncle,
Luis

[PS] Love to all your lot, without forgetting Damián.

Spa Als, FR; *BVMC* f

From Jean-Claude Carrière

[Paris, May 1982]

Dear maestro,

Yesterday I took part in a public round table at the Mexican Cultural Centre[1] on Cesarman's[2] book, he was there as well. To be honest, I find the book fairly bad. I wonder why? Anyway, he's a nice person your psychoanalyst.[3] Berzosa[4] was there too, and the photographer[5] who published that wonderful book on you (Gálvez?).

Our book[6] is going very well. The latest I heard (yesterday) was that 19,000 copies have 'gone out', although that doesn't mean 'been sold'. They expect to sell, provisionally, somewhere between 12 and 15,000 copies. As I mentioned, we only get anything if it goes over 20 or 22,000 copies, then we might get additional payments. I hope the copies and the reviews have arrived.

There are more now (in particular, a wonderful and very favourable one in *L'Humanité*) that I'll send shortly. I'm getting lots of responses, all very candid; I imagine you'll be getting lots of letters as well, perhaps from the odd lunatic even.

Otherwise, everything is going well. Wajda is filming *Danton*[7] and sends his regards. He's delighted, of course, with what you said about him in the book. As for me, I'm comfortable working with Volker Schlöndorff.[8] Iris has her first job as an apprentice assistant director in Carlos's[9] film (on the section they are shooting in Paris), she's really happy and seems to be really getting on with things. I'll be going to a 'colloquium' in Cannes for a couple of days and then I'll be back. I keep my eyes open for any possible excuse to get back to Mexico and see you. Perhaps I'll come up with an idea for another film over there.

Any news of you – particularly if it is good – would make me very happy. Much love to Jeanne from the three of us, and to the little dog as well.[10]

Un gran, gran abrazo,[11]
[Jean-Claude]

Fre Als Od, AB/646.4

[1] In Paris.
[2] The French edition of Cesarman's book, *L'oeil de Buñuel*, published by Dauphin in Paris, May 1982 (AB/776).
[3] Cesarman.
[4] José María Berzosa, documentary film-maker, exiled to France in 1956, actor in *The Milky Way*.
[5] Antonio Gálvez.
[6] *My Last Breath*.
[7] *Danton* (1983), script co-written by Carrière about the death of the French revolutionary leader Georges Danton.
[8] On an adaptation of *Un amour de Swann* (1984), dir. Schlöndorff.
[9] *Antonieta* (1982), dir. Carlos Saura.
[10] Tristana, LB's dog, drawn by Carrière in the letter.
[11] Spanish in the original (A huge, huge, hug).

To José Rubia Barcia

Mexico City, 6 August 1982

My dear Don Pepe,

Of course, I got your book,[1] but I was prevented from writing back when I wanted to by my laziness, poor eyesight and innate agraphia. I thought your '*cantigas*' were exquisite, tender and original. I read them in Spanish and in Galician, the latter out aloud, to enjoy their sweet sound, a daring task for someone from Aragon. You've become a good and very subtle writer of the erotic blended with nostalgia for your homeland. It's a lovely edition and the drawings are excellent. Congratulations, I'm so delighted for you. As for that Rubín[2] Barcia you mention, that's my fault for my bad eyesight and for correcting the proofs at top speed. I was sick of it after five weeks reciting my 'adventures' to Carrière. A friend[3] wrote from Spain and gave me, along with other things, a list of all the names misspelt in the French text. I imagine they'll be corrected in subsequent editions in France and in Spain. Here's the list: *Rubin* Barcia, Ramón Gómez de la *Cerna* (Serna), Corpus *Vaga* (Barga), Evelyn *Vaugh* (Waugh), the painter *Quintilla* (Quintanilla[4]), *Arnices* (Arniches), *Cosio* (Cossío), *Filmosono* (Filmófono), *Lara* (Larra), etc.

The book has now been sold to twelve countries with different languages, but not yet to the United States of America.[5]

I also congratulate you on the birth of your first grandchild. Love to the mother and 'grandma' Eva, and my warmest regards to you,

Luis

Spa Als, CBC; *CLB* 103–104

¹ *Cantigas de bendicer.*
² Rubia Barcia's name misspelt in *Mon Dernier soupir.*
³ Sanz de Soto.
⁴ Luis Quintanilla (1893–1978), painter.
⁵ English translation by Abigail Israel published in the United States, *My Last Sigh* (New York: Alfred Knopf, 1983).

To Luís de Pina¹

Luís de Pina, Secretary of State for Culture Cinemateca Portuguesa,
Lisbon

Mexico City, 28 August 1982

Dear Mr Luís de Pina,

My sincere thanks for your kind letter, and I am deeply sorry not be able to accept your invitation,² as a trip to Portugal – a country I love – would be an indescribable pleasure for me. The reasons I have to decline are as follows: my age, 82 years, which has prevented me from taking any kind of trip now for three years; I also have very deficient eyesight and hearing, which makes it difficult for me to communicate with people I don't know, which, in this case, would be inevitable.

If my son Juan Luis, who lives in Paris, is not working on a film, I'm sure he would be delighted to represent me in Lisbon.

I remain very cordially yours,
Luis Buñuel

Spa Tls, Od; *CILB* 11 f

¹ Portuguese film critic, director of the Lisbon Cinemateca (founded 1948), 1982 to 1991.
² To attend the LB retrospective at the Cinemateca, October 1982 (AB/295).

To Alfredo Guevara

Mexico City, 20 September 1982

Alfredo Guevara
Ministry of Culture, Havana

My dear friend Alfredo Guevara,

How could I forget you when we saw one another every day for over a month filming *Nazarín*! Afterwards, I often had news of you and your work organizing Cuban cinema, because no friend of mine from that city arrives without news of you and your activities.

I am very grateful for the kind letter you sent with García Márquez and for the honour of your invitation to do a recorded interview for your film archive. Unfortunately, and mostly for health reasons, I am COMPLETELY removed from the 'vain world's uproar'.

I have scarcely left home for three years and it's now more than five since I set foot in a cinema. I never watch television. I feel my 82 years and every day brings a new physical defect. My eyesight is so bad I can barely read. My legs are failing and ... that's enough of my clinico-medical confessions. My dear friend Guevara, I am no longer up to *interviews*[1] of any kind. Although all that, should you come to Mexico one day, would not prevent me taking great pleasure in seeing you and exchanging views on your activities,

Most friendly greetings,
Buñuel

Spa, Od; *NCL* 69

[1] English in the original.

To Homero Aridjis[1]

[Mexico City, November 1982][2]

Dear friend,

I'm putting into a few lines what I have already told you of my impressions on reading your book *El último Adán*. You can take out anything you don't find useful:

Mankind will bring about the apocalypse, not God, that is in my view an absolute truth. This is the vast difference between the apocalyptic delirium of *El último Adán* and the mediocre description of the Apocalypse by Saint John. There is no doubt that human creativity has been enriched by the passing of the centuries.

The last Adam, his Eve already lost, wanders the ruined cities and barren fields in dense smoke under a dark sky, coming across groups of terrified humans with singed hair and eyebrows, blankly staring eyes and loosely hanging bellies. His progress is hampered by volcanoes erupting and clashing earth tremors, smoke, ash, skeletons, scattered human limbs and, above all, the fetid smell of putrefying flesh that I call 'the sweet smell of eternity'.

Greek Homer's 'endlessly smiling sea'[3] has been extinguished, leaving only darkness and chaos.

To my mind, the constant and obsessive reiteration offers a powerful contribution to Aridjis's narrative of delirious apocalypse, an alternative title for which might be: *Dies irae, dies illa, solvet saeclum in favilla.** [4]

Luis Buñuel

* I crossed out the bit about *teste David cum sibylla*[5] because I think it's stupid.

Spa Tlsps, HA

[1] Mexican writer (born 1940).
[2] The asterisked note at the end is LB's; he is writing in response to having seen Aridjis's play *Moctezuma*, premiered in Mexico City in 1982.
[3] 'La sonrisa innumerable del mar' in the original.
[4] First line of thirteenth-century Latin hymn, attributed to Italian Franciscan Thomas of Celano: 'Dies iræ, dies illa / Solvet sæclum in favilla / Teste David cum Sibylla (Day of wrath and doom impending / Heaven and earth in ashes ending / David's word with Sibyl's blending)'.
[5] Reference to the third line (translated above).

From Joaquín Aranda

Zaragoza, [October 1982]

DEAR JEANNE AND LUIS,
    OBRA LITERARIA[1] HAS GONE TO PRESS. IT'S GOING TO BE WONDERFUL. PLEASE SEND ME LIST OF PEOPLE YOU WANT TO RECEIVE A COPY. THE FIRST TWO WILL OF COURSE BE FOR YOU. WE WILL LAUNCH THE BOOK AT THE TRIBUTE TO YOU IN PARIS.[2]

LOVE.
WILL WRITE SOON,
JOAQUÍN ARANDA

Spa Tel AB/1403.07

[1] *Luis Buñuel: Obra literaria.*
[2] Organized by the Georges Pompidou Centre and the Mexican Cultural Centre in Paris, November 1982.

To Jean-Claude Carrière

Mexico City, 3 November 1982

My dear Jean-Claude,
    That long letter, so full of interesting information, you wrote on your return to Paris has arrived. Thank you. I'm really sorry to hear about Benayoun and Scola.[1] And I fervently hope they will recover soon.
    I also got your postcards from India,[2] a truly fascinating country and more habitable, of course, than Mexico where state and presidential larceny have reached 'sublime' heights running into dozens of billions of dollars. They have put exchange controls in place and travellers can only take $500 out of the country. I had $18,000 saved up for an emergency and they've exchanged them for pesos. The people celebrated the president[3] as a 'national hero' when he nationalized the banks. *Quousque tandem*[4] will the masses put up with it? Not much longer I think. I, of course, would leave tomorrow if I were well. It's too late now.
    As for the ridiculous tribute to me in Paris,[5] I'd rather not mention it. I'm genuinely embarrassed.
    Everyone says the book has sold well in Spain. It was a *bestseller*[6] for two weeks. I haven't heard from Laffont, but he has sent fourteen international contracts.
    My health: dreadful, but I'd rather not go into that. I just hope my last illness will come soon, and that it won't make me suffer. I've told my children to come and see me without the grandchildren to sort everything out before my final journey.

Kisses for Auguste and Iris, and a big hug for you,
Luis

[PS] Letters take *months* to arrive. Will you ever get this one I wonder? My poor eyesight makes it very difficult for me to write.

Spa Als, JCC

1   Ettore Scola (1931–2016), Italian director who took part in a six-hour TV mini-series directed by Benayoun on the life of Jerry Lewis, *Bonjour Mr. Lewis* (1982).
2   Carrière went to India to prepare for his stage adaptation of the *Mahabharata* for Peter Brooks, premiered at the Avignon Festival, 1985.
3   López Portillo.
4   'How long?', Latin, from '*Quousque tandem abutere, Catilina, patientia nostra*? (For how long, O Catiline, will to continue to abuse our patience?), attributed to Cicero in response to the Catiline conspiracy to overthrow the Roman Republic.
5   Margarita and Conchita Buñuel took part in the homage with a group of drummers from Calanda and a wax effigy of LB.
6   English in the original.

From Salvador Dalí

[Castillo de Púbol,[1] November 1982]

DEAR BUÑUEL,
    EVERY TEN YEARS I SEND YOU A LETTER YOU DISAGREE WITH, BUT I HAVE COME UP WITH A FILM TONIGHT WE COULD MAKE IN TEN DAYS. NOT ABOUT THE PHILOSOPHICAL DEVIL, BUT ABOUT OUR VERY OWN LITTLE DEVIL. IF YOU ARE INTERESTED COME AND SEE ME AT THE CASTILLO DE PÚBOL.

REGARDS,
DALÍ

Spa Tel, AB/577.3; *VID* 740

1   Medieval Castle of Pubol, Girona, Catalonia, Spain, bought by Dalí for his wife Gala in 1969.

From Salvador Dalí

[Púbol Castle, November 1982]

I AM WAITING FOR YOU TO SEND TELEGRAM TO MY ADDRESS WHICH I FORGOT: PÚBOL CASTLE, GIRONA PROVINCE.

REGARDS,
DALÍ

Spa Tel, AB/577.2

To Salvador Dalí

[Mexico City, November 1982]

I got both your telegrams. Wonderful idea about little devil film, but I gave up making films five years ago and don't leave home now. Shame.

Regards ...
[Buñuel]

Spa Tel, FSD/348

Figure 88 Buñuel, with Jeanne and children, Rafael and Juan Luis, Mexico City, 1982.

To Juan Luis Buñuel

Mexico City, 28 November 1982

Dear Juan Luis,

I know that the catastrophic economic situation may mean financial trouble for you two and your mother in the future. This has me concerned about Jeanne's peace of mind.

You should use my archive and Dalí's[1] painting as a possible source of income. I think it would be best to try and sell them in Spain but WATCH YOURSELF!! with the riffraff in charge of public institutions, you know I've *never* trusted them, but they do come in handy at times like this.[2]

I warn you, they are a force to be reckoned with, but you decide.

Love, Luis

Spa Tls, JLB

[1] *Portrait of Luis Buñuel.*
[2] Painting acquired by Reina Sofía Museum, Madrid, in 1988.

To Agustín Sánchez Vidal

Mexico City, 7 February 1983

Mr Agustín Sánchez Vidal,

Luis Buñuel has serious problems with his eyesight and is almost completely unable to read and write.

His removal from all social interaction also means that he is unable to keep up with his correspondence, as he has no secretary.

He asks you forgive his decision and hopes that you understand his reasons. By order:

Jeanne Buñuel

[PS] Your round the world trip, incredible.[1] Your introduction to the book,[2] magnificent.

You will see the extent of my decrepitude from this letter.

Warm regards,
Luis

Spa Tlsps, ASV

[1] Postcard from Sánchez Vidal to LB, sent from Sydney, Australia, 8 July 1982 (AB/1382.29).
[2] *Luis Buñuel: Obra literaria.*

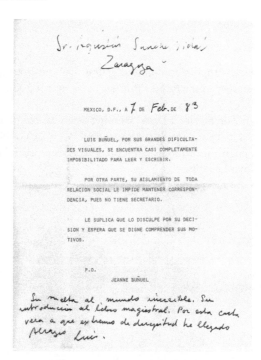

Figure 89 Letter from Rucar and Buñuel to Sánchez Vidal, 7 February 1983.

To Jean-Claude Carrière

Mexico City, 10 April 1983

My dear Jean-Claude,

Albeit briefly and with great difficulty, I am typing this letter to you. IMPORTANT: please tell Laffont in future to send only TWO COPIES of each foreign edition of my *famous* book. Ten copies of the Portuguese edition arrived, which I was going to burn, but I sent eight on to the Portuguese embassy in the end. Please don't forget to tell him.

The last two months have been very bad, but I am getting slowly better, although I'm far from what I once was. My diabetes is completely under control thanks to an excellent doctor I have. My peripheral vision isn't bad, but I have no central vision. Hence my difficulties reading and writing.

I've had no word from Serge, although he did say six months ago he was going to send royalties on my last two films, which are the only two on which I get 10% of the profits.

I see you are as busy as ever. Happy you.[1] I never go out now, I just breathe in dust laden with excrement, a terrible year in Mexico, the worst ever. This country has everything against it.

I would be very happy to see you over here if you decide to come, even if my physical, and even more so, my mental deficiencies might try to drive you from my side.

Multiple kisses for the mother and daughter, and any left over for you,
Luis

[PS] I'm not re-reading this letter. It's going off whatever state it's in.

Spa Tls, JCC

---

[1]   Possible allusion to Golden Age poet Francisco de Quevedo's poem 'Dichoso tú'.

From Costa-Gavras[1] to Jeanne Rucar de Buñuel

Mrs Luis Buñuel
27 Cerrada Félix Cuevas, Mexico City

Paris, 2 August 1983

I am deeply saddened by the passing of Luis Buñuel,[2] one of the last giants of cinema and an old friend of the Cinémathèque Française. On behalf of the Board and all staff at the Cinémathèque, I send my most heartfelt condolences. Please be assured that Luis Buñuel will live on among us on the screens of the Cinémathèque,

Costa-Gavras

Fre Tel C, CIN

---

[1]   Greek–French film-maker (born 1933), President of the Cinémathèque française from 1982 to 1987.
[2]   LB died in Mexico City in the early hours of 29 July1983, of cardiac, liver and kidney failure associated with cancer.

To his friends

[Mexico City, 1983]

Luis Buñuel's last will and testament to his friends

Dry Martini: gin, drops of vermouth, preferably Noilly-Prat. Perhaps Angostura. Ice, very hard, so it doesn't melt too quickly.

Buñueloni: Carpano, gin and sweet Cinzano. More gin than other ingredients.

Surrealists' drink: beer, Picon and grenadine.

Spa Tlu, RMS; *CUA* 638 f

Index